May Your Journey with Food Flavor, Laughter, Friends & Abundan...

Experience the Whole Journey with Food with the companions!

<u>Our Journey with Food Cookery Book</u> takes you through the next journey with food with more History, Science, and Recipes – this is no average Cookbook!

ISBN: 979-8-9864312-3-9

This isn't just an Empty Plate ~ It is a Full Banquet of Food, Sustainability and Mindfulness!

The Journey with Food would not be complete without an in depth look at food history and myth, science and inspiring individuals with Mindfulness Knowledge!

<u>Empty Plate</u>
<u>Food ~ Sustainability ~ Mindfulness</u>
ISBN: 978-1-7329072-3-2

Our Journey with Food

Reviews

Wow! I feel like I've been on a whirlwind tour through health's medical, political, and historical underpinnings as we know it today. Dr. Karr's meticulous and unapologetic storytelling, weaving research, current events, and historical documents stirred many emotions and convictions in my heart. I especially appreciate all the nutritional information about vitamins and minerals. She includes historical information, the latest research on the relationship between deficiencies and certain chronic health conditions, and populations that are at risk. Her extensive coverage of vitamins D and K, including clinical trials, history, and other important information, is the most comprehensive I've seen. *Our Journey with Food* is an engaging and current reference, much better than my old textbook! I will repeatedly refer to this volume as I educate my clients on their health choices and remind myself of the new research that Dr. Karr has diligently unearthed and included.

~ Julie Brow-Polanco,
Health Coach, Herbalist, Aromatherapist

This book provides individuals with an understanding of how food as "medicine" contributes to overall health and wellbeing. The weaving of the origins of food, as our ancestors consumed, with how holistic practitioners integrate food as a healing modality make this a rich book for all to read. Dr. Karr writes that holistic nutrition is a way of life that considers each individual's unique physical, emotional, cultural, psycho-social, and spiritual responses. The chapter titled "How we get what we need" provides a comprehensive and holistic overview to those who desire to take the journey with food to promote health and healing.

~Lynne King, DNS, MSN, MS, RN, AHN-BC, Caritas Coach®

Modern Americans often compare our evolving bodies to machines, which necessarily reduces food's purpose to serving as fuel. Dr. Tammera Karr's contrasting view encourages us to renew our intimate and holistic relationship with food. This updated and comprehensive look at how and what we eat reminds us of the philosophy that governs Tammera's practice: "Our cells carry the memory of our ancestors." Exploring our food's history, Dr. Karr calls us back to the wisdom of our ancestors and indigenous peoples who grew and knew their food much better than most of us do today. Explaining anatomy/physiology, pathologic conditions, and neuroimmunology as understandably as she lists ingredients in favorite whole-food recipes, Tammera's writing weaves together current scientific data with poignant quotations from ancient physicians and scholars. Her deep love and respect for herbs and foods as healing medicine and nutritional support for holistic well-being are apparent throughout.

~ Kathleen Bell RN, MSN, CNM, AHN-BC®

Tammera writes like she talks. Weaving history into today's relevant awareness is Tam's special knack. She has a robust and insatiable appetite in her personal quest for answering questions that drive her. I say thank you for distilling the complexities of food and diet into usefulness! Thank you for sharing the treasures that you have gathered over the years with all of us!

~ Lorrie Amitrano, FNP-C, AHN, CNP

Our Journey with Food

Our Journey with Food is an honest and enlightening look at the healthful aspects of our food. Tammera presents a wealth of information about how food impacts our physical health, making this a must-have resource for everyone.

~ *Rebekah Fedrowitz, MHN, BCHN®*

Much of our population has moved from rural America to the cities and has radically changed their diet from farmed fresh food to corporate prepared food. *Our Journey with Food*, by Tammera Karr, is a fascinating account of our history of food that explains this process. Tammera captures this information and, with interest and relevant examples, provides the reader with insights into health and disease. This edition has included important information on medical cannabis and the brain's plasticity as it relates to aging. This book is such an important resource on nutrition that it has been implemented into our required reading for the curriculum at American College of Healthcare Sciences. We are pleased to be able to provide our students with this perspective on nutrition and health.

~ *Janet Ludwig, Ph.D.*
Education Director - Director of Doctoral Studies – American College of Healthcare Sciences

This book is absolutely wonderful, inclusive, yet easy to understand how food is truly the foundation of wellness. Bringing us through the history of our food, we begin to see a startling picture emerge that shows us how much our food has been compromised. And how in turn that impacts our bodies and our health. With easy to understand, commonsense information (plus delicious recipes), this book should be required reading for anyone who wants to really understand their food and improve their health.

~ *Mira Dessy, NE, BCHHP*
The Ingredient Guru

Wow! I just had fine dining at a full buffet reading Tammera Karr's book, *Our Journey with Food!* Tammera offers many selections of great nutrient-dense chapters explaining proteins, fats, and carbohydrates. Then she delves into nutrients such as minerals and vitamins, deeply explaining their importance in our health and very existence. She touches on so many aspects of our health and lives that I feel loved and nourished by her book. As a holistic nutritionist, I work mainly with clients struggling to conceive and women concerned about getting breast cancer. I so appreciate Dr. Karr writing this book and sharing with all of us her wisdom and how we need to reconnect with our ancestors 'wisdom of eating and food preparation. Her recipes are so delicious, just reading them got me salivating! A must read!

~ *Donna M. McIntosh, MS, CHFS*
Stop Breast Cancer NOW - The Goddess of Natural Fertility

Here we are at the top of the food chain, and we're more confused about what to eat than ever before. In *Our Journey with Food*, Tammera Karr provides us with a glimpse into the past and explains how and why we've lost our connection with healthy food. This book is not only a fascinating and fresh look at past culinary traditions but also a wake-up call to get back to basics; unprocessed, healthful, wholesome foods.

~ Melissa McLean-Jory, MNT
The Gluten-Free Edge

This book is absolutely wonderful, inclusive, yet easy to understand how food is truly the foundation of wellness. Bringing us through the history of our food, we begin to see a startling picture emerge that shows us how much our food has been compromised. And how in turn that impacts our bodies and our health. With easy to understand, commonsense information (plus delicious recipes) this book should be required reading for anyone who wants to really understand their food and improve their health.

~ Mira Dessy, NE, BCHHP
The Ingredient Guru

Our Journey with Food is a must-have for health-minded consumers, holistic health practitioners, as well as students of nutrition and health sciences. With the creativity of an artist and the insight of a historian, Dr. Tammera Karr takes you on a thought-provoking journey with food and how we eat. For anyone who wants a deeper understanding of the psychology of eating, an up-to-date description of the human digestive process and vital organs, the importance and often little-known facts about micro- and macronutrients, or perhaps simply to take advantage of the plethora of helpful nutritional recommendations and tips that are found throughout -- this book is one you can't be without.

~ Barbara Rodgers, NC, BCHN®
Baby Maker -- A complete, holistic guide to nutrition for fertility, conception and pregnancy

Our Journey with Food shines as a bright and unique light in a world filled with disinformation. Tammera Karr's brilliantly synergistic approach makes this a book you cannot put down. Her contagious love of history and our rich connection with food, along with a textbook-like exhaustive commentary on nutrition is why I believe this book should be in every institute of learning. Tammera's inclusion of toxicity and the chemicals that are killing us, as well as very current research on brain preservation and the looming threat of Alzheimer's disease, places this book in the "must read" category for anyone serious about their health and the health of others.

Our Journey with Food covers it all, along with fabulous recipes that you know you can make time and time again! Bravo Tammera, for a book destined to bear the dog-eared, well-worn, often-used look of our most beloved books.

~ Christine Wokowsky, CN, BCHN®, CGP
Radiant Detox: Your 21-Day Gateway to Vitality

Our Journey with Food

Tammera Karr's *Our Journey with Food* is jam-packed with relevant and important information about nutrition and real health (not just the absence of disease). It also contains loads of fun facts about our sources of nourishment. Did you know that onion skins' thickness has been used to predict the severity of the oncoming winter? Of course, Tammera would know that; she's the most down-to-earth, Farmer's Almanac, foodie-nutritionist around!

Thanks, Tam, for creating this awesome resource that will not only help save lives with the well-researched information it contains but will provide great fodder for interesting discussion around many a dinner table.

~ Susan Barendregt, Functional Nutritionist

Tammera Karr's *Our Journey with Food* is a must-read. Tammera has the uncanny ability to take complicated physiology, vitamins, minerals, statistics, and the confusion over what to eat, and break it down into easy-to-understand-and-digest chunks. A resource you will refer to over and over.

Americans are some of the unhealthiest citizens in the world. How did this happen? Why did this happen? Tammera answers these questions and so many more as she takes you on a journey through the history of our food. Full of facts and interesting statistics that will blow your mind.

Learn which foods are best for the prevention of cancer, fatigue, diabetes, and hormonal health challenges; the why is backed with the latest research, which now supports what holistic nutrition practitioners have always known. Consume chocolate, eggs (including the yolks), meat, and alcohol in confidence once again while taking in all the great tips and anecdotes. Yes, you heard me right! What nutritionist covers alcohol? Learn the health effects and benefits connected to alcohol and how to make wassail! Wow! This is one powerhouse, fact-packed book.

~ Karen Langston CNCP, CN, LM, SIT
Holistic Nutritionist specializing in digestive health @ KarenLangston.com

This book is a cornucopia of food and nutrition information! *Our Journey with Food 3rd Edition* and the companion books in the series are cutting-edge science, entertaining, inspiring, thought-provoking, and empowering. A true, comprehensive, in-depth look at holistic health and nutrition, these books contain valuable historical insights, tips, and tools for holistic educators, practitioners, and students. Well-referenced is an understatement. Dr. Karr and her collaborators have packed this 3rd edition with over 1,500 current scientific citations that are beautifully organized, taking the reader through our full lifespan. Dr. Karr and her team have outdone themselves!

~Nicole Hodson, NC, BCHN®, CDSP™
NANP Executive Director

Our Journey with Food

3rd Edition Revised & Expanded

Tammera J. Karr, PhD, BCHN®, CDSP™, CNW®, CGP
Kathleen Bell, RN, MSN, CNM, AHN-BC®
Leana Susan Guptha, ND, DO, MS, MBA, PhD

Forewords by
James L. Wilson, ND, DC, PhD
&
Sarica Cernohous, DACM, L.Ac., BSBA

Summerland Publishing ~ Summerland, CA

Cover Design by JVMedia Design™ 2014, 2018, 2023
Kitchen life in the 18th century, Skansen, Stockholm, Sweden – Neracc

Photography, Graphs/Illustration Credits
Michael W. Karr, Tammera J. Karr
National Archives, Washington, DC
Oregon Historical Society, Portland, Oregon
Adobe iStock license

Copy Editor & Content Advisor
Julie A. Thenell, BS, MS, NC, BCHN®, CDSP™

Content Expert Advisors
Kathleen Bell, RN, MSN, CNM, AHN-BC®
Leena S. Guptha, ND, DO, MS, MBA, PhD
Soneil Guptha MD FACC FESC FCCP FICA MFPM GFMD

Paperback **First Edition 2015** – ISBN: 978-0-9904864-0-4
Library of Congress Control Number: 2015931833

Paperback **Second Edition 2018** – ISBN: 978-0-9995562-1-4
Library of Congress Control Number: 2018933169

Paperback **Third Edition** Revised and Expanded 2023 – ISBN: 979-8-9864312-6-0
Library of Congress Control Number: 2023914567

All rights reserved ©2015-2023 by Tammera J. Karr
and Holistic Nutrition for the Whole You

    Disclaimer: The contents of this book are intended as educational information for a wide variety of individuals and knowledge levels. This book is not intended to prescribe, diagnose or treat any form of health challenge. Any dietary approach or nutritional therapies must be done under the supervision of a qualified health provider in accordance with state and federal laws. **The authors of this book do not accept any responsibility for how individuals may use the enclosed information – they do so at their own discretion and risk.**

As much as possible, the authors adhered to the original text and regional spelling of works for historical preservation. The authors of this book do not endorse or subscribe to any set "dietary" approach. The emphasis is on empowering educators and consumers to embrace healthy lifestyles and utilize locally produced, genetically, and culturally appropriate foodstuffs. This book does not wholly represent the complexity of nutrition science.

Author's Note

This book intends to provide historical and nutritional information about the foods we eat and have been traditionally eaten as a society. It includes direct quotes from original case studies, scientific journals, and other reputable sources. The research sources are in the endnotes for each chapter, and a bibliography of historical and educational texts can be found at the back. We have endeavored to provide this information in a manner accessible to individuals from a wide background; consumers, students, educators, and clinicians.

If you are viewing this book in an electronic version, <u>we cannot guarantee</u> all the research article hyperlinks will function. If you are viewing an electronic copy of this work, we ask you to **not share** this copy as the sales proceeds from this book make it possible for the author to place electronic copies in college libraries and make them available to students at no cost.
To purchase an electronic copy, go to: https://yourwholenutrition.com/e-books/

Historical images and photographs from archives, libraries, and museums supplement the text.

This text also includes nutrition research from a wide range of scientific papers and journals on multiple subjects.

~

Sheepherders Wagon, Shanako, Oregon
Photo by Tammera Karr

The Basque and Irish traveled the remote areas of Washington, Oregon, Idaho, Nevada, Montana, and Wyoming from the late 19th century to modern times in sheepherder wagons. The Basque are world-renowned for their food, and it is an essential part of their culture. They cooked over wood fires and collected wild herbs and foods to supplement wild game for their meals. These herders enjoyed rich, "one-pot meals" and dense, hardy yeast bread cooked in Dutch ovens or old coffee cans over hot coals. They moved, rested, and dreamed under the sun and stars, keeping with the natural cycles.

Sheep were taken to high-elevation mountain meadows during the summer and early fall to graze on nutrient-rich grass, lichens, and moss. Even today, many of these high meadows are in roadless areas and are difficult to reach. A herder would live alone for months with his dogs out of their wagon, surrounded by nature. Today these wagons are pulled behind a four-wheel drive pick-up truck and have rubber tires or have been replaced by travel trailers. Soon, they may not exist outside of museums.

As this lifestyle vanishes in the West, volumes of information from history, immigrants, and the cultures they encountered in the Americas, pass through the vale, lost and often forgotten. Worldwide, food is still used as medicine, and this book's pages hopefully illustrate just how relevant *Food as Medicine* remains in the 21st century.

Dedication

For my family, past, present, and future.
Michael, Brendan, and grandson Michael,
Nephews Matthew and Donald,
Great Niece Neveah, Great Nephew Christian, and all those who follow.

Gratitude to my many mentors for their patience, guidance, and inspiration, and to my medical oversight and coauthor Kathleen Bell. My heartfelt and profound thanks.

A book is only as good as those who edit the work. It is impossible to fully express my gratitude for Julie Thenell, who has gracefully guided me and the content contributors without losing her mind. 😊

Special thanks to JV Media Design and Shery Holub, who developed cover designs, marketing tools, and the YourWholeNutrition.com website.

For the students at Portland Community College, American College of Healthcare Science, Pacific College of Health Sciences, and clients over the years, thank you for sharing a part of your life with me.

To the editors of the Roseburg Beacon who took a chance on a fledgling writer.

This book has been made possible by the generous donations of:

Matthew M. Davies	Susan & Lee Tyler
Michael W. Karr	Charlie Goe
Mercy Armer	Jean Hunnecutt
Linda E. Fallon	Ruth Kummrow
Jean Caskey	Lorrie Amitrano
Julie Thenell	Shirley & Clyde Pyle
Karen Gibbons	Jacque Everden
Anonymous Angel	M. A. Hansen
Betty Sitz	Mary L. Hagood
Kathleen Bell	Dr. Darryl B. George
Leena & Soneil Guptha	Carol Rodríguez

In Memory of Mary L. Hagood, FNP-C
She flies with dragons now.
1955-2023

Mary believed in me and the power of integrative health care and nutrition. Much of what is shared in this book was learned under her supervision and she is deeply missed.

What Calls Me

My cells carry the memories of my ancestors—
they call out to be remembered and to remind.

My blood surges with the song of family—
the past whispers, the present sings, and the future dances on the fringes of the mind.

I sing out what I have learned, of remembrance and tell the story of our history, tradition,
family, and of responsibility.

My cells carry the memory of our ancestors,
our past, present and our hope in what is yet to come.

by Tammera J. Karı

Our Journey with Food

Contents

FOREWORD ~ FIRST EDITION 2015 — XVII

FOREWORD ~ SECOND EDITION 2018 — XIX

INTRODUCTION — 1

CHAPTER ONE ~ PEEK INTO FOOD HISTORY — 7

CHAPTER TWO ~ PARADIGM SHIFT: WELLNESS CARE — 31

CHAPTER THREE ~ PARADIGM SHIFT ~ DIET: A MANNER OF LIFE — 41

CHAPTER FOUR ~ DIGESTION CONNECTION — 61

CHAPTER FIVE ~ RESEARCH OXALATES — 85

CHAPTER SIX ~ HOW TO GET WHAT WE NEED — 95

CHAPTER SEVEN ~ FOOD OUR FIRST MEDICINE — 115

CHAPTER EIGHT ~ FIBER & FAT — 151

CHAPTER NINE ~ PROTEIN — 189

CHAPTER TEN ~ MINERALS: THE FOUNDATION OF HEALTH — 217

CHAPTER ELEVEN ~NUTRIENTS	249
CHAPTER TWELVE ~ HERBS TO NOURISH & SUPPORT	279
CHAPTER THIRTEEN ~ WHEN FOOD BECOMES THE ENEMY	303
CHAPTER FOURTEEN ~ FOREVER CHEMICALS: EXCITOTOXINS & PFAS	327
CHAPTER FIFTEEN ~ HYDRATION	345
CHAPTER SIXTEEN ~ ALCOHOL	361
CHAPTER SEVENTEEN ~ PRECONCEPTION NOURISHMENT	371
CHAPTER EIGHTEEN ~ RESEARCH: NOURISHMENT	387
CHAPTER NINETEEN ~ NUTRITION FOR OUR GOLDEN YEARS	401
CHAPTER TWENTY ~NEW PARADIGM FOR BUILDING BETTER HEALTH	423
CHAPTER TWENTY-ONE ~ MAXIMIZING WELLNESS AND LONGEVITY	443
PRINCIPLES	467
BIBLIOGRAPHY OF HISTORICAL & PUBLISHED TEXTS	471
INDEX	474

> "If you are planning for a year, sow rice; if you are planning for a decade, plant trees; if you are planning for a lifetime, educate people."
>
> — *Confucius*

Foreword ~ *First Edition 2015*

We live in an age in which doctors and scientists specialize more and more, building their reputations and careers around being experts in ever-narrowing areas of expertise. This has allowed us to make significant advances in medicine and science but has also left us drowning in a tsunami of often conflicting bits of information that are too overwhelming and confusing. What is lacking but greatly needed are generalists who can meaningfully integrate all the bits of information generated by specialists and impart that understanding in a practical way to the rest of us. A vital area desperately in need of unbiased, knowledgeable generalists is the connection between food, nutrition, and health because it plays such a central role in our ability to lead whole and healthy lives.

I believe Dr. Karr is one of these much needed but rare generalists with no vested interest or ulterior motive except to integrate and synthesize information in a way that both makes sense and is useful. In *Our Journey with Food*, Dr. Karr has provided a sourcebook integrating extensive scientific, historical, and traditional information from the fields of food, nutrition, and health. She writes from the perspective of one who loves and understands the subject based on her academic training, clinical expertise, and hands-on experience living in the wilds of Oregon.

With a grassroots style that is almost folksy at times, she tells it like it is, as a person who has *real* experience with food—growing, storing, cooking, and studying it—and as a professional with academic knowledge and a clear grasp of practical applicability. This is an unusual book combining many scientific facts, anecdotes, folk tales, history, and photos, as well as political issues and fallacies around food and specific nutrients. She does a nice job of debunking the cholesterol and fat myths and emphasizes the devastating effects of white sugar and flour while revealing the influences of agribusiness and politics on our daily food intake without being too sinister or fatalistic.

So this book is indeed a "Journey with Food" that also provides a succinct rundown on each of the major vitamins and minerals and their roles in health, plus the medicinal uses of some foods. It makes for entertaining reading!

When so much of the United States' gross domestic product (GDP) depends upon sickness, you know that overall health in this country is not nearly as good as we would like to believe. One significant reason for this is that many people no longer recognize good food when they see or taste it, let alone know how to grow, store and cook it. Their taste buds have become so distorted with the excess sugar and artificial sweeteners and flavors present in much of the typical North American diet that if they shift to a diet of natural foods, it takes them approximately six weeks to be able to taste fully the natural flavors. Food has been defined and redefined to fit so many political and economic purposes, but for me the definition of food is simple: Real food is that which comes from or runs around on the ground, or lives in the water. In short, if it does not look like it was once alive, it probably is not real food.

Most of you familiar with my writing know that stress and its effects on endocrine function and the overall balance of the body (homeostasis) is a central topic of my work. I can attest from decades of clinical and research experience that without making real food the major component of daily consumption, it is almost impossible to recover from stress, adrenal fatigue, or other forms of debilitation and illness. It is also true that without the essential ingredient of good food, it is very difficult to be and remain healthy and withstand the stresses of life. Food is the raw material that becomes the body. Just as in building a house, substandard raw materials cannot produce a house that will withstand the storms of life.

Too many people drive themselves with caffeine and quick energy concoctions instead of obtaining real energy from good quality foods. Most cannot even imagine functioning properly without their caffeine and sugar fixes. Combine this with the high consumption of over the counter, prescription and street drugs, and it is not surprising that a large portion of the population no longer knows what it is like to wake up feeling refreshed, healthy and eager to meet the day. We are on a runaway train careening from fast food restaurants to doctor's offices while accepting these diminished or debilitated states of life as normal. Because we have forgotten or never knew we could be healthy by eating real food and leading less stressful lives, we continue to exist in desensitized overloaded states, just striving to remain functional. This is now so common we do not even recognize how unusual it is to live life unencumbered by sickness, partial disability, or degeneration before our time. We must change!

So, thank you, Dr. Karr, for writing this book! It is a place where people can find practical guidance on how to incorporate real food as the major portion of their daily diet, as well as answers that lead the way back to health. With the shift in healthcare currently taking place in the U.S., there will be an even greater divide between the people who know how to live a healthy lifestyle and take care of themselves, and those who depend on the medical system for their "health" (i.e., sick) care. Over time, the former will fare much better. We would all greatly benefit from having more generalists like Dr. Karr who have lived their subjects as she has lived food, nutrition, and health.

James L. Wilson, DC, ND, Ph.D., author of
Adrenal Fatigue: The 21st Century Stress Syndrome

> Good bread is the most fundamentally satisfying of all foods; good bread with fresh butter, the greatest of feasts!
>
> -James Beard

Foreword ~ *Second Edition 2018*

Suppose you are ready to engage a deeper level of understanding around food, health, and happiness. In that case, you are in the right place—welcome to a fun and full handbook to looking after yourself and your loved ones, using the sage wisdom of our ancestors and the knowledge of our modern-day experience.

In this wonderful tome, you will find what has been largely missing from the human experience of passing down wisdom from one generation to the next. It has not been but a hundred years in the making, this turn toward greater isolation, the development of the nuclear family unit, often hundreds (if not thousands) of miles from their larger family structure.

What has been gained in independence, self-reliance and mobility has come at a price. The deeper connections to the people we know, the communities that know us, and the hand-me-down practices of how to best take care of ourselves, our land, and how that land can best take care of us.

This trade-off has resulted in a culture that has lost out on sharing the wisdom of the ages in many respects. This moves away from the land, the animals and plants and how to best work with them has allowed us to use our bodies and minds differently than any humans who have come before this industrial and technological age.

Being freed from the incredibly demanding and daunting experience of leaning on our self-sufficiency and self-reliance abilities has allowed for a different use of the human capacity. Were it not for being freed from the yoke of farming, animal husbandry, food preparation, preservation, and all that is required to maintain a household; there would not be the Internet, automobiles, space travel, and so many countless other activities, goods, and services we take for granted in the 21st-century.

For as much as we may bemoan the loss of species' habitat, nutrient density, unpolluted and replete waterways and seemingly predictable weather patterns; I am not here to paint a rosy picture of days gone

Our Journey with Food

by. There is much in the human history that I cannot fathom as being part of humanity, and I am eternally grateful for the advent of clean, hot water coming from a faucet in my home (and climate control, especially when it is below zero in the winter). I am grateful for the access to modern medicine when needed, and I also appreciate the ability to drop into the natural food store and pick up a few sticks of grass-fed butter, imported from Europe and available to me in Arizona for the ridiculously reasonable price of $3.50 per package.

That is all, truly, amazing.

However, despite the accolades, I think most of us can agree there have been some significant tradeoffs. (A quick glance at the news will remind you of many, should you need a refresher.) Thankfully, it does not have to be a mutually exclusive deal. We can have our proverbial cake and eat it in many ways.

We live in an incredible information age, and the ability to share wisdom and knowledge is more accessible than at any time in human history. The book you hold in your hands is a grand example of this. It is a lovely blend of folksy good sharing—peppered with photos from days gone by—it is a delightful reference of how our ancestors looked at the world around them and put it to best use for the human body (which, interestingly, was often good for the earth itself as well).

I love this kind of sharing, and Dr. Karr does a fantastic job of imparting what your great grandma would have loved for you to have known, to look after yourself, your loved ones, your community, and your land.

However, it does not stop there—in good 21st-century fashion, Dr. Karr infuses this traditional wisdom with modern research—which more often than not confirms what tradition has suggested, affirming good practices for the best expression of health and happiness.

So good for you for reading this book—may its pages accumulate yellow highlights, bent corners, and a few tea splatters as you enjoy and learn from the wisdom and the knowledge that is shared, and see how easily and joyfully you can incorporate some of the suggestions—and, when you get used to those suggestions and reap their benefits, choose another place to add in some additional changes.

I have been in the natural health industry for over two decades, and I learned A LOT from Dr. Karr's loving efforts here, and I know you will too.

Moreover, be a good friend and share this book with the people you love—they will benefit in untold ways as well—treat it like the tool of wisdom that it is.
Wishing you and yours the very best, with love!

Sarica Cernohous, DACM, MSTOM, BSBA, L.Ac.
Author of *The Funky Kitchen—Easy Techniques from Our Ancestors for Improved Digestion, Enhanced Vitality, and Joy*

"All good men and women must take responsibility to create legacies that will take the next generation to a level we could only imagine."

~ *Jim Rohn*

Left: William Nelson Armer 1875-1958
Center: Amy Francis Armer 1901-1992
Right: Margaret "Mag" Oletha Petree Armer 1875-1965

Introduction

My journey into the world of natural health began in the 1970s when my great-aunt Amy took me to her homemade camper and treated my stinging nettle burns with lemon juice. It was magic and firmly placed her as a heroine in my young heart from then on. Later she gave my mother a copy of *Back to Eden* by Jethro Kloss, published in 1939. Kloss (1863-1946) was an herbalist, speaker, teacher, and food researcher who pioneered the food-combining diet. (We will look at this more in Chapter 3 on Diets.) Jethro was an avid believer in cooperation with Nature's healing resources. For my great-aunt, Amy Francis Armer Sisco, *Nature* medicine was the *common* medicine in 1901 when she was born in Arkansas and would remain her medicine of choice until she died in Idaho at 91 in 1992.

It would be only four years after Amy had passed before I entered school to study holistic nutrition and two more decades before I learned nutrition and herbalism reached back over four generations in my maternal family line. Did an unspoken passing of a family legacy transpire in the camper by the Snake River all those years ago? What if a cellular connection to history is as strong as ancient ponderosa pine, facing seasonal change anchored in bedrock? Before I knew anything about DNA and generational transcription through science, I intuitively understood those who came before share knowledge and memories through family lines.

In 2002, an opportunity arose to work with a small alternative medical group in rural Southern Oregon. The first week at the clinic was a crash course in chronic illnesses. Clients presented with auto-immune illnesses, amputations, debilitating migraines, glaucoma, type 2 diabetes, hepatitis C, thyroid, and endocrine diseases. Within the next few months, the list grew to include PTSD, depression, bipolar disorder, failed gastric bypasses, drug addiction, chronic pain clients with more titanium in their backs than bone, and cancer.

The "School of Real Life" was now in session, and these folks were desperate. For most, holistic nutrition was a last-ditch try for help. I would like to say every client had success, but that would be a lie. There were personality clashes, the clients who came for the wrong reasons, and those just going through the motions. These clients were the hardest to work with because I knew "if" they would "change," they would get better. It turned out it wasn't they who needed to change; it was me. In my youthful passion, I overlooked the difference between flooding the client with information, and learning to listen—to be open to what was important to the client. None of them had developed their conditions overnight; disease had been decades in the making, maybe even generations.

During the next dozen years, there was no shortage of clinical training with a host of dedicated healthcare providers and more work to earn a doctorate by 2011. Thanks to those who shared their medical, herbal, acupuncture, naturopathic, and psychology knowledge, I learned to listen more and talk less over time.

Changing the Paradigm

In practicing natural health care, especially in Holistic Nutrition and Nursing, the name of a disease is not the primary focus of care. The focus is on the client, their story, and their journey. Many conditions share symptoms which vary over time, including everything from brain fog, leg cramps, neuropathy, night

sweats, fatigue, rashes, and hair loss to digestive complaints. These symptoms can be precursors to more severe illnesses such as Crohn's, Parkinson's, multiple sclerosis, cancer, and Pick's Disease (rapid deterioration of the brain's frontal lobe). Modern medical opinions say there is no way to prevent these illnesses; at best, a slowing of the progression is all that can be expected, and they are accepted as a *normal* function of aging.

Holistic approaches through nutrition, functional medicine and holistic nursing provide a different paradigm on health. One of giving the body critical elements found in whole natural foods, clean water, a supportive environment, and restorative rest in order to achieve homeostasis – balance. It sounds like 1939 and Jethro Kloss advocating for *nature's healing resources*, right? Today a culturally responsible *Holistic Wellness* approach is providing a greater understanding of how to empower individuals toward improved health earlier in life. Chronic illnesses **do not** have to be an expected *normal* part of aging. Degenerative and chronic illnesses can be down-regulated by optimizing lifestyle choices and individualized or targeted nutrition. The 21st century has opened the door to a greater understanding of up/down-regulating genetic receptors; from the Human Genome research, we are learning how to deactivate many conditions through diet and lifestyle. This nutritional therapy is available economically and empowers every client – food in a natural, local, unrefined state and daily lifestyle choices were my great-aunt's prescribed choices, and they can be ours as well.

> ***Principle 1:*** Individuals can improve their health without drugs by changing their lifestyle and diet.

Introduction

Science Confirming it Wasn't Quackery

Over time, I developed a theory, and in 2010, I began sharing it with clients and colleagues ~ *"Our cells carry the memories of our ancestors,"* I would say; some would agree while others would roll their eyes. By 2017, genetic studies in publications that supported my theory became more frequent, especially on how nutrition and events in the lives of grandparents 'can affect the health of their children and grandchildren.[1, 2, 3]

We all suffer from *progressive generational malnutrition* is yet another theory I repeated to all. The year 2023 finds North American populations in the fourth and fifth generations being raised on highly processed foods. Each successive generation that deviates further from cultural and "*real*" whole foods suffers added genetic and nutritional imbalances, resulting in chronic, life-shortening illnesses. One of my trusted mentors on this topic, Elizabeth Lipski, Ph.D., made the following statement at a conference in 2015, *"It takes four generations to damage genes and four generations to repair genes."* Dr. Liz has shared volumes of credible research with students and the public over the years, reaffirming the truth of her words in 2015, while the emerging field of nutrigenomics is still in the early days of understanding.

Research on multiple sclerosis and diet by Terry Wahls, MD, a clinical professor of Internal Medicine at the University of Iowa and the Wahls Foundation, validates natural foods' superiority over manufactured and synthesized food-like items. Dr. Wahls and her team conduct clinical trials testing the effect of therapeutic diet and lifestyle to treat multiple sclerosis–related symptoms. Kara Fitzgerald, ND, pioneered methylation challenges and how natural foods activate positive genetic receptor sites better than nutraceuticals. This new knowledge began a huge paradigm shift as supplementation was believed to be the best way to address nutrition insufficiencies.

Traditional salmon fishing at Celilo Falls on the Columbia River in the 1950s provided nutrient-dense food for multiple first peoples of the Pacific Northwest. The roughly horseshoe-shaped falls 14 miles upstream from present-day The Dalles, Oregon, was one of two crucial fishing and trading places on the Columbia River for the Yakima, Nez Perce, Warm Springs, and Umatilla peoples. Celilo Falls disappeared under the water behind The Dalles Dam in 1957. Bonneville Hydro-electric Power Agency operates and maintains about three-fourths of the high-voltage transmission in its service territory, including Idaho, Oregon, Washington, western Montana, and parts of eastern Montana, California, Nevada, Utah, and Wyoming. Photo by Benjamin Gifford – OHS Image BB001038.

Medical biases abound and are not limited to Western medical views. They occur for many reasons, from misinterpreting data and research, repeating outdated information and concepts, or anger and fear due to discrimination. In Western medical interpretation, ignoring the role and power of whole food nutrition in health may be the single largest bias. Every year, research and clinical science open more doors to understanding the wisdom and medicine of our ancestors. The validity of cultural healing approaches from Traditional Chinese Medicine (TCM) and Ayurveda from India date back thousands of years and helped the respective cultures flourish. These cultures practiced healing arts and understood the power of food before Western civilization had coined the word science.[4] Ancient people did not need a microscope or mass spectrometer to determine what foods and herbs to eat; they learned from observation, experience, and the passing on of knowledge. The tides are turning, and those who benefit from holistic and integrative nutrition and traditional healing can receive care in the armed forces, Veterans Administration hospitals, and a growing number of clinics across the globe. This knowledge of *nature's* medicine common in my aunt Amy's childhood, almost lost, is once more being used openly by a growing number of trained wellness healthcare professionals, health coaches, massage therapists, and traditional Asian practitioners. Members of First Peoples 'nations are taking back their sacred medicine and food practices to heal the mind, body and spirit of their people.

What May Surprise You

Alcoholic drinks are in corner markets, homes, camper vans, backpacks, and in secret stashes. Alcohol remains a controversial subject for nutritionists to write about. Still, the fact remains, clinicians tell clients countless times a year to eliminate alcohol for their blood sugar, hypertension, kidney function, waistline, inflammation, and liver health, but they rarely do. I found myself wondering about all the reasons why. There are obvious historical reasons relating to its use with unsafe water, food preservation, and other culinary uses. However, the modern views on addiction do not explain the cultural demand for a

hearty ale, wee dram, or tropical drink in Margaritaville. There had to be more to this question, and I began looking into the history of spirits, beer, cider, and wine; how they affect our health, social and medical biases, and our innate desire to imbibe. The story is long and may be surprising.

Additionally, the following pages of *Our Journey with Food* will contain information from nutrition, medical, cellular biology, environmental studies, and clinical research. I have also included two new opinion research papers.

I can't imagine sharing all this information without putting it into historical context and perspective. You will learn how vital understanding history is when it comes to food and the forgotten healing properties associated with it. I will challenge your understanding of dietary programs, eating trends, recommendations, and what defines nourishment.

Our conversations will also include how food affects our culture and how we interact and view the world around us. Food and all things involved with food drive economies, politics, and beliefs.

Our search for *nourishment* continues to drive a hunger that prompts movement to new perspectives, communities, or returning to cultural foods that connect us to those who have come before us.

> ***Principle 2***: Food is foundational to culture and history, and understanding the power of food is essential to human wellness.

Introduction

It is Time for Our Journey with Food. Are you ready?

For thousands of years, food and herbs were humankind's only "medicine" sources; the volume of information lost to time on this subject is immeasurable. Hopefully, we can regain some of this lost knowledge with the aid of science, technology, and a resurgence in natural and cultural health. Food is very much a part of our history and our health.

1918 Ford Model T camper.

Not pictured: The first know motor home still in existence was built on a Model T chassis in 1914 by Dunton of Reading in the UK. It had been abandoned in the 1920s and was discovered in Shepperton, not far from downtown London in the 1970s. The custom bodywork for the camper included a big picture window and a leather sofa for the driver, polished pine floors and timbers for support, four berths, a large table, gobs of storage space including a massive wood dresser, and a wood-burning stove for cooking and heating.

"No matter what accomplishments you make, somebody helped you."

- Althea Gibson

Our Journey with Food

---

1 We Inherit More Than Just Genes, December 28, 2017: Knowridge Science Report
2 Your Diet Affects Your Grandchildren's DNA, Scientists Say by Christopher Wanjek, July 27, 2012
3 Grandma's Experiences Leave a Mark on Your Genes, June, 2015 by Dan Hurley: Discovery Magazine
4 The predominant modern use, "natural and physical science," generally restricted to study of the phenomena of the material universe and its laws, is by mid-19c. https://www.etymonline.com/word/science

> "If you are going to live, leave a legacy. Make a mark on the world that can't be erased."
>
> ~ Maya Angelou

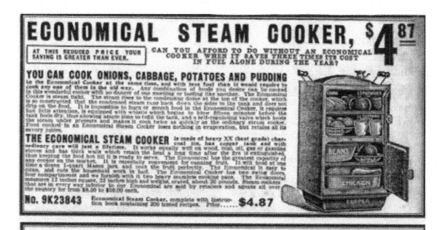

Catalogue advertisement provided by Bowman Museum Prineville, Oregon

Chapter One ~ *Peek into Food History*

In 1973, Reay Tannahill wrote a book that is still today considered one of the most comprehensive works on food history. Aptly titled *Food in History,* the book covers man's selections of foods from prehistoric to the modern age. At last, here was a book that spoke to my love of history and food. I began collecting works such as *Near a Thousand Tables: A History of Food* by Felipe Fernandez-Armesto, *Empires of Food* by Evan D.G. Fraser, and similar historical tomes. Eventually, my collection grew to included cookbooks from the mid-1800s, vintage copies of J.H. Kellogg and F.M. Pottenger, and nursing texts from the 1920s and 30s. One day I came across *The Taste of War* by Lizzie Collingham and *Botany of Desire* by Michael Pollan, and my focus changed from the past to the present.

As I read different perspectives and met more people from around the world, I realized we are all immigrants. Humankind has always traveled from the beginning of our history, following food and finding shelter. With each location and season, new skills developed, knowledge grew, and advances in all aspects occurred due to our pursuit and attainment of food. As travels took us across continents and oceans, culture developed and formed our ideas about food – now considered a *resource* – and the landscape changed with ox and plow. I learned about our ancestors 'quest for new foods, farmland, commercial enterprise, and methods of food preservation. It became clear just how much food has shaped the heritage and history of each continent. Nourishment, sustenance, food; no matter what you call it, it has been sought out by explorers long before the works of Frank N. Meyer and P.H. Dorsett coined the term *agricultural explorers* in the late 1800s.[1,2]

With no baking or business experience, Margaret Rudkin in 1937 began experimenting with preservative-free bread with all-natural ingredients for her son with allergies. By 1948, her bakery was producing 50,000 loaves a week.

In 1961, Rudkin sold the business to the Campbell Soup Company and became a member of the Board of Directors.

Rose Totino launched a frozen pizza business in 1962 just as frozen foods were gaining national prominence. Totino's sold to Pillsbury in 1975 for $22 million. Totino was named the first female vice president at Pillsbury, and she was the first woman inducted in the Frozen Food Hall of Fame.

As individuals within our countries and cultures, we are dirt farmers, ranchers, truck drivers, educators, homemakers, students, nurses, doctors, and stockbrokers, *all* living our lives and building the future because of one ingredient: the foundation of life—*food*.

Culture & Change

Many parts of the world view food as a role in healing and a source of primal nourishment. Unfortunately, most individuals living in the contemporary United States have lost sight of food's role as both medicine and a cultural treasure. The industries and *food-like* products developed in the United States are affecting global food culture and health, and not in a good way; all the more reason to look at food's history so we can protect and restore our food legacy.

An important part of history is the acknowledgment of those who changed history for the right reasons. We gain insight and perspective by remembering a small handful of innovators and influencers. Those born after World War II came into a world of speed. Trains, vehicles, and jets all set speed records. The food manufacturing industry kept pace, delivering increasingly industrially processed foods to consumers at dizzying speed. The famines of the Great Depression and wars influenced our need for more of everything. By the 1960s, food industrialists began launching frozen meals that tasted good, and drive-through restaurant franchises sprouted like weeds. Opportunities, abundance, convenience, and wealth came for those willing to take risks.

The frozen food selection went from bland vegetables to pizza and pastry through the chemical magic of edible food stabilizers thanks to two women entrepreneurs, Margaret Rudkin of Pepperidge Farms and Rose Totino, who developed frozen pizza.

These women joined Marjorie Merriweather Post in becoming the first female CEOs of multi-billion-dollar industrial food corporations in the United States. Sixty years later, in 2023, Fortune 500 companies with women CEOs account for 9%, largely through the efforts of those who risked everything to have a chair at the table.

Train transportation was still significant in the postwar era; well before Clarence Birdseye developed flash freezing and jet transport, refrigerated rail cars delivered food from far and wide to cities, increasing the feel of "modern" abundance.[3, 4] Gerry Thomas, a Swanson & Sons salesman, was traveling from Pittsburgh to Nebraska on Pan American Airways in 1950. When the stewardess served his meal, the aluminum tray sparked an idea that would become a signature of TV dinners. At the time, Pan Am was testing single-compartment foil trays used to serve warm in-flight meals to passengers. Thomas "borrowed" one of the trays, conveniently slipping it into his coat pocket. Upon returning to Pittsburg, Thomas presented plans for a three-compartment version, ensuring the peas and gravy would remain separated.[5]

Unlike older European countries still reeling from World War I and II, the United States had a surplus of industry in need of new markets. And thousands of veterans needed jobs upon returning home; jobs done only months before by women. These jobs had given women a taste of freedom, independence, and equality.[6] Politicians took steps to ensure returning male veterans had jobs with added incentives to hiring veterans[7] and removed support for women in the workplace. A cultural shift from *Rosie the Riveter* to *Mrs. Cleaver* with an apron and pearls ensued.

Magazine Ad from 1950s – Note the color choices.

Innovation and marketing grabbed our food and how we prepared meals in the 1950s. The *little woman* was back in the home where she belonged, *according to the male-dominated work world and political climate of the day*. Postwar prosperity meant manufacturers faced a growing market – one was the family household, especially kitchen appliances, which were in high demand by women. With a booming economy and demand for convenience, sales of refrigerators, freezers and appliances in feminine colors exploded. Ads for electric mixers, coffee pots, and toasters were in magazines for women, interspersed with articles on how to be a "modern wife" and recipes for entertaining your husband's boss.[8, 9]

In the 1950s, 20% of North American households had televisions. Ten years later in 1960, 86% of the population had TVs. Television brought a new opportunity for advertising firms, a way to introduce consumers to TV dinners, and the beginning of mindless eating habits as meals moved from table to *TV-tray*. Food product development and marketing became an exciting, fast-growing field, and with the move from radio to television, commercials and program sponsorship took on an active in-person feel. Programs like *I Love Lucy*, *Ed Sullivan*, *The Lone Ranger*, and *Leave it to Beaver* incorporated new products into episodes, generated millions of dollars, and swayed how Americans began to view the *modern* world including the foodstuffs we brought into our homes. The influence was so great that a well-known cartoon caricature was invented to promote a breakfast cereal on Saturday mornings – Fred Flintstone and the Flintstone cartoon show hit the air on September 30, 1960.

Invention and Innovation

Corning Ware®, the white cookware decorated with blue cornflowers, has been a fixture at family gatherings and potlucks for decades. S. Donald Stookey, the father of glass–ceramics, pioneered the understanding of internal nucleation phenomena in glass. Initially, the white ceramic, Pyroceram®, developed by CorningWare was for military applications in World War II. Don Stookey and the Corning researchers also proved the ceramic-glass was perfect for bakeware in the home after the war. This non-toxic/porous material could safely withstand sudden temperature changes, was resistant to stains and odors, and it was versatile. The same dish could be used for cooking, freezing, and serving food; a boon to cooks looking for kitchen shortcuts. In 1965, the blue and white corn flower cookware changed how we cooked once more.[10, 11]

An obscure plastic container invented in 1946 by Earl Tupper became an essential kitchen staple called Tupperware® in American kitchens in the 1950s.[12] It took a clever woman named Brownie Wise to convince Mr. Tupper that home parties would bring his product into homes faster and cheaper than typical sales options. Tupperware home sales allowed struggling homemakers to launch a home business with a product everyone could use. With an almost cult-like following, Brownie catapulted plasticware into everyday life, and the success would foster a dozen competing brands by the 21st century. No other product has been as successful as Tupperware in-home party sales during Brownie Wise's time with Tupperware. From the 1940s to the present, plastic has become a foundation of daily life; everything from storage containers and clothing to computers and jet aircraft contains or is made of plastics. It would not be until 2022 that dangers to human health from plastics, along with those associated with *forever chemicals* (endocrine systems) would be reported by researchers calling for regulatory policies.[13]

Influencers Changing Culture

Before the microwave oven became a fixture in homes in the 1960s, *The I Hate to Cook Book* impacted millions of kitchens in the United States and abroad. Peg Bracken's cookbook quickly became a staple of suburban homes, introducing prepackaged industrial food products to family meals. In her role as an editor for the New York Times, Bracken had a readymade audience to share her views on cooking. She believed ingredients should be cheap, common, convenient, ideally frozen, or tinned. Canned soups were the staple ingredient in her recipes. So were crushed cornflakes, powdered onion soup mix, and Spam®. Alcohol also had its place, though in many cases, Bracken's instructions called for it to bypass the cooking process entirely and proceed straight down the cook's throat.[14, 15]

While the intent was to market primarily to the "lower economic class" of consumers, the middle class with more disposable income bought the lion's share of processed foods.[16] Bracken's book opened the doors of home kitchens to mega-food manufacturers; Rice-a-Roni, American Cheese, and Hamburger Helper are still prevalent in stores and homes. Unfortunately, these highly refined products once used for convenience cooking are now the mainstay for college students and working families.

Most people have no idea about the food revolutions in 1960s kitchens, the opposing views of Julia Child and Adelle Davis, and the results that Bracken's quick-fix recipes had on Americans 'health.

In 1955, the Tappan Stove Company, under a licensing agreement with Raytheon, brought the first consumer microwave ovens to the U.S. market with a price tag of $1,300. In 1965, Raytheon acquired Amana Refrigerators, Inc. In 1967, it introduced to the U.S. market the first countertop model of microwave ovens (it sold for $495 retail and was smaller, safer, and more reliable than previous models). Only 1% of households in America in 1971 had a microwave; by 1986, the number had risen to 25% of U.S. households. *(Microwave Oven Regression Model, U.S. Bureau of Labor Statistics)*.[17, 18]

During this period, science and technology seemed to promise an ever more convenient, beautiful future for the denizens of post-war America. Each product was better, faster and sleeker than the last. With the increase of premade, packaged and convenience foods, and economic growth came ever-expanding landfills and islands of plastic floating in the oceans. News revealed in 2022 of microplastics in foods, water, and humans (even newborn babies), confirmed this author's opinion on plastic pollution contributing to a growing list of health problems, including sterility.[19]

KFC was incorporated in 1955. Largest QFR in 1963. Acquired by R.J. Reynolds in 1982. Pre-tax 1992 profits from international operations = $92 million; U.S. $86 million. By 1993, Asian outlets grew 30%. By 2020, KFC had 22,600 stores in 135 countries = value of $8.3 billion; and sales = $27.9

The 1970s to1990s became the age of snacking, and a new fast food and candy market erupted into one of the largest food industry sectors. Without realizing it, individuals became hooked on the easy and fast, sweet high-carb rush to the brain from highly refined food-like products. Celebrities told us what we should eat to be *trendy and sexy*. The influence on food choices came from the entertainment and marketing industries through popular TV shows and gritty movies: Star Trek, Good Morning America, Fred Flintstone, and Oprah Winfrey. Chemicals used in food manufacturing replaced recognizable food substances, creating a whole new food additive industry. Artificial sweeteners, colors and flavors, along with sugar-free and no-fat snacks, promised consumers lean trim bodies.

In thirty years, America became a culture of fast food and snacks; within 70 years, fast food and its accompanying chemicals would become a global phenomenon. By the end of the 20th century, the United States population was chronically ill and confused about food. Third-world countries fell victim to greedy international corporations, promising economic independence to women and nutrition for their children. By 2020, inner city food deserts reflected the disparity between food production/availability and meal preparation within low-income populations. Individuals no longer knew what or how to cook the foods of the past — arguably, foods that had been responsible for building a nation.

When I found *Soylent* meal replacements in the grocery store in 2020, I was stunned that anyone would think Soylent a good product name. Out of curiosity, I looked into the company founded in 2013 by a tech industry entrepreneur. The tech industry and Silicon Valley are now influencing food trends and policy. Rob Rhinehart, a soy plant-based diet proponent, felt consumers were too attached to the idea of flavor and wasted time with meal preparation. His reported view was that the role of food was to provide nutrients and that flavor had no importance; not an unusual opinion for many males in the software and gaming industry. While the company is still producing a selection of powder and premade meal replacement drinks, a string of CEOs have struggled to win over consumers who shop outside of Walmart, fast-stop markets, and 7-Elevens. Sadly, these outlets are prevalent in low-income areas and food deserts, resulting in poor quality selection of fresh and whole foods for children, teens, and adults working and living in food deserts.

In 2023 the Washington Post published an article on the role of influencers being paid by the food industry to shape eating habits. In particular the attack on the World Health Organizations positions and warning on Sucralose. [20] We will look at this study in a later chapter.

Farm to Table

National Archives Washington, D.C.

Farming has changed dramatically since the 1970s according to the latest U.S. census (2017 published in 2019) comprised of 820 pages on American agriculture.[21] A National Geographic article, *The Making of Megafarms, A Mixture of Pride and Pain*, says, "Large corn and soy farms in the Midwest may cover up to 16,000 acres, which equates to 25 square miles of farmland." At one time, dozens of smaller farms covered the same land area, and their agrarian lifestyle supported tens of families. Today, two men with seven full-time employees are doing the work that hundreds did decades ago. Those seven to ten workers plant the seeds, spread the fertilizer, and keep the irrigation water flowing. The farm managers spend as much time inside their offices monitoring crops on computers as they once did in the field, deliberating what seeds to buy, when to plant, and when to sell their harvest.

There seems to be a slight rebounding of small, family farms due to lifestyle preference of the modern *homesteader* movement, and health benefits of locally produced food. For small family-owned farms and ranches in many areas, both husband and wife hold down outside employment to make ends meet. However, a growing agricultural movement for sustainable farming reduces the dependence of small family farms on industrialized crops for food.

2017 U.S.A. Agriculture Data[22]

Of the 2.4 million farms and ranches, 76,865 made $1 million or more in 2017, representing just over 2/3 of the $389 billion in the total value of production, while the 1.56 million operations making under $50,000 represent just 2.9%.

Average farm income is $43,053. A total of 43.6% of farms had positive income in 2017.

96% of farms and ranches are family owned.

In 2017, 130,056 farms sold directly to consumers = $2.8 billion.

Military veterans = 11% of all farmers. Average age is 67.9.

36% of producers are female, and 56% of all farms have at least one female decision maker.

Hispanic, Latino, and Spanish producers = 86,278.

American Indian and Native Alaskan producers = 42,705.

Asian producers average = 15,826.

African American producer = 32,910.

Hawaiian/Pacific Islander producers = 3,018.

A Return to Farming Heritage

Every culture in the world can lay claim to farming, animal husbandry, and herding. Along with capturing fire, these pursuits are viewed as the reason for human success. Worldwide, each location and microclimate introduced humans to new foods. In 2005 a grant from Oxfam America launched the *Native American Food Sovereignty Alliance*. This program supports food sovereignty and culinary mentorship within the vast indigenous culture. According to the *United Nations Food and Agricultural Organization*, 75% of the world's food comes from approximately 12 plants and 5 animal species. [23, 24] Growing culturally diverse food crops like *Fonio*, a drought-resistant ancient grain from West Africa and *Kernza* a grain from the United States, adds to farming resiliency and protects plant diversity in the food supply. Farming today is gaining in diversity in the number of ethnically, gender, and culturally diverse growers providing *farm-to-table foods*, education and businesses. The new generation of farmers is challenging not only how food is grown but also how it is bought and sold.

While the term *organic* is relatively new regarding farming in America – as everything was organic before the *chemical* age, there were 14,093 certified organic farms and countless others listed in tilth and sustainable directories, and 8,669 registered farmers markets in 2020.[25, 26] A niche market for handmade personal and durable goods is on the rise in American culture, similar to what was seen during the Great Depression and World War II. Farmers' markets can be found from coast to coast, and whole food activists are introducing the public to healthy foods via mobile farm market vans on college campuses and turning vacant land into community gardens. The buy-local movement shows no sign of slowing. There is a push to move away from the large box stores that have overrun small local businesses. Community-supported agriculture (CSA) programs are thriving in many areas. The direct-to-consumer CSA model shortens the distance, both geographically and personally, between growers and consumers, ensuring higher quality and safer foods for individuals.

People are also learning how to prepare and preserve their homegrown produce. Canning, fermenting, and other food preservation methods are returning in American kitchens. The era of the "prepper" impacts the economy in many Pacific Northwest communities. To learn more read *Our Journey with Food Cookery Book* Chapter 2 *the Pantry*.

Politics and Food

When we look back at the food history of legislation and agriculture, we gain insight into how we have gotten into the mess we are in today. The adage, *good intentions pave the way to hell,* aptly describes American Food Policy. The implementation of the Pure Food and Drug Act of 1906 made it illegal to sell products doctored with toxic chemicals. [27] John McMonigle and Charles Wille served one year in Leavenworth Prison, in 1886 and 1915, respectively, for the crime of selling margarine, or oleo recorded as *crimes against butter*. American dairy farmers quickly demanded protection from imitation butter in the late 1880s when margarine began affecting market sales.

This resulted in raising margarine's price through taxes and licensing fees. Amendments to the Margarin Act of 1886 taxed colored margarine at an even higher rate. Public outcry against margarine taxes mounted as the supply of butter dwindled during and after World War II and federal margarine taxes were repealed in 1950.[28] In today's world there are dozens of margarine products for consumers to buy, yet at the turn of the 20th century, it was considered a health hazard. This opinion has been proven by the second decade of the 21st century. Research has shown that refined plant oils in the form of margarine are linked to inflammation and chronic illnesses, consequently natural unrefined fats and oils are increasing in popularity.[29]

The Hatch Act of 1887 was designed to "sow the seeds of creativity in every state" through land grants and research stations dedicated to improving agricultural and food production methods. In a way, it was a success—but not without a cost.

Solely in terms of productivity and efficiency, a cumulative increase in the use of chemical fertilizers, herbicides, and pesticides makes perfect sense. The ensuing loss of thousands of drought/cold resistant and heritage foods belonging to a 12,000-year-old food legacy for humans was not taken into consideration. These valuable heritage plants and their seeds are vital in preserving gastronomy, the health of our human genetics, and the environment we all live in. To name the obvious, countless varieties of cabbage, corn, wheat, and greens that do not require tons of chemicals, water or genetic modification (GMO) to grow.[30]

Subsequent agricultural bills passed in the 1930s helped regulate supply and demand.[31] The race for bigger, faster and better production has moved beyond the application of chemicals into the realm of altering the genetic code of living organisms. Multi-billion-dollar agribusinesses such as Bayer/Monsanto®, Eli Lilly®, ConAgra® and Cargill® are actively researching genetic modification and

CRISPR editing of food crops and livestock including splicing dog DNA into corn and cholera DNA into potatoes.[32]

Too bad the Pure Food and Drug Act of 1906 [33, 34] has been buried in a quicksand of time, politics and "progress." Undoubtedly, the writers of that bill would balk at the number of chemicals — many with little to no safety data — being introduced into our food supply. While large corporate mega-giants are without a doubt "doing what it takes" to make billions, consumer responsibility also plays a role in deciding what's found on our grocery store shelves.

The Internet has made it possible for activists and average citizens critical of GMOs and industrial-chemical farming methods to rally millions of supporters to their cause. However, these rally cries are not always supported by unbiased or factual information. As an author researching and fact-checking claims, I have learned social media is a poor substitute for reading statements in valid context. Social media, podcasts and blogs can also prove to be a fertile field for frauds and charlatans hawking the next *miracle* cure or diet. The mantle of due diligence ultimately resides on the shoulders of the consumer.

Library of Congress ~ Political cartoon, The World evening (New York, N.Y.) June 9, 1906, Final Results Edition, Page 3, Image 3. Chronicling America.

Principle 3: Informed consumerism is the responsibility of the individual; reliance on government agencies, news sources or social media for reliable information is fraught with bias.

Responsibility

Keep in mind efforts to combat obesity, diabetes, and other health conditions can be a threat to businesses that produce and sell food: If people eat less, profits will decline. Because the food industry can't appear to be nonresponsive to what has been termed a public health crisis, it employs several tactics to maintain legitimacy and position itself as "part of the solution" while also protecting profits. Food companies tend to frame obesity as solely the consequence of people's choices rather than the choices they are being offered, say researchers at George Washington University. [35] Buzzwords like *antioxidant*, *gluten-free* and *whole grain* deceive consumers into thinking food products are healthier than they actually are, according to a new research study – a *false sense of health* and failure to understand the information presented in nutrition facts panels may contribute to the obesity epidemic in the United States, say researchers at the University of Houston. [36]

Historical Perspective

National Archives, Washington, D.C.

In 1894, *Farmer's Bulletin* promoted the USDA's first food recommendations. The suggestions were for men and focused on carbohydrates, protein, fat, and minerals. In 1916, a nutritionist, Caroline Hunt wrote the first USDA food guide, *Food for Young Children*. Then *How to Select Foods* USDA guidelines, introduced 5 food groups – successfully targeting the issue of gross malnutrition in the United States.

Victory Gardens were an essential part of the war effort in 1917, similarly, during the Great Depression and circa 1942. Every household was expected to plant a garden to keep food on the table and support the troops. The home farm extension program provided free seeds to families who couldn't buy them.

In 1943, the USDA updated its guidelines to the "Basic 7," a noble attempt at food grouping by micronutrients; food science was still in its infancy. The second Food Recommendation Chart to be published by the USDA was in 1945, the precursor to today's food guides. Food guidelines made their next transformation in 1992 when foods were grouped by protein, dairy, grain, fruits/vegetables. The Food Wheel (1984) followed and was a collaboration between the American Red Cross and the USDA. The Food Wheel was the basis for the Food Pyramid (1992-2011) that followed and the My Plate (2011). The 2015-2020 Dietary Guidelines for America are a shift back to the micronutrient model and will be looked at more in Chapter 3. [37]

Chapter 1 ~ Peek into Food History

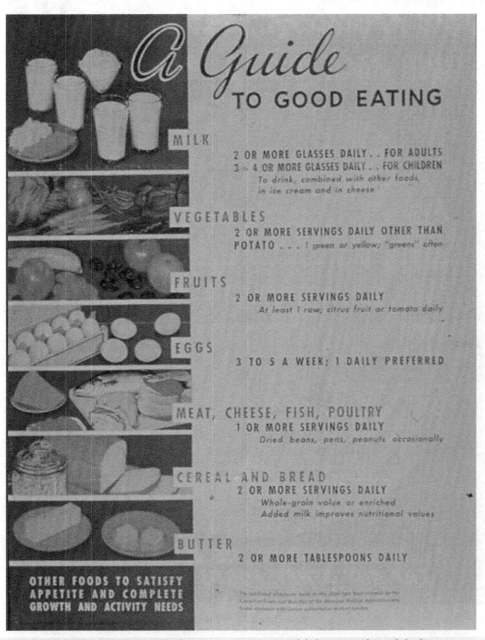

Basic 7 Food Guide 1943 was the first government suggested daily servings for each food group.
Source: National Agricultural Library, Agricultural Research Service, U.S. Department of Agriculture

Basic 7 Food Guide 1945
Source: National Agricultural Library, Agricultural Research Service, U.S. Department of Agriculture

Chapter 1 ~ Peek into Food History

Photo of a kitchen in an upscale home in Oregon City, Oregon, circa 1900. Due to Oregon Falls on the Willamette River and the hydroelectric plant established in the 1800s, Oregon City was the first area to transmit commercial electricity in the United States (in 1889, to Portland, Oregon).

Oregon City was established in 1842 by Dr. John McLoughlin, the "Father of the Oregon Territory"
Historical Photograph print by Alex Blendl).

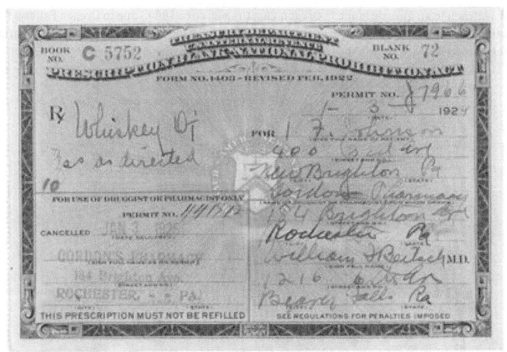

During prohibition, two classes of alcohol were still legally permitted: sacramental and medicinal. According to Sections 6 of the Volstead Act, a person may, without a permit, purchase and use liquor for medicinal purposes when prescribed by a physician as herein provided. The 1920s were still the era when alcohol could be taken "medicinally," in 1917 the American Medical Association had taken alcohol off the list of permitted medical therapies. By 1922, two years into the 13-year dry spell of Prohibition, the AMA changed its mind, and booze was back on the prescription pad.

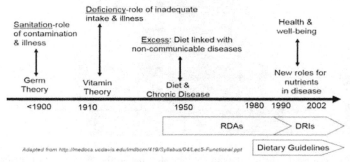

Public health messages in the United States during the 20th century can be divided into two general categories. The policies and nutrition research of the first half of the 20th century (1900-1950) was focused on deficiency of nutrients. Research and public health policies in the second half of the 20th century (1950 - 2000) began to focus on the role of diet in chronic disease. In particular, the focus was on excessive, rather than inadequate, dietary intake.

Chapter 1 ~ Peek into Food History

Christmas, 1930 – children eating homemade bread, boiled turnips, and cabbage. The Great Depression pushed many to the brink of starvation; home gardens provided the poor in rural areas with higher quality food than those in cities. Whenever I ask older clients who grew up in America's rural areas in the 1930s and 1940s about food, they all respond, "We were poor but never went hungry."

Sample School Lunch Menu 1936

THE SCHOOL LUNCH

With very simple equipment and limited assistance for preparation and service, it is possible to provide a school-lunch menu consisting of one nourishing and appetizing hot dish, a glass or two of milk, a fruit or tomatoes or some uncooked vegetable, and bread and butter or sandwiches. With more equipment, the lunch can be improved by adding a choice of main dishes, or expanding the menu in other ways. Day-to-day planning can be done to best advantage from the standpoint of nutrition if the teacher or lunch director knows something about the kind of meals the children get at home, and whether there are deficiencies in their usual diet. With this knowledge, the school lunch can be made to safeguard the children's health by providing the kind of foods most needed to make up an adequate diet.

Another safeguard is to plan lunches far enough ahead to make sure that the main dishes of any given week are sufficiently varied to include, all told, all the kinds of food essential for good nutrition—as listed just above. This precaution is good practice in general, but is especially helpful to children whose meals at home may not supply enough of some essential food constituent. Posting the menu a day or two in advance also helps the children who bring a part of their lunch from home, because their mothers can then plan better to supplement what the children get at school.

MAIN DISHES

The food value of any dish depends, of course, upon the ingredients and the method of preparation. The main dish should always be nourishing and appetizing. Creamed vegetables, meat and vegetable stews, nourishing soups rich in vegetables or milk or both, beans or peas of some kind, eggs prepared in some simple way, cheese prepared in white sauce or with tomatoes, and scalloped dishes

Our Journey with Food

In the 1930s, the Civilian Conservation Corps (CCC) built roads, trails, and buildings all over the nation. Our national parks all benefited from these young men and their labors. This civilian army had to be fed. But the food that fueled this labor-intensive work was not modern institutional food. Companies like Kellogg's provided the CCC with tin boxes filled with recipes and menus for every day of the week. Foods were purchased in nearby communities to use in the recipes.

Tennessee CCC menu February 3, 1937[38]

Breakfast: Stewed Peaches - Boiled Rice - Fresh Milk - Hot Biscuits - Fried Bacon - Scrambled Eggs - Coffee

Lunch: Macaroni & Cheese - Cold Tomatoes - Lima Beans - Fried Cabbage - Dried Peach Cobbler - Coffee

Supper: Fried Beef Steak - Brown Gravy - Fried Eggplant - Green Beans - Cream Cauliflower - Butter & Jam with Bread

Chapter 1 ~ Peek into Food History

In 1940, brothers Richard and Maurice McDonald opened their first restaurant in San Bernardino, California.[39] Fast food chain restaurants like McDonald's started becoming prevalent in the 1960s. One of the first Ronald McDonald clown mascots was designed in 1963. Ray Kroc later took the franchise global; today, there are more than 40,000 locations worldwide.

The fast-food industry is the most heavily advertised sector of the U.S. economy, spending over $4.6 billion in 2012.[40] A 2013 AdAge compilation of the 25 largest U.S. advertisers ranked McDonald's as the fourth largest advertiser, spending $957,000,000 globally.[41] In 2023, McDonald's increased its marketing budget to $1.1 billion.

Fast-food restaurants spent $5 billion on advertising in 2019, a 9% increase from 2012, with preschoolers, children, and teens viewing an average of 2.1 to 2.3 fast-food TV ads per day. 63% of fast-food restaurants in the US use social media for promotional purposes. In the US alone, over 40 million customers visit Taco Bell every week and sales for the company were $13.28 billion in 2021.

In 2021, Domino's Pizza became the biggest spender on advertising in the United States, reaching $510 million, outspending McDonald's in the same advertising sector. Fast food TV ads disproportionately target Black and Hispanic youth. Black youth view 75% more fast food TV ads than their White peers. Ads targeting Hispanics significantly increase their interest in purchasing products. Spanish language TV ads increased 33%.[42]

As of 2022, McDonald's has 13,500 locations in 118 countries including the U.S. and is the most profitable fast-food restaurant in the world, with nationwide sales of $46.0 billion. Starbucks comes in second at $24 billion, Chick-fil-A at $16.7 billion, and Taco Bell in fourth place with $12.6 billion. As of June 2022, the fast-food industry was worth $331.4 billion, roughly 1/3 of the global market. Every day advertisers place colorful images and messages in front of consumers to entice them to buy.

In the 1950s, women had been shoved back into the home after working in a wide variety of jobs during World War II. Following the war, women were expected to look beautiful and have the kiddies all clean and well-behaved with a delicious meal waiting when the men arrived home after work.

Advertisers soon saw an opportunity to meet the growing demand of American women for easier and more convenient pre-made foods. The postwar economic boom was a perfect time to change American's ideas about food, science, and health.

Magazine ad for Swanson TV Diners 1950

7UP ad 1950 & 1955 - Women's Home Journal

March 1951 Women's Home Companion

7-Up was created in 1929 and contained *lithium citrate,* giving the drinker a mental lift. The U.S. Food and Drug Administration banned the use of lithium in beer and soft drinks in 1948, and 7-Up was reformulated two years later.

West Bend Aluminum Company is one of the oldest appliance manufacturers in America, founded in 1911. To learn more about aluminum cookware see *Our Journey with Food Cookery Book.* The *Women's Home Journal* circa. 1958 ad to the left is an example of colorful marketing to grab the reader's visual focus.

Women's Home Journal 1958

Chapter 1 ~ Peek into Food History

November 10, 1940. Mrs. Ella Worthington (left), champion cranberry picker of the peninsula in Pacific County, Washington, and Mrs. Joe Weisner display measures of cranberries. Mrs. Worthington averages 20 measures a day.
– OHS Image bb012654

Lucille Stewart, Port Adams Packing Company Newport, OR. Packing first of the season Dungeness crab at Yaquina Bay packing plant. December 1, 1963

– OHS Image bb012650

Verboort Sausage Festival, Woodburn, OR October 1962.
Packing Cabbage – OHS Image bb12658

Our Journey with Food

In the 1950s, Julia Child splashed onto the global culinary scene and radically changed how American women entertained and cooked. In 1963, this remarkable lady took over TV sets with the first of many cooking shows. In 1966, Julia Child won a Primetime Emmy Award for "Achievement in Educational Television" for *The French Chef*, becoming the first educational television personality to receive an Emmy in an open competition. She cooked pasta for Mr. Rogers in 1974. Her energetic and free spirit laid the foundation for today's cooking programs, networks, websites, bloggers, and authors.

Photo American History Museum Smithsonian, Washington D.C

James Beard, born in Portland, Oregon, in 1903, was a dear friend and cooking companion of Julia Child. James never called himself a chef even though he was instrumental in training some of the most famous chefs in America. Anointed the "Dean of American cookery" by the New York Times in 1954, James Beard laid the groundwork for the food revolution that put America at the forefront of global gastronomy. He was a pioneer *foodie* and host of the first food program on the fledgling medium of television in 1946. In 1955, Beard established the James Beard Cooking School. He continued to teach cooking to men and women for the next 30 years at his schools in New York City and Seaside, Oregon.[43]

US Postal Service Forever Stamps
Released in 2014
Authors Collection

In 2022 and 2023 Sean Sherman – *The Sioux Chef* became the first Native American to win the James Beard and Julia Child Awards. Chef Sean Sherman focuses on the revitalization and evolution of Indigenous foods systems throughout North America. Through his activism and advocacy, Sean is helping to reclaim and celebrate the rich culinary heritage of Indigenous communities around the world.

Photo Credit: Nancy Bundt

Chapter 1 ~ Peek into Food History

By the 1970s, magazines were filled with ads for processed foods like Cheeze Whiz®, Nutella®, Coke®, Hungry Man®, Denty Moore®, and the biggest advertiser by far, McDonald's®.

Slogans like "Kentucky Fried Chicken makes everyday Mother's Day," "Cheetos, a Wealth of Real Cheese Taste," "Sugar Keeps Your Energy Up and Your Weight Down," and New Irish Mocha Mint "Lucky us" from International Coffees®, a General Mills product, accompanied eye-catching ads providing enticement with words and images.

Fast-Food Industry Era – 1960 to present

Franchise fast food has been part of the landscape my entire life, as is the case for many. Kentucky Fried Chicken and Popeyes were regional "quick service" restaurants (QSR) until the beef shortages of the 1970s.

Within 20 years, franchise QSR took over the world. Taco Bell, Little Caesars, and Domino's Pizza sprang up in the Midwest as entrepreneurial college students with no culinary training changed how Americans ate; and unknowingly launched a health pandemic that would exceed $237 billion per year in direct medical costs with another $90 billion lost on reduced productivity.[44] The total consumer spending in the QSR sector in the United States was $304.8 billion in 2021, up from the previous year's total of $272 billion.[45]

The plant-based meals market reached $29.4 million in 2020. Plant-based protein is projected to increase by 7.7% globally by 2030, with a value of $162 billion. Digital ordering of fast foods took off with the COVID pandemic, a 67% increase that will likely triple in 2023.

More Disturbing Statistics Emerged in 2022

The most frequently advertised food and beverage category to children and teens is fast food, representing 40% of all youth-directed food marketing expenditures.

In 2019, Black preschoolers, children, and teens watched 75% more fast-food advertisements on TV than White children and teens.

Those exposed to food advertising chose 28% more unhealthy snacks than those exposed to non-food advertising.

Kids watching educational YouTube videos are under the more subliminal impact of ads using M&Ms and Coke bottles to teach counting.[46]

With a global fast food market expected to reach $931.7 billion by 2027, it isn't a surprise that over 50 million Americans are consuming fast food.

These economic numbers would be unimaginable to my parents and in-laws, who were depression-era babies.

> ***Principle 4:*** The priority of food manufacturers and marketing is growth; market share and profit, not health or equity. Due diligence is the consumers' responsibility.

---

1 Dorsett-Morse Oriental Agricultural Exploration Expedition Collection; USDA National Agricultural Library: https://www.nal.usda.gov/exhibits/speccoll/collections/show/12

Chapter 1 ~ Peek into Food History

2. Dorsett-Morse Oriental Agricultural Exploration Expedition Collection; https://www.nal.usda.gov/collections/special-collections/dorsett-morse-oriental-agricultural-exploration-expedition-collection
3. Inland Northwest Rail Museum, Reardan Washington
4. Western Union Railroad Museum in Portola California
5. Biakolo, K., (2020) A Brief History of the TV Dinner, Smithsonian Magazine: https://www.smithsonianmag.com/arts-culture/brief-history-tv-dinner-180976039/
6. "Interventions, Social Policy ." International Encyclopedia of the Social Sciences. . Retrieved March 20, 2023 from Encyclopedia.com: https://www.encyclopedia.com/social-sciences/applied-and-social-sciences-magazines/interventions-social-policy
7. "Government, Federal ." International Encyclopedia of the Social Sciences. Retrieved March 20, 2023 from Encyclopedia.com: https://www.encyclopedia.com/social-sciences/applied-and-social-sciences-magazines/government-federal
8. The American Magazine – New York, NY 1952, 1953
9. Good Housekeeping Vol. 134 January – June 1952
10. Beall, G. H. (2016). Dr. S. Donald (Don) Stookey (1915–2014): Pioneering Researcher and Adventurer. Frontiers in Materials, 3. https://doi.org/10.3389/fmats.2016.00037
11. CorningWare Casserole Dish; National Museum of American History: https://americanhistory.si.edu/collections/search/object/nmah_1425270
12. Blakemore, E., (2019) History Chanel; Tupperware Parties: Suburban Women's Plastic Path to Empowerment; https://www.history.com/news/tupperware-parties-brownie-wise
13. Plastics pose threat to human health, December 15, 2020; Endocrine Society press release: https://www.endocrine.org/news-and-advocacy/news-room/2020/plastics-pose-threat-to-human-health
14. Bracken, P., (1960) The I Hate To Cook Book; Harcourt, Brace and Company Library of Congress # 60-10919
15. http://www.nytimes.com/2007/10/23/arts/23bracken.html?_r=0
16. Food Fights Culture and War by Tom Nealon, 2016 ISBN # 978 1 4683 14410 0
17. http://www.bls.gov/cpi/cpimwo.htm
18. http://www.bls.gov/cpi/cpimwo.htm_truncated
19. Karr, T., Bell, K., (2020); Summerland, Empty Plate: Food-Sustainability-Mindfulness
20. https://www.washingtonpost.com/wellness/2023/09/13/dietitian-instagram-tiktok-paid-food-industry/
21. Census of Agriculture, USDA (2017) http://www.agcensus.usda.gov/
22. 2017 Census of Agriculture Data Now Available, USDA released April 2019: https://www.usda.gov/media/press-releases/2019/04/11/2017-census-agriculture-data-now-available
23. Pollinators vital to our food supply under threat (2019); Food and Agriculture Organization of the United Nations: https://www.fao.org/news/story/en/item/384726/icode/
24. UN Biodiversity Convention partners with Slow Food International in celebrating the International Day for Biological Diversity, (2019): https://www.cbd.int/doc/press/2019/pr-2019-05-22-idb-en.pdf
25. https://www.wsj.com/articles/the-transformation-of-the-american-farm-in-18-charts-1514474480?mod=e2fb
26. USDA Census of Agriculture. https://www.agcensus.usda.gov/Publications/Local_Food/index.php
27. What's Cooking Uncle Sam? Records from the National Archives pg. 28
28. What's Cooking Uncle Sam? Records from the National Archives pg. 13
29. Research and Markets (2021) Worldwide Animal and Marine Fats and Oils Industry to 2026- Featuring Darling Ingredients, Tallow Products & York Foods Among Others: https://www.globenewswire.com/news-release/2021/10/21/2318024/28124/en/Worldwide-Animal-and-Marine-Fats-and-Oils-Industry-to-2026-Featuring-Darling-Ingredients-Tallow-Products-York-Foods-Among-Others.html
30. Seed; The Untold Story – Botanical Explorer, Independent Lens April 17, 2017
31. Agricultural Adjustment Act 1933
32. CRISPR in Livestock and Food Safety: Beyond Genome Editing (2022): https://www.beefresearch.org/resources/beef-safety/fact-sheets/crispr-in-livestock-and-food-safety-beyond-genome-editing
33. http://www.loc.gov/rr/news/topics/purefood.html
34. http://www.encyclopedia.com/topic/Food_and_Drug_Act_of_1906.aspx
35. George Washington University. "Is the food industry really concerned with obesity? If people eat less, profits will decline." ScienceDaily. ScienceDaily, 2 June 2014. www.sciencedaily.com/releases/2014/06/140602150703.htm.
36. University of Houston. "How food marketing creates false sense of health." ScienceDaily. ScienceDaily, 13 June 2014. www.sciencedaily.com/releases/2014/06/140613130717.htm.
37. https://www.cnpp.usda.gov/dietary-guidelines
38. "Favorite Recipes of the United States Conservation Corps 1933-1942" (Spiral-bound)
39. TIME Dec 29, 2014: 2015 The Year Ahead, pg 112
40. Fast Food Marketing Ranking Tables 2012-2013. Yale. Retrieved January 25, 2014
41. Meet America's 25 biggest advertisers. AdAge. Retrieved July 8, 2013

42 Yaqub, M. (2022), 10 Craving Fast Food Advertising Statistics to Understand the Food Advertising Industry; https://www.businessdit.com/junk-food-advertising-statistics/
43 https://www.jamesbeard.org/about/james-beard
44 CDC Health and Economic Benefits of Diabetes Interventions: https://www.cdc.gov/chronicdisease/programs-impact/pop/diabetes.htm
45 Fast food restaurants in the U.S.- statistics & facts: https://www.statista.com/topics/863/fast-food/
46 Yaqub, M. (2022), 10 Craving Fast Food Advertising Statistics to Understand the Food Advertising Industry; https://www.businessdit.com/junk-food-advertising-statistics/

> "Legacy is not leaving something for people. It's leaving something in people."
>
> ~ Peter Strople

Celebrating Nutrition at the NANP Conference 2017, Portland, Oregon

Dr. Janet Ludwig, Julie Thenell, Dr. Sarica Cernohous, Dr. Tammera and CC Raeside

Chapter Two ~ Paradigm Shift: Wellness Care

The 21st century began with a resistive reaction within the medical establishment to a growing grassroots movement of changing health practices among many Americans; headlines for everything from nutrition to vampire movies contained holistic as the catchword. Many of my clients felt they couldn't honestly share information about their herbs, supplements, diet, or lifestyle with their primary care provider due to fear of ridicule. Although it felt wonderful when they openly expressed their trust in my recommendations, using natural remedies can place holistic providers in opposition to Western evidence-based pharmaceutically oriented healthcare. How individuals view healthcare relates to their belief system, culture, and lifestyle. Relabeling treatment recommendations with adjectives such as Alternative, Integrative, Functional, Ancestral, and Wisdom may be trendy, but is it accurate or ethical for wellness approaches including herbalism, nutrition, health coaching, acupuncture or Ayurvedic?

Semantics

Andrew Weil, MD, has been a modern influencer of healthcare and acceptance of mainstream *Biomedicine*.[1] Before Biomedicine replaced traditional Western medicine (the term used in mainstream healthcare), the descriptors *traditional, allopathic*, and *Western* medicine were used to distinguish alternatives from mainstream medicine. Biomedicine, in 2023, is the hypothetical umbrella term covering most health science, education, training, and technology in academic and government settings. Biomedicine, however, does not capture the cultural and historical value of *wellness management* through mind-body approaches from India, China, Native American, and Western/holistic herbology. These views can be seen as stand-alone approaches to health care within the perspectives of their various cultures.[2, 3, 4, 5]

In 2022, the World Health Organization (WHO) set up a *Global Centre for Traditional Medicine* in Jamnagar, India and in 2019 included some traditional medicines in its *International Classification of Diseases-11*, a compendium used by doctors to diagnose medical conditions. In the summer of 2023, the WHO convened its first summit dedicated to traditional medicine.

> "With billions of people already using traditional medicines, the organization needs to explore how to integrate them into conventional healthcare and collaborate scientifically to understand their use more thoroughly. Currently, the WHO considers traditional and complementary medicines to include disciplines as wide-ranging as Ayurveda, yoga, homeopathy, and complementary therapies.
>
> "For some people in some countries, it's their only source of interventions or services for health and well-being," says Shyama Kuruvilla, WHO lead for the *Global Centre for Traditional Medicine*.
>
> "A lot has changed over the past 15 years," says Lisa Susan Wieland, director of *Cochrane Complementary Medicine at the University of Maryland School of Medicine in Baltimore*. "Where there was previously insufficient good-quality research to determine what does and doesn't work, we are now seeing more and better research on some traditional medicine," she says.[6]

It is critical to carefully address health's social and environmental determinants beyond conventional notions of healthcare limited to sick care. The *Shanghai Declaration 2016* and WHO *Traditional Medicine Strategy* acknowledge the growing importance of Indigenous Knowledge (IK) and Cultural Traditional Medicine (CTM) in advancing health goals. There is a growing consensus to decolonize the restrictive idea of IK/CTM and expand its vision to include traditional, complementary, and integrative medicine and health systems. As the WHO recognizes the value and diversity of the cultures of Indigenous Peoples and local communities, along with their traditional knowledge, modern medicine will face growing changes in how it approaches research and patient care.[7]

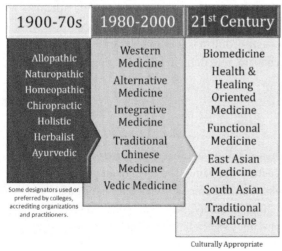

Indigenous and Cultural Traditional Medicine focuses on prevention and lifestyle interventions as part of the WHO-established health equity targets. Herbal medicine, fasting, forest and nature-based therapies, and practices like yoga, tai chi, qigong, and mindfulness meditation have been used for centuries to strengthen the body's resistance and enhance resilience. Prioritizing prevention empowers healthy living, good nutrition, coping with stress-reducing chronic diseases, and enhancing well-being. In contrast to the typically reductionist approach of conventional medicine, indigenous and cultural medicine emphasizes the interconnectedness of mind, body, and spirit, considering the relationship between the planetary environment and the social and political systems in which we live.

The words we use are critical to how we interact in healthcare; they influence the "feel" of any given situation and affect the degree of trust in the information being presented. The questions asked of us and by us during client interactions either facilitate an open and collaborative client experience or a frustrating and failed encounter. The client's culture and location must play a central role in how clinicians, nurses, acupuncturists, massage therapists, health coaches, and nutritionists convey information.

Cultural sensitivity was not a consideration in the 1800s or 1900s when a patient entered a doctor's office or a hospital. The perspectives and beliefs of my great grandparents and parents, accepted in their day, may be viewed today as biased, even racist. A downside to working with older clients is the lack of shared life experiences and perspectives that aid in communication. Equally, working with clients from different countries can bring communication challenges due to language and cultural differences. How my German client poses a question differs from my student from India, not only because of the language but also the syntax and context. My perspective on diet and lifestyle may be vastly different from theirs. For example, fast food is pervasive in America but not as much in Germany or India. When we allow clients to share their perspectives, communication becomes collaborative. The volume of information I have learned teaching students from many countries and cultures has broadened my understanding of nutrition and how food connects us all.

> ***Principle 5***: "There is a deep yearning for a human (whole) approach to medicine."   ~Bill Moyers

Should Labels be Used as Descriptors

During the years of my education, being in private practice, and later as an instructor, the names and ways of referring to ideas, symptomology, and clients have evolved. This evolution has included a growing, albeit slow, acceptance of natural medicine and traditional health practices. As is often the case, changes are initially imperfect, and new terminology sometimes adds to confusion and communication challenges. Trying to keep up with the appropriate terminology of the day can be frustrating for both the client and the provider.

Throughout this updated and revised edition of *Our Journey with Food*, my contributors and I have endeavored to use descriptors that respect culture, community, and gender. While including historical information has not always been easy, the question arises: "*Do you change historical context language, or do you represent historical information intact according to its timeline?*" After much thoughtful consideration and consultation with individuals of varying ages, backgrounds, and ethnicities, I decided to represent historical information as it is found. While it may be filled with biases, it also represents the perspective of another time and place, without which continued growth in understanding, meaning, and perspective cannot happen.

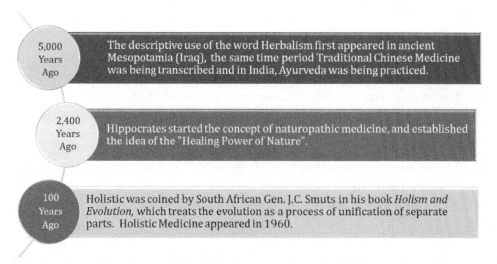

Here is an example: Jethro Kloss, Weston A. Price, and Frances Pottenger are major influencers of the natural health movements in North America and Europe. They were also educated Protestant White males of a modest to wealthy socioeconomic status. When I read their original works, as an educated woman in 2023, it is with great difficulty. Today, I can see the injustice of their views. However, when I approach the writings from a broader historical perspective, I see the groundbreaking science and vision of the authors. This does not justify their views; it is simply personal insight allowing differing perspectives. Learning in this way, it is my hope that healing science can move forward. There are many views of the past as seen by multiple cultures that are exclusive, abusive, racist and — *in my own view* — just plain wrong.

Eugenics permeates Western medical standards, contributing to implicit biases in 2023.[8, 9, 10, 11] Scholars believe Plato was the first person to promote the idea of eugenics, but it wasn't until Sir Frances Galton coined the word and concept in his book *Inquiries into Human Faculty and its Development* in 1883 that it caught fire in the minds of 19th century influencers. Now the part that has been removed from history so as not to offend: "Eugenics encouraged people of so-called healthy, "superior" stock to reproduce and discouraged reproduction of the physically or mentally challenged—or anyone who fell outside the social norm. Eugenics was popular in America during much of the first half of the twentieth century. Adolf Hitler embraced eugenics and orchestrated its use to create an advanced Aryan race." [12]

Eugenic views and connections within North American and European governments, religions, education, and medicine,[13] have resulted in crimes and unjust biases against a great many people, which laid the foundation for the mistrust of vaccines, drugs, medical intervention, social services, and other treatments in use in 2023.

To Understand You Must Learn Perspective

By the beginning of the COVID pandemic in 2020, cultural sensitivity was influencing how healthcare providers referred to themselves and their services. Research conducted during this time began illuminating healthcare disparities amongst Indians of the Americas, Latin Americans, African Americans, older adults, and women.[14]

A study from the University of Miami in 2020 revealed that when a physician or provider is the same culture as the client, anxiety and pain are reduced, especially in Black populations.[15, 16] A growing number of studies are showing a level of *implicit bias*[17] and lack of diversity in healthcare, resulting in individuals either not getting care or seeking out other options. This bias does not come without risk. If providers or their employing healthcare systems are influenced by unscrupulous marketers, social posts, or incomplete/outdated information, clients can find themselves in a dangerous situation. Such situations include physical impossibility for clients to reach care and/or fill prescriptions or clients cutting their medication dosages so they last longer. People with diabetes need wounds checked and cared for to prevent amputations, especially in the aging population. I cannot stress the importance of evidence-informed practices, continuing education requirements, and certifications to protect clients and holistic/integrative care providers.

> ***Principle 6***: The boundaries between conventional biomedicine and alternative health and wellness therapies are imprecise and continually changing.

Change Brings Empowerment

Achieving health involves more than taking a pill, eating a particular diet, or having lab tests done. To develop sustainable health, individuals have to change. Changes can include any number of habits, views or biases as well as overcoming barriers that interfere with wellness.

Functional MRI research has shown a strong connection between speakers' and listeners' brains that vanishes when communication is poor. In good communication, the listener can anticipate what will be communicated before speech is produced, resulting in greater understanding.[18, 19]

The energetic connection visible through the use of technology during storytelling or when having personal conversations does not end with neurological function. Researchers in 2021 shared a four-stage study that showed individuals unconsciously synchronize body functions as well. Today neuroscience is experiencing a paradigm shift regarding our previous understanding of the brain as only one part of the physical body. Continued research is important for increased understanding about the mind-body connection, mindfulness, and looking more broadly at how the brain-mind-body relationship affects every aspect of wellness.[20]

> ***Principle 7***: Being open to sharing perspectives and beliefs can create collaborative relationships and improve communication.

The Wellness Paradigm

Each person is unique, the sum of many parts, contributed by inner and outer influences. Our unique environment is made up of many influences: the world around us, culture, the home, and our internal sense of self. When our personal environment changes, it can bring growth or create turmoil that erodes our well-being.

The personal environment directly affects the choices we make about nutrition and diet. Some of our diet choices are based on cultural foods, others on trends and popularity. Ideally, they should be chosen because of how they foster wellness. We feel bright and alive when we consume foods that nourish us on a cellular level. From our personal environment springs forth lifestyle and movement. Lifestyle is made up of choices that support health and well-being. Movement springs from lifestyle. When you feel good it is natural to move. Movement supports detoxification along with mental and physical wellness.

Our personal environment also is home to our beliefs, which influence the ability to be mindful. The choice to be mindful involves action. When we consciously choose organic or locally produced foods, it involves developing a habit that forms a lifestyle component. The beliefs we hold can support or damage wellness. Research has shown those with a belief system have better mental and physical health and a sense of wellness. This sense of wellness builds resiliency that supports individuals during periods of heightened stress.[21]

> ***Principle 8***: Food connects us all.

Good relationships and healthy communication can support and bind us, while toxic interactions can equally damage and tear us down. When relationships are supportive, individuals have improved well-being resulting in meaningful longevity. To have supportive relationships, there must be communication stemming from shared experiences or beliefs. When positive, the exchange verbally and physically through body language and facial cues releases a wave of feel-good neurotransmitters in the brain that signal countless interconnected systems within the body. These systems govern immune functions and are used by the microbiome to disseminate nourishment so the digestive system can transport it into the bloodstream for cellular uptake.[22] This biochemical cycle of release and uptake brings the personal wellness environment into balance, allowing critical functions to come full circle in order to maintain and support homeostasis — the body's dynamic dance of balance — all over again.

In 2020, Kathleen Bell and I wrote *Empty Plate: Food~Sustainability~Mindfulness*, where we dove deeply into such topics as how food insecurity directly influences morbidity due to multiple causes, the mind-body connection, and what constitutes a wellness lifestyle. Our work led us to a personal shift in perspective; increasing our awareness and understanding of what constitutes nourishment, and that it goes far beyond only the calories from food.

> ***Principle 9:*** Health-related changes in lifestyle are made incrementally. Results are seen if new behaviors are sustained over time.

A study released in mid-2023 opened our awareness to a new term – *food swamp*. This study from the U.S. looked at how food inequities across the country translate to increased risks of dying from obesity-related cancers, such as breast, bowel, and liver cancer. The term *food deserts* was coined in the early 1990s and some have questioned the accuracy of this theory. The 2023 study confirmed wealthy, White neighborhoods in the U.S. average three to four more supermarkets over poor, Black suburbs – limiting the latter's choice of affordable fresh food, especially if public transit is lacking. But when fruits and vegetables are made available in local stores, real-world studies show residents are quick to pick them up.[23] Additionally, studies have found that urban residents who purchase groceries at small neighborhood stores pay between 3-37% more than suburbanites buying the same products at supermarkets.[24] *Food swamps* were defined as places where fast-food outlets and convenience stores outnumber farmers markets and grocery stores, with no supermarkets within a 1-mile radius.

> "Food deserts and food swamps mainly exist in the south or southeastern region, where chronic disease rates are the highest among U.S. adults, including clusters for breast, lung, colorectal, and prostate cancers. Among the 3,038 counties studied – representing 96.7% of the U.S. – those with high rates of obesity-related cancer deaths had a greater fraction of older people, Black residents, low-income families, and higher rates of diabetes and obesity. Overall, age-matched residents in underserved communities have 77% greater odds of dying from obesity-related cancer than people residing in areas with ample healthy food options." [25]

The *Association of Food Deserts and Food Swamps with Obesity-Related Cancer Mortality in the U.S.* study questions the idea that diet is a modifiable risk factor when where people live and work seriously shapes their health because they may not know how to improve their choices.[26]

These papers affirm our dedication to sharing nourishment and food sovereignty information that can empower clients, students, and providers. For a paradigm shift to occur, information, knowledge, skills, and beliefs must be part of the conversation. Kathleen and I took on the challenge and now have added esteemed colleagues in shifting the paradigm. You will read their stories and learn from their perspectives in later chapters on hydration and living to your potential, as well as in new collaborative published research. While a book is quite an accomplishment for everyone involved, moving into writing a peer-reviewed abstract/poster and accompanying research papers can be a new kind of daunting. Dispersal of new concepts and ideas gives extra importance to the words selected for the illumination of evidence. Words can become vehicles of change or catastrophe, either catalyzing inspiration for change as a kite is lifted by the wind or sinking scholars under waves of disagreement and crushing new perspectives into the sand. We are confident we have provided ample scientific, cultural, and historical evidence of the relevance of *Food As Medicine* to float a paradigm battleship of a new perspective.

> **Principle 10:** In order to achieve and sustain wellness, multiple elements of each human's being must co-operate in good relationship and proper balance: mind/body/brain/spirit/environment/energy systems.

---

1 Philosophy of Biomedicine: First published Thu Apr 9, 2020; Stanford Encyclopedia of Philosophy; https://plato.stanford.edu/entries/biomedicine/

2 The History of Naturopathy: https://societyofnaturopaths.org/about-naturopathy/history-of-naturopathy/

3 Carlock D. (2006). Native American health: traditional healing and culturally competent health care internet resources. Medical reference services quarterly, 25(3), 67–76. https://doi.org/10.1300/J115v25n03_06

4 Medicine Ways, Native Peoples' Concepts of Health and Illness: https://www.nlm.nih.gov/nativevoices/exhibition/healing-ways/medicine-ways/healing-plants.html

5 Han, S. Y., Lee, S. H., & Chae, H. (2022). Developing a best practice framework for clinical competency education in the traditional East-Asian medicine curriculum. BMC medical education, 22(1), 352. https://doi.org/10.1186/s12909-022-03398-4

6 Vaidyanathan, G. (2023). WHO's first traditional medicine summit splits opinions. https://doi.org/10.1038/d41586-023-02636-z

7 Patwardhan, B., Wieland, L. S., Aginam, O., Chuthaputti, A., Ghelman, R., Ghods, R., Soon, G. C., Matsabisa, M. G., Seifert, G., Tu'itahi, S., Chol, K. S., Kuruvilla, S., Kemper, K., Cramer, H., Nagendra, H., Thakar, A., Nesari, T., Sharma, S., Srikanth, N., . . . Acharya, R. (2023). Evidence-based traditional medicine for transforming global health and well-being. Journal of Ayurveda and Integrative Medicine, 14(4), 100790. https://doi.org/10.1016/j.jaim.2023.100790

8 Iredale, R. (2000). Eugenics and its Relevance to Contemporary Health Care. Nursing Ethics. https://doi.org/10.1177/096973300000700303

9 21st century eugenics? Hansen, N. E., Janz, H. L., Sobsey, D. J.; Published:December, 2008 DOI:https://doi.org/10.1016/S0140-6736(08)61889-9

10 Allen G. E. (2011). Eugenics and modern biology: critiques of eugenics, 1910-1945. Annals of human genetics, 75(3), 314–325. https://doi.org/10.1111/j.1469-1809.2011.00649.x

11 DeSesso J. M. (2019). The arrogance of teratology: A brief chronology of attitudes throughout history. Birth defects research, 111(3), 123–141. https://doi.org/10.1002/bdr2.1422

12 History.com

Chapter 2 ~ Paradigm Shift: ~ Wellness Care

13 Magno, G., Boer, L. L., Oostra, R. J., & Zanatta, A. (2022). The role of the University of Padua medical school in the study of conjoined twins between 18th and early 19th century. American journal of medical genetics. Part A, 188(12), 3423–3431. https://doi.org/10.1002/ajmg.a.62938

14 2021 National Healthcare Quality and Disparities Report [Internet]. Rockville (MD): Agency for Healthcare Research and Quality (US); 2021 Dec. DISPARITIES IN HEALTHCARE. Available from: https://www.ncbi.nlm.nih.gov/books/NBK578532/

15 University of Miami. (2020, August 24). Having a doctor who shares the same race may ease patient's angst: New research suggests that Black patients may have less pain and anxiety when treated by a physician of their own race. ScienceDaily. Retrieved April 1, 2023 from www.sciencedaily.com/releases/2020/08/200824144315.htm

16 Takeshita J, Wang S, Loren AW, et al. Association of Racial/Ethnic and Gender Concordance Between Patients and Physicians With Patient Experience Ratings. JAMA Netw Open. 2020;3(11):e2024583. doi:10.1001/jamanetworkopen.2020.24583

17 Implicit bias is thought to be shaped by experience and based on learned associations between particular qualities and social categories, including race and/or gender. Individuals' perceptions and behaviors can be influenced by the implicit biases they hold, even if they are unaware they hold such biases. Implicit bias is an aspect of implicit social cognition: the phenomenon that perceptions, attitudes, and stereotypes can operate prior to conscious intention or endorsement. https://www.apa.org/topics/implicit-bias

18 Stephens, G. J., Silbert, L. J., & Hasson, U. (2010). Speaker–listener neural coupling underlies successful communication. Proceedings of the National Academy of Sciences, 107(32), 14425-14430. https://doi.org/10.1073/pnas.1008662107

19 Drexel University. (2017, February 27). Brain imaging headband measures how our minds align when we communicate. ScienceDaily. Retrieved April 1, 2023 from www.sciencedaily.com/releases/2017/02/170227082207.htm

20 Cell Press. (2021, September 14). People synchronize heart rates while listening attentively to stories. ScienceDaily. Retrieved April 1, 2023 from www.sciencedaily.com/releases/2021/09/210914111238.htm

21 Karr, T., Bell, K., (2020) Empty Plate: Food~Sustainability~Mindefulness; Summerland Publishing ISBN: 978-1-7329072-3-2

22 Karr, T., Bell, K., (2020) Empty Plate: Food~Sustainability~Mindefulness; Summerland Publishing: ISBN: 978-1-7329072-3-2

23 Peng, K., Rodríguez, D. A., Peterson, M., Braun, L. M., Howard, A. G., Lewis, C. E., Shikany, J. M., & Gordon-Larsen, P. (2020). GIS-Based Home Neighborhood Food Outlet Counts, Street Connectivity, and Frequency of Use of Neighborhood Restaurants and Food Stores. Journal of urban health : bulletin of the New York Academy of Medicine, 97(2), 213–225. https://doi.org/10.1007/s11524-019-00412-x

24 Peng, K., Rodriguez, D. A., Hirsch, J. A., & Gordon-Larsen, P. (2021). A method for estimating neighborhood characterization in studies of the association with availability of sit-down restaurants and supermarkets. International journal of health geographics, 20(1), 15. https://doi.org/10.1186/s12942-020-00257-7

25 Bevel MS, Tsai M, Parham A, Andrzejak SE, Jones S, Moore JX. Association of Food Deserts and Food Swamps With Obesity-Related Cancer Mortality in the US. JAMA Oncol. Published online May 04, 2023. doi:10.1001/jamaoncol.2023.0634

26 Phillips, A. Z., & Rodriguez, H. P. (2019). Adults with diabetes residing in "food swamps" have higher hospitalization rates. Health services research, 54 Suppl 1(Suppl 1), 217–225. https://doi.org/10.1111/1475-6773.13102

Our Journey with Food

> "Take care of yourself, be healthy, and always believe you can be successful in anything you truly want."
>
> ~Alessandra Ambrosio

Chapter Three ~ *Paradigm Shift* ~

Diet: A Manner of Life

By the 19th century, magazines were becoming influencers of public opinion. Thin was in and companies aligned themselves with *modern* medicine. There was never a more lucrative alliance than the medical and tobacco industries. Cigarettes were prescribed for asthmatics, stress, and weight loss. In 1929, Lucky Strikes launched an advertising campaign against obesity. Slogans read: "When tempted to nibble, remember your middle." "Light up a Lucky … be smart, be slender!" "Reach for a Lucky instead of a Sweet." The latter sparked a lawsuit from the growing candy industry. Lucky Strike dropped the word "sweet," telling consumers to "Reach for a Lucky instead." The power of advertising and government contracts placed Lucky Strikes, Marlboro and Camel as the iconic cigarettes on the market by the end of World War II. From that era through the Vietnam War, military troops would find the following in government-issued C-rations: hardtack biscuits, corned beef, bacon, salt and pepper, ground coffee, and tobacco.

Image: New York National Guard Food Service 2014.

Following World War II, changes in body image and views on food became the foundation for new ways to be slim: anorexia, bulimia, orthorexia, liposuction, tummy tucks, and more. Our contemporary opinions about food can be traced to the *Clean Food* movement of the 1960s and *the diet age*, which took off in the 1970s. The Age of Aquarius introduced us to the *grapefruit diet* (revived from the 1950s). In the mid-1970s, Elvis Presley popularized the *Sleeping Beauty Diet* in which he was heavily sedated for several days, hoping to wake up thinner. British actress-model Twiggy introduced us to vegetarianism which, although seen as faddish at the time, a plant-based diet is now a popular and effective lifestyle choice when done in balance.

Extreme low-calorie plans were promoted by actresses Farah Fawcett and Jane Fonda; simultaneously, and perhaps not coincidentally, a startling increase in anorexia began during the 1970s. Anorexia, bulimia nervosa, orthorexia, and binge eating were considered rare eating disorders until the latter half of the 20th century. A research study in 2023 showed individuals experiencing binge-eating disorder exhibit severe symptomology, but symptoms in those who experienced binge-eating disorder plus anorexia nervosa are even more severe.[1] Research published in 2021 on U.S. military veterans reported approximately one-third of women and one-fifth of men had symptoms consistent with an eating disorder diagnosis.[2,3]

Changing Times, Changing Perspectives

The Jack LaLanne Show began in 1951 and ran for 34 years. Jack LaLanne produced fitness and nutrition videos until his death at 96 in 2011.

Widespread interest in Asian philosophy and lifestyle, which increased in popularity in the 1970s, introduced the ancient vegetarian macrobiotic diet principles to mainstream America by the 1990s. Dating back to the 4th century B.C. and re-popularized many times throughout history,[4] macrobiotic and Ayurvedic[5] approaches over the next two decades introduced new foods to *hip* consumers.[6] The protocols of these ancient — but new — diets were undoubtedly far healthier than the snazzy processed "diet" and weight-loss foods appearing on grocery store shelves resembling desserts, such as the low-fat "chocolate" chews and drinks.

Low-fat diets were all the rage in the 1980s, with Jane Fonda, Raquel Welch, Olivia Newton-John, Tamilee Webb, and supermodel Christie Brinkley producing workout videos to thin us down. While the ladies were jazzercising with Jane, the guys headed to the gym to work out with Arnold Schwarzenegger and his *Shape with Arnold* workout. Copies of *Arnold's Encyclopedia of Modern Bodybuilding* are still used 41 years later.

We should note that long before Arnold came Jack Lalanne, born in 1914 and considered the Godfather of workout routines and diet plans. Jack was diagnosed with bulimia at 14 and had to drop out of school. He would go on to accomplish superhuman fitness feats well into his 80s. We will look more at his legacy later. Home fitness equipment became vogue; stationary bikes, NordicTrack, and who can forget the original *ThighMaster* endorsed by Suzanne Somers? This still present and misguided dietary approach ignores our bodies 'need for a vital nutrient found in real, unprocessed food — fat. Saturated fats are necessary for hormone production. Hormones will be covered in a later chapter.

> ***Principle 11:*** The health and wellness of our bodies is dependent on consuming a wholesome nutritious diet; food is one integral component, but diet encompasses more than food. Diet is an entire way of life.

Diet Confusion

It is time to change how we think about the word *diet* as being only about weight loss. Aristotle is believed to be the first to use the word *diaita* as specifically meaning a *way of living* prescribed by a physician. In its original context, *diaita* wasn't solely focused on foods to achieve weight loss; it was meant to represent an entire way of life; sensible, moderate, encompassing food, drink, lifestyle and exercise. The Greek philosophers and citizens understood that a healthy mind and body created a healthy society. Then it all went wrong …. By the 3rd century B.C. Hippocrates believed being fat was morally and physically detrimental, the result of luxury and corruption. He recommended a diet of light and emollient foods, slow running, hard work, wrestling, sea-water enemas, walking about naked, and vomiting after lunch.[7]

As the 21st century introduced more science with each diet program, medical professionals became increasingly involved in nutrition. An upside to medical research entering the diet industry is that a paradigm change occurred in the *why* and *how* of obesity and metabolic syndrome, a term first described in 1988 as *syndrome X*. The syndrome hinges on the existence of insulin resistance and results in glucose intolerance, hypertension, and dyslipidemia. The *World Health Organization* (WHO) produced the first formalized definition of metabolic syndrome in 1998.[8] By 2023, the understanding of metabolic syndrome as a significant sign of hormone dysfunction, chronic illness and inflammation in predominantly Westernized cultures is well known.

The Dawn of Hormone Balance for Weight Loss

Dr. Barry Sears was a researcher at Boston University and MIT before forming his own biotechnology company. By the 1990s, he had developed *The Zone Diet* and was an author and sought-after speaker. What was unique about the Zone diet, as compared to all other diets, was hormones. The Zone diet looked at how foods affected blood sugar and insulin production. Here was a diet that said you could eat more, not less, if your foods were balanced. As of 2023, Dr. Berry Sears is still actively researching on cellular senescence and inflammation at Arizona State University.

Gene and Joyce Daoust took the *Zone Diet's* complex information on activating the metabolism by balancing hormones to stimulate weight loss to a consumer-friendly level by publishing recipes and meal plans. In *The Formula: A Personalized 40-30-30 Weight Loss Program,* published in 2001, the nutritional science is reasonably well covered, considering when it was written. I had the honor of meeting the Daousts on several occasions and saw firsthand how the 40-30-30 dietary approach worked with clients. In 2023 the 40-30-30 balancing of carbohydrates, fats and proteins still works; however, its reliance on fructose and meal replacement shakes and bars is problematic. Remember *that The Zone Diet is an anti-inflammatory* rather than a weight loss diet; weight loss ensues because of lowering inflammatory markers. A positive for health coaches: the Zone is not a deprivation diet; most clients complain they can't eat all the food measured out for their metabolism, and it includes desserts.

> **The Zone Diet & 40-30-30**
>
> The *U.S. News & World Report's* listed the Zone Diet, 13th best diet of 2023.[9]
>
> <u>Positives</u>
> - ✓ Filling – it's rich in high-fiber foods.
> - ✓ No off-limit foods or food groups.
> - ✓ A clearly defined plan with recipes.
> - ✓ Diverse foods and flavors.
>
> <u>Challenges</u>
> - ⇨ Tedious portioning, meal planning or prep.
> - ⇨ Lots of rules to remember.
> - ⇨ Research dated.

At the beginning of the 21st century, Robert Atkins, MD (1972)[10] and Ann Louise Gittleman, PhD, additionally illustrated the need for a balance between the macronutrient's protein, fat, and carbohydrates. Dr. Atkins fat-centric low-carbohydrate approach was later revived and promptly followed by the scorn of TV health experts, dietetics and American Medical Association spokespeople. As is often the case with medical celebrities promoting dietary change; they become targets when their opinion is not the *accepted medical standard of care*, which can lead to misinterpretation and misquotes by both media and the celebrity, equally. To maintain media standing, celebrity health gurus can sensationalize their message, embellish the research and/or repeat false information. I watched this happen with Steven Gundry, MD, and T. Colin Campbell PhD, both of whom began well and still have their followings; however, I have found too many times their information and research is either seriously outdated or exaggerated, bringing their credibility into question. Fortunately, many dietary approaches - minus the celebrity - while in opposition to each other, actually do have evidence-based and informed practice research to support usage for some individuals when done sensibly.

> ***Principle 12:*** The same dietary approach does not suit everyone. The key is to find a pattern of eating that leads to metabolic balance for each person.

First Ladies in Wellness Care

Dynamic female medical celebrities ruled the early days of the 21st century. Dr. Ann Louise Gittleman, wrote on women's hormonal health and electromagnetic fields (EMF) well before others. Her book *ZAPPED,* illuminating EMFs effects on health is, in my opinion, the most credible information available to date on the subject. I was impressed with a book written by Diana Schwarzbein, MD in 2005 and later had the great privilege of meeting Diana over lunch and learning from her at conferences. As an endocrinologist working with diabetics, Diana brought hard science on metabolic syndrome to the table.

With a thriving practice in central California, Diana feels the best way to help clients isn't with a prescription pad but health education. Diana's philosophy and approach to helping clients with metabolic syndrome has heavily influenced how I discuss diabetes and metabolic syndrome with clients and students.

I first met Terry Wahls, MD in 2015, and like Diana Schwarzbein, MD, she has become a significant influencer in my practice and writing. I feel confident the *Wahls Protocol Diet* is today's best approach to chronic health challenges. As of 2023, Terry has authored more than 60 peer-reviewed papers on dietary treatments for multiple sclerosis (MS) and auto-immune conditions.[11] As a Clinical Professor of Medicine at the University of Iowa, Dr. Wahls conducts clinical trials that test the effect of nutrition and lifestyle interventions to treat MS and other progressive health problems. Dr. Wahls is an expert on *Paleo, Intermittent Fasting and Keto diets* and therapeutic lifestyle changes. Her protocol blends these dietary approaches for optimum benefit to the individual.

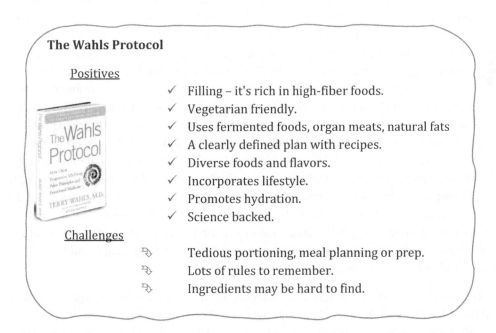

The Wahls Protocol

<u>Positives</u>
- ✓ Filling – it's rich in high-fiber foods.
- ✓ Vegetarian friendly.
- ✓ Uses fermented foods, organ meats, natural fats
- ✓ A clearly defined plan with recipes.
- ✓ Diverse foods and flavors.
- ✓ Incorporates lifestyle.
- ✓ Promotes hydration.
- ✓ Science backed.

<u>Challenges</u>
- ➯ Tedious portioning, meal planning or prep.
- ➯ Lots of rules to remember.
- ➯ Ingredients may be hard to find.

The Paleolithic diet (PD) has one big challenge – its name. This is largely because there is no way for anthropologists and archaeologists to know for sure what humans ate during early history. Using the *paleo* name has created vocal criticism from anthropologists and archaeological communities as pseudoscience. However, one presentation presented a different perspective at the 2013 anthropology/archaeology symposium on the ancient human diet. The researchers shared that the long-used data graphs supporting a high animal protein diet for archaic humans were wrong. The data on high-protein (solely from animal sources) diets did not consider proteins found in plants and insects or fire and cooking, once believed to develop later, was a significant advance in archaic cultures. This advance allowed for plants and insects to account for significant protein beyond animal sources in the diet. [12] Current research by anthropologists and archaeologists indicates that the ancient diets of early humans were diverse and not limited to meat and insects, as once thought. The widespread use of fire and cooking increased food diversity, calories and digestibility during the paleo periods. [13, 14]

Even with this information the Paleo Diet was the butt of jokes and ridicule amongst anthropologists and medical circles. The typical take was that paleo was an unhealthy high, protein fad diet. By 2018, the paleo diet had research confirming health benefits and by 2023, it had been evaluated in side-by-side comparison studies with the Mediterranean, DASH and SWANK diets. The caveman and carnivore craze moved from the paleo model to an almost exclusive meat and fat-centered approach, more closely following the Ketogenic model. To learn more on the history and diversity of the ancient diet, see *Empty Plate: Food~Sustainability~Mindfulness* and *Our Journey with Food Coookery Book*.

Walter Lyle Voegtlin was an American gastroenterologist and pioneer of the Paleolithic diet.

The ideas behind the PD came from *primitive* diets advocated in the 19th century by Walter L. Voegtlin (1904 – 1975).[15] The philosophy of eugenics is reflected in Voegtlin's research and writing on primitive diets. The specter of eugenics influences on the researchers and authors who modernized Voegtlin hypothesis and developed the PD is unknown and should not overshadow the effectiveness and safety of the PD for inflammation and auto-immune diseases. In the 21st century Dr. Loren Cordain a fellow Oregonian, popularized the PD in his best-selling books, which has led to a food industry worth approximately $500 million. Dr. Cordain is a Professor Emeritus in the Department of Health and Exercise Science at Colorado State University. During the past 20 years, his research has focused on the evolutionary and anthropological basis for modern humans' diet, health and well-being. The Jönsson PD study (2009) was the first to assess the potential benefit compared to a diabetes diet for patients. Likened to the *diabetes diet*, the Paleolithic diet resulted in statistically significant lowering of hemoglobin A1c, triglycerides, diastolic blood pressure, weight, body mass index, and waist circumference. Unfortunately, the small size of the Jönsson PD study limited the power of statistical data correlation.[16] Another PD study from 2019 corroborated Jonsson's findings of positive benefits to diabetic weight loss.[17] The conclusion stated that the PD may assist in controlling weight and waist circumference and managing chronic diseases.[18, 19]

Researchers in 2021 looked at the PD and performance athletes. Their conclusion, in the long term: among the diets reviewed the Paleo diet was the only one resulting in a decrease in fasting plasma (fP) glucose and fasting plasma (fP) insulin.[20] The most promising research conclusions published in 2022 reported that better insights gained into the effect of the PD on the modulation of glucose and lipid metabolism factors in patients with metabolic disorders will advance future research.[21]

> ***Principle 13:*** Nutritional needs are never static, but constantly changing to accommodate the demands of normal processes (growth, development, and aging) as well as specialized needs for healing and recovery from illness, insult or injury.

Sarah Ballantyne, PhD, published *Paleo Principles* in 2017, providing extensive evidence-informed and science-based PD text followed by detailed consumer cookbooks.

> **The Paleo Diet** [22, 23]
>
> Positives
> - Rich in high-fiber vegetables and fruits.
> - High in potassium and antioxidants
> - Naturally raised meat, fish, organ meats, natural fats
> - A clearly defined plan with recipes.
> - Diverse foods and flavors.
> - Diabetic friendly with low-carb, and sodium
> - Promotes hydration.
>
> Challenges
> - Science is limited but favorable.
> - Tedious meal planning or prep.
> - Dairy, grain, and legume restricted.
> - Challenging for vegetarians.
> - Ingredients may be hard to find.

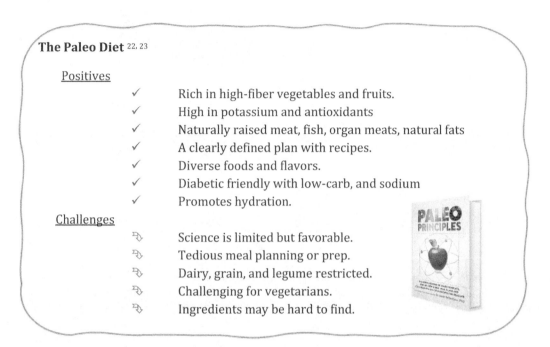

Deanna Minich is the next female influencer in how I think about diet, food, and the microbiome. Her understanding of nutrition science has placed Deanna as a leading academic on the subject. Dr. Minich, with the title of Chief Science Officer at *Symphony Natural Health*, has authored four book chapters and fifty scientific publications. She leads their medical advisory team, oversees scientific communication, and provides educational leadership for the company's plant-derived nutraceuticals. Deanna is a perfect example of a practitioner in *Integrative Nutrition Medicine*; she creatively blends her understanding of Ayurvedic and Western Bioscience medicine, bringing a colorful and inclusive balanced approach. Mistakenly referred to as pseudoscience for too long, Ayurveda is a 3,000-year-old wellness model which is increasingly science supported; a PubMed search generated 7,240 research papers in 2023. Ayurveda in *Sanskrit* means *The Science of Life and* is heavily practiced in India and Nepal by 80% of the population.[24]

Deanna's understanding of color as an artist led her to explore food's colors in combination with traditional Ayurvedic chakras, or energy centers in the body. Deanna recognized the correlation of organ and endocrine systems as being aligned with the chakras' colors and how the same colorful foods contained nutrients that support the body systems. [25, 26] *The Rainbow Diet*,[27, 28] takes a deeper look at the colors of plant and fungi foods, explaining both what and how they influence in our bodies and microbiome. Skillfully blending Eastern and Western science traditions, her book contains cutting-edge discoveries about how the brain recognizes phytonutrients in foods by color, then communicates with and sends preferred chemicals to various parts of the microbiome.[29] The entire spectrum of the human microbiome can then feed on the potent colors found in polyphenol and phytochemical-rich foods. [30, 31]

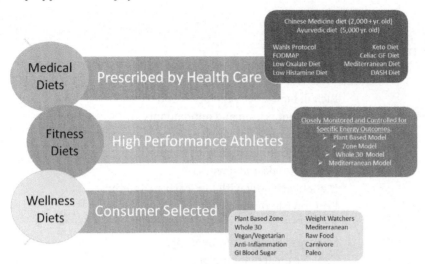

When reviewed dietary models generally fit into one or more of the three categories of medical, fitness and wellness approaches. Aspects of a diet may be used on its own or in totality of a lifestyle plan. Dietary models contain elements of gastronomy reflecting historic and modern knowledge.

The Mediterranean Diet

The Mediterranean Diet (MD) is the most researched and validated dietary plan to date. [32, 33] However, do not be fooled into thinking what is reported as a MD is a culturally correct approach. True Mediterranean gastronomy consists of a wide range of natural foods from varied landscapes within the Mediterranean region. Often the MD, when subjected to research, is limited in food sources, cooking methods and environmental cofactors. Science is clear that a MD is beneficial for weight loss, heart health and inflammation. In fact, when you look at the multitude of diets recommended for consumers, they all have a common foundation in the MD.

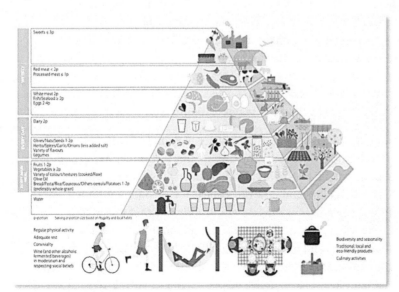

A Better Pyramid[34]

A study led by researchers from Stanford University in 2023 revealed cellular effects of the Mediterranean diet for the first time, based on how one of its healthy fats influenced lifespan.

Chapter 3 ~ Paradigm Shift ~ Diet: A Mannar of Life

The new study focused on one healthy fat, oleic acid, which is the main monounsaturated fatty acids (MUFAs) in olive oil and some nuts.[35]

The Mediterranean diet is truly a manner of life; encompassing a shared cultural heritage widely recognized for its contribution to health and well-being and evolving because of modern technology, food processing, and globalization. According to MD researchers, ongoing developments and innovations worldwide have changed the scope of foods available globally throughout the year. The inclusiveness of the new MD pyramid caught my attention when Jeffery, a nurse in Anchorage, Alaska, shared research published in 2020. I loved how it includes sweets, wine, processed meats which have cultural significance, culinary activities, and rest! The previous graph comes from *Updating the Mediterranean Diet Pyramid towards Sustainability: Focus on Environmental Concerns.* A link to the published paper can be found in the chapter endnotes #32.

Medical Diets Keto and Intermittent Fasting

It is sometimes a challenge to remember that the ketogenic diet (KD) is neither new nor a popular weight loss diet. Keto is a highly restrictive diet and not suitable for everyone. The KD has primarily been used as a medical diet for epileptic and brain tumor patients. Dietary approaches have been used to treat epilepsy since 500 B.C.; the historical accounts refer primarily to fasting. Mark Twain reportedly said, "A little starvation can do more for the average sick man than can the best medicines and doctors. I do not mean a restricted diet. I mean total abstention from food for one or two days."

Mark Twain (Samuel Langhorne Clemens), 1835-1910

The ketogenic diet is a science-based, low-carbohydrate, moderate-protein, high-fat diet with a history dating back to the 1920s. In the 1920s, the KD was introduced by modern physicians as a treatment for epilepsy. The high-fat diet was found to mimic the fasting metabolism and was used for two decades until the advent of antiepileptic drugs. By the end of the 20th century, ketogenic therapy was available in a small number of children's hospitals. Beginning in 1993, there was a resurgence in scientific interest about the KD and clinical use began by 2012. This brief review traces the history of one of the most effective treatments for childhood epilepsy.

The KD switches the body's primary fuel source from glucose to fats and ketones, which offers health benefits by amply supplying the brain with energy while lowering blood sugar and insulin levels.[36] Glucose normally stimulates pancreatic β cells to release insulin, allowing glucose to enter cells and provide energy. With high carbohydrate and glucose intake from industrially processed foods, the pancreas increasingly secretes more insulin, which promotes the interaction of growth hormone receptors and growth hormones IGF-1 in the liver. This promotes cell growth and proliferation, which can be detrimental to individuals with diabetic, cardiovascular, and cancer conditions. When glucose is scarce, the body senses the need to make an alternative form of energy for cells. The liver then produces ketones and fatty acids, which provide energy to healthy cells.[37]

Dom D'Agostino, PhD, is a tenured Associate Professor at the University of South Florida, where he studies metabolic-based therapies such as the ketogenic diet. He has published numerous peer-reviewed papers and articles on exogenous ketones.[38] Dr. D'Agostino's research delves into the possibility of reducing the KD-restrictive nature through ketogenic supplements called exogenous ketones. This would remove dietary limitations and a person could ingest ketones in pill form instead of producing it within the body. Supplementations can come from synthetic or naturally derived ketones, and there are three types: ketone esters, ketone salts, and medium-chain triglycerides (MCTs).[39, 40]

> *Principle 14:* Local organically grown, minimally processed whole foods are the proven choices for a healthful diet.

Intermittent Fasting (Sort of the New Kid on the Block)

One approach to improving weight and metabolic outcomes is intermittent fasting (IF), which consists of multiple different timing schedules for temporary food avoidance, including alternate-day fasting, other similar full-day fasting patterns, and time-restricted feeding (where the day's food is consumed over a 6-hour period, allowing for 18 hours of fasting). These feeding schedules have favorable metabolic effects by intermittently inducing the metabolism of fatty acids to ketones. The regimens overall lead to a decrease in weight and have been linked to improvements in dyslipidemia and blood pressure.[41] Intermittent fasting is often utilized in conjunction with Paleo and ketogenic approaches. Most of the available research demonstrates that IF is effective at reducing body weight, decreasing fasting glucose, decreasing fasting insulin, reducing insulin resistance, decreasing leptin levels, and increasing adiponectin levels.[42, 43] Research published in 2020 about fasting from dawn to sunset on anti-cancer effects confirmed circadian clock rhythm as one of the causes of metabolic syndrome and metabolic syndrome-induced cancers. Pharmacologic treatments are insufficient to reduce the risk of developing metabolic syndrome-induced cancers.[44] The research findings on intermittent fasting from dawn to sunset for four consecutive weeks, which is in synchrony with the circadian rhythm and earth's rotation, was a positive adjunct treatment in metabolic syndrome. Future research will further look at the effects of IF for prevention and treatment of metabolic syndrome-induced cancers.[45]

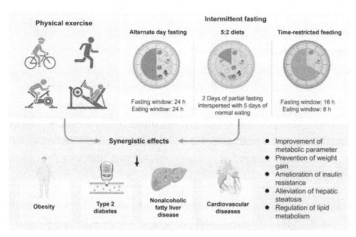

Intermittent fasting is an alternative dietary strategy for reducing energy intake (EI) that involves >60% energy restriction on 2-3 days per week or on alternate days. While numerous studies have evaluated IF as a weight loss strategy, there are several limitations, including lack of a standard-of-care control, failure to provide guideline-based behavioral support, and failure to rigorously evaluate dietary and adherence using objective measures.[46] A 2023 systematic research review found that IF interventions produced similar beneficial effects for weight loss and chronic disease risk factors compared with daily caloric restriction (DCR). Very limited evidence suggests that IF may be more effective than DCR for fat loss and insulin sensitivity, but conclusions cannot be drawn based on the current evidence.[47]

A paper published in 2023 on preventing metabolic disorders through interaction with gut microbiota found that IF and regular physical exercise can improve several metabolic and inflammatory parameters, resulting in stronger beneficial actions for metabolic health.[48, 49]

Do *Ph* Diets Work?

I'm frequently asked what I think of acid/alkaline balancing plans. This protocol has a fascinating food history and secured a position in pseudoscience in 2023. *The alkaline diet* is based on the theory that certain foods, when consumed, leave an alkaline or acid residue or ash. The acid ash hypothesis says that excessive acid in the diet may cause several diseases in modern society and the alkaline diet could prevent and cure these diseases. The minerals calcium, iron, magnesium, zinc, and copper are said to be the principal components of the residual ash. Food is thus classified as alkaline, acid, or neutral according to the *pH* of the solution created with its ash in water. This diet is promoted by some naturopaths, chiropractors, and integrative health practitioners.[50] Research released in 2021 on the effects of acid or base interventions on bone health concluded that it is unnecessary to emphasize the adverse impact of acidic diets on bone health. This study showed that future research should focus more on whether urinary calcium excretion is related to bone calcium loss that is caused by an acidic diet and whether protein can offset the adverse effects of acid on bones.[51] In 2021, a larger study looking at the Mediterranean diet reported that both high and low dietary acid were associated with a higher risk of osteoporotic fractures, and only high dietary acid was found to have a negative relation to bone mineral density in senior adults with existing chronic health conditions.[52] Dietary acid load association with hip fractures was looked at again in 2022. Data collected through a food frequency questionnaire given to 1,070 71-year-old individuals from Guangdong, China, found a positive association in individuals with a lower body mass index. However, the association of *pH* in the diet is only one factor and does not equate to either cause or correlation in statistical significance.[53]

History for perspective on *pH* diet: In 1863, Dr. James Caleb Jackson operated the Dansville Sanitarium in Dansville, New York. Dr. Jackson was a staunch vegetarian. One of Dr. Jackson's patrons was Ellen G. White (1827-1915). Ms. White co-founded the Seventh Day Adventist religion, which advocates a vegetarian lifestyle. I have no doubt that White and John H. Kellogg were influenced by the German vegetarian physician and author Louis Kuhne (1835-1901). His conceptual view of the cause for disease was that the average human body was overburdened with toxins that eventually led to degenerations of the internal organs. He stressed the importance of proper digestion and of avoiding constipation.

Dr. John Harvey Kellogg's (1852-1943) vocation was in the health spa and hospital business.[54] He was the superintendent of Battle Creek Sanitarium in Battle

Creek, Michigan. While history has relegated John H. Kellogg's medical status to that of a "bowel-obsessed" quack (as noted in the novel and film *Road to Wellville*), he was considered a highly skilled surgeon in his day. He was a devout man known for developing the *Religion of Biologic Living*.[55]

While recuperating in 1893, Charles William Post became impressed with the new-fangled "health" foods being served at the Battle Creek Sanitarium. His stay at the sanitarium revived a passing interest in food development. The following year, he founded his own sanitarium, La Vita Inn. For more of the Post story, go to *Our Journey with Food Cookery Book*.

These events occurred during the Victorian era, known for producing idiosyncratic views about health and morality. Dr. Kellogg, for example, believed that sexual relations were sinful and detrimental to one's health. He reported that he and his wife had been married for over forty years and had never once "polluted" themselves with fornication. He later went on to say that *he had 100% success with his patients*. Any who were not cured, he claimed, must have foiled their own recovery because of "self-pollution" (sex or masturbation) and/or because they ate "animal flesh"—actions which were, to his mind, both sinful and the cause of disease. A somewhat similar dietary approach, the Hay diet, was developed by the American physician William Howard Hay in the 1920s.

The late 19th century and early 20th century saw the birth of neo-naturopathy, particularly in Germany. Henry Lindlahr (1862-1924) opened the book *The New Science of Healing* by Louis Kuhne, which became instrumental in promoting a philosophical law – *when we ignore and eschew healthy options in our lives, Nature has a way of leveling the score. Deceiving Nature indefinitely is not sustainable*.[56]

Without the natural health movement of the late 1900s, we would not have naturopathic providers today.

Vis medicatrix naturae ~ there is Healing in the Power of Nature.

"I reached the limits of Nature's endurance and began to suffer greatly from the results of my ignorance and foolishness."..."At the age of 35, I found myself a physical and mental wreck without faith in God, in Nature, or myself."

~ Henry Lindlahr
Founder of Naturopathic
Medicine

Another theory, called *nutripathy*, was developed by American Gary A. Martin in the 1970s. Others who have advocated alkaline-acid balancing diets include D.C. Jarvis, Robert Young, Herman Aihara, Fred Shadian, and Victor A. Marcial-Vega. *The Acid-Alkaline Diet* (2006) by Dr. Christopher Vasey, a Swiss naturopath, recommends a vegetarian (predominately raw food) lifestyle and restricts the consumption of grain, sugar, fruit, dairy, eggs, mushrooms, alcohol, caffeine, condiments, fermented foods, fat, nuts, and even many vegetables. Both Dr. Young and Dr. Vasey claim that one can obtain all the protein necessary for muscle, tissue, bone, and brain health from plant sources like soy. For some, this protocol may be somewhat beneficial if they are highly sensitive to sugars, gluten, yeasts, and molds. Others may feel better when these items are restricted due to their histamine-promoting agents. Also, weight loss can occur because of what is called a catabolic state (not to be confused with ketosis), which results in the destruction of cells, tissues, and hormones; basically, one is feeding off their own body. Some of the restricted foods such as broccoli, berries, organic meats, and fish oils have since been scientifically proven to be effective in preventing cancer, heart disease, depression, and diabetes.

The *pH* diets promote a strict limited food approach which is unsustainable and even counterproductive. In my view, the *pH* dietary approach does not hold up to scrutiny or agree with evidence-informed dietary approaches of nutrigenomics, cancer nutrition sciences, and phytochemical studies. Please don't end up eliminating healthy foods because you think it will balance your *pH*. The human *pH* system is complicated, with both acid and alkaline activity needed to maintain healthy digestion and elimination processes.

Weston A. Price: Un-Refined Food Diet

Like Kellogg and others from the Victorian and Edwardian periods, eugenics colored the understandings at this time of human history and genetics. Dr. Price's research investigated what was healthy and normal for the human body. His need for stable controls led him to investigate *primitive* populations isolated from *modern* influences. He never found a native population who were primarily vegetarian, much to his and his contemporaries 'dismay. The closest he would have found were the followers of *Jainism* in India, however, they were not a primitive population. Dr. Price found that native groups who followed their traditional nature-based diet enjoyed good health and vigor, and those that turned to the *civilized* diet of processed, sugar-laden foods soon developed a variety of illnesses. Dr. Price and his wife documented how the conditions worsened with each successive generation. Their research took them to six continents. Dr. Price consistently found that it was not the meat, fat, dairy, or fruit that individuals ate that created health issues. Instead, it was processed foods and refined sugars, grains, fats, and salt that rapidly damaged the human body.[57, 58, 59]

> "If civilized man is to survive, he must incorporate the fundamentals of primitive nutritional wisdom into his modern life-style."
>
> – *Dr. Weston A. Price*

Dr. Price wrote in a 1935 article, that was read at the New York Dental Centennial Meeting, "In no instance have I found the change from a high immunity to dental caries [cavities] to a high susceptibility… to be associated with a change from a diet with a high potential alkalinity to a high potential acidity." In fact, Dr. Price adds that his data show, if anything, that good tooth health is the result of an acidifying diet. Dr. Price further discounts the notion that an alkalizing diet promotes general health and stresses the importance of eating whole foods rich in vitamins and minerals, particularly the fat-soluble vitamins so abundant in animal foods.[60]

The research conducted by Weston A. Price and his wife Florence in the 1920s and 1930s would be difficult, if not impossible, for us to recreate today. First, the populations he studied lived in remote areas that were untouched by modern lifestyles. Today it is unlikely that such a vast collection of first people's communities exist. Additionally, the research methodology would be difficult to replicate, and it may not satisfy modern ethical standards—just as Dr. Keys 'work with conscientious objectors and low-calorie diets in the 1940s is not likely to be reproduced today.[61] While these studies are antiquated, the Weston Price diet is used by millions of individuals worldwide. Many of the research findings by Dr. Price and his wife are being confirmed by nutrition science in the 21st century.

From 1932-42, Francis M. Pottenger, Jr., MD, conducted what is known as the *Pottenger's Cats Study* involving over 900 cats.[62] This study sparked interest in a diet high in uncooked organ meats and unpasteurized dairy. According to the Price-Pottenger Nutrition Foundation, Dr. Pottenger discovered only diets containing raw milk and raw meat produced optimal health, good bone structure and density, wide palates with plenty of space for teeth, shiny fur, no parasites or disease, reproductive ease, and gentleness. The degenerative health of the cats on cooked meat/cooked milk diets continued and appeared to be passed from generation to generation. After several generations of degeneration, Pottenger attempted to test the potential "regeneration" of health by means of replacing a cooked diet with a raw one. He found that this was indeed possible, though minor health problems persisted even into the third generation.

Dr. Pottenger's longitudinal study of nutrients and what is now recognized as the enzymes present in raw foods was decades ahead of its time. While Pottenger did not fully realize the significance of the study conclusions at the time, Pottenger and his cats paved the way for modern epigenetics.[63, 64]

The *Pottenger's Cats Study* clearly supported eating real, natural foods loaded with enzymes to prevent degeneration and illness. Dr. Pottenger applied the principles of nutrition and endocrinology early in his practice,[65] using crude extracts of adrenal cortex as supplements to treat allergic states and exhaustion. At his hospital, he served liberal amounts of liver, butter, cream, and eggs to convalescing patients.[66] In his treatment of respiratory diseases such as tuberculosis, asthma, allergies, and emphysema, he highlighted proper diet based on the principles discovered by Weston A. Price.

Developer of the Myers Cocktail

Another contemporary of Dr. Price and Dr. Pottenger was Dr. John A. Myers (1900-1984), a forward-thinking clinical doctor from Baltimore, Maryland. Dr Myers pioneered intravenous therapies.[67] His research interest was in trace minerals and the interrelationships of the biochemistry of cellular function. Myers found the application of specific nutritional elements could be used to improve the metabolism of body systems. Dr. Myers was noted for his unique way of blending mineral components to control metabolic balance in the body. The Myers cocktail was a noted formula that boosted the immune system and is still in use in IV hydration therapy.[68, 69]

Today we may not fully appreciate the work done by Dr. Harold Hawkins, a noted dental surgeon and a former Associate Professor of Bacteriology at University of Southern California. Dr. Hawkins work on human dental health answered many questions on how nutrition and the digestion of carbohydrates led to tooth decay and supported the groundbreaking work of Dr. Weston A. Price and Dr. Francis M. Pottenger, Jr.

Dr. Hawkins 'research was on nutritional biochemistry during the 1930s and 1940s of more than eight thousand individual human cases. Improved patient dental health was accomplished principally with food, supplemented by a small percentage of vitamin concentrates.

His work helped to establish a theory, widely accepted today, that tooth decay is the result of fermentation of carbohydrates by bacteria in the mouth, forming acids which in turn dissolve the mineral salts found in tooth enamel. Hawkins noted an important variable was the level of a digestive enzyme secreted in saliva. His study showed that 66% of those who were decay-prone were deficient in ptyalin, a form of amylase found in the saliva of humans.

The level of ptyalin was found to be related to two factors.

- ➢ The amount of B vitamins in the diet, which contributed to increased ptyalin production.
- ➢ The percentage of carbohydrates or sugars which tear it down. [70, 71, 72]

Plant vs. Animal

When it comes to plant-based diets, emotions can run high, and it has been a topic hotly debated for almost 200 years. Perspective on both sides is valuable. Key to the conversation is the individual's belief system. In a later chapter, we will dive deeper into protein benefits from animal and plant sources.

The Good Housekeeper, dated 1844 and written in 1830 with over 5,000 copies sold, says it follows the Andrew Comb Method and brought Andrew Comb (1797-1847) to my attention. Comb was the personal physician to King Leopold I of Belgium and Queen Victoria of England. He was known for his ability to listen and his exceptional professional courtesy. He was also a critic of the vegetarian ideas of Sylvester Graham. In his book *The Physiology of Digestion*, he commented:

> "The arguments of Mr. Graham and Dr. Alcott in favour of exclusive vegetable diet, are not based on sound physiological principles, and the broad assertions which they make of the superior strength of vegetable-eating savages in comparison with civilised Europeans, rest on insufficient evidence, and are not supported by the experience of trustworthy observers."[73]

While humans may not have had an ancient vegan predecessor, the vegan and vegetarian approaches to diet have been part of human history for over 4,000 years. The original concept of having a plant-based

diet can be traced to ancient India, China, Korea, the Arab world, and eastern Mediterranean societies. The term "veganism" began in the 1940s, while the first vegetarian society had previously formed in England in 1847. Three years later, Sylvester Graham, a minister who also invented the childhood favorite Graham crackers (1880), officially brought vegetarianism to America. Graham and his followers led lives that relied on four virtues: temperance, abstinence, hygiene, and vegetarianism. Sounds very similar to the views of J. H. Kellogg and Ellen G. White.

For individuals with strong vegan ideologies and histories, including animal foods is unnecessary. There are Hindus, Jains, and Buddhists who have cultural and religious precepts for a well-balanced diet. When a culture has a dietary history dating back for centuries, their microbiome and digestive factors (intrinsic factors: stomach acid, enzymes, microbiome) are not well suited for a radical change to eating meat. The areas for the greatest health concern for strict vegans are anemia, sarcopenia (muscle loss), and osteoporosis.[74]

There is ample research to support a well-balanced vegetarian or plant-based diet.[75, 76] However, there are occasions when a plant-based diet can be detrimental.[77] Individuals with small intestinal bacteria overgrowth (SIBO), candida overgrowth, celiac disease, and histamine illnesses cannot eat the most common staple foods or garner enough calories to support health from strict vegan or vegetarian diets.[78] Based on an individuals constitution and blood type a strict plant based approach may worsen their conditions.[79] There are also challenges for hormone balance, especially regarding conception, pregnancy, and postpartum health for female vegetarians relying on processed foods.[80] In a later chapter, we will look at the dietary needs for fertility (preconception) through lactation. Based on genetics, gender, age, and blood type, the plant-based diets can turn around chronic health challenges.[81] If an individual chooses to include animal proteins for health reasons, it should be introduced slowly with simple broths and gradually increased to mild poultry and fish. For those with type 2 diabetes, a carefully monitored plant-based diet can lower both body weight and hypertension. As with all carbohydrate-centric approaches, challenges with controlling blood sugars can occur on a low protein vegan diet.

In conclusion, even after decades of dietary research and reviewing pertinent history, it is clear that views that may be construed as quackery or pseudoscience will continue to be up for debate. Research can find merit in the dietary approaches of Kellogg, Kloss, Price, and Pottenger even when their views and recommendations appear to be in opposition. All of these dietary approaches have in common the endorsement of locally grown, minimally processed natural, and whole foods that lay the foundation for diet diversity in the 21st century. Our lesson is that ***diet matters*** in preventing, slowing, and correcting countless chronic diseases.

> ***Principle 15***: Diet Matters.

Enter Big Food Manufactures

As we continue to learn more about the nutritional superiority of whole foods over processed and refined ingredients, the food industry attunes to the market, quickly responding to consumer food demands. The food industry takes advantage of consumers living in food deserts and swamps by providing merchants with food products with lengthy expiration dates. This allows the merchant in low-income areas to maintain an inventory more affordably. By 2017, the *natural food* market, comprised of natural and organic food brands, was owned by the big giants of food: General Mills®, Campbell®, Mars®, Coke®, Pepsi®, Frito-Lay®, Cargill®, and Bayer-Monsanto®. The largest growth area of the natural foods market was food and beverage, contributing 70% of sales in 2020 alone. Current information on sales reflects a 6.6% increase in this area, accounting for $271 billion. This corner of the food market is expected to surpass $300 billion by the end of 2023. Natural foods and drinks is one area where the COVID pandemic positively impacted individuals, as more people changed to consuming whole foods to support immune health.[82]

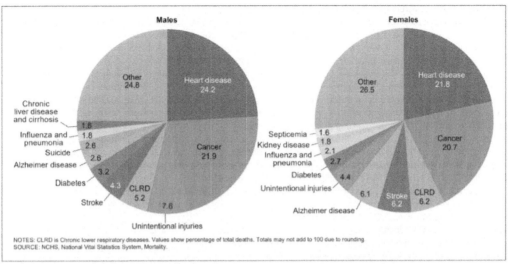

Figure 1. Percent distribution of the 10 leading causes of death, by sex: United States, 2017

---

1 Pawar, P. S., Thornton, L. M., Flatt, R. E., Sanzari, C. M., Carrino, E. A., Tregarthen, J. P., Argue, S., Bulik, C. M., & Watson, H. J. (2023). Binge-eating disorder with and without lifetime anorexia nervosa: A comparison of sociodemographic and clinical features. The International journal of eating disorders, 56(2), 428–438. https://doi.org/10.1002/eat.23858

2 Masheb, R. M., Ramsey, C. M., Marsh, A. G., Snow, J. L., Brandt, C. A., & Haskell, S. G. (2021). Atypical Anorexia Nervosa, not so atypical after all: Prevalence, correlates, and clinical severity among United States military Veterans. Eating behaviors, 41, 101496. https://doi.org/10.1016/j.eatbeh.2021.101496

3 Masheb, R. M., Ramsey, C. M., Marsh, A. G., Decker, S. E., Maguen, S., Brandt, C. A., & Haskell, S. G. (2021). DSM-5 eating disorder prevalence, gender differences, and mental health associations in United States military veterans. The International journal of eating disorders, 54(7), 1171–1180. https://doi.org/10.1002/eat.23501

4 History of Macrobiotic, The Macrobiotics Association; macrobiotics.org.uk

5 Origin and development of Ayurveda: A Brief History by V. Narayanaswamy, Anceient Science of Life 1981: https://www.ncbi.nlm.nih.gov/pmc/articles/PMC3336651/pdf/ASL-1-1.pdf

6 https://ideas.ted.com/what-americans-can-learn-from-other-food-cultures/?utm_campaign=social&utm_medium=referral&utm_source=facebook.com&utm_content=ideas-blog&utm_term=humanities

7 Foxcroft, L. (2012), Calories and Corsets: A history of dieting over two thousand years; ISBN: 1846684250

8 Lam DW, LeRoith D. Metabolic Syndrome. [Updated 2019 Feb 11]. In: Feingold KR, Anawalt B, Blackman MR, et al., editors. Endotext [Internet]. South Dartmouth (MA): MDText.com, Inc.; 2000-. Available from: https://www.ncbi.nlm.nih.gov/books/NBK278936/

9 Esposito, L. (2023), U.S. News Health; https://health.usnews.com/best-diet/zone-diet#expert-sources

10 http://www.shape.com/blogs/weight-loss-coach/dieting-through-decades-what-weve-learned-fads

11 PubMed search (2023) https://pubmed.ncbi.nlm.nih.gov/?term=Terry%20Wahls&page=2

12 CARTA: The Evolution of Human Nutrition: University of California Television (2013): https://www.youtube.com/watch?v=e_NYyDcsEPQ

13 Kabukcu C. (2022) The real Paleo diet: new archaeological evidence changes what we thought about how ancient humans prepared food: https://theconversation.com/the-real-paleo-diet-new-archaeological-evidence-changes-what-we-thought-about-how-ancient-humans-prepared-food-195127

14 Hendy, J., Welker, F., Demarchi, B. et al. A guide to ancient protein studies. Nat Ecol Evol 2, 791–799 (2018). https://doi.org/10.1038/s41559-018-0510-x

15 Voegtlin, W., (1975)The Stone Age Diet: Based On In Depth Studies Of Human Ecology And The Diet Of Man

16 Lindeberg, S., Jönsson, T., Granfeldt, Y. et al. A Palaeolithic diet improves glucose tolerance more than a Mediterranean-like diet in individuals with ischaemic heart disease. Diabetologia 50, 1795–1807 (2007). https://doi.org/10.1007/s00125-007-0716-y

17 Klonoff DC. The beneficial effects of a Paleolithic diet on type 2 diabetes and other risk factors for cardiovascular disease. J Diabetes Sci Technol. 2009 Nov 1;3(6):1229-32. doi: 10.1177/193229680900300601. PMID: 20144375; PMCID: PMC2787021.

18 Gupta, L., Khandelwal, D., Lal, P. R., Kalra, S., & Dutta, D. (2019). Palaeolithic Diet in Diabesity and Endocrinopathies- A Vegan's Perspective. European endocrinology, 15(2), 77–82. https://doi.org/10.17925/EE.2019.15.2.77

19 Sohouli, M. H., Fatahi, S., Izze da Silva Magalhães, E., Rodrigues de Oliveira, B., Rohani, P., Ezoddin, N., Roshan, M. M., & Hekmatdoost, A. (2022). Adherence to a Paleolithic Diet in Combination With Lifestyle Factors Reduces the Risk for the Presence of Non-Alcoholic Fatty Liver Disease: A Case-Control Study. Frontiers in nutrition, 9, 934845. https://doi.org/10.3389/fnut.2022.934845

20 Frączek, B., Pięta, A., Burda, A., Mazur-Kurach, P., & Tyrała, F. (2021). Paleolithic Diet-Effect on the Health Status and Performance of Athletes?. Nutrients, 13(3), 1019. https://doi.org/10.3390/nu13031019

21 Sohouli, M. H., Fatahi, S., Lari, A., Lotfi, M., Seifishahpar, M., Găman, M. A., Rahideh, S. T., AlBatati, S. K., AlHossan, A. M., Alkhalifa, S. A., Alomar, S. A., & Abu-Zaid, A. (2022). The effect of paleolithic diet on glucose metabolism and lipid profile among patients with metabolic disorders: a systematic review and meta-analysis of randomized controlled trials. Critical reviews in food science and nutrition, 62(17), 4551–4562. https://doi.org/10.1080/10408398.2021.1876625

22 de Menezes, E. V. A., Sampaio, H. A. C., Carioca, A. A. F., Parente, N. A., Brito, F. O., Moreira, T. M. M., de Souza, A. C. C., & Arruda, S. P. M. (2019). Influence of Paleolithic diet on anthropometric markers in chronic diseases: systematic review and meta-analysis. Nutrition journal, 18(1), 41. https://doi.org/10.1186/s12937-019-0457-z

23 M. Ryberg, S. Sandberg, C. Mellberg, O. Stegle, B. Lindahl, C. Larsson, J. Hauksson, T. Olsson (2013); A Palaeolithic-type diet causes strong tissue-specific effects on ectopic fat deposition in obese postmenopausal women. https://onlinelibrary.wiley.com/doi/10.1111/joim.12048

24 Nepal Population (2023) https://countrymeters.info/en/Nepal

25 Yao, J., Zhang, Y., Zhao, J., Wang, X. Z., Lin, Y. P., Sun, L., Lu, Q. Y., & Fan, G. J. (2022). Efficacy of flavonoids-containing supplements on insulin resistance and associated metabolic risk factors in overweight and obese subjects: a systematic review and meta-analysis of 25 randomized controlled trials. Frontiers in endocrinology, 13, 917692. https://doi.org/10.3389/fendo.2022.917692

26 Tovar-Palacio, C., Noriega, L. G., & Mercado, A. (2022). Potential of Polyphenols to Restore SIRT1 and NAD+ Metabolism in Renal Disease. Nutrients, 14(3), 653. https://doi.org/10.3390/nu14030653

27 Minich, D., (2018) The Rainbow Diet: A Holistic Approach to Radiant Health Through Foods and Supplements (Nutrition, Healthy Diet & Weight Loss)

28 The Rainbow Diet: eating by colour to boost health and longevity, (2022): https://longevity.technology/lifestyle/the-rainbow-diet-eating-by-colour-to-boost-health-and-longevity/

29 Pérez-Jiménez, J., Neveu, V., Vos, F., & Scalbert, A. (2010). Systematic analysis of the content of 502 polyphenols in 452 foods and beverages: an application of the phenol-explorer database. Journal of agricultural and food chemistry, 58(8), 4959–4969. https://doi.org/10.1021/jf100128b

30 Rakhi, N. K., Tuwani, R., Mukherjee, J., & Bagler, G. (2018). Data-driven analysis of biomedical literature suggests broad-spectrum benefits of culinary herbs and spices. PloS one, 13(5), e0198030. https://doi.org/10.1371/journal.pone.0198030

31 Yao, J., Zhao, J., Wang, X., Yang, Z., Lin, Y., Sun, L., Zhang, Y., Lu, Q., & Fan, G. (2022). Flavonoids for viral acute respiratory tract infections: protocol for a systematic review and meta-analysis of randomised controlled trials. BMJ open, 12(9), e056919. https://doi.org/10.1136/bmjopen-2021-056919

32 Guasch-Ferré, M., & Willett, W. C. (2021). The Mediterranean diet and health: a comprehensive overview. Journal of internal medicine, 290(3), 549–566. https://doi.org/10.1111/joim.13333

33 Galbete, C., Schwingshackl, L., Schwedhelm, C., Boeing, H., & Schulze, M. B. (2018). Evaluating Mediterranean diet and risk of chronic disease in cohort studies: an umbrella review of meta-analyses. European journal of epidemiology, 33(10), 909–931. https://doi.org/10.1007/s10654-018-0427-3

34 Serra-Majem, L., Tomaino, L., Dernini, S., Berry, E. M., Lairon, D., Ngo de la Cruz, J., Bach-Faig, A., et al. (2020). Updating the Mediterranean Diet Pyramid towards Sustainability: Focus on Environmental Concerns. International Journal of Environmental Research and Public Health, 17(23), 8758. MDPI AG. Retrieved from http://dx.doi.org/10.3390/ijerph17238758

35 Conger, K., (2023) Mediterranean diet's cellular effects revealed: https://med.stanford.edu/news/all-news/2023/05/mediterranean-diet-fat.html

36 Wilson JM, Lowery RP, Roberts MD, Sharp MH, Joy JM, Shields KA, Partl JM, Volek JS, D'Agostino DP. Effects of Ketogenic Dieting on Body Composition, Strength, Power, and Hormonal Profiles in Resistance Training Men. J Strength Cond Res. 2020 Dec;34(12):3463-3474. doi: 10.1519/JSC.0000000000001935. PMID: 28399015.

37 Tan-Shalaby J. (2017). Ketogenic Diets and Cancer: Emerging Evidence. Federal practitioner : for the health care professionals of the VA, DoD, and PHS, 34(Suppl 1), 37S–42S.

Chapter 3 ~ Paradigm Shift ~ Diet: A Mannar of Life

38. Ari, C., Kovács, Z., Murdun, C., Koutnik, A. P., Goldhagen, C. R., Rogers, C., Diamond, D., & D'Agostino, D. P. (2018). Nutritional ketosis delays the onset of isoflurane induced anesthesia. BMC anesthesiology, 18(1), 85. https://doi.org/10.1186/s12871-018-0554-0
39. Poff AM, Moss S, Soliven M, D'Agostino DP. Ketone Supplementation: Meeting the Needs of the Brain in an Energy Crisis. Front Nutr. 2021 Dec 23;8:783659. doi: 10.3389/fnut.2021.783659. PMID: 35004814; PMCID: PMC8734638.
40. Norwitz NG, Mindrum MR, Giral P, Kontush A, Soto-Mota A, Wood TR, D'Agostino DP, Manubolu VS, Budoff M, Krauss RM. Elevated LDL-cholesterol levels among lean mass hyper-responders on low-carbohydrate ketogenic diets deserve urgent clinical attention and further research. J Clin Lipidol. 2022 Nov-Dec;16(6):765-768. doi: 10.1016/j.jacl.2022.10.010. Epub 2022 Nov 2. PMID: 36351849.
41. Vasim, I., Majeed, C. N., & DeBoer, M. D. (2022). Intermittent Fasting and Metabolic Health. Nutrients, 14(3), 631. https://doi.org/10.3390/nu14030631
42. Templeman, I., Gonzalez, J. T., Thompson, D., & Betts, J. A. (2020). The role of intermittent fasting and meal timing in weight management and metabolic health. The Proceedings of the Nutrition Society, 79(1), 76–87. https://doi.org/10.1017/S0029665119000636
43. Rynders, C. A., Thomas, E. A., Zaman, A., Pan, Z., Catenacci, V. A., & Melanson, E. L. (2019). Effectiveness of Intermittent Fasting and Time-Restricted Feeding Compared to Continuous Energy Restriction for Weight Loss. Nutrients, 11(10), 2442. https://doi.org/10.3390/nu11102442
44. Russo A, Autelitano M, Bisanti L. Metabolic syndrome and cancer risk. Eur J Cancer. 2008 Jan;44(2):293-7. doi: 10.1016/j.ejca.2007.11.005. Epub 2007 Dec 4. PMID: 18055193.
45. Mindikoglu, A. L., Abdulsada, M. M., Jain, A., Jalal, P. K., Devaraj, S., Wilhelm, Z. R., Opekun, A. R., & Jung, S. Y. (2020). Intermittent fasting from dawn to sunset for four consecutive weeks induces anticancer serum proteome response and improves metabolic syndrome. Scientific reports, 10(1), 18341. https://doi.org/10.1038/s41598-020-73767-w
46. Ostendorf, D. M., Caldwell, A. E., Zaman, A., Pan, Z., Bing, K., Wayland, L. T., Creasy, S. A., Bessesen, D. H., MacLean, P., Melanson, E. L., & Catenacci, V. A. (2022). Comparison of weight loss induced by daily caloric restriction versus intermittent fasting (DRIFT) in individuals with obesity: study protocol for a 52-week randomized clinical trial. Trials, 23(1), 718. https://doi.org/10.1186/s13063-022-06523-2
47. Ezzati, A., Rosenkranz, S. K., Phelan, J., & Logan, C. (2023). The Effects of Isocaloric Intermittent Fasting vs Daily Caloric Restriction on Weight Loss and Metabolic Risk Factors for Noncommunicable Chronic Diseases: A Systematic Review of Randomized Controlled or Comparative Trials. Journal of the Academy of Nutrition and Dietetics, 123(2), 318–329.e1. https://doi.org/10.1016/j.jand.2022.09.013
48. Zhang, L., Liu, Y., Sun, Y., & Zhang, X. (2022). Combined Physical Exercise and Diet: Regulation of Gut Microbiota to Prevent and Treat of Metabolic Disease: A Review. Nutrients, 14(22), 4774. https://doi.org/10.3390/nu14224774
49. Zhang, L., Wang, Y., Sun, Y., & Zhang, X. (2023). Intermittent Fasting and Physical Exercise for Preventing Metabolic Disorders through Interaction with Gut Microbiota: A Review. Nutrients, 15(10), 2277. https://doi.org/10.3390/nu15102277
50. Schwalfenberg G. K. (2012). The alkaline diet: is there evidence that an alkaline pH diet benefits health?. Journal of environmental and public health, 2012, 727630. https://doi.org/10.1155/2012/727630
51. Han, Y., An, M., Yang, L., Li, L., Rao, S., & Cheng, Y. (2021). Effect of Acid or Base Interventions on Bone Health: A Systematic Review, Meta-Analysis, and Meta-Regression. Advances in nutrition (Bethesda, Md.), 12(4), 1540–1557. https://doi.org/10.1093/advances/nmab002
52. García-Gavilán, J. F., Martínez, A., Konieczna, J., Mico-Perez, R., García-Arellano, A., Basora, J., Barrubés, L., Goday, A., Canudas, S., Salas-Salvadó, J., & Bulló, M. (2021). U-Shaped Association between Dietary Acid Load and Risk of Osteoporotic Fractures in 2 Populations at High Cardiovascular Risk. The Journal of nutrition, 151(1), 152–161. https://doi.org/10.1093/jn/nxaa335
53. Li, C. F., Liu, Y. P., Liu, C. Y., Zhu, H. L., Wu, B. H., Li, B. L., & Chen, Y. M. (2022). Dietary Acid Load Was Positively Associated with the Risk of Hip Fracture in Elderly Adults. Nutrients, 14(18), 3748. https://doi.org/10.3390/nu14183748
54. John Harvey Kellogg Papers, 1832-1965, (Majority of material found within 1874-1943): https://findingaids.lib.umich.edu/catalog/umich-bhl-851724
55. http://www.amazon.com/Harvey-Kellogg-Religion-Biologic-Living/dp/0253014476/ref=pd_sim_sbs_b_1?ie=UTF8&refRID=00AMH5K1T99PXZ7S4Y1P
56. Czeranko S. (2019). Henry Lindlahr (1862-1924). Integrative medicine (Encinitas, Calif.), 18(3), 49.
57. Price, W. A., (2004) Nutrition and Physical Degeneration 6th Edition
58. https://www.westonaprice.org/health-topics/nutrition-greats/weston-a-price-dds/
59. https://price-pottenger.org/why-traditional-diet
60. Price, W. A (1933) Acid-Base Balance of Diets That Produce Immunity to Dental Caries Among the South Sea Islanders and Other Primitive Races
61. http://www.bcmj.org/article/ancel-keys-and-lipid-hypothesis-early-breakthroughs-current-management-dyslipidemia
62. Pottenger F. M., (1983) Pottenger's Cats, a study in nutrition
63. Price Pottenger Foundation (1952-2023) https://price-pottenger.org/blog/pottengers-cats-early-epigenetics-and-implications-for-your-health/

64 Graham, Gray, Kesten, Deborah, and Scherwitz, Larry. 2011. Pottenger's Prophecy: How Food Resets Genes for Wellness or Illness. Amherst, Mass.: White River Press.
65 http://ifnh.org/product-category/educational-materials/pioneers-of-nutrition/dr-francis-m-pottenger-jr/
66 http://en.wikipedia.org/wiki/Francis_M._Pottenger,_Jr.
67 Gaby A. R., (2002) Intravenous Nutrient Therapy: the "Myers' Cocktail" Alternative Medicine Review Volume 7, Number 5 pg. 389
68 http://ifnh.org/product-category/educational-materials/pioneers-of-nutrition/dr-john-a-myers/
69 Levy T., E. (2002) Vitamin C, Infectious Diseases, and Toxins ISBN# 1-4010-6964-9
70 http://ifnh.org/product-category/educational-materials/pioneers-of-nutrition/dr-harold-f-hawkins/
71 http://www.dentalbytes.com/dental-treatments/dental-care/dentist-dietetic-service-3.htm
72 Hawkins, H.F., Applied Nutrition ISBN-13: 978-0878810697
73 Combe, Andrew. (1860). The Physiology of Digestion. Edinburgh: Maclachan & Stewart. pp. 145-146
74 The Endocrine Society. (2022, August 4). Vegans who lift weights may have stronger bones than other people on a plant-based diet: Vegans and omnivores who do resistance training may have similar bone structure. ScienceDaily. Retrieved April 21, 2023 from www.sciencedaily.com/releases/2022/08/220804102619.htm
75 Miles, F. L., Lloren, J. I. C., Haddad, E., Jaceldo-Siegl, K., Knutsen, S., Sabate, J., & Fraser, G. E. (2019). Plasma, Urine, and Adipose Tissue Biomarkers of Dietary Intake Differ Between Vegetarian and Non-Vegetarian Diet Groups in the Adventist Health Study-2. The Journal of nutrition, 149(4), 667–675. https://doi.org/10.1093/jn/nxy292
76 Medawar, E., Huhn, S., Villringer, A., & Veronica Witte, A. (2019). The effects of plant-based diets on the body and the brain: a systematic review. Translational psychiatry, 9(1), 226. https://doi.org/10.1038/s41398-019-0552-0
77 University of Helsinki. (2021, January 21). Vegan diet significantly remodels metabolism in young children: Statuses of Vitamin D and A require special attention. ScienceDaily. Retrieved April 21, 2023 from www.sciencedaily.com/releases/2021/01/210121132300.htm
78 Devrim-Lanpir, A., Hill, L., & Knechtle, B. (2021). Efficacy of Popular Diets Applied by Endurance Athletes on Sports Performance: Beneficial or Detrimental? A Narrative Review. Nutrients, 13(2), 491. https://doi.org/10.3390/nu13020491
79 Klein L, Dawczynski C, Schwarz M, Maares M, Kipp K, Haase H, Kipp AP. Selenium, Zinc, and Copper Status of Vegetarians and Vegans in Comparison to Omnivores in the Nutritional Evaluation (NuEva) Study. Nutrients. 2023 Aug 11;15(16):3538. doi: 10.3390/nu15163538. PMID: 37630729; PMCID: PMC10459941.
80 Gajski G, Matković K, Delić L, Gerić M. Evaluation of Primary DNA Damage in Young Healthy Females Based on Their Dietary Preferences. Nutrients. 2023 May 8;15(9):2218. doi: 10.3390/nu15092218. PMID: 37432334; PMCID: PMC10181164.
81 American College of Cardiology. (2020, March 18). To reap heart benefits of a plant-based diet, avoid junk food: Plant-based diet found to reduce cardiovascular risk, but only if foods are healthful. ScienceDaily. Retrieved April 21, 2023 from www.sciencedaily.com/releases/2020/03/200318104449.htm
82 Crawford, E (2021) Sales growth of natural, organic products slows, but still on track to surpass $300bn by 2023: https://www.foodnavigator-usa.com/Article/2021/09/24/Sales-growth-of-natural-organic-products-slows-but-still-on-track-to-surpass-300bn-by-2023

Victor Lindlahr, the son of Dr Henry Lindlahr, considered the founder of American Naturopathy, or more accurately, the bringer of the German Nature Cure to the United States. Copy 1942 authors collection.

> "Healthy citizens are the greatest asset any country can have."
>
> ~Winston Churchill

Chapter Four~ Digestion Connection

To live, we must eat. But what we eat and why, and numerous cumulative effects of lifestyle on our body systems can create a complicated story. Let's begin by first looking at the amazing digestive system.

Everything ingested into and processed within the digestive tract becomes more than defined macronutrients (carbohydrates, fats, and protein); it becomes a sea of chemicals, minerals, enzymes, vitamins, and beneficial bacteria, many of which are still being explored by modern science. These compounds are combined intelligently to make up every structure, reaction, and function within the human body. Because of the innate intelligence that connects all cell functions in the body, one organ system's nutrient supply cannot be easily separated from another — if blood flows to it, then the food you eat and the chemicals contained in that food will go there.

Every culture on the planet has its distinct food history. As humans evolved, they learned from observation which foods were safe, satisfying, strengthening, and enlightening (ceremonial foods). Because of this, each population developed the ability to digest and utilize foods unique to its environment.

We are dependent on the digestive system to process and absorb nutrients regardless of whether they come from nutraceuticals or whole natural foods.[1] This critical body system is comprised of the brain, mouth, pharynx, esophagus, stomach, small and large intestine, liver, gallbladder, pancreas, kidneys, bladder, and the microbiome.

The word "*digestion*" means "*to take apart.*" It is the process whereby food is broken down mechanically and chemically in the gastrointestinal tract and converted into absorbable substances. Before diving into aspects of the lower digestive system, let's first look at the brain, where the digestive process begins. The cephalic phase ("*cephalic*" means "*relating to the head*") starts in the brain. It explains why you may feel hungry after walking by a bakery or seeing a TV commercial, or why some individuals will start to sweat when entering a restaurant. Preparation for food to enter the physical digestive tract all starts happening when we look at, smell, or even think about food. This concept was first described by Ivan Pavlov, who demonstrated that his dogs would start salivating at the anticipation of a meal.[2] There is a constant dynamic interplay between the mind and the digestive process, as emotions profoundly influence the functioning and structure of tissues in the stomach and intestines. These sensitive tissues display immediate responses to anger, anxiety, fear, and all forms of stress and worry.

> ***Principle 16:*** Our cells carry the memory of our ancestors. It is well to learn your own family history: place of origin, cultural food preferences, and preparation, so you can eat those things that will be familiar to the genetics of your body's cells.

Miracle Cure

Whenever someone recounts a miraculous improvement after using a new supplement, I instinctively know the individual has significant nutritional issues and, in a matter of time, their dramatic results will fade. The primary physiological reason for this dramatic response is that as cell receptor sites open and receive long missing or insufficient nutrients, they at first respond in an over-excited manner, which can result in sudden, dramatic improvements in well-being. As time passes, generally after 90-180 days, the receptor sites *reset* and the response moderates. Awareness of improved health diminishes as a new normal (set point) is achieved. This set point is not permanent, and when we stop taking supplemental nutrients and consuming healthy whole foods, a deficiency will once more result. Notably, some individuals will experience positive results for extended periods depending on the dietary approach, the health of the microbiome, and the quality of nutrients taken as supplements.

The other side of this coin comes with no obvious sign of improvement. When our cells are nourished, we have an upturn in energy, mental alertness, and motivation. However, when chronic illness is involved, it can take weeks, months, or years to replenish the needed nutrients to optimal levels. Deep healing, which occurs on the microscopic level, takes time — during which individuals may feel small improvements — but then revert to how they felt before. The chronically ill require higher than recommended levels of nutrition in easily digestible forms, primarily as food for the mitochondria within cells to have adequate energy for healing and remission of symptoms. To recover from injury (including surgery) or an illness, recommended dietary allowances (RDA) are not enough; and handfuls of vitamin supplements cannot replace the nutritional value of real foods and the symphony of biochemical interactions that are required to truly feed our bodies. Dr. Terry Wahls does an excellent job of explaining this process in her book *The Wahls Protocol*.

The Gut

Healthy Gut Advisor, Karen Langston, tells clients: **the gut is the home to all health and the throne of all illness**. The distinct organs that make up the gut all play a role in the transportation of nutrients, fostering a flourishing microbiome and protective barrier to pathogens and parasites. When the single-cell lining of the gut (epithelium) becomes damaged, particles of undigested food and harmful pathogens enter our bloodstream, where they can trigger auto-immune reactions and damage the liver, nerves, and even the brain. This condition is called increased intestinal permeability (IIP) or leaky gut syndrome. Tight junctions between intestinal epithelial cells that line the digestive tract serve major protective function. When these junctions become weakened, they cannot successfully control intestinal and/or bowel permeability, losing their critical protective function. Minerals, water, and monosaccharides can be absorbed as-is without needing molecular changes by the digestive tract. These compounds are directly absorbed into the bloodstream. However, fats, starches, and proteins must be broken down into smaller molecules.

As a general rule, mainstream Western medicine does not support the theory behind *leaky gut syndrome*. An individual can suffer for decades with increasing health challenges associated with IIP. However, according to the Director of the Center for Human Nutrition at the Cleveland Clinic, Donald Kirby, MD, this attitude does not mean the theory is invalid. "From an MD's standpoint, it's a very gray area," he says. "Physicians don't know enough about the gut, which is our biggest immune system organ. We can say, however, that leaky gut reflects an unknown diagnosis that still needs to be made."[3] In 2023, leaky gut syndrome or IIP is not taught in standard medical curricula.

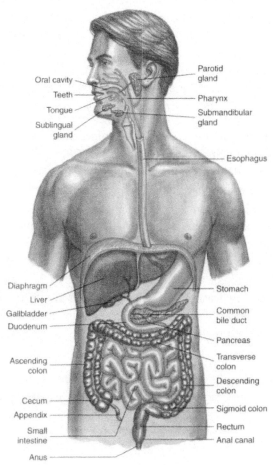

When I interviewed *Healthy Gut Advisor* Karen Langston, she shared, "Interesting to note, leaky gut is not something new. What has changed is the terminology." Originally referred to as *intestinal hyperpermeability*, it has morphed into *intestinal permeability* and now *leaky gut*. A paper published in 2021 reported that the onset of metabolic disorders depends on the damage to the integrity of the intestinal barrier, resulting in intestinal permeability. A growing body of research supports intestinal microbiota as an environmental factor crucial to obesity and associated metabolic disorders. Chronic inflammation due to endotoxemia is now believed to be a key contributor to the development of obesity.[4] Metabolic disorders are associated with dysregulation of the microbiota-gut-brain axis and an altered gut flora composition.[5, 6, 7]

Research published in 2023 revealed that *microplastics may pose a serious danger to the intestine.* Researchers found signs of potential inflammatory effects, including the release of cytokines linked to human inflammatory bowel disease (IBD). We unwittingly eat, drink, and inhale microplastics on a regular basis, with the average person now ingesting an estimated 74,000 tiny plastic particles every year. The experiments showed different cell types absorbing different sizes of particles. The smallest nanoplastics were taken in by epithelial cells, which line the interior walls of the intestines, while microfold cells, which play a role in the gut's immune response, absorbed larger particles and sent them into the intestinal tissue.[8]

> ***Principle 17:*** Food is medicine.

When Medication Interferes with Digestion

Western medicine treats symptoms with targeted medications, surgeries, or appliances. However, side effects and complications from pharmaceuticals can result in more drugs being prescribed, with polypharmacy as the outcome. One common, but rarely addressed, side effect of medication use is nutritional deficiencies, which can lead to cascading symptomology and health degradation. According to a paper published in 2018, the number of research studies examining potential drug-nutrient interactions is limited. The long-term use of prescription and over-the-counter drugs can induce both subclinical and clinically relevant micronutrient deficiencies that develop over months or years.[9] A paper published following COVID-19 concluded that elderly patients with chronic diseases who used nutrient-depleting medications were at high risk for micronutrient deficiency when the inflammatory insult of COVID-19 is present.[10] A deficiency of micronutrients impairs immune responses, which results in inappropriate secretion of cytokines, decreased antibody response and antibody affinity, and increased susceptibility to viral infection.[11] To maintain a healthy level of circulating nutrients in the body we must be able to extract them from the food we ingest. If there is an incomplete nutrient profile in the food consumed, deficiency occurs. According to the *National Institute of Health* (NIH), 60-70 million people report being affected by a digestive disease. As of 2023, *drugs.com* listed 81 medications for indigestion alone.

Many patients are under the impression that their healthcare providers have training in nutrition and are keeping up with current research. Often, this is not the case. Extensive pharmacologic training prepares providers to know more about drug interactions than subsequent nutrient deficiencies caused by drugs. One example is the need to supplement with coenzyme Q10 when placing clients on cholesterol medications or advising them to take red yeast rice.[12, 13] Another hazard is patients becoming victims of *standard practices* or *routines*, often due to physicians 'workload and decision-making being driven by insurance companies 'formularies/reimbursements and government protocols. The current age of *electronic medical records* (mandated by the Obamacare Act) often confuses practitioners and clients alike. Individuals today have greater access to over-the-counter (OTC) medications, many that were available only by prescription five or ten years ago. With this ease of access and the incessant influence of TV commercials, individuals may be using drugs that adversely affect their digestion and general health without realizing it.

> ***Principle 18:*** A healthy gut is necessary for good health.

Chapter 4 ~ Digestion Connection

The (outdated) published information on the NIH website lists acid reflux as weekly affecting 20% of the U.S. population, with 64.6 million related prescriptions given in 2004. The 2023 version of the Johns Hopkins website lists the following drugs as the most prescribed for a host of digestive conditions.

> Over the counter and prescribed medications that increase the severity of reflux:
> - Nonsteroidal anti-inflammatory agents (NSAIDs)
> - Nitrates
> - Theophylline
> - Calcium channel blockers
> - Oral antibiotics
> - Birth control pills

One of medication's most common side effects is constipation. Various drugs can cause constipation by affecting the nerve and muscle activity in the colon (large intestine).[14, 15] In 2000, 63 million people in North America suffered from chronic constipation.[16] This resulted in 5.3 million prescriptions by 2004.[17, 18]

> Medicines that may cause constipation include the following:
> - Antihypertensives
> - Anticholinergics
> - Cholestyramine
> - Iron
> - Antacids containing mostly aluminum
> - Narcotics/pain medicines

Diarrhea is another very common side effect of medication and is frequently caused by antibiotics, all of which affect bacteria normally present in the large intestine. At its worst, the deleterious antibiotic effect on intestinal bacteria allows the overgrowth of Clostridium difficile (*C. difficile*), causing severe antibiotic-induced diarrhea. This bacterium is associated with colitis, an inflammation of the bowel, resulting in very loose, watery stools.

> The most common antibiotics to cause this type of diarrhea:
> - Penicillin, including ampicillin and amoxicillin
> - Clindamycin
> - Cephalosporins

Over the past few decades, the significantly increased use of pharmaceuticals, combined with a diet consisting of predominately manufactured foods, has placed the United States 35th in the world for health. According to the 2019 Bloomberg Global Health Index ranking, Spain's overall score of 92.75 qualified it as the healthiest country in the world.[19]

> ***Principle 19:*** Medication use (especially long-term and polypharmacy) can contribute to nutritional deficiencies and degradation of health.

Digestive health and cannabis

An epidemic of pain medication (opioid) abuse hit the media spotlight in 2015. By 2023, twenty states and the District of Columbia had legalized *cannabis* (marijuana) for medical and recreational use. Cannabis in several forms is currently viewed as a viable herb for mitigating chronic pain associated with glaucoma, migraines, back pain, Crohn's disease, nerve pain, and cancers. Research on cannabis and turmeric for inflammatory bowel disease (IBD) looked at the ability of cannabinoids to modulate gut motility and visceral pain due to their anti-inflammatory properties. Clinical trials are evaluating the therapeutic role of cannabinoid therapy in the treatment of IBD, irritable bowel syndrome (IBS), nausea and vomiting, and GI motility disorders.[20, 21] A growing body of research notes that tetrahydrocannabinol (THC) can bind to the primary cannabinoid receptors as it has a similar chemical structure to anandamides, a group of cannabinoids naturally produced in the body known as endogenous cannabinoids or endocannabinoids.[22]

While this research looks promising, the use of cannabis does not come without side effects. Regarding the digestive system, opioid pain medications and inhaled cannabis can interfere with intrinsic factors, mucosal linings, digestion, microbiome, and transit time. Research is highlighting growing concerns over these side effects.[23] *Marijuana use disorder* and *cannabinoid hyperemesis syndrome* can affect 30% of those who use inhalant cannabis.[24, 25, 26] Much like opioids, cannabis can hijack neural pathways and "light up" the dopamine reward system in the brain.[27] According to the *National Institute on Drug Abuse*, mild withdrawal symptoms include grouchiness, sleeplessness, decreased appetite, anxiety, and cravings, which are typical central nervous system substance withdrawal symptoms.[28] However, more distressing symptoms are not discussed as openly such as increased paranoia, hallucinations, cardiac damage, and loss of cognition.[29, 30] How many of these unspoken symptoms result from nutritional deficiencies, cannabis use/abuse, or the chemicals used in commercial and illegal grows has not been adequately investigated. Much like prescription pain medications, cannabis also carries risks of addiction and adverse reactions depending on the person's age and constitution.[31] It is essential to note that cannabidiol (CBD), derived from hemp, has nutritional benefits and is produced for dietary and topical use. Cannabis is a complex plant with over 400 chemical entities of which more than 60 are cannabinoid compounds, some of them with opposing effects.[32] Delta-9-tetrahydrocannabinol (THC) is most plentiful in many forms of cannabis, while CBD is found in higher quantities in hemp.[33, 34]

While I have seen this herb being used responsibly and with efficacy for several conditions, such as nausea and pain associated with cancer treatments, PTSD, migraines, and Crohn's, I have also seen the darker side effects in clients who use cannabis. Many of the symptoms for cannabinoid hyperemesis syndrome can be the same as those in an individual who may be using cannabis as treatment for nausea, vomiting, and anxiety. Consumers and clinicians alike must exercise caution when reading media websites, blogs, commercial flyers, and marketing information about the use of cannabis.

In 2020, the University of Alberta published research on more than 100 toxic chemicals present in cannabis smoke. For individuals purchasing through dispensaries, there is a growing risk that the product purchased for pain management is potentially worsening their condition due to fertilizer, insecticides, and fungicides.[35] Chemicals such as nitrogen oxides, hydrogen cyanide, and aromatic amines were found in marijuana smoke at concentrations three to five times higher than tobacco smoke.[36] Unfortunately, many individuals seeking care for chronic pain management also suffer from severe nutritional deficiencies. These individuals can be so consumed with their pain and the added depression and stress associated with chronic illness that the thought of making radical dietary changes to natural organic food is overwhelming. We live in a society that does not value food as medicine, nor do we completely understand digestion and its impact on our health, especially as a contributor to chronic pain.[37, 38, 39]

The *cannabinoid* receptors in the human brain (CB1) outnumber other neurochemical receptor types. CB1 acts like a traffic control for the levels and activity of most other neurotransmitters. Our bodies produce endocannabinoids, structurally like molecules in the cannabis plant. The first endocannabinoid discovered was named *anandamide* after the Sanskrit word *Ananda*, meaning *bliss*. A second cannabinoid receptor, CB2, exists primarily in our immune system and is critical to helping control immune function and modulating intestinal inflammation, contractions, and pain in inflammatory bowel conditions.[40]

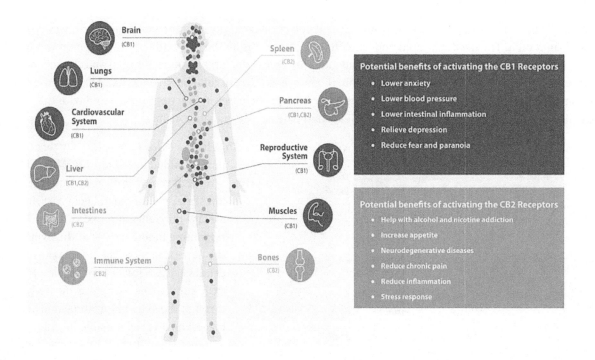

Genetic Testing

In 2015 genetic testing became available to physicians to assist with appropriate drug determination. These tests allow providers and clients to learn early on in selected therapies which medications individuals will respond to positively. A similar approach is beneficial for natural healthcare practitioners in understanding the nutrient needs of individuals. Genetic laboratories such as 23andMe, combined with a growing number of gene interpreting companies, provide information on the methylenetetrahydrofolate (MTFHR) gene associated with many illnesses: heart disease, Alzheimer's, macular degeneration, attention deficit hyperactivity disorder (ADHD), and some cancers. Additionally, these reports provide information on caffeine metabolism and whether cilantro tastes like soap. We will look more at the growing world of bioindividual nutrition and the new information gene research is bringing to light in an upcoming chapter.

> ***Principle 20:*** Dietary recommendations should be determined by individual needs: genetics, cultural background, beliefs, lifestyle choices, family and community norms, and available resources.

Liver

Most of us spend very little time thinking about our liver. Much attention is focused on the heart and the brain, and for a good reason, but the liver is equally as important.

Where is the liver in relation to everything else? If you're an anatomy student, you can probably lay your hand right on it. The liver is located underneath the bottom ribs on the right side of the abdomen and is only inches from the heart, lungs, kidneys and gut. The liver is the largest internal organ and the second largest organ in the whole body, after the skin. It comprises 2.5% of total body weight and is the only organ able to regenerate after injury or illness. The liver participates in functions associated with the cardiovascular, digestive, and excretory systems and plays a role in metabolism.

The liver stores and filters the blood to remove infectious organisms. It processes approximately three pints of blood every minute. Most blood arrives at the liver directly from the intestines via the portal vein carrying dietary nutrients and toxins. The remaining blood arrives at the liver via the hepatic artery. The liver is the primary organ for detoxification of toxic substances that enter the body through the skin, respiration, and ingestion. It is responsible for the metabolism of 90% of ingested alcohol, 25% of basal metabolism, and for the conversion of stored glycogen into glucose for release into the bloodstream.

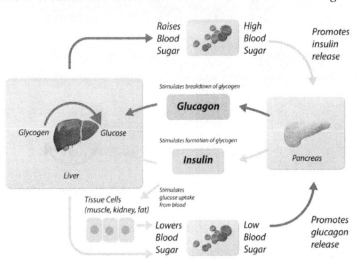

Intestinal permeability may be an underlying cause of liver malfunction. This can occur due to the additional workload placed on the liver of detoxifying antigens that enter the body because of poor gut health. This is an especially important consideration for children and adults with gluten sensitivity and autism spectrum. Systemic lupus erythematosus (SLE), a form of the grave autoimmune disease lupus erythematosus (LE), and hepatitis A, B and C infections cause degeneration and death of the liver. Additionally, impaired liver function may occur because of adrenal insufficiency and gluten sensitivity.

Geneticists have discovered that approximately 40% of the population are poor methylators. Affected individuals have difficulty collecting and utilizing nutrients like B vitamins and sulfur compounds, substances that aid in metabolic conversion to co-factors. Poor methylation by the liver may also cause reduced carbohydrate metabolism, which would also affect the liver's ability to control glycogen, leptin, and cholesterol production and utilization. Could this be part of the reason for increases in the incidence of diabetes and non-alcoholic fatty liver disease which have occurred since the COVID pandemic? Time will tell us more. But these are things we know now: if your liver is bogged down with high fructose corn sweetener, medications, and chemicals, you are increasing your risk factors for type 2 diabetes, fatty liver disease, hormone disruption, and obesity.

The liver stores several vitamins and minerals for the body to use: cobalt, 15% of the body's copper, manganese, ferritin (the endogenous form of iron), coenzyme Q10, biotin, and folic acid. Vitamins A, C, D, E, K, B1, B2, B5, B6, and B12 all concentrate in the liver. But that's not all. Endogenous phospholipids (healthy fats) and proteins are manufactured in the liver as well as cholesterol, which protects the brain and heart, and is necessary for hormone production.

For those with thyroid disease, approximately 80% of triiodothyronine (T3) is produced in the liver from the conversion of thyroxine (T4) to T3, and T3 accounts for 20% of thyroid hormone production. T3 is approximately ten times more potent than T4. A healthy liver is central to hormone production and utilization of all hormones: insulin, testosterone, progesterone, estrogens [estrone (E1), estradiol (E2), estriol (E3)], melatonin, DHEA, and others.

People with liver ailments should avoid carnitine, "smart drugs" (Adrafinil, Propranolol only with caution), xanthinol nicotinate, the herbs coltsfoot, licorice, and valerian, and high iron-containing foods such as watermelon, strawberries, sesame seeds, pumpkin seeds, liver, molasses, and prunes. Beneficial herbs for liver health are artichoke leaf, green tea, jiaogulan, Korean ginseng, Lycium, and milk thistle as well as black cherry (juice), grape (juice), lemon (juice, drink upon awakening in the morning), pear (juice), and reishi mushrooms. Many of these herbs and foods are found in high-quality liver detox products and plans.

I encourage you to do a liver detox twice a year and follow in your ancestors' footsteps by eating grass-fed, sustainably raised pork, beef, or poultry liver 1-4 times a month (if you do not have hepatitis C or elevated ferritin levels). Liver is nature's multi-vitamin, and eating liver helps your liver to be healthier. Our ancestors knew this. It's time to return to those old-fashioned food values that kept all of us more vigorous.

> Liver malfunction may cause adult acne, rosacea, halitosis (bad breath), and psoriasis.

The Pancreas

The pancreas is comprised of an endocrine and an exocrine portion. The endocrine part consists of the Islets of Langerhans, which are responsible for the secretion of insulin, glucagon, and somatostatin. Pancreatic exocrine tissues (the acini) produce inactive digestive enzymes that are mixed with sodium bicarbonate from the ductules connecting the acini to the pancreatic duct. This pancreatic "juice" flows through the pancreatic duct, connecting with the hepatic duct, and ultimately emptying into the duodenum via the sphincter of Oddi. Once in the duodenum, the inactive enzymes come into contact with enterokinase and enteropeptidase, which activate pancreatic trypsinogen zymogen to its active form (trypsin), activating all other pancreatic enzymes.

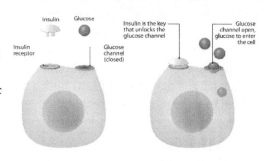

Pancreatic enzymes play a vital role in breaking down carbohydrates, proteins, and fats. Sodium bicarbonate neutralizes the acidic chyme created in the stomach that will make its way from the stomach to mix with the juice in the duodenum [thus also increasing the *pH* of the small intestine] and start the enzyme-activating process.[41]

Digestion and absorption are virtually impossible without enzymes. Enzymes are the essential building blocks of life. They are the key to the body's ability to correctly digest and benefit from the foods we eat. Enzymes provide the energy we need to rebuild muscles, cells, nerves, tissues, bones, and glands. They spark the chemical reactions responsible for breathing, digestion, growth, and reproduction. They are currently being studied for their roles in anti-aging and cognition.[42] America's foremost integrative cancer pioneer, Nicholas Gonzalez, MD, utilized enzymes heavily in his cancer protocols.

The Gallbladder

Did you know you can have gallbladder stones after removing your gallbladder? You can still develop stones in the ducts that lead to the gallbladder from the liver. While getting gallstones after a cholecystectomy (removal of the gallbladder) is rare, it can occur and will require medical treatment. To understand how gallstones can return after gallbladder surgery, it is essential to comprehend the function of the gallbladder and how gallstones are formed.

Your gallbladder is a small pear-shaped organ in the abdomen that holds a digestive fluid called bile, which is made up of 70% cholesterol. People suffering from gallbladder disease or who have recently had gallstone surgery may benefit from following a low-fat and low-cholesterol diet;[43, 44] family history should also be considered.

Located just under the liver, the gallbladder is connected by the common bile duct to the liver. The liver produces bile that drains into the gallbladder, which serves as a reservoir. When we consume food, the gallbladder contracts and releases the bile through the common bile duct, which travels into the small intestine. Bile is a fluid-like substance that helps digest the fats in the foods we consume.

Cholesterol in the bile forms stone-like deposits ranging in size from a tiny grain of sand to a golf ball. These deposits are known as gallstones. While almost everyone has gallstones, a portion of the population will develop complications from having these deposits. Complications occur when the gallstones block or become lodged in the ducts, blocking the flow of bile. Gallstones can also form in the bile ducts. This condition, known as choledocholithiasis, can cause the stones to travel and block the pancreatic duct if left untreated.

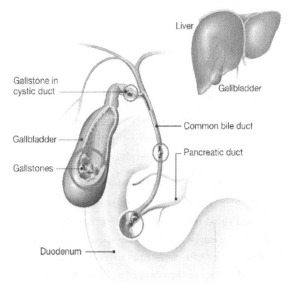

Symptoms can include minor to severe pain in the upper abdomen, upper back pain, nausea and/or vomiting. Often, individuals believe they are experiencing indigestion and do not seek medical attention until the pain becomes unbearable.[45]

Because bile aids in the digestion of fats, after the gallbladder has been removed, the body may not produce enough bile to digest fats properly, resulting in upset stomach and diarrhea. To help prevent this, the diet should avoid hydrogenated oils, margarine, saturated fats, and fried foods. You should not eliminate all fats from your diet. Healthy fats such as olive oil and omega-3 fatty acids should be included in small amounts as the body benefits from these healthy fats.

Fiber, with proper fluid intake, moves through the digestive tract with little effort, helping to keep the tract free of blockages. High-fiber choices include whole-wheat pasta, oatmeal, split peas, lentils, and black beans. According to the Mayo Clinic, you should try to consume 25-38 grams of fiber per day.[46]

After the gallbladder has been removed, a diet that includes plenty of fresh, organic fruits and vegetables is beneficial to help you heal. In addition to providing fiber, fresh fruits and vegetables are naturally low in fat and contain valuable vitamins and minerals. Recommended fruits and vegetables include beets, cucumbers, onions, garlic, grapes, lemons, tomatoes, apples, and berries.[47, 48, 49]

The Mayo Clinic recommends taking a vitamin supplement due to deficiencies in vitamin C, vitamin E or calcium that may cause you to experience digestive discomfort. You can add turmeric and ginger to meals to aid in bile production and fat digestion. When dining at restaurants, keep dressing off salads, select grilled chicken or fish, and order rice or potatoes without butter and sour cream. When dining out remember to add a pancreatic digestive enzyme product before eating. This aids the gallbladder in triggering the pancreas to release enzymes. When the trigger is not there, pancreatic enzymes become deficient.

The Appendix

This maligned and overlooked organ is a worm-like appendage attached to the cecum and closed at the other end, floating below the junction of the small and large intestines. It's a thin tube about four inches long.

The appendix has become the subject of renewed study as we research the microbiome and its role in the lymphatic and immune system of adults. We know that the appendix serves a vital role in the fetus and in young adults. Endocrine cells appear in the appendix of the human fetus at around the 11th week of development. These endocrine cells of the fetal appendix have been shown to produce various biogenic amines and peptide hormones, compounds that assist with various biological control (homeostatic) mechanisms. Up until recently, there had been little prior evidence of this particular or any other role of the appendix in animal research because the appendix does not exist in domestic mammals.

The appendix is now thought to be primarily involved in immune functions among adult humans. Lymphoid tissue begins to accumulate in the appendix shortly after birth and reaches a peak between the second and third decades of life, decreasing rapidly thereafter and practically disappearing after the age of 60. During the early years of growth and development, however, the appendix has been shown to function as a lymphoid organ, assisting with the maturation of B lymphocytes (one variety of white blood cell) and in the production of the class of antibodies known as immunoglobulin A (IgA) antibodies. Researchers have also shown that the appendix is involved in the production of molecules that help to direct the movement of lymphocytes to various other locations in the body.

In the past, the appendix was often routinely removed and discarded during other abdominal surgeries to prevent any possibility of a later attack of appendicitis. These days an appendix is spared if it appears to be healthy in case it is needed later for reconstructive surgery if the urinary bladder is removed. In such surgery, a section of the intestine is formed into a replacement bladder, and the appendix is used to re-create a urethral "sphincter muscle" so that the patient remains continent (able to retain urine). In addition, the appendix has been successfully fashioned into a makeshift replacement for a diseased ureter, allowing urine to flow from the kidneys to the bladder. As a result, the appendix, once regarded as a nonfunctional tissue, is now regarded as an important "back-up" tissue that can be used in a variety of reconstructive surgical techniques.[50]

The appendix acts as a storehouse for good bacteria capable of "rebooting" the digestive system after diarrheal illnesses. When chyme passes through the ileocecal valve entering into the cecum, the first part of the large intestine, the appendix is triggered to release commensal bacteria and then promote fermentation of contents into vital nutrients such as B vitamins, vitamin K2, iron, coenzyme Q10, fatty acids, and energy.[51]

Enzymes the Catalyst for Health

Enzymes are proteins that act as catalysts, speeding the rate of biochemical reactions. Enzymes are found in every cell of every living plant, microorganism, and animal, including humans. They can only be formed from organic living matter. Enzymes are required for the healthy functioning of every organ system. They direct, accelerate, modify, or retard all body functions. They do so in a unique, step-by-step, highly efficient, safe, and remarkably economical manner.

Enzymes serve as the body's labor force and help perform every single function required for our daily activities. They also support our immune system. As biocatalysts, they either begin a reaction or cause a reaction to speed up. Without enzymes, life would not exist.

> **Enzymes** - specialized proteins designed to break apart a specific molecule type in your food **Lipase** – breaks down fat
> **Amylase** – breaks down large carbohydrate chains
> **Cellulase** – helps break down fiber for optimal nutrition from plant foods
> **Invertase** – breaks down simple sugars
> **Alpha Galactosidase** – helps break down amylase-resistant carbohydrates
> **Protease** (also called proteolytic enzymes) – breaks down protein
> **Papain** – works with bromelain and protease
> **Bromelain** – derived from pineapple; one of the strongest, safest, and most tested way to break down proteins

The Enzymatic Process

Enzymes work by virtue of their shape. Enzyme molecules can be compared in structure to short lengths of pearls (amino acids) strung and wound together. This long string folds in on itself as specific sequences of amino acids are more attracted to each other than to other sequences, thus giving the enzymes a

particular shape. At one point on the surface of the string of "pearls," there is something resembling a keyhole. This is called the active site on the enzyme. When matched with its particular coenzyme (vitamin, mineral or trace element), this "lock" accepts the key contained in the molecule of the enzyme's substrate. The molecular structure is transformed into a different structure; both the enzymes and the newly transformed molecule are free to part.

Dr. Max Wolf, MD, researched enzymes and hormones at Columbia University from the 1930s through the 1960s. Dr. Wolf determined that enzyme production diminishes in humans after age 27. Humans have historically supplemented their enzyme levels by consuming fresh, raw foods. Modern preservation and preparation techniques often destroy the enzymes these foods contain. *Raw-foodism,* also called the raw food diet, uses this as a foundational tenet in promoting raw over cooked foods for health. As defined in a 1923 *American Raw Food, Health and Psychological Club* publication, raw food has not "been subjected to the devastating heat of the flame and the consequent devitalizing changes which destroy its freshness and render it so much waste when taken into the human system."[52]

Enzyme deficiency can cause the body's functions to become less efficient. And yet, in the past, the medical establishment paid only limited attention to this vital biological component. When enzymes were traditionally studied in medical school, the emphasis was placed primarily on their digestive functions in the pancreas and gastrointestinal tract. Sports medicine has taken the lead in using proteolytic enzymes for injuries and the reduction of inflammation and scar tissue.

Clinicians used to be taught that oral enzymes were indicated only for digestive problems and not for any other medical conditions, as they were not readily absorbed. Unfortunately, in the United States and in other countries this was generally accepted as medical dogma, and the potential importance of enzymes for other conditions was overlooked for decades.

In addition to being used for digestive disorders, enzymes are now widely utilized to treat various types of blood clots (particularly those causing heart attacks, strokes, and occlusions of the leg veins), cancer, allergies, chronic inflammatory illnesses, and several congenital deficiency diseases.[53, 54]

Proteolytic/Systemic Enzymes vs. Digestive Enzymes

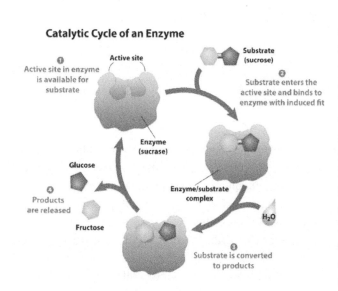

Digestive enzymes start in the mouth. In the saliva (which increases via thoughts about food, smells or feeling hunger) there are two digestive enzymes; amylase to break down simple carbohydrates and lingual lipase to break down large chain fatty acids into shorter ones. In the stomach, pepsin enzyme breaks down protein structures, and in the small intestine pancreatic enzymes and brush border enzymes help digest food particles. Supplemental digestive enzymes are found in a couple of forms and combinations. Betaine HCl is usually found with the enzyme pepsin to aid in supporting protein breakdown in the stomach. Plant digestive enzymes are grown on plant medium and are functional over a wide range of *pH* levels from the mouth to the small intestine.

Animal-based enzymes typically extracted from pancreatic or stomach enzymes in cows or pigs work in a narrow alkaline *pH* range and are thus most efficient in the small intestine.[55] Systemic or proteolytic enzymes are programmed to survive stomach acid and only activate at the right *pH* level. These enzymes need to be taken on an empty stomach to direct their action toward reducing inflammation, not aiding digestion. In this way, they can pass through the stomach into the small intestines, where they are activated and can be absorbed into the bloodstream. Animal-based pancreatic enzymes are the accepted form of supplementation for pancreatic insufficiency, providing benefit to individuals with gallbladder insufficiency or removal and gastrointestinal disorders. The safety and efficacy of these enzymes in the treatment of malabsorption and lactose intolerance is well documented.

Serratia peptidase or serrapeptase[56, 57] commonly used for chronic pain is a proteolytic enzyme isolated from the non-pathogenic enterobacteria Serratia E15. Research shows serrapeptase induces fibrinolytic, anti-inflammatory, and anti-endemic (preventing swelling and fluid retention) activity in tissues.[58, 59, 60] Its anti-inflammatory effects are believed to be eighteen times more efficient than chymotrypsin in terms of bradykinin-decomposing activity.[61] Bradykinin is a protein in the body that causes a severe inflammatory response. Additionally, serrapeptase's role in the reduction of pain is attributed to the enzyme's ability to block the release of amines from inflamed tissues. Physicians in Europe and Asia use serrapeptase as an alternative to aspirin, ibuprofen, and other NSAIDs.[62]

Bromelain: A major sulfhydryl proteolytic (protein-digesting) enzyme found in pineapple plants that exhibits anti-inflammatory properties, having multiple activities in many areas of medicine. Due to its low toxicity, high efficiency, high availability, and relative simplicity of acquisition, it is the object of inexhaustible interest of scientists. Bromelain was found to be of benefit during COVID infections by inhibiting or preventing symptoms of the disease.[63] Its anti-inflammatory and anticoagulatory properties make it a potential agent that may slow the progression of the disease. Diosmin, a flavone glycoside of *diosmetin* found mainly in citrus fruits, combined with bromelain significantly increased total thiols and glutathione in the RBCs.[64]

Papain and Rutin: Proteolytic enzymes obtained from unripe papaya. Due to their flavonoid properties, these enzymes are beneficial for strengthening capillaries and other connective tissue; some function as anti-inflammatory, antihistaminic, and anti-viral activity.[65, 66]

Amylase: A group of enzymes found in saliva, produced by the pancreas, and by parts of plants. Salivary and pancreatic amylase (encoded by AMY1 and AMY2 genes, respectively) are responsible for digesting starchy foods.[67] Some individuals produce forms of amylase that increase carbohydrate absorption, increasing susceptibility to type 2 diabetes. The genetic variant determining starch metabolism influences the response to weight-loss dietary intervention.[68, 69] Research is looking at how amylase inhibitors can reduce carbohydrate uptake. Several classes of phytochemicals, including polyphenols and flavonoids, have been shown to inhibit amylase.[70] A paper released in 2018 looked at how cooking affected the digestibility of starches. The phenolic compounds found in legumes contributes to the α-amylase inhibitory properties.[71]

Protease: Enzymes that catalyze the splitting of proteins into smaller peptide fractions and amino acids by a process known as proteolysis necessary for digestion of proteins. Regulated proteolysis is a pivotal regulatory mechanism in all living organisms, from bacteria to mammalian cells and viruses.[72]

Lipase: An enzyme secreted in the digestive tract that catalyzes the breakdown of fats into individual fatty acids that can be absorbed into the bloodstream. Lipases are water-soluble enzymes that hydrolyze water-insoluble lipid molecules, such as triglycerides, phospholipids, and galactolipids. They are ubiquitous in nature and are present in humans, animals, insects, plants, fungi, and microorganisms.[73]

Additional enzymes include **pancreatin**, **trypsin**, and **chymotrypsin**.

Clinicians and patients need to remember that enzymes speed activity. This is especially important for those who are taking pharmaceutical medications like Coumadin and prescription painkillers. Enzymatic activity can work so powerfully on the medicine's efficacy (pharmacokinetics) that it can be as if you had doubled the dosage. Proteolytic enzymes may help increase pain medication's impact without taking additional pills. IMPORTANT: DO NOT take pain medications and enzymes simultaneously, and DO NOT attempt to combine both treatments without the supervision of your pain specialist.

> **Benefits of Systemic Proteolytic Enzymes**
> ➢ Supplementation speeds recovery from exercise and injury
> ➢ Prevents the buildup of excess fibrin and scar tissue
> ➢ Digests dead tissue, blood clots, cysts and arterial plaque
> ➢ Reduces inflammation, speeds healing from bruises and other tissue injuries, including fractures; reduces overall recovery time
> ➢ Unblocks arteries in coronary patients

Probiotics

The immune system comprises all structures and processes involved in defending against outside entities that attempt to infiltrate or degrade any part of the body. Specifically, it is comprised of anatomic barriers such as the skin and mucous membranes which physically block the entry of antigens into the body, and physiological barriers (body temperature and acidity) that inhibit the growth of or kill damaging microorganisms, as well as the various organs and cells of the immune system itself. Overall coordination of the immune system takes place in the hypothalamus and pineal glands.

When the digestive tract becomes compromised by poor eating habits, stress, chemicals, environmental toxins and/or heavy metals, the entire body's health is jeopardized. Our immune system protects us from viruses, bacterial overgrowth, yeasts, and naturally occurring mutant cells that can evolve into cancer.

BENEFICIAL BACTERIA

lactococcus lactobacillus balgaricus

streptococcus thermophilus bifidobacterium propionibacterium

Beneficial microorganisms, or probiotics, are small organisms beneficial to human health and too small to be visible to the naked eye. Around 30 years ago, the GI tract, with its microflora of bacteria, was like a black box of the unknown. Research was not aware of the role, complexity, and versatility of all the microbes in the human body because they could not each be grown individually in a petri dish. Today we have technology allowing us to explore the microbiome frontier. Today, scientists can easily identify bacteria from fragments of their DNA.

Researchers are uncovering a vast, largely unexplored world that may play a critical role in the body and our health. Our gut bacteria help digest fiber and synthesize vitamin K, B vitamins, iron, and coenzyme Q10. Some "good bacteria" even secrete antibacterial compounds and lactic acids that can attack "nasty" bugs.[74] And there is evidence that our intestinal microflora may influence whether we become overweight or are susceptible to diabetes.[75, 76, 77]

The collection of microorganisms in the gut, our microbiome, is unimaginably large. By some estimates, as many as 500-1,000 species of bacteria inhabit our intestines, and the roughly 100 trillion microorganisms in those species are around 10 times greater than the number of cells in our body.[78]

The human digestive system contains approximately eight pounds of commensal bacteria, all involved in a multitude of activities necessary for the human body to thrive. We are only beginning to understand the interaction and communication with the microbiome and the rest of the body including the immune system. Through gut microbe activity and interaction, they have the ability to influence chemical reactions and functions in the body from hormones to behavior and emotions to weight and detoxification functions in the liver.

An imbalance in the ratio of beneficial microorganisms and detrimental microorganisms in the body is known as dysbiosis. Probiotics comprise approximately 90% of the digestive tract bacteria in healthy persons.

> ***Principle 21:*** Bacterial DNA in the microbiome accounts for 90% of the DNA in a human body.

An imbalance or overgrowth of certain bacteria can affect liver detoxification. The human liver has three phases of detoxification. β-glucuronidase is a phase II enzyme that is highly important in enterohepatic cycling and is responsible for the activation of foodborne carcinogens in the gut.[79] β-glucuronidase can also be produced by certain commensal bacteria. A dysbiosis or overgrowth situation may result in producing excessive levels of β-glucuronidase. In turn, high levels of β-glucuronidase can result in the deconjugation of toxins during phase II. This enzyme imbalance will also affect hormones: deconjugating estrogen causes recirculation (through enterohepatic uptake) leading to an estrogen-dominant state in the body and elevating risks for estrogen-sensitive cancers, including breast and prostate.[80]

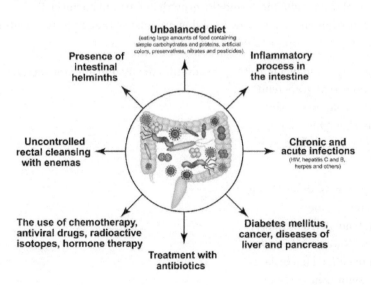

In the small intestine, which makes up 56% of the intestinal tract, bacterium imbalances can lead to small intestinal bacterial overgrowth or SIBO for short. Small intestinal bacterial overgrowth (SIBO) is defined as the presence of excessive bacteria in the small intestine. SIBO is frequently implicated as the cause of chronic diarrhea and malabsorption. Patients with SIBO may also suffer from unintentional weight loss, nutritional deficiencies, and osteoporosis.[81] According to a study published in the *American Journal of Gastroenterology*, these symptoms are common features of many other GI diseases such as celiac disease, food intolerances, food allergies, parasitic infestations, and bacterial infections of both the small and large intestines.

When SIBO happens, both digestion and absorption can be interrupted, particularly for nutrients like iron and other fat-soluble vitamins. Symptoms can range from bloating, gas, abdominal pain and/or diarrhea, to chronic constipation. These symptoms occur when the bacteria of the small intestine feed on the nutrients that the small intestine is supposed to be sending into the bloodstream.[82] SIBO is specifically diagnosed by lactulose breath testing, a method that takes six breath samples over the course of a few hours and analyzes which bacteria are present. In some cases, stool analysis and urine testing may also be done to confirm diagnosis or to get further information.[83, 84]

Probiotics in the colon can lower total serum cholesterol levels. Additionally, commensal bacterium helps heal ulcerative colitis and urinary tract infections (UTIs) by producing hydrogen peroxide, which is utilized by the body to "extinguish" neutralized antigen/antibody complexes. Probiotics ferment insoluble fiber, starch, and undigested carbohydrates in the colon. The short-chain saturated fatty acids produced by this fermentation are the principal energy source for the colon's epithelial cells.[85, 86] Also, probiotics manufacture vitamins that not only help with energy and nerve function[87] but are necessary for brain health:[88] biotin, choline, folic acid, inositol, PABA (para-aminobenzoic acid), vitamin B2, vitamin B5, vitamin B6 and vitamin K. Additionally, gut bacteria play an important role in hormone balance, especially estriol, progesterone, serotonin, and dopamine.[89]

According to a 2022 study on microbiota in the stomach and the application of probiotics to gastroduodenal diseases, using a probiotic strain (LG21) demonstrated a significant improving effect on major functional dyspepsia symptoms (*h. pylori* infection resulting in ulcers). One of the possible mechanisms of this effect is protection of the duodenal mucosa from injurious intestinal bacteria through the resolution of SIBO.[90]

Fructooligosaccharides (FOS) are considered a soluble fiber and a prebiotic that support the growth of beneficial microorganisms in the intestinal tract while inhibiting the growth of harmful bacteria. FOS nourishes most beneficial bacteria; because beneficial bacteria are living organisms, they require nutrition like any living organism. Note that FOS are NOT a source of nourishment for toxic bacteria.

Pharmaceutical antibiotics destroy the body's beneficial bacteria in addition to any detrimental bacteria. Long-term usage (e.g., more than one month) of grapefruit seed extract, large amounts of raw garlic, goldenseal, silver protein, and pasteurized foods have also been found to destroy the body's endogenous probiotics in the digestive tract.

Ideally, retailers of beneficial bacteria products should keep their products refrigerated up to the point of sale; beneficial bacteria die much faster when not refrigerated. A recent survey conducted by the National Nutritional Foods Association (U.S.A.) found that 50% of beneficial bacteria supplements in retail stores contained significantly fewer

INDICATIONS FOR USE

malnutrition

allergy

after antibiotics therapy

decreased immunity

intestinal infections

overweight

viable beneficial bacteria than claimed on the label. Freeze-dried (lyophilized) beneficial bacteria supplements, usually powder-based, have a longer shelf-life than non-freeze-dried products.

Caution should be exercised when recommending probiotic products grown in a yeast matrix. My clinical experience is that these products can increase yeast overgrowth (thrush, athlete's foot, jock itch and vaginal irritation) in clients with candida albicans overgrowth.

> **Principle 22:** When using probiotics and fermented foods – more is not always better.

Feed Your Microbiome Resistant Starch

In the last century, starch present in foods was thought to be wholly digested. However, during the 1980s, studies on starch digestion showed that besides digestible starch, which could be rapidly or slowly hydrolyzed, a variable fraction resisted hydrolysis by digestive enzymes. That fraction was named resistant starch (RS). It encompasses those forms of starch that are not accessible to human digestive enzymes but can be fermented by the colonic microbiota, producing short-chain fatty acids.[91] Resistant starch (RS) benefits human health by interacting with gut microbiota. However, aligning RS structures with gut microbiota profiles and consequentially health benefits is difficult. The current definition of RS types is strongly associated with starch digestion behaviors in the small intestine, which does not precisely reflect their interactions with human gut microbiota. Distinct alterations of gut microbiota could be related to the same RS type.[92] Rice is the main staple food for a large population around the world, and it generally has a high glycemic index and low resistant starch (RS) content. Although many strategies have been applied to develop healthier rice products with increased RS contents, their actual effects on gut microbiota and human health remain elusive.[93, 94]

Resistant Starch has been associated with general physiological effects such as reduced postprandial insulin levels and higher high-density lipoprotein cholesterol levels. Consumption of low glycemic index foods is related to a reduced risk of type 2 diabetes.[95] RS enters the large intestine fermented by the microbiome leading to the synthesis of short-chain fatty acids as major end products, which in turn have systemic health effects.[96] Dietary approaches with inclusion of resistant starches include a traditional Mediterranean diet and the Wahls Protocol.[97]

The most common resistant starch foods are purple and red potatoes (raw potatoes, cooked and then cooled and peeled – think potato salad), green and purple sting beans, snap peas, Jerusalem artichokes (like wild camas), tigernut, and yams. If an individual is from the tropics, green bananas and plantain also provide resistant starch in the diet.

How you cook your resistant starch foods matters because heat can affect the structure of starch molecules. Lightly sauté or steam string beans and snap peas and consume cold during warmer months in a salad with potatoes and Jerusalem artichokes. Resistant starch feeds the friendly bacteria in your intestine, positively affecting the type of bacteria and their number.

If in doubt some individuals benefit from supplementing with 2-4 tablespoons of raw potato starch. Raw potato starch contains about 8 grams of resistant starch per tablespoon and almost no usable carbohydrates.

---

1 Digestive Wellness, Elizabeth Lipski, PhD, CCN
2 Power ML, Schulkin J. Anticipatory physiological regulation in feeding biology: cephalic phase responses. Appetite. 2008 Mar;50(2-3):194–206.
3 Donald Kirby, MD, gastroenterologist, director, Center for Human Nutrition, Cleveland Clinic.
4 Ságodi, L., Sólyom, E., Ságodi, L., & Almási, A. (2022). Összefüggés a bél-hiperpermeabilitás és az elhízás között [Relationship between intestinal hyperpermeability and obesity]. Orvosi hetilap, 163(32), 1261–1267. https://doi.org/10.1556/650.2022.32542
5 Gasmi, A., Mujawdiya, P. K., Pivina, L., Doşa, A., Semenova, Y., Benahmed, A. G., & Bjørklund, G. (2021). Relationship between Gut Microbiota, Gut Hyperpermeability and Obesity. Current medicinal chemistry, 28(4), 827–839. https://doi.org/10.2174/0929867327666200721160313
6 Fülöp, V., Demeter, J., & Cseh, Á. (2021). A praenatalis és postnatalis mikrobiom jelentősége és hatásai a korai egyedfejlődés időszakában és az intervenciós kezelés lehetőségei [Significance and effects of prenatal and postnatal microbiome in the period of early individual development and options for interventional treatment]. Orvosi hetilap, 162(19), 731–740. https://doi.org/10.1556/650.2021.32082
7 Meng, X., Zhang, G., Cao, H., Yu, D., Fang, X., de Vos, W. M., & Wu, H. (2020). Gut dysbacteriosis and intestinal disease: mechanism and treatment. Journal of applied microbiology, 129(4), 787–805. https://doi.org/10.1111/jam.14661
8 Chen, Y., Williams, A. M., Gordon, E. B., Rudolph, S. E., Longo, B. N., Li, G., & Kaplan, D. L. (2023). Biological effects of polystyrene micro- and nano-plastics on human intestinal organoid-derived epithelial tissue models without and with M cells. Nanomedicine: Nanotechnology, Biology and Medicine, 50, 102680. https://doi.org/10.1016/j.nano.2023.102680
9 Mohn, E. S., Kern, H. J., Saltzman, E., Mitmesser, S. H., & McKay, D. L. (2018). Evidence of Drug-Nutrient Interactions with Chronic Use of Commonly Prescribed Medications: An Update. Pharmaceutics, 10(1), 36. https://doi.org/10.3390/pharmaceutics10010036
10 Lewis, S. L., Chizmar, L. R., & Liotta, S. (2022). COVID-19 and micronutrient deficiency symptoms- is there some overlap?. Clinical nutrition ESPEN, 48, 275–281. https://doi.org/10.1016/j.clnesp.2022.01.036
11 Muthuvattur Pallath, M., Ahirwar, A. K., Chandra Tripathi, S., Asia, P., Sakarde, A., & Gopal, N. (2021). COVID-19 and nutritional deficiency: a review of existing knowledge. Hormone molecular biology and clinical investigation, 42(1), 77–85. https://doi.org/10.1515/hmbci-2020-0074
12 Qu, H., Guo, M., Chai, H., Wang, W. T., Gao, Z. Y., & Shi, D. Z. (2018). Effects of Coenzyme Q10 on Statin-Induced Myopathy: An Updated Meta-Analysis of Randomized Controlled Trials. Journal of the American Heart Association, 7(19), e009835. https://doi.org/10.1161/JAHA.118.009835
13 Kennedy, C., Köller, Y., & Surkova, E. (2020). Effect of Coenzyme Q10 on statin-associated myalgia and adherence to statin therapy: A systematic review and meta-analysis. Atherosclerosis, 299, 1–8. https://doi.org/10.1016/j.atherosclerosis.2020.03.006
14 Xu, Y., Amdanee, N., & Zhang, X. (2021). Antipsychotic-Induced Constipation: A Review of the Pathogenesis, Clinical Diagnosis, and Treatment. CNS drugs, 35(12), 1265–1274. https://doi.org/10.1007/s40263-021-00859-0
15 Singh, G., Haileselassie, Y., Briscoe, L., Bai, L., Patel, A., Sanjines, E., Hendler, S., Singh, P. K., Garud, N. R., Limketkai, B. N., & Habtezion, A. (2022). The effect of gastric acid suppression on probiotic colonization in a double blinded randomized clinical trial. Clinical nutrition ESPEN, 47, 70–77. https://doi.org/10.1016/j.clnesp.2021.11.005
16 Mikulic, M. (2022) Number of bupropion prescriptions in the U.S. from 2004 to 2020: https://www.statista.com/statistics/782139/bupropion-prescriptions-number-in-the-us/
17 Berardi, R., Clinical Update on the Treatment of Constipation in Adults (2004): https://www.pharmacytimes.com/authors/rosemary-r-berardi-pharmd-fccp-fashp
18 Daniali, M., Nikfar, S., & Abdollahi, M. (2020). An overview of interventions for constipation in adults. Expert review of gastroenterology & hepatology, 14(8), 721–732. https://doi.org/10.1080/17474124.2020.1781617
19 Healthiest Countries 2023: https://worldpopulationreview.com/country-rankings/healthiest-countries
20 Quezada, S. M., & Cross, R. K. (2019). Cannabis and Turmeric as Complementary Treatments for IBD and Other Digestive Diseases. Current gastroenterology reports, 21(2), 2. https://doi.org/10.1007/s11894-019-0670-0

Chapter 4 ~ Digestion Connection

21 Kienzl, M., Storr, M., & Schicho, R. (2020). Cannabinoids and Opioids in the Treatment of Inflammatory Bowel Diseases. Clinical and translational gastroenterology, 11(1), e00120. https://doi.org/10.14309/ctg.0000000000000120

22 Scherma M, Masia P, Satta V, Fratta W, Fadda P, Tanda G. Brain activity of anandamide: a rewarding bliss? Acta Pharmacol Sin. 2019 Mar;40(3):309-323. doi: 10.1038/s41401-018-0075-x. Epub 2018 Jul 26. PMID: 30050084; PMCID: PMC6460372.

23 Marian Wilson, Hannah Y. Gogulski, Carrie Cuttler, Teresa L. Bigand, Oladunni Oluwoye, Celestina Barbosa-Leiker, MaryLee A. Roberts. Cannabis use moderates the relationship between pain and negative affect in adults with opioid use disorder. Addictive Behaviors, 2018; 77: 225 DOI: 10.1016/j.addbeh.2017.10.012

24 https://www.ncbi.nlm.nih.gov/pubmed/26502112

25 Chu F, Cascella M. Cannabinoid Hyperemesis Syndrome. [Updated 2022 Jul 4]. In: StatPearls [Internet]. Treasure Island (FL): StatPearls Publishing; 2023 Jan-. Available from: https://www.ncbi.nlm.nih.gov/books/NBK549915/

26 Khattar, N., & Routsolias, J. C. (2018). Emergency Department Treatment of Cannabinoid Hyperemesis Syndrome: A Review. American journal of therapeutics, 25(3), e357–e361. https://doi.org/10.1097/MJT.0000000000000655

27 https://legislature.vermont.gov/assets/Documents/2016/WorkGroups/Corrections%20Oversight/Marijuana%20Legalization/W~Kalev%20Freeman~Powerpoint-%20Evidence%20for%20Cannabis%20as%20a%20Substitute%20for%20Opioids~9-23-2016.pdf

28 https://www.drugabuse.gov/publications/drugfacts/marijuana

29 Marijuana and heart health: What you need to know: 2017, https://www.health.harvard.edu/heart-health/marijuana-and-heart-health-what-you-need-to-know

30 Marijuana and Public Health: CDC- https://www.cdc.gov/marijuana/health-effects.htm

31 Karen Langston, CNH Healthy Gut Advisor

32 Atakan Z. (2012). Cannabis, a complex plant: different compounds and different effects on individuals. Therapeutic advances in psychopharmacology, 2(6), 241–254. https://doi.org/10.1177/2045125312457586

33 Rezende, B., Alencar, A. K. N., de Bem, G. F., Fontes-Dantas, F. L., & Montes, G. C. (2023). Endocannabinoid System: Chemical Characteristics and Biological Activity. Pharmaceuticals (Basel, Switzerland), 16(2), 148. https://doi.org/10.3390/ph16020148

34 VanDolah, H. J., Bauer, B. A., & Mauck, K. F. (2019). Clinicians' Guide to Cannabidiol and Hemp Oils. Mayo Clinic proceedings, 94(9), 1840–1851. https://doi.org/10.1016/j.mayocp.2019.01.003

35 Border Pesticide Initiative Results in Prosecution of 50 defendants for Smuggling Dangerous Chemicals (2021): https://www.justice.gov/usao-sdca/pr/border-pesticide-initiative-results-prosecution-50-defendants-smuggling-dangerous

36 Moir, D. et al. A comparison of minstream and sidestream marijuana and tobacco cigarette smoke produced under two machine smoking conditions. Chemical Research in Toxicology 21, 494–502, https://doi.org/10.1021/tx700275p (2007).

37 Rondanelli, M., Faliva, M. A., Miccono, A., Naso, M., Nichetti, M., Riva, A., Guerriero, F., De Gregori, M., Peroni, G., & Perna, S. (2018). Food pyramid for subjects with chronic pain: foods and dietary constituents as anti-inflammatory and antioxidant agents. Nutrition research reviews, 31(1), 131–151. https://doi.org/10.1017/S0954422417000270

38 Kurowska, A., Ziemichód, W., Herbet, M., & Piątkowska-Chmiel, I. (2023). The Role of Diet as a Modulator of the Inflammatory Process in the Neurological Diseases. Nutrients, 15(6), 1436. https://doi.org/10.3390/nu15061436

39 McGrattan, A. M., McGuinness, B., McKinley, M. C., Kee, F., Passmore, P., Woodside, J. V., & McEvoy, C. T. (2019). Diet and Inflammation in Cognitive Ageing and Alzheimer's Disease. Current nutrition reports, 8(2), 53–65. https://doi.org/10.1007/s13668-019-0271-4

40 Rezende, B., Alencar, A. K. N., de Bem, G. F., Fontes-Dantas, F. L., & Montes, G. C. (2023). Endocannabinoid System: Chemical Characteristics and Biological Activity. Pharmaceuticals (Basel, Switzerland), 16(2), 148. https://doi.org/10.3390/ph16020148

41 Alternative Medicine Review Volume 13, Number 4 2008; The Role of Enzyme Supplementation in Digestive Disorders – Roxas Mario, ND

42 http://www.nutraingredients-usa.com/Consumer-Trends/Huge-opportunities-in-the-emerging-cognitive-health-market-Enzymotec-USA-CEO

43 http://www.livestrong.com/article/346199-diet-after-gallstone-surgery/

44 http://www.helium.com/items/1169768-gallstones-after-having-the-gallbladder-removed

45 http://voices.yahoo.com/preventing-gallstones-after-gallbladder-removal-2102510.html

46 Nicola Veronese and others, Dietary fiber and health outcomes: an umbrella review of systematic reviews and meta-analyses, The American Journal of Clinical Nutrition, Volume 107, Issue 3, March 2018, Pages 436–444, https://doi.org/10.1093/ajcn/nqx082

47 http://www.livestrong.com/article/346199-diet-after-gallstone-surgery/

48 http://www.webmd.com/digestive-disorders /open-gallbladder-surgery-for-gallstones

49 http://www.gastromdg astromd.com/education/bileductstones.html

50 What is the function of the human appendix? By Loren G. Martin, professor of physiology at Oklahoma State University; Scientific America 2018

51 Cai S, Fan Y, Zhang B, Lin J, Yang X, Liu Y, Liu J, Ren J and Xu H (2021) Appendectomy Is Associated With Alteration of Human Gut Bacterial and Fungal Communities. Front. Microbiol. 12:724980. doi: 10.3389/fmicb.2021.724980

52 The Raw Truth, Jordan Rubin, 2010

53 VTT Technical Research Centre of Finland. (2020, April 15). A more plant-based diet without stomach troubles: Getting rid of FODMAPs with enzymes. ScienceDaily. Retrieved May 15, 2023 from www.sciencedaily.com/releases/2020/04/200415110457.htm
54 University of Pennsylvania. (2019, April 9). Everyday enzymes, now grown in plants. ScienceDaily. Retrieved May 15, 2023 from www.sciencedaily.com/releases/2019/04/190409153633.htm
55 Karen Langston, CHN Healthy Gut Advisor
56 Jadhav SB, Shah N, Rathi A, Rathi V, Rathi A. Serratiopeptidase: Insights into the therapeutic applications. Biotechnol Rep (Amst). 2020 Oct 17;28:e00544. doi: 10.1016/j.btre.2020.e00544. PMID: 33134103; PMCID: PMC7585045.
57 Dhiman, A., & Purohit, R. (2023). Profiling the disintegration of BRPs released by massive wasp stings using serratiopeptidase: An in-silico insight. Computers in biology and medicine, 159, 106951. Advance online publication. https://doi.org/10.1016/j.compbiomed.2023.106951
58 Tiwari M. (2017). The role of serratiopeptidase in the resolution of inflammation. Asian journal of pharmaceutical sciences, 12(3), 209–215. https://doi.org/10.1016/j.ajps.2017.01.003
59 Proceedings of the National Academy of Sciences of the United States of America, 1988 May; 85(9): 3245-3249
60 https://www.astenzymes.com/study-shows-serrapeptase-stronger-trypsin-chymotrypsin-and-aspirin
61 Proceedings of the National Academy of Sciences of the United States of America, 1988 May; 85(9): 3245-3249
62 Nair, S. R., & C, S. D. (2022). Serratiopeptidase: An integrated View of Multifaceted Therapeutic Enzyme. Biomolecules, 12(10), 1468. https://doi.org/10.3390/biom12101468
63 Owoyele, B. V., Bakare, A. O., & Ologe, M. O. (2020). Bromelain: A Review on its Potential as a Therapy for the Management of Covid-19. Nigerian journal of physiological sciences : official publication of the Physiological Society of Nigeria, 35(1), 10–19.
64 Hikisz, P., & Bernasinska-Slomczewska, J. (2021). Beneficial Properties of Bromelain. Nutrients, 13(12), 4313. https://doi.org/10.3390/nu13124313
65 Pitsillou, E., Liang, J., Ververis, K., Hung, A., & Karagiannis, T. C. (2021). Interaction of small molecules with the SARS-CoV-2 papain-like protease: In silico studies and in vitro validation of protease activity inhibition using an enzymatic inhibition assay. Journal of molecular graphics & modelling, 104, 107851. https://doi.org/10.1016/j.jmgm.2021.107851
66 Pitsillou, E., Liang, J., Karagiannis, C., Ververis, K., Darmawan, K. K., Ng, K., Hung, A., & Karagiannis, T. C. (2020). Interaction of small molecules with the SARS-CoV-2 main protease in silico and in vitro validation of potential lead compounds using an enzyme-linked immunosorbent assay. Computational biology and chemistry, 89, 107408. https://doi.org/10.1016/j.compbiolchem.2020.107408
67 Heianza, Y., Sun, D., Wang, T., Huang, T., Bray, G. A., Sacks, F. M., & Qi, L. (2017). Starch Digestion-Related Amylase Genetic Variant Affects 2-Year Changes in Adiposity in Response to Weight-Loss Diets: The POUNDS Lost Trial. Diabetes, 66(9), 2416–2423. https://doi.org/10.2337/db16-1482
68 Heianza, Y., Sun, D., Wang, T., Huang, T., Bray, G. A., Sacks, F. M., & Qi, L. (2017). Starch Digestion-Related Amylase Genetic Variant Affects 2-Year Changes in Adiposity in Response to Weight-Loss Diets: The POUNDS Lost Trial. Diabetes, 66(9), 2416–2423. https://doi.org/10.2337/db16-1482
69 Farrell, M., Ramne, S., Gouinguenet, P., Brunkwall, L., Ericson, U., Raben, A., Nilsson, P. M., Orho-Melander, M., Granfeldt, Y., Tovar, J., & Sonestedt, E. (2021). Effect of AMY1 copy number variation and various doses of starch intake on glucose homeostasis: data from a cross-sectional observational study and a crossover meal study. Genes & nutrition, 16(1), 21. https://doi.org/10.1186/s12263-021-00701-8
70 Lin Q, Qiu C, Li X, Sang S, McClements DJ, Chen L, Long J, Jiao A, Tian Y, Jin Z. The inhibitory mechanism of amylase inhibitors and research progress in nanoparticle-based inhibitors. Crit Rev Food Sci Nutr. 2022 Jul 13:1-10. doi: 10.1080/10408398.2022.2098687. Epub ahead of print. PMID: 35822304.
71 Chinedum, E., Sanni, S., Theressa, N., & Ebere, A. (2018). Effect of domestic cooking on the starch digestibility, predicted glycemic indices, polyphenol contents and alpha amylase inhibitory properties of beans (Phaseolis vulgaris) and breadfruit (Treculia africana). International journal of biological macromolecules, 106, 200–206. https://doi.org/10.1016/j.ijbiomac.2017.08.005
72 Fink, T., & Jerala, R. (2022). Designed protease-based signaling networks. Current opinion in chemical biology, 68, 102146. https://doi.org/10.1016/j.cbpa.2022.102146
73 Lim, S. Y., Steiner, J. M., & Cridge, H. (2022). Lipases: it's not just pancreatic lipase!. American journal of veterinary research, 83(8), ajvr.22.03.0048. https://doi.org/10.2460/ajvr.22.03.0048
74 Dixit, K., Chaudhari, D., Dhotre, D., Shouche, Y., & Saroj, S. (2021). Restoration of dysbiotic human gut microbiome for homeostasis. Life sciences, 278, 119622. https://doi.org/10.1016/j.lfs.2021.119622
75 Portincasa, P., Bonfrate, L., Vacca, M., De Angelis, M., Farella, I., Lanza, E., Khalil, M., Wang, D. Q., Sperandio, M., & Di Ciaula, A. (2022). Gut Microbiota and Short Chain Fatty Acids: Implications in Glucose Homeostasis. International journal of molecular sciences, 23(3), 1105. https://doi.org/10.3390/ijms23031105
76 Duan, Y., Zhong, Y., Xiao, H., Zheng, C., Song, B., Wang, W., Guo, Q., Li, Y., Han, H., Gao, J., Xu, K., Li, T., Yin, Y., Li, F., Yin, J., & Kong, X. (2019). Gut microbiota mediates the protective effects of dietary β-hydroxy-β-methylbutyrate (HMB) against obesity induced by high-fat diets. FASEB journal : official publication of the Federation of American Societies for Experimental Biology, 33(9), 10019–10033. https://doi.org/10.1096/fj.201900665RR

Chapter 4 ~ Digestion Connection

77 Cândido, F. G., Valente, F. X., Grześkowiak, Ł. M., Moreira, A. P. B., Rocha, D. M. U. P., & Alfenas, R. C. G. (2018). Impact of dietary fat on gut microbiota and low-grade systemic inflammation: mechanisms and clinical implications on obesity. International journal of food sciences and nutrition, 69(2), 125–143. https://doi.org/10.1080/09637486.2017.1343286
78 Should You Take a Probiotic Every Day?, Center for Science in the Public Interest, May 2016
79 Humblot, C., Murkovic, M., Rigottier-Gois, L., Bensaada, M., Bouclet, A., Andrieux, C., Anba, J., & Rabot, S. (2007). Beta-glucuronidase in human intestinal microbiota is necessary for the colonic genotoxicity of the food-borne carcinogen 2-amino-3-methylimidazo[4,5-f]quinoline in rats. Carcinogenesis, 28(11), 2419–2425. https://doi.org/10.1093/carcin/bgm170
80 Mroczynska M, Galecka M, Szachta P, Kamoda D, Libudzisz Z, Roszak D. Polish journal of microbiology / Polskie Towarzystwo Mikrobiologow. The Polish Society of Microbiologists. 2013;62:319-325.
81 Small Intestinal Bacterial Overgrowth; Gastroenterol Hepatol (N Y). 2007 Feb; 3(2): 112–122.
82 Small intestinal bacterial overgrowth and symptoms of irritable bowel syndrome; The American Journal of Gastroenterology; Cambridge Vol. 96, Iss. 7, (Jul 2001): 2281-2282. Cuoco, Lucio; Cammarota, Giovanni; Jorizzo, Reginanna; Gasbarrini, Giovanni.
83 https://blog.paleohacks.com/sibo/#
84 Healthy Gut Healthy You, Dr. Michael Ruscio, The Ruscio Institute 2018 pp 39-50
85 Norwich BioScience Institutes. "How bacteria with a sweet tooth may keep us healthy." ScienceDaily. ScienceDaily, 25 October 2013. www.sciencedaily.com/releases/2013/10/131025185704.htm.
86 Norwich BioScience Institutes. "Sticky solution for identifying effective probiotics." ScienceDaily. ScienceDaily, 25 November 2009. www.sciencedaily.com/releases/2009/11/091124113611.htm
87 Wiley-Blackwell. "A gut-full of probiotics for your neurological well-being." ScienceDaily. ScienceDaily, 5 July 2011. www.sciencedaily.com/releases/2011/07/110705210737.htm.
88 University of Michigan Health System. "Probiotics reduce stress-induced intestinal flare-ups, study finds." ScienceDaily. ScienceDaily, 14 March 2013. www.sciencedaily.com/releases/2013/03/130314110256.htm.
89 https://www.hormonesbalance.com/articles/how-the-gut-bacteria-impact-your-hormones/
90 Koga Y. (2022). Microbiota in the stomach and application of probiotics to gastroduodenal diseases. World journal of gastroenterology, 28(47), 6702–6715. https://doi.org/10.3748/wjg.v28.i47.6702
91 Bello-Perez, L. A., Flores-Silva, P. C., Agama-Acevedo, E., & Tovar, J. (2020). Starch digestibility: past, present, and future. Journal of the science of food and agriculture, 100(14), 5009–5016. https://doi.org/10.1002/jsfa.8955
92 Li, C., & Hu, Y. (2023). Align resistant starch structures from plant-based foods with human gut microbiome for personalized health promotion. Critical reviews in food science and nutrition, 63(15), 2509–2520. https://doi.org/10.1080/10408398.2021.1976722
93 Cao, S., & Li, C. (2022). Influence of Resistant Starch in Whole Rice on Human Gut Microbiota—From Correlation Implications to Possible Causal Mechanisms. Journal of agricultural and food chemistry, 70(40), 12760–12771. https://doi.org/10.1021/acs.jafc.2c05380
94 Wen, J. J., Li, M. Z., Hu, J. L., Tan, H. Z., & Nie, S. P. (2022). Resistant starches and gut microbiota. Food chemistry, 387, 132895. https://doi.org/10.1016/j.foodchem.2022.132895
95 Jenkins, D. J., & Kendall, C. W. (2000). Resistant starches. Current opinion in gastroenterology, 16(2), 178–183. https://doi.org/10.1097/00001574-200003000-00014
96 Cione, E., Fazio, A., Curcio, R., Tucci, P., Lauria, G., Cappello, A. R. R., & Dolce, V. (2021). Resistant Starches and Non-Communicable Disease: A Focus on Mediterranean Diet. Foods (Basel, Switzerland), 10(9), 2062. https://doi.org/10.3390/foods10092062
97 Liu, H., Zhang, M., Ma, Q., Tian, B., Nie, C., Chen, Z., & Li, J. (2020). Health beneficial effects of resistant starch on diabetes and obesity via regulation of gut microbiota: a review. Food & function, 11(7), 5749–5767. https://doi.org/10.1039/d0fo00855a

> You don't have to cook fancy or complicated masterpieces ~ just good food from fresh ingredients.
>
> ~ Julia Child

Chapter Five ~

Literature Review ~ Oxalates: Dietary Oxalates and Kidney Inflammation

Karr, T., Guptha, L., Bell, K., Thenell, J

Pacific College of Health and Science – The National Association of Nutrition Professionals, and The American Holistic Nurses Association

Abstract

This literature review explores the role of dietary oxalate in the development of chronic inflammatory kidney disease in middle age and older individuals. The authors pose the following questions: Is oxalate produced endogenously? If food sources contribute to chronic kidney disease and inflammation, what are those foods? What role does cultural food preparation and cooking play in denaturing food oxalates?

Oxalates are not limited to edible plants; normal human metabolic processes of breaking down ascorbic acid may create up to 30mg of oxalate daily. Research supports urolithiasis as a common urologic disease in industrialized societies. Approximately 80% of kidney stones are calcium oxalate resulting in hyperoxaluria. Endogenous oxalate sources include ascorbic acid, amino acids, and glyoxal metabolism. Additional research estimates the daily endogenous production of oxalate to be 10–25mg. Suboptimal colonization of oxalate-degrading bacteria and malabsorptive disease are also contributing factors to the development of kidney disease. Oxalate transcellular processes, though poorly understood, rely on multifunctional anion exchangers and are being investigated.

A review of research showed that including foods high in oxalate may contribute approximately 50–80% of the urinary oxalate in compromised individuals with liver glycation, bacterial insufficiencies, malabsorption and anion exchange challenges. Traditional cooking processes reduced food oxalate levels by 30-40%. Juicing of raw foods increased oxalate levels. Food combined with red and white wine provides protective compounds, reducing epithelial damage in the urologic tract.

For persons with a family history of kidney stones, foods high in oxalates may be eaten in moderation, provided there is adequate calcium intake in the diet to decrease the absorption of oxalates from the meal ingested.

Introduction

Public interest in dietary oxalates and their role in developing chronic inflammatory conditions, including kidney disease in middle age and older individuals, led the authors to review oxalate research. The authors reviewed and compared statistical information from >60 studies and medical texts published between 1962-2023 on kidney function, disease, and dietary oxalate sources. After excluding research dated by more than ten years, the authors pose the following questions:

Is oxalate produced endogenously? [1, 2, 3, 4, 5]

Urolithiasis is a <u>common</u> urologic disease in <u>industrialized societies</u> with kidney stones as the most prevalent form of kidney inflammation.[6] Hyperoxaluria is excessive urinary excretion of oxalate. Primary hyperoxaluria characterized by recurrent kidney and bladder stones (≈12% of population) caused by overproduction of oxalates filtered through the kidneys and excreted as waste in urine.[7] Oxalate levels are not limited to the ingestion of plants. Normal human metabolic processes,[8] including the breakdown of ascorbic acid, account for 35-55% of circulating oxalates and can create ≤30mg of serum oxalate daily.[9] Glyoxylic acid accounts for 50-70% of urinary oxalate. Oxalate and calcium bind together in the intestine and are excreted in the stool.[10] Kidney stones are generally comprised of calcium salts (75-85%) and uric acid (5-8%).[11] Approximately 80% of kidney stones contain calcium oxalate, resulting from hyperoxaluria.[12, 13, 14, 15]

> ***Principle 23:*** Normal physiologic processes in the body depend on complex, multifunctional biochemical reactions.

What causes hypercalciuria? Elevated calcium in the urine can result from elevated calcium absorption from the intestines or bones into the blood. Chronic hypercalciuria may result in impaired renal function, nephrocalcinosis, and chronic kidney disease. Impaired calcium regulation in the kidneys subsequently results in elevations of oxalate in the urine. Malabsorption conditions and unabsorbed fatty acids that bind calcium in the digestive tract increase oxalate absorption, resulting in elevated urine and serum oxalate levels.[16]

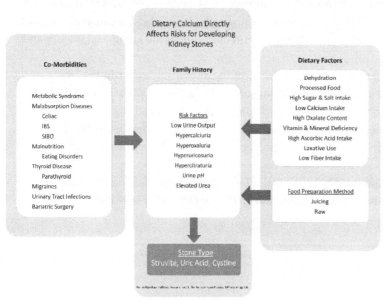

Malabsorption due to conditions such as Crohn's disease, ulcerative colitis, celiac disease, IBD, IBS, SIBO, disordered eating, and bariatric surgery increases risk for kidney stones.

For individuals who produce calcium oxalate stones, adequate dietary calcium consumption is vital to maintain bone calcium stores (800-1200mg/day).[17]

Chapter 5 ~ Oxalate Literature Review Research

Research does not support calcium restriction for individuals with kidney stones. Nutrition science texts <u>do not</u> recommend reducing protein to lower the risk of stone formation; increased protein does not lead to increased oxalate synthesis due to pyridoxine (B6) acting as a cofactor converting glyoxylate to glycine.

Endogenous oxalate sources include ascorbic acid, tyrosine, tryptophan, phenylalanine, hydroxyproline, and glyoxal metabolism.[18] Suboptimal colonization of oxalate-degrading bacteria due to malnutrition and antibiotic use contributes to the endogenous production of oxalate.[19] Oxalate transcellular processes, though poorly understood, rely on multifunctional anion exchangers and are being investigated.[20, 21]

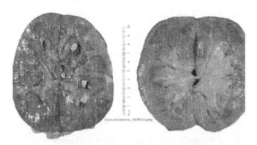

Males have higher risks (≤12%) for developing kidney stones than females (≤7%) until women enter menopause. At this time, hormonal changes, primarily in estradiol availability, lead to metabolic syndrome, tissue friability in the urinary tract, and increased antibiotic use for UTIs, resulting in incidences equalizing.[22] Exposure to ethylene glycol, heavy metals,[23] chemotherapy drugs, NSAIDs, and antacids increases inflammatory kidney risks.[24, 25] High blood pressure, hypothyroidism, diabetes, and obesity (common in metabolic syndrome) can increase kidney stone risk.[26] <u>Note:</u> Kidney disease can occur without the overconsumption of oxalate foods or the development of stones.

> What is the role of oxalate in plants? Calcium oxalate (CaOx) crystals are distributed among all photosynthetic organisms' taxonomic levels, from small algae to angiosperms and giant gymnosperms, occurring as crystals of various shapes.[27] Recent work indicates that calcium oxalate formation is generally a mechanism for regulating bulk-free calcium levels in tissues and organs.[28] A novel function in light regulation during photosynthesis the crystals help to evenly distribute light to the chloroplasts lining the radial wall. The crystals might also help to dissipate excess light by reflecting light back up to the window tissue. Recent evidence suggested that CaOx crystals function as carbon reservoirs since its decomposition provides CO^2 that may be used as carbon source for photosynthesis.[29] The protection offered by CaOx crystals against herbivory may be overstated, as claims have been mainly based on their shapes and hard and indigestible nature rather than on experimental evidence. [30]

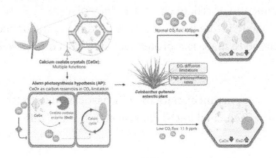

> ***Principle 24:*** It is neither useful nor logical to pinpoint a singular chemical substance and posit either its absence or excess as the cause of a particular pathophysiologic problem.

If food sources contribute to chronic kidney disease and inflammation, what are those foods?

Metabolic syndrome is the leading co-morbidity (25.2% among U.S. seniors [≥65 years]) for kidney disease.[31] Metabolic syndrome corresponds with type 2 diabetes, increased fructose consumption, and decreased fiber consumption, all consistent with the industrialized diet. The bioavailability of food and urine oxalate are affected by oxalate salt forms, food processing, and cooking methods with meal composition; a 70% reduced risk is associated when *Oxalobacter formigenes* is in the GI tract.[32, 33, 34] *O. formigenes* is an anaerobic bacterium that relies solely on oxalate for growth and is crucial in oxalate-degrading bacterium in the intestinal tract. Degradation of oxalate in the gut by *O. formigenes* plays a critical role in preventing renal toxicity.

It is important to note that whole-natural foods has the advantage of metabolic checks and balances. According to nutrition texts, the human body absorbs between 3-8% of the soluble oxalate in food.[35] Research on rice bran in 1984 showed reduced oxalate absorption when calcium-rich foods were in the diet.[36] Evidence of stones decreased among patients treated with rice bran for ≥3 years.[37] Oxalates do not occur in foods as single anti-nutrients. Oxalates are found with vitamin cofactors, minerals, and the organic acids citrate and malate, which control acidity.[38] Research published in 2016 on hydroxycitrate (HCA), a substance isolated from *Malabar tamarind*, under certain conditions, effectively inhibits calcium oxalate crystal growth and dissolves crystals.[39, 40] Additionally, consuming a fiber-rich diet has been shown to reduce kidney inflammation and stone formation incidences.[41]

In 2021, researchers reviewed data from 18,436 participants finding no significant association between coffee consumption and renal function or risk of chronic kidney disease.[42] Research published in 2022 on coffee consumption in predominately White populations related to the incidence of kidney stones found decreased risk in women compared to men. The protective effects of coffee itself were greater than that of caffeine alone.[43]

The authors found limited studies reporting oxalate toxicity associated with two Chinese herbs. A 2015 study found that different Chinese medicinal herbs contain significantly different amounts of oxalate, even from the same family. Using medicinal herbs with the highest oxalate content for susceptible individuals might increase the risk of kidney stone formation.[44, 45, 46, 47]

Recognized research on dietary inclusion of spinach, strawberries, raspberries, beets, rhubarb, tea, nuts, wheat bran, chocolate, sorrel, sesame, carambola, amaranth, almonds, and soybean high oxalate foods may contribute ≈40-50% of the urinary oxalate in individuals with compromised liver glycation, malnutrition, metabolic syndrome, bacterial insufficiencies, fat and mineral malabsorption, and anion exchange challenges.[48, 49, 50, 51] Researchers found that the riper the fruit consumed, the lower the oxalate content and dietary absorption.[52] A 2015 review of dietary treatments for renal stone formation found that a diet low in oxalate and containing average calcium intake (800-1200mg/day for adults) decreased the urinary excretion of oxalate and a diet high in oxalates and low in calcium increased oxalate urinary output.[53]

Presently no consensus exists on the effects of dietary oxalate on stone formation, even in clients with hyperoxaluria.[54] Examining research and management protocols revealed a range of interventions for clients with kidney inflammation.[55] Protocols included reducing highly refined processed foods, excess phosphorus, sugar (fructose), purines and increasing water intake with unsweetened citrus, cranberry, and black cherry juices to balance urine *pH*.

What role does cultural food preparation play in denaturing oxalates present in foods?[56, 57, 58, 59]

The accepted statistical data reviewed was older than 20yr and contained numerous errors. Statistical data sources included the Harvard T.H. Chan School of Public Health oxalate chart (2004), the Food Standards Australia New Zealand oxalate levels in foods data, and USDA agricultural data on oxalate content. Food preparation methods included research on oxalate content following boiling, stir-frying, soaking, fermentation, juicing, and raw.[60, 61, 62]

Cultivation in calcium-rich soils and combining high oxalate foods with animal protein for oxalate mitigation is supported by reviews of gastronomy traditions.[63] Traditional cooking processes of soaking, fermenting, [64, 65] sprouting, [66] blanching, boiling, and wok-frying reduce oxalate levels. [67, 68] Food combining provides protective compounds for reducing the epithelial damage that affects renal function.[69] Oxalate levels increase with some forms of cooking, such as deep-frying high starch (russet potatoes used in potato chips and fries) foods.[70] With raw parsley, spinach, chard, celery, beet greens and roots, juicing increased oxalate levels due to concentration.[71, 72] In the case of spinach, cooking appeared to increase oxalate levels when boiled but decreased when blanched. The authors postulate the decrease in oxalate results from removing the oxalate-rich liquid and the effects of freezing. [73, 74]
In general, absorbed food levels of soluble oxalate depend on many factors; each variety of spinach can contain a wide range of oxalate. Agriculture research identified over 300 spinach cultivars with oxalate levels ranging from 647.2–1286.9mg/100g by raw weight (200% variability by cultivar). Eight spinach varieties contain >780mg/100g of oxalate. This is one example of the wide inconsistencies due to the lack of cultivar distinction in oxalate content data.[75]

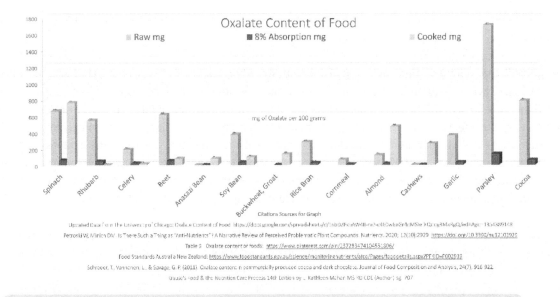

> ***Principle 25:*** Plants may contain substances that can be potentially harmful along with others that are beneficial.

Clinical Tools [76]

Health and wellness coaches unless a licensed healthcare professional do not diagnose or treat, they partner with clients or patients in a thought-provoking and creative process that inspires them to maximize their personal and professional potential.[77] The coach approaches kidney inflammation from a whole health perspective, aiding the client in assessing areas of health on a scale of 1-10. The client and coach explore the importance, readiness and safety on agreed goals. The coach assists the client in their exploration of the feasibility of options and obstacles, dietary, lifestyle and success in reaching goals.[78] The coach facilitates the journey through active listening, brainstorming, reflection and accountability using positive affirmation to support well-being.[79,80]

The American Kidney Fund is another resource for a free community health education program and provides information about preventing, managing, and treating kidney disease, as well as living a healthy lifestyle.[81]

Conclusion

Oxalates' role in affecting kidney health is complex and poorly understood. One area of confusion pertains to outdated research on soluble and insoluble oxalate content in raw and cooked foods. The most up-to-date data comes from agriculture research and creates the greatest opportunity for misinterpretation of food oxalate levels due to the influence of cultivars, climate, and location of specific foods. Traditional cultivation, harvesting, preparation, and combining of foods can reduce risks due to seasonal dietary use and synergistic combining of cofactors that bind and remove oxalates from the body. Specific cofactors that bind or inhibit oxalate content in foods (calcium, malic acid, potassium, magnesium, vitamin C, fatty acids, probiotics) lower the risks of developing kidney stones and overall inflammatory effects on kidneys.

Chapter 5 ~ Oxalate Literature Review Research

An individual's age, gender, and overall health play the most central role in developing kidney stones and inflammation. Overall health is impacted by hydration, processed food consumption, especially those high in sugar (fructose).

For individuals with a family history of kidney stones, oxalate foods may be eaten in moderation provided calcium intake and probiotics are adequate to decrease absorption of oxalates from the meal. The data suggest a dietary approach that includes whole, unrefined foods, food diversity, hydration, cooking vegetables, and coaching can be effective in reducing the uptake of oxalates in predisposed individuals.

> ***Principle 26:*** Traditional and ethnocultural methods of cultivating plants and preparing meals often serve to mitigate the effects of harmful substances that may exist in raw foods.

---

1 Noonan, S. C., & Savage, G. P. (1999). Oxalate content of foods and its effect on humans. Asia Pacific journal of clinical nutrition, 8(1), 64–74.

2 Yilmaz, M. I., Carrero, J. J., Axelsson, J., Lindholm, B., & Stenvinkel, P. (2007). Low-grade inflammation in chronic kidney disease patients before the start of renal replacement therapy: sources and consequences. Clinical nephrology, 68(1), 1–9. https://doi.org/10.5414/cnp68001

3 Ermer, T., Eckardt, K. U., Aronson, P. S., & Knauf, F. (2016). Oxalate, inflammasome, and progression of kidney disease. Current opinion in nephrology and hypertension, 25(4), 363–371. https://doi.org/10.1097/MNH.0000000000000229

4 Johnson, R. J., Perez-Pozo, S. E., Lillo, J. L., Grases, F., Schold, J. D., Kuwabara, M., Sato, Y., Hernando, A. A., Garcia, G., Jensen, T., Rivard, C., Sanchez-Lozada, L. G., Roncal, C., & Lanaspa, M. A. (2018). Fructose increases risk for kidney stones: potential role in metabolic syndrome and heat stress. BMC nephrology, 19(1), 315. https://doi.org/10.1186/s12882-018-1105-0

5 Petroski, W., & Minich, D. M. (2020). Is There Such a Thing as "Anti-Nutrients"? A Narrative Review of Perceived Problematic Plant Compounds. Nutrients, 12(10), 2929. https://doi.org/10.3390/nu12102929

6 Alelign, T., & Petros, B. (2018). Kidney Stone Disease: An Update on Current Concepts. Advances in urology, 2018, 3068365. https://doi.org/10.1155/2018/3068365

7 Alelign, T., & Petros, B. (2018). Kidney Stone Disease: An Update on Current Concepts. Advances in urology, 2018, 3068365. https://doi.org/10.1155/2018/3068365

8 Ermer, T., Eckardt, K. U., Aronson, P. S., & Knauf, F. (2016). Oxalate, inflammasome, and progression of kidney disease. Current opinion in nephrology and hypertension, 25(4), 363–371. https://doi.org/10.1097/MNH.0000000000000229

9 Knight, J., Madduma-Liyanage, K., Mobley, J. A., Assimos, D. G., & Holmes, R. P. (2016). Ascorbic acid intake and oxalate synthesis. Urolithiasis, 44(4), 289–297. https://doi.org/10.1007/s00240-016-0868-7

10 Kidney Stones | Johns Hopkins Medicine. https://www.hopkinsmedicine.org/health/conditions-and-diseases/kidney-stones

11 Pizzorno, J., Murray, M., Joiner-Bey, H., (2016). The Clinician's Handbook of Natural Medicine, 3rd edition pg 588-599

12 Huang Y, Zhang Y, H, Chi Z, P, Huang R, Huang H, Liu G, Zhang Y, Yang H, Lin J, Yang T, Cao S, Z: The Handling of Oxalate in the Body and the Origin of Oxalate in Calcium Oxalate Stones. Urol Int 2020;104:167-176. doi: 10.1159/000504417

13 Chai and Liebman, "Effect of Different Cooking Methods on Vegetable Oxalate Content."

14 Martin-Higueras, C., Ludwig-Portugall, I., Hoppe, B., & Kurts, C. (2019). Targeting kidney inflammation as a new therapy for primary hyperoxaluria?. Nephrology, dialysis, transplantation : official publication of the European Dialysis and Transplant Association- European Renal Association, 34(6), 908–914. https://doi.org/10.1093/ndt/gfy239

15 Kidney Stone Disease: An Update on Current Concepts (2018) https://www.ncbi.nlm.nih.gov/pmc/articles/PMC5817324/

16 Expert Digs Deep Into Research of Kidney Stones Causes and Treatments (2020): https://pubmed.ncbi.nlm.nih.gov/37176022/

17 Kidney Stones, Health, Johns Hopkins Medicine, Retrieved 03/23/2023: https://www.hopkinsmedicine.org/health/conditions-and-diseases/kidney-stones

18 Huang Y, Zhang Y, H, Chi Z, P, Huang R, Huang H, Liu G, Zhang Y, Yang H, Lin J, Yang T, Cao S, Z: The Handling of Oxalate in the Body and the Origin of Oxalate in Calcium Oxalate Stones. Urol Int 2020;104:167-176. doi: 10.1159/000504417

19 Liebman, M., & Al-Wahsh, I. A. (2011). Probiotics and other key determinants of dietary oxalate absorption. Advances in nutrition (Bethesda, Md.), 2(3), 254–260. https://doi.org/10.3945/an.111.000414

20 Rozenfeld, J., Tal, O., Kladnitsky, O., Adler, L., Efrati, E., Carrithers, S. L., Alper, S. L., & Zelikovic, I. (2012). The pendrin anion exchanger gene is transcriptionally regulated by uroguanylin: a novel enterorenal link. American journal of physiology. Renal physiology, 302(5), F614–F624. https://doi.org/10.1152/ajprenal.00189.2011

21 National Center for Biotechnology Information (2023). PubChem Pathway Summary for Pathway R-HSA-427601, Multifunctional anion exchangers, Source: Reactome. Retrieved March 28, 2023 from https://pubchem.ncbi.nlm.nih.gov/pathway/Reactome:R-HSA-427601.

22 Hill, A. J., Basourakos, S. P., Lewicki, P., Wu, X., Arenas-Gallo, C., Chuang, D., Bodner, D., Jaeger, I., Nevo, A., Zell, M., Markt, S. C., Eisner, B. H., & Shoag, J. E. (2022). Incidence of Kidney Stones in the United States: The Continuous National Health and Nutrition Examination Survey. The Journal of urology, 207(4), 851–856. https://doi.org/10.1097/JU.0000000000002331

23 The Merck Manual 18th edition pg 2021-20211

24 Pizzorno, J., Murray, M., Joiner-Bey, H. (2016), The Clinician's Handbook of Natural Medicine, 3rd edition pg 590

25 Taber's Cyclopedic Medical Dictionary, (2005) 20th edition, pg 1876-1877

26 University of Houston. (2016, August 8). Researchers propose new treatment to prevent kidney stones: Modifier appears to dissolve crystals of the most common kidney stone. ScienceDaily. Retrieved March 23, 2023 from www.sciencedaily.com/releases/2016/08/160808115447.htm

27 Franceschi, V. R., & Nakata, P. A. (2005). Calcium oxalate in plants: formation and function. Annual review of plant biology, 56, 41–71. https://doi.org/10.1146/annurev.arplant.56.032604.144106

28 Paiva E. A. S. (2019). Are calcium oxalate crystals a dynamic calcium store in plants?. The New phytologist, 223(4), 1707–1711. https://doi.org/10.1111/nph.15912

29 Gómez-Espinoza, O., González-Ramírez, D., Bresta, P., Karabourniotis, G., & Bravo, L. A. (2020). Decomposition of Calcium Oxalate Crystals in Colobanthus quitensis under CO2 Limiting Conditions. Plants, 9(10), 1307. MDPI AG. Retrieved from http://dx.doi.org/10.3390/plants9101307

30 Paiva É. A. S. (2021). Do calcium oxalate crystals protect against herbivory?. Die Naturwissenschaften, 108(3), 24. https://doi.org/10.1007/s00114-021-01735-z

31 Saklayen M. G. (2018). The Global Epidemic of the Metabolic Syndrome. Current hypertension reports, 20(2), 12. https://doi.org/10.1007/s11906-018-0812-z

32 Daniel, S. L., Moradi, L., Paiste, H., Wood, K. D., Assimos, D. G., Holmes, R. P., Nazzal, L., Hatch, M., & Knight, J. (2021). Forty Years of Oxalobacter formigenes, a Gutsy Oxalate-Degrading Specialist. Applied and environmental microbiology, 87(18), e0054421. https://doi.org/10.1128/AEM.00544-21

33 Chamberlain, C. A., Hatch, M., & Garrett, T. J. (2020). Oxalobacter formigenes produces metabolites and lipids undetectable in oxalotrophic Bifidobacterium animalis. Metabolomics : Official journal of the Metabolomic Society, 16(12), 122. https://doi.org/10.1007/s11306-020-01747-2

34 Tavasoli, S., Alebouyeh, M., Naji, M., Shakiba Majd, G., Shabani Nashtaei, M., Broumandnia, N., & Basiri, A. (2020). Association of intestinal oxalate-degrading bacteria with recurrent calcium kidney stone formation and hyperoxaluria: a case-control study. BJU international, 125(1), 133–143. https://doi.org/10.1111/bju.14840

35 Mahan, L. K., Raymond, J. 14th edition (2017). Krause's Food & The Nutrition Care Process, pg 700-708

36 Ala-Opas, M., Elomaa, I., Porkka, L., & Alfthan, O. (1987). Unprocessed bran and intermittent thiazide therapy in prevention of recurrent urinary calcium stones. Scandinavian journal of urology and nephrology, 21(4), 311–314. https://doi.org/10.3109/00365598709180789

37 Ohkawa, T., Ebisuno, S., Kitagawa, M., Morimoto, S., Miyazaki, Y., & Yasukawa, S. (1984). Rice bran treatment for patients with hypercalciuric stones: experimental and clinical studies. The Journal of urology, 132(6), 1140–1145. https://doi.org/10.1016/s0022-5347(17)50065-8

38 A. Etienne, M. Génard, P. Lobit, D. Mbeguié-A-Mbéguié, C. Bugaud, What controls fleshy fruit acidity? A review of malate and citrate accumulation in fruit cells, Journal of Experimental Botany, Volume 64, Issue 6, April 2013, Pages 1451–1469, https://doi.org/10.1093/jxb/ert035

39 University of Houston. (2016, August 8). Researchers propose new treatment to prevent kidney stones: Modifier appears to dissolve crystals of the most common kidney stone. ScienceDaily. Retrieved March 23, 2023 from www.sciencedaily.com/releases/2016/08/160808115447.htm

40 Kim, D., Rimer, J. D., & Asplin, J. R. (2019). Hydroxycitrate: a potential new therapy for calcium urolithiasis. Urolithiasis, 47(4), 311–320. https://doi.org/10.1007/s00240-019-01125-1

Chapter 5 ~ Oxalate Literature Review Research

41 Dreher, M.L. (2018). Fiber-Rich Diets in Chronic Kidney Disease. In: Dietary Fiber in Health and Disease. Nutrition and Health. Humana Press, Cham. https://doi.org/10.1007/978-3-319-50557-2_15

42 Mazidi, M., Mikhailidis, D. P., Dehghan, A., Jóźwiak, J., Covic, A., Sattar, N., & Banach, M. (2021). The association between coffee and caffeine consumption and renal function: insight from individual-level data, Mendelian randomization, and meta-analysis. Archives of medical science : AMS, 18(4), 900–911. https://doi.org/10.5114/aoms/144905

43 Geng, J., Qiu, Y., Kang, Z., Li, Y., Li, J., Liao, R., Qin, Z., Yang, Q., & Su, B. (2022). The association between caffeine intake and risk of kidney stones: A population-based study. Frontiers in nutrition, 9, 935820. https://doi.org/10.3389/fnut.2022.935820

44 Huang, J., Huang, C., & Liebman, M. (2015). Oxalate contents of commonly used Chinese medicinal herbs. Journal of traditional Chinese medicine = Chung i tsa chih ying wen pan, 35(5), 594–599. https://doi.org/10.1016/s0254-6272(15)30145-x

45 Assimos D. G. (2016). Re: Oxalate Contents of Commonly Used Chinese Medicinal Herbs. The Journal of urology, 196(1), 137–138. https://doi.org/10.1016/j.juro.2016.04.008

46 Phytotherapy and Herbal Medicines for Kidney Stones: https://pubmed.ncbi.nlm.nih.gov/32990535/

47 Efficacy of a Multicomponent Nutraceutical Formulation for the Prevention and Treatment of Urinary Tract Stones (2023) https://www.research.chop.edu/cornerstone-blog/expert-digs-deep-into-research-of-kidney-stones-causes-and-treatments

48 Garland, V., Herlitz, L., & Regunathan-Shenk, R. (2020). Diet-induced oxalate nephropathy from excessive nut and seed consumption. BMJ case reports, 13(11), e237212. https://doi.org/10.1136/bcr-2020-237212

49 Massey L. K. (2003). Dietary influences on urinary oxalate and risk of kidney stones. Frontiers in bioscience : a journal and virtual library, 8, s584–s594. https://doi.org/10.2741/1082

50 University of Chacago Oxalic Acid food chart https://docs.google.com/spreadsheets/d/1p4YNGC5ybKyt8Kr1ovG_YVTYf1Hn3Z8lyP-f7-icuBg/edit?pli=1#gid=0

51 Liu, M., & Nazzal, L. (2019). Enteric hyperoxaluria: role of microbiota and antibiotics. Current opinion in nephrology and hypertension, 28(4), 352–359. https://doi.org/10.1097/MNH.0000000000000518

52 Ramírez-Rodríguez, Y., Martínez-Huélamo, M., Pedraza-Chaverri, J., Ramírez, V., Martínez-Tagüeña, N., & Trujillo, J. (2020). Ethnobotanical, nutritional and medicinal properties of Mexican drylands Cactaceae Fruits: Recent findings and research opportunities. Food chemistry, 312, 126073. https://doi.org/10.1016/j.foodchem.2019.126073

53 Prezioso, D., Strazzullo, P., Lotti, T., Bianchi, G., Borghi, L., Caione, P., Carini, M., Caudarella, R., Ferraro, M., Gambaro, G., Gelosa, M., Guttilla, A., Illiano, E., Martino, M., Meschi, T., Messa, P., Miano, R., Napodano, G., Nouvenne, A., Rendina, D., ... CLU Working Group (2015). Dietary treatment of urinary risk factors for renal stone formation. A review of CLU Working Group. Archivio italiano di urologia, andrologia : organo ufficiale [di] Societa italiana di ecografia urologica e nefrologica, 87(2), 105–120. https://doi.org/10.4081/aiua.2015.2.105

54 Rakel, D., (2012). Integrative Medicine, 3rd edition pg. 544-548

55 https://www.kidneycareuk.org/about-kidney-health/conditions/kidney-stones/

56 Wołyniec, W., Szwarc, A., Kasprowicz, K., Zorena, K., Jaskulak, M., Renke, M., Naczyk, M., & Ratkowski, W. (2022). Impact of hydration with beverages containing free sugars or xylitol on metabolic and acute kidney injury markers after physical exercise. Frontiers in physiology, 13, 841056. https://doi.org/10.3389/fphys.2022.841056

57 Brigide, P., , de Toledo, N. M. V., , López-Nicolás, R., , Ros, G., , Frontela Saseta, C., , & de Carvalho, R. V., (2019). Fe and Zn in vitro bioavailability in relation to antinutritional factors in biofortified beans subjected to different processes. Food & function, 10(8), 4802–4810. https://doi.org/10.1039/c9fo00199a

58 Lan Shi, Susan D. Arntfield, Michael Nickerson,Changes in levels of phytic acid, lectins and oxalates during soaking and cooking of Canadian pulses,Food Research International,Volume 107,2018,Pages 660-668,ISSN 0963-9969,https://doi.org/10.1016/j.foodres.2018.02.056. https://www.sciencedirect.com/science/article/abs/pii/S0963996918301492

59 Makinde, F. M., & Akinoso, R. (2014). Comparison between the nutritional quality of flour obtained from raw, roasted and fermented sesame (Sesamum indicum L.) seed grown in Nigeria. Acta scientiarum polonorum. Technologia alimentaria, 13(3), 309–319. https://doi.org/10.17306/j.afs.2014.3.9

60 Petroski, W., & Minich, D. M. (2020). Is There Such a Thing as "Anti-Nutrients"? A Narrative Review of Perceived Problematic Plant Compounds. Nutrients, 12(10), 2929. MDPI AG. Retrieved from http://dx.doi.org/10.3390/nu12102929

61 Effect of cooking and germination on bioactive compounds in pulses and their health benefits https://www.sciencedirect.com/science/article/abs/pii/S1756464617301226

62 Park, K. Y., Jeong, J. K., Lee, Y. E., & Daily, J. W., 3rd (2014). Health benefits of kimchi (Korean fermented vegetables) as a probiotic food. Journal of medicinal food, 17(1), 6–20. https://doi.org/10.1089/jmf.2013.3083

63 Quinteros, A., Farré, R., & Lagarda, M. J. (2003). Effect of cooking on oxalate content of pulses using an enzymatic procedure. International journal of food sciences and nutrition, 54(5), 373–377. https://doi.org/10.1080/09637480310001595270

64 Wadamori, Y., Vanhanen, L., & Savage, G. P. (2014). Effect of Kimchi Fermentation on Oxalate Levels in Silver Beet (Beta vulgaris var. cicla). Foods (Basel, Switzerland), 3(2), 269–278. https://doi.org/10.3390/foods3020269

65 Park, K. Y., Jeong, J. K., Lee, Y. E., & Daily, J. W., 3rd (2014). Health benefits of kimchi (Korean fermented vegetables) as a probiotic food. Journal of medicinal food, 17(1), 6–20. https://doi.org/10.1089/jmf.2013.3083

66 Suma PF, Urooj A. Influence of germination on bioaccessible iron and calcium in pearl millet (Pennisetum typhoideum). J Food Sci Technol. 2014 May;51(5):976-81. doi: 10.1007/s13197-011-0585-8. Epub 2011 Nov 23. PMID: 24803707; PMCID: PMC4008749.
67 Savage, G., & Vanhanen, L. (2018). Oxalate Contents of Raw, Boiled, Wok-Fried and Pesto and Juice Made from Fat Hen (Chenopodium album) Leaves. Foods (Basel, Switzerland), 8(1), 2. https://doi.org/10.3390/foods8010002
68 Chai, W., & Liebman, M. (2005). Effect of different cooking methods on vegetable oxalate content. Journal of agricultural and food chemistry, 53(8), 3027–3030. https://doi.org/10.1021/jf048128d
69 Gisela Gerardi, Cecilia I. Casali, Mónica Cavia-Saiz, María D. Rivero-Pérez, Cecilia Perazzo, María L. González-SanJosé, Pilar Muñiz, María C. Fernández Tome, Bioavailable wine pomace attenuates oxalate-induced type II epithelial mesenchymal transition and preserve the differentiated phenotype of renal MDCK cells, Heliyon, Volume 6, Issue 11, 2020, e05396, ISSN 2405-8440, https://doi.org/10.1016/j.heliyon.2020.e05396.
70 Bong, W. C., & Savage, G. (2018). Oxalate content of raw, wok-fried, and juice made from bitter gourd fruits. Food science & nutrition, 6(8), 2015–2019. https://doi.org/10.1002/fsn3.706
71 Leo Vanhanen, Geoffrey Savage, Comparison of oxalate contents and recovery from two green juices prepared using a masticating juicer or a high speed blender,
NFS Journal, Volume 1, 2015, Pages 20-23, ISSN 2352-3646, https://doi.org/10.1016/j.nfs.2015.07.002.
72 Jane E. Getting, James R. Gregoire, Ashley Phul, Mary J. Kasten, Oxalate Nephropathy Due to 'Juicing': The American Journal of Medicine, Volume 126, Issue 9, 2013, Pages 768-772, ISSN 0002-9343, https://doi.org/10.1016/j.amjmed.2013.03.019.
73 Lubem, R., Omenka, A.J., Mchihi, Msenhemba, M., & Sughnen, F. (2019). EFFECT OF BLANCHING TIME ON OXALATE AND PHYTATE CONTENT OF NON-CONVENTIONAL LOCAL VEGETABLES IN BENUE STATE, NIGERIA Tyohemba,.
74 Radek, M., & Savage, G. P. (2008). Oxalates in some Indian green leafy vegetables. International journal of food sciences and nutrition, 59(3), 246–260. https://doi.org/10.1080/09637480701791176
75 Durham, S (2017). Making Spinich with Low Oxalate Levels: https://agresearchmag.ars.usda.gov/2017/jan/spinach/
76 Image 5: Duke Wheel of Health (2022) URL: https://guides.mclibrary.duke.edu/integrativecoachingpatients
77 International Coaching Federation, All thing Coaching (2023): https://coachingfederation.org/about#:~:text=ICF%20defines%20coaching%20as%20partnering,their%20personal%20and%20professional%20potential.
78 Kidney Coach Playbook, Mount Sinai, Recanati/Miller Transplantation Institute: https://www.mountsinai.org/files/MSHealth/Assets/HS/Care/Transplant/Kidney-Pancreas/KidneyCoachPlaybook17copy%20-%205.22.15.pdf
79 Guptha, L., (2018) https://2bwell.solutions/to-affirm-or-not-to-affirm/
80 Guptha, L., (2017) Psychology Today; To Affirm or Not Affirm? https://www.psychologytoday.com/us/blog/embodied-wellness/201704/affirm-or-not-affirm
81 American Kidney Fund (2023): https://www.kidneyfund.org/get-involved/kidney-health-coach

"In our fast-forward culture, we have lost the art of eating well. Food is often little more than fuel to pour down the hatch while doing other stuff - surfing the Web, driving, walking along the street. Dining at a desk is now the norm in many workplaces. All this speed takes a toll. Obesity, eating disorders and poor nutrition are rife."

~Carl Honore
Author of *Praise of Slow*

Science in the Kitchen. A Scientific Treatise on Food Substances and Their Dietetic Properties, together with a Practical Explanation of the Principles of Healthful Cookery. by Mrs. E. E. Kellogg 1892 ~ Authors private collection.

Chapter Six ~ *How to Get What We Need*

Research in the 21st century is opening the door to understanding the role of nourishment as not only coming from our food but also from being affected by nature, wavelengths, movement, beliefs, and culture. Indigenous populations with a rich gastronomy history may well understand the interplay of these elements of nourishment better than individuals of AngloCelt heritage like mine. Losing our essential connection with the elements of nourishment can happen quickly. The past three generations in the United States have lived with suppressed knowledge about nourishing influences from outside an individual's gastronomy, which is all it takes for such knowledge to disappear. A growing movement in ethnobotany in North America is slowly returning cultural foods to First Peoples and African Americans.[1]

> Ethnobotany research is the study of a region's plants and their practical uses through the traditional knowledge of a local culture and people. It aims to document the local customs involving the practical uses of local flora for many aspects of life.

In the Western tradition there is a recognized hierarchy of beings, with the human being on top and the plants at the bottom. In First Peoples's ways of knowing, humans are often referred to as *the younger brothers of Creation*. The perspective is that humans have the least experience with how to live and thus the most to learn – *we must look to our teachers among the other species for guidance...They've been on the earth far longer than we have been and have had time to figure things out*.[2]

In 2008, Chef Jamie Oliver began a campaign in Australia to encourage people to learn how to prepare simple, fresh, and healthy food. It was based on an initiative launched by the British government during World War II, which aimed to educate the public on how to continue to eat healthily despite food rationing. Oliver's 10-week program was proven in a 2014 study to change peoples 'attitudes towards food. Published in the open-access journal *BMC Public Health,* the research found that these changes persisted up to six months after completion of the program.[3]

Research supports that a society that consumes copious calories found in the highly industrialized food market but receives little nourishment from gastronomy and lives in a state of heightened stress and inadequate sleep predisposes its members to increased chronic illness, premature aging, a decline in cognitive abilities, and more years in assisted living.[4, 5, 6]

Food insecurity reports in 2021 began reflecting more focus on well-being through nutritional security in addition to food insecurity itself. The concept of food security focuses on access to and affordability of safe, *nutritious* food plus respect for personal heredity and preferences. However, national policies and solutions have lost equal focus on this concept's "nutritious" portion, fostering institutional emphasis on quantity over quality of food. Tufts University Health Sciences Campus has reported, "Traditionally marginalized minority groups, as well as people living in rural and lower-income counties, are most likely to experience disparities in nutrition quality, food insecurity, and corresponding diet-related diseases."[7]

We no longer live in a state of hunger like the state of affairs in the late 19th century, the Great Depression of the 1930s, or famine from war. Instead, once affordable in inner city areas, fresh foods are now replaced with packaged foods with high calorie content and indeterminant shelf life. These highly processed foods and the epidemic availability of franchise "fast foods" are at the heart of the Western world's health pandemic.[8] In North America, we sarcastically call a diet filled with industrial foods the SAD (Standard American Diet). Unfortunately, SAD has become the Western diet, which is now taking over numerous countries that are rushing to be part of a perceived affluent first-world culture. It makes one think of the old saying so many have heard from parents: "*If your friends jump off a cliff, are you going to do it also?*" We understand this question was meant to encourage us to think before jumping. Hopefully, once we think about available choices, we can see how easily and economically we can turn the Western SAD into a *NEW* (nourished, energized, wellness) lifestyle.

Join Us in a
Nourished
Energized
Wellness
Lifestyle
Paradigm

> ***Principle 27:*** Nourishment must be redefined beyond the diet to include the influences of culture, lifestyle, and the environment.

Vitamins from Food

Vitamins were discovered not because of idle curiosity but because of the scourge of disease. In 1905, William Fletcher was the first scientist to determine that if particular factors (later dubbed "vitamins") were removed from food, illness and disease soon followed. Dr. Fletcher was searching for the cause of beriberi when he discovered that eating unpolished rice prevented beriberi because it contains vitamin B1 (thiamine).

In 1912, the Polish scientist Casimir Funk named the nutritional parts of food "vitamins" — after *vita*, meaning *life* and *amine* — from compounds found in the thiamine he isolated from rice husks. Hopkins and Funk formulated the vitamin hypothesis of deficiency disease: a lack of vitamins could make you sick.

We find several layers when we look at a seed such as wheat or rice. It is within these layers that Casimir Funk found the nutrients he later named vitamins. The layers are comprised of the **bran** (the outer "wrapper"), which contains lots of fiber and minerals such as iron and vitamin B1; the **germ** or embryo, which includes many of the B vitamins and the fat-soluble vitamins like A, D and E, several minerals, and high-quality protein; and the **endosperm**, which is primarily short-chain starch, a small quantity of low-quality protein, and almost no vitamins or minerals.

When wheat is milled into white flour, the bran and germ are removed, leaving only the endosperm. These isolated short-chain starches are readily converted to sugar, creating dangerous blood sugar surges for diabetics and hypoglycemics. When the remaining endosperm is further chemically treated (bleached) to make it appear even whiter, more nutrients are destroyed. Some researchers believe this pre-digested starch plays a role in fatty liver disease, as it can quickly pass through the gut directly into the liver with little or no digestive action beyond freeing up the saccharides it contains.[9]

Hildegard of Bingen, a 12th century abbess, poet, author, mystic, musician, and renowned healer, whose work *Physica* was translated into English by Priscilla Throop, reminds us that processed wheat has been known for centuries to be harmful to human health. She wrote:

> "If anyone sifts out the bran from the flour and then makes bread from that flour, the bread is weaker and feebler than if it had been made from the proper flour. Without its bran, the flour loses its strength somewhat and produces more mucous in a person than that made from whole wheat flour. "Whosoever cooks grain, or wheat without the entire grain, or wheat not ground in the mill, it is as if he eats another food, for this wheat furnishes neither correct blood nor healthy flesh, but more mucous. It is scarcely digested."

In 1943, the United States government admitted that modern processing might cause nutritional deficiencies. So, by law, manufacturers of white flour must manually add back three specific B vitamins (thiamine or B1, riboflavin or B2, and niacin or B3) and iron. Thus, the bleached white flour is "enriched." Unprocessed whole wheat contains around 16 minerals and 11 vitamins that are mostly removed during processing, yet only these three synthetically produced vitamins and iron are *all* that must be added back into flour.

Our Journey with Food

> ***Principle 28:*** You are not what you eat. You are what your body assimilates from what you eat.

Carbohydrate Confusion

Carbohydrates are organic compounds of carbon, hydrogen, and oxygen in which (with few exceptions) the ratio of hydrogen to oxygen is 2:1. The body uses carbohydrates as a source of energy and heat (after conversion to glucose via glycogen which reverts to glucose). Dietary carbohydrates are initially converted to and stored as glycogen until their subsequent conversion to glucose or adipose tissue (fat). Carbohydrates account for 1% of the human body weight. The optimal human diet would consist of 60% carbohydrates, of which 45% would be polysaccharides and 15% would be simple sugars.[10, 11]

The optimal total daily intake of carbohydrates is 75-150 grams per day; the present average consumption in Western nations is 250-400 grams per day. The FDA recommends a maximum daily intake of 300-375 grams of dietary carbohydrates.[12] Could an over-consumption of carbohydrates account for our ever-increasing waistlines and an epidemic of mood disorders? Remember, more carbohydrates equal more calories, many of which come from refined #2 field corn products like high fructose corn sweetener.[13, 14, 15]

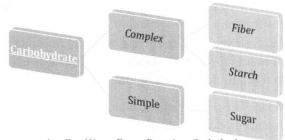

Any Food Not a Fat or Protein = Carbohydrate

> **Simple carbohydrates** are found in fruits, vegetables, and milk products, as well as in sweeteners like sugar, honey, syrup, and foods like candy, soft drinks, and frosting or icing.
>
> **Complex carbohydrates** are found in breads, cereals, pasta, rice, beans, peas, and starchy vegetables such as potatoes, turnips, cruciferous, green peas, and fresh corn.

"Good" and" Bad" Carbohydrates

Carbohydrates come in all colors, sizes, and shapes. The rich, buttery orange of winter squash is due to the healthy carotenoids activated by cooking. With the sweet tang of Bing cherries and the refreshing zest of savory herbs, these flavorful foods do not elevate blood sugars, and the flavonoids they contain reduce inflammation in the joints and muscular tissues like the heart.

Generally, the fresher your fruits and vegetables, the higher their nutritional quality. If you are overweight or diabetic, your health will improve if you select fruits and vegetables low on the glycemic scale like cherries, berries, mixed greens, beans, fennel, bok choy, onion, garlic, and asparagus. The carbohydrates that have the highest impact on blood sugars are starches: corn, potatoes, winter squash, beets, oats, rice,

Chapter 6 ~ How to Get What We Need

and wheat. Also, fruits like melon, pineapple, banana, and mango can spike blood sugar, increasing insulin levels that lead to inflammation.[16]

Alcohol will rapidly convert to sugar and elevate blood glucose levels. Thus, alcohol and the foods mentioned above should be consumed only occasionally and in limited quantities by individuals trying to lose/maintain weight or who have heart disease or diabetes. This is due to their influence on the metabolic hormones leptin and insulin. The higher insulin levels rise to meet the increase in blood sugar, the more inflammation affects your body, increasing your risk of heart disease, type 2 diabetes, and other chronic inflammatory illnesses.[17, 18]

The more processed a carbohydrate is, the faster it will adversely affect the body.[19] Eating three saltine crackers can elevate blood sugars faster than table sugar. This is because the flour in the crackers is refined to almost pure glucose, which can be absorbed quickly through the mouth and throat mucous membranes. Bread made of white or whole wheat flour will also convert rapidly, bouncing blood sugar levels up and down like a yo-yo. Often during food processing, sugars and starches are added that the body does not know what to do with, like high fructose corn sweetener (HFCS), now referred to as simply corn sugar.

The liver manufactures the hormone leptin, a neuropeptide which signals satisfaction to the brain when you are eating and getting full. HFCS (high fructose corn sweetener) blocks this hormone, and the brain fails to get the signal you have eaten or consumed sufficient calories. Twenty years after leptin was found to regulate metabolism and weight through brain cells called neurons, researchers found that the hormone also acts on other types of cells to control appetite.[20] Leptin is also known for its hunger-blocking effect on the hypothalamus, a region in the brain. Food intake is influenced by signals that travel from the body to the brain. Leptin is a molecule that signals the brain to modulate food intake.[21]

Research shows that a woman aged 40 or above who consumes one 12oz soft drink daily (made with HFCS) increases her diabetes risk factors by 50%.[22] HFCS has been one of the most insidious chemicals in our food supply since 1980. Obesity and diabetes rates have sky-rocketed over the 43 years of replacing sugar with HFCS in the food industry.[23]

In 2009, the corn product manufacturers of America started an ad campaign to protect their production of HFCS. These ads, endorsed by the American Dietetic Association, now the Academy of Nutrition and Dietetics (AND), informed consumers that HFCS was no different from sugar and that it was not more harmful if consumed in moderation. By the end of 2010, the corn industry had decided to discontinue the use of the name high fructose corn sweetener and changed the name to corn sugar. Nothing has changed but the name; this chemically derived sweetener can still damage your liver.[24, 25, 26, 27, 28]

> *"Carbohydrates may cause more harm than fat to the heart,"* researchers from the 2017 Prospective Urban Rural Epidemiology (PURE) study concluded after examining the eating habits of 135,335 individuals aged 35-70 in 18 countries with an average follow-up period of 7.4 years assigned to each subject.

> Study findings challenge long-held beliefs on fat's harmfulness in the diet, naming high carbohydrate intake as a bigger culprit in the risk of developing heart disease. "During follow-up, we documented 5,796 deaths and 4,784 major cardiovascular disease events. Higher carbohydrate intake was associated with an increased risk of total mortality but not with the risk of cardiovascular disease or cardiovascular disease mortality," says the report published in the medical journal *The Lancet*.[29]

A study from 2022 suggests eating later in the day can directly impact weight regulation in three keyways: the number of calories we burn, our hunger levels, and how our bodies store fat. This study shows that eating earlier in the day can impact three critical drivers of how our bodies balance energy and the subsequent obesity risk – and it's a change that's perhaps simpler for some people to manage than sticking to a diet or exercise regime.[30]

Many believe non-sugar sweeteners (NSS) are a free pass to indulge in sweet carbohydrates such as cookies, sodas, and candy. In May 2023, the World Health Organization (WHO) published a statement on non-sugar sweeteners for weight control. While the information on the detrimental effects of non-calorie sweeteners may not surprise most, the WHO's position now places a level of awareness and accountability on food companies. "Results of the review also suggest that there may be potential undesirable effects from long-term use of NSS, such as an increased risk of type 2 diabetes, cardiovascular diseases, and mortality in adults." The statement goes on to say that NSS does not help people with weight control over the long term. "NSS are not essential dietary factors and have no nutritional value. People should reduce the sweetness of the diet, starting early in life, to improve their health."[31] In 2023, *The Journal of Toxicology and Environmental Health, Part B* published that when a person consumes sucralose, the body produces *sucralose-6-acetate* one of the several fat-soluble compounds produced in the gut following sucralose is *genotoxic* and is linked to leaky gut syndrome. The researchers found sucralose causes DNA to break apart, increasing disease risk. The researchers found that in food products the amounts were so high, they exceeded the current European safety levels.[32]

> *Principle 29:* If a choice is available, always choose whole, fresh, and locally grown foods.

Phytonutrients Found in Carbohydrates: Challenging the Paradigm

Fruits and vegetables contain phytonutrients, which are not considered essential for keeping you alive, unlike the vitamins and minerals that plant foods have; or so we may have learned from a recognized medical blog post or page. However, research in the 21st century has challenged this opinion dating from the 1970s. When you eat or drink phytonutrient-rich foods, current research shows they help prevent disease and increase longevity. A 6-week dietary intervention with 333mg of polyphenols from strawberries and cranberries improved insulin sensitivity in overweight and obese non-diabetic, insulin-resistant individuals.[33] Plant-derived foods are rich in phytonutrients and polyphenols associated with several cardiometabolic health benefits, such as reduced postprandial hyperglycemia (lowering blood sugar after meals). A 2019 abstract published on PubMed concluded: "The development of a science-based personalized nutrition approach focusing on plant foods rich in specific bioactive compounds could contribute to alleviating the dramatic burden of metabolic and cardiovascular diseases."[34]

Pomegranate juice is a potent anti-inflammatory due to its high concentration of antioxidants. The juice has been found to reduce inflammation and prevent oxidative stress damage. Flavonols in pomegranate juice may help block inflammation contributing to osteoarthritis and cartilage damage. The juice is currently being studied for its potential effects on osteoporosis, rheumatoid arthritis, and other types of arthritis and joint inflammation. Pomegranate was traditionally used to treat diabetes in the Middle East and India. Researchers believe the effects of pomegranate on diabetes may help decrease insulin resistance and lower blood sugar.

Polyphenols are challenging to separate from the term phytonutrients. Polyphenols are a diverse and widely distributed class of secondary metabolites with numerous beneficial properties, including modulation of glucose, lipid metabolism, and DNA integrity.[35] Cranberries are high in polyphenols, and epidemiological studies have shown that a high-polyphenol diet may reduce risk factors for diabetes and cardiovascular disease. Researchers in 2020 reported in a double-blind placebo-controlled study on cranberry juice; participants consumed 450ml of low-energy cranberry beverage or placebo daily for eight weeks. Levels of *8*-isoprostane (a biomarker of lipid peroxidation) decreased in the cranberry group but increased in the placebo group. Peroxidation is a chain reaction that occurs in fat metabolism, leading to the production of free radicals, which are known to cause cell damage. Study participants with high levels of the polyphenol CRP benefited the most. The polyphenol helped lower oxidative stress biomarkers in individuals with obesity and a pro-inflammatory state.[36] Cranberries are just one food being looked at for their beneficial and supportive properties. Strawberries, blackberries, blueberries, cherries, and pomegranates are all part of the antioxidant superfood group.[37, 38, 39]

According to an abstract on PubMed published in 2023, polyphenols have anticancer capabilities, destroying altered or malignant cells without harming normal cells. Flavonoids are a class of polyphenols that demonstrate antioxidant, antiviral, anticancer, and anti-inflammatory effects. Bioavailability and chemical processes determine the biological actions of flavonoids. These low-cost naturally occurring nutritional components have significant biological activities and are beneficial for several chronic disorders, including cancer.[40]

More than 25,000 phytonutrients, including polyphenols, are found in plant foods. More than 600 carotenoids provide yellow, orange, and red colors in fruits and vegetables. *Carotenoids* act as antioxidants in your body: alpha-carotene, beta-carotene, and beta-cryptoxanthin. A healthy body can convert all of these to vitamin A, providing the conversion process is functional and your microbiome is healthy. Carotenoids help keep the immune system working correctly and protect the eyes from degenerative blindness. Yellow and orange foods like yams, winter squash, pumpkin, and carrots are good alpha- and beta-carotene sources. They also contain beta-cryptoxanthin, as do sweet red peppers. *Ellagic acid* found with carotenoids is beneficial in reducing the risk of cancer and may slow the growth of cancer cells. Additionally, it may help your liver neutralize cancer-causing chemicals normally found in the human body.[41]

Green tea (*Camellia sinesis*) is widely known for its anticancer and anti-inflammatory properties. Among the biologically active compounds in *Camellia sinesis*, the main antioxidant agents are catechins. C*atechins* are a form of flavonoids. They exhibit the robust property of neutralizing reactive oxygen and nitrogen molecules during metabolism. Green tea catechin derivatives include *epicatechin*, *epigallocatechin*, *epicatechin gallate,* and *epigallocatechin gallate*. The last of these has the most potent anti-inflammatory and anticancer potential. Their antioxidant properties vary depending on the type and origin of the green tea leaves.[42, 43] Cancer is a significant cause of death worldwide, with multiple pathophysiological manifestations. Genetic abnormalities, inflammation, bad eating habits, radiation exposure, work stress, and toxin consumption are linked to cancer disease development and progression.

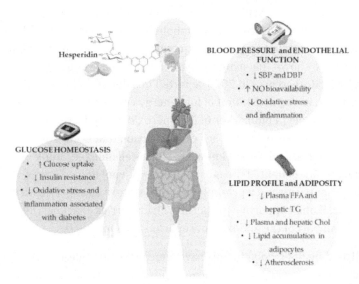

Research emerged by 2020 on other phytonutrients like *hesperidin* (a flavonoid in citrus fruits), a potential therapeutic agent able to modulate several cardiovascular disease (CVD) risk factors.[44] The hesperidin flavonoid works as an antioxidant reducing inflammation in the body to help prevent chronic disease.[45] Research also suggests that *resveratrol* (a natural polyphenol) might play a role in reducing the risk of heart disease and certain cancers, and help extend life.[46]

Broadly, cruciferous vegetables belong to the Cruciferae family, which mainly contains the Brassica genus, but does include a few other genera. In general, cruciferous vegetables are cool-weather vegetables with flowers that have four petals to resemble a cross. In most cases, the leaves or flower buds of cruciferous vegetables are eaten, but there are a few where the roots or seeds are also eaten.

Glucosinolates are found in cruciferous vegetables. Both the cooking and digesting process of foods convert and metabolize glucosinolates into cofactor compounds. Cruciferous foods positively affect genetic receptor sites by turning on positive aspects and turning off negative receptors, thereby reducing the development and growth of cancer.

Plant-derived compounds have caught the scientific community's attention due to their chemo-preventive and anti-cancer effects. *Sulforaphane* (SFN) is a phytocompound belonging to the isothiocyanate family. Although also found in seeds and mature plants, SFN is mainly present in the sprouts of many cruciferous vegetables, including cabbage, broccoli, cauliflower, and Brussels sprouts. SFN is produced by converting glucoraphanin through the enzyme *myrosinase*, which leads to the formation of this isothiocyanate.[47] Research in 2020 began looking at the efficacy of SFN in the treatment of neurodegenerative diseases, including Alzheimer's disease (AD), Parkinson's disease (PD), and multiple sclerosis (MS). Additionally, medical researchers have extensively investigated sulforaphane for other health benefits. It has been shown that sulforaphane may protect against various types of cancer, decrease the risk of cardiovascular disease, and help with autism and osteoporosis.[48] Sulforaphane studies have shown that SFN can target a specific cancer cell population displaying stem-like properties, known as cancer stem cells (CSCs).[49]

Arugula	Bok choy	Broccoli	Broccoli rabe
Broccoli romanesco	Brussel sprouts	Cabbage	Cauliflower
Chinese broccoli	Chinese cabbage	Collard greens	Daikon
Garden cress	Horseradish	Kale	Kohlrabi
Komatsuna	Land cress	Mizuna	
Mustard, seeds/leaves		Radish	Rutabaga
Tatsoi	Turnips, root/greens		Wasabi
Watercress			

Dietary *phytoestrogens* are bioactive compounds with estrogenic activity. With the growing popularity of plant-based diets, the intake of phytoestrogen-rich legumes (especially soy) and legume-derived foods has increased. Evidence from preclinical studies suggests these compounds may affect hormones and health. *Phytoestrogens* can exert estrogen-like effects and block the effects of endogenous estrogens found within the body.[50] Soy foods contain isoflavones, a type of phytoestrogen. Flaxseeds and sesame seeds are high in lignans, a different kind of phytonutrient, into chemicals with some estrogen-like effects.[51] Moderate soy isoflavone intake was associated with favorable predictive outcomes in Chinese early-stage breast cancer survivors.[52] As previously discussed, the microbiome is variable; up to two-thirds of human microflora differ between individuals.[53,54] This variety of intestinal microflora is responsible for differences in metabolic, hormonal, and immunological processes in humans. Meaningful differences have been observed in the metabolism of phytoestrogens with estrogenic or anti-estrogenic activity.[55,56]

> ***Principle 30:*** A "balanced diet" includes all the colors of the rainbow and all the tastes available to the human palate: sweet, salty, sour, bitter, and savory.

Antioxidants

Antioxidants come in a rainbow of colors: purple, red, orange, yellow, and green. It is the consumption of antioxidant-rich foods that keep us healthy. Studies over the last three decades have shown that this group of nutrients can protect against cancers, cataracts, macular degeneration, allergies, heart disease, inflammatory diseases, and more than 80 age-related illnesses. They can also slow the aging process.

Chronic inflammation is associated with various chronic diseases, including cardiovascular disease, neurodegenerative disease, and cancer, all of which severely affect people's health. Importantly, both the quantity and quality of oxidative stress induced by unbalanced production and elimination of reactive oxygen species (ROS) is one of the essential risk factors for chronic inflammation.[57]

Antioxidants comprise a growing group of minerals, herbs, and vitamins, such as vitamins C, A, and E; beta-carotene; *bioflavonoids*; selenium, germanium, lycopene, and proanthocyanidins. Antioxidants are found in all fruits and vegetables, and it is easy to use food concentrates or nutraceuticals to ensure adequate intake of disease-fighting antioxidants.

One food we may not associate with antioxidant properties is mushrooms. Mushrooms grow worldwide, and we are still learning to cultivate mushrooms for commercial sustainability. Humans have consumed mushrooms as part of indigenous cultures worldwide since the beginning of time. So far, more than 350 types have been identified in China — with countless more in regions of the Pacific Northwest, Canada, and Europe. Mushrooms are rich in *polysaccharides*, *peptides*, *polyphenols*, *alkaloids*, and *terpenoids*, all compounds associated with healthy biological functions, especially due to their *antioxidant* properties.[58] As such, the extracts purified from mushrooms could activate the expression of antioxidant enzymes.

Oxidative stress (OS), an imbalance resulting from excessive production of reactive oxygen species, represents a common characteristic in the brains of older adults.

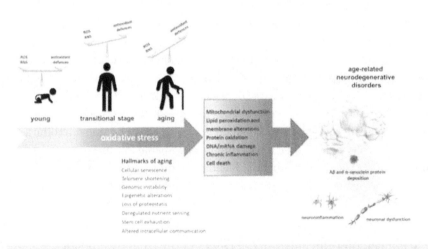

Liu, Z., Ren, Z., Zhang, J., Chuang, C., Kandaswamy, E., Zhou, T., & Zuo, L. (2018). Role of ROS and Nutritional Antioxidants in Human Diseases. Frontiers in Physiology, 9, 360203. https://doi.org/10.3389/fphys.2018.00477

Antioxidant supplementation or dietary intake could be effective preventive and therapeutic interventions in maintaining the integrity and survival of neurons and counteracting neurodegenerative pathologies associated with aging.[59]

Mushroom polysaccharides have received growing attention in anti-diabetes fields due to their advantages in broad resources, structure diversity, and multiple bioactivities. These substances are considered an unlimited source of healthy active components potentially applied in functional foods and nutraceuticals.[60] According to research underway in 2023, mushroom polysaccharides may alleviate metabolic diseases, inflammatory bowel diseases, cancers, and other symptoms by changing the intestinal microenvironment, regulating gut microbiota, increasing the production of short-chain fatty acids, improving the intestinal mucosal barrier, regulating lipid metabolism, and activating specific signaling pathways.[61]

Antioxidant-Rich Foods

Here are just a few examples of antioxidant-rich foods: blueberries, cherries, raspberries, blackberries, greens, tomatoes, plums, peppers, grapes, winter squash, açaí, pomegranate, beer, wine, spirulina, propolis, miso, tempeh, cranberries, kiwifruit, grapefruit, olives, oranges, lemons, limes, elderberries, mushrooms, herbs, cocoa, grape seeds, sesame seeds, green tea, garlic, and onions. Alaskan salmon contains the antioxidant *astaxanthin,* which comes from the krill the salmon feed on; this makes their flesh a bright red-pink.[62, 63]

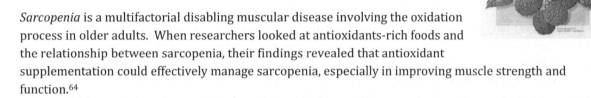

Sarcopenia is a multifactorial disabling muscular disease involving the oxidation process in older adults. When researchers looked at antioxidants-rich foods and the relationship between sarcopenia, their findings revealed that antioxidant supplementation could effectively manage sarcopenia, especially in improving muscle strength and function.[64]

Many recognized bioactive components have been isolated and identified in Traditional Chinese Medicine. Traditional Chinese herbs have recently attracted more attention within the science community, especially in the treatment efficacy for diseases affected by bioactive components of herbs. Researchers have isolated bioactive substances with strong antioxidant functions in fungi, yeast, and algae.[65]

Free Radical Theory

The free radical theory of aging was first described in 1954 by Dr. Denham Harman. He stated that "a single standard process, modifiable by genetic and environmental factors, was responsible for aging and death in all living things." He continues, "Aging is caused by free radical reactions, which may be caused by the environment, from disease and intrinsic reactions within the aging process."

It has taken 55 years for Dr. Harman's work to be taken seriously by the medical community. The conventional Western medical wisdom states that disease must come from outside man, not as a by-product of normal biological functions. Many still do not fully understand the importance of antioxidants in disease prevention. A 2022 study confirmed the role of *Bacillus licheniformis* and *Astragalus membranaceus* extract on blood glucose by regulating antioxidation activity. The study showed supplementation of the bacterium and herb improved diabetic melitus, prolonged lifespan, and enhanced anti-aging enzyme activity.[66]

Nutrigenetics (the science of how genetic variations influence a person's nutritional status) studies show that whole foods are the best way to obtain antioxidants. Nutrigenomics focuses on how nutrients and food can impact gene expression. On a cellular level, whole foods interface with DNA highly efficiently. Nutrients such as vitamins or minerals from foods can activate or deactivate genes linked to risk for Alzheimer's disease, heart disease, or other health issues. In contrast, separated from their whole food source, isolated nutrients may have little or no effect on mitochondrial energy function.[67, 68] It follows, then, that any malnutrition (any nutrient deficiency or excess in your diet) can affect gene expression.[69] These effects on gene expression are known as *epigenetic influences*. Each environmental factor that can turn our genes *on* or *off* is considered epigenetic. *Epi* means *on top of*, describing an influence *on top of genetics*.[70, 71]

Methylation, a chemical process in the body during which a small molecule (called a methyl group) gets added to DNA, protein, or other molecules, affects the activity of various genes. A metabolic deficiency in methyl donors, such as folate, vitamin B12, choline, and methionine which "donate" methyl groups in this process, can hinder methylation. Nutrigenomics deals with these and other epigenetic influences of diet and nutrients.[72, 73, 74]

Free Radicals

No matter how many antioxidants we consume, normal metabolic free radical production will always exist.[75] Free radicals can come from normal metabolic processes in the body or from exposure to cancer-causing substances (carcinogens) or other harmful substances in the environment. The body makes free radicals while breaking down nutrients to give us the energy we need to function. Free radicals have a lifespan of only a fraction of a second but during that time can damage DNA, sometimes causing mutations that can increase your risk of health conditions like heart disease and cancer. Antioxidants in our foods can neutralize unstable molecules and reduce the chances of them becoming free radicals.

Some common oxidative triggers include: [76]

- Stress: Emotional or physical, stress makes you breathe less and burn more energy. Stress feeds on anaerobic metabolism, not oxygen.
- Ozone in the air: A way to produce superoxide.
- Auto exhaust: You breathe carbon monoxide and hydrochloric acid instead of oxygen.
- Cigarette and wood smoke: Same as auto exhaust.
- Inflammation: Your body's immune system creates free radicals to fight germs. Very effective as an immediate response to injury or acute illness but damaging over time if the condition becomes chronic.
- Radiation: Alters molecules, so they throw off more free radicals.
- Sunlight: A form of radiation; *necessary for vitamin D production.*
- Contaminated water: Heavy metals, medications, petroleum, herbicides, and pesticides are commonly found in municipal water supplies (from your tap). Be aware that store-bought bottled water may be only minimally filtered city water.
- Processed foods: Shift your body into anaerobic metabolism, trying to make something useful out of the fake food you just consumed.
- Toxic metals and industrial chemicals are in the soil, water, and air. Some professionals, such as welders, fabricators, auto/aircraft detailers, herbicide applicators, gas station attendants, mechanics, janitors, and landscapers, have higher-than-average exposure rates.
- Drugs: They can alter the body's ability to metabolize oxygen.

> **The Free Radical Theory**
>
> of aging asserts that many of the changes that occur as our bodies age are caused by cellular damage due to free radicals. Damage to DNA, protein cross-linking and other changes have been attributed to free radicals. Over time, this damage accumulates and causes us to experience aging.[77]

Principle 31: Antioxidants – GOOD; Free radicals – BAD

Anti-Nutrients

Despite the need to increase plant-food consumption, some concerns have been raised about whether dietary change is beneficial because of the various "antinutrient" compounds plants contain. Some of the antinutrients called into question include lectins, oxalates, goitrogens, phytoestrogens, phytates and tannins. Antinutrients do not form in plants in isolation; they are only one of many chemical structures found in a wide variety of plants. Beans contain the antinutrients tannins, lectins, phytic acid, and oligosaccharides. Antinutrients influence the bioavailability and digestibility of nutrients and minerals. The phenolic composition of beans promotes several benefits including reduction in the incidence of cancer, cardiovascular diseases, and antioxidant and anti-inflammatory effects. Phenolic acids and *flavan-3-ol* reduce the risk of diseases in the digestive tract, and the high amount of resistant starch reduces the glycemic index.[78] Traditional cultivation and gastronomy may be the answer to neutralizing antinutrients, allowing for greater inclusion of beneficial foods. Individuals with specific health conditions may elect to decrease their plant food intake despite potential benefits.[79]

Exception to Every Rule

Fermented foods are defined as foods or beverages produced through controlled microbial growth, allowing the conversion of food components through enzymatic action. In recent years, fermented foods have grown in popularity due to their proposed health benefits. There is limited clinical evidence for the effectiveness of most fermented foods in gastrointestinal health and disease. However, there is always an exception to every rule.

Kimchi is a traditional Korean food manufactured by fermenting vegetables with probiotic lactic acid bacteria. Kimchi can be considered a probiotic vegetable food with health benefits, similar to yogurt as a probiotic dairy food. Further, the significant ingredients of kimchi are cruciferous vegetables combined with other healthy functional foods, such as garlic, ginger, and red pepper powder. The health benefits of kimchi, based on research done in 2014 and 2016, include anticancer, anti-obesity, anti-constipation, colorectal health promotion, probiotic properties, cholesterol reduction, fibrinolytic effect, antioxidative and anti-aging properties, brain health, immune support, and skin health.[80,81]

> Omics sciences refer to various fields of study in biological sciences that end with -omics, such as genomics, transcriptomics, proteomics, metabolomics, metagenomics, phenomics, and epigenomics. These fields aim to study the collective characterization and quantification of biological molecules that translate into the structure, function, and dynamics of an organism or organisms.

From a research perspective, analyzing the functional role of microbial communities is difficult, especially regarding the conversation over antinutrient reduction through fermentation. The omics sciences of fermented foods provides metabolic and functional understanding of microbial communities and their impact on nutritional properties.[82, 83] High-quality clinical trials investigating the health benefits of fermented foods remain promising in understanding how traditional food preparations reduce inflammatory reactions from anti-nutrients.[84]

THE TRAINING OF THE SCHOOL DIETITIAN.[1]

LILLIAN A. KEMP.

Drexel Institute.

The training of the school dietitian is a subject which makes a strong appeal to all who are interested in the school feeding movement, as so much depends upon the person bearing this title and the character of her work.

Ten years ago the school dietitian was practically unknown; today there is a constant and ever increasing demand for the capable, well trained woman who can efficiently direct the system of food administration in the school dining hall. This position requires a woman especially qualified and well trained, one with definite ideas concerning her field and with ability to execute them. It is an ideal profession for a woman, demanding personality and enthusiasm, which are as essential here as in the home.

A woman of mature years and general experience is undoubtedly the best person for a position of this character. The course which Drexel Institute has offered for some time has brought together in each succeeding year, women from twenty-one to forty-five years of age—teachers, bookkeepers, secretaries, nurses, housekeepers, and others who wished a change in occupation.

> Early dietitians were also known as nutritionists or home economists. By the 1940s many of these women had chemistry degrees, and worked in food labs, or schools. Their research was often published in the Journal of Home Economics.
>
> The Training of the School Dietitian
> Vol. V, No. 5, Pg 442
> Journal of Home Economics
> December (1913)

Chapter 6 ~ How to Get What We Need

Additional supporting citations [85, 86, 87]

Nutritional antioxidant	Common dietary sources	Supplemental effects on human diseases or aging
Anthocyanin	Strawberries, black rice (Peng et al., 2014; Winter et al., 2017).	• Alleviated astrogliosis and preserved neuromuscular junctions and muscle function in ALS (Winter et al., 2017). • Extended lifespan in animal models (Peng et al., 2014).
Lipoic acid	Muscle meats, kidney, liver, and heart; low content in fruits and vegetables (Shay et al., 2009).	• Protected neurons against OS-induced mitochondrial dysfunction (Moreira et al., 2010; Zuo and Motherwell, 2013).
Lycopene	Tomatoes, watermelon, papaya, apricot, and pink grapefruit (Sesso et al., 2005; Wood et al., 2012).	• Improved clinical asthma outcomes by suppressing airway inflammation (Wood et al., 2012). • Reduced LDL oxidation in blood (Ignarro et al., 2007). • Intake of lycopene was inversely correlated with CVD incidence (Kohlmeier and Hastings, 1995; Arab and Steck, 2000; Rao and Agarwal, 2000).
Melatonin	White mustard (seed), black mustard (seed), almond (seed), celery, walnuts, sweet corn, rice (Bonnefont-Rousselot and Collin, 2010).	• Attenuated OS-related lung deterioration in lung diseases (Gumral et al., 2009).
Phytochemicals	Fruits (Mazo et al., 2017).	• Potentially prevent or delay the development of PD (Mazo et al., 2017).
Polyphenols	Fruit, vegetables, coffee, tea, and cereals (Ignarro et al., 2007).	• Higher polyphenol intake was linked with reduced risk of CVD (Vita, 2005). • Anti-cancer activity against lung, breast, tongue, gastric, larynx, colon, and prostate cancers (Manikandan et al., 2012; Sak, 2014). • Extended lifespan in animal models (Peng et al., 2014).
Resveratrol	Purple wine and peanuts (Anekonda, 2006).	• Protected neurons from Aβ and OS-induced toxicity (Anekonda, 2006; Bellaver et al., 2014).
Selenium	Tuna, oyster, salmon, eggs, green peas, pepper, onion, pork, beef (Navarro-Alarcon and Cabrera-Vique, 2008).	• A combination of selenium and vitamin E protected against oxidative damage in the colon of rats with ulcerative colitis (Bitiren et al., 2010).
Theaflavins	Black tea (Peng et al., 2014).	• Extended lifespan in animal models (Peng et al., 2014).
Vitamin A	Eggs, dairy products, orange-colored fruits, green leafy and yellow-colored vegetables (Tang, 2010).	• Intake of vitamins A and C was inversely associated with the incidence of asthma (Allen et al., 2009).
Vitamin C	Strawberry, Grapefruit, broccoli, and orange (Proteggente et al., 2002).	• Reduced airway inflammation and exercise-induced bronchoconstriction in asthma (Tecklenburg et al., 2007). • Intake of vitamins A and C was inversely associated with the incidence of asthma (Allen et al., 2009).
Vitamin D	Fatty ocean fish, sunlight (Holick et al., 2011).	• Improved respiratory muscle function and exercise capability in COPD (Hornikx et al., 2012). • Increased the bone mineral density and reduced the risk of hip and other fractures in the elderly (Lips, 2001).
Vitamin E	Wheat germ oil, sunflower oil, hazelnut, and almonds (Reboul et al., 2006)	• Reduced the incidence of CVD death and non-fatal myocardial infarction (Stephens et al., 1996). • Attenuated functional decline associated with AD (Sano et al., 1997). • A combination of vitamin E and coenzyme Q10 improved energy generation in some cases of Friedreich ataxia (Lodi et al., 2001). • A combination of selenium and vitamin E protected against oxidative damage in the colon of rats with ulcerative colitis (Bitiren et al., 2010).

Aβ, amyloid-β; AD, Alzheimer disease; ALS, amyotrophic lateral sclerosis; COPD, chronic obstructive pulmonary disease; CVD, cardiovascular diseases; LDL, low-density lipoprotein; OS, oxidative stress; PD, Parkinson's disease.

---

1 Penn State. (2021, August 19). Researchers help track the growth of ginseng forest farming in Pennsylvania. ScienceDaily. Retrieved May 15, 2023 from www.sciencedaily.com/releases/2021/08/210819195051.htm

2 Kimmerer, Robin W. (2013) Braiding Sweetgrass, p.9. Milkweed Editions, Canada.

3 Jessica Herbert, Anna Flego, Lisa Gibbs, Elizabeth Waters, Boyd Swinburn, John Reynolds, Marj Moodie. Wider impacts of a 10-week community cooking skills program- Jamie's Ministry of Food, Australia. BMC Public Health, 2014; 14 (1): 1161 DOI: 10.1186/1471-2458-14-1161

4 Washington State University. (2022, May 9). Food insecurity risk related to diabetes later in life. ScienceDaily. Retrieved May 15, 2023 from www.sciencedaily.com/releases/2022/05/220509100931.htm

5 University of Texas at San Antonio. (2019, January 23). Those with inadequate access to food likely to suffer from obesity. ScienceDaily. Retrieved May 15, 2023 from www.sciencedaily.com/releases/2019/01/190123144522.htm

6 University of California- Berkeley. (2022, September 9). Food insecurity has lasting impacts on the brains and behavior of mice: Results suggest young people may suffer long-term consequences, in particular in the area of cognitive flexibility. ScienceDaily. Retrieved May 15, 2023 from www.sciencedaily.com/releases/2022/09/220909160331.htm

7 Tufts University, Health Sciences Campus. (2021, April 1). Time to shift from 'food security' to 'nutrition security' to increase health and well-being. ScienceDaily. Retrieved May 10, 2023 from www.sciencedaily.com/releases/2021/04/210401123921.htm

8 Michigan Medicine- University of Michigan. (2022, September 29). Rate of food insecurity skyrockets for Americans with cardiovascular disease: Diet is the greatest contributor to death from cardiovascular disease. ScienceDaily. Retrieved May 15, 2023 from www.sciencedaily.com/releases/2022/09/220929133445.htm

9 Patel, A. H., Peddu, D., Amin, S., Elsaid, M. I., Minacapelli, C. D., Chandler, T. M., Catalano, C., & Rustgi, V. K. (2023). Nonalcoholic Fatty Liver Disease in Lean/Nonobese and Obese Individuals: A Comprehensive Review on Prevalence, Pathogenesis, Clinical Outcomes, and Treatment. Journal of clinical and translational hepatology, 11(2), 502–515. https://doi.org/10.14218/JCTH.2022.00204

10 An International Journal of Molecular Glycoscience: 2023, Carbohydrate Research publishes reports of original research in the following areas of carbohydrate science. https://www.sciencedirect.com/journal/carbohydrate-research

11 Klammer, C., Schindler, K., Bugl, R., Plazek, D., Vötter, M., Kirchner, T., Martino, C., Klammer-Martin, J., Brix, J., Dämon, S., Hoppichler, F., Kautzky-Willer, A., Kruschitz, R., Toplak, H., Clodi, M., & Ludvik, B. (2023). Ernährungsempfehlungen für Menschen mit Diabetes (Update 2023) [Nutrition for diabetic patients (Update 2023)]. Wiener klinische Wochenschrift, 135(Suppl 1), 62–77. https://doi.org/10.1007/s00508-023-02170-y

12 Ludwig, D. S., Hu, F. B., Tappy, L., & Brand-Miller, J. (2018). Dietary carbohydrates: role of quality and quantity in chronic disease. BMJ (Clinical research ed.), 361, k2340. https://doi.org/10.1136/bmj.k2340

13 Monson, K. R., Peters, B. A., Usyk, M., Um, C. Y., Oberstein, P. E., McCullough, M. L., Purdue, M. P., Freedman, N. D., Hayes, R. B., & Ahn, J. (2022). Elevated dietary carbohydrate and glycemic intake associate with an altered oral microbial ecosystem in two large U.S. cohorts. Cancer research communications, 2(12), 1558–1568. https://doi.org/10.1158/2767-9764.crc-22-0323

14 Millen, A. E., Dahhan, R., Freudenheim, J. L., Hovey, K. M., Li, L., McSkimming, D. I., Andrews, C. A., Buck, M. J., LaMonte, M. J., Kirkwood, K. L., Sun, Y., Murugaiyan, V., Tsompana, M., & Wactawski-Wende, J. (2022). Dietary carbohydrate intake is associated with the subgingival plaque oral microbiome abundance and diversity in a cohort of postmenopausal women. Scientific reports, 12(1), 2643. https://doi.org/10.1038/s41598-022-06421-2

15 Casarin, M., da Silveira, T. M., Bezerra, B., Pirih, F. Q., & Pola, N. M. (2023). Association between different dietary patterns and eating disorders and periodontal diseases. Frontiers in oral health, 4, 1152031. https://doi.org/10.3389/froh.2023.1152031

16 Nicoară, D. M., Munteanu, A. I., Scutca, A. C., Mang, N., Juganaru, I., Brad, G. F., & Mărginean, O. (2023). Assessing the Relationship between Systemic Immune-Inflammation Index and Metabolic Syndrome in Children with Obesity. International journal of molecular sciences, 24(9), 8414. https://doi.org/10.3390/ijms24098414

17 Kolb, H., Kempf, K., Röhling, M., & Martin, S. (2020). Insulin: too much of a good thing is bad. BMC medicine, 18(1), 224. https://doi.org/10.1186/s12916-020-01688-6

18 Luo, T. T., Wu, Y. J., Yin, Q., Chen, W. G., & Zuo, J. (2023). The Involvement of Glucose and Lipid Metabolism Alteration in Rheumatoid Arthritis and Its Clinical Implication. Journal of inflammation research, 16, 1837–1852. https://doi.org/10.2147/JIR.S398291

19 Pagliai, G., Dinu, M., Madarena, M. P., Bonaccio, M., Iacoviello, L., & Sofi, F. (2021). Consumption of ultra-processed foods and health status: a systematic review and meta-analysis. The British journal of nutrition, 125(3), 308–318. https://doi.org/10.1017/S0007114520002688

20 Obradovic, M., Sudar-Milovanovic, E., Soskic, S., Essack, M., Arya, S., Stewart, A. J., Gojobori, T., & Isenovic, E. R. (2021). Leptin and Obesity: Role and Clinical Implication. Frontiers in endocrinology, 12, 585887. https://doi.org/10.3389/fendo.2021.585887

21 Yale University. "Leptin also influences brain cells that control appetite, researchers find." ScienceDaily. ScienceDaily, 1 June 2014. www.sciencedaily.com/releases/2014/06/140601150930.htm.

22 Sigala, D. M., Widaman, A. M., Hieronimus, B., Nunez, M. V., Lee, V., Benyam, Y., Bremer, A. A., Medici, V., Havel, P. J., Stanhope, K. L., & Keim, N. L. (2020). Effects of Consuming Sugar-Sweetened Beverages for 2 Weeks on 24-h Circulating Leptin Profiles, Ad Libitum Food Intake and Body Weight in Young Adults. Nutrients, 12(12), 3893. https://doi.org/10.3390/nu12123893

23 Sigala, D. M., Hieronimus, B., Medici, V., Lee, V., Nunez, M. V., Bremer, A. A., Cox, C. L., Price, C. A., Benyam, Y., Chaudhari, A. J., Abdelhafez, Y., McGahan, J. P., Goran, M. I., Sirlin, C. B., Pacini, G., Tura, A., Keim, N. L., Havel, P. J., & Stanhope, K. L. (2021). Consuming Sucrose- or HFCS-sweetened Beverages Increases Hepatic Lipid and Decreases Insulin Sensitivity in Adults. The Journal of clinical endocrinology and metabolism, 106(11), 3248–3264. https://doi.org/10.1210/clinem/dgab508

24 Naomi, N. D., Ngo, J., Brouwer-Brolsma, E. M., Buso, M. E. C., Soedamah-Muthu, S. S., Pérez-Rodrigo, C., Harrold, J. A., Halford, J. C. G., Raben, A., Geleijnse, J. M., Serra-Majem, L., & Feskens, E. J. M. (2023). Sugar-sweetened beverages, low/no-calorie beverages, fruit juice and non-alcoholic fatty liver disease defined by fatty liver index: the SWEET project. Nutrition & diabetes, 13(1), 6. https://doi.org/10.1038/s41387-023-00237-3

25 Mayer-Davis, E., Leidy, H., Mattes, R., Naimi, T., Novotny, R., Schneeman, B., Kingshipp, B. J., Spill, M., Cole, N. C., Bahnfleth, C. L., Butera, G., Terry, N., & Obbagy, J. (2020). Beverage Consumption During Pregnancy and Birth Weight: A Systematic Review. USDA Nutrition Evidence Systematic Review.

26 Anderson, J. J., Gray, S. R., Welsh, P., Mackay, D. F., Celis-Morales, C. A., Lyall, D. M., Forbes, J., Sattar, N., Gill, J. M. R., & Pell, J. P. (2020). The associations of sugar-sweetened, artificially sweetened and naturally sweet juices with all-cause mortality in 198,285 UK Biobank participants: a prospective cohort study. BMC medicine, 18(1), 97. https://doi.org/10.1186/s12916-020-01554-5

27 Naomi, N. D., Brouwer-Brolsma, E. M., Buso, M. E. C., Soedamah-Muthu, S. S., Harrold, J. A., Halford, J. C. G., Raben, A., Geleijnse, J. M., & Feskens, E. J. M. (2023). Association of sweetened beverages consumption with all-cause mortality risk among Dutch adults: the Lifelines Cohort Study (the SWEET project). European journal of nutrition, 62(2), 797–806. https://doi.org/10.1007/s00394-022-03023-6

28 Stanhope, K. L., Medici, V., Bremer, A. A., Lee, V., Lam, H. D., Nunez, M. V., Chen, G. X., Keim, N. L., & Havel, P. J. (2015). A dose-response study of consuming high-fructose corn syrup-sweetened beverages on lipid/lipoprotein risk factors for cardiovascular disease in young adults. The American journal of clinical nutrition, 101(6), 1144–1154. https://doi.org/10.3945/ajcn.114.100461

29 Scientists raise alarm over high carbohydrate intake: https://www.nation.co.ke/news/Scientists-raise-alarm-over-high-carbohydrate-intake-/1056-4238210-1qd19wz/index.html

30 Late isocaloric eating increases hunger, decreases energy expenditure, and modifies metabolic pathways in adults with overweight and obesity (2022); DOI:https://doi.org/10.1016/j.cmet.2022.09.007

31 WHO advises not to use non-sugar sweeteners for weight control in newly released guideline (2023); https://www.who.int/news/item/15-05-2023-who-advises-not-to-use-non-sugar-sweeteners-for-weight-control-in-newly-released-guideline

32 Schiffman SS, Scholl EH, Furey TS, Nagle HT. Toxicological and pharmacokinetic properties of sucralose-6-acetate and its parent sucralose: in vitro screening assays. J Toxicol Environ Health B Crit Rev. 2023 May 29:1-35. doi: 10.1080/10937404.2023.2213903. Epub ahead of print. PMID: 37246822.

33 Leitzmann C. (2016). Characteristics and Health Benefits of Phytochemicals. Forschende Komplementarmedizin (2006), 23(2), 69–74. https://doi.org/10.1159/000444063

34 Morand, C., & Tomás-Barberán, F. A. (2019). Contribution of plant food bioactives in promoting health effects of plant foods: why look at interindividual variability?. European journal of nutrition, 58(Suppl 2), 13–19. https://doi.org/10.1007/s00394-019-02096-0

35 Rahn, C., Bakuradze, T., Stegmüller, S., Galan, J., Niesen, S., Winterhalter, P., & Richling, E. (2023). Polyphenol-Rich Beverage Consumption Affecting Parameters of the Lipid Metabolism in Healthy Subjects. International journal of molecular sciences, 24(1), 841. https://doi.org/10.3390/ijms24010841

36 Hsia, D. S., Zhang, D. J., Beyl, R. S., Greenway, F. L., & Khoo, C. (2020). Effect of daily consumption of cranberry beverage on insulin sensitivity and modification of cardiovascular risk factors in adults with obesity: a pilot, randomised, placebo-controlled study. The British journal of nutrition, 124(6), 577–585. https://doi.org/10.1017/S0007114520001336

37 Parekh, N., Garg, A., Choudhary, R., Gupta, M., Kaur, G., Ramniwas, S., Shahwan, M., Tuli, H. S., & Sethi, G. (2023). The Role of Natural Flavonoids as Telomerase Inhibitors in Suppressing Cancer Growth. Pharmaceuticals (Basel, Switzerland), 16(4), 605. https://doi.org/10.3390/ph16040605

38 Ullah, A., Munir, S., Badshah, S. L., Khan, N., Ghani, L., Poulson, B. G., Emwas, A. H., & Jaremko, M. (2020). Important Flavonoids and Their Role as a Therapeutic Agent. Molecules (Basel, Switzerland), 25(22), 5243. https://doi.org/10.3390/molecules25225243

39 Paquette, M., Medina Larqué, A. S., Weisnagel, S. J., Desjardins, Y., Marois, J., Pilon, G., Dudonné, S., Marette, A., & Jacques, H. (2017). Strawberry and cranberry polyphenols improve insulin sensitivity in insulin-resistant, non-diabetic adults: a parallel, double-blind, controlled and randomised clinical trial. The British journal of nutrition, 117(4), 519–531. https://doi.org/10.1017/S0007114517000393

40 Farhan, M., Rizvi, A., Aatif, M., & Ahmad, A. (2023). Current Understanding of Flavonoids in Cancer Therapy and Prevention. Metabolites, 13(4), 481. https://doi.org/10.3390/metabo13040481

41 Rahn, C., Bakuradze, T., Stegmüller, S., Galan, J., Niesen, S., Winterhalter, P., & Richling, E. (2023). Polyphenol-Rich Beverage Consumption Affecting Parameters of the Lipid Metabolism in Healthy Subjects. International journal of molecular sciences, 24(1), 841. https://doi.org/10.3390/ijms24010841

42 Musial, C., Kuban-Jankowska, A., & Gorska-Ponikowska, M. (2020). Beneficial Properties of Green Tea Catechins. International journal of molecular sciences, 21(5), 1744. https://doi.org/10.3390/ijms21051744

43 Farhan M. (2022). Green Tea Catechins: Nature's Way of Preventing and Treating Cancer. International journal of molecular sciences, 23(18), 10713. https://doi.org/10.3390/ijms231810713

44 Mas-Capdevila, A., Teichenne, J., Domenech-Coca, C., Caimari, A., Del Bas, J. M., Escoté, X., & Crescenti, A. (2020). Effect of Hesperidin on Cardiovascular Disease Risk Factors: The Role of Intestinal Microbiota on Hesperidin Bioavailability. Nutrients, 12(5), 1488. https://doi.org/10.3390/nu12051488

45 Rajput, A., Sharma, P., Singh, D., Singh, S., Kaur, P., Attri, S., Mohana, P., Kaur, H., Rashid, F., Bhatia, A., Jankowski, J., Arora, V., Tuli, H. S., & Arora, S. (2023). Role of polyphenolic compounds and their nanoformulations: a comprehensive review on cross-talk between

chronic kidney and cardiovascular diseases. Naunyn-Schmiedeberg's archives of pharmacology, 396(5), 901–924. https://doi.org/10.1007/s00210-023-02410-y

46 Terao J. (2023). Potential Role of Quercetin Glycosides as Anti-Atherosclerotic Food-Derived Factors for Human Health. Antioxidants (Basel, Switzerland), 12(2), 258. https://doi.org/10.3390/antiox12020258

47 Schepici G, Bramanti P, Mazzon E. Efficacy of Sulforaphane in Neurodegenerative Diseases. Int J Mol Sci. 2020 Nov 16;21(22):8637. doi: 10.3390/ijms21228637. PMID: 33207780; PMCID: PMC7698208.

48 Vanduchova A, Anzenbacher P, Anzenbacherova E. Isothiocyanate from Broccoli, Sulforaphane, and Its Properties. J Med Food. 2019 Feb;22(2):121-126. doi: 10.1089/jmf.2018.0024. Epub 2018 Oct 27. PMID: 30372361.

49 Coutinho LL, Junior TCT, Rangel MC. Sulforaphane: An emergent anti-cancer stem cell agent. Front Oncol. 2023 Jan 23;13:1089115. doi: 10.3389/fonc.2023.1089115. PMID: 36776595; PMCID: PMC9909961.

50 Domínguez-López, I., Yago-Aragón, M., Salas-Huetos, A., Tresserra-Rimbau, A., & Hurtado-Barroso, S. (2020). Effects of Dietary Phytoestrogens on Hormones throughout a Human Lifespan: A Review. Nutrients, 12(8), 2456. https://doi.org/10.3390/nu12082456

51 Linus Pauling Institute » Micronutrient Information Center; α-Carotene, β-Carotene, β-Cryptoxanthin, Lycopene, Lutein, and Zeaxanthin retrieved May 2023; https://lpi.oregonstate.edu/mic/dietary-factors/phytochemicals/carotenoids

52 Ho, S. C., Yeo, W., Goggins, W., Kwok, C., Cheng, A., Chong, M., Lee, R., & Cheung, K. L. (2021). Pre-diagnosis and early post-diagnosis dietary soy isoflavone intake and survival outcomes: A prospective cohort study of early stage breast cancer survivors. Cancer treatment and research communications, 27, 100350. https://doi.org/10.1016/j.ctarc.2021.100350

53 Kolátorová, L., Lapčík, O., & Stárka, L. (2018). Phytoestrogens and the intestinal microbiome. Physiological research, 67(Suppl 3), S401–S408. https://doi.org/10.33549/physiolres.934022

54 McKenney EA, Hale AR, Anderson J, Larsen R, Grant C, Dunn RR. 2023. Hidden diversity: comparative functional morphology of humans and other species. PeerJ 11:e15148 https://doi.org/10.7717/peerj.15148

55 Santos-Marcos, J. A., Mora-Ortiz, M., Tena-Sempere, M., Lopez-Miranda, J., & Camargo, A. (2023). Interaction between gut microbiota and sex hormones and their relation to sexual dimorphism in metabolic diseases. Biology of sex differences, 14(1), 4. https://doi.org/10.1186/s13293-023-00490-2

56 Brettle, H., Tran, V., Drummond, G. R., Franks, A. E., Petrovski, S., Vinh, A., & Jelinic, M. (2022). Sex hormones, intestinal inflammation, and the gut microbiome: Major influencers of the sexual dimorphisms in obesity. Frontiers in immunology, 13, 971048. https://doi.org/10.3389/fimmu.2022.971048

57 Xia, Y., Wang, D., Li, J., Chen, M., Wang, D., Jiang, Z., & Liu, B. (2022). Compounds purified from edible fungi fight against chronic inflammation through oxidative stress regulation. Frontiers in pharmacology, 13, 974794. https://doi.org/10.3389/fphar.2022.974794

58 Xia, Y., Wang, D., Li, J., Chen, M., Wang, D., Jiang, Z., & Liu, B. (2022). Compounds purified from edible fungi fight against chronic inflammation through oxidative stress regulation. Frontiers in pharmacology, 13, 974794. https://doi.org/10.3389/fphar.2022.974794

59 Liuzzi, G. M., Petraglia, T., Latronico, T., Crescenzi, A., & Rossano, R. (2023). Antioxidant Compounds from Edible Mushrooms as Potential Candidates for Treating Age-Related Neurodegenerative Diseases. Nutrients, 15(8), 1913. https://doi.org/10.3390/nu15081913

60 Liu, X., Luo, D., Guan, J., Chen, J., & Xu, X. (2022). Mushroom polysaccharides with potential in anti-diabetes: Biological mechanisms, extraction, and future perspectives: A review. Frontiers in nutrition, 9, 1087826. https://doi.org/10.3389/fnut.2022.1087826

61 Zhao, J., Hu, Y., Qian, C., Hussain, M., Liu, S., Zhang, A., He, R., & Sun, P. (2023). The Interaction between Mushroom Polysaccharides and Gut Microbiota and Their Effect on Human Health: A Review. Biology, 12(1), 122. https://doi.org/10.3390/biology12010122

62 Chen, Y. C., Chia, Y. C., & Huang, B. M. (2021). Phytochemicals from Polyalthia Species: Potential and Implication on Anti-Oxidant, Anti-Inflammatory, Anti-Cancer, and Chemoprevention Activities. Molecules (Basel, Switzerland), 26(17), 5369. https://doi.org/10.3390/molecules26175369

63 Nyero, A., Anywar, G. U., Achaye, I., & Malinga, G. M. (2023). Phytochemical composition and antioxidant activities of some wild edible plants locally consumed by rural communities in northern Uganda. Frontiers in nutrition, 10, 1070031. https://doi.org/10.3389/fnut.2023.1070031

64 Besora-Moreno, M., Llauradó, E., Valls, R. M., Tarro, L., Pedret, A., & Solà, R. (2022). Antioxidant-rich foods, antioxidant supplements, and sarcopenia in old-young adults ≥55 years old: A systematic review and meta-analysis of observational studies and randomized controlled trials. Clinical nutrition (Edinburgh, Scotland), 41(10), 2308–2324. https://doi.org/10.1016/j.clnu.2022.07.035

65 https://doi.org/10.1016/j.fshw.2014.11.002

66 Wang, D., Zhang, Y., Xu, M., Sun, X., Cui, X., Wang, X., & Liu, D. (2022). Dietary Bacillus licheniformis improves the effect of Astragalus membranaceus extract on blood glucose by regulating antioxidation activity and intestinal microbiota in InR[E19]/TM2 Drosophila melanogaster. PloS one, 17(7), e0271177. https://doi.org/10.1371/journal.pone.0271177

67 Corella, D., Barragán, R., Ordovás, J. M., & Coltell, Ó. (2018). Nutrigenética, nutrigenómica y dieta mediterránea: una nueva visión para la gastronomía [Nutrigenetics, nutrigenomics and Mediterranean diet: a new vision for gastronomy]. Nutricion hospitalaria, 35(Spec No4), 19–27. https://doi.org/10.20960/nh.2120

68 Caradonna, F., Consiglio, O., Luparello, C., & Gentile, C. (2020). Science and Healthy Meals in the World: Nutritional Epigenomics and Nutrigenetics of the Mediterranean Diet. Nutrients, 12(6), 1748. https://doi.org/10.3390/nu12061748

69 Mead MN. Nutrigenomics: the genome--food interface. Environ Health Perspect. 2007 Dec;115(12):A582-9. doi: 10.1289/ehp.115-a582. PMID: 18087577; PMCID: PMC2137135.

70 Fenech M, El-Sohemy A, Cahill L, Ferguson LR, French TA, Tai ES, Milner J, Koh WP, Xie L, Zucker M, Buckley M, Cosgrove L, Lockett T, Fung KY, Head R. Nutrigenetics and nutrigenomics: viewpoints on the current status and applications in nutrition research and practice. J Nutrigenet Nutrigenomics. 2011;4(2):69-89. doi: 10.1159/000327772. Epub 2011 May 28. PMID: 21625170; PMCID: PMC3121546.

71 Castejon-Vega B, Cordero MD, Sanz A. How the Disruption of Mitochondrial Redox Signalling Contributes to Ageing. Antioxidants (Basel). 2023 Mar 29;12(4):831. doi: 10.3390/antiox12040831. PMID: 37107206; PMCID: PMC10135186.

72 Gasmi A, Mujawdiya PK, Noor S, Piscopo S, Menzel A. Lifestyle Genetics-Based Reports in the Treatment of Obesity. Arch Razi Inst. 2021 Oct 31;76(4):707-719. doi: 10.22092/ari.2021.356057.1768. PMID: 35096307; PMCID: PMC8790989.

73 Guevara-Ramírez P, Cadena-Ullauri S, Ruiz-Pozo VA, Tamayo-Trujillo R, Paz-Cruz E, Simancas-Racines D, Zambrano AK. Genetics, genomics, and diet interactions in obesity in the Latin American environment. Front Nutr. 2022 Dec 1;9:1063286. doi: 10.3389/fnut.2022.1063286. PMID: 36532520; PMCID: PMC9751379.

74 Marcum JA. Nutrigenetics/Nutrigenomics, Personalized Nutrition, and Precision Healthcare. Curr Nutr Rep. 2020 Dec;9(4):338-345. doi: 10.1007/s13668-020-00327-z. PMID: 32578026.

75 Alkadi H. (2020). A Review on Free Radicals and Antioxidants. Infectious disorders drug targets, 20(1), 16–26. https://doi.org/10.2174/1871526518666180628124323

76 Li, T. T., Wang, H. Y., Zhang, H., Zhang, P. P., Zhang, M. C., Feng, H. Y., Duan, X. Y., Liu, W. B., Wang, X. W., & Sun, Z. G. (2023). Effect of breathing exercises on oxidative stress biomarkers in humans: A systematic review and meta-analysis. Frontiers in medicine, 10, 1121036. https://doi.org/10.3389/fmed.2023.1121036

77 Castejon-Vega B, Cordero MD, Sanz A. How the Disruption of Mitochondrial Redox Signalling Contributes to Ageing. Antioxidants (Basel). 2023 Mar 29;12(4):831. doi: 10.3390/antiox12040831. PMID: 37107206; PMCID: PMC10135186.

78 Carbas, B., Machado, N., Oppolzer, D., Ferreira, L., Queiroz, M., Brites, C., Rosa, E. A., & Barros, A. I. (2020). Nutrients, Antinutrients, Phenolic Composition, and Antioxidant Activity of Common Bean Cultivars and their Potential for Food Applications. Antioxidants (Basel, Switzerland), 9(2), 186. https://doi.org/10.3390/antiox9020186

79 Petroski, W., & Minich, D. M. (2020). Is There Such a Thing as "Anti-Nutrients"? A Narrative Review of Perceived Problematic Plant Compounds. Nutrients, 12(10), 2929. MDPI AG. Retrieved from http://dx.doi.org/10.3390/nu12102929

80 Park, K. Y., Jeong, J. K., Lee, Y. E., & Daily, J. W., 3rd (2014). Health benefits of kimchi (Korean fermented vegetables) as a probiotic food. Journal of medicinal food, 17(1), 6–20. https://doi.org/10.1089/jmf.2013.3083

81 Patra JK, Das G, Paramithiotis S, Shin HS. Kimchi and Other Widely Consumed Traditional Fermented Foods of Korea: A Review. Front Microbiol. 2016 Sep 28;7:1493. doi: 10.3389/fmicb.2016.01493. PMID: 27733844; PMCID: PMC5039233.

82 Rizo, J., Guillén, D., Farrés, A., Díaz-Ruiz, G., Sánchez, S., Wacher, C., & Rodríguez-Sanoja, R. (2020). Omics in traditional vegetable fermented foods and beverages. Critical reviews in food science and nutrition, 60(5), 791–809. https://doi.org/10.1080/10408398.2018.1551189

83 Omics-Based Clinical Discovery: Science, Technology, and Applications (2022) https://www.ncbi.nlm.nih.gov/books/NBK202165/

84 Dimidi, E., Cox, S. R., Rossi, M., & Whelan, K. (2019). Fermented Foods: Definitions and Characteristics, Impact on the Gut Microbiota and Effects on Gastrointestinal Health and Disease. Nutrients, 11(8), 1806. https://doi.org/10.3390/nu11081806

85 Carlsen MH, Halvorsen BL, Holte K, Bøhn SK, Dragland S, Sampson L, Willey C, Senoo H, Umezono Y, Sanada C, Barikmo I, Berhe N, Willett WC, Phillips KM, Jacobs DR Jr, Blomhoff R. The total antioxidant content of more than 3100 foods, beverages, spices, herbs and supplements used worldwide. Nutr J. 2010 Jan 22;9:3. doi: 10.1186/1475-2891-9-3. PMID: 20096093; PMCID: PMC2841576.

86 Jeganathan, B., Punyasiri, P. A., Kottawa-Arachchi, J. D., Ranatunga, M. A., Abeysinghe, I. S., Gunasekare, M. T., & Bandara, B. M. (2016). Genetic Variation of Flavonols Quercetin, Myricetin, and Kaempferol in the Sri Lankan Tea (Camellia sinensis L.) and Their Health-Promoting Aspects. International journal of food science, 2016, 6057434. https://doi.org/10.1155/2016/6057434

87 Mahmud, A. R., Ema, T. I., Siddiquee, M. F., Shahriar, A., Ahmed, H., Mosfeq-Ul-Hasan, M., Rahman, N., Islam, R., Uddin, M. R., & Mizan, M. F. R. (2023). Natural flavonols: actions, mechanisms, and potential therapeutic utility for various diseases. Beni-Suef University journal of basic and applied sciences, 12(1), 47.

"We know that food is a medicine, perhaps the most powerful drug on the planet with the power to cause or cure most diseases."

~Dr. Mark Hyman

Chapter Seven ~ *Food Our First Medicine*

Lucille Meeks cooks a big meal on a woodstove for a branding party on her ranch near Bend, Oregon, in 1952. Gas stoves, along with refrigerators and freezers, changed food preparation methods for individuals living on ranches in the eastern half of the Pacific Northwest following the development of the Bonneville Power Agency. –OHS image bb012655

Food should always be your first medicine regardless of your family history, genetic markers, and unique living environment. Modern inventions have undoubtedly made food preparation and preservation more convenient. Still, as technology progresses, we are more inclined to make our food the *Star Trek* way, thus sacrificing health for convenience.

Biotechnology & Food

Let's look at CRISPR and genetically modified foods (GMOs). The first question is: Will these modified structures interface with human genetics in a beneficial or harmful way? This is highly controversial and fraught with opinion, incomplete science, and more questions than answers.[1, 2]

> CRISPR/Cas9 is a tool that can be used to precisely cut and remove or replace a specific genetic sequence. The Cas9 protein serves as a pair of molecular scissors, guided to the specific genetic target by an easily swapped RNA guide. Basically, it seeks out a specific genetic sequence and, when it finds that sequence, cuts it out. Once the target DNA is snipped, it can be deleted or replaced.
>
> Deleting or turning down a gene, such as the one responsible for turning sliced apples brown, does not introduce foreign DNA and thus is a non-GMO method. Similarly, altering the expression of a gene related to pest resistance in a variety of sweet potato to make it more resistant, could be a non-GMO method.

The age of genetic modification began in the 1970s when scientists would take a gene that conferred desirable properties in one species (cold tolerance in flounder) and blast it into the genome of another species (tomato). The foreign gene would incorporate randomly into a host plant's DNA. This bioengineering resulted in the famous frost-resistant fish tomatoes, symbolizing what was wrong with genetically modified foods. The next bioengineering development is CRISPR, promising to be far more precise, faster, and cheaper. Researchers are already using it to edit a wide variety of foods—not just commodity crops such as soy and corn, but also more minor vegetables and fruits. DuPont's yogurt-culture facility in Madison, Wisconsin, perfected CRISPR's ubiquitous presence in dairy, predominately cheese and yogurt, in 2005.[3, 4]

> **Hybridization** is growing two plants together in a special way to help the plants develop sought-after natural traits. Because of the importance of plant hybridization in evolution, it is important to accurately identify hybrid. Selective breading is another term used for animals and plants.
>
> Genetically Modified Organisms (GMOs) unlike hybridization taking advantage of natural traits, GMOs insert traits that are not natural into the genetic strand of a plant or animal.
>
> In plants, scientific identification of hybrids is thought to have begun in 1716, when Cotton Mather described corn/maize and squash plants as being of hybrid origin (Zirkle, 1934).

Moving forward from 2020, Africa faces food safety and security challenges. *The World Food Programme (WFP)* of the United Nations (UN) estimates that 20% of Africa's population of 1.2 billion people face the highest level of undernourishment in the world. Factors such as insecurity and conflict, poverty, climate change, and population growth have been identified as critical contributors to the food security challenges on the continent. Researchers, government agencies, and corporations insist that GMO crops are the only way to feed the world's poorest populations.[5] While some African nations are updating their laws to allow GMOs, others are debating whether they are worth the risk. Currently, Tanzania and Uganda do not accept GMOs, but Kenya does.[6]

The European Union's (EU) 2019 legislative position on genetically modified organisms GMOs aims to ensure a high level of human, animal, and environmental health protection and a well-functioning EU internal market. The EU has authorized the placing on the market of 118 GMOs. These have been obtained through long-standing techniques of genetic modification, namely transgenesis.[7, 8] The first field trial of a CRISPR-Cas-9 gene-edited crop began in 2018 at *Rothamsted Research* in the UK. In late July 2018, after the trial had started, the European Court of Justice ruled that techniques such as gene editing (CRISPR) fall within the *European Union's 2001 GMO* directive, meaning that gene-edited plants should be considered genetically modified (GM), and the trial ended.[9] As of June 2023, the EU has not changed its position on CRISPR and GMO crops, even under fire from researchers and multinational corporations.[10]

In contrast to the confusing European directives and position, and the industry driven policies of the United States FDA, organic and indigenous organizations, farmers and their communities see the increased use of GMO and CRISPR biotechnology as an unsustainable approach for the poor. The loss of cultural foods and gastronomy adapted to local, regional soils and climates allows for diversity and better nutrition that is local and not dependent on corporations. When corporations hold the rights to food crops, food inequity and insecurity can just as easily happen as when governments, war, and climates bring about change.

Before the food is approved for a country's population, the research data is reviewed, hopefully in its entirety. GMO and CRISPR foodstuffs are banned in Japan as well as in many other countries.[11] In Japan, inspectors read the complete company-provided study on the genetically modified soy health risk assessment and denied its safety for public use. In the United States, 98% of the soy produced is genetically modified, along with corn.

I frequently tell clients, *"Your cells carry the memories of your ancestors."* If your great-great-great-great grandmother wouldn't recognize the food on your plate or its core ingredients, how do you expect your cells to? How will these biotechnology methods change hormones in humans and animals is still emerging. GMOs are considered hormone modifiers and are linked to damaging the digestive system and microbiome. Unlike the United States, the information has convinced many countries to block GMO and CRISPR foods. These technologies may have unintended consequences that pave the way to a mountain of health problems over time.

> ***Principle 32:*** If it takes a chemistry set to make or a chemistry book to figure out ingredients, don't buy it to eat.

Foods & Hormones

Evidence has emerged that endocrine-disrupting chemicals (EDCs) can produce adverse effects, even at low doses that are assumed safe. A 2018 paper on the evidence and harm of EDCs concluded that living without EDCs is impossible due to their omnipresence. Notably, some lifestyles can increase the excretion of EDCs or mitigate their harmful effects through the activation of mitohormesis or xenohormesis. The effectiveness of lifestyle interventions should be evaluated as practical ways against EDCs in the real world.[12] A published study in 2020 went further in alerting individuals and those in healthcare on the growing dangers of chemicals used in agriculture, sewage runoff, pharmaceuticals, and industry. All of which impact human health and the foods we consume. Increased awareness of EDCs is due to altered human health documented by several epidemiological and experimental studies. EDCs are associated with deleterious effects on male and female reproductive health; they cause diabetes, obesity, metabolic disorders, thyroid homeostasis, and increase the risk of hormone-sensitive cancers.[13]

Sewage effluents used in agriculture and forestry are a significant source of several EDCs, contaminating drinking water supplies. Similarly, water storage in types of plastics leaches EDCs into drinking water. Domestic wastewater containing pharmaceutical ingredients, metals, pesticides, and personal care product additives also contributes to chemical exposure.[14] These EDCs act via various receptors through known and unknown mechanisms, including epigenetic modification.[15]

Individuals can select certified organic foods and install quality water filters to reduce the concern over xenoestrogen and phytoestrogen's effect on breast and prostate health.[16] Since food is often a significant route of exposure to EDCs, awareness of potential EDCs in food and food packing is necessary. Their potential link to breast and prostate cancer development should be carefully evaluated if a multi-generational history or a lifestyle high in exposure to EDCs.[17]

I recommend avoiding soy foods that are not fermented (and maybe even those that are), as soy contains phytoestrogen. Remember that the opinion on estrogen and cancer proliferation is still hotly debated.[18] If an individual is dealing with estrogen-driven breast health challenges, phytoestrogens are viewed by many American medical providers as problematic or equally dangerous as synthetic forms. While many choose to use phytoestrogens for menopause,[19] their undisclosed use could compound hormone challenges due to not being used properly or providing the needed phytohormone. Use caution when having any conversation with clients regarding phytoestrogenic food and hormones.

Flax, like soy, is another food that has gotten tremendous attention for its health properties. A 2020 study looked at the traditional use of flax fibers for wound care. The tested flax fibers did not have a pro-proliferative effect on the neoplastic cell line. Interestingly, flax with genetic modifications had a stronger impact on the proliferative activity of fibroblasts, keratinocytes, and microvascular endothelium than the traditional flax fiber used.[20, 21] Did you know that linseed oil used in painting is made by letting flax oil go rancid? When you read about flax and talk to those familiar with its use, you learn that flax oil should be freshly pressed each day. [22] Flax oil is so sensitive to heat, light, and air that Dr. Udo Erasmus, one of the world's foremost oil experts, designed and custom-ordered specialized equipment for pressing flax to achieve medicinal-quality oil. Flax, like soy, is a phytoestrogen and elevates estradiol levels in both men and women.[23]

Plants take minerals from the soil and water and chelate them through photosynthesis, allowing animals and humans to digest and incorporate minerals for health. Dietary trace minerals are pivotal and critical in numerous metabolic processes. Trace mineral deficiencies (except for iodine, iron, and zinc) do not often develop spontaneously in adults on ordinary diets; infants are more vulnerable because their growth is rapid and intake varies. However, if the minerals are not in the soil, they will unlikely be present in the diet, especially for populations reliant on industrial food products. Over time the trace mineral stores decline further, opening the door to chronic health challenges. Trace mineral imbalances can result from hereditary disorders (e.g., hemochromatosis, Wilson disease), kidney dialysis, parenteral nutrition, restrictive diets prescribed for people with inborn errors of metabolism, or various popular diet plans.[24] The trace mineral selenium is critical in cancer prevention.[25] Selenium (Se), a natural mineral trace element, is an essential component of *selenoproteins* that plays a vital role in antioxidant defense. The activity of the enzyme glutathione peroxidase (GPx), a highly efficient antioxidant enzyme, is closely dependent on the presence of Se.[26] Three to four Brazil nuts contain the minimum daily recommendation of 200 mcg of selenium daily. It is not wise to go over 400 mcg of selenium daily without consulting a healthcare provider knowledgeable in nutrient protocols.

Mushrooms

Mushroom production and consumption have significantly increased in recent decades. This trend is driven mainly by their nutritional value and the presence of bioactive and nutraceutical components associated with health benefits. These benefits have now moved mushrooms into the category of functional food. Mushrooms contain vitamins and minerals (vitamins B, C, and D, iron, phosphorus, copper, potassium and selenium) and are low in calories and fiber. Mushrooms are high in protein and low in cholesterol. Consuming mushrooms may help prevent or treat severe health conditions like cancer, diabetes, and cardiac diseases. Commonly consumed mushroom species exposed to a source of ultraviolet (UV) radiation, such as sunlight or a UV lamp, can generate nutritionally appropriate amounts of vitamin D. The most common form of vitamin D in mushrooms is D2, with lesser amounts of vitamins D3 and D4. In contrast, Vitamin D3 is the most common form in animal foods.

Dried or fresh mushrooms, provide trace minerals and immune-building properties.[27] <u>Note</u>: raw mushrooms are indigestible see *Our Journey with Food Cookery Book* for more information. Most breast, prostate, colon, stomach, and liver health protocols call for the incorporation of mushrooms, provided you are not allergic or sensitive to fungus/mold.

The immune-enhancing properties of many plants and fungi are due to containing bioactive phytoconstituents such as polyphenols, terpenoids, β-glucans, and vitamins. Probiotics and prebiotics can be innovative tools to reduce intestinal inflammation and downregulate hypersensitivity reactions. Plant sources of melatonin, a multifunctional molecule with proven anti-inflammatory and immunomodulatory properties, have been discovered relatively recently in mushrooms.[28, 29]

A study released in 2017 shows mushrooms are filled with antioxidants known for their anti-aging benefits. Researchers found mushrooms have high amounts of ergothioneine and glutathione, both essential antioxidants; the amounts of the two compounds varied significantly between mushroom species.

> "What we found is that, without a doubt, mushrooms are the highest dietary source of these two antioxidants taken together and that some types are packed with both of them," said Beelman, a researcher at Penn State.
>
> "The free radical theory of aging has been around for a long time…when we oxidize our food to produce energy, there's a number of free radicals that are produced as side products of that action, and many of these are quite toxic," said Beelman. "The body has mechanisms to control most of them, including ergothioneine and glutathione, but eventually enough accrue to cause damage, which has been associated with many of the diseases of aging, like cancer, coronary heart disease, and Alzheimer's." [30]

Findings reported in *Food Chemistry* indicate the amounts of ergothioneine and glutathione in mushrooms vary by species, with the porcini species, a wild variety, containing the highest measure of the two compounds among the 13 species tested. The more common mushroom type known as the white button, had fewer antioxidants but higher amounts than most other foods.

Not all edible mushrooms are used for cooking; many have been found to contain medicinal benefits and are sold as supplements, teas, or herbs. Eastern cultures have used mushrooms for food and medicine for thousands of years. Ancient Egyptians believed that eating mushrooms would make one live forever. France was one of the first countries renowned for the cultivation of fungi. After King Louis XIV's reign, mushrooms gained popularity in England; in the late 19th century, cultivated mushrooms came to the United States.

Mushrooms are the fruit of fungi called mycelium, which grows in soil, wood, or decaying matter. There are thousands of known varieties and still more to be found. The most popular varieties are black trumpet, chanterelle, clown ear, lobster, morel, oyster, porcini, portobello, shiitake, truffle, white button, and wood ear mushrooms. Mushrooms convey a fifth taste sense, called *umami* in Japanese, which translates as savory or meaty.

After being harvested, mushrooms' quality continues to deteriorate, showing signs of discoloration, moisture loss, texture changes, increased microorganisms, nutrient and flavor loss. Maintaining postharvest quality and extending the shelf life of mushrooms requires postharvest preservation techniques, such as physical, chemical, and thermal processes.[31, 32]

The mushroom of the gods, Agaricus blazei Murill, is a type of Brazilian mushroom. It is now grown in large quantities in Japan. *Agaricus blazei Murill* may help to prevent and treat various types of cancer. It may inhibit the formation of new blood vessels that feed tumors, help to prevent liver cancer, enhance NK lymphocytes' function, and improve NK lymphocytes' ability to destroy cancer cells. It also may help normalize liver function in hepatitis B patients.

Mushroom sugar, trehalose, is a disaccharide comprised of two glucose molecules. Trehalose is a nonreducing disaccharide with two glucose molecules. It is 45% as sweet as sucrose. Mushroom sugar may alleviate Huntington's disease. It is present in a wide variety of organisms, including bacteria, yeast, fungi, insects, invertebrates, and lower and higher plants, where it may serve as a source of energy and carbon. Trehalose has received attention for its role in neuroprotection, especially in animal models of various diseases.[33]

Dancing mushrooms (maitake) are a type of Japanese mushroom. Maitake mushrooms may improve immune system function with the onset of AIDS and inhibit HIV from killing helper T-cells by up to 97% in 50% of AIDS patients. Maitake mushrooms may help prevent many types of bacterial and viral diseases. They may contain and treat breast, liver, lung, and prostate cancer. Maitake mushrooms are believed to help treat chronic fatigue syndrome (CFS). They also help to lower elevated blood sugar levels and high serum triglycerides and may support weight loss. They also facilitate the growth of bone marrow and may reduce blood pressure.

The oyster mushroom is another type of Japanese mushroom. It is cream and gray, with fluted caps. The mushroom is valued in culinary circles, where it is often used in salads to provide a soft meaty texture and delicate flavor. Oyster mushrooms may lower blood pressure, help prevent and treat ulcerative colitis, improve kidney function, prevent and treat some forms of cancer, and stimulate cell death of prostate cancer cells.

There are thousands of research articles, herbal citations, and folk remedies that attest to the healing properties of mushrooms. **Culinary information** on mushrooms can be found in *Our Journey with Food Cookery Book* pg 169-180.

> ***Principle 33:*** Mushrooms provide unique vital compounds for health and vitality.

So Why Should You Eat Broccoli?

Mother always said to eat your broccoli, and she was right. Broccoli contains vitamins B1, B2, A, C, E, and K, folic acid, calcium, chromium, indoles, isothiocynates (heavy-duty cancer fighters), and sulforaphane glucosinolate. The best way to obtain broccoli's health benefits is to consume it freshly steamed or as sprouts regularly. A handful of three-day-old sprouts contain 50 times the sulforaphane glucosinolate as 114 pounds of regular broccoli. For those who use broccoli as a cancer-preventive food, I'd go with broccoli sprouts in my juice or salads daily. Bladder cancer is the 7th most common cancer worldwide, accounting for 3.2% of all cancers. In 2000, there were an estimated 260,000 new cases in men and 76,000 in women.[34]

Benefits of Broccoli

- Cancer prevention (breast, bladder, stomach, colon and prostate cancer)
- Antioxidant (prevention of ophthalmic disorders/AMDR, anti-aging)
- Anti-inflammatory (prevention of cardiovascular disease, lowers LDL cholesterol, lowers blood pressure, helps prevent headaches and cramps, repairs damaged gastrointestinal mucosa)
- Enhances detoxification of heavy metals (arsenic), endogenous estrogens, and xenoestrogens
- Neuro-protective (Parkinson's disease, Alzheimer's disease)
- Antibiotic (kills *helicobacter pylori*, sinus problems, herpes outbreaks, due to the indol-3-carbonal)

Cruciferous vegetables are the most beneficial when steamed or lightly cooked. They may cause digestive distress and slow thyroid function when consumed raw (although thyroid disruption is unlikely and may be based more on myth than fact).

Cruciferous vegetables have the highest cancer-fighting properties when cooked, fermented, or pickled. This could be why traditional dishes that incorporate the Brassica family are usually pickled, fermented, steamed, or cooked in some fashion. Grandmother did know best.

Broccoli for Just about Everything

The whole Brassica family contains essential ingredients for fighting cancer. How these ingredients work is still mostly a mystery. Researchers have learned there are over 2,000 different nutrients and co-factors in any one food; they can identify about 200. These agents interact with human genes, turning gene response and expression on and off.

> "Almost all aspects of life are engineered at the molecular level, and without understanding molecules, we can only have a very sketchy understanding of life itself," said Francis Crick, PhD, co-discoverer of the DNA double helix.
>
> " An increasing body of evidence has demonstrated that individual compounds —as well as complex mixtures of chemicals—derived from food, alter the expression of genes in the human

body. Studies based on ethnopharmacology and phytotherapy concepts showed that nutrients and botanicals could interact with the genome causing marked changes in gene expression".[35]

Broccoli is a green cruciferous vegetable and a member of the *italic cultivar* group. There are two main types of broccoli, heading and sprouting. Broccoli has been around for over 2,000 years and was first seen in Turkey. The Italian immigrants of the early 19th century carried broccoli to North America. It took another century for broccoli to become available outside the Italian communities and develop into a commercial crop. 90% of the broccoli grown in the United States comes from the Salinas Valley in California. Arizona, Texas, Florida, and Washington take over production during the winter months.

Sulforaphane and Kaempferol

A clinical trial in one of China's most polluted regions involving nearly 300 Chinese men and women found daily consumption of a half cup of broccoli sprout juice produced significant and sustained excretion of benzene, a known human carcinogen, and acrolein, a lung irritant. Johns Hopkins Bloomberg, School of Public Health researchers, working with colleagues in the U.S. and China, used a plant compound called sulforaphane that had already demonstrated cancer-preventative properties in animal studies.[36]

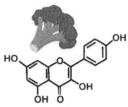

Kaempferol (KP), as a natural anti-inflammatory compound, has been reported to have curative effects on alleviating senile osteoporosis (SOP), an inflammation-related musculoskeletal disease.

Senile osteoporosis (SOP) is an inflammation-related musculoskeletal disease with serious complications, including spine deformation, osteoporotic fracture, and bone pain.[37, 38] Osteoporotic vertebral fracture (OVF) is the worst-affected complication in SOP patients, with about 1.8 million vertebral fractures estimated to happen every year in China with the number of vertebral fractures predicted to increase to 3 million in 2050.[39]

Kaempferol is a flavonoid identified in various natural products and used in traditional Chinese medicine (*Drynariae Rhizoma*).[40] Studies have illustrated that KP exerts the antiosteoporotic function via upregulating microRNA-101 and activating the Wnt/β-catenin pathway, which promotes osteoblast differentiation, proliferation, and migration.[41] Kaempferol is just one of many compounds found in broccoli being studied that supports a higher consumption to reduce associated risks of type 2 diabetes.[42, 43, 44, 45]

> ***Principle 34:*** Sulforaphane and Kaempferol rich foods are the key ingredients in upregulating positive cell receptor sites and down regulating negative cell receptor.

How do I get the most out of my broccoli?

The way you prepare and consume your broccoli matters, according to a study from the University of Illinois. The study provides convincing evidence and suggests steaming broccoli with broccoli sprouts may make the vegetable's anti-cancer effect almost twice as powerful.

"Broccoli prepared correctly is an extremely potent cancer-fighting agent—three to five servings a week are enough to have an effect. To get broccoli's benefits, though, the enzyme *myrosinase* must be present; if it's not there, sulforaphane, broccoli's cancer-preventive and anti-inflammatory component, doesn't form," said Elizabeth Jeffery, a University of Illinois professor of nutrition.[46]

Remember to buy from a reputable local farm, farmers market, or the organic section at your favorite grocery store. Steam until it is tender but still crisp and bright green. You can also stir-fry or wrap it in foil with other vegetables like peppers, tomatoes, onions, and garlic. Add a pinch of thyme, basil, and oregano, and place it on your grill to steam in its natural juices and enjoy with your chicken or steak.

Turnips

The first vegetable carved for Halloween was not the pumpkin but the turnip. The turnip is a member of the cruciferous family, including broccoli and cabbage. Both the root and the greens are eaten; the greens are smaller and more tender than their more prominent family member, collard greens. Rutabagas are a cross between turnips and wild cabbage (collard greens or wild cabbage are in the *Acephala* (kale) cultivar group).

Turnips were cultivated almost 4,000 years ago in Asia. The Greeks and Romans further cultivated turnips into several varieties. They were widely grown throughout Europe in the Middle Ages until potatoes became popular in the 18th century.
In Scotland and Ireland, turnips were carved and placed at doorways on All Hallows 'Eve to ward off evil spirits.

Early European settlers brought the turnip to America; they grew well in the South and became a favorite food in local cooking. The greens from the turnip became a mainstay in African American households. This may be because the traditional West African diet utilized a wide selection of greens.

Purple turnip *Brassica rapa ssp. rapa* is highly appreciated by consumers.[47] Although turnips are starch, they provide only a third of the calories as an equal number of potatoes. They are an excellent source of fiber, vitamin C, folic acid, pantothenic acid, thiamine, niacin, potassium, magnesium, riboflavin, vitamin E, manganese, and copper. The greens have a higher concentration of nutrients than the root itself.

Like all members of the cruciferous family, turnips are excellent cancer fighters.

Watercress

In traditional medicine, watercress (WC) is a known remedy for hypercholesterolemia, hyperglycemia, hypertension, arthritis, bronchitis, diuresis, odontalgia, and scurvy. It also acts as an antiestrogenic and can be a nutritional supplement. It has been reported that these therapeutic effects are due to primary metabolites such as isothiocyanates, glucosinolates, polyphenols (flavonoids, phenolic acids, and proanthocyanidins), vitamins (B_1, B_2, B_3, B_6, E, and C), terpenes (including carotenoids), and bio-elements which exist in this plant.[48] Many pharmacological studies confirm the antioxidant, antibacterial, anticancer, antipsoriatic, anti-inflammatory, cardioprotective, renoprotective, hepatoprotective, and antigenotoxicity effects of WC.[49] The consumption of WC extract can help reduce the complications of hypercholesterolemia and hyperglycemia.[50]

Watercress has been cultivated in Europe, Central Asia, and the Americas for millennia for use as both food and medicine. Hippocrates, the father of medicine, is thought to have decided on the location for his

first hospital because of its proximity to a stream so he could use only the freshest watercress to treat his patients. Watercress is believed by many to be an aphrodisiac. In Crete, islanders swear by its powers and ancient recipes are handed down from generation to generation.

A myriad of microorganisms colonizes the oral cavity, some of which are proven to be detrimental to human health. Numerous efforts have been made to control the population of pathogenic agents in the oral cavity, including using natural phytochemicals from medicinal plants. *Nasturtium officinale* has long been used in traditional medicine to manage hypertension, respiratory infections, and hyperglycemia, and its effectiveness against some microbes has been reported. A 2022 study showed antibacterial activity of *N. officinale extract* effectively inhibited the growth of the tested oral bacteria at different concentrations but was more effective against *S. mutans*, *E. faecalis* and *S. aureus* and may be effective in managing some oral microbial infections.[51] Oral health and the associated bacteria have been linked to a growing number of chronic illnesses and cognitive decline.[52]

Irish monks were said to have survived for long periods eating only bread and watercress and referred to watercress as "pure food for sages." Watercress is a rich source of vitamin C; historically it was chiefly valued as an antiscorbutic (to prevent scurvy).[53]

Watercress was used as a salad vegetable and added to stews. The juice pressed from the watercress was used for gravies to accompany roast meats in medieval France. Watercress was often eaten in-between courses to cleanse the palate. Watercress was promoted during World War I as an essential health-giving homegrown food. One of Britain's best-known dishes, watercress soup, became very popular in the 17th century when it was claimed to cleanse the blood. Victorians thought the plant was a cure for toothache, hiccups and even freckles! Watercress is often mentioned as an ingredient in detox vegetable juice recipes and a cure for various ills. It could virtually be viewed as a staple part of the regime for those wishing to juice their way to health.[54, 55]

Watercress is versatile; it can be used as a salad green with romaine lettuce or fresh spinach, steamed and eaten as a vegetable, and in soups, sandwiches, and wraps for a subtle, peppery flavor.

Health Benefits of Watercress

Modern science has identified more than 15 essential vitamins and minerals in this herb – more iron than spinach, calcium than milk, and vitamin C than oranges. Watercress is low in calories but contains phytonutrients like isothiocyanates and antioxidants with a plethora of disease-preventive properties.[56] *Gluconasturtiin* and *glucosinolate* compounds provide the peppery flavor and are the antioxidants included in the leaves and stems. Phenethyl isothiocyanate, shown to inhibit carcinogens, is also present.[57]

Vitamin K is the most prominent nutrient in watercress, with 312% of the daily recommended value. It forms and strengthens the bones and limits neuronal damage in the brain, which helps treat Alzheimer's disease. There's also vitamin C, with 72% of the daily value, closely followed by vitamin A, with 64%. Vitamin C provides top-notch infection-fighting power to stave off colds and flu, helps maintain healthy connective tissue, and prevents iron deficiency. Vitamin A, also known as retinol, is essential for a properly functioning immune system and produces pigments in the retina of the eye, an absence of which can cause night blindness.

Manganese is a cofactor for high doses of the antioxidant enzyme superoxide dismutase and calcium when you eat watercress. Antioxidant flavonoids, ß carotene, zeaxanthin, and lutein protect from lung and mouth cancers. B-complex vitamins include riboflavin, niacin, vitamin B_6 (pyridoxine), thiamin, and pantothenic acid, which are essential for keeping cellular metabolic functions at peak performance.

According to a two-year research project at the University of Ulster, eating watercress daily can significantly reduce DNA damage to blood cells and further resist DNA damage caused by free radicals.[58,59]

Scientists found significant anticancer properties in a watercress-derived compound called phenylethyl isothiocyanate (PEITC). Single-blind, randomized crossover trials involved 60 healthy men and women eating about 1½ cups of fresh watercress daily for eight weeks. Positive results included a reduction in blood triglyceride levels by an average of 10% and a significant (33% - 100%) increase in lutein and beta-carotene content associated with higher intake levels resulting in a lowered incidence of eye diseases such as cataracts and macular degeneration.

Scientific research found that the PEITC in watercress may suppress breast cancer cell development. Studies at the University of Southampton found PEITC may starve tumor growth of blood and oxygen by "turning off" a signal in the body. Researchers explained that "as tumors develop, they rapidly outgrow their existing blood supply, so they send out signals that make surrounding normal tissues grow new blood vessels into the tumor, which feed them oxygen and nutrients."

Onion: A Fine Lily

When fall approaches, my thoughts turn to warm and savory foods like onions. The thickness of the onion skin has been used to predict how severe the next winter may be; thin skins mean a mild winter and thick skins indicate a rough winter ahead. Onions, garlic, chives, shallots, leeks, and green onions (scallions) are in the *Amaryllis* family—often incorrectly referred to as the Lily family. There are two basic types: the bulb-forming favorites like Walla Walla, Vidalia and Spanish red onions, and the perennials that produce clusters of onions that can be replanted. Cluster onions include shallots, Egyptian onions, and garlic. This family of vegetables is cultivated worldwide and has been used for health and culinary purposes for millennia.

Onions originated in Central Asia—from Iran to Pakistan and northward to the Slavic countries. Onion gardens have been excavated that date back 5,000 years; Pharaohs were buried with onions to symbolize immortality—documents dating back to the 6th century show onions being used medicinally in India. The Romans believed that onions could cure almost any ailment. Even though the onion was not spicy enough for the Greeks and Romans, they were heavily used for its pungency. They were widely available to the more impoverished populations worldwide.

Christopher Columbus and other explorers brought onions to the Americas. The three top vegetables of European cuisine from the Middle Ages to the present are beans, cabbage, and onions. Onions have been used as currency and given as wedding gifts.

Wild onions have grown in North America since the arrival of the Pilgrims. The Native Americans used wild onions for cooking, as a seasoning in syrups, and for dyeing textiles. Official onion cultivation began in America in 1629 and is now one of the top ten vegetable crops grown in the United States. China, India, the United States, Turkey, and Pakistan are the world's leading producers of onions. Idaho, Oregon, Washington, California, and Texas are the largest onion producers in the United States.

Vitamin C, fiber, biotin, folate, chromium, vitamin K, and thiamine are found in members of the onion family, along with potent anti-cancer phytochemicals like quercetin, phenolic acid, sterols, pectin, volatile oils, sulfur compounds, and the enzyme *alliinase*. This enzyme's release and conversion to trans-S-cystine causes the cook's eyes to water.

Onion peel is a common bio-waste, occasionally used in traditional medicine to treat liver ailments and inflammation.[60] While not quite as highly valued medicinally as garlic, onions are widely used for similar purposes because they possess the same properties. Studies have shown that onion extracts, like those of garlic, decrease blood sugar and lipid levels, prevent clots, lower blood pressure, reduce inflammation (onions are one of the only foods that contain prostaglandin E1), improve asthma and allergies, and retard viruses by strengthening the immune system. The blood sugar-lowering effects of onions have been clinically comparable to prescription drugs *tolbutamide* and *phenformin*, commonly given to type 2 diabetics. Onions have been found to help the liver process glucose more efficiently by increasing the availability and natural secretion of insulin.

Historically, onions have been used in the treatment of asthma due to their ability to inhibit the production of compounds that cause bronchial spasms and mucous production. Onion extracts have been found to inhibit the formation of tumor cells, and shallots exhibit significant activity against leukemia.

Maintaining and enhancing testosterone levels in men is a constant target for researchers. From 1967 until now, numerus research studies have revealed the effect of onion on testosterone. A 2019 review on testosterone in males, as enhanced by onion, found evidence that onions enhance the testosterone level in males. The mechanisms by which this occurs are mainly by increasing the production of luteinizing hormone, improving the antioxidant defense mechanism in the tests, neutralizing the damaging effects of the generated free radicals, ameliorating insulin resistance, promoting nitric oxide production, and altering the activity of adenosine 5'-monophosphate-activated protein kinase.[61]

Health Benefits of Onions [62, 63]

- Onions help prevent lung, breast, ovary, kidney, prostate, skin, mouth, esophageal, stomach, colon, and liver cancer.
- They help prevent and treat diabetes, hypoglycemia, metabolic syndrome, and insulin resistance.
- Onions help lower cholesterol and reduces the risk of atherosclerosis, cardiovascular disease, heart attack, and stroke.
- They help to increase bone density and possibly decreases the risk of osteoporosis.

Onions are available in fresh, frozen, canned, and dehydrated forms. I prefer fresh as this form has the most nutritional benefit. Store your onions in a cool (55 degrees), dry location to help them retain their vitamin C content for six months.

If incorrectly stored, onions are prone to contamination by aflatoxin produced by *aspergillus parasiticus*. Onions are often subjected to food irradiation to inhibit their sprouting potential; food irradiation can have various toxic effects. Onions may cause food allergies and trigger migraines in some people.

Onion Allergy Symptoms

Anaphylactic shock	Asthma
Breathing difficulties	Bloating
Burning sensation mouth	Diarrhea
Fainting	Fatigue Gas/burping
Gum blisters	Hives/itching
Lip swelling	Mental disorientation
Mouth blisters	Nausea
Puffy eyes and face	Rashes or dry skin flakes

Onion Allergy

Onion allergy is triggered by eating or having direct contact with onions. A study in 2019 confirmed that cooked onion can induce severe allergic reactions, suggesting the presence of thermostable components.[64] True onion allergy is rare. Studies show that only 3% of adults may have this allergy. Despite the statistics, a considerable number of people suffer from onion intolerance. People with onion intolerance don't show as many adverse reactions as those with allergies.[65] Moreover, patients with onion intolerance can consume small amounts of cooked onion, whereas some who have an allergy can't even stand the smell of onions. In most cases, raw onion is the culprit for the allergic reaction.

Allergic reactions to onions can be internal or external. External reactions usually result from direct contact with or smelling onions, while internal reactions come from ingesting onions.

An individual's response or allergic reaction may appear at different times and degrees. Some people react immediately, while others don't exhibit symptoms for at least 24 hours. The degree of their allergic reaction depends on their sensitivity to onions. As for the healing time, most people feel better when the allergen is expelled from their body. In rare cases, though, the allergic reaction lasts for days, even after the onion has been out of the system.[66, 67, 68]

Onion Allergy from Food

Broth/stock	Chicken frozen
Chives	Crackers
Flavored cheese, especially Mexican cheese	
Gravy/sauces	Garlic
Gardener's garlic	Garlic powder
Leeks	Meat, canned/processed
Marinades	Onion juice
Onion powder	Pre-made pizza crusts
Pre-made sauces	Pre-made soups
Salad Dressings	Shallots

Beets

In my home, we had canned and pickled sugar beets with greens. For me, the beet greens were (and sometimes still are) the only edible part of the plant, but many people love beets in all their forms. Recently, there has been a growing interest in the biological activity of red beetroot (*Beta vulgaris rubra*) and its potential utility as a health-promoting and disease-preventing functional food. As a source of nitrate, beetroot ingestion provides a natural means of increasing in vivo nitric oxide (NO) availability. It has emerged as a potential strategy to prevent and manage pathologies associated with diminished NO bioavailability, notably hypertension and endothelial function.[69, 70]

Like many modern vegetables, beetroot was first cultivated by the Romans. In the 19th century, it gained significant commercial value when it was discovered that beets could be converted into sugar. The Amalgamated Sugar Company was founded in 1897 in Logan, Utah, and is now in Boise, Idaho. The company markets its sugar under the White Satin brand.

By the 1950s, White Satin sugar was in every grocery store in the Pacific Northwest. The company was listed on the New York Stock Exchange in 1950. A new distribution center in Portland, Oregon, was finished in 1951. The distribution silo could hold 2,500 tons of sugar and supply it in bulk, liquid, blended, or packaged. Classic beetroot recipes like borscht are associated with Central and Eastern Europe. A traditional borscht recipe from Ukraine can be found in the *Our Journey with Food Cookery Book*. Beets are in the same family as chard and spinach, and the leaves and roots can be eaten. The leaves have a bitter taste, whereas the round root is sweet. Beets come in various colors, including white and creamy yellow. Beets can be eaten raw, cooked, or pickled.

Beets are exceptionally healthy, especially the greens, which are rich in calcium, iron, and vitamins A and C. Beetroots are an excellent source of folic acid and a splendid source of fiber, manganese, and potassium. Beets help the liver to detoxify harmful chemicals from the body. The greens can be cooked up and enjoyed in the same ways as spinach.

A unique source of phytonutrients called *betalains* is found in beets. Betanin and vulgaxanthin are the best-studied betalains found in beets, and both have been shown to provide antioxidant, anti-inflammatory, detoxification, anticancer, blood pressure, lipid-lowering, anti-diabetic, and anti-obesity effects. Betanin, the main component of the red beetroot, is a betalain glycosidic pigment used as a food additive. Betalain's red-colored pigments are found in other foods like the stems of chard and rhubarb, but the peel and flesh of beets offer an unusually high concentration.[71]

An estimated 10-15% of U.S. adults experience beeturia, a reddening of the urine, after consumption of beets; this phenomenon is not harmful. Beeturia may indicate problems with iron metabolism for some individuals. Persons with iron deficiency, iron excess, or particular issues with iron metabolism are much more likely to experience beeturia than individuals with healthy iron metabolism. Red beetroot betalains have great potential as a functional food ingredient in the food and medical industry due to their diverse health-promoting effects. Betalains from red beetroot are natural pigments, mainly yellow-orange betaxanthins or red-violet betacyanins. However, betalains are sensitive to heat, *pH*, light, and oxygen, leading to poor stability during processing and storage.[72]

Winter Vegetables High in Vitamin A

The word "pumpkin" comes from the Greek word "pepon" or "big melon." Pumpkins are members of the melon family, along with cantaloupes and watermelon. Pumpkins that make good jack-o'-lanterns are not necessarily the best for pie-making. For pies, my personal favorites are sweet meat or Hubbard squashes. Pumpkins come in various colors in addition to orange, such as white, blue, and red.

Pumpkin seeds found in Mexico are estimated to be at least 7,500 years old. The pumpkin was a mainstay of Native American culture; it was used for food, and the shell was used for making mats and other products. Early American settlers made the first pumpkin pie; they filled the hollowed-out pumpkin with honey, milk, spices, and baked it.

The largest pumpkin producers are the United States, India, China, and Mexico. The pumpkin capital of the world is reported to be in Morton, Illinois, the location of the Libby processing plant.

Pumpkins play a role in preventing cancer, diabetes, hypertension, and asthma. Findings in 2017 on glucose release from winter vegetables concluded that with sweet potato and winter squash, the glucose content and the released glucose during digestive simulation depends on the variety and the storage time. These factors strongly affect the supply of glucose for human nutrition and should be considered for adjusting a diet according to consumer needs.[73]

Ipomoea batatas, also known as sweet potato, is a highly versatile and delicious vegetable with high nutritional value. It is also a valuable medicinal plant having anti-cancer, antidiabetic, and anti-inflammatory activities. Sweet potato is now considered a valuable source of unique natural products, including some that can be used to develop medicines against various diseases and make industrial products.[74, 75] Sweet potato (*Ipomoea batatas*) leaves provide a dietary source of nutrients and different bioactive compounds. These constituents of sweet potato leaves (SPL) vary among varieties and play essential roles in treating and preventing various diseases.[76]

Potatoes: Red, White, Purple and Brown

Today, the potato is the most consumed vegetable in America. The potato has a long history that started long before it accidentally washed up on the beaches of Ireland. Potatoes were cultivated for food for more than 2,000 years in South America. The Inca, it is believed, cultivated potatoes since 3000 B.C.

In the ancient ruins of Peru and Chile, archeologists have found potatoes dating back to 500 B.C. The Inca had many uses for potatoes, which varied in size from a small nut to an apple and in color from red and gold to blue and black. The Inca buried potatoes with their dead, stashed them in concealed bins in case of war or famine, dried them, and carried them on long journeys. They placed raw potato slices on broken bones, carried them to prevent rheumatism, and ate them with other foods to avoid indigestion. The Inca also used potatoes to measure time by observing how long potatoes took to grow.

Spanish explorer Gonzalo Jiminez de Quesada (1499-1579) took the potato instead of gold to Spain. The Spanish believed the potato to be a type of truffle and called them "tartuffo." Potatoes were used on Spanish ships to prevent scurvy due to their high vitamin C content, and it was noted that the sailors who ate potatoes did not suffer from scurvy.

By 1585, the potato traveled to Italy and England, to Belgium and Germany by 1587, to Austria in 1588, and to France around 1600. The potato was considered odd, poisonous, or evil wherever the potato was introduced. In France and England, the potato was believed to cause leprosy, syphilis, narcosis, scrofula, early death, sterility, rampant sexuality, and poor soil.

An Irish legend claims that when ships of the Spanish Armada wrecked off the Irish coast in 1588, the ships were carrying potatoes that washed ashore. Other historical accounts report that Sir Walter Raleigh first brought potatoes to Ireland and planted them at his Irish estate at Myrtle Grove, Youghal, near Cork, Ireland. Legend has it that he made a gift of the potato plant to Queen Elizabeth I. The local gentry was invited to a banquet featuring the potato in every course. Unfortunately, the cooks had no clue what to do with the potatoes and tossed out the lumpy-looking tubers. They instead brought to the royal table a dish of boiled stems and leaves (which are poisonous) and promptly made everyone deathly ill. The potatoes were then banned from court.

French military chemist and botanist Antoine-Augustin Parmentier, while searching for food to reduce famine, persuaded the king of France to let him plant 100 useless acres outside Paris, France, with potatoes. He asked the king to place troops around the fields to increase the interest of the local farmers. When the crop was ready for harvest, the troops were allowed the night off; the local farmers, as hoped, stole and planted the potatoes. This began potato farming, even if they were primarily used as hog food for many years.

The "Great Famine" or "Great Starvation" in Ireland resulted from potato blights, a fungal infection in the soil. A book written in 1962 called *The Great Hunger: Ireland 1845-1849* by Cecil Woodham-Smith reads: *That cooking any food other than a potato had become a lost art. Women hardly boiled anything but potatoes. The oven had become unknown after introducing the potato before the Great Starvation.*

Although potatoes are grown throughout the United States, no state is more associated with the potato than Idaho. In the 1850s, most Americans considered potato food for animals rather than humans. As late as the middle of the 19th century, the *Farmer's Manual* recommended that potatoes "be grown near the hog pens as a convenience towards feeding the hogs." It was not until the Russet Burbank potato was developed by American horticulturist Luther Burbank in 1872 that the Idaho potato industry took off. A whole chapter was dedicated to potato storage in the 1943-1947 *USDA Science in Farming Yearbook*. The storage of table stock potatoes also has become more complex. Potatoes for early consumption can be kept in warm-temperature storage with minimal air circulation, and it is now known that this treatment retains a higher vitamin content.[77] So those old-fashioned root cellars that were already in use influenced food's quality.

The effects of domestic cooking methods (boiling, baking, steaming, microwaving, frying, stir-frying, air-frying) on the composition of phytochemicals (phenolics, anthocyanins, and carotenoids) and the antioxidant activity in purple-fleshed potatoes were investigated in 2016. Among all the cooking methods, stir-frying retained only slight levels of the phytochemicals and antioxidant activity observed in raw potatoes. In contrast, steaming and microwaving retained most of the health-promoting compounds found in raw potatoes.[78] Boiling peeled tubers decreased contents of total glycoalkaloids (α-chaconine and αsolanine) and appeared as the most favorable cooking method. Red- and purple-fleshed cultivars retained higher amounts of antioxidants (ascorbic acid, chlorogenic acid, and total anthocyanin) after boiling and may be healthier than white or yellow cultivars.[79] Potatoes were the most significant contributors of vegetable phenolics to the American diet.[80, 81] A 2022 study on cooking methods of potatoes and the effects on nutrients found that all cooking methods showed negative effects on the contents of vitamin C, total phenolic, phenolic acids, and DPPH radical-scavenging activity, but the effects depended on the cooking methods; frying, air-drying, and roasting showed a more intense decrease of total phenolic, phenolic acids, and antioxidant activities than that of steaming or microwaving, regardless of the potato verities.[82] Research published in 2023 on French fry production confirmed potatoes with different flesh colors contain health-promoting compounds (i.e., *hydroxycinnamic acids*), which vary in content and stability during thermal processing. While producing French fries, samples of unpeeled, peeled, cut, blanched, pre-dried and fried potatoes were collected. After peeling, colored potatoes, especially purple ones, had more *hydroxycinnamic acids* remaining in the flesh than in the flesh of the light-yellow variety.[83]

This food has increased America's waist considerably because of its high glycemic rating and the addition of fat used in frying. Research published in 2018 confirmed a significant positive association between high potato consumption and risk of type 2 diabetes, especially the consumption of French fries.[84] Again in 2021, research found a positive relationship between potatoes and type 2 diabetes in Western populations.[85, 86] We seem to forget that northern Europeans have only consumed the potato for a few hundred years and, as such, their DNA structure is not entirely adapted to this starchy food.

Berries

My favorites are blackberries, but strawberries, raspberries, blueberries, currants, gooseberries, cranberries, huckleberries, and marionberries also have incredible health benefits. Strawberries and blueberries are two of the most commonly consumed berries. Berries, in general, are characterized by their highly nutritional compounds, including minerals, vitamins, fatty acids, and dietary fiber, as well as their high content of and wide diversity of bioactive compounds, such as phenolic compounds and organic acids.[87] These bioactive compounds have been associated with protective effects against chronic diseases, such as cardiovascular disease, cancer, Alzheimer's, and other disorders.

Less than 10% of Western populations consume adequate whole fruits and dietary fiber; the typical intake is about half the recommended. Evidence of the beneficial health effects of consuming sufficient whole fruits has been steadily growing, especially regarding their bioactive fiber prebiotic impact and role in improved weight control, wellness and healthy aging.[88] These low-glycemic berries are great for those with diabetes; they help prevent cancer and support heart and eye health. Strawberries help curb your appetite; they contain vitamin C and iron, making them a perfect food for those who struggle with anemia.

A 2023 study on fruit intake and adiposity confirmed what holistic nutritionists have shared with clients for over 30 years; fruit intake per serving is paradoxically related to general body adiposity and central fat distribution, while fruit salad intake is negatively associated with central distribution adiposity. However, consuming fruit in the form of juices is positively associated with a significant increase in BMI and waist circumference.[89, 90]

According to Deanna Minich, PhD, berries belong to "insight," and the dark indigo and purple colors of berries support the pituitary gland, brain, neurons/neurotransmitters, sleep, mood, thoughts, and intuition.[91] The darker the color, the richer the resveratrol, the powerhouse antioxidant that protects the brain and nerves. Blue and purple foods also are established to promote neuronal plasticity, which means your brain's ability to create new pathways, improving cognition, learning, and memory.[92]

Strawberries have been described by the Fat Resistance Diet (FRD) as a fruit that can increase a hormone that stimulates metabolism, suppresses appetite, and controls blood sugar after starchy meals while inhibiting inflammation. This hormone that strawberries trigger, *adiponectin*, is the fat-burning hormone that works with leptin, which regulates weight. High levels of adiponectin in the bloodstream have been shown to lower the risk of heart attack, while lower levels of adiponectin indicate obesity.[93]

Blackberries have been found to have the highest antioxidant capacity among fruits and vegetables. They are rich in vitamin C, fiber, phytochemicals, tannins, flavonoids, and catechins. Blackberries also help alleviate allergies as they stop the action of histamine. If you are out camping and get burned, gently rub blackberry leaves on the area to soothe the skin. Blackberries have been found in human cell studies to prevent lung, esophageal, liver, and colon damage/cancer.[94]

Blueberries have been held in high regard by Native Americans for centuries. They believed they possessed magical powers and were sent by the "Great Spirit" to feed children during famine. They are native to North America, as are two other berries, cranberry and Concord grape. Blueberries are rich in antioxidants, phytochemicals, and ellagic acid, a natural chemical that may inhibit tumor growth. Fresh or frozen blueberries contain the highest levels of anthocyanins, whereas dried ones have almost none. Blueberries are supportive of brain health, cognition, and memory. They are antibacterial and are beneficial to the urinary tract system. As with other berries, they have high cancer-fighting properties. Blueberries have also been found to be good for the heart and circulatory system.[95]

Elderberries contain more vitamin C than any other fruit except rose hips and black currants. They also contain vitamin A, carotenoids, flavonoids, tannins, polyphenols, and anthocyanins. These chemicals fight cancer, heart disease, diabetes, infection, and inflammation.[96] Since Hippocrates, healers have used elderberries as a diuretic and laxative to treat stomach ailments and promote urinary tract health. Studies have shown elderberries can efficiently prevent influenza and the common cold.[97] They are recommended to treat colitis; in one study, there was a 50% reduction in colon damage after one month.

A review of elderberry extracts confirmed the traditional herb's effectiveness. Elderberry is highly reputed for its health-improving effects. Multiple pieces of evidence indicate that the consumption of berries is linked to enhancing human health and preventing or delaying the onset of chronic medical conditions. Compared with other fruit, elderberry is a rich source of anthocyanins (approximately 80% of the polyphenol content). These polyphenols are the principals that essentially contribute to the high antioxidant and anti-inflammatory capacities and the health benefits of elderberry fruit extract. Health effects include attenuation of cardiovascular, neurodegenerative, and inflammatory disorders and anti-diabetic, anticancer, antiviral, and immuno-stimulatory effects.[98]

Raspberries are similar to their cousins, blackberries and strawberries. There are over 200 known species of raspberries. Xylitol, the sugar substitute, is made from raspberries. Blackberries and raspberries are bramble fruits formed by aggregating several smaller fruits called drupelets. Raspberries are a good source of vitamin C, fiber, selenium, and phosphorus and are rich in various antioxidants and phytochemicals associated with cancer and diabetes prevention.[99] Diet is an essential factor that affects the risk of modern-day metabolic diseases, including cardiovascular disease, diabetes mellitus, obesity, and Alzheimer's disease. The potential ability of certain foods and their bioactive compounds to reverse or prevent the progression of the pathogenic processes that underlie these diseases has attracted research attention.[100] They have been found to avoid fatty liver disease and reduce obesity.[101]

Freezing destroys much of the vitamin C in raspberries, so enjoy them fresh when possible.

<u>A note on xylitol</u>: Although this sweetener is extracted from natural sources, this does not necessarily mean the processed substance is healthy or safe. Some individuals have adverse reactions to xylitol because it has an alcohol base.

Cranberries were first used by Native Americans. Cranberries, blueberries, and Concord grapes are North America's three native fruits that are commercially grown. Today, cranberries are commercially grown throughout the northern part of the United States and are available in fresh and processed forms.

Cranberries are commonly used to treat urinary tract infections. Their ability to protect the delicate lining of the bladder and the urethra from bacteria and damage from the acidic properties of urine has been known for centuries. Stress, aging, hormonal imbalance, and low water consumption contribute to kidney and bladder issues.

Phytonutrients present in cranberries include phenolic acids, proanthocyanidins, anthocyanins, flavonoids, and triterpenoids. They are also high in fiber, vitamin C, and manganese, all of which are central to the maintenance of tissue elastin, cell permeability, tissue flexibility, and are anti-inflammatory. In the vascular system, cranberries inhibit plaque formation on the vessel walls.

The essential nutrients in cranberries help prevent premature aging and degenerative conditions like dementia. Studies have confirmed that cranberries help prevent breast, colon, prostate, and lung cancer. Incorporating nutrient-rich cranberries into your diet through easy-to-make sauces, dried fruit, and juice can promote overall health and longevity. Be aware that canned cranberry products and commercial juices may contain added sugar and may be missing vital nutrients.

Organic versus Conventional Cranberries

Supporters of the use of pesticides to grow cranberries claim that the pesticides are necessary since the bogs are rife with natural pests and the wetlands encourage fungi. The *What's On My Food* website reveals 13 pesticides commonly found on conventional cranberries. Of these, three are known or are probable carcinogens, six are suspected hormone disruptors, five are neurotoxins, one is a developmental or reproductive toxin, and six are honeybee toxins. One contraindication for cranberries is that they may exacerbate your condition if you suffer from kidney stones, especially calcium-oxalate stones. Cranberry juice has enormous health benefits, but whole berries pack a much greater nutritional punch.

Pomegranates are one of the few foods I can eat every day for months and never get tired of the flavor.

Today they are available in whole fruit form or husked, cleaned seeds and juice almost year-round. For those who grew up in southern California, you may have had a tree in your yard and remember the beautiful deep red jellies made by family members from the pomegranate fruit.

The pomegranate is one of the "seven kinds" mentioned in the Bible, which Israel was blessed with. Humankind has revered the pomegranate since the dawn of recorded history. Ancient Greeks, Romans, and the peoples of China, India, and the Middle East found its properties to be life-giving and invigorating. As befits a fruit with many seeds, the pomegranate traditionally represents fertility and originates everywhere.

The pomegranate tree is native from Iran to the Himalayas in northern India and has been cultivated throughout the Mediterranean region of Asia, Africa, and Europe since ancient times. The tree was introduced in California by Spanish settlers in 1769. It is grown for its fruit, mainly in the dry zones of California and Arizona.

Health Benefits

Pomegranates have three times more antioxidants than red wine and green tea. The antioxidants in pomegranate juice can help remove free radicals, protect cells from damage, and reduce inflammation.[102] Pomegranate (*Punica granatum L.*) is a polyphenol-rich food and medicinal plant containing flavonols, anthocyanins, and tannins. Ellagitannins (ETs) are the most abundant polyphenols in pomegranates. A growing body of research shows that polyphenol-rich pomegranate extracts and their metabolites target multiple types of brain cells and support their redox balance, proliferation and survival, and cell signaling.[103]

The juice of a single pomegranate has more than 40% of your daily requirement of vitamin C. Vitamin C can be broken down when pasteurized, so opt for homemade or fresh pomegranate juice to get most of the nutrients. In addition to vitamins C and E, pomegranate juice is an excellent source of folate, potassium, and vitamin K.[104]

Pomegranate juice made a splash when researchers found it helped stop the growth of prostate cancer cells. The antioxidants in the juice and their high concentration are believed to stall the progress of Alzheimer's disease and protect memory. Pomegranate juice can reduce inflammation in the gut and improve digestion. It may benefit people with Crohn's disease, ulcerative colitis, and other inflammatory bowel diseases.[105, 106]

Pomegranate juice is in the running as the most heart-healthy juice. It appears to protect the heart and arteries. Small studies have shown that the juice improves blood flow and keeps the arteries from becoming stiff and thick. It may also slow plaque growth and cholesterol buildup in the arteries.[107] Drinking pomegranate juice may lower systolic blood pressure. Pomegranates have also been shown to be antibacterial and antiviral in lab tests. It is being studied for its effects on common infections and viruses.[108]

> ***Principle 35:*** There is no such thing as too many veggies, so "eat the rainbow" of colors in foods.

Citrus

Late one night in 2017, I traveled back in time with *"Food Fights – Culture and War"* by Tom Nealon. Reading some little tidbit of history that gives you an aha moment is always exciting. That is the case with lemons and citrus, utilized heavily in Mediterranean diets.

I found an interesting section on lemonade and the plague; it turns out lemonade became a trendy drink in the 1640s in Italy and Paris. When the plague hit in the 1660s, cities like Venice, Naples, and Paris were

relatively untouched. Author Tom Nealon tracked down the role of lemonade, a trendy beverage of the time. Lemonade was sold from street stalls and made in homes; the peel and citrus off-cast went into the street/alley and dock trash piles frequented by rats that carry the flea that hosts the bacteria responsible for the plague. The rats fed on the citrus filled with limonene (*limonene is a clear, colorless liquid hydrocarbon classified as a cyclic monoterpene and is the major component in the oil of citrus fruit peels*), which it turns out kills the bacterium responsible for the plague. So, the population was saved due to the rats and people being healthier from eating and drinking lemons. Now I understand why the Italians have such a big citrus drink culture.

Citrus are native to southeastern Asia but have been grown in the Mediterranean for centuries. The citrus trees and fruit are of great importance in Mediterranean countries, and, in the case of orange, mandarin, and lemon trees, they found the Mediterranean area soil and climatic conditions perfect for developing high fruit quality.[109]

Of all citrus fruits, lemons and limes have the highest citric acid content, about 1.4 grams per ounce, or about 8% of their dry weight. Lemons and limes also contain ascorbic acid, vitamin C, and malic acid. Citric acid from lemons and limes is often used as an additive in food preparation to add a tart flavor and as a preservative. For example, citric acid helps prevent fresh vegetables from browning and maintains the color of meat during storage. It also contains the crystallization of sucrose in candy and promotes flexibility and separation of cheese slices.

Lemons also contain a small amount of malic acid, which is tart but enhances the sweetness of sucrose in fruit, according to an article published in the *Journal of Experimental Botany* in March 2006. The human body also produces malic acid. According to *NYU Langone Medical Center*, malic acid may have therapeutic benefits for individuals with fibromyalgia. People with fibromyalgia may have trouble using or producing malic acid, which can affect normal muscle function.[110] However, a 2019 study review on the use of malic acid supplements for fibromyalgia found little or no improvement for individuals. This may have resulted from a lack of microbiome bacteria that break down malic acid, making it available to cells.[111, 112]

Epidemiological studies have shown an inverse relationship between dietary flavonoid intakes and cardiovascular diseases. Citrus are the main winter fruits consumed in the Mediterranean diet and are the primary source of dietary flavonoids.[113] The possible beneficial effects are due to the high amounts of vitamins and minerals and the antioxidant properties of their flavonoids.[114] Dietary flavonoids may help to supplement the body's antioxidant defenses against free radicals. The beneficial effects of these compounds are due to their antioxidant activity related to atherosclerosis and cancer development and their anti-inflammatory and antimicrobial activity.[115, 116]

A Japanese study found a positive correlation between lowering blood pressure in walking and lemon ingestion, and a study on mice found lemon juice helped protect the liver from alcohol injury.[117, 118]

Grapefruit juice can block the action of enzymes that break down some medications. (FDA /Michael J. Ermarth/ CC BY-SA 4.0/Wikimedia Commons)

Caution: Grapefruit in, canned, juiced and fresh form has been shown to negatively interfere with some prescription medications, primarily those for hypertension.

Peaches and Plums

Peaches are originally from China. They belong to the genus *Prunus* and the *Rosaceae* family; their scientific name is *Prunus persica*. Technically, the peach is a "drupe," having similar features to other family members of Prunus, including plums, nectarines, almonds, and damson.

Peaches are low in calories (100 grams provide 39 calories) and contain no saturated fats. They are packed with minerals and vitamins. The total measured antioxidant strength (ORAC value) of 100 grams of peach fruit is 1814.

Fresh peaches are a moderate source of vitamin A and ß-carotene. ß-carotene is a pro-vitamin that converts to vitamin A in the body. Consumption of fruits rich in vitamin A is known to offer protection from lung and oral cavity cancers. Additionally, peaches contain potassium, fluoride, and iron. Potassium is essential to cells and body fluids that help regulate heart rate and blood pressure. Fluoride is a component of bones and teeth and helps to prevent dental caries. Fluoride found in foods (unlike what is found in oral health products) does not have harmful side effects. Iron is required for red blood cell formation.

Commercial peach packing c. 1905; Thompson Fruit Company. OHS Image bb012659

Peaches contain health-promoting flavonoid polyphenolic antioxidants such as lutein, zeaxanthin, and ß-cryptoxanthin. These compounds help protect against the oxygen-derived free radicals and reactive oxygen species (ROS) that play a role in aging and various disease processes.

In the past, we ate in season. We enjoyed berries, peaches, greens, and sweet peas in the spring. Summer brought delicious tomatoes, melons, carrots, bitter greens, beans, sweet corn, and onions. Fall gave us more substantial fare like grains, squash, and potatoes. The saying "everything has its season" is especially true of food.

Organic versus Commercial

The fruits and vegetables listed by the Environmental Working Group (EWG) as the "Dirty Dozen" tested positive, when conventionally grown, for at least 47 different chemicals; some tested positive for as many as 67. Unless you relish consuming a chemical cocktail, it will help if you go organic for produce on the "dirty" list.[119] The produce on the "Clean 15" list contained none or negligible traces of pesticides and may be safe to consume in non-organic form.[120]

"Clean 15"

Asparagus	Avocados	Cabbage
Carrots	Corn sweet	Honeydew Melon
Kiwi	Mango	Mushrooms
Onions	Peas sweet, frozen	Pineapples
Potatoes sweet	Watermelon	Papayas

"Dirty Dozen"

Apples	Celery
Bell Peppers Sweet	Blueberries Domestic
Cherries	Collard Greens
Grapes Imported	Green Beans
Lettuce	Kale
Mustard Greens	Nectarines
Peaches	Pears
Peppers Hot	Potatoes

The lists of "dirty" and "clean" produce were compiled after the USDA washed the produce using high-power pressure water systems that most of us could only dream of having in our kitchens. The complete list contains 49 types of produce rated on a scale from least to most contaminated. You can check out the full list at www.foodnews.org.

Why are some types of produce more prone to absorbing pesticides than others? Pineapple and sweet corn, for example, have a protective barrier in their outer layer of skin. Strawberries and lettuce do not. The President's Cancer Panel recommends washing conventionally grown produce to remove residues. Researchers, however, say that while washing won't hurt and may help, it is impossible to eliminate all chemical residues.

Principle 36: Eat organic: food should always be your first medicine.

Chocolate

The cacao tree is aptly named Theobroma cacao by the famous botanist Carl von Linnaeus. The cacao tree only grows within twenty degrees of the equator in the damp tropics. Once mature, the tree will produce small, white flowers that can only be pollinated by midges, a fly no larger than a pencil's tip. When cacao pods are mature, they are harvested by hand using a machete. Each pod is broken open to expose the beans and white pulp and collected into a pile. The beans and pulp remain outside in the heat and high humidity to undergo fermentation.

Fermentation is a metabolic process that occurs with microorganisms. Bacteria and yeast thrive in hot, moist climates, and the cacao pulp is an excellent nutrient source. In this case, the bacteria and yeast are needed to produce the precursor compounds necessary for chocolate's characteristic flavor and aroma. Bacteria eat some sugar and acid content, converting it into other molecules. Fermentation typically lasts for about a week. Once fermentation is complete, the farmers will separate the beans from the pulp, used as a nutrient source during fermentation. Next, the beans are left to dry in the sun.

In Greek, Theobroma translates to the *food of the gods*. Chocolate connoisseurs know there is more than a gustatory pleasure in this food. In 1753, Carl von Linnaeus, a Swedish scientist, thought cacao was so important he named the genus and species of tree *Theobroma cacao*, which means *cacao, the food of the gods*. This food dates to prehistoric times and was extensively cultivated in Mexico and Central and South America centuries before Europeans arrived. The Mayan Indians began cultivating cacao about 600 AD. The indigenous populations ate only the fruit, which contains numerous health benefits. The seed or cacao nib was set aside for a psychedelic brew called *ayahuasca* and for medicines. According to Aztec myth, cacao awakened power and wisdom. When the explorer Cortes brought cacao back to Spain in 1528, it was sequestered and enjoyed only by the nobility and the wealthy.[121] In medieval times, chocolate was viewed as a luxury item and an indulgence. In modern times chocolate is used as gifts for mothers and sweethearts. It is made into cocktails, cold and hot drinks, candies, powders, wines, and lotions. The Spanish are widely responsible for introducing and developing chocolate foods and beverages.

The Making of Chocolate Foods

The most critical step in chocolate making is roasting. Roasting generates hundreds of the flavor compounds associated with chocolate. The beans are roasted at high temperatures for roughly one hour. Many chemical reactions are responsible for cocoa color, flavor, and aroma. Cocoa naturally has a strong, pungent/bitter taste from flavanols. Without roasting, the cacao beans would never obtain the

flavor profile we associate with modern chocolate. Cacao nibs are crushed to form cocoa butter and cocoa liquor. There are several processing steps involved in reducing cacao's bitter taste. Cocoa liquor has a very concentrated, chocolatey flavor with a trace of bitterness and acidity. Other ingredients like sugar, milk solids, vanilla, and emulsifiers are added to the pure cocoa liquor. Adding these ingredients to the liquor results in a course, heterogeneous mixture that must still be further processed. The more cocoa is processed (through fermentation, alkalizing, roasting, etc.), to form what we think of as chocolate, the more flavanols are lost.

What Science Tells Us About the Health Properties of Chocolate

Flavonoids are naturally occurring compounds in plant-based foods offering specific health benefits. They are part of the polyphenol group (chemicals found in plants). Flavanols are a type of flavonoid found explicitly in cocoa and chocolate. More than 4,000 flavonoid compounds are found in various foods and beverages, such as cranberries, apples, peanuts, chocolate, onions, tea, and red wine. Most popular commercial chocolates are highly processed, providing little, if any, health benefits.[122, 123] Dark chocolate contains a large number of antioxidants (nearly eight times the amount found in strawberries). Flavonoids also help lower blood pressure nitric oxide production; they can also balance certain hormones. Intervention studies on healthy and metabolically dysfunctional

volunteers have suggested that cocoa improves blood pressure, platelet aggregation, and endothelial function. The effect of chocolate is more convoluted since the sucrose and lipid may transiently and negatively impact endothelial function, partly through insulin signaling and nitric oxide bioavailability.[124] The fats in chocolate ($1/3$ oleic acid, $1/3$ stearic acid, and $1/3$ palmitic acid) do not impact your cholesterol.[125] Dark chocolate helps restore flexibility to arteries while preventing white blood cells from sticking to the walls of blood vessels. Oxidative stress, inflammation, and endothelial function define three biological mechanisms that have shown sensitivity to chocolate. Moreover, the consumption of chocolate has been involved in the protective modulation of blood pressure, lipid profile, activation of platelets, and insulin sensitivity. Dark chocolate seems more protective than milk or white chocolate.[126, 127] The high-flavanol cocoa and dark chocolate treatment was associated with enhanced vasodilation in both conduit and resistance arteries and was accompanied by significant reductions in arterial stiffness in women.[128]
Cocoa bean shell (CBS) is one of the primary solid wastes derived from the chocolate industry. This residual biomass could be an exciting source of nutrients and bioactive compounds due to its high content in dietary fibers, polyphenols, and methylxanthines. Specifically, CBS can be employed as a raw material for recovering, for example, antioxidants, antivirals, and/or antimicrobials.[129]

Benefits of Dark Chocolate

- Oleic acid is a monounsaturated fat; also found in olive oil.
- Stearic acid is saturated fat, which research shows has a neutral effect on cholesterol.
- Lowers blood pressure: Studies have shown that consuming a small portion of dark chocolate daily can reduce blood pressure.
- Lowers cholesterol: Dark Chocolate has been shown to reduce LDL cholesterol by up to 10%.
- Stimulates endorphin production, which gives a feeling of pleasure.
- It contains serotonin, which acts as an antidepressant.
- Source of theobromine, caffeine, and other stimulants. Benefits include diuretic effects, widening arteries and boosting blood flow, lifting mood, improving focus/concentration, and possibly having aphrodisiac effects. Theobromine has a more profound effect on our cardiovascular system, with muscle-calming properties, than on the central nervous system. It works as a cardiac stimulant and vasodilator by widening blood vessels, managing blood pressure, increasing oxygen supply, reducing coronary vasospasm, improving blood flow, and supporting healthy circulation.

Chocolate is a complex food with over 300 compounds and chemicals in each bite. Look for pure dark chocolate or dark chocolate with nuts, orange peel, or other natural flavorings. To enjoy and appreciate chocolate, take the time to taste it. Most studies used no more than 100 grams, or about 3.5 ounces, of dark chocolate daily. One bar of dark chocolate has around 400 calories.[130]

Enjoy moderate portions of chocolate (e.g., one ounce) a few times per week, and don't forget to consume other flavonoid-rich foods like apples, red wine, tea, onions, and cranberries. Your best choices are dark chocolate instead of milk chocolate (especially milk chocolate loaded with other fats and sugars) and cocoa powder without Dutch processing (cocoa treated with an alkali to neutralize its natural acidity).

Caution: According to the National Hazardous Substances Database: I*n large doses,* theobromine may cause nausea and anorexia, and the daily intake of 50-100g cocoa (1.5 g theobromine) has been associated with sweating, trembling, and severe headaches. Occasionally, people (mostly the elderly) need hospital treatment for a theobromine reaction.[131, 132]

Coffee: Black If You Please

After oil, coffee is the second most traded commodity in the world. Coffee is globally one of the most widely consumed beverages. Due to the high economic importance for the countries that produce, export, and import it, its purity and detection of external impurities have been a constant concern. In some cases, visual inspection is unreliable in roasted ground coffee because of the resemblance in color and the texture of the cheapest fillers.[133] Coffee comes from an evergreen tree that produces red cherries or beans. Most coffee comes from Arabica or Robusta varieties of beans. Arabica beans comprise 70% of the world's coffee production. Robusta coffee comes from southeast Asia and Brazil, contains about 50% more caffeine than Arabica, and has a more pungent, bitter taste. The adulteration of roasted coffee is a strategy used to reduce costs. Conventional methods employed to identify adulteration in roasted and ground coffee involve optical and electron microscopy, which require the pretreatment of samples and are time-consuming and subjective.[134]

Africans fueled up on protein-rich coffee-and-animal-fat balls—primitive PowerBars ®—and unwound with wine from coffee berry pulp. Coffee traveled across the Red Sea to Arabia, where roasted beans were brewed around 1000 AD. By the 13th century, Muslims were drinking coffee religiously. The "bean broth" powered dervishes, kept worshippers from falling asleep during prayers, and was part of daily life. Wherever Islam went, coffee went —from North Africa to the eastern Mediterranean to India.[135, 136]

1916 Crystal coffee grinder and 1920s Hills Brothers coffee glass jar. Authors collection.

Arabia made beans infertile by parching or boiling them before exporting, and it is said that no coffee seed sprouted outside Africa or Arabia until the 1600s when an Indian pilgrim-cum-smuggler left Mecca with fertile seeds strapped to his belly. A merchant of Venice introduced Europe to coffee in 1615. The Dutch were the first to successfully transport a coffee plant into Europe in 1616. In 1696, they founded the first European-owned coffee estates in colonial Java, now part of Indonesia. Coffee came to the new world in 1727. Brazil's government wanted a chunk of the coffee market and used a spy to smuggle seeds from a coffee country. Lt. Col. Francisco de Melo Palheta accomplished the task and is referred to by coffee historians as the *James Bond of Beans.* The Lieutenant Colonial traveled to French Guiana, ostensibly to mediate a border dispute, emissary Palheta chose a path of pleasant resistance—the governor's wife. At a state farewell dinner, she presented him with a sly token of affection: a bouquet spiked with seedlings. By the 1800s, Brazil's monster harvests would turn coffee from an elite indulgence into a drink for the people.

Dangers and Benefits

The downsides of coffee are related to the caffeine content that makes the drink so appealing in the morning. Dangerous caffeine overdoses generally don't occur with coffee, but the unpleasant effects of too much caffeine – like anxiety, GI upset, and palpitations – can occur. Caffeine withdrawal can be uncomfortable, causing headaches, fatigue, and irritability. Independent of caffeine content, coffee can also exacerbate gastroesophageal reflux disease (GERD) in certain people. So, discontinue coffee for a while if you get heartburn or an upset stomach after drinking coffee.[137] Many worry that coffee can induce arrhythmias in susceptible individuals, but this has never been shown to be true in moderate amounts (up to four cups per day).

On the other hand, the coffee habit has significant potential upsides. In observational studies, people who drink coffee regularly appear to have lower rates of diabetes, stroke, heart disease, certain cancers, and dementia. Metabolic syndrome, with its increasing prevalence, is becoming a major public health problem worldwide. Coffee contains over 1,000 components, such as caffeine, chlorogenic acid, diterpenes, and trigonelline. It has been proven in many studies that coffee consumption has a positive effect on chronic diseases. And more recent studies have even shown coffee drinkers seem to have lower all-cause mortality – that is, death from any cause – than non-coffee drinkers.[138] Studies like these show association, not causation, but many experts think that a causative relationship between coffee drinking and improved health is plausible, given coffee's high antioxidant content.[139]

In the short term, coffee can also boost mood, alertness, mental energy, and concentration, which should surprise almost everyone.[140]

A moderate intake of coffee is about three 6 oz cups per day or 18 oz daily. Coffee doesn't contain significant amounts of vitamins or minerals but contains more antioxidants than most other foods. An average cup of coffee contains between 60 -130 mg of caffeine.[141]

Does Roasting Damage the Antioxidants?

In the article *Cellular Antioxidant and Anti-inflammatory Effects of Coffee Extracts with Different Roasting Levels,* researchers evaluated the effects of *Coffea arabica* green coffee extracts of light, medium, and French roasted beans. Whereas the caffeine levels did not differ significantly between the various roasting levels, the levels of chlorogenic acid did vary and correlate with the differences in antioxidant and anti-inflammatory activity.[142]

"When people think of coffee, they associate it with caffeine. However, coffee beans have many other chemicals that could help fight chronic inflammatory diseases," says *Journal of Medicinal Food* Editor-in-Chief Sampath Parthasarathy, MBA, PhD. "Coffee drinkers are passionate about different roasts – light, medium, and dark."[143]

Coffee is a stimulant, as are soda pops and energy drinks. Stimulants affect the brain and central nervous system, which can be good and bad depending on the situation and extent. Asthmatics may find they can breathe better, and headache sufferers can speed the relief provided by aspirin with coffee or black tea. Coffee consumption reduces inflammation and prevents heart disease in non-caffeine-sensitive postmenopausal women. One study found that older men had less memory loss when consuming three cups of coffee daily. The University of Arizona found that drinking decaffeinated coffee had the reverse effect.[144]

On the other hand, coffee consumption can increase fibrocystic breast disease, hypertension, dehydration, sleep disturbances, and acid indigestion.[145] Added artificial flavorings, cream, and sugar can increase asthma restriction, raise blood sugars, and cause weight gain by increasing stress hormones and counting calories. If these added flavors are the only way to drink coffee, find a better way to wake up—one that helps your brain work better, not more jittery.

For every cup of coffee you drink, your kidneys may need one quart of water to flush and prevent kidney stone formation. As with everything, enjoy that cup (6-12 oz) of coffee in moderation. Select high-quality, fragrant, organic brands and go easy on artificial flavors and refined sugars.

Dump the Plastic Coffee Maker and Pods

Past research on hot beverage appliances has shown raised quantities of nickel, copper, zinc, chromium, and lead in coffee. Müller tested 11 electric kettles and eight coffee machines to release elemental ions three times on three separate days, both before and after the manufacturer-recommended decalcification of the device.

Kettles showed leaching to be well within the specified release limit; however, coffee machines showed, in some cases, alarmingly high levels of lead, especially post-decalcification, with one device giving results 150 times the recommended limit. Nickel, manganese, chromium, and zinc levels exceeded limits up to fourfold. Conversely, concentrations of leached elements did reduce each day and throughout the three days of testing combined.[146, 147]

---

1 Benjamin E. Goulet and others, Hybridization in Plants: Old Ideas, New Techniques, Plant Physiology, Volume 173, Issue 1, January 2017, Pages 65–78, https://doi.org/10.1104/pp.16.01340
2 López-Caamal, A., Tovar-Sánchez, E. Genetic, morphological, and chemical patterns of plant hybridization. Rev. Chil. de Hist. Nat. 87, 16 (2014). https://doi.org/10.1186/s40693-014-0016-0
3 Szalinski, C (2014) Science, ASCB: https://www.ascb.org/science-news/yogurt-shows-the-way-for-a-revolution-in-genome-editing/
4 Enhanced Bacteriophage Management in Yogurt Production: https://www.mdpi.com/2079-6382/10/3/308/pdf
5 Gbashi, S., Adebo, O., Adebiyi, J. A., Targuma, S., Tebele, S., Areo, O. M., Olopade, B., Odukoya, J. O., & Njobeh, P. (2021). Food safety, food security and genetically modified organisms in Africa: a current perspective. Biotechnology & genetic engineering reviews, 37(1), 30–63. https://doi.org/10.1080/02648725.2021.1940735
6 Mmbando G. S. (2023). The legal aspect of the current use of genetically modified organisms in Kenya, Tanzania, and Uganda. GM crops & food, 14(1), 1–12. https://doi.org/10.1080/21645698.2023.2208999
7 Bruetschy C. (2019). The EU regulatory framework on genetically modified organisms (GMOs). Transgenic research, 28(Suppl 2), 169–174. https://doi.org/10.1007/s11248-019-00149-y

8 Ruffell D. (2018). The EU Court of Justice extends the GMO Directive to gene-edited organisms. FEBS letters, 592(22), 3653–3657. https://doi.org/10.1002/1873-3468.13293

9 Faure, J. D., & Napier, J. A. (2018). Europe's first and last field trial of gene-edited plants?. eLife, 7, e42379. https://doi.org/10.7554/eLife.42379

10 Marone, D., Mastrangelo, A. M., & Borrelli, G. M. (2023). From Transgenesis to Genome Editing in Crop Improvement: Applications, Marketing, and Legal Issues. International journal of molecular sciences, 24(8), 7122. https://doi.org/10.3390/ijms24087122

11 Japan GM Food Update (2022): https://www.foodnavigator-asia.com/Article/2022/07/05/japan-issues-tighter-labelling-regulations-for-products-with-genetically-modified-components?utm_source=copyright&utm_medium=OnSite&utm_campaign=copyright

12 Lee DH. Evidence of the Possible Harm of Endocrine-Disrupting Chemicals in Humans: Ongoing Debates and Key Issues. Endocrinol Metab (Seoul). 2018 Mar;33(1):44-52. doi: 10.3803/EnM.2018.33.1.44. PMID: 29589387; PMCID: PMC5874194.

13 Gonsioroski, A., Mourikes, V. E., & Flaws, J. A. (2020). Endocrine Disruptors in Water and Their Effects on the Reproductive System. International journal of molecular sciences, 21(6), 1929. https://doi.org/10.3390/ijms21061929

14 Czarnywojtek, A., Jaz, K., Ochmańska, A., Zgorzalewicz-Stachowiak, M., Czarnocka, B., Sawicka-Gutaj, N., Ziółkowska, P., Krela-Kaźmierczak, I., Gut, P., Florek, E., & Ruchała, M. (2021). The effect of endocrine disruptors on the reproductive system- current knowledge. European review for medical and pharmacological sciences, 25(15), 4930–4940. https://doi.org/10.26355/eurrev_202108_26450

15 Kumar, M., Sarma, D. K., Shubham, S., Kumawat, M., Verma, V., Prakash, A., & Tiwari, R. (2020). Environmental Endocrine-Disrupting Chemical Exposure: Role in Non-Communicable Diseases. Frontiers in public health, 8, 553850. https://doi.org/10.3389/fpubh.2020.553850

16 Wan, M. L. Y., Co, V. A., & El-Nezami, H. (2022). Endocrine disrupting chemicals and breast cancer: a systematic review of epidemiological studies. Critical reviews in food science and nutrition, 62(24), 6549–6576. https://doi.org/10.1080/10408398.2021.1903382

17 Wan, M. L. Y., Co, V. A., & El-Nezami, H. (2022). Endocrine disrupting chemicals and breast cancer: a systematic review of epidemiological studies. Critical reviews in food science and nutrition, 62(24), 6549–6576. https://doi.org/10.1080/10408398.2021.1903382

18 Maharjan, C. K., Mo, J., Wang, L., Kim, M. C., Wang, S., Borcherding, N., Vikas, P., & Zhang, W. (2021). Natural and Synthetic Estrogens in Chronic Inflammation and Breast Cancer. Cancers, 14(1), 206. https://doi.org/10.3390/cancers14010206

19 Tanwar, A. K., Dhiman, N., Kumar, A., & Jaitak, V. (2021). Engagement of phytoestrogens in breast cancer suppression: Structural classification and mechanistic approach. European journal of medicinal chemistry, 213, 113037. https://doi.org/10.1016/j.ejmech.2020.113037

20 Gębarowski T, Wiatrak B, Janeczek M, Żuk M, Pistor P, Gąsiorowski K. Were our Ancestors Right in Using Flax Dressings? Research on the Properties of Flax Fibre and Its Usefulness in Wound Healing. Oxid Med Cell Longev. 2020 Nov 24;2020:1682317. doi: 10.1155/2020/1682317. PMID: 33299521; PMCID: PMC7707976.

21 Gębarowski, T., Jęśkowiak, I., & Wiatrak, B. (2022). Investigation of the Properties of Linen Fibers and Dressings. International journal of molecular sciences, 23(18), 10480. https://doi.org/10.3390/ijms231810480

22 He, Y., Zhu, X., Ning, Y., Chen, X., Sen, B., & Wang, G. (2023). Saturated and Polyunsaturated Fatty Acids Production by Aurantiochytrium limacinum PKU#Mn4 on Enteromorpha Hydrolysate. Marine drugs, 21(4), 198. https://doi.org/10.3390/md21040198

23 Chi, G., Xu, Y., Cao, X., Li, Z., Cao, M., Chisti, Y., & He, N. (2022). Production of polyunsaturated fatty acids by Schizochytrium (Aurantiochytrium) spp. Biotechnology advances, 55, 107897. https://doi.org/10.1016/j.biotechadv.2021.107897

24 Muchenje, V., Mukumbo, F. E., Descalzo, A. M., & Schönfeldt, H. C. (2018). Introduction to the special issue on Balanced diets in food systems: emerging trends and challenges for human health and wellbeing. Food research international (Ottawa, Ont.), 104, 1–3. https://doi.org/10.1016/j.foodres.2018.01.033

25 Tako E. (2019). Dietary Trace Minerals. Nutrients, 11(11), 2823. https://doi.org/10.3390/nu11112823

26 Fernández-Lázaro, D., Fernandez-Lazaro, C. I., Mielgo-Ayuso, J., Navascués, L. J., Córdova Martínez, A., & Seco-Calvo, J. (2020). The Role of Selenium Mineral Trace Element in Exercise: Antioxidant Defense System, Muscle Performance, Hormone Response, and Athletic Performance. A Systematic Review. Nutrients, 12(6), 1790. https://doi.org/10.3390/nu12061790

27 Cardwell, G., Bornman, J. F., James, A. P., & Black, L. J. (2018). A Review of Mushrooms as a Potential Source of Dietary Vitamin D. Nutrients, 10(10), 1498. https://doi.org/10.3390/nu10101498

28 Gasmi, A., Shanaida, M., Oleshchuk, O., Semenova, Y., Mujawdiya, P. K., Ivankiv, Y., Pokryshko, O., Noor, S., Piscopo, S., Adamiv, S., & Bjørklund, G. (2023). Natural Ingredients to Improve Immunity. Pharmaceuticals (Basel, Switzerland), 16(4), 528. https://doi.org/10.3390/ph16040528

29 Arunachalam, K., Sasidharan, S. P., & Yang, X. (2022). A concise review of mushrooms antiviral and immunomodulatory properties that may combat against COVID-19. Food chemistry advances, 1, 100023. https://doi.org/10.1016/j.focha.2022.100023

30 Penn State. "Mushrooms are full of antioxidants that may have antiaging potential." ScienceDaily. ScienceDaily, 9 November 2017. www.sciencedaily.com/releases/2017/11/171109100409.htm.

31 Castellanos-Reyes, K., Villalobos-Carvajal, R., & Beldarrain-Iznaga, T. (2021). Fresh Mushroom Preservation Techniques. Foods (Basel, Switzerland), 10(9), 2126. https://doi.org/10.3390/foods10092126

32 Dawadi, E., Magar, P. B., Bhandari, S., Subedi, S., Shrestha, S., & Shrestha, J. (2022). Nutritional and post-harvest quality preservation of mushrooms: A review. Heliyon, 8(12), e12093. https://doi.org/10.1016/j.heliyon.2022.e12093

33 Collins, J., Danhof, H., & Britton, R. A. (2019). The role of trehalose in the global spread of epidemic Clostridium difficile. Gut microbes, 10(2), 204–209. https://doi.org/10.1080/19490976.2018.1491266

34 (Ferlay et al., 2001)

35 (Phenolics, inflammation and nutrigenomics" J Sci Food Agric, 2006, Vol 86(15): 2503-1509)

36 Johns Hopkins Bloomberg School of Public Health. "Broccoli sprout beverage enhances detoxification of air pollutants in clinical trial." ScienceDaily. ScienceDaily, 16 June 2014. www.sciencedaily.com/releases/2014/06/140616102410.htm.

37 Liu Z. Z., Hong C. G., Hu W. B., et al. Autophagy receptor OPTN (optineurin) regulates mesenchymal stem cell fate and bone-fat balance during aging by clearing FABP3. Autophagy . 2021;17(10):2766–2782. doi: 10.1080/15548627.2020.1839286.

38 Guo Y., Jia X., Cui Y., et al. Sirt3-mediated mitophagy regulates AGEs-induced BMSCs senescence and senile osteoporosis. Redox Biology . 2021;41 doi: 10.1016/j.redox.2021.101915.10191

39 Si L., Winzenberg T. M., Jiang Q., Chen M., Palmer A. J. Projection of osteoporosis-related fractures and costs in China: 2010–2050. Osteoporosis International . 2015;26(7):1929–1937. doi: 10.1007/s00198-015-3093-2.

40 Xu Z. L., Xu M. Y., Wang H. T., et al. Pharmacokinetics of eight flavonoids in rats assayed by UPLC-MS/MS after oral administration of Drynariae rhizoma extract. Journal of Analytical Methods in Chemistry . 2018;2018:11. doi: 10.1155/2018/4789196.4789196

41 Wang Y., Chen H., Zhang H. Kaempferol promotes proliferation, migration and differentiation of MC3T3-E1 cells via up-regulation of microRNA-101. Artificial Cells, Nanomedicine, and Biotechnology . 2019;47(1):1050–1056. doi: 10.1080/21691401.2019.1591428.

42 Jia, X., Zhong, L., Song, Y., Hu, Y., Wang, G., & Sun, S. (2016). Consumption of citrus and cruciferous vegetables with incident type 2 diabetes mellitus based on a meta-analysis of prospective study. Primary care diabetes, 10(4), 272–280. https://doi.org/10.1016/j.pcd.2015.12.004

43 Chen, G. C., Koh, W. P., Yuan, J. M., Qin, L. Q., & van Dam, R. M. (2018). Green leafy and cruciferous vegetable consumption and risk of type 2 diabetes: results from the Singapore Chinese Health Study and meta-analysis. The British journal of nutrition, 119(9), 1057–1067. https://doi.org/10.1017/S0007114518000119

44 Pokharel, P., Kyrø, C., Olsen, A., Tjønneland, A., Murray, K., Blekkenhorst, L. C., Bondonno, C. P., Hodgson, J. M., & Bondonno, N. P. (2023). Vegetable, but Not Potato, Intake Is Associated With a Lower Risk of Type 2 Diabetes in the Danish Diet, Cancer and Health Cohort. Diabetes care, 46(2), 286–296. https://doi.org/10.2337/dc22-0974

45 Jiang, Z., Sun, T. Y., He, Y., Gou, W., Zuo, L. S., Fu, Y., Miao, Z., Shuai, M., Xu, F., Xiao, C., Liang, Y., Wang, J., Xu, Y., Jing, L. P., Ling, W., Zhou, H., Chen, Y. M., & Zheng, J. S. (2020). Dietary fruit and vegetable intake, gut microbiota, and type 2 diabetes: results from two large human cohort studies. BMC medicine, 18(1), 371. https://doi.org/10.1186/s12916-020-01842-0

46 University of Illinois College of Agricultural, Consumer and Environmental Sciences. "Sprouts? Supplements? Team them up to boost broccoli's cancer-fighting power." ScienceDaily. ScienceDaily, 31 January 2011. www.sciencedaily.com/releases/2011/01/110127110707.htm.

47 Zhuang, H., Lou, Q., Liu, H., Han, H., Wang, Q., Tang, Z., Ma, Y., & Wang, H. (2019). Differential Regulation of Anthocyanins in Green and Purple Turnips Revealed by Combined De Novo Transcriptome and Metabolome Analysis. International journal of molecular sciences, 20(18), 4387. https://doi.org/10.3390/ijms20184387

48 Mostafazadeh, M., Sadeghi, H., Sadeghi, H., Zarezade, V., Hadinia, A., & Panahi Kokhdan, E. (2022). Further evidence to support acute and chronic anti-inflammatory effects of Nasturtium officinale. Research in pharmaceutical sciences, 17(3), 305–314. https://doi.org/10.4103/1735-5362.343084

49 Sadeghi, H., Azarmehr, N., Razmkhah, F., Sadeghi, H., Danaei, N., Omidifar, N., Vakilpour, H., Pourghadamyari, H., & Doustimotlagh, A. H. (2019). The hydroalcoholic extract of watercress attenuates protein oxidation, oxidative stress, and liver damage after bile duct ligation in rats. Journal of cellular biochemistry, 120(9), 14875–14884. https://doi.org/10.1002/jcb.28749

50 Panahi Kokhdan, E., Khodabandehloo, H., Ghahremani, H., & Doustimotlagh, A. H. (2021). A Narrative Review on Therapeutic Potentials of Watercress in Human Disorders. Evidence-based complementary and alternative medicine : eCAM, 2021, 5516450. https://doi.org/10.1155/2021/5516450

51 Tabesh, M., Sh, M. E., Etemadi, M., Naddaf, F., Heidari, F., & Alizargar, J. (2022). The antibacterial activity of nasturtium officinale extract on common oral pathogenic bacteria. Nigerian journal of clinical practice, 25(9), 1466–1475. https://doi.org/10.4103/njcp.njcp_1887_21

52 Beydoun, M. A., Beydoun, H. A., Hossain, S., El-Hajj, Z. W., Weiss, J., & Zonderman, A. B. (2020). Clinical and Bacterial Markers of Periodontitis and Their Association with Incident All-Cause and Alzheimer's Disease Dementia in a Large National Survey. Journal of Alzheimer's disease : JAD, 75(1), 157–172. https://doi.org/10.3233/JAD-200064

53 https://link.springer.com/article/10.1007%2FBF01762872

54 http://www.watercress.co.uk/about/did-you-know/

55 http://www.libraryireland.com/SocialHistoryAncientIreland/III-XVII-8.php

56 Hanschen, F. S., & Rohn, S. (2021). Advanced Research on Glucosinolates in Food Products. Foods (Basel, Switzerland), 10(12), 3148. https://doi.org/10.3390/foods10123148

57 Schulze, H., Hornbacher, J., Wasserfurth, P., Reichel, T., Günther, T., Krings, U., Krüger, K., Hahn, A., Papenbrock, J., & Schuchardt, J. P. (2021). Immunomodulating Effect of the Consumption of Watercress (Nasturtium officinale) on Exercise-Induced Inflammation in Humans. Foods (Basel, Switzerland), 10(8), 1774. https://doi.org/10.3390/foods10081774

58 Gill, C. I., Haldar, S., Boyd, L. A., Bennett, R., Whiteford, J., Butler, M., Pearson, J. R., Bradbury, I., & Rowland, I. R. (2007). Watercress supplementation in diet reduces lymphocyte DNA damage and alters blood antioxidant status in healthy adults. The American journal of clinical nutrition, 85(2), 504–510. https://doi.org/10.1093/ajcn/85.2.504

59 Fogarty, M. C., Hughes, C. M., Burke, G., Brown, J. C., & Davison, G. W. (2013). Acute and chronic watercress supplementation attenuates exercise-induced peripheral mononuclear cell DNA damage and lipid peroxidation. The British journal of nutrition, 109(2), 293–301. https://doi.org/10.1017/S0007114512000992

60 Ahmed, A. F., Al-Yousef, H. M., Al-Qahtani, J. H., & Al-Said, M. S. (2017). A hepatonephro-protective phenolic-rich extract from red onion (Allium cepa L.) peels. Pakistan journal of pharmaceutical sciences, 30(5(Supplementary)), 1971–1979.

61 Banihani S. A. (2019). Testosterone in Males as Enhanced by Onion (Allium Cepa L.). Biomolecules, 9(2), 75. https://doi.org/10.3390/biom9020075

62 Marefati, N., Ghorani, V., Shakeri, F., Boskabady, M., Kianian, F., Rezaee, R., & Boskabady, M. H. (2021). A review of anti-inflammatory, antioxidant, and immunomodulatory effects of Allium cepa and its main constituents. Pharmaceutical biology, 59(1), 287–302. https://doi.org/10.1080/13880209.2021.1874028

63 Ahmed, A. F., Al-Yousef, H. M., Al-Qahtani, J. H., & Al-Said, M. S. (2017). A hepatonephro-protective phenolic-rich extract from red onion (Allium cepa L.) peels. Pakistan journal of pharmaceutical sciences, 30(5(Supplementary)), 1971–1979.

64 Albanesi, M., Pasculli, C., Giliberti, L., Rossi, M. P., Di Bona, D., Caiaffa, M. F., & Macchia, L. (2019). Immunological characterization of onion (Allium cepa) allergy. Postepy dermatologii i alergologii, 36(1), 98–103. https://doi.org/10.5114/ada.2019.82829

65 Beigoli, S., Behrouz, S., Memar Zia, A., Ghasemi, S. Z., Boskabady, M., Marefati, N., Kianian, F., Khazdair, M. R., El-Seedi, H., & Boskabady, M. H. (2021). Effects of Allium cepa and Its Constituents on Respiratory and Allergic Disorders: A Comprehensive Review of Experimental and Clinical Evidence. Evidence-based complementary and alternative medicine : eCAM, 2021, 5554259. https://doi.org/10.1155/2021/5554259

66 http://allergysymptomsx.com/onion-allergy.php

67 https://www.anaphylaxis.org.uk/knowledgebase/onion-and-garlic-allergy/

68 https://www.celiac.com/gluten-free/topic/38231-onion-intolerance/

69 Clifford T, Howatson G, West DJ, Stevenson EJ. The potential benefits of red beetroot supplementation in health and disease. Nutrients. 2015 Apr 14;7(4):2801-22. doi: 10.3390/nu7042801. PMID: 25875121; PMCID: PMC4425174.

70 Platko, K., Lebeau, P. F., Nederveen, J. P., Byun, J. H., MacDonald, M. E., Bourgeois, J. M., Tarnopolsky, M. A., & Austin, R. C. (2023). A Metabolic Enhancer Protects against Diet-Induced Obesity and Liver Steatosis and Corrects a Pro-Atherogenic Serum Profile in Mice. Nutrients, 15(10), 2410. https://doi.org/10.3390/nu15102410

71 Hadipour, E., Taleghani, A., Tayarani-Najaran, N., & Tayarani-Najaran, Z. (2020). Biological effects of red beetroot and betalains: A review. Phytotherapy research : PTR, 34(8), 1847–1867. https://doi.org/10.1002/ptr.6653

72 Fu, Y., Shi, J., Xie, S. Y., Zhang, T. Y., Soladoye, O. P., & Aluko, R. E. (2020). Red Beetroot Betalains: Perspectives on Extraction, Processing, and Potential Health Benefits. Journal of agricultural and food chemistry, 68(42), 11595–11611. https://doi.org/10.1021/acs.jafc.0c04241

73 Zaccari, F., Cabrera, M. C., & Saadoun, A. (2017). Glucose Content and In Vitro Bioaccessibility in Sweet Potato and Winter Squash Varieties during Storage. Foods (Basel, Switzerland), 6(7), 48. https://doi.org/10.3390/foods6070048

74 Mohanraj, R., & Sivasankar, S. (2014). Sweet potato (Ipomoea batatas [L.] Lam--a valuable medicinal food: a review. Journal of medicinal food, 17(7), 733–741. https://doi.org/10.1089/jmf.2013.2818

75 Nogueira, A. C., Sehn, G. A. R., Rebellato, A. P., Coutinho, J. P., Godoy, H. T., Chang, Y. K., Steel, C. J., & Clerici, M. T. P. S. (2018). Yellow sweet potato flour: use in sweet bread processing to increase β-carotene content and improve quality. Anais da Academia Brasileira de Ciencias, 90(1), 283–293. https://doi.org/10.1590/0001-3765201820150804

76 Nguyen, H. C., Chen, C. C., Lin, K. H., Chao, P. Y., Lin, H. H., & Huang, M. Y. (2021). Bioactive Compounds, Antioxidants, and Health Benefits of Sweet Potato Leaves. Molecules (Basel, Switzerland), 26(7), 1820. https://doi.org/10.3390/molecules26071820

77 The Yearbook of Agriculture 1943-1947 – Science in Farming, USDA, by Alfred D. Edgar page 871

78 Tian J, Chen J, Lv F, Chen S, Chen J, Liu D, Ye X. Domestic cooking methods affect the phytochemical composition and antioxidant activity of purple-fleshed potatoes. Food Chem. 2016 Apr 15;197 Pt B:1264-70. doi: 10.1016/j.foodchem.2015.11.049. Epub 2015 Nov 12. PMID: 26675866.

79 Lachman J, Hamouz K, Musilová J, Hejtmánková K, Kotíková Z, Pazderů K, Domkářová J, Pivec V, Cimr J. Effect of peeling and three cooking methods on the content of selected phytochemicals in potato tubers with various colour of flesh. Food Chem. 2013 Jun 1;138(2-3):1189-97. doi: 10.1016/j.foodchem.2012.11.114. Epub 2012 Dec 5. PMID: 23411230.

80 Song W, Derito CM, Liu MK, He X, Dong M, Liu RH. Cellular antioxidant activity of common vegetables. J Agric Food Chem. 2010 Jun 9;58(11):6621-9. doi: 10.1021/jf9035832. PMID: 20462192.

81 Cebulak T, Krochmal-Marczak B, Stryjecka M, Krzysztofik B, Sawicka B, Danilčenko H, Jarienè E. Phenolic Acid Content and Antioxidant Properties of Edible Potato (Solanum tuberosum L.) with Various Tuber Flesh Colours. Foods. 2022 Dec 25;12(1):100. doi: 10.3390/foods12010100. PMID: 36613318; PMCID: PMC9818533.

82 Fang H, Yin X, He J, Xin S, Zhang H, Ye X, Yang Y, Tian J. Cooking methods affected the phytochemicals and antioxidant activities of potato from different varieties. Food Chem X. 2022 May 21;14:100339. doi: 10.1016/j.fochx.2022.100339. PMID: 35634223; PMCID: PMC9133768.

83 Tajner-Czopek A, Rytel E, Kita A, Sokół-Łętowska A, Kucharska AZ. Content and Stability of Hydroxycinnamic Acids during the Production of French Fries Obtained from Potatoes of Varieties with Light-Yellow, Red and Purple Flesh. Antioxidants (Basel). 2023 Jan 29;12(2):311. doi: 10.3390/antiox12020311. PMID: 36829870; PMCID: PMC9951911.

84 Zhang Y, You D, Lu N, Duan D, Feng X, Astell-Burt T, Zhu P, Han L, Duan S, Zou Z. Potatoes Consumption and Risk of Type 2 Diabetes: A Meta-analysis. Iran J Public Health. 2018 Nov;47(11):1627-1635. PMID: 30581777; PMCID: PMC6294859.

85 Guo F, Zhang Q, Jiang H, He Y, Li M, Ran J, Lin J, Tian L, Ma L. Dietary potato intake and risks of type 2 diabetes and gestational diabetes mellitus. Clin Nutr. 2021 Jun;40(6):3754-3764. doi: 10.1016/j.clnu.2021.04.039. Epub 2021 May 1. PMID: 34130021.

86 Schwingshackl L, Schwedhelm C, Hoffmann G, Boeing H. Potatoes and risk of chronic disease: a systematic review and dose-response meta-analysis. Eur J Nutr. 2019 Sep;58(6):2243-2251. doi: 10.1007/s00394-018-1774-2. Epub 2018 Jul 9. PMID: 29987352; PMCID: PMC6689281.

87 Mustafa, A. M., Angeloni, S., Abouelenein, D., Acquaticci, L., Xiao, J., Sagratini, G., Maggi, F., Vittori, S., & Caprioli, G. (2022). A new HPLC-MS/MS method for the simultaneous determination of 36 polyphenols in blueberry, strawberry and their commercial products and determination of antioxidant activity. Food chemistry, 367, 130743. https://doi.org/10.1016/j.foodchem.2021.130743

88 Dreher M. L. (2018). Whole Fruits and Fruit Fiber Emerging Health Effects. Nutrients, 10(12), 1833. https://doi.org/10.3390/nu10121833

89 Guerra Valencia, J., Ramos, W., Cruz-Ausejo, L., Torres-Malca, J. R., Loayza-Castro, J. A., Zeñas-Trujillo, G. Z., Guillen Ponce, N. R., Zuzunaga-Montoya, F. E., Valladares-Garrido, M. J., Vera-Ponce, V. J., & De La Cruz-Vargas, J. A. (2023). The Fruit Intake-Adiposity Paradox: Findings from a Peruvian Cross-Sectional Study. Nutrients, 15(5), 1183. https://doi.org/10.3390/nu15051183

90 Guerra Valencia, J., Saavedra-Garcia, L., Vera-Ponce, V. J., Espinoza-Rojas, R., & Barengo, N. C. (2023). Factors Associated with Normal-Weight Abdominal Obesity Phenotype in a Representative Sample of the Peruvian Population: A 4-Year Pooled Cross-Sectional Study. Journal of clinical medicine, 12(10), 3482. https://doi.org/10.3390/jcm12103482

91 Whole Detox: A 21 day Personalized Program by Deanna Minich, PhD HarperCollins 2016, pg 36

92 Whole Detox: A 21 day Personalized Program by Deanna Minich, PhD HarperCollins 2016, pg 41

93 Miller, K., Feucht, W., & Schmid, M. (2019). Bioactive Compounds of Strawberry and Blueberry and Their Potential Health Effects Based on Human Intervention Studies: A Brief Overview. Nutrients, 11(7), 1510. https://doi.org/10.3390/nu11071510

94 Skrovankova, S., Sumczynski, D., Mlcek, J., Jurikova, T., & Sochor, J. (2015). Bioactive Compounds and Antioxidant Activity in Different Types of Berries. International journal of molecular sciences, 16(10), 24673–24706. https://doi.org/10.3390/ijms161024673

95 Wilder-Smith, C. H., Materna, A., & Olesen, S. S. (2023). Blueberries Improve Abdominal Symptoms, Well-Being and Functioning in Patients with Functional Gastrointestinal Disorders. Nutrients, 15(10), 2396. https://doi.org/10.3390/nu15102396

96 Osman, A. G., Avula, B., Katragunta, K., Ali, Z., Chittiboyina, A. G., & Khan, I. A. (2023). Elderberry Extracts: Characterization of the Polyphenolic Chemical Composition, Quality Consistency, Safety, Adulteration, and Attenuation of Oxidative Stress- and Inflammation-Induced Health Disorders. Molecules (Basel, Switzerland), 28(7), 3148. https://doi.org/10.3390/molecules28073148

97 Liu, D., He, X. Q., Wu, D. T., Li, H. B., Feng, Y. B., Zou, L., & Gan, R. Y. (2022). Elderberry (Sambucus nigra L.): Bioactive Compounds, Health Functions, and Applications. Journal of agricultural and food chemistry, 70(14), 4202–4220. https://doi.org/10.1021/acs.jafc.2c00010

98 Osman, A. G., Avula, B., Katragunta, K., Ali, Z., Chittiboyina, A. G., & Khan, I. A. (2023). Elderberry Extracts: Characterization of the Polyphenolic Chemical Composition, Quality Consistency, Safety, Adulteration, and Attenuation of Oxidative Stress- and Inflammation-Induced Health Disorders. Molecules (Basel, Switzerland), 28(7), 3148. https://doi.org/10.3390/molecules28073148

99 Zhang, X., , Sandhu, A., , Edirisinghe, I., , & Burton-Freeman, B., (2018). An exploratory study of red raspberry (Rubus idaeus L.) (poly)phenols/metabolites in human biological samples. Food & function, 9(2), 806–818. https://doi.org/10.1039/c7fo00893g

100 Zhang, X., Sandhu, A., Edirisinghe, I., & Burton-Freeman, B. M. (2020). Plasma and Urinary (Poly)phenolic Profiles after 4-Week Red Raspberry (Rubus idaeus L.) Intake with or without Fructo-Oligosaccharide Supplementation. Molecules (Basel, Switzerland), 25(20), 4777. https://doi.org/10.3390/molecules25204777

101 Burton-Freeman, B. M., Sandhu, A. K., & Edirisinghe, I. (2016). Red Raspberries and Their Bioactive Polyphenols: Cardiometabolic and Neuronal Health Links. Advances in nutrition (Bethesda, Md.), 7(1), 44–65. https://doi.org/10.3945/an.115.009639

102 Moga, M. A., Dimienescu, O. G., Bălan, A., Dima, L., Toma, S. I., Bîgiu, N. F., & Blidaru, A. (2021). Pharmacological and Therapeutic Properties of Punica granatum Phytochemicals: Possible Roles in Breast Cancer. Molecules (Basel, Switzerland), 26(4), 1054. https://doi.org/10.3390/molecules26041054

103 Aleksandrova, S., Alexova, R., Dragomanova, S., Kalfin, R., Nicoletti, F., Fagone, P., Petralia, M. C., Mangano, K., & Tancheva, L. (2023). Preventive and Therapeutic Effects of Punica granatum L. Polyphenols in Neurological Conditions. International journal of molecular sciences, 24(3), 1856. https://doi.org/10.3390/ijms24031856

104 http://nutritiondata.self.com/facts/fruits-and-fruit-juices/2038/2
105 Ferreira, Mandy. "15 health benefits of pomegranate juice." Medical News Today. MediLexicon, Intl., 12 Jul. 2017. Web. 12 Jan. 2018. https://www.medicalnewstoday.com/articles/318385.php
106 Vučić, V., Grabež, M., Trchounian, A., & Arsić, A. (2019). Composition and Potential Health Benefits of Pomegranate: A Review. Current pharmaceutical design, 25(16), 1817–1827. https://doi.org/10.2174/1381612825666190708183941
107 Saeed, M., Naveed, M., BiBi, J., Kamboh, A. A., Arain, M. A., Shah, Q. A., Alagawany, M., El-Hack, M. E. A., Abdel-Latif, M. A., Yatoo, M. I., Tiwari, R., Chakraborty, S., & Dhama, K. (2018). The Promising Pharmacological Effects and Therapeutic/Medicinal Applications of Punica Granatum L. (Pomegranate) as a Functional Food in Humans and Animals. Recent patents on inflammation & allergy drug discovery, 12(1), 24–38. https://doi.org/10.2174/1872213X12666180221154713
108 Alexova, R., Alexandrova, S., Dragomanova, S., Kalfin, R., Solak, A., Mehan, S., Petralia, M. C., Fagone, P., Mangano, K., Nicoletti, F., & Tancheva, L. (2023). Anti-COVID-19 Potential of Ellagic Acid and Polyphenols of Punica granatum L. Molecules (Basel, Switzerland), 28(9), 3772. https://doi.org/10.3390/molecules28093772
109 ciTrUS aS a comPonenT of The meDiTerranean DieT: https://www.researchgate.net/publication/311911612_Citrus_as_a_Component_of_the_Mediterranean_Diet
110 https://www.livestrong.com/article/164362-difference-between-citric-acid-and-ascorbic-acid/
111 Ferreira, I., Ortigoza, Á., & Moore, P. (2019). Magnesium and malic acid supplement for fibromyalgia. Suplemento de magnesio y ácido málico para fibromialgia. Medwave, 19(4), e7633. https://doi.org/10.5867/medwave.2019.04.7632
112 Haddad, H. W., Mallepalli, N. R., Scheinuk, J. E., Bhargava, P., Cornett, E. M., Urits, I., & Kaye, A. D. (2021). The Role of Nutrient Supplementation in the Management of Chronic Pain in Fibromyalgia: A Narrative Review. Pain and therapy, 10(2), 827–848. https://doi.org/10.1007/s40122-021-00266-9
113 Barreca, D., Gattuso, G., Bellocco, E., Calderaro, A., Trombetta, D., Smeriglio, A., Laganà, G., Daglia, M., Meneghini, S., & Nabavi, S. M. (2017). Flavanones: Citrus phytochemical with health-promoting properties. BioFactors (Oxford, England), 43(4), 495–506. https://doi.org/10.1002/biof.1363
114 Ortiz, A. C., Fideles, S. O. M., Reis, C. H. B., Bellini, M. Z., Pereira, E. S. B. M., Pilon, J. P. G., de Marchi, M. Â., Detregiachi, C. R. P., Flato, U. A. P., Trazzi, B. F. M., Pagani, B. T., Ponce, J. B., Gardizani, T. P., Veronez, F. S., Buchaim, D. V., & Buchaim, R. L. (2022). Therapeutic Effects of Citrus Flavonoids Neohesperidin, Hesperidin and Its Aglycone, Hesperetin on Bone Health. Biomolecules, 12(5), 626. https://doi.org/10.3390/biom12050626
115 Citrus flavonoids: Molecular structure, biological activity and nutritional properties: A review: https://doi.org/10.1016/j.foodchem.2006.11.054
116 https://www.sciencedirect.com/science/article/pii/S0308814606009356
117 Kato Y, Domoto T, Hiramitsu M, Katagiri T, Sato K, Miyake Y, Aoi S, Ishihara K, Ikeda H, Umei N, Takigawa A, Harada T. Effect on blood pressure of daily lemon ingestion and walking. J Nutr Metab. 2014;2014:912684. doi: 10.1155/2014/912684. Epub 2014 Apr 10. PMID: 24818015; PMCID: PMC4003767.
118 Protective Effects of Lemon Juice on Alcohol-Induced Liver Injury in Mice: https://www.ncbi.nlm.nih.gov/pmc/articles/PMC5439254/
119 EWG Dirty Dozen for 2017
120 https://www.ewg.org/foodnews/clean_fifteen_list.php#.WlgHHjdG1hE
121 Rusconi, M., & Conti, A. (2010). Theobroma cacao L., the Food of the Gods: a scientific approach beyond myths and claims. Pharmacological research, 61(1), 5–13. https://doi.org/10.1016/j.phrs.2009.08.008
122 Rosas-Campos, R., Meza-Rios, A., Rodriguez-Sanabria, J. S., la Rosa-Bibiano, R., Corona-Cervantes, K., García-Mena, J., Santos, A., Sandoval-Rodriguez, A., & Armendariz-Borunda, J. (2022). Dietary supplementation with Mexican foods, Opuntia ficus indica, Theobroma cacao, and Acheta domesticus: Improving obesogenic and microbiota features in obese mice. Frontiers in nutrition, 9, 987222. https://doi.org/10.3389/fnut.2022.987222
123 Escutia-Gutiérrez, R., Sandoval-Rodríguez, A., Galicia-Moreno, M., Rosas-Campos, R., Almeida-López, M., Santos, A., & Armendáriz-Borunda, J. (2023). Mexican Ancestral Foods (Theobroma cacao, Opuntia ficus indica, Persea americana and Phaseolus vulgaris) Supplementation on Anthropometric, Lipid and Glycemic Control Variables in Obese Patients: A Systematic Review and Meta-Analysis. Foods (Basel, Switzerland), 12(6), 1177. https://doi.org/10.3390/foods12061177
124 Kerimi, A., & Williamson, G. (2015). The cardiovascular benefits of dark chocolate. Vascular pharmacology, 71, 11–15. https://doi.org/10.1016/j.vph.2015.05.011
125 Jaćimović, S., Popović-Djordjević, J., Sarić, B., Krstić, A., Mickovski-Stefanović, V., & Pantelić, N. Đ. (2022). Antioxidant Activity and Multi-Elemental Analysis of Dark Chocolate. Foods (Basel, Switzerland), 11(10), 1445. https://doi.org/10.3390/foods11101445
126 Vertuani, S., Scalambra, E., Vittorio, T., Bino, A., Malisardi, G., Baldisserotto, A., & Manfredini, S. (2014). Evaluation of antiradical activity of different cocoa and chocolate products: relation with lipid and protein composition. Journal of medicinal food, 17(4), 512–516. https://doi.org/10.1089/jmf.2013.0110
127 Fernández-Murga, L., Tarín, J. J., García-Perez, M. A., & Cano, A. (2011). The impact of chocolate on cardiovascular health. Maturitas, 69(4), 312–321. https://doi.org/10.1016/j.maturitas.2011.05.011

128 West, S. G., McIntyre, M. D., Piotrowski, M. J., Poupin, N., Miller, D. L., Preston, A. G., Wagner, P., Groves, L. F., & Skulas-Ray, A. C. (2014). Effects of dark chocolate and cocoa consumption on endothelial function and arterial stiffness in overweight adults. The British journal of nutrition, 111(4), 653–661. https://doi.org/10.1017/S0007114513002912

129 Sánchez, M., Laca, A., Laca, A., & Díaz, M. (2023). Cocoa Bean Shell: A By-Product with High Potential for Nutritional and Biotechnological Applications. Antioxidants (Basel, Switzerland), 12(5), 1028. https://doi.org/10.3390/antiox12051028

130 Flanagan, A., Bechtold, D. A., Pot, G. K., & Johnston, J. D. (2021). Chrono-nutrition: From molecular and neuronal mechanisms to human epidemiology and timed feeding patterns. Journal of neurochemistry, 157(1), 53–72. https://doi.org/10.1111/jnc.15246

131 Judelson, D. A., Preston, A. G., Miller, D. L., Muñoz, C. X., Kellogg, M. D., & Lieberman, H. R. (2013). Effects of theobromine and caffeine on mood and vigilance. Journal of clinical psychopharmacology, 33(4), 499–506. https://doi.org/10.1097/JCP.0b013e3182905d24

132 Garbarino, S., Garbarino, E., & Lanteri, P. (2022). Cyrcadian Rhythm, Mood, and Temporal Patterns of Eating Chocolate: A Scoping Review of Physiology, Findings, and Future Directions. Nutrients, 14(15), 3113. https://doi.org/10.3390/nu14153113

133 Sezer, B., Apaydin, H., Bilge, G., & Boyaci, I. H. (2018). Coffee arabica adulteration: Detection of wheat, corn and chickpea. Food chemistry, 264, 142–148. https://doi.org/10.1016/j.foodchem.2018.05.037

134 Toci, A. T., Farah, A., Pezza, H. R., & Pezza, L. (2016). Coffee Adulteration: More than Two Decades of Research. Critical reviews in analytical chemistry, 46(2), 83–92. https://doi.org/10.1080/10408347.2014.966185

135 Cortes, the Secret History of Coffee, Cocca & Cola

136 http://www.serdas.com/coffee-history/

137 Paz-Graniel, I., & Salas-Salvadó, J. (2023). Coffee and health. El café y la salud. Medicina clinica, 160(8), 352–354. https://doi.org/10.1016/j.medcli.2023.01.010

138 Baspinar, B., Eskici, G., & Ozcelik, A. O. (2017). How coffee affects metabolic syndrome and its components. Food & function, 8(6), 2089–2101. https://doi.org/10.1039/c7fo00388a

139 Stefanello, N., Spanevello, R. M., Passamonti, S., Porciúncula, L., Bonan, C. D., Olabiyi, A. A., Teixeira da Rocha, J. B., Assmann, C. E., Morsch, V. M., & Schetinger, M. R. C. (2019). Coffee, caffeine, chlorogenic acid, and the purinergic system. Food and chemical toxicology : an international journal published for the British Industrial Biological Research Association, 123, 298–313. https://doi.org/10.1016/j.fct.2018.10.005

140 Why Your Coffee Habit May Have Major Upsides For Your Health by Forbes; https://www.forbes.com/sit es/quora/2017/08/08/why-your-coffee-habit-may-have-major-upsides-for-your-health/#4e65be1c938d

141 Gökcen, B. B., & Şanlier, N. (2019). Coffee consumption and disease correlations. Critical reviews in food science and nutrition, 59(2), 336–348. https://doi.org/10.1080/10408398.2017.1369391

142 Soohan Jung, Min Hyung Kim, Jae Hee Park, Yoonhwa Jeong, Kwang Suk Ko. Cellular Antioxidant and Anti-Inflammatory Effects of Coffee Extracts with Different Roasting Levels. Journal of Medicinal Food, 2017; 20 (6): 626

143 Nerurkar, P. V., Yokoyama, J., Ichimura, K., Kutscher, S., Wong, J., Bittenbender, H. C., & Deng, Y. (2023). Medium Roasting and Brewing Methods Differentially Modulate Global Metabolites, Lipids, Biogenic Amines, Minerals, and Antioxidant Capacity of Hawai'i-Grown Coffee (Coffea arabica). Metabolites, 13(3), 412. https://doi.org/10.3390/metabo13030412

144 Wu L, Sun D, He Y. Coffee intake and the incident risk of cognitive disorders: A dose-response meta-analysis of nine prospective cohort studies. Clin Nutr. 2017;36(3):730-736.

145 Hutachok, N., Angkasith, P., Chumpun, C., Fucharoen, S., Mackie, I. J., Porter, J. B., & Srichairatanakool, S. (2020). Anti-Platelet Aggregation and Anti-Cyclooxygenase Activities for a Range of Coffee Extracts (Coffea arabica). Molecules (Basel, Switzerland), 26(1), 10. https://doi.org/10.3390/molecules26010010

146 Frederic D. Müller, Christin Hackethal, Roman Schmidt, Oliver Kappenstein, Karla Pfaff, Andreas Luch. Metal release from coffee machines and electric kettles. Food Additives & Contaminants: Part A, 2015; 32 (11): 1959 DOI: 10.1080/19440049.2015.1086929

147 Socała, K., Szopa, A., Serefko, A., Poleszak, E., & Wlaź, P. (2020). Neuroprotective Effects of Coffee Bioactive Compounds: A Review. International journal of molecular sciences, 22(1), 107. https://doi.org/10.3390/ijms22010107

"All life is an experiment. The more experiments you make, the better."

~ Ralph Waldo Emerson

Chapter Eight ~ *Fiber & Fat*: Overlooked & Under-Appreciated

Healthy carbohydrates contain soluble and insoluble fibers. Fiber is our housekeeping team; not only does it keep our bowels moving, reducing the risk factors for colon cancer, but it also removes toxins and transports hormone metabolites, lowering blood sugars, blood pressure, and cholesterol. There is also evidence that fibers play a vital role in weight management by slowing the absorption of simple carbohydrates (high glycemic flash fuels from fructose and sucrose).

Consumers in the United States spend roughly $30 billion annually on weight loss and an estimated $1-2 billion on weight loss programs. Research supports the idea that reducing the number of flash fuel calories consumed, managing stress, and becoming more active is the only way to lose weight sustainably. What is not often discussed, however, is nature's built-in environmental protection agent, fiber.[1, 2]

Not all the nutrients in food are digestible to humans. Fiber is the indigestible part of fruits, vegetables, seeds, whole grains, and herbs. Dietary fiber performs various roles in the digestive tract. It provides good satiety value, thus decreasing energy (calorie) intake. It increases peristalsis, facilitates bowel movement, and prevents constipation. Fibers are usually polysaccharides and can be soluble or insoluble in water. Short-chain fatty acids (SCFAs) are the major anions in the large intestine. Bacterial fermentation of dietary fiber produces them. SCFAs are known to have various physiological and pathophysiological effects on the intestine.[3]

Soluble fiber is found in oat bran, barley, nuts, seeds, beans, lentils, peas, and some fruits and vegetables. The types of soluble fiber are primarily pectin, beta-glucans, and inulin.

Insoluble fiber is found in foods such as wheat bran, vegetables, and whole grains. Types of insoluble fibers are cellulose, hemicellulose, and psyllium. Fiber serves as food to the gut microflora for the fermentation process, producing short-chain fatty acids. Short-chain fatty acids help to reduce circulating cholesterol.

Dietary fiber consumption absorbs glucose in the digestive tract and retards its release rate to the bloodstream, maintaining the body's blood glucose level.[4] Fiber and fiber-rich foods are natural regulators and efficiently remove unneeded fats, sugar, toxins, and intestinal congestion. All these critical processes serve to reduce inflammation, a primary contributor to chronic illness.[5]

Nutrition has been demonstrated as a means to modulate epigenetic markers linked to increased disease risks or to protect against diseases. Overnutrition (obesity) and undernutrition (famine) have been observed to alter prenatal epigenetic tags that may increase the risk of offspring developing disease later in life. Exposure to environmental pollution also alters epigenetic markers and may contribute to inflammation and disease. It has been demonstrated that pollutants, via epigenetic modulations, can increase the activation of NF-κB and upregulate microRNAs (genetic transcription factors) associated with inflammation, cardiac injury, and oxidative damage. Importantly, recent evidence suggests that nutritional components, including epigallocatechin gallate (EGCG) found in green tea, white tea, oolong tea, strawberries, raspberries, blackberries, plums, peaches, kiwi, cocoa, and avocado can protect against pollutant-induced inflammation through epigenetic regulation of pro-inflammatory target genes, such as NF-κB.[6,7] All of the above-listed foods except tea contain both soluble and insoluble fiber.

> Nuclear factor kappa-light-chain-enhancer of activated B cells (NF-κB) is a protein complex that controls DNA transcription, cytokine production, and cell survival.
>
> MicroRNAs are small, single-stranded, non-coding RNA molecules that play a crucial role in regulating gene expression.

America's escalating cancer, diabetes, heart disease, and obesity rates reflect a population consuming a high-calorie diet essentially devoid of fiber. Will you eat cake or carrots? What will most people pick when choosing between indulgent and healthy foods? The answer may depend on what other foods sit nearby on the grocery shelf, suggests research published in *Psychological Science,* a journal of the Association for Psychological Science.[8] Paradoxically, the nearby presence of an indulgent treat can cause more people to opt for healthy food, said study coauthor Scott Huettel, professor of psychology and neuroscience at Duke University. Context, in other words, affects food choices.

> "When people choose foods, they don't simply reach into their memory and pick the most-preferred food. Instead, how much we prefer something depends on what other options are available," Huettel said.
>
> "If you see one healthy food and one unhealthy food, most people will choose the indulgent food," he said. "But if you add more unhealthy foods, it seems, suddenly the healthy food stands out." There are so many widely varying opinions about nutrients like fats and fiber that it's hard to find a definitive answer. Researchers at the *California Institute of Technology* assumed the healthiness of food is not factored into a person's food choice until aftertaste. And for those individuals who exercised less self-control, they hypothesized, health would factor into the choice even later.[9]

Chapter 8 ~ Fiber & Fat Overlooked and Under Appreciated

By consuming more soluble and insoluble forms of fiber through healthy food choices, you can improve the health of your entire body, from your brain to your bowels. Fiber is not usually thought of as a nutrient, but it should be, especially when you look at the fifteen ways fiber helps the human digestive system work:

1. Weight loss and maintenance
2. Increase energy
3. Reduce heart disease
4. Lower or maintain healthy cholesterol levels
5. Reduce diabetes risk and regulate blood sugars
6. Reduce cancer risk
7. Maintain bowel regularity
8. Reduce diverticulitis
9. Regulate IBS (irritable bowel syndrome)
10. Reduce body odor; improve skin and hair
11. Improve immune function
12. Balance brain chemistry
13. Reduce headaches and allergies
14. Prevent GERD and/or stomach nausea associated with slow transit time (constipation)
15. Detoxify the body of hormone-disrupting chemicals and environmental toxins found in foods, water, the environment, and body care products

The average American consumes 4-8 grams of fiber per day. The American Diabetic Association recommends as much as 40 grams of fiber per day, and the daily recommended dietary allowance (RDA) for fiber is 20 grams.[10] Although I may disagree with the RDA on many things, this is clear: Americans of all ages are not eating enough fiber-rich foods.

How do you know if your bowels are not "up to speed?" Take a transit time test. Eat an "indicator food" that will show up in the stool, such as corn, beets, dark chocolate, or sesame seeds. Then, time how long it takes to see the indicator food in the toilet bowl. The ideal time ranges from 12-15 hours. Daily, two to three bowel movements are optimum if well-formed and easy.

> The complex relationship between dietary fiber intake, the gastrointestinal tract, and host metabolism cannot be understood if not viewed in its entirety. Viscous fibers increase gastric emptying rate, inhibit nutrient absorption, and contribute to short-chain fatty acid (SCFA) fermentation. These effects may lead to a reduced postprandial glucose level in the bloodstream and an increased release of *incretin* glucagon-like peptide 1 (GLP-1) and *satiety-stimulating hormones* peptide YY (PYY), influencing energy intake and peripheral tissue metabolism. Prebiotics found in fiber-rich foods modulates microbiota composition and SCFA production, affecting energy homeostasis and insulin sensitivity.[11]

Fiber for Health

As all fibers have differing properties, they also exert different functional effects in the GI tract contributing to metabolic alterations such as modifying cholesterol levels and improving glycemic control.[12] Insoluble fibers, such as *cellulose* and *hemicellulose*, are not fermented but act as bulking fibers, instigating faster transit times and improved stool regularity, provided an individual is well hydrated and is not using over-the-counter anti-inflammatory medications or exhibits thyroid imbalance.[13]

Gut bacteria secrete enzymes that can break down specific *glycosidic bonds* in the structure of undigestible fibers. Bacteria vary in the type and number of enzymes they produce and the fibers they ferment, consequently, the metabolites produced also differ. Therefore, a diet rich in various fibers supports a diverse gut microbiome in humans.[14] Bacteria profit from fiber fermentation by obtaining energy to keep the process going. Without insoluble and soluble fiber, bacteria would use the glycoprotein-rich mucus layer of the gut as an alternative energy source, thereby disrupting this protective barrier.[15]

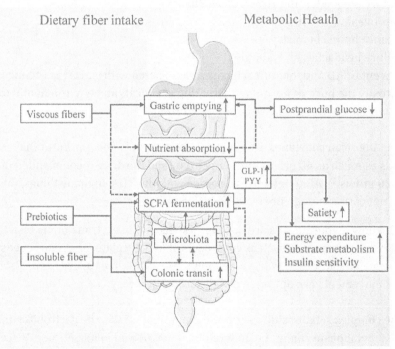

Müller M, Canfora EE, Blaak EE. Gastrointestinal Transit Time, Glucose Homeostasis and Metabolic Health: Modulation by Dietary Fibers. Nutrients. 2018; 10(3):275. https://doi.org/10.3390/nu10030275

How to Get More Fiber in Your Diet

Eating natural foods like berries, cherries, apples, and greens is the most beneficial and nutrient-dense method to increase dietary fiber. If an individual has slow transit time (time between food consumption and evacuation), consider adding a natural fiber supplement to your daily program: psyllium seed, acacia fiber, chia seeds, or flax seed (add flax only if you are female and not concerned about phytoestrogen).

Chapter 8 ~ Fiber & Fat Overlooked and Under Appreciated

When introducing clean forms of fiber supplements, (psyllium seed, acacia) start with half the recommended dose for two weeks to give your gut time to adjust to the increase in fiber. If you develop gas, bloating, or cramps, increase the amount of water you consume or change the type of fiber supplement. Be advised that other beverages do not have the same effect as water. They can contribute to adverse symptoms by acting as diuretics and preventing your digestive system from supplying adequate fluid. Fiber adds bulk to your meals and creates a sense of fullness, naturally reducing your calorie consumption and slowing down the eating process. This allows your digestive system, hormones, and brain to take the time required for efficiency. Bowels are soft muscle and, like every other muscle, require exercise to stay healthy. Fiber traps chemicals, fats, prescription medications, oil-soluble nutrients like omega 3, 6 and 9, water, and undigested food particles as it moves through the small and large intestines. This is why fiber effectively reduces diarrhea for those with IBS, ulcerative colitis, or ileostomies. The

> 1 cup cooked black beans = 19.4 grams
> ¾ cup lightly cooked broccoli = 7.0 grams
> ½ cup cooked spinach = 7.0 grams
> 1 cup red lentils = 6.4 grams
> 1 medium yam cooked = 6.8 grams
> ¾ cup Heritage™ heirloom whole grains organic cereal = 6 grams
> 1 cup whole grain spaghetti = 5.6 grams
> 1 teaspoon psyllium seed = 5 grams
> ¼ cup uncooked quinoa = 5 grams
> 1 tablespoon golden flax seed meal = 5 grams
> 1 Cliff™ bars = 5 grams
> ½ cup raspberries = 4.6 grams
> ½ cup raw blackberries = 4.4 grams
> ½ cup cooked greens = 4.0 grams

following list shows how much fiber you can add to your diet via everyday foods.

***Skip the Metamucil**, which contains artificial dyes, flavors, and chemicals and costs more than whole foods or other fiber supplements.*

Principle 37: Fiber is your friend; it feeds the gut microbiota.

Safer Alternatives: Acacia

Acacia has been used in medicines, baking ingredients, tools, and woodwork for centuries. It has a long history in civilizations as ancient as the Egyptians and the aboriginal tribes of Australia.

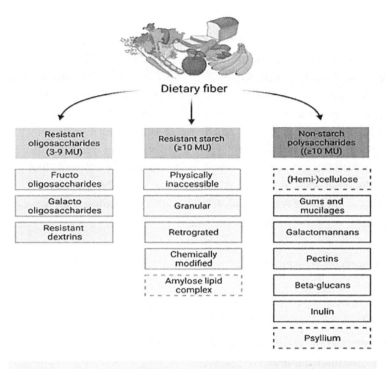

Verstegen, R. E. M., Kostadinova, A. I., Merenciana, Z., Garssen, J., Folkerts, G., Hendriks, R. W., & Willemsen, L. E. M. (2021). Dietary Fibers: Effects, Underlying Mechanisms and Possible Role in Allergic Asthma Management. Nutrients, 13(11), 4153. MDPI AG. Retrieved from http://dx.doi.org/10.3390/nu13114153

Acacia gum has a naturally sticky texture. Materials with this property are often used to reduce irritation and inflammation. The gum is especially effective in easing stomach or throat discomfort. Acacia is often used in topical skin treatments to help wounds heal. Doctors, scientists, and researchers believe this effect may be due to some of acacia's chemicals, such as alkaloids, glycosides, and flavonoids. In one study, a species of acacia known as *Acacia caesia* was tested on rats as part of a topical wound treatment. It led to quicker wound healing than the standard treatment.[16] Another animal study suggested that acacia may also help heal ulcers. Polysaccharides show protective effects on intestinal barrier function due to their effectiveness in mitigating oxidative damage, inflammation, and probiotic effects.[17]

A laboratory aide measures out the right amount of apple essence to give candy an apple flavor.

Yearbook of Agriculture 1943-1947 Science in Farming

Acacia gum contains water-soluble dietary fibers (WSDF) that are not only good fiber for your diet but also helpful in keeping your cholesterol under control. One study showed that taking 15 grams of acacia gum in the liquid form daily helped manage the plasma cholesterol concentration in blood. Although published in 1992, this is the most comprehensive study to date on the effects of acacia gum on the blood. WSDF can also help you maintain a healthy weight and is good for cardiovascular health. The Food and Drug Administration (FDA) has even changed regulations to recognize the beneficial use of acacia as a good fiber source in many popular foods, including cereals, juice, and yogurt.[18, 19, 20]

Fiber & Kidney Health

Although diet is the cornerstone of managing the patient with chronic kidney disease (CKD), it remains a relatively underused component of the clinician's armamentarium. The ecosystem of the human gut consists of trillions of microorganisms forming an authentic metabolically active non-human organ fueled by the nutrients consumed, whose function is to produce bioactive compounds. These microbiota-derived metabolites may either be protective for kidney function (e.g., short-chain fatty acids from the fermentation of dietary fibers) or deleterious (e.g., gut-derived uremic toxins such as trimethylamine N-oxide, p-cresyl sulfate, and indoxyl sulfate from the fermentation of amino acids).[21, 22, 23]

The gut microbiome is composed of diverse bacteria that have beneficial and adverse effects on human health. The microbiome has recently gained attention and is increasingly noted to play a significant role in health and several disease states. Increasing urea concentration during chronic kidney disease (CKD) leads to alterations in the intestinal flora that can increase the production of gut-derived toxins and alter the intestinal epithelial barrier.[24] Intestinal microbiota plays a vital role in collecting uremic toxins because numerous uremic solutes are generated in the process of protein fermentation by the colonic microbiota. Numerous studies have indicated that chronic kidney disease (CKD) progression to end-stage renal disease (ESRD) is firmly associated with the accumulation of toxic metabolites in blood and other metabolic compartments. Some disease states, including CKD, are associated with dysbiosis.[25, 26] Patients with CKD have a higher cardiovascular risk than the average population, partially due to the accumulation of solutes known as uremic toxins in the blood plasma. Although the impact of diet on uremic toxicity in CKD is difficult to quantify, nutrient intake plays an important role. Indeed, most uremic toxins are gut-derived compounds, including Maillard reaction products, hippurates, indoles, phenols, and polyamines.[27]

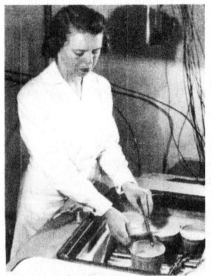

To study changes in freezing food at home, Equipment Specialist Dorothy Skinner inserts a thermocoupler into a carton of liquid. Soluble fibers would be added to improve texture and creaminess.

Yearbook of Agriculture 1943-1947 Science in Farming

> The Maillard reaction is a non-enzymatic browning process that occurs in foods when proteins and/or amino acids chemically react with carbohydrates of reducing sugars. Applying heat during cooking accelerates and continues this intricate process, elevating the taste, aromas, and appearance of food.

MiraLAX®

The medical community has advised that MiraLAX® is a safe, over-the-counter remedy for constipation in adults and children. As it turns out, MiraLAX may contain or degrade into some of the same toxins found in anti-freeze; thousands of adverse event reports have been filed with the FDA over the last decade.[28] In December 2011, the FDA placed MiraLAX — a *polyethylene glycol*-containing blockbuster drug marketed by Merck & Co., Inc. — on its Adverse Event Reporting System (AERS) concerning "neuropsychiatric events."

Besides MiraLAX, this warning also applies to Movicol, Dulcolax, Colyte, Colovage, Co-Lav, Clensz-Lyte, ClearLax, GoLYTELY, GaviLyte C, GlycoLax, Go-Evac, GlycoPrep, E-Z-Em Fortrans, Halflytely, Lax-a-Day, LaxLyte, MoviPrep, Macrogol, NuLytely, OCL, Peg-Lyte, Prep Lyte, Softlax, TriLyte, and all other brands with polyethylene glycol 3350 (PEG for short) as their active ingredient. The "3350" qualifier refers to this particular PEG variant's molecular weight.[29]

Polyethylene glycol combines ethylene glycol molecules into a large polymer chain, hence the prefix poly, (Greek for *many*). On its own, ethylene glycol is used in automotive antifreeze and brake fluid. According to the *National Institute for Occupational Safety and Health*, it is a highly toxic substance.

> "Ethylene glycol is chemically broken down in the body into toxic compounds. Its toxic byproducts first affect the central nervous system (CNS), the heart, and the kidneys. Ingestion of sufficient amounts [as little as 30ml] can be fatal."[30]

The "neuropsychiatric events" in the FDA's safety alert refer to neurologic disorders of the central and peripheral nervous systems, such as autism, dementia, depression, schizophrenia, multiple sclerosis, Alzheimer's, and Parkinson's.[31]

Buckwheat – A Pioneer Food

Buckwheat (BW) is a gluten-free crop in the *Polygonaceae* family, abundant with beneficial phytochemicals that provide significant health benefits. It has been cultivated and adapted in diverse ecological zones all over the world. Recently its popularity is expanding as a nutrient-rich healthy food with low calories. The bioactive compounds in buckwheat are flavonoids (i.e., rutin, quercetin, orientin, isoorientin, vitexin, and isovitexin), fatty acids, polysaccharides, proteins, amino acids, iminosugars, dietary fiber, fagopyrins, resistant starch, vitamins, and minerals. Buckwheat possesses high nutritional value due to these bioactive compounds. Additionally, several essential bioactive factors have long been gaining interest because these compounds are beneficial for healing and preventing numerous diseases.[32]

Buckwheat is a highly nutritional food that has been shown to provide a wide range of beneficial health effects, including plasma cholesterol level reduction, neuroprotection, anti-cancer, anti-inflammatory, anti-diabetic effects, and improvement of hypertension conditions.[33,34] Buckwheat protein is of outstanding quality and — unlike popular cereals — is rich in the essential amino acid lysine. Buckwheat is also used in gluten-free diets for people with celiac disease and non-celiac gluten sensitivity. It has also been recognized that buckwheat has prebiotic and antioxidant activity.[35] Buckwheat is not related to wheat or other grains within the grass family. Instead, buckwheat is related to sorrel, knotweed, and rhubarb. Because its seeds are eaten, it is referred to as a pseudo-cereal. Seeds like quinoa, amaranth, and buckwheat, used for centuries in traditional cuisine, are trendy in culinary circles as alternatives to wheat and other grains.

Researchers from Japan have found that a traditional liquor made from buckwheat could even be used medicinally. In a study published in the journal *Antioxidants*, researchers from Osaka University revealed that an ingredient in Chinese buckwheat liquor containing various herbal medicine extracts could induce autophagy, a process that cells use to clean up damaged or non-essential proteins. Autophagy plays a vital role in diseases such as cancer, alcoholic liver disease, and Alzheimer's disease, so finding a way to encourage this process is a topic of considerable interest. Herbal substances are an intriguing potential source of compounds that could be used in this type of treatment.[36]

Common buckwheat was domesticated and first cultivated inland in Southeast Asia, possibly around 6000 BC, and spread to the Middle East and Europe. Buckwheat arrived in Finland by 5300 BC, then to the Balkans circa 4000 BC as the first sign of agriculture in the region. Buckwheat is called "*grechka*" in Russian and Ukrainian, meaning *Greek*, due to its introduction in those regions by the Byzantine Greeks.

In the northeastern United States, buckwheat was a common crop in the 18th and 19th centuries. More than 1,000,000 acres were harvested in the United States in 1918. Cultivation declined sharply in the 20th century due to commercial use of nitrogen fertilizer, which maize and wheat thrived on. In 1954, production had declined to 150,000 acres; by 1964, production was only 50,000 acres. However, an "explosion in popularity of ancient grains" increased domestic production from 2009–2014.

Unlike grains from the grass family, Buckwheat contains all eight essential amino acids in excellent proportions—including lysine. Accordingly, buckwheat is a surprisingly rich source of protein. One cup of buckwheat delivers 23 grams of high-quality protein. Buckwheat contains riboflavin (vitamin B_2), niacin (vitamin B_3), phosphorus, zinc, iron, calcium, potassium, selenium, copper, magnesium, and manganese. Each of these minerals plays a significant role in health. Copper is required for red blood cell production. Magnesium relaxes blood vessels, lowers blood pressure, and serves as a cofactor for more than 300 enzymes, including those involved in the body's use of glucose and insulin secretion. Manganese supports bone and skin health, as well as critical biochemical processes.

A glucoside called rutin, a phytochemical that strengthens capillary walls, is found in buckwheat. One clinical study showed mixed results in the treatment of chronic venous insufficiency. Buckwheat contains D-chiro-inositol, a component of the secondary messenger pathway for insulin signal transduction found deficient in type 2 diabetes and polycystic ovary syndrome. It is being studied for use in treating type 2 diabetes. High-protein buckwheat flour is being investigated for possible use as a functional ingredient in foods to reduce plasma cholesterol, body fat, and cholesterol gallstones.[37, 38, 39]

One cup of buckwheat delivers 68% of the recommended daily fiber intake (for a 2,000 calorie a day diet), substantially inhibiting the rate of glucose absorption, which is essential for maintaining balanced blood sugar levels. The fiber content provided by one serving of buckwheat represents 300% of the fiber found in an equivalent serving of quinoa.

Groats from buckwheat are commonly used in Western Asia and Eastern Europe. Roasted groats cooked with broth to a texture like rice or bulgur made porridge, a typical and definitive peasant dish. The dish was brought to America by Ukrainian, Russian, and Polish immigrants who called it *kasha*. They mixed it with pasta or used it as a filling for cabbage rolls, knishes, and blintzes; hence buckwheat prepared in this fashion is most commonly called "kasha" in America. The groats can also be sprouted and eaten raw or cooked.

Buckwheat pancakes, sometimes raised with yeast, are known as buckwheat *blinis* in Russia and *galettes* in France. Similar pancakes were an ordinary food in American pioneer days. The buckwheat flour gives them an earthy, mildly mushroom-like taste.

Adverse Reactions

Buckwheat can be a potent allergen for some individuals; buckwheat can provoke IgE-mediated anaphylaxis. Cases of anaphylaxis induced by buckwheat ingestion have been reported in Korea, Japan, and Europe, where it is more often described as a "hidden allergen."

Light sensitivity, called "fagopyrism," can result from the fagopyrin in buckwheat. The symptoms are a rash on exposure to sunlight. The leaves of buckwheat contain far more fagopyrin than the grain. This condition primarily occurs in animals that graze on buckwheat and in individuals who eat large amounts of buckwheat sprouts or drink buckwheat sprout juice.

Beans

There are over one thousand varieties of beans (also known as pulses or legumes), and three main types of beans; snap, shell and dry. Some of the "Baby Boomer generation" may have earned summer money by picking pole or snap beans. No doubt, the pickers participated in bean fights as the season wore on. Beans were discovered to have existed 20,000 years ago. Lima and pinto beans were cultivated by Mexican and Peruvian civilizations more than 7,000 years ago. As these people migrated to North America, they brought beans with them. Spanish explorers, in turn, introduced beans to Europe in the 1500s. From there, the Spanish and Portuguese traders carried beans into Africa and Asia.

The United States is currently the sixth largest producer of dry beans after Brazil, India, China, Burma, and Mexico. The top producing states are North Dakota and Michigan.

There are several species of beans, all of which provide proteins, carbohydrates, dietary fiber, vitamins, minerals, and phenolic compounds. More recently, the complexity of phytochemical components has expanded, including the role of anti-nutritional factors in nutrient bioavailability and immune responses. Experimental and clinical studies have shown that the consumption of beans results in less food consumption, control of body weight, and improved metabolic biochemical parameters.[40]

In terms of safe and healthy food, beans play a relevant role. The bean species of *Phaseolus vulgaris* L. is the most consumed legume worldwide in both poor and developed countries. *Phaseolus vulgaris* stands out in this arena as a vital source of protein, vitamins, essential minerals, soluble fiber, starch, and phytochemicals, plus being low in fat.[41, 42]

Great Northern, pinto, garbanzo, peas, and lentils benefit your health. Nutritionally, beans count both as a vegetable and a protein source. They are rich in fiber (soluble and insoluble) and help promote bowel regularity, lower cholesterol and blood pressure, and reduce cancer risk. Beans are an excellent source of potassium, folate, magnesium, manganese, molybdenum, and thiamine.

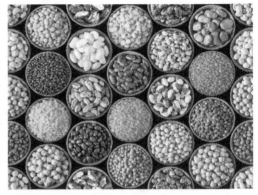

Research shows that those who eat beans regularly, more so than other foods, seem to live longer regardless of ethnicity. Europeans have been eating beans for centuries, and many diverse and tasty dishes reflect various cultures. According to the 1999-2002 *National Health Survey*, bean-eaters were less likely to be obese. There is also conclusive data linking bean consumption and heart health. One study that followed 16,000 middle-aged men for 25 years showed that higher bean consumption resulted in a lower risk for heart disease by an astounding 82%.[43, 44]

The consumption of beans is also associated with reducing breast cancer in postmenopausal women. For those with type 2 diabetes, beans are beneficial for lowering and controlling blood sugars due to their fiber content. The daily recommendation for fiber intake for a person with diabetes is 50 grams.

Dark beans, like black beans, are rich in antioxidants called *anthocyanins,* which are also found in grapes, blueberries, cherries, and cranberries. Of the top twenty antioxidant foods, four of them are beans. Beans have been prescribed as a remedy for constipation for centuries. If you are one of the unfortunate ones who suffer from flatulence, you may have avoided this healthy food group. In our family, we have found that soaking dry beans with 1-2 tablespoons of baking soda for twenty-four hours, then rinse and cook on the stove top, instant pot or can in glass jars in a pressure canner, make beans a fast and gas-free food.[45, 46, 47] For more on beans see Our Journey with Food Cookery Book pg. 22-24, 119-134

Ways to Improve the Digestibility of Beans

To help your digestive system adjust to beans and reduce flatulence, start slowly by cooking them in a stainless-steel pressure pan or Instant Pot® and consume small amounts such as a ¼-½ cup serving.[48] Gas is often the result of introducing fiber into a gut that is used to working without it. The necessary bacterium needed to properly ferment and digest the starches found in the fiber-rich food take time to develop and populate. Products like Beano® and digestive enzymes help break down fiber and protein, which reduces gas and discomfort.[49, 50, 51]

<u>It is worth the effort to cook whole beans properly. Do not compromise your health with improperly cooked canned beans.</u>

Lectins

What are "lectins," and why should you pay attention to them? Lectins are a protein that can bind to cell membranes. Lectins offer a way for molecules, especially sugars, to stick together without involving the immune system, which can influence cell-to-cell interaction. Lectins can bind specific carbohydrates in glyco-complexes. Lectins have been used in many biological fields as a protein-carbohydrate exchange.[52]

Lectins are abundant in raw legumes (beans, peas, alfalfa, peanut, lentils) and grains, commonly found in the seed part, which then becomes the leaves when planted. Additionally, lectins are found in dairy products and some vegetables. While lectin content in food is usually relatively constant, genetic modification has created fluctuations in many legumes and grass grains such as soy, alfalfa, wheat, corn, and rice.

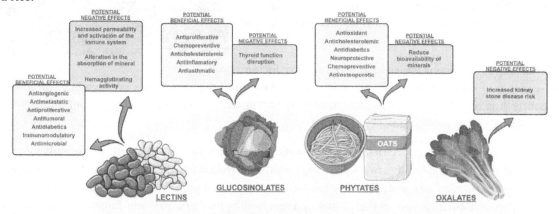

López-Moreno, M., Garcés-Rimón, M., & Miguel, M. (2022). Antinutrients: Lectins, goitrogens, phytates and oxalates, friends or foe? Journal of Functional Foods, 89, 104938. https://doi.org/10.1016/j.jff.2022.104938

In plants, lectins are a defense against microorganisms, pests, and insects. The evolution of lectin formation in plants allows the vital chemistry of seeds to remain intact as they pass through the digestive systems of animals. Lectins are resistant to human digestion, especially in today's world of the compromised digestive microbiome, and they enter the bloodstream unchanged. Any food component that passes through the digestive lining unaltered into the bloodstream jeopardizes our health.[53]

Are lectins bad?

"In 1988, a hospital launched a 'healthy eating day' in its staff canteen at lunchtime. One dish contained red kidney beans, and 31 portions were served. At 3 p.m., one of the customers, a surgical registrar, vomited in the theatre. Over the next four hours, ten more customers suffered profuse vomiting, some with diarrhea. All had recovered by the next day. No pathogens were isolated from the food, but the beans contained an abnormally high concentration of the lectin *phytohaemagglutinin*."[54]

In a study with rats, researchers at Penn State College of Medicine found that after ingesting paraquat, a once widely used herbicide banned in the U.S. since 2007, along with lectins -- sugar-binding proteins found widely in nature -- the animals developed Parkinsonism. The researchers were able to track the formation and spread of a misfolded protein called *alpha-synuclein*, which previous research has linked with Parkinson's disease. Lectins, used in medications to help deliver substances into the brain or stomach, have also been associated with certain rare forms of Parkinsonism. But the researchers weren't sure if the lectins were causing Parkinsonism or helping different substances get into the body that triggered the symptoms.[55]

A National Institutes of Health report published in the *British Medical Journal* in April 1999 provides valuable information on the validity of reducing lectins in your diet. "Lectins are carbohydrate-binding proteins present in most plants, especially seeds and tubers like cereals, potatoes, and beans. Until recently, their main use was as histology and blood transfusion reagents, but in the past two decades we have realized that many lectins are (a) toxic, inflammatory, or both; (b) resistant to cooking and digestive enzymes; and (c) present in much of our food. It is thus no surprise that they sometimes cause "food poisoning." However, the alarming finding came with the discovery in 1989 that some food lectins get past the gut wall and deposit themselves in distant organs."[56]

Winter is when conditions like seasonal affective disorder (SAD), reduced immunity, and chronic inflammation increase. Winter is the time of year we are most likely to feel our worst mentally and physically, and increasingly tempted by comfort food. A review published in *Nutrients* in March 2013 describes lectins as "anti-nutrients" and a leading contributor to many health challenges." Inflammation is the innate immune system response triggered by noxious stimuli, microbial pathogens, and injury. When a trigger remains or when immune cells are continuously activated, an inflammatory response may become self-sustainable and chronic. Chronic inflammation has been associated with many medical and psychiatric disorders, including cardiovascular disease, metabolic syndrome, cancer, autoimmune diseases, schizophrenia, and depression."[57, 58, 59, 60]

Our understanding of the C-type lectin-like receptors (CTLRs) and their functions in immunity has continued to expand from their initial roles in pathogen recognition. There are now clear examples of CTLRs acting as scavenger receptors, cell death and cell transformation sensors, and regulators of immune responses and homeostasis.[61] Traditional Chinese Medicine (TCM) research has examined the water extract of *Artemisia argyi* leaves that selectively inhibited the podoplanin-induced platelet aggregation. Tumor cell-induced platelet aggregation (TCIPA) is a mechanism that protects tumor cells in circulation and the promotion of tumor cell invasion and metastases. The C-type lectin-like receptor 2 (CLEC-2) binds podoplanin (PDPN) on the platelet surface and facilitates the TCIPA.[62] Lectins were valued in TCM for reducing tumor formation through eating traditional foods containing C-type lectin.

Regarding lectins, the research is not as straightforward as we might hope. Chronic inflammatory and auto-immune conditions may be "too much of a good thing" when lectins are combined with agricultural biotechnology, resulting in heightened inflammation. When we utilize traditional gastronomy approaches, lectins (like other antinutrients) may become our friend, not our foe.[63]

> ***Principle 37:*** Fiber is your friend. It feeds the gut microbiome, detoxifies and reduces illnesses.

Popcorn, The Fun Fiber

Our family has always reached for the economical and fun popcorn as a snack. Long before bags of chips, we had popcorn. Popcorn's popularity is not limited to the United States. Today, snacking in Western countries contributes to one-third of daily calorie-dense intake, with many snacks consisting of energy-dense and nutrient-poor foods. Choices about snacking are affected by many individual, social, and environmental factors. Social norms, for example, that emphasize healthful eating are likely to increase the intake of nutrient-rich snacks. In addition, satiety, the feeling of fullness that persists after eating, is a critical factor in suppressing overconsumption, which can lead to overweight and obesity.

Aflatoxins are secondary metabolites produced mainly by the molds *Aspergillus flavus, A. parasiticus,* and *A. nomius.* They contaminate cereals, dry fruits, oilseeds, and spices. Aflatoxins harm animals and humans, inducing vomiting, diarrhea, hepatitis, cirrhosis, immunosuppression, miscarriages, and mutagenic and teratogenic effects, resulting in different cancers. Popcorn (*Zea mays everta*) is a cereal susceptible to aflatoxin contamination, and there are no reports about the risk of its consumption. A study released in 2020 did a random sampling of 30 popcorn samples from 253 surveys on the frequency of popcorn consumption.

> **Results**: Aflatoxins were found in 47% of the 30 samples. The results show that 9.5% of the consumers of AFB1-contaminated popcorn are at risk, and 52.2% are at risk for total aflatoxin exposure. Popcorn is accessible to children with lower weight, increasing the risk.[64]

Acrylamide, a probable human carcinogen, can be produced via the Maillard reaction between asparagine and reducing sugars at high temperatures during food processing. Acrylamide is a known neurotoxic compound for humans. One of the food products containing acrylamide is popcorn. Popcorn is a vital source of snacks for children, especially students. Microwaved popcorn contains lower amounts of acrylamide than other methods of preparation. Meta-regression data analysis shows the type of popcorn also influences the amount of acrylamide. It was found that sweet popcorn contains higher amounts of acrylamide. The overall value of acrylamide concentration in popcorn was calculated to be 459.6 ±220.3 μg/kg.[65] A study in 2022 looked at industrial and traditional popcorn sold in Tehran, Iran, in the spring of 2021. Industrial popcorn is popcorn that has a manufacturing license from the health authorities. Retailers in entertainment centers sell traditional popcorn. The amount of acrylamide ranged from non-detectable up to 14.8 mg/kg. Acrylamide was detected in 86% of samples. A significant difference was observed between industrial and traditional popcorn samples.[66] Whether these differences between Industrial and home-prepared popcorn were due to the oil, cookware, and/or type and duration of heat during preparation remain unanswered questions.

Chapter 8 ~ Fiber & Fat Overlooked and Under Appreciated

You may be avoiding popcorn based on recommendations from a provider due to diverticular disease concerns. A 2020 study debunked this myth about popcorn. The role of diet in preventing diverticular disease has long been debated, however a high-fiber diet appears to decrease the likelihood of symptomatic diverticulitis.

> The myth of avoiding nuts, corn, popcorn, and seeds to prevent episodes of diverticulitis has been debunked with current data. Overall, the "diverticulitis diets" recommendations mirror those for a healthy lifestyle – high fiber, focusing on whole grains, fruits, and vegetables.[67]

A Little History and Fun

Biblical accounts of "corn" stored in the pyramids of Egypt reference other grains such as barley. The word "corn" was commonly used to refer to various European grains, such as wheat, barley, and rye. In Scotland and Ireland, the term "corn" referred to oats. Maize was the ordinary American corn.

The first use of wild and early cultivated corn was believed to be popping. Archeologists have found traces of popcorn in 1,000-year-old Peruvian tombs.[68] The oldest ears of popcorn ever seen were discovered in the Bat Cave of west central New Mexico in 1948 and 1950, ranging in size from a penny to about 2 inches; the oldest Bat Cave ears are about 4,000 years old. According to archaeologists, 7,000-year-old maize husks found at archaeological sites in Peru and Mexico are the remnants of ancient indigenous peoples 'popcorn preparations and consumption.[69] Aztecs and Mayans are thought to have used popcorn in Central America and Mexico, and the Incans are supposed to have used it in South America. Before the Americas were discovered, it was common in parts of India, China, and Sumatra. By the time Columbus discovered the Caribbean Islands (the start of colonial period 1492-1773), popcorn had grown in more than 700 countries of the ancient world.[70] Leif Ericsson's landing in North America was five centuries prior to Columbus (history.com). Since archaeologists discovered popcorn, we can safely consider it the first snack food.

Popcorn was integral to early 16th century Aztec Indian ceremonies. In 1519, Cortes first saw popcorn when he invaded Mexico and encountered the Aztecs. Writings of Peruvian Indians in 1650, the Spaniard Cobo says, "They toast a certain kind of corn until it bursts. They call it *pisancalla*, and they use it as a confection."

The moldboard plow became commonplace in the mid-1800s and led to the widespread planting of maize in the United States. Popcorn was very popular from the 1890s until the Great Depression. Street vendors used to follow crowds around, pushing steam or gas-powered poppers through fairs, parks, and expositions.

According to the Popcorn Board website, "Charles Cretors, founder of C. Cretors and Company in Chicago, introduced the world's first mobile popcorn machine at the World's Columbian Exposition in Chicago in 1893." Scientific American reported:

> 'This machine ... was designed to move to any location where the operator would likely do a good business. The apparatus, which is light and strong and weighing but 400 or 500 pounds, can be drawn readily by a boy or by a small pony to any picnic ground, fair, political rally, etc., and to many other places where a good business could be done for a day or two.'

Popcorn at 5 to 10 cents a bag was among the few luxuries down-and-out families could afford. During the Great Depression, the popcorn business thrived while other companies failed. A slump did happen during the early 1950s with the arrival of television. Attendance at movie theaters dropped and with it popcorn consumption; a new relationship between television and popcorn was formed.

Many of us have fond memories of making Jiffy Pop®. Developed in 1958 by Frederick C. Mennen of LaPorte, Indiana, Jiffy Pop® made it big in the 1970s when the stage magician Henri Bouton Fils, better known as Harry Blackstone, Jr., was endorsing the television commercial jingle "the magic treat—as much fun to make as it is to eat."[71]

Did you know that microwave popcorn was the first use of microwave heating in the 1940s? Percy Spencer of Raytheon Manufacturing Corporation® figured out how to mass produce magnetrons to generate microwaves for service in World War II. Looking for post-war applications of Raytheon technology, Spencer spurred the development of the microwave oven. Popcorn was vital to many of Spencer's experiments.

The first patent for a microwave popcorn bag was issued to General Mills® in 1981, and home popcorn consumption increased by tens of thousands of pounds in the years following. According to the National Popcorn Board, about 17 billion quarts of popcorn are popped yearly in the United States. That's about 54 quarts for every man, woman, and child. The average American eats about six quarts of popped popcorn per year. Nebraska is the most productive state regarding crop production, with neighboring states such as Illinois, Indiana, Kansas, Michigan, Missouri, and Ohio rounding out the top six producers of 90% of the unpopped popcorn for consumers' use at home.

According to the non-GMO shopping guide, available for free at www.nongmoshoppingguide.com, there is no GMO popcorn.[72]

Our family likes to sit outdoors on a summer night, hang a sheet on the shop wall and use the projector to screen movies while we enjoy our organic buttered popcorn. Sort of like the ol 'fashioned drive-in, but better.

Fat

Growing evidence shows that nutrition can positively and negatively modulate the toxic effects of pollutant exposure. Diets high in pro-inflammatory fats, such as linoleic acid, can exacerbate pollutant toxicity, whereas diets rich in bioactive and anti-inflammatory food components, including omega-3 fatty acids and polyphenols, can attenuate toxicant-associated inflammation. How is it that our ancestors consumed large quantities of high-fat foods for centuries and never fell victim to the health challenges of

Chapter 8 ~ Fiber & Fat Overlooked and Under Appreciated

current generations? To answer this, we must look at the lifestyle, food, and preparation methods commonly used by past generations. The foods they consumed came from their garden or local farms. They sometimes had periods of fasting or calorie reduction due to weather, income, and harvest, too. The terms "processed" and "organic" were unheard of; everything from condiments to the main course was made from scratch.

Lifestyle and environmental factors have also dramatically changed over time. Every human in history must deal with some stress and trauma, but today we suffer from background stressors we may not even be fully aware of, such as noise pollution, electromagnetic fields (EMF), and artificial light. In addition to our modern food preparation and farming practices, these stressors contribute to the growing variety of chronic health challenges we now face.

Many believe that people live much longer now than they used to, which is true, but what has changed is childhood life expectancy. Because more infants and children survive to adulthood, the average adult reflects a longer life expectancy. Americans are only living 5 to 7 years longer than they did 100 years ago.[73] And many now consume more plastic and petroleum byproducts than wholesome natural foods.

The next question is, do those years represent an increase in the quality of life or only in quantity? The American lifestyle has dramatically changed over the past century; we are now primarily a sedentary society which consumes, on average, 900-2,500 more calories daily than we can burn. And when did we begin to develop intrinsic deficiencies requiring cholesterol-lowering medications? I'm convinced that an excess of highly processed synthetic fats and devitalized foods combined with widespread medical misconceptions regarding the role of cholesterol in the body have led to the overuse of cholesterol-lowering medications.

Over the past few decades, most Americans replaced so-called "bad" saturated fats from animal and plant sources with polyunsaturated fats like corn, cottonseed, sunflower, and canola oil. Today these oils are predominately from GMO crops, are loaded with chemicals, and are processed at high temperatures with chemical solvents. These highly processed oils have been shown to elevate prostaglandin, along with two chemical markers in the bloodstream that exacerbate inflammation and increase cancer risk.[74, 75] In current studies reviewed for this book's revision, these oils were found to initially cause cholesterol levels to decrease, while increasing markers for inflammation, diabetes, liver enzyme dysfunction, and cancer.

Fat is the generic term for fats (solid) and oils (liquid) in foods. All fats are triglycerides composed of mixtures of saturated, unsaturated, and polyunsaturated fatty acids. Fatty acids are the building blocks of fat. Two of these fatty acids are required in the diet, making them essential fatty acids: *linolenic acid* and *alpha-linolenic acid*. These fats are commonly found in cold water fish such as Alaska salmon, free-range grass-fed beef and poultry, wild game, and high-quality omega-3 oil supplements.

Fat is necessary to add flavor and moisture to the diet. It is a crucial macronutrient for energy, brain function, hormonal balance, nerve development, insulation, and weight control. For the past thirty years, Americans have been led to believe (by the media and those who have the most to gain financially) that fat is wrong and that a carbohydrate diet is heart-healthy and better for you. Instead, we have replaced healthy fats like coconut oil, olive oil and yes, real butter and eggs, with highly processed fats that metabolize into prostaglandin 2 (found in polyunsaturated, hydrogenated omega-6 vegetable oils), an inflammation driver that leads to heart disease, high cholesterol, type 2 diabetes, and inflammatory illnesses such as arthritis, gout, fibromyalgia, and maybe dementia.

In 2018, one of the most extensive systematic assessments of the effects of omega-6 fats on cardiovascular health, mortality, blood lipid profiles, and adiposity was completed using unpublished data. No evidence was found that increasing omega-6 fats reduces cardiovascular outcomes other than myocardial infarction (MI). Although the benefits of omega-6 fats remain proven, increasing omega-6 fats may only benefit people at high risk of MI. Increased omega-6 fats reduce total serum cholesterol but not other blood fat fractions or adiposity.[76] Plant-based diets (PBDs) are increasingly popular. Thus far, the literature has focused on their association with lipid profiles, with less investigation of lipoprotein and inflammatory profiles. Because pro-atherogenic lipid, lipoprotein, and inflammatory processes may facilitate the development of atherosclerosis, understanding the relation between PBDs and these processes is essential to inform risk mitigation strategies.[77]

No longer is it advisable to render your fats from poultry, beef and pork, primarily due to the commercial use of large quantities of antibiotics, petroleum, and hormone-disrupting chemicals in the industrial production of these meats; both animals and humans store these substances in body fat. Humans are omnivores, thus we are designed to consume natural fats in eggs, flesh, and plant foods. Fat provides energy and insulation, slowing the conversion of carbohydrates like rice, corn, bread, sugar, dairy, and potatoes to glucose (sugar). This gives the pancreas time to determine how much insulin the body needs. By keeping these two chemicals in check with healthy "real" fats, the human body can control inflammation, which is the root cause of degenerative illnesses like type 2 diabetes and heart disease.

Fat has been considered the enemy of good nutrition, but it boasts several potential health benefits when included in a healthy diet. In the September 2014 issue of *Food Technology* magazine, published by the Institute of Food Technologists (IFT), Linda Milo Ohr wrote about how fatty acids and nutritional oils may benefit cognition, weight management, heart health, mood, and eye and brain development.

Here are some of the benefits of fat:

- Omega-3 fatty acids: Associated with brain development, cognition, eye health, dementia, heart health, and depression.
- Pinolenic acid: Based on pine nut oil derived from a Korean pine tree, is rich in long-chain fatty acids, suppressing appetite and promoting a feeling of fullness.
- Conjugated linoleic acid: Weight management.
- Hemp oil: Contains a balanced ratio of omega-6 and omega-3 linolenic essential fatty acids and also includes vitamin E. *(Clients who are regularly drug tested should be alerted they may have a false positive test if consuming hemp foods. While unlikely, "better safe than sorry.")*[78, 79]
- Fish oil: Beneficial effects on cardiovascular, neurological, and cognitive health.
- Coconut oil: Aids in energy production, skin and dental health.[80]

> ***Principle 38:*** Fat is necessary in a healthy diet, but all fats are not created equal.

Von Willebrand - Being Aware

Over the years, I have learned to pay attention to clients with rapid heart rates when recommending omega-3, -6 and -9 oil supplements. Besides being a source of blood-thinning nutrients like vitamins E and C, fish oils can be a problem for individuals with "thin" blood. If clients take a daily blood thinner medication or have a history of mitral valve prolapse, tachycardia, or arrhythmias, be aware of blood thinning nutrients, enzymes, herbs, and hormones (such as progesterone) which can worsen the client's situation. Using proteolytic enzymes and non-steroidal anti-inflammatory drugs (NSAIDs) can start noticeable trouble for individuals who do not know their family history for being "easy" bleeders. NSAIDs, in particular their over-the-counter versions, break down necessary blood clotting proteins.[81]

According to the National Heart, Lung, and Blood Institute, Von Willebrand disease (VWD) is a bleeding disorder affecting blood clotting ability. Von Willebrand is a condition inherited from a parent.[82, 83] Heavy and hard-to-stop bleeding may occur in the affected person if blood doesn't clot after an injury. The bleeding can damage internal organs, and microbleeds can create joint damage and inflammation. Most people with von Willebrand are born with it, though its warning signs may not show for years. Some people may suspect a bleeding disorder when they have heavy bleeding after a dental procedure or, for women, during a menstrual period.[84]

General Symptoms
Many people with von Willebrand disease don't know it because the signs are mild or absent. The most common symptom of the condition is abnormal bleeding. The severity of the bleeding varies from one person to another.

If you have von Willebrand disease, you might experience:
- Excessive bleeding from an injury or after surgery or dental work
- Nosebleeds that don't stop within 10 minutes
- Heavy or prolonged menstrual bleeding
- Blood in your urine or stool
- Easy bruising or lumpy bruises

Signs and Symptoms of von Willebrand in Women
Signs and symptoms of a heavy period that may indicate von Willebrand disease include:
- The presence of blood clots in your menstrual flow more significant than 1 inch (2.5 centimeters) in diameter.
- The need to change your menstrual pad or tampon more often than hourly.
- The need to use double sanitary protection to control menstrual flow.
- Symptoms of anemia including tiredness, fatigue, or shortness of breath.

Principle 39: Use fish oil and omega 3 and 6 oil supplements with care.

Olive Oil

The olive-oil-centered Mediterranean diet has been associated with extended life expectancy and reduced risk of age-related degenerative diseases. Extra virgin olive oil (EVOO) itself has been proposed to promote "successful aging," being able to virtually modulate all the features of the aging process because of its great monounsaturated fatty acids content and its minor bioactive compounds, the polyphenols above all.[85] Extra virgin olive oil (EVOO), a popular functional food and a major source of fat in the Mediterranean diet possesses a variety of healthful components, including monounsaturated fatty acids and bioactive phenolic compounds that, individually and collectively, exert beneficial effects on cardiometabolic markers of health and act as neuroprotective agents through their anti-inflammatory and antioxidant activities. The gut microbiota and health of the intestinal environment are now considered essential factors in the development of obesity, metabolic disease, and even certain neurodegenerative conditions via the gut-brain axis.[86] There is increasing evidence that a diet rich in EVOO is linked to a significant reduction in the diversity of gut microbiome (GM), causing a switch from predominant bacteria to a more protective group of bacteria.[87]

The biological activity of polyphenols is strongly related to their antioxidant properties. They tend to reduce the pool of reactive oxygen species (aka: free radicals) and to neutralize potentially carcinogenic metabolites. The broad spectrum of health-promoting properties of plant polyphenols comprises antioxidant, anti-inflammatory, anti-allergic, anti-atherogenic, anti-thrombotic, and anti-mutagenic effects. Scientific studies present the ability of polyphenols to modulate the human immune system by affecting the proliferation of white blood cells and the production of cytokines or other factors that participate in the immunological defense.[88]

Oxysterols, the oxidized products of cholesterol present in cholesterol-containing foodstuffs, have been shown to exert pro-oxidant and pro-inflammatory effects, altering the intestinal epithelial layer and thus contributing to the pathogenesis of human inflammatory bowel diseases and colon cancer. Polyphenols in extra virgin olive oil possess antioxidant and anti-inflammatory properties and concentrate in the intestinal lumen, which may help prevent intestinal diseases. Study results from 2018 suggest a protective effect of extra virgin olive oil polyphenols at the intestinal level, helping to avoid or limit redox unbalance and the onset and progression of chronic intestinal inflammation.[89]

Research has been accumulating on olive oil's health-protective properties. EVOO presents several protective effects on the liver, reducing hepatic steatosis, hepatocyte ballooning, fibrogenesis, and preventing lipid peroxidation, among other effects. Due to its high levels of monounsaturated fatty acids, mainly oleic acid and phenolic compounds, such as hydroxytyrosol and oleuropein, EVOO can participate in the activation of different signaling hepatocyte pathways involved in the prevention of inflammation, oxidative stress, endoplasmic reticulum stress, mitochondrial dysfunction, and insulin resistance, allowing the prevention or resolution of liver damage.[90] The phytonutrient components in olive oil are effective against breast cancer cells, and studies suggest the abundance of olive oil in the Mediterranean way of eating may account for why the diet helps prevent depression.[91]

Recently, scientists have discovered that phenolic compounds in olive oil directly repress genes linked to inflammation.[92, 93] A research team took blood samples after meals to check for the expression of over 15,000 human genes. The results? The high phenol olive oil impacted the regulation of almost 100 genes, many of which have been linked to obesity, high blood fat levels, type 2 diabetes, and heart disease.[94, 95]

> "We identified 98 differentially expressed genes when comparing the intake of phenol-rich olive oil with low-phenol olive oil. Several of the repressed genes are known to be involved in pro-inflammatory processes, suggesting that the diet can switch the activity of immune system cells to a less deleterious inflammatory profile, as seen in metabolic syndrome," Dr. Perez-Jimenez said in a statement to the press. "These findings strengthen the relationship between inflammation, obesity, and diet and provide evidence at the most basic level of healthy effects derived from virgin olive oil consumption in humans." The ability of olive oil's phenolic compounds to reduce or prevent inflammation also provides a molecular basis for the reduction of heart disease observed in Mediterranean countries, where virgin olive oil represents a primary source of dietary fat.[96]

These findings could be especially important in halting the dangerous effects of metabolic syndrome. Characterized by excess abdominal fat, high cholesterol, high blood pressure, and high blood glucose levels, metabolic syndrome is linked to type 2 diabetes, heart disease, and early death.

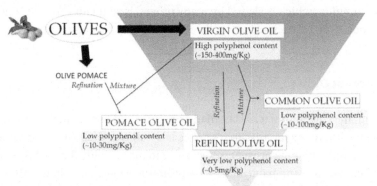

Gorzynik-Debicka, M., Przychodzen, P., Cappello, F., Kuban-Jankowska, A., Marino Gammazza, A., Knap, N., Wozniak, M., & Gorska-Ponikowska, M. (2018). Potential Health Benefits of Olive Oil and Plant Polyphenols. International journal of molecular sciences, 19(3), 686. https://doi.org/10.3390/ijms19030686

But the next time you reach for a bottle of extra virgin olive oil, beware. A study from the University of California-Davis found more than two-thirds of imported extra virgin olive oil bottles are not what they seem. To be classified as extra virgin, olive oil can't be rancid or doctored with lesser oils. The fruit must be a perfect size, color, and ripeness. When UC-Davis's lab tested the most common 14 brands, all of them failed one or more trials, showing sophisticated adulteration practice of olive oil are worldwide. The lab can identify defects, degradation, and dilution in olive oil beyond what human taste buds can detect. Often, olive oil is cut or blended with other oils like hazelnut, soybean, sunflower, and different types of oil. There is no legal definition in the U.S. for grades of olive oil, but mounting concern over truth-in-olive-oil-labeling has drawn in the USDA. Since October 2010, regulations have conformed to international standards. Olive oil from every olive oil-producing country, including the U.S., is subject to random sampling off retail shelves.

Over 60% of the brain is made up of cholesterol; all of our hormones, too. Without healthy fats in our diet, the liver must make cholesterol to meet the body's needs for these essential components. There is a direct correlation between lower cholesterol and increases in depression, impaired immune function, muscle weakness, and hormone imbalances. All-natural oils have health benefits when fresh and free from heavy metal contamination. So whether or not you are of Mediterranean descent, take up the fun of olive oil tasting.

Many consumers believe that manufacturers 'proclamations of "fat-free," "no trans-fats," "heart healthy," and "zero cholesterol" equal "good for you." The corn industry and the companies that profit from such claims (McDonald's®, Coke®, Monsanto®, Cargill®, et al.) may be partly responsible for many of the modern health problems in America. The consumer must take their share of the blame also, however.

A local egg farmer, on average, receives 40 cents on every dollar of eggs sold. In contrast, a corn farmer only receives 2 cents on every dollar. According to Michael Pollan, in his book *The Omnivore's Dilemma*, most of the profit in food production goes to large companies like McDonald's and Coca-Cola. High fructose corn sweetener, only one of the hundreds of products made from #2 corn, is the leading cause of non-alcoholic fatty liver disease, obesity, and elevated cholesterols — not the healthy fats in natural foods like organic butter, eggs, meats, and fresh whole grains and vegetables.

My opinion, which is shared by many others, is that cholesterol is one of the most unfairly maligned and unnecessarily "treated" naturally occurring blood components in healthcare today.[97]

Coconut Oil

Initially, coconut oil was classified as a saturated fatty acid food item and criticized for its negative impact on health. However, research studies have shown that coconut oil is a rich source of medium-chain fatty acids, opening new prospects for its use in many fields. Those born in the 1940s or 1950s may remember when coconut and palm oil were in prepared foods. Then in the 1970s and 1980s, we were told these oils were terrible for us and a leading cause of heart disease. Before we knew it, new "healthy oils" were contained in our favorite foods; canola and soybean oils had taken over the market almost overnight.

The coconut provides a nutritious source of meat, juice, milk, and oil and has fed and nourished populations worldwide for generations. Nearly one-third of the world's population depends on coconut to some degree for their food and economy. In these cultures, the coconut has a long and respected history. Coconut is highly nutritious and rich in fiber, vitamins, and minerals. It is classified as a "functional food" because it provides many health benefits beyond its nutritional content.

In traditional medicine around the world, coconut is used to treat a wide variety of health problems, including abscesses, asthma, baldness, bronchitis, bruises, burns, colds, constipation, cough, dropsy, dysentery, earache, fever, flu, gingivitis, gonorrhea, irregular or painful menstruation, jaundice, kidney stones, lice, malnutrition, nausea, rash, scabies, scurvy, skin infections, sore throat, swelling, syphilis, toothache, tuberculosis, tumors, typhoid, ulcers, upset stomach, weakness, and wounds.

Some of these treatments may not be effective, but the jury is still out until the research is done.

Modern Health Uses

Published studies in medical journals show that coconut, in one form or another, may provide a broad range of health benefits. Some of these are summarized below. However, it is still unclear just how coconut oil kills many viruses and bacterium.

- Anti-parasitic, viral, bacterial, and fungal
- Improves digestion and absorption of nutrients, and insulin secretion and utilization of blood glucose
- Relieves pain and irritation caused by hemorrhoids
- Anti-inflammatory
- Helps prevent periodontal disease and tooth decay
- Reduces epileptic seizures
- Applied topically, forms a chemical barrier on the skin to ward off infection and reduces symptoms associated with psoriasis, eczema, and dermatitis
- It prevents wrinkles, sagging skin, and age spots; protection from ultraviolet radiation from the sun, and helps control dandruff

Medium-chain triglycerides (MCT) are naturally found in coconut oil, milk fat, and palm kernel oil. They are synthetically produced by esterification and interesterification reactions. Due to MCT's numerous health benefits, it is used as a functional or nutraceutical oil in various food and pharmaceutical formulations.[98] Medium-chain fatty acids (MCFA) can be used along with polyunsaturated fatty acids to increase their nutraceutical benefits and food applications to synthesize structured lipids. While much is debated about the role of MCT oil in human health and wellness, there is limited information on daily requirements, impact on specific population groups, and effects of long-term consumption. Coconut oil, due to its unique absorption and metabolism characteristics, has been used therapeutically since the 1950s in treating fat malabsorption, cystic fibrosis, epilepsy, weight control, and to increase exercise performance. In a study done on triglyceride levels in healthy men, researchers found that:

> "Medium-chain triglycerides are readily hydrolyzed in the intestines, and the fatty acids are transported directly to the liver via the portal venous system, in contrast to long-chain fatty acids (LCFA), which are incorporated into chylomicrons for transport through the lymphatic system or peripheral circulation. Medium-chain fatty acids (MCFA) do not require carnitine to cross the double mitochondrial membrane of the hepatocyte. Thus they quickly enter the mitochondria and undergo rapid beta-oxidation, whereas most LCFA are packaged into triglycerides in the hepatocyte. Mean triglyceride values after canola oil increased 47% above baseline. At the same time, mean triglyceride values after CT oil decreased 15% from the baseline, consistent with several other studies involving short- and longer-term feeding with MCT oil."[99]

Coconut oil is being promoted as a healthy oil with heart health benefits. Observational evidence suggests that consuming coconut flesh or squeezed coconut in traditional dietary patterns does not lead to adverse cardiovascular outcomes. However, these findings cannot be applied to a typical Western diet due to significant dietary and lifestyle pattern differences.[100] Butter and coconut oil, predominantly saturated fats, appear to have other effects on blood lipids. The impact of different dietary fats on lipid profiles, metabolic markers, and health outcomes vary not just according to the general classification of their main component fatty acids as saturated or unsaturated but possibly according to different profiles in individual fatty acids, processing methods, as well as the foods in which they are consumed or dietary patterns.[101] A 2022 meta-analysis review on coconut oil intake revealed no clinically relevant improvement in lipid profile and body composition compared to other oils/fats.[102, 103]

Avocado Oil

Avocado oil (AO) has antioxidants and anti-inflammatory effects. Researchers looked at the effects of avocado oil on insulin sensitivity, cognition, and inflammatory markers in 2022. These results suggest that AO supplementation has the potential to be an effective strategy for combating the effects of obesity.[104]

Avocados have thousands of years of traditional use and benefits; however, the extracted oil is relatively new. Avocados are native to South Central Mexico, with humans consuming them since around 5000 BC. Several traditional cultures in the New World enjoyed avocados for food, including the Aztecs, Incas, and Mayans. Since the flesh of an avocado is nearly one-third of oil, it seems inconceivable that food manufacturers only began mass-producing avocado oil for the world market in modern times.[105]

The extraction of fat from avocados is similar to olive oil. The resulting oil and water separate via a high-speed decanting centrifuge. Unrefined avocado oil retains the odor and taste of the fruit pulp from which it was extracted. It is also more nutritious than refined. Extra virgin avocado oil and cold-pressed avocado oil are both unrefined choices. These two avocado oils are optimal and widely available for cooking and salad dressings.

The oil is very similar to olive oil in that both contain high levels of oleic acid, a healthy monounsaturated omega-9 fat. Oleic acid has "a beneficial effect on cancer, autoimmune and inflammatory diseases, besides the ability to facilitate wound healing."[106] The saturated-to-monounsaturated fatty acid ratio affects the regulation of cell growth and differentiation. Alteration in this ratio has been implicated in various diseases, such as liver dysfunction and intestinal inflammation. In 2019, researchers found vitamin A deficiency increases the oleic acid levels in the kidney when a high fructose diet is consumed.[107] This again illustrates the need for a holistic, balanced approach to the diet to prevent vital nutrient deficiencies. Eight preliminary clinical studies suggest that avocado consumption helps support human cardiovascular health, weight management, and healthy aging.[108, 109]

Chapter 8 ~ Fiber & Fat Overlooked and Under Appreciated

> ***Principle 40:*** Epigenetic regulation in the body is related to what you eat.

An Alert from the World Health Organization

Canola oil is one of the world's most widely consumed vegetable oils, yet surprisingly little is known about its effects on health. I have always believed this oil would be found to be harmful to humans. <u>As of 2023, the following is hotly contested research</u>: A study published online in December 2017 in the *Journal Scientific Reports* by researchers at the Lewis Katz School of Medicine (LKSOM) at Temple University associates the consumption of canola oil in the diet with worsened memory, worsened learning ability, and weight gain in mice, which model Alzheimer's disease. The study is the first to suggest that canola oil is more harmful than healthful for the brain.

> "Canola oil is appealing because it is less expensive than other vegetable oils and advertised as healthy. Very few studies, however, have examined that claim, especially regarding the brain."[110]

Dr. Pratico's laboratory at LKSOM and the study's co-author focused their work on memory impairment and the formation of amyloid plaques and neurofibrillary tangles in Alzheimer's disease. Amyloid plaques and phosphorylated tau, responsible for the construction of tau neurofibrillary tangles, contribute to neuronal dysfunction and degeneration and memory loss in those with Alzheimer's disease. What may be a surprising connection between canola oil and Alzheimer's comes from research released in 2020 on gum bacteria. How canola oil affects the microbiome has yet to be thoroughly investigated.[111] Bacteria populating the gut microbiota can release significant amounts of amyloids and lipopolysaccharides, which might play a role in the modulation of signaling pathways and the production of proinflammatory cytokines related to the pathogenesis of Alzheimer's disease.[112, 113]

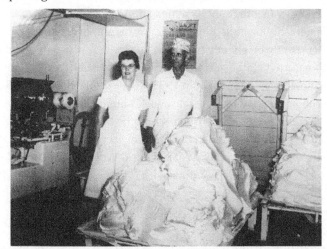

Virgi Fallon with fresh sweet butter before packaging.
Jerome Creamery, Idaho circ. 1960

The Cholesterol Question
by Soneil Guptha, MD, FACC, FESC

A disease (atherosclerosis) considered a scourge of modern civilization is not so modern after all. Researchers performed CT scans on 137 mummies and found plaques in all populations studied, from hunter-gatherers to the southwestern United States.[114] The same researcher, in his seminal publication, quoted from various sources. "Human remains from elite Chinese burials to Canadian Eskimos to Egyptian mummies have been reported to have vascular calcification," Professor Caleb Finch at the USC Davis School of Gerontology said. "The oldest individual may be the Tyrolean iceman, Ötzi, (and was discovered frozen in a glacier in the Italian Alps in 1991) as he's called, — 3000 BC, lived during the Copper Age, and both of his carotid arteries were calcified. He died because of a wound from a weapon, in addition to the wound multiple compounding conditions have been identified . But I think it's a robust conclusion that they're, at least in the last 10,000 years in the Neolithic era, people who have had some level of atherosclerosis. Although, it may not have been a major cause of death or disability."[115, 116, 117]

As cardiovascular disease (CVD) emerged as the prime cause of mortality in the 20th century in the Western world, Ancel Keys, a pioneering American Physiologist in 1947, conducted a prospective cohort study of 12,000 men aged 40-59 years from 18 areas of seven countries (Italy, Greek Islands, Yugoslavia, Netherlands, Finland, Japan, and the United States).[118] After 15 years of follow-up, the study confirmed the predictive value of heart attack to blood pressure, blood cholesterol, and cigarette smoking.[119] Keys and his colleagues determined that in societies where fat was a major component of every meal (i.e., the U.S. and Finland), the blood cholesterol levels and heart-attack death rates were highest. Conversely, blood cholesterol was low in cultures where diets were based on fresh fruit and vegetables, bread, pasta, and plenty of olive oil (i.e., the Mediterranean region), and heart attacks were rare.[120]

Historically it was Nikolai N. Anitschkow, an experimental pathologist born in 1885 from St. Petersburg, who in 1913 reported that simply feeding rabbits a high cholesterol diet (egg yolk dissolved in sunflower oil) can and did produce lesions duplicating atherosclerosis in human disease.[121] Sadly his "cholesterol hypothesis," which would currently be eligible for a Nobel Prize and was published in a reputable science journal, did not get attention until its English translation was published in 1983 despite his publishing a complete and comprehensive details of his work in 1933.[122, 123, 124] Earlier in 1938, Carl Muller demonstrated a link between hereditary heart disease in 17 families in Oslo, where xanthomatosis and hypercholesterolemia were common.[125] The problem could be that Anitschkow may have been far ahead of the times. The "cholesterol hypothesis" gained momentum 40 years later in the 1950s as metabolic studies from various researchers sparked interest after World War II. The Anitschkow dictum *"no atherosclerosis with cholesterol"* became synonymous with *"diet-cholesterol-heart disease theory/lipid hypothesis"* and the likely discovery of the Watanabe strain of rabbits in 1980 that have mutations of LDL-receptor genes with blood cholesterol levels over 600mg/dL.[126]

In the 1950s, higher disproportionate mortality rates with CVD prompted studies on the role of diet and CVD risk. By the 1960s, John Yudkin identified added sugar as the prominent agent, while Ancel Keys disagreed and identified fat as the primary agent for the risk of CVD.[127, 128] In 1965, a literature review sponsored by the Sugar Research Foundation (SRF) published in the *New England Journal of Medicine* singled out fat and cholesterol as the dietary causes of coronary heart disease (CHD). It downplayed evidence that sucrose consumption was also a risk factor. In 2016, an analysis of the SRF documents combined with documents from the sugar industry concluded that:[129]

> "(1) Because CHD is the leading cause of death globally, the health community should ensure that CHD risk is evaluated in future risk assessments of added sugars.
> (2) Policymaking committees should consider giving less weight to food industry–funded studies and include mechanistic and animal studies as well as studies appraising the effect of added sugars on multiple CHD biomarkers and disease development."[130]

Is Cholesterol Bad?

Cholesterol is an essential molecule in humans; its excess can cause disease, BUT its deficiency in circulation may result in an inability to distribute vitamins K and E to vital organs with serious consequences. Most clinicians appreciate cholesterol's role in stabilizing cellular plasma membranes, but there are other important biological functions that cholesterol serves.

- Cholesterol is a sterol synthesized by animal cells that regulates fluidity, permeability, and gene transcription.[131]

- Cholesterol serves as a molecule of regulation and forms the backbone of all steroid hormones and vitamin D analogs.[132]

- Cholesterol is responsible for growth and development throughout life and may be useful as an anticancer facilitator.[133]

Cholesterol is also a component of the diet, present in animal food, such as meat, fish, poultry, egg yolks, butter, cheese, and other dairy products made from whole milk.[134] Its primary function is to maintain the integrity and fluidity of cell membranes and to serve as a precursor for the synthesis of substances that are vital for the organism, including steroid hormones, bile acids, and vitamin D. Cholesterol undergoes metabolic conversion into oxygenated sterols (oxysterols).

Dysfunction in the metabolism and transport of cholesterol, sterol intermediates, and oxysterols occurs in various pathophysiological settings such as atherosclerosis, cancers, and neurodegenerative diseases.[135]

Although a high dietary cholesterol intake was considered a risk factor for cardiovascular diseases (CVD), recent evidence suggests that it does not significantly increase the levels of low-density lipoprotein cholesterol (LDL-C) in circulation. It is well known that ~75% of the LDL-cholesterol (the main ingredient of the atheromatous plaque) is produced by the liver.[136] Research from 2019 showed a surprising connection with the diurnal rhythm in the body. The relationship with the circadian system is still being investigated.[137]

What Is Good Cholesterol, Bad Cholesterol, and Their Applications?

Proteins called "lipoproteins" carry the cholesterol, triglycerides, and other remnants in our blood. These and many of their subgroups can be measured in the labs and helps healthcare providers understand their value/use in the body. Each lipoprotein contains a mixture of protein, cholesterol, and triglycerides in varying amounts. It should be recognized the triglycerides that make the major component of very low-density lipoprotein are a type of fat that our body uses for energy.[138,139]

For nutritionists, the following three subtypes of lipoproteins are important for dietary applications.

- LDL (low-density lipoprotein) cholesterol, sometimes called "bad" cholesterol, makes up most of your body's cholesterol. High levels of LDL cholesterol raise your risk for heart disease and stroke.

- HDL (high-density lipoprotein) cholesterol, sometimes called "good" cholesterol, absorbs cholesterol in the blood and carries it back to the liver. The liver then flushes it from the body. High HDL cholesterol levels can lower your risk for heart disease and stroke.

- VLDL (very low-density lipoprotein) cholesterol is made by the liver, is a prime carrier of triglycerides, and is like the LDL-cholesterol. It also contributes to the build up of the plaques (also called atherosclerosis) in the vascular system. This buildup is called "plaque," and it can cause health problems, such as heart attacks and strokes.

Dyslipidemia and Atherosclerosis

Primary disorders of lipid metabolism such as familial hypercholesterolemia (FH), chylomicronemia, familial combined hyperlipidemia, familial dysbetalipoproteinemia classify according to Fredrickson phenotype.[140]

Secondary dyslipidemia can result from diabetes mellitus, hypothyroidism, obstructive liver diseases, chronic renal failure, drugs that increase LDL-C including retinoids, cyclosporine A, and phenothiazines, and drugs that decrease HDL-C including progestins, androgens, beta-blockers, and anabolic steroids.

Based on the types of lipid abnormalities, dyslipidemias can be categorized into high total cholesterol (TC), high low-density lipoprotein cholesterol (LDL-C), high non-high-density lipoprotein cholesterol (non-HDL-C), high triglycerides (TG), and low high-density lipoprotein cholesterol (HDL-C). According to the Adult Treatment Panel III (ATP III), the standard levels per guidelines follow.[141]

- ➢ Fasting triglyceride level:
    - Normal: <150 mg/dL
    - Mild hypertriglyceridemia: 150 to 499 mg/dL
    - Moderate hypertriglyceridemia: 500 to 886 mg/dL
    - Very high or severe hypertriglyceridemia: >886 mg/dL

- LDL-C level:
  - Optimal: <100 mg/dL
  - Near optimal/above optimal: 100 to 129 mg/dL
  - Borderline high: 130 to 159 mg/dL
  - High: 160 to 189 mg/dL
  - Very high: >190 mg/dL

- HDL level:
  - Low: <40
  - High: equal to or >60

Dyslipidemia is multifactorial and related to poor glycemic control, insulin resistance, inflammation, and genetic susceptibility. Oxidative stress associated with type 2 diabetes can be implicated in insulin resistance, inflammation in neural tissues, and lipid metabolism disorders affecting cognitive dysfunction in diabetics. However, all the above-stated elements are beyond the scope of this chapter for nutritionists or for those interested in non-pharmacological/holistic/nutritional management of dyslipidemia.[142]

Principles of Holistic Nutrition or Integrative Management of Dyslipidemia

Nies LK and colleagues in 2006 reported that effective therapeutic options for lipid-lowering include intake of fiber, intake of plant stanols/sterols, replacement of animal protein with soy protein, and substitution of foods high in saturated fat with those with monounsaturated fatty acids (e.g., dry roasted almonds).[143] Adding omega-3 fatty acids is effective for reducing triglycerides in patients with hypertriglyceridemia. Well designed studies with long-term outcome data are necessary to further define the role for guggul, red yeast rice, policosanol, garlic, and flaxseed in the management of dyslipidemia.

Finally, an individual's other medical conditions and their medications are important variables in the consideration of any integrative approach to holistic nutrition.

For a good review and understanding of medicinal, edible plants, the reader may wish to browse a recent publication titled *Medicinal and edible plants in the treatment of dyslipidemia: advances and prospects*.[144] Carrie Dennett, MPH, RDN, CD, in her blog, suggests that nutraceuticals can be beneficial to integrate since nutraceuticals are fortified foods or supplements that can synergistically complement nutritional value. These could be artichoke leaf extract, berberine, bergamot, flaxseed, garlic, plant sterols, red yeast rice, soy foods, and fiber.[145]

A holistic and integrative approach or non-pharmacological management of dyslipidemia may be useful. It can be considered with careful attention to other medical conditions and their treatments in collaboration with the family or treating physician in the following circumstances.

- Those who are at low CV risk require minimal reduction in LDL or triglycerides.

- Those who are statin sensitive or have statin side effects and/or wish to reduce the dose of statins that they are being administered.

A diet that avoids trans fats entirely, limits saturated fats, and the complete avoidance of foods with high sugar or processed carbohydrates is an important step in nutritional counseling as are strategies to incorporate olive oil, nuts, avocado, beans, lentils, fruits and vegetables, and less reliance on commercial baked goods or snack foods along with exercise to increase HDL and burn the sugar/calorie consumed.

NOTE: A patient's additional medical conditions and medications are important variables when considering any integrative approach to holistic nutrition.

> ***Principle 41:*** Cholesterol does not have to be a "dirty" word.

Author's Reflection

The United States, unlike other countries, does not have a single, longstanding food tradition. Our food history is a "mulligan stew" where one nationality's dietary traditions blend into another's. We view food as fuel or substance; we only "eat to live." We look to government agencies, health professionals, diet books, television, and commercial food vendors to tell us what to eat. The result is fast food chains, processed foods, and no deep, abiding connection with food.

For many in the modern world, our senses of taste, smell, and texture are programmed to prefer processed and synthesized foods over the homegrown meals our mothers or grandparents prepared. Food preparation, by and large, focuses on convenience and is modeled after examples set by authors like Peg Bracken in the 1960s. The current trend for the millennial generation is even more concerning; research reveals this generation has moved into the world of consumer versus preparer.

Their lack of connection with traditional food preparation, unrefined oils, nutrient-dense grains, fiber-rich vegetables, and fruits has resulted in devastating health consequences at younger and younger ages. At this juncture in history, we must ask whether the price paid for this cultural change will be too great?

Additional studies[146]

1) A 2023 study examined the association between low-density lipoprotein cholesterol and sudden cardiac arrest (SCA) in people with diabetes. A total of 2,602,577 patients were included. The conclusions: Low LDL-cholesterol level can be a surrogate marker for increased risk of SCA in people with diabetes mellitus. This paradoxical association should be recognized and extended to clinical preventive measures.[147]

2) *Hellenic National Nutrition and Health Survey* (HNNHS) confirmed other studies' findings that eggs, a primary source of dietary cholesterol, do not increase the risk of dyslipidemia. Results were even better when fiber was included in the diet. Interestingly, the results of the HNNHS indicated that the risk of dyslipidemia could even decrease with moderate egg consumption of less than five per week, possibly due to a balanced diet.[148]

3) A study from 2019 assessed the effects of a high-fiber cereal at dawn (Sohor) during the month of Ramadan on satiety, bowel habits, body composition, blood glycemia, and blood lipidemia. It was found that this consumption had a positive effect on satiety, and it improved bowel functions and blood lipid levels.[149]

4) The 2019 *Relationship Between HDL Functional Characteristics and Cardiovascular Health and Potential Impact of Dietary Patterns* was a review of selected functions of high-density lipoprotein (HDL) particles and ways that various dietary patterns may affect cardiovascular health biomarkers, focusing on HDL functionality. HDL cholesterol efflux capacity (an important measure of HDL function in humans) and paraoxinase 1 are also associated with several food groups, such as virgin olive oil, lycopene-rich diet, nuts, and eggs.[150]

5) A paper in 2018 published in *Nutrients* looked at calorie restriction and its effects on lipids. The results showed that a negative energy balance induced by calorie restriction and aerobic exercise could reduce triglyceride levels by decreasing circulating large and medium, very low-density lipoprotein (VLDL) particles, reducing the risk of CVD.[151]

---

1 Rozman K. (1985). Intestinal excretion of toxic substances. Archives of toxicology. Supplement. = Archiv fur Toxikologie. Supplement, 8, 87–93. https://doi.org/10.1007/978-3-642-69928-3_10

2 Jandacek, R. J., & Genuis, S. J. (2013). An assessment of the intestinal lumen as a site for intervention in reducing body burdens of organochlorine compounds. TheScientificWorldJournal, 2013, 205621. https://doi.org/10.1155/2013/205621

3 Tazoe H, Otomo Y, Kaji I, Tanaka R, Karaki SI, Kuwahara A. Roles of short-chain fatty acids receptors, GPR41 and GPR43 on colonic functions. J Physiol Pharmacol. 2008 Aug;59 Suppl 2:251-62. PMID: 18812643.

4 Jahan, K., Qadri, O.S., Younis, K. (2020). Dietary Fiber as a Functional Food. In: Ahmad, S., Al-Shabib, N. (eds) Functional Food Products and Sustainable Health. Springer, Singapore. https://doi.org/10.1007/978-981-15-4716-4_10

5 Verstegen, R. E. M., Kostadinova, A. I., Merenciana, Z., Garssen, J., Folkerts, G., Hendriks, R. W., & Willemsen, L. E. M. (2021). Dietary Fibers: Effects, Underlying Mechanisms and Possible Role in Allergic Asthma Management. Nutrients, 13(11), 4153. MDPI AG. Retrieved from http://dx.doi.org/10.3390/nu13114153

6 Hoffman, J. B., Petriello, M. C., & Hennig, B. (2017). Impact of nutrition on pollutant toxicity: an update with new insights into epigenetic regulation. Reviews on environmental health, 32(1-2), 65–72. https://doi.org/10.1515/reveh-2016-0041

7 Cione, E., La Torre, C., Cannataro, R., Caroleo, M. C., Plastina, P., & Gallelli, L. (2019). Quercetin, Epigallocatechin Gallate, Curcumin, and Resveratrol: From Dietary Sources to Human MicroRNA Modulation. Molecules (Basel, Switzerland), 25(1), 63. https://doi.org/10.3390/molecules25010063

8 Sullivan, N. J., Fitzsimons, G. J., Platt, M. L., & Huettel, S. A. (2019). Indulgent Foods Can Paradoxically Promote Disciplined Dietary Choices. Psychological Science, 30(2), 273–287. https://doi.org/10.1177/0956797618817509

9 California Institute of Technology. "Cake or carrots? Timing may decide what you'll eat." ScienceDaily. ScienceDaily, 15 December 2014. www.sciencedaily.com/releases/2014/12/141215154633.htm.

10 https://www.dietaryguidelines.gov/resources/2020-2025-dietary-guidelines-online-materials/food-sources-select-nutrients/food-0

11 Müller, M., Canfora, E., & Blaak, E. (2018). Gastrointestinal Transit Time, Glucose Homeostasis and Metabolic Health: Modulation by Dietary Fibers. Nutrients, 10(3), 275. MDPI AG. Retrieved from http://dx.doi.org/10.3390/nu10030275

12 Holscher, H.D. Dietary fiber and prebiotics and the gastrointestinal microbiota. Gut Microbes 2017, 8, 172–184. [Google Scholar] [CrossRef]

13. Stephen, A.M.; Champ, M.M.; Cloran, S.J.; Fleith, M.; van Lieshout, L.; Mejborn, H.; Burley, V.J. Dietary fibre in Europe: Current state of knowledge on definitions, sources, recommendations, intakes and relationships to health. Nutr. Res. Rev. 2017, 30, 149–190. [Google Scholar] [CrossRef] [PubMed]
14. Holscher, H.D. Dietary fiber and prebiotics and the gastrointestinal microbiota. Gut Microbes 2017, 8, 172–184. [Google Scholar] [CrossRef]
15. Desai, M.S.; Seekatz, A.M.; Koropatkin, N.M.; Kamada, N.; Hickey, C.A.; Wolter, M.; Pudlo, N.A.; Kitamoto, S.; Terrapon, N.; Muller, A.; et al. A Dietary Fiber-Deprived Gut Microbiota Degrades the Colonic Mucus Barrier and Enhances Pathogen Susceptibility. Cell 2016, 167, 1339–1353.e1321. [Google Scholar] [CrossRef] [PubMed][Green Version]
16. Evaluation of wound healing activity of Acacia caesia in rats; https://doi.org/10.1016/j.wndm.2015.03.001
17. Zeng S, Cao J, Chen Y, Li C, Wu G, Zhu K, Chen X, Xu F, Liu Q, Tan L. Polysaccharides from Artocarpus heterophyllus Lam. (jackfruit) pulp improves intestinal barrier functions of high fat diet-induced obese rats. Front Nutr. 2022 Nov 3;9:1035619. doi: 10.3389/fnut.2022.1035619. PMID: 36407513; PMCID: PMC9669604.
18. Water-Soluble Dietary Fiber In the Management of Elevated Plasma Cholesterol In Healthy Subjects; http://healthresourceshakleecom.c.presscdn.com/wp-content/uploads/2014/03/Haskell-1992.pdf?2de911
19. https://www.regulations.gov/document?D=FDA-2011-F-0765-0003
20. https://www.healthline.com/health/7-uses-for-acacia#good-source-of-fiber
21. Koppe, L., & Soulage, C. O. (2022). The impact of dietary nutrient intake on gut microbiota in the progression and complications of chronic kidney disease. Kidney international, 102(4), 728–739. https://doi.org/10.1016/j.kint.2022.06.025
22. Castillo-Rodriguez, E., Fernandez-Prado, R., Esteras, R., Perez-Gomez, M. V., Gracia-Iguacel, C., Fernandez-Fernandez, B., Kanbay, M., Tejedor, A., Lazaro, A., Ruiz-Ortega, M., Gonzalez-Parra, E., Sanz, A. B., Ortiz, A., & Sanchez-Niño, M. D. (2018). Impact of Altered Intestinal Microbiota on Chronic Kidney Disease Progression. Toxins, 10(7), 300. https://doi.org/10.3390/toxins10070300
23. Liu, L., Xu, J., Zhang, Z., Ren, D., Wu, Y., Wang, D., Zhang, Y., Zhao, S., Chen, Q., & Wang, T. (2022). Metabolic Homeostasis of Amino Acids and Diabetic Kidney Disease. Nutrients, 15.
24. Hobby, G. P., Karaduta, O., Dusio, G. F., Singh, M., Zybailov, B. L., & Arthur, J. M. (2019). Chronic kidney disease and the gut microbiome. American journal of physiology. Renal physiology, 316(6), F1211–F1217. https://doi.org/10.1152/ajprenal.00298.2018
25. Rysz, J., Franczyk, B., Ławiński, J., Olszewski, R., Ciałkowska-Rysz, A., & Gluba-Brzózka, A. (2021). The Impact of CKD on Uremic Toxins and Gut Microbiota. Toxins, 13(4), 252. https://doi.org/10.3390/toxins13040252
26. El Amouri, A., Snauwaert, E., Foulon, A., Vande Moortel, C., Van Dyck, M., Van Hoeck, K., Godefroid, N., Glorieux, G., Van Biesen, W., Vande Walle, J., Raes, A., & Eloot, S. (2021). Dietary Fibre Intake Is Associated with Serum Levels of Uraemic Toxins in Children with Chronic Kidney Disease. Toxins, 13(3), 225. https://doi.org/10.3390/toxins13030225
27. Lauriola, M., Farré, R., Evenepoel, P., Overbeek, S. A., & Meijers, B. (2023). Food-Derived Uremic Toxins in Chronic Kidney Disease. Toxins, 15(2), 116. https://doi.org/10.3390/toxins15020116
28. https://pbmattorneys.com/prescription-drug-injuries/miralax/
29. https://www.gutsense.org/gutsense/the-role-of-miralax-laxative-in-autism-dementia-alzheimer.html
30. National Institute for Occupational Safety and Health (NIOSH), "ETHYLENE GLYCOL : Systemic Agent," The Emergency Response Safety and Health Database, last reviewed May 12, 2011, accessed January 16, 2013,
31. The Merck Manual for Healthcare Professionals, "Neurologic Disorders," Accessed January 16, 2013
32. Huda, M. N., Lu, S., Jahan, T., Ding, M., Jha, R., Zhang, K., Zhang, W., Georgiev, M. I., Park, S. U., & Zhou, M. (2021). Treasure from garden: Bioactive compounds of buckwheat. Food chemistry, 335, 127653. https://doi.org/10.1016/j.foodchem.2020.127653
33. Giménez-Bastida JA , Laparra-Llopis JM , Baczek N , Zielinski H . Buckwheat and buckwheat enriched products exert an anti-inflammatory effect on the myofibroblasts of colon CCD-18Co. Food Funct. 2018 Jun 20;9(6):3387-3397. doi: 10.1039/c8fo00193f. PMID: 29870039; PMCID: PMC6597957.
34. Giménez-Bastida, J. A., & Zieliński, H. (2015). Buckwheat as a Functional Food and Its Effects on Health. Journal of agricultural and food chemistry, 63(36), 7896–7913. https://doi.org/10.1021/acs.jafc.5b02498
35. Noreen, S., Rizwan, B., Khan, M., & Farooq, S. (2021). Health Benefits of Buckwheat (Fagopyrum Esculentum), Potential Remedy for Diseases, Rare to Cancer: A Mini Review. Infectious disorders drug targets, 21(6), e170721189478. https://doi.org/10.2174/1871526520999201224122605
36. Osaka University. (2021, August 16). The good her b: Buckwheat liquor helps cells clean house. ScienceDaily. Retrieved June 2, 2023 from www.sciencedaily.com/releases/2021/08/210816102545.htm
37. The Kitchen Cookbook- Recipes, Kitchens & Tips to Inspire Your Cooking by Sara Kate Gillingham and Faith Durand. http://www.care2.com/greenliving/10-health-benefits-of-buckwheat.html
38. Buckwheat- Wikipedia, the free encyclopedia. (n.d.). Retrieved from, http://en.wikipedia.org/wiki/Buckwheat_flour
39. Buckwheat- Wikipedia, the free encyclopedia. (n.d.). Retrieved from http://en.wikipedia.org/wiki/Buckwheat_flour.
http://www.sare.org/Learning-Center/Books/Managing-Cover-Crops-Profitably-3rd-Edition/Text-Version/Nonlegume-Cover-Crops/Buckwheat

Chapter 8 ~ Fiber & Fat Overlooked and Under Appreciated

40 Vieira, N. M., Peghinelli, V. V., Monte, M. G., Costa, N. A., Pereira, A. G., Seki, M. M., Azevedo, P. S., Polegato, B. F., de Paiva, S. A. R., Zornoff, L. A. M., & Minicucci, M. F. (2023). Beans comsumption can contribute to the prevention of cardiovascular disease. Clinical nutrition ESPEN, 54, 73–80. https://doi.org/10.1016/j.clnesp.2023.01.00

41 Rodríguez, L., Mendez, D., Montecino, H., Carrasco, B., Arevalo, B., Palomo, I., & Fuentes, E. (2022). Role of Phaseolus vulgaris L. in the Prevention of Cardiovascular Diseases-Cardioprotective Potential of Bioactive Compounds. Plants (Basel, Switzerland), 11(2), 186. https://doi.org/10.3390/plants11020186

42 Alcázar-Valle, M., Lugo-Cervantes, E., Mojica, L., Morales-Hernández, N., Reyes-Ramírez, H., Enríquez-Vara, J. N., & García-Morales, S. (2020). Bioactive Compounds, Antioxidant Activity, and Antinutritional Content of Legumes: A Comparison between Four Phaseolus Species. Molecules (Basel, Switzerland), 25(15), 3528. https://doi.org/10.3390/molecules25153528

43 Marventano, S., Izquierdo Pulido, M., Sánchez-González, C., Godos, J., Speciani, A., Galvano, F., & Grosso, G. (2017). Legume consumption and CVD risk: a systematic review and meta-analysis. Public health nutrition, 20(2), 245–254. https://doi.org/10.1017/S1368980016002299

44 Qin, L. Q., Xu, J. Y., Han, S. F., Zhang, Z. L., Zhao, Y. Y., & Szeto, I. M. (2015). Dairy consumption and risk of cardiovascular disease: an updated meta-analysis of prospective cohort studies. Asia Pacific journal of clinical nutrition, 24(1), 90–100. https://doi.org/10.6133/apjcn.2015.24.1.09

45 Khatoon, N., & Prakash, J. (2004). Nutritional quality of microwave-cooked and pressure-cooked legumes. International journal of food sciences and nutrition, 55(6), 441–448. https://doi.org/10.1080/09637480400009102

46 Khrisanapant, P., Leong, S. Y., Kebede, B., & Oey, I. (2021). Effects of Hydrothermal Processing Duration on the Texture, Starch and Protein In Vitro Digestibility of Cowpeas, Chickpeas and Kidney Beans. Foods (Basel, Switzerland), 10(6), 1415. https://doi.org/10.3390/foods10061415

47 Duijsens, D., Verkempinck, S. H. E., De Coster, A., Pälchen, K., Hendrickx, M., & Grauwet, T. (2023). How Cooking Time Affects In Vitro Starch and Protein Digestibility of Whole Cooked Lentil Seeds versus Isolated Cotyledon Cells. Foods (Basel, Switzerland), 12(3), 525. https://doi.org/10.3390/foods12030525

48 Redondo-Cuenca, A., Pedrosa, M. M., Sanz, M. D. T., Alvarado López, A. N., & Garcia-Alonso, A. (2022). Influence of high-pressure processing on nutritional composition and bioactive compounds of Phaseolus coccineus L. Journal of food science, 87(12), 5289–5302. https://doi.org/10.1111/1750-3841.16361

49 The Wahls Protocol, by Terry Wahls, M.D., Avery 2014

50 Barampama, Z., & Simard, R. E. (1995). Effects of soaking, cooking and fermentation on composition, in-vitro starch digestibility and nutritive value of common beans. Plant foods for human nutrition (Dordrecht, Netherlands), 48(4), 349–365. https://doi.org/10.1007/BF01088494

51 Chatur, P., Johnson, S., Coorey, R., Bhattarai, R. R., & Bennett, S. J. (2022). The Effect of High Pressure Processing on Textural, Bioactive and Digestibility Properties of Cooked Kimberley Large Kabuli Chickpeas. Frontiers in nutrition, 9, 847877. https://doi.org/10.3389/fnut.2022.847877

52 Mishra, A., Behura, A., Mawatwal, S., Kumar, A., Naik, L., Mohanty, S. S., Manna, D., Dokania, P., Mishra, A., Patra, S. K., & Dhiman, R. (2019). Structure-function and application of plant lectins in disease biology and immunity. Food and chemical toxicology : an international journal published for the British Industrial Biological Research Association, 134, 110827. https://doi.org/10.1016/j.fct.2019.110827

53 Vojdani, A., Afar, D., & Vojdani, E. (2020). Reaction of Lectin-Specific Antibody with Human Tissue: Possible Contributions to Autoimmunity. Journal of immunology research, 2020, 1438957. https://doi.org/10.1155/2020/1438957

54 Gilbert RJ. Healthy eating day. Communicable Disease Report. 1988;33:3–4.

55 Penn State. (2018, December 4). A toxin that travels from stomach to brain may trigger Parkinsonism. ScienceDaily. Retrieved June 2, 2023 from www.sciencedaily.com/releases/2018/12/181204131105.htm

56 Nutrients 2013, 5, 771-787; doi:10.3390/nu5030771

57 http://www.unexplainedinfertilityinfo.com/autoimmune-causes/

58 Freed D. L. (1999). Do dietary lectins cause disease?. BMJ (Clinical research ed.), 318(7190), 1023–1024. https://doi.org/10.1136/bmj.318.7190.1023

59 Freed D L J. Do dietary lectins cause disease? The evidence is suggestive—and raises interesting possibilities for treatment BMJ 1999; 318 :1023 doi:10.1136/bmj.318.7190.1023

60 de Punder, K., & Pruimboom, L. (2013). The dietary intake of wheat and other cereal grains and their role in inflammation. Nutrients, 5(3), 771–787. https://doi.org/10.3390/nu5030771

61 Scur, M., Parsons, B. D., Dey, S., & Makrigiannis, A. P. (2023). The diverse roles of C-type lectin-like receptors in immunity. Frontiers in immunology, 14, 1126043. https://doi.org/10.3389/fimmu.2023.1126043

62 Tseng, C. P., Huang, Y. L., Chang, Y. W., Liao, H. R., Chen, Y. L., & Hsieh, P. W. (2020). Polysaccharide-containing fraction from Artemisia argyi inhibits tumor cell-induced platelet aggregation by blocking interaction of podoplanin with C-type lectin-like receptor 2. Journal of food and drug analysis, 28(1), 115–123. https://doi.org/10.1016/j.jfda.2019.08.002

63 Urugo, M. M., & Tringo, T. T. (2023). Naturally Occurring Plant Food Toxicants and the Role of Food Processing Methods in Their Detoxification. International journal of food science, 2023, 9947841. https://doi.org/10.1155/2023/9947841

64 Morales-Moo, T., Hernández-Camarillo, E., Carvajal-Moreno, M., Vargas-Ortiz, M., Robles-Olvera, V., & Salgado-Cervantes, M. A. (2020). Human Health Risk Associated with the Consumption of Aflatoxins in Popcorn. Risk management and healthcare policy, 13, 2583–2591. https://doi.org/10.2147/RMHP.S274767

65 Abedini, A., Zirak, M. R., Akbari, N., Saatloo, N. V., Badeenezhad, A., & Sadighara, P. (2022). Acrylamide; a neurotoxin in popcorns: a systematic review and meta-analysis. Reviews on environmental health, 10.1515/reveh-2022-0085. Advance online publication. https://doi.org/10.1515/reveh-2022-0085

66 Akbari-Adergani, B., Shahbazi, R., Esfandiari, Z., Kamankesh, M., Vakili Saatloo, N., Abedini, A., Ramezankhani, R., & Sadighara, P. (2023). Acrylamide content of industrial and traditional popcorn collected from Tehran's market, Iran: A risk assessment study. Journal of food protection, 86(1), 100001. https://doi.org/10.1016/j.jfp.2022.10.001

67 Hawkins, A. T., Wise, P. E., Chan, T., Lee, J. T., Glyn, T., Wood, V., Eglinton, T., Frizelle, F., Khan, A., Hall, J., Ilyas, M. I. M., Michailidou, M., Nfonsam, V. N., Cowan, M. L., Williams, J., Steele, S. R., Alavi, K., Ellis, C. T., Collins, D., Winter, D. C., … Lightner, A. L. (2020). Diverticulitis: An Update From the Age Old Paradigm. Current problems in surgery, 57(10), 100862. https://doi.org/10.1016/j.cpsurg.2020.100862

68 http://www.history.com/news/hungry-history/a-history-of-popcorn

69 Early History of Popcorn, USDA National Agricultural Library, Retrieved June 4, 2023: https://www.nal.usda.gov/exhibits/speccoll/exhibits/show/popcorn/early-history

70 The Different Types Of Pots You Can Use To Cook Popcorn by Loyola Martinez | Nov 11, 2022 https://popcorncarnival.com/the-different-types-of-pots-you-can-use-to-cook-popcorn/

71 http://www.history.com/news/hungry-history/a-history-of-popcorn

72 http://www.nongmoshoppingguide.com/

73 Life Expectancy in the U.S. Dropped for the Second Year in a Row in 2021 (2022): https://www.cdc.gov/nchs/pressroom/nchs_press_releases/2022/20220831.htm

74 DiNicolantonio, J. J., & O'Keefe, J. H. (2018). Omega-6 vegetable oils as a driver of coronary heart disease: the oxidized linoleic acid hypothesis. Open heart, 5(2), e000898. https://doi.org/10.1136/openhrt-2018-000898

75 Liu, Z., Yuan, J., Wen, P., Guo, X., Li, K., Wang, Y., Liu, R., Guo, Y., & Li, D. (2023). Effect of Lard or Plus Soybean Oil on Markers of Liver Function in Healthy Subjects: A Randomized Controlled-Feeding Trial. Foods (Basel, Switzerland), 12(9), 1894. https://doi.org/10.3390/foods12091894

76 Hooper, L., Al-Khudairy, L., Abdelhamid, A. S., Rees, K., Brainard, J. S., Brown, T. J., Ajabnoor, S. M., O'Brien, A. T., Winstanley, L. E., Donaldson, D. H., Song, F., & Deane, K. H. (2018). Omega-6 fats for the primary and secondary prevention of cardiovascular disease. The Cochrane database of systematic reviews, 7(7), CD011094. https://doi.org/10.1002/14651858.CD011094.pub3

77 Elliott, P. S., Kharaty, S. S., & Phillips, C. M. (2022). Plant-Based Diets and Lipid, Lipoprotein, and Inflammatory Biomarkers of Cardiovascular Disease: A Review of Observational and Interventional Studies. Nutrients, 14(24), 5371. https://doi.org/10.3390/nu14245371

78 Evaluating the impact of hemp food consumption on workplace drug tests. https://www.ncbi.nlm.nih.gov/pubmed/11765026

79 These foods can make you test positive for drugs- http://www.bbc.co.uk/bbcthree/article/bf2caf17-55e1-4708-87b6-e9cd3bf4321d

80 http://www.ift.org/food-technology/past-issues/2014/september/columns/nutraceuticals.aspx

81 RCSI. (2022, November 3). New role for blood clotting protein in triggering inflammation: Discovery has potential to lead to new treatments for patients with inflammatory and blood clotting disorders. ScienceDaily. Retrieved June 6, 2023 from www.sciencedaily.com/releases/2022/11/221103104941.htm

82 NIH/National Heart, Lung and Blood Institute. (2008, February 29). First US Von Willebrand Disease Clinical Practice Guidelines Issued. ScienceDaily. Retrieved June 5, 2023 from www.sciencedaily.com/releases/2008/02/080229141836.htm

83 Lehigh University. (2019, May 21). A better understanding of the von Willebrand Factor's A2 domain. ScienceDaily. Retrieved June 6, 2023 from www.sciencedaily.com/releases/2019/05/190521084926.htm

84 https://www.mayoclinic.org/diseases-conditions/von-willebrand-disease/symptoms-causes/syc-20354978

85 Serreli, G., & Deiana, M. (2020). Extra Virgin Olive Oil Polyphenols: Modulation of Cellular Pathways Related to Oxidant Species and Inflammation in Aging. Cells, 9(2), 478. https://doi.org/10.3390/cells9020478

86 Millman, J. F., Okamoto, S., Teruya, T., Uema, T., Ikematsu, S., Shimabukuro, M., & Masuzaki, H. (2021). Extra-virgin olive oil and the gut-brain axis: influence on gut microbiota, mucosal immunity, and cardiometabolic and cognitive health. Nutrition reviews, 79(12), 1362–1374. https://doi.org/10.1093/nutrit/nuaa148

87 Memmola, R., Petrillo, A., Di Lorenzo, S., Altuna, S. C., Habeeb, B. S., Soggiu, A., Bonizzi, L., Garrone, O., & Ghidini, M. (2022). Correlation between Olive Oil Intake and Gut Microbiota in Colorectal Cancer Prevention. Nutrients, 14(18), 3749. https://doi.org/10.3390/nu14183749

88 Gorzynik-Debicka, M., Przychodzen, P., Cappello, F., Kuban-Jankowska, A., Marino Gammazza, A., Knap, N., Wozniak, M., & Gorska-Ponikowska, M. (2018). Potential Health Benefits of Olive Oil and Plant Polyphenols. International journal of molecular sciences, 19(3), 686. https://doi.org/10.3390/ijms19030686

89 Serra, G., Incani, A., Serreli, G., Porru, L., Melis, M. P., Tuberoso, C. I. G., Rossin, D., Biasi, F., & Deiana, M. (2018). Olive oil polyphenols reduce oxysterols-induced redox imbalance and pro-inflammatory response in intestinal cells. Redox biology, 17, 348–354. https://doi.org/10.1016/j.redox.2018.05.006

90 Soto-Alarcon, S. A., Valenzuela, R., Valenzuela, A., & Videla, L. A. (2018). Liver Protective Effects of Extra Virgin Olive Oil: Interaction between Its Chemical Composition and the Cell-signaling Pathways Involved in Protection. Endocrine, metabolic & immune disorders drug targets, 18(1), 75–84. https://doi.org/10.2174/1871530317666171114120552

91 Moral, R., & Escrich, E. (2022). Influence of Olive Oil and Its Components on Breast Cancer: Molecular Mechanisms. Molecules (Basel, Switzerland), 27(2), 477. https://doi.org/10.3390/molecules27020477

92 Santangelo, C., Vari, R., Scazzocchio, B., De Sanctis, P., Giovannini, C., D'Archivio, M., & Masella, R. (2018). Anti-inflammatory Activity of Extra Virgin Olive Oil Polyphenols: Which Role in the Prevention and Treatment of Immune-Mediated Inflammatory Diseases?. Endocrine, metabolic & immune disorders drug targets, 18(1), 36–50. https://doi.org/10.2174/1871530317666171114114321

93 Gorzynik-Debicka, M., Przychodzen, P., Cappello, F., Kuban-Jankowska, A., Marino Gammazza, A., Knap, N., Wozniak, M., & Gorska-Ponikowska, M. (2018). Potential Health Benefits of Olive Oil and Plant Polyphenols. International journal of molecular sciences, 19(3), 686. https://doi.org/10.3390/ijms19030686

94 Vazquez-Martin, A., Fernández-Arroyo, S., Cufí, S., Oliveras-Ferraros, C., Lozano-Sánchez, J., Vellón, L., Micol, V., Joven, J., Segura-Carretero, A., & Menendez, J. A. (2012). Phenolic secoiridoids in extra virgin olive oil impede fibrogenic and oncogenic epithelial-to-mesenchymal transition: extra virgin olive oil as a source of novel antiaging phytochemicals. Rejuvenation research, 15(1), 3–21. https://doi.org/10.1089/rej.2011.1203

95 Albrahim, T., Alotaibi, M. H. M., Altamimi, N. M. M., Albariqi, A. M. A., Alqarni, L. A. O., Alassaf, S. N. A., Aloudah, H. S., Alahmed, M., Almnaizel, A. T., Aldraihem, M. R., & Alonazi, M. (2022). The Impact of Dietary Consumption of Palm Oil and Olive Oil on Lipid Profile and Hepatocyte Injury in Hypercholesterolemic Rats. Pharmaceuticals (Basel, Switzerland), 15(9), 1103. https://doi.org/10.3390/ph15091103

96 King's College London. "Why you need olive oil on your salad." ScienceDaily. ScienceDaily, 19 May 2014. www.sciencedaily.com/releases/2014/05/140519160712.htm.

97 Yan, S., Zhou, H., Liu, S., Wang, J., Zeng, Y., Matias, F. B., & Wen, L. (2020). Differential effects of Chinese high-fat dietary habits on lipid metabolism: mechanisms and health implications. Lipids in health and disease, 19(1), 30. https://doi.org/10.1186/s12944-020-01212-y

98 Jadhav, H. B., & Annapure, U. S. (2023). Triglycerides of medium-chain fatty acids: a concise review. Journal of food science and technology, 60(8), 2143–2152. https://doi.org/10.1007/s13197-022-05499-w

99 Nimbkar, S., Leena, M. M., Moses, J. A., & Anandharamakrishnan, C. (2022). Medium chain triglycerides (MCT): State-of-the-art on chemistry, synthesis, health benefits and applications in food industry. Comprehensive reviews in food science and food safety, 21(2), 843–867. https://doi.org/10.1111/1541-4337.12926

100 Eyres, L., Eyres, M. F., Chisholm, A., & Brown, R. C. (2016). Coconut oil consumption and cardiovascular risk factors in humans. Nutrition reviews, 74(4), 267–280. https://doi.org/10.1093/nutrit/nuw002

101 Khaw, K. T., Sharp, S. J., Finikarides, L., Afzal, I., Lentjes, M., Luben, R., & Forouhi, N. G. (2018). Randomised trial of coconut oil, olive oil or butter on blood lipids and other cardiovascular risk factors in healthy men and women. BMJ open, 8(3), e020167. https://doi.org/10.1136/bmjopen-2017-020167

102 Duarte, A. C., Spiazzi, B. F., Zingano, C. P., Merello, E. N., Wayerbacher, L. F., Teixeira, P. P., Farenzena, L. P., de Araujo, C., Amazarray, C. R., Colpani, V., & Gerchman, F. (2022). The effects of coconut oil on the cardiometabolic profile: a systematic review and meta-analysis of randomized clinical trials. Lipids in health and disease, 21(1), 83. https://doi.org/10.1186/s12944-022-01685-z

103 Unhapipatpong, C., Shantavasinkul, P. C., Kasemsup, V., Siriyotha, S., Warodomwichit, D., Maneesuwannarat, S., Vathesatogkit, P., Sritara, P., & Thakkinstian, A. (2021). Tropical Oil Consumption and Cardiovascular Disease: An Umbrella Review of Systematic Reviews and Meta Analyses. Nutrients, 13(5), 1549. https://doi.org/10.3390/nu13051549

104 de Oliveira Marques, S., Muller, A. P., Luciano, T. F., Dos Santos Tramontin, N., da Silva Caetano, M., Luis da Silva Pieri, B., Amorim, T. L., de Oliveira, M. A. L., & de Souza, C. T. (2022). Effects of Avocado Oil Supplementation on Insulin Sensitivity, Cognition, and Inflammatory and Oxidative Stress Markers in Different Tissues of Diet-Induced Obese Mice. Nutrients, 14(14), 2906. https://doi.org/10.3390/nu14142906

105 Avocado oil production and chemical characteristics: https://link.springer.com/article/10.1007/BF02542007

106 An overview of the modulatory effects of oleic acid in health and disease. https://www.ncbi.nlm.nih.gov/pubmed/23278117

107 Gopal Reddy, M. R., Kumar, M. S., Acharya, V., Venkata, S. M., Putcha, U. K., & Jeyakumar, S. M. (2019). Vitamin A deficiency increases the oleic acid (C18:1) levels in the kidney of high fructose diet-fed rats. The Indian journal of medical research, 150(6), 620–629. https://doi.org/10.4103/ijmr.IJMR_1574_17

108 Piccinin, E., Cariello, M., De Santis, S., Ducheix, S., Sabbà, C., Ntambi, J. M., & Moschetta, A. (2019). Role of Oleic Acid in the Gut-Liver Axis: From Diet to the Regulation of Its Synthesis via Stearoyl-CoA Desaturase 1 (SCD1). Nutrients, 11(10), 2283. https://doi.org/10.3390/nu11102283

109 Hass Avocado Composition and Potential Health Effects https://www.ncbi.nlm.nih.gov/pmc/articles/PMC3664913/

110 Lauretti, E., Praticò, D. Effect of canola oil consumption on memory, synapse and neuropathology in the triple transgenic mouse model of Alzheimer's disease. Sci Rep 7, 17134 (2017). https://doi.org/10.1038/s41598-017-17373-3

111 Yamashima T. (2023). Implication of Vegetable Oil-Derived Hydroxynonenal in the Lysosomal Cell Death for Lifestyle-Related Diseases. Nutrients, 15(3), 609. https://doi.org/10.3390/nu15030609

112 Beydoun, M. A., Beydoun, H. A., Hossain, S., El-Hajj, Z. W., Weiss, J., & Zonderman, A. B. (2020). Clinical and Bacterial Markers of Periodontitis and Their Association with Incident All-Cause and Alzheimer's Disease Dementia in a Large National Survey. Journal of Alzheimer's disease : JAD, 75(1), 157–172. https://doi.org/10.3233/JAD-200064

113 Yamashima, T., Ota, T., Mizukoshi, E., Nakamura, H., Yamamoto, Y., Kikuchi, M., Yamashita, T., & Kaneko, S. (2020). Intake of ω-6 Polyunsaturated Fatty Acid-Rich Vegetable Oils and Risk of Lifestyle Diseases. Advances in nutrition (Bethesda, Md.), 11(6), 1489–1509. https://doi.org/10.1093/advances/nmaa072

114 Heagerty AH. Scanning ancient history for evidence of modern illness. Lancet 2013;381,1165-1166. DOI:https://doi.org/10.1016/S0140-6736(13)60639-X).

115 https://lifespanhealth.usc.edu/professor-caleb-finch-aging-genes-and-the-environment/

116 Nerlich, A. G., Egarter Vigl, E., Fleckinger, A., Tauber, M., & Peschel, O. (2021). Der Mann aus dem Eis : Lebensszenario und Pathologische Befunde aus 30 Jahren Forschung an der Gletschermumie „Ötzi" [The Iceman : Life scenarios and pathological findings from 30 years of research on the glacier mummy "Ötzi"]. Der Pathologe, 42(5), 530–539. https://doi.org/10.1007/s00292-021-00961-6

117 Madjid, M., Safavi-Naeini, P., & Lodder, R. (2019). High prevalence of cholesterol-rich atherosclerotic lesions in ancient mummies: A near-infrared spectroscopy study. American heart journal, 216, 113–116. https://doi.org/10.1016/j.ahj.2019.06.018

118 Keys A (ed). Coronary heart disease in seven countries. Circulation 1970;41(4S1):1-198

119 Keys, A (1980). Seven Countries: A Multivariate Analysis of Death and Coronary Heart Disease. Harvard University Press. ISBN 978-0-674-80237-7

120 Keys, A (1980). Seven Countries: A Multivariate Analysis of Death and Coronary Heart Disease. Harvard University Press. ISBN 978-0-674-80237-7).

121 Anitschkow N. N., Chalatow S. 1913. Ueber experimentelle Cholesterinsteatose und ihre Bedeutung fur die Entstehung einiger pathologischer Prozesse. Zentralbl. Allg. Pathol. 24: 1–9 [Google Scholar

122 Steinberg D. 2013. Anitschkow: birth of the lipid hypothesis of atherosclerosis. In Missed Nobel Prizes. G. Thompson, editor. [Google Scholar

123 No authors listed]. 1983. Classics in arteriosclerosis research: On experimental cholesterin steatosis and its significance in the origin of some pathological processes by N. Anitschkow and S. Chalatow, translated by Mary Z. Pelias, 1913. Arteriosclerosis. 3: 178–182 [PubMed]

124 Anitschkow N. N. 1933. Experimental atherosclerosis in animals. In Arteriosclerosis. E. V. Cowdry, editor. Macmillan, New York. 271–322. [Google Scholar

125 No authors listed. Nutrition classics. Archives of Internal Medicine. Angina pectoris and Hereditary Xanthomatosis. 1939; 64- in Nutr Rev. 1987 Apr;45(4):113-5. doi: 10.1111/j.1753-4887.1987.tb02723.x.PMID: 3295605 No abstract available. PMID: 3295605, DOI: 10.1111/j.1753-4887.1987.tb02723.x).

126 Watanabe Y: Serial inbreeding of rabbits with hereditary hyperlipidemia (WHHL-rabbit). Atherosclerosis, 1980; 36: 261-268 [PubMed] [Google Scholar]

127 Yudkin J. Dietary fat and dietary sugar in relation to ischemic heart-disease and diabetes. Lancet. 1964;2(7349):4–5. [PubMed] [Google Scholar])

128 Keys A. Sucrose in the diet and coronary heart disease. Atherosclerosis. 1971;14:193-202

129 Kearns, C. E., Schmidt, L. A., & Glantz, S. A. (2016). Sugar Industry and Coronary Heart Disease Research: A Historical Analysis of Internal Industry Documents. JAMA internal medicine, 176(11), 1680–1685. https://doi.org/10.1001/jamainternmed.2016.5394

130 Papers of Roger Adams. Urbana: University of Illinois; Roger Adams: an inventory of the papers of Roger Adams at the University of Illinois Archives, 1889–1971. Record Series No. 15/5/23. [Google Scholar]; Papers, 1952–1999 (inclusive), 1960–1978 (bulk) Boston, MA: Harvard Medical Library, Francis A. Countway Library of Medicine; Finding aid Hegsted, D. Mark (David Mark), 1914–2009. H MS c54. [Google Scholar]; Cheek DW. Sugar Research, 1943–1972. Bethesda, MD: International Sugar Research Foundation; 1974. [Google Scholar]; Sugar Research Foundation Inc. Papers of Roger Adams at the University of Illinois Archives, 1889–1971. Urbana: University of Illinois; Minutes of a meeting of the Scientific Advisory Board (November 9, 1962) Record Series No. 15/5/23. [Google Scholar]; Hickson JL. Papers of Roger Adams at the University of Illinois Archives, 1889–1971. Urbana: University of Illinois; Memoranda to Neil Kelly regarding possible activities of the Sugar Association Inc (December 14, 1964) Record Series No. 15/5/23. [Google Scholar])

131 Yamauchi Y, Rogers MA. Sterol Metabolism and Transport in Atherosclerosis and Cancer. Front Endocrinol (Lausanne). 2018 Sep 19;9:509. doi: 10.3389/fendo.2018.00509. PMID: 30283400; PMCID: PMC6157400.

132 Schroor M., Sennels H., Fahrenkrug J., Jørgensen H., Plat J., Mensink R. Diurnal Variation of Markers for Cholesterol Synthesis, Cholesterol Absorption, and Bile Acid Synthesis: A Systematic Review and the Bispebjerg Study of Diurnal Variations. Nutrients. 2019;11:1439. doi: 10.3390/nu11071439.

Chapter 8 ~ Fiber & Fat Overlooked and Under Appreciated

133 Schade, D. S., Shey, L., & Eaton, R. P. (2020). Cholesterol Review: A Metabolically Important Molecule. Endocrine practice : official journal of the American College of Endocrinology and the American Association of Clinical Endocrinologists, 26(12), 1514–1523. https://doi.org/10.4158/EP-2020-0347

134 University of California San Francisco; Cholestrol Content of Foods (2023) https://www.ucsfhealth.org/education/cholesterol-content-of-foods

135 Sunil B, Ashraf AP. Dyslipidemia in Pediatric Type 2 Diabetes Mellitus. Curr Diab Rep. 2020 Sep 9;20(10):53. doi: 10.1007/s11892-020-01336-6. PMID: 32909078; PMCID: PMC7481147.

136 Stellaard, F. (2023). From Dietary Cholesterol to Blood Cholesterol. Nutrients, 15(14), 3086. MDPI AG. Retrieved from http://dx.doi.org/10.3390/nu15143086

137 Li H, Ren J, Li Y, Wu Q, Wei J. Oxidative stress: The nexus of obesity and cognitive dysfunction in diabetes. Front Endocrinol (Lausanne). 2023 Apr 3;14:1134025. doi: 10.3389/fendo.2023.1134025. PMID: 37077347; PMCID: PMC10107409.

138 Mahley, R. W., Innerarity, T. L., Rall, S. C., Jr, & Weisgraber, K. H. (1984). Plasma lipoproteins: apolipoprotein structure and function. Journal of lipid research, 25(12), 1277–1294.

139 Wang, H. P., Zhang, N., Liu, Y. J., Xia, T. L., Chen, G. C., Yang, J., & Li, F. R. (2023). Lipoprotein(a), family history of cardiovascular disease, and incidence of heart failure. Journal of lipid research, 64(7), 100398. https://doi.org/10.1016/j.jlr.2023.100398

140 (Fredrickson DS. An international classification of hyperlipidemias and hyperlipoproteinemias. Ann Intern Med. 1971 Sep;75(3):471-2. [PubMed])

141 (Expert Panel on Detection, Evaluation, and Treatment of High Blood Cholesterol in Adults. Executive Summary of The Third Report of The National Cholesterol Education Program (NCEP) Expert Panel on Detection, Evaluation, And Treatment of High Blood Cholesterol In Adults (Adult Treatment Panel III). JAMA. 2001 May 16;285(19):2486-97. [PubMed]):

142 Nies LK, Cymbala AA, Kasten SL, Lamprecht DG, Olson KL. Complementary and alternative therapies for the management of dyslipidemia. Ann Pharmacother. 2006 Nov;40(11):1984-92. doi: 10.1345/aph.1H040. Epub 2006 Oct 17. PMID: 17047144)

143 (Nies LK, Cymbala AA, Kasten SL, Lamprecht DG, Olson KL. Complementary and alternative therapies for the management of dyslipidemia. Ann Pharmacother. 2006 Nov;40(11):1984-92. doi: 10.1345/aph.1H040. Epub 2006 Oct 17. PMID: 17047144)

144 Hu Y, Chen X, Hu M, Zhang D, Yuan S, Li P, Feng L. Medicinal and edible plants in the treatment of dyslipidemia: advances and prospects. Chin Med. 2022 Sep 29;17(1):113. doi: 10.1186/s13020-022-00666-9. PMID: 36175900; PMCID: PMC9522446)

145 Integrative Nutrition: Holistic Cholesterol Management By Carrie Dennett, MPH, RDN, CD Today's Dietitian Vol. 19, No. 11, P. 16

146 Zampelas, A., & Magriplis, E. (2019). New Insights into Cholesterol Functions: A Friend or an Enemy?. Nutrients, 11(7), 1645. https://doi.org/10.3390/nu11071645

147 Kim YG, Jeong JH, Han KD, Roh SY, Min K, Lee HS, Choi YY, Shim J, Choi JI, Kim YH. Association between low-density lipoprotein cholesterol and sudden cardiac arrest in people with diabetes mellitus. Cardiovasc Diabetol. 2023 Feb 20;22(1):36. doi: 10.1186/s12933-023-01769-9. PMID: 36803488; PMCID: PMC9940386.

148 Magriplis E., Mitsopoulou A., Karageorgou D., Bakogianni I., Dimakopoulos I., Micha R., Michas G., Chourdakis M., Chrousos G., Roma E., et al. Frequency and Quantity of Egg Intake Is Not Associated with Dyslipidemia: The Hellenic National Nutrition and Health Survey (HNNHS) Nutrients. 2019;11:1105. doi: 10.3390/nu11051105.

149 Jarrar A., Beasley J., Ohuma E., Cheikh Ismail L., Qeshta D., Mohamad M., Al Dhaheri A. Effect of High Fiber Cereal Intake on Satiety and Gastrointestinal Symptoms during Ramadan. Nutrients. 2019;11:939. doi: 10.3390/nu11040939.

150 Bardagjy A., Steinberg F. Relationship Between HDL Functional Characteristics and Cardiovascular Health and Potential Impact of Dietary Patterns: A Narrative Review. Nutrients. 2019;11:1231. doi: 10.3390/nu11061231

151 Chooi Y., Ding C., Chan Z., Lo J., Choo J., Ding B., Leow M., Magkos F. Lipoprotein Subclass Profile after Progressive Energy Deficits Induced by Calorie Restriction or Exercise. Nutrients. 2018;10:1814. doi: 10.3390/nu10111814.

> "Cultural legacies are powerful forces. They have deep roots and long lives. They persist, generation after generation, virtually intact, even as the economic and social and demographic conditions that spawned them have vanished, and they play such a role in directing attitudes and behavior that we cannot make sense of our world without them."
>
> ~ Malcolm Gladwell, Outliers

Chapter Nine ~ *Protein*

At no time has an essential element of nourishment been so hotly debated as the type of protein consumers should eat and the effects on the environment.

I unabashedly confess to being a red meat eater. Like millions of individuals worldwide, more than my health is connected to the beef, bison, elk, venison, pork, poultry, or fish I consume. It is easy to declare this or that form of protein the healthiest or most detrimental to the planet. My personal belief is that no one dietary dogma or rule benefits everyone. Like the foods we eat, we humans are diverse and are products of the culture, region, climate, and soils that our food and water come from. BUT….There always seems to be a *but* when discussing the sustainability, pros, and cons associated with dietary choices. Over the following pages, we will explore protein and some of the challenges related to branding any whole food as good or bad.

> Both plant and animal foods contain protein. Foods that provide all nine essential amino acids are called high quality proteins. Animal foods like meat, fish, poultry, eggs, and dairy products are all high-quality protein sources, and the essential amino acids in animal products are in the right balance.

Not all protein comes from livestock, fish, or fowl. By 2023, consumers have a wide selection of protein from fungi, legumes, algae, nuts, seeds, and dairy sources other than bovine. How well an individual digests various forms of protein may be the more important question. If an individual is vegan or vegetarian, the intrinsic factors for digesting complex animal proteins become absent. As I visit various authors of historic cookbooks and nursing texts in my collection, there is a common theme. When ill, especially for vegetarians or vegans, foods should be easy to digest, nutritious, warm, and often animal bone broth. For those on strict plant-based approaches, it takes time to slowly introduce animal base foods into the diet if required for health.

Nutritional factors, including low protein intake and poor dietary variety, affect age-associated impairment in physical performance resulting in physical frailty. In particular, dietary protein intake, necessary for muscle protein synthesis, has been the focus of several epidemiologic investigations.[1, 2, 3] It is fascinating how much the science of today is supporting the wisdom and knowledge of times gone by regarding food as medicine.

> Plant foods contain lower quality proteins, with fruits and vegetables being poor sources. Other plant foods, like baked beans, split peas, lentils, peanuts, nuts, seeds, and grains like wheat, are better sources; however, each type of plant protein is low in one or more of the essential amino acids.

All your body's cells contain protein, which is continually broken down and remodeled to meet your growth and maintenance needs. Dietary protein ingestion stimulates muscle protein synthesis by providing amino acids to the muscle. Many substances that control body functions, such as enzymes and hormones, also are made from protein. Other functions of protein include forming blood cells and producing antibodies to protect us from illness and infections.[4] Protein digestion, in which your body breaks down dietary protein into usable amino acids, makes these nutrients available to your cells to support muscle maintenance, immune function, hormone synthesis, red blood cell formation, and tissue repair. There are 20 amino acids in the protein that we eat every day. Many proteins are made of thousands of amino acids strung together.

Another factor determining the muscle protein synthetic response to protein ingestion is age.[5] A study released in 2022 reviewed protein digestion and absorption following food processing. Dietary protein digestion and absorption rates can be significantly increased or decreased by food processing treatments such as heating, gelling (a semirigid jelly-like colloid in which a liquid is dispersed in a solid), and enzymatic hydrolysis with subsequent metabolic impacts on muscle synthesis and glucose homeostasis. Food processing at extremely high temperatures at alkaline *pH* and/or in the presence of reducing sugars can modify amino acid side chains, leading to loss of bioavailability. Some protein-rich food ingredients are deliberately aggregated, gelled, or hydrolyzed during manufacture. Hydrolysis accelerates protein digestion/absorption and increases *splanchnic* utilization.[6]

> Splanchnic refers to organs in the abdominal cavity, including the stomach, small intestine, large intestine, pancreas, spleen, liver, and may also include the kidney. The splanchnic circulation receives >25% of cardiac output and contains a similar percentage of the total blood volume under normal conditions. It can act as a site of regulation of distribution of cardiac output and also as a blood reservoir.

Chapter 9 ~ Protein

> ***Principle 42:*** Eating meat and/or eggs does not cause heart disease.

Milk: Our First Food

In the century of research chronicled between 1917 and 2017, dairy goats have gone from simply serving as surrogates for cows to serving as transgenic carriers of human enzymes. Goat milk has been an essential part of human nutrition for millennia, in part because of the more remarkable similarity of goat milk to human milk, softer curd formation, a higher proportion of small milk fat globules, and different allergenic properties when compared with cow milk. However, critical nutritional deficiencies limit its suitability for infants. Great attention has been given to protein differences between goat and cow milk, fat and enzyme differences, and their effects on the physical and sensory properties of goat and cow milk products. Physiological differences between the species necessitate different techniques for analyzing somatic cell counts (any cell of an animal or plant other than a germ cell), which are naturally higher in goat milk. The high value of goat milk throughout the world has generated a need for various techniques to detect the adulteration of goat milk products with cow milk.[7]

Cow milk is the most common dairy milk. Most infant formulas are based on cow milk protein ingredients. Consumers now seek alternatives such as goat milk, which has increasingly been used in the last 30 years to manufacture infant, follow-on, and young child formulas. While similar in many aspects, compositional and functional differences exist between cow and goat milk. The use of whole goat milk as the only source of protein in formulas allows levels of milk fat, short- and medium-chain fatty acids, sn-2 palmitic acid, and milk fat globule membrane (MFGM) to be maximized, providing similarities to the complex human milk fat globules. Research on complex human milk fat globules from 2020 demonstrates benefits for infant digestion and cognitive and immune development.[8, 9]

Human milk is uniquely optimized for the needs of the developing infant. Its composition is complex and dynamic, driven primarily by gestational age of the infant, maternal genetics and, to a lesser extent, the mother's nutritional status and environment. One crucial component gaining attention is the milk fat globule (MFG). The MFG comprises a triglyceride-rich core surrounded by a tri-layer membrane, also known as the milk fat globule membrane (MFGM) which originates from mammary gland epithelia. The MFGM is enriched with glycerophospholipids, sphingolipids, cholesterol, and proteins, some of which are glycosylated and are known to fulfill numerous biological roles.[10, 11]

As We Age

Older age is associated with a lower muscle protein synthetic response to food ingestion, also called anabolic resistance. Anabolic resistance to protein intake is believed to be one of the factors responsible for the loss of muscle mass observed with increasing age.[12]

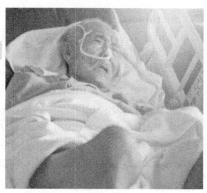

Malnutrition is associated with increased mortality and poor functional recovery after stroke. Malnutrition during hospitalization affects the functional recovery and post-discharge destinations of elderly stroke patients.[13] A 2022 study showed that nutritional supplementation with protein, amino acids, vitamins, and minerals positively affected recovery after stroke, with improvements in motor function, cognition, activities of living, and mood.[14] Progressive age-related reductions in muscle mass and strength (sarcopenia) can cause substantial morbidity. Data suggest that milk and other dairy products containing different bioactive compounds (i.e., protein, leucine) can enhance muscle protein synthesis, particularly when combined with resistance exercise.[15] Protein supplementation on top of resistance training is recommended to increase muscle mass and strength, particularly for obese persons.[16]

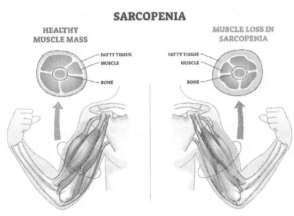

Sarcopenia is one of the main issues associated with the process of aging. Sarcopenia is the loss of muscle strength, mass, and function, often exacerbated by chronic comorbidities, including cardiovascular diseases, chronic kidney disease, and cancer. Although the pathophysiologic mechanisms are complex, the broad underlying cause of sarcopenia includes an imbalance between anabolic and catabolic muscle homeostasis, which occurs with or without neuronal degeneration. The intrinsic molecular mechanisms of aging, chronic illness, malnutrition, and immobility are associated with the development of sarcopenia.[17] According to the World Health Organization (WHO), a 38% increase in the number of older individuals worldwide is expected by 2025.[18] A decrease in muscle mass and function with advancing age exacerbates the likelihood of mobility impairments, disease development, and early mortality.[19] A 2023 study of chronic kidney disease (CKD) showed that when a chronic catabolic state exists, sarcopenia commonly occurs through various mechanisms, resulting in muscle wasting and decreased muscle endurance. Sarcopenic patients with CKD have high morbidity and mortality rates. Indeed, the prevention and treatment of sarcopenia are mandatory for preserving health and function in older age.[20]

Crosstalk Between Protein and the Microbiome

Gut microbiota, the largest symbiont community hosted in human organisms, is emerging as a pivotal player in the relationship between dietary habits and health. Oral and, primarily, intestinal microbes metabolize dietary components, affecting human health by producing harmful or beneficial metabolites involved in the incidence and progression of diseases. Accumulated research has revealed that the gut microbiota mediates the crosstalk between protein metabolism and immune response. Gut microbes are involved in the digestion, absorption, metabolism, and transformation process of dietary protein in the gastrointestinal tract. Amino acids can be metabolized into numerous microbial metabolites, which participate in various physiological functions related to health and diseases. The components of dietary protein impact the gut microbiota composition, concentration, and amino acid balance. In other words, dietary protein is a primary factor contributing to the function of gut microbes.[21]

Habitual diet (Western, Agrarian and Mediterranean omnivore diets, vegetarian, vegan, and gluten-free diets) drives the composition of the gut microbiota and metabolome. Within the dietary components, polymers (mainly fibers, proteins, fats, and polyphenols) that are not hydrolyzed by human enzymes are the main leads in the metabolic pathways of gut microbiota, which in turn directly influence the human metabolism.[22]

How Much Protein?
How much protein an individual needs depends on his or her body size and special needs, like growth. Some forms of protein are easier to digest than others, depending on the person's gastric health and cultural/typical types of protein consumed.

Children need more protein per pound of body weight than adults because they are growing and building new protein tissue. Pregnant and nursing women need more protein for the baby's growth and to produce milk.

Combining foods from any two of the following plant groups will make a higher-quality protein:

- ✓ Legumes, such as dry beans, peas, peanuts, lentils, and soybeans
- ✓ Grains such as wheat, rye, rice, corn, oats, and barley
- ✓ Seeds and nuts, such as sunflower and pumpkin seeds, pecans, and walnuts

Combining a small amount of animal products with any of the plant groups listed above will make a higher-quality protein:

- ✓ Eggs
- ✓ Dairy products, such as milk, cheese, and yogurt
- ✓ Meat, such as beef, poultry, fish, lamb, and pork

Amino Acids: All the Biochemistry You Never Knew!

Amino acids are a large group of organic molecules that contain both an acid group (-COOH) and an amino group (-NH2). In most amino acids, both chemical structures are attached to the same carbon atom. All amino acids are white, crystalline, and soluble in water. Dietary amino acids are typically consumed as dietary proteins, which are broken down into individual amino acids by the digestive system and then re-synthesized into endogenous proteins.

Individual amino acids are classified according to whether they are required as an essential part of the diet or not, and also according to their chemical structure.

Spent and excessive amino acids are eliminated from the body via the urea cycle; conversion of the nitrogen component of amino acids to ammonia, which then combines with carbon dioxide for excretion in the urine as urea.

> **Acidic Amino Acids** ~ aspartic and glutamic acids
>
> **Basic Amino Acids** are a component of *protamines* ~ arginine, histidine, lysine
>
> **Branch Chain Amino Acids** (BCAA) arise from the fact that BCAAs have carbon atoms that deviate (branch from) the main linear carbon backbone of the specific branched-chain amino acid molecule ~ isoleucine, leucine, valine
>
> **Essential Amino Acids** are essential for the maintenance of human health and must be supplied via the diet ~ isoleucine, leucine, lysine, methionine, phenylalanine, threonine, tryptophan, valine, histidine
>
> **Glucogenic Amino Acids** are amino acids that form metabolic intermediates, which then form glucose after they have lost their amino group ~ alanine, arginine, aspartic acid, cysteine, glutamic acid, glycine, histidine, methionine, phenylalanine, proline, serine, threonine, tyrosine, valine
>
> **Ketogenic Amino Acids** form *ketones* after losing their amino group ~ leucine, phenylalanine, tyrosine
>
> **Large Neutral Amino Acids** are amino acids with comparatively large but neutral molecules that share a common transport method through the *blood-brain barrier* and compete for entry into the brain.
>
> **Non-Essential Amino Acids** theoretically can be synthesized endogenously from essential amino acids ~ alanine, arginine, asparagine, aspartic acid, citrulline, cysteine, cystine, glutamic acid, glutamine, glycine, histidine, serine, tyrosine
>
> **Sulfur-Containing Amino Acids** ~ cysteine, cystine, methionine, taurine
>
> **Urea Cycle Amino Acids** facilitate the excretion of ammonia from the body through urea ~ arginine, citrulline, ornithine

Amines are organic compounds containing the amino functional group (-NH2) known for their strong, pungent odors. Amines occur in foods and in the bloodstream from the breakdown (*decarboxylation*) of amino acids ~ catecholamines, diphenylamine, heterocyclic aromatic amines, hexosamines, methylhexaneamine, neurine, nitrosamines, phenethylamines, polyamines, protamines, ptomaines, tryptamine.

A study released in 2023 on the amino acid *taurine* revealed how deficiencies impact our health and lifespan. This study found that the semi-essential amino acid taurine naturally decreased with age. Supplementing with taurine slowed key markers of aging, such as increased DNA damage, telomerase deficiency, impaired mitochondrial function, and cellular senescence. Declining taurine levels in humans was associated with aging-related diseases; however, its metabolites increased with exercise. In animal studies, taurine supplementation improved lifespan.[23] Some of the best dietary sources of taurine are scallops, turkey, chicken, seaweed, and beef. It may be worth thinking about how much of these foods you're eating as part of a well-rounded diet.

> ***Principle 43:*** Not all proteins are created equal, and how much a body requires is related to age.

Plant-based Protein

Plant-based diets are often touted as healthier than their meat-eating counterparts; existing research doesn't always support those claims, however. It is important to note that all dietary preferences have pros and cons—vegan, vegetarian, and meat-eaters. A systematic review of observational and intervention studies published between 2000 and 2020 was conducted to assess and compare nutrient status and intake in adult populations consuming plant-based diets (mainly vegetarian and vegan) with that of meat-eaters. One hundred forty-one studies were included, mainly from Europe, South/East Asia, and North America. Protein intake was lower in people following plant-based diets than meat-eaters but well within recommended intake levels. Vegans had the lowest vitamin B_{12}, calcium, and iodine intake and status, with lower bone mineral density. Meat-eaters were at risk of inadequate intakes of fiber, PUFA, α-linolenic acid (ALA), folate, vitamins D and E, calcium, and magnesium. <u>There were nutrient inadequacies across all dietary patterns, including vegan, vegetarian, and meat-based diets</u>.[24]

Plant Protein Concentrates and Dairy Substitutes

Plant protein concentrates and isolates are alternatives to meat, dairy and eggs; fractionation of ingredients and subsequent processing modifies proteins' techno-functional and nutritional properties. The differences in composition and structure of plant proteins and the wide range of processing steps and conditions can have uncertain results on protein digestibility. A study on the digestibility of plant proteins in 2022 examined the effect of fractionation. The researchers reviewed data on enzymatic hydrolysis, alkaline treatment, heating, high pressure, fermentation, complexation, extrusion, and gelation, as well as oxidation and interactions with starch or fiber for protein-rich soybean, yellow peas, and lentils. The data confirmed temperature and type of processing can improve protein digestibility, while more extensive processing can be detrimental.[25, 26]

Among the plant-based proteins, both lentils and quinoa have received attention as dairy-based protein alternatives. Fermentation is recognized as an effective technique in enhancing the functional properties, nutritional values, and protein digestibility of quinoa and lentils for potential options for dairy-based proteins.[27]

Considering the Challenges

Information from the studies discussed previously, presents me with some challenges and brings me back to considering not only the costs but also controls over the availability of processed plant-based proteins. As with so many other food-like substances, they are highly processed, and extensive resources are required to grow, process, and ship. All of these issues usually fail to make it into the conversation on climate change. These expensively processed foods are only available to the poorest populations in Africa, India, and South America when relief agencies supply them. They are not at all similar to foods that populations anywhere on the planet have prepared for centuries and are ill-suited to the unique climates of its many regions. Instead, these man-made products are used to augment protein content in commercially made foods and meat-free substitutes and marketed as trendy for vegetarians and weight loss. I cannot shake the gut feeling that the natural balance of whole foods is skewed here somehow, and the perception of using these protein products contributing to reducing climate change is no more than a feel-good exercise. There are countless traditionally-made and culturally appropriate plant-based foods for consumers to select and make without increasing costs or industrialization.[28] Once you have learned how to prepare foods correctly, you can enjoy their authentic flavor and nutrition while truly supporting stainable environmental practices.

Protein and Protecting Our Brain

The ketogenic diet—high in protein—may not be for everyone. However, a study reported in December 2014 by the American Epilepsy Society illustrates the ketogenic approach is highly beneficial for clients with epilepsy. By 2017, researchers found fasting and ketogenic diets were protective to the brain as well as having anti-aging benefits.[29, 30, 31, 32]

Researchers at John Hopkins University conducted a four-year study at their Adult Epilepsy Diet Center. The authors followed 134 adults with epilepsy, including 21 participants who were already following a ketogenic diet (KD). Their findings suggest that dietary therapy may benefit some adults with epilepsy. Of the 78 patients with drug-resistant epilepsy who began, the median seizure frequency was 10 seizures per week. The authors analyzed one month of data from 78 study participants and found that 43 (55%) had a greater than 50% seizure reduction. Of these, 28 (36%) patients became seizure-free. Patients who became seizure-free had been diagnosed with focal epilepsy, generalized epilepsy (10, including 5 with juvenile myoclonic epilepsy), and Doose syndrome. Also, 58 participants supplied three-month calendars of self-reported seizure activity.[33, 34, 35, 36]

Paradigm Shift in When to Eat Protein

Most Americans eat a diet that consists of little or no protein at breakfast, a bit of protein at lunch, and an overabundance of protein at dinner. It is common, even for vegans and vegetarians, for one daily meal to be more protein than others.[37]

Those who are chronically ill or elderly may only eat one meal daily and consume almost no protein. Research now supports what holistic nutrition practitioners have always known: lean, organic protein is necessary for the body to heal and repair itself. Some individuals do best with plant-based proteins, fish, or poultry, while others prefer lean red meats. Either way, 30 grams of protein is the current daily recommendation from noted functional medical authors and clinicians Terry Wahls, MD and Mark Hyman, MD.

> A female with a low to moderate activity level, weighing 135 pounds, requires between 86 and 143 grams of protein daily for normal blood sugar and metabolic function. If she is very active, her protein requirements increase.
>
> 1.5 grams (g) of protein are required to make 1 pound of muscle.
>
> The formula: Divide the body weight by .4536, then divide that answer by 2.
>
> This number will equal the number of grams per day of protein needed for health.
> (135 /.4536 = 297 / 2 = 149 g / 3 (number of average meals daily) = 49 g approximate total protein per meal = approx. 3 oz (1 oz = 28.34 g)

The time of day we consume our protein is also problematic, according to research from a team of scientists at the University of Texas Medical Branch at Galveston.

As it turns out, Dr. Barry Sears and others who promoted the "40-30-30" intake approach for blood sugar and weight control in the 1990's were right; corroborated by the research at the University of Texas Medical Branch at Galveston in the spring of 2014.

> This study shows the typical cereal or carbohydrate-dominated breakfast, a sandwich or salad at lunch, and an overly generous serving of meat/protein for dinner may not provide the best metabolic environment to promote healthy aging and maintenance of muscle size and strength. The potential for muscle growth is less than optimal when protein consumption is skewed toward the evening meal instead of being evenly distributed throughout the day.
>
> Age-related conditions such as osteoporosis (bone weakening) and sarcopenia (muscle wasting) do not suddenly develop. Instead, they are insidious processes precipitated by suboptimal lifestyle practices, such as diet and exercise, in early middle age.
>
> The study's results were obtained by measuring muscle protein synthesis rates in healthy adults who consumed two similar diets that differed in protein distribution throughout the day. One of the diets contained 30 grams of protein at each meal, while the other had 10 grams at breakfast, 15 grams at lunch, and 65 grams at dinner. Lean beef was the primary nutrient-dense source of protein for each daily menu. Using blood samples and thigh muscle biopsies, the researchers determined the subjects' muscle protein synthesis rates over 24-hour periods.
>
> The researchers provided volunteers with a generous daily dose of 90 grams of protein—consistent with the average amount currently consumed by healthy adults in the United States.
>
> When study volunteers consumed the evenly distributed protein meals, their 24-hour muscle protein synthesis was 25% greater than subjects who ate according to the skewed

protein distribution pattern. This result was not altered by several days of habituation to either protein distribution pattern.

The study results indicate that a more effective protein consumption pattern will likely differ dramatically from many Americans' daily eating habits.

> "Usually, we eat very little protein at breakfast, a bit more at lunch, and then consume a large amount at night. So we're not taking enough protein on board for efficient muscle building and repair during the day, and at night we often take in more than we can use. We risk having this excess oxidized and ending up as glucose or fat."[38]

Researchers suggest that a more efficient eating strategy for making muscle and controlling total caloric intake would be to shift some of the extra protein consumed at dinner to lunch and breakfast.

> *Principle 44:* When (time of day) you eat protein is equally important as how much and what kind is eaten.

Collagen Powder

Collagen is made from an amino acid protein, gelatin, which is collagen before it is broken down. In the early 1990s, Knox® Gelatin became a popular joint support food, leading to the development of glucosamine/chondroitin products, which are hydrolyzed. Collagen is broken down via water and various blending techniques into collagen peptides, making the amino acids shorter; the thought is that if they are broken down, they are easier to absorb (*bioavailability*). Additionally, this processing keeps collagen from forming back into gelatin — so when it is put into water with ice it doesn't thicken.

> When choosing the right powder supplement for your needs, the critical factors are purity, taste, texture, and origin.
>
> 1. Purity – The best collagen contains a high protein content and all nineteen specific amino acids, thus restoring bone density, improving concentration, balancing emotions, and maintaining mobile and healthy joints.
>
> 2. Taste and Texture – You want to be sure the powder will dissolve readily and be easily masked by whatever you blend with it.
>
> 3. Origin – You will be putting quite a bit of this stuff in your body daily and want it to be well-sourced and ethically produced.[39]

At present, for me, the product is too new, with little actual research and a lot of marketing hype; time will tell. I prefer old-school cooking methods that bring collagen into my diet without needing an industrial manufacturing plant.

Ahead of His Time

The awareness of influencers like Jack LaLanne reminds us that health and physical fitness can be achieved without processed food products, collagen supplements, or gyms. LaLanne followed a pescatarian dietary approach, pioneered juicing to get nutrients from vegetables, and invented the first-ever protein powders. It could be argued that Jack LaLanne singlehandedly kickstarted the American fitness revolution; opening his fitness studio in 1936 and commonly saying on his TV show, *"Exercise is king, nutrition is queen; put them together and you've got a kingdom."* Our mothers took time to follow along with Jack LaLanne on television during the 1960s. He had you use whatever was on hand to move those muscles and strengthen your body. Canned goods were held as hand weights, and chair backs were often used for support/balance. During his lifetime, he set countless world records in strength and endurance. In 1984, Jack, at 70 years of age, swam while handcuffed, shackled, fighting winds and currents, towing 70 boats with 70 people from the Queen's Way Bridge in the Long Beach Harbor to the ship Queen Mary — 1½ miles. Jack passed away in 2011 at 96; quite a story for a kid with an eating disorder and health problems.

> "Jack LaLanne was thirty years ahead of his time. He is truly the terminator of unhealthy living. He possesses the secret formula for the fountain of youth."
>
> ~Arnold Schwarzenegger

Overconsumption

Asian societies learned long ago that for soy protein to be beneficial, it had to be fermented or predigested. Even then, other foods were necessary as balance to its phytoestrogens to prevent thyroid, prostate, and breast diseases. The average Japanese consumes over 15mg of iodine in seafood and sea vegetables daily. The iodine protects against the estrogenic and goitrogenic properties of the soy. In addition to soy, an Asian diet consists of meat, bones, eyes, glands, skin, and internal organs, all of which provide a broad range of amino acids and nutrients. By the way, the Japanese refuse to eat American soy foods and do not let Monsanto® sell GMO soy in their country.[40]

Most Americans overeat highly processed foods, including protein powders filled with GMO ingredients, alternative sweeteners, and artificial flavors. Overloading with any one food can lead to health problems, especially for children who are still developing. If you are using a protein product, research the ingredients and the brand you selected, or buy from a practitioner who has investigated the product, and only use them for a short time.

Teach your teens how to shop for and cook real food, buying good sources of protein and fresh foods. Adopt the practice of making family meals from scratch or cook together for a family event that everyone can get involved in at least once a week. As a parent, don't let your teens use protein powders without supervision; they will need their kidneys and liver for many years.

A Little History

So how has red meat from cattle and other flesh foods become such an integral yet controversial part of the American diet?

> "Although cattle have been domesticated for less than 10,000 years, they are the world's most valuable animal, as judged by their multiple contributions of draft power, meat, milk, hides, and dung. Evidence for the domestication of cattle dates from between 8,000 and 7,000 years ago in southwestern Asia; dating suggests cattle were not domesticated until cereal domestication, whereas sheep and goats entered the barnyard of humans with the beginning of agriculture. Domestication would have initially required a supply of animals by capturing them from the wild. In the holding pens, some captive bulls and cows bred, and from these matings calves were born. Their overall size was smaller, and their temperament more docile. The next generation to follow reinforced the characteristics of the parents, and a gene pool that distinguished these bovines from their wild forebears gradually formed. No longer were they aurochs, but rather cattle."[41]

At the end of the Little Ice Age (roughly the 18th century), the use of salt to preserve meat became more frequent. City dwellers and seafarers could carry dried preserved meats instead of traveling with living animals. The quality and taste were less than the best.

From 1870 to 1920, livestock ranching provided the meat for boom towns, logging camps, and railway development. Transportation of fresh foods, especially meat, was a problem; the dilemma of how to get fresh meat to European markets affected price and demand. In the 1942 *Yearbook of Agriculture— Keeping Livestock Healthy*, sub-par livestock nutrition is cited as "responsible for significant economic losses" for decades.[42] The U.S. was at the forefront of new advances in meat canning processes, but many products were far from palatable in the 19th and early 20th centuries. The Shaker ice houses and their expertise in layered insulation made transportation in railroad ice cars possible over vast distances. In the 1850s, a Scottish immigrant to Australia designed and improved an ether compressor, making ice manufacturing possible for the first time; this was the advent of refrigeration.[43]

Over a century ago, the federal government passed the *Meat Inspection Act of 1906* to protect consumers from tainted meat products. Back then, meat was commonly adulterated with sulfate, boric acid, formaldehyde, coal tar, and saltpeter. And it wasn't just meat—questionable additives like coal dust and kerosene were used to fool consumers into thinking that green coffee beans were roasted (if it was even coffee!). It wasn't until 1965 that manufacturers were required to list ingredients on food products meant for human consumption.[44]

Today's Reality Could Turn Anyone Off Meat

The consumer often thinks very little about how the food arrived at the point of purchase or where it originated. We assume that the quality of food at our fingertips is far superior to that of our ancestors; we like to believe it is cleaner, fresher and safer. However, every year food recalls result in millions of pounds of potentially dangerous foods being discarded.

In addition to the risks of contamination and spoilage, there is also the issue of added chemicals. According to a study from Sweden, men who eat moderate amounts of processed red meat may have an increased risk of incidence and death from heart failure, according to a 2014 study in *Circulation: Heart Failure*, a journal of the American Heart Association. Processed meats are preserved by smoking, curing, salting, or adding preservatives. Examples include cold cuts (ham, salami, bologna, lunch meat, jerky, pepperoni), sausage, bacon and hot dogs.

> "Processed red meat commonly contains sodium, nitrates, phosphates and other food additives, and smoked and grilled meats also contain polycyclic aromatic hydrocarbons, all of which may contribute to the increased heart failure risk," said Alicja Wolk, DMSc, senior author of the study and professor in the Division of Nutritional Epidemiology at the Institute of Environmental Medicine, Karolinska Institute in Stockholm, Sweden. "Unprocessed meat is free from food additives and usually has less sodium." [45]

Pink Slime Renamed

In 2010, the great "pink slime" scandal erupted. The Modesto Meat Company recalled about one million pounds of ground beef after seven people were sickened by *E. coli* contamination. The U.S. Department of Agriculture announced that the Valley Meat Company had sold the potentially contaminated meat in California, Texas, Oregon, Arizona, and internationally.

Suddenly, news about "pink slime" was everywhere. On *FoodNavigator.com*, a website for those in the food industry, I saw the headline: "Pink slime: Safe, nutritious and icky." It said, "Scary junk science about ammonium hydroxide has led to a safe, nutritious product being pulled from stores. Beef Products Inc, the nation's leading manufacturer of 'pink slime '(aka: lean finely textured beef) is suspending product production at three of four plants after major retailers said they would stop buying it. The move follows a storm of media hysteria spewed onto a largely ignorant public."

The news report said, "If the Beef Products manufacturing company can't clear itself from this pink slime PR mess, it will mean 1.5 million cattle will need to be slaughtered to meet demands for ground beef, pink slime free." ABC News later settled with a South Dakota meat producer in 2017 after it filed a $1.9 billion lawsuit against the network over its reports on the company's lean, finely textured beef product dubbed 'pink slime.' The United States Department of Agriculture (USDA) in 2019 reclassified the product once referred to as "pink slime" or "lean finely textured beef" as "ground beef." The reclassification was based on a review of the company's processing and production facility in Dakota City, Nebraska. The USDA still recognizes "lean finely textured beef" as a category, but the label *pink slime* no longer applies.[46]

What about ammonium hydroxide used in the manufacture of pink slime? The *Material Safety Data Sheet* reports: Very hazardous in case of skin contact (corrosive, irritant, permeator), eye contact (irritant), or ingestion. Non-corrosive to the eyes. Non-corrosive for lungs. Liquid or spray mist may damage tissue, particularly on mucous membranes of the eyes, mouth, and respiratory tract. Skin contact may produce burns. Inhalation of the spray mist may produce severe irritation of the respiratory tract, characterized by coughing, choking, or shortness of breath. Severe over-exposure can result in death.

> "Inflammation of the eye is characterized by redness, watering, and itching. Skin inflammation is characterized by itching, scaling, reddening, or occasionally blistering. Repeated or prolonged exposure to the substance can produce target organ damage. Ingestion: If swallowed, do not induce vomiting unless directed to do so by medical personnel. Never give anything by mouth to an unconscious person. Loosen tight clothing such as a collar, tie, belt, or waistband. Get medical attention immediately."

I can see a long list of problems calling a product derived by highly mechanized means "ground beef." This slippery slope paved the way for cell-cultured chicken meat companies to use the term for their products. The USDA approved cell-cultured chicken in May of 2023.[47, 48] I am thankful for the availability of unprocessed real meat through local ranchers. I've never had my T-bones or bison ossobuco recalled due to contamination.

Lamb and Mutton

Only sheep flesh food is unique in containing some of the most bioavailable amino acids and omega-3 compared to other foods.

Historically, mutton or sheep has provided an easy, portable flesh food for many cultures dating from antiquity to modern times. Shepherds could easily guard sheep; they browse on a wider variety of grasses and brush and are adaptable to cold, high elevation climates.

In regions of some countries without access to a coastline and fish, lamb has sometimes been shown to provide more omega-3 than any other food in the diet. In Australia, where both children and adults frequently eat lamb, recent studies have shown lamb to rank among the top omega-3 foods in the daily diet. Grass-fed lamb has been shown to average at least 25% more omega-3 than conventionally fed lamb, including as much as 49% more ALA (alpha-linolenic acid), the basic building block for omega-3. In the nutritional profile of grass-fed lamb, we use a conservative average estimate of 40 milligrams of omega-3 per ounce of roasted lamb loin. That's 50% of the omega-3 in an ounce of baked codfish or broiled tuna, and 67% of the amount in an ounce of sesame seeds.[49]

Sheep were among the first animals ever to be domesticated by humans, occurring more than 10,000 years ago. The domestication of sheep started in the Middle East, in what is now Turkey. Sheep were introduced as a source of food and textiles (wool) and became popular throughout many regions of the world. Over 2,000 years ago, the Romans introduced sheep into Great Britain, where lamb remains very popular. Lamb was not introduced into the Western Hemisphere until the early 16th century when the armies of Spanish explorer Hernán Cortés brought sheep with them on their explorations. Since ancient times, the lamb has been regarded as a religious symbol. In various religions, including Judaism, it was commonly used as a sacrifice and a symbol of sacrifice. Jesus is often referred to as the "Lamb of God." In many countries, lamb is a traditional Easter dish commemorating the Last Supper, at which lamb was likely served.

Lamb farming peaked in the U.S. in 1884 with 51 million head of sheep. Today, lamb farming involves about 6 million head. Half of all lamb consumed in the U.S. is imported, and within this category of imported lamb, nearly 68% comes from Australia and 30% from New Zealand.[50, 51]

Here is a hint for cooking with lamb: After roasting on a rack or grilling your lamb, squeeze fresh lime on to the meat just before eating. All the flavor associated with lanolin or gamey mutton vanishes.

Pork

Wild and domesticated pork is the most consumed red meat worldwide, especially in eastern Asia, but its consumption is forbidden in certain religions, such as Islam and Judaism.

Being high in protein and rich in many vitamins and minerals, lean pork can be an excellent addition to a healthy diet. The protein content of lean, cooked pork is around 26% by fresh weight. By dry weight, the protein content of lean pork can be as high as 89%, making it one of the richest dietary sources of protein.[52, 53] Pork contains all the essential amino acids necessary for the growth and maintenance of our bodies. For this reason, eating pork, or other meats, may benefit bodybuilders, recovering athletes, post-surgical patients, or other people who need to build up or repair their muscles.

The proportion of fat in pork usually ranges from 10-16%, but it can be much higher depending on the level of trimming and various other factors. Clarified pig fat, called lard, is used as a cooking fat.[54, 55, 56] Like other types of red meat, pork is mainly composed of saturated and unsaturated fats, present in approximately equal amounts. The fatty acid composition of pork is slightly different from the meat of ruminant animals, such as beef and lamb. Pork is low in conjugated linoleic acid (CLA) and is slightly richer in unsaturated fats.

Heart Health and Pork Meat

Heart disease, also called cardiovascular disease (CVD), is the leading cause of premature death worldwide. Some studies have shown an increased risk for CVD in both processed and unprocessed red meat eaters, whereas others showed an increased risk for processed meat only. However, there is no clear-cut evidence that meat, in itself, actually causes heart disease. Observational studies can only reveal possible associations but cannot provide evidence for a direct cause-and-effect relationship. It is clear that high meat intake is linked with unhealthy lifestyle factors, such as low consumption of fruits and vegetables, less physical activity, smoking, and overeating; most observational studies try to statistically correct for these factors.[57] The link between saturated fats and heart disease is also unclear, and many high-quality studies have not found any significant association.[58, 59]

> ***Principle 45:*** Nutritional deficiencies can result from all dietary patterns: vegan, vegetarian, meat/flesh-eaters.

Fish

Do you buy fish from the store? How about that favorite basket of fish'n chips from the local fast food joint? Are you sure you are getting the fish named on the menu or label? Nearly half of the seafood samples in restaurants and grocery stores in four major Canadian cities were mislabeled, according to a new Oceana Canada report released in 2021. The mislabeling rate among retailers was 6.5%, lower than the 25% combined average from Oceana Canada's previous studies. The mislabeling rate among restaurants increased from 56% - 65%.[60] Oceana Canada's research found ten instances where products labeled as butterfish or tuna were escolar. Of the 13 samples labeled snapper, seven were tilapia. And 24 of the butterfish, yellowtail, and white tuna samples were mislabeled.

Seafood mislabeling is common in New York and Boston. The report, released on February 21, 2013, shows fraudulent labeling is happening across the country and is just as likely to occur in Texas and Colorado as in Boston or New York. Some 49% of the retail outlets sampled in Austin and Houston sold mislabeled seafood; in Colorado, 36%. The highest mislabeling rates occurred with snapper and tuna; 87% and 59% respectively. The report found that only seven of the 120 samples of red snapper purchased nationwide were red snapper.

So what's the big deal? Mislabeling can put consumers at risk when species such as king mackerel, high in mercury, or escolar, which contains a naturally occurring toxin that can cause gastrointestinal problems, are marketed as grouper and white tuna. The U.S. imports 90% of its seafood; less than 2% is inspected for fraud. The Food and Drug Administration regularly updates its list of seafood approved for sale. In 2012, 19 new species were added, including cornetfish, sampa, and claresse.[61] Ever heard of these fish? Dust off your poles and fishing gear or take a drive to the coast and visit a U.S.-owned fish cannery. Buy fresh fish off the boat, can or freeze it yourself, and support our local U.S. fisheries.

> Be especially wary of fish from Thailand, Vietnam, and China. These countries have posted health advisories to their own citizens regarding the dangers of eating their domestically farmed fish.
>
> Seafood Watch provides a free consumer guide to best seafood choices.
> www.seafoodwatch.org

Chapter 9 ~ Protein

Incredible Edible Eggs

Eggs are an ancient food, and gastronomy has many recipes worldwide utilizing the remarkable chicken egg, but the recipes are not limited to chicken eggs alone. Summer in many areas brings out dishes of Eggs Benedict, deviled eggs, egg salad, boiled, fried, scrambled, and poached eggs. Yet the health benefits of eggs have been questioned.

Eggs and chickens remind me of my 4-H days and conversations about poultry feed and commercial egg production. Eggs get their color from the feed given to the birds, and they especially love baby grass, which is rich in chlorophyll. Corn and wheat add more yellow coloring to the yolks. Chickens are far from vegetarian and can be cannibalistic, especially when their diets are protein deficient. Worms, bugs, slugs, spiders, broken eggs, meat scraps; the list of what chickens will eat is long, and chickens left to their own devices will consume protein-rich foods before grain. It is these foods that add nutritional value to eggs. Yes, they'll gobble up grains and seeds, but what they really want is found in a three-day-old cow pie or compost pile. Just like cows, the digestive system of chickens was not designed to subsist solely on grain. Everything an animal eats becomes part of their flesh and DNA. If you are allergic to wheat, corn, or soy and consume products from animals fed on these grains, you might suffer an allergic or inflammatory response that could lead to chronic illness.

Here is an example: I have a 67-year-old client who reacts to corn and dairy. Most commercial milk comes from cows that were fed corn. Also, when this client eats store-bought eggs — whether cage-free, organic, or commercial — he immediately suffers from gas, cramping, and diarrhea. There is no distress when this client eats truly free-range eggs; chickens fed only cracked peas and whatever they can find on their own. Do you see the connection here? It isn't just about what we eat, but also about what is consumed by what we eat. The same line of reasoning applies to our soils, vegetables, fruits, and fish.

Why Do Americans Wash and Chill Their Eggs?

Americans, Japanese, Australians, and Scandinavians tend to be squeamish about chicken eggs, so they are washed, which removes the natural protective wax coating on the shell that keeps bacteria from invading the egg. Once eggs have been washed, they have to be refrigerated.

To understand this practice, let's rewind. About a hundred years ago, many people worldwide washed their eggs. But there are a lot of ways to do it wrong, so the method got a bad reputation in certain parts of the world. A batch of rotten eggs, washed in Australia, left a bad impression on its British importers. By 1970, the USDA had perfected the art of the wash with the help of machines, and it required all egg producers to wash eggs for sale. Meanwhile, many European countries prohibited washing, and Asian countries never got on board with it. The exception was Japan, which joined the egg-washers after a bad spate of salmonella in the 1990s.

Washing and Refrigeration

"The egg is a marvel in terms of protecting itself, and one of the protections is this coating, which prevents them from being porous," says food writer Michael Ruhlman, author of *Egg: A Culinary Exploration of the World's Most Versatile Ingredient.* "Once you start refrigeration, you must have it through the whole value chain, from farm to store. Once you stop — if the eggs are cold and you put them in a warm environment — they'll start sweating, which becomes a breeding ground for bacteria." Another perk of consistent refrigeration is shelf life. It jumps from about 21 days to almost 50 days. In many countries, constant refrigeration just isn't possible.

In North America, we like to have everything super clean, so they probably initiated the washing of the egg very early on, leading down the refrigeration path. But in a lot of places, a dirty egg with poop on it is no big deal. You brush it off when you get home.[62, 63]

Medical Myth Meets the Incredible Egg

Next, we move into the fairytale world of medical mythology. Doctors told patients to stop eating eggs for years because they are high in cholesterol and could lead to heart disease.

On July 19, 2013, a study that would make my great-grandmother smack her forehead was published. To her, it was common sense that eggs were good for a growing child. The news headline read: "*Eating Eggs Is Not Linked to High Cholesterol in Adolescents*, Study Suggests." It stated, "Although in the late 20th century it was maintained that eating more than two eggs a week could increase cholesterol, in recent years, experts have begun to refute this myth. A new study has found that eating more eggs is not associated with higher serum cholesterol in adolescents, regardless of how much physical activity they do."[64]

There is more. Let's look at information from Dr. Niva Shapira of Tel Aviv University's School of Health Professions. In a study published on August 2, 2011, she stated that eggs are not created equal. "Eggs high in omega-6 fatty acids heighten cholesterol's tendency to oxidize, which forms dangerous plaque in arteries." Dr. Shapira's research shows eggs laid by hens with a healthier feed can lessen oxidation of LDL (low-density lipoprotein), the body's "bad cholesterol."

> "But healthier eggs cost more," Dr. Shapira says. "The price of chicken feed varies from region to region, and in many areas, feed containing products high in omega-6 fatty acids, such as wheat, corn or maize, soy, and their oils, are much cheaper for egg producers to purchase."

A 2022 study published on the role of eggs in a healthy diet confirmed, "Epidemiologic evidence and clinical trials have found no links between egg intake and increased risk for heart disease. Eggs are a good source of high-quality protein. Eggs, in addition to numerous vitamins and minerals, contain compounds including choline, lutein, and zeaxanthin with functions that go beyond nutrition as they protect against chronic disease."[65] In a 2022 study, eggs were found to improve plasma biomarkers in patients with metabolic syndrome when included as part of a plant-based diet.[66] Additionally, in 2018, and article titled *Compared to an Oatmeal Breakfast, Two Eggs/Day Increased Plasma Carotenoids and Choline without*

Increasing Trimethyl Amine N-Oxide Concentrations was published.[67] These few facts are a small portion of research contained in >20 articles on the benefits of eggs.

Poultry eggs from different species varied significantly due to their divergent process of evolution. However, the information on egg characteristics has been mainly limited to chicken. A study published in 2019 reported that egg albumen of turkey had the highest quantity of essential amino acids (EAA) and total amino acids (TAA), while duck and goose eggs had relatively higher EAA/TAA ratios.[68, 69]

So the bottom line is that buying from the farmers market or a local farmer is best. Look them in the eye and ask if they are feeding their chickens commercial egg mixtures or if their birds are free-range? Are they washing the eggs or wiping them off? I know my egg providers by name and sight. They live in our community, and I know they depend financially on the quality of the food they produce, just like I rely on it for my health.

Turkey

Today's domesticated turkey is descended from the wild turkey. It was the Mesoamericans who first domesticated the wild turkey. For the Aztecs, it was an essential source of protein; the feathers were used for decorative purposes. Additional evidence suggests the Hopi Indians may have domesticated the turkey even before the Aztecs. Spanish explorers, who had found them among the Aztecs and other Mesoamerican peoples, introduced the turkey to Europe.

Turkeys are often eaten as the main course in Christmas feasts (stuffed turkey) and for Thanksgiving in the United States and Canada. This tradition has its origins in modern times rather than colonial. Before the 20th century, pork ribs were the most common food on the holiday menu, as the animals were usually slaughtered in November. Turkeys were once so abundant in the wild that they were eaten regularly and considered commonplace, whereas pork ribs were rarely available outside of the Thanksgiving-New Year season. Turkey also displaced the traditional Christmas roast goose or beef of the United Kingdom and Europe. Before World War II, the turkey was a luxury in the United Kingdom. In Charles Dickens's *A Christmas Carol*, Bob Cratchit had a goose before Scrooge bought him a turkey.

Intensive turkey farming from the late 1940s dramatically reduced the price, shifting turkey to the most common Thanksgiving and Christmas dinner meat. With the availability of refrigeration, whole turkeys could be shipped frozen to distant markets. Disease control increased production, allowing the domesticated turkey to be eaten year-round. Ground turkey is often marketed as a beef substitute.

Wild turkeys, while technically the same species as domesticated turkeys, have a very different taste from farm-raised turkeys. Almost all of the meat is dark, even the breast, with a more intense flavor. The flavor can also vary seasonally with changes in forage, often leaving wild turkey meat with a gamier taste in late summer due to the more significant number of insects in its diet. A wild turkey fed predominantly on grass and grain has a milder flavor. Older heritage breeds also differ in taste.

The poultry industry produces approximately two to four billion pounds of feathers yearly. Most are ground into a protein source for ruminant animal feed. Additionally, poultry feathers are used in the manufacture of amino acid supplements and inclusion in protein powders.

Health Benefits

Turkey contains amino acids with high levels of L-lysine and leucine. Wild turkey also contains essential fatty acids, iron, chromium, and zinc with the peptide anserine. The highest levels of essential fatty acids are found in the skin at 39.3%. Roasted turkey contains about 29% protein per 100 grams of meat, almost 40% less than an equal amount of soy protein. This high-protein content may partially account for the dangers of soy isolate products and their potential to cause kidney and liver damage.

> ***Principle 46:*** Dietary protein is a key factor in gut microbiota functioning.

Traditional Christmas Foods – Return of the Mincemeat Pie

Mincemeat is a favorite seasonal food for our family; it brings back the unique flavor and smells of the holidays in Northern Idaho and Eastern Oregon. Every year come November, we put together a considerable bowl to marinate and blend mincemeat, full of ground meat, apples, wild huckleberries, cranberries, currents, spices, fat, and brandy. Once the flavors are blended and we have had our fill of fresh pie, the remainder goes into jars for canning and is used on special occasions in the coming year. In today's modern world of refrigeration and the international food commerce world, most people have never tasted a real old-fashioned mincemeat pie or are even sure of what mincemeat is!

In the food culture of the Pacific Northwest, this holiday food originated from the employees of the Hudson Bay Company and Native peoples; everyone brought with them flavors and traditions from his or her native cultures. In this case, the mincemeat pie from England melded with the Native Peoples' *pemican* to form what is viewed as traditional mincemeat here in the western part of America. Coveted handwritten recipes from grandmothers and mothers are tucked into cookbooks and recipe boxes in ranch kitchens, dating back to the mid-1800s. The flavor of real mincemeat pie (not the sticky, bland version in glass jars at stores) is a blend of Middle Eastern spices and meat. This meat mixture, traditionally mutton, was made into a pie and formed the main course of a meal, not a dessert. Traditional mincemeat has a rich, meaty taste and texture, with a festive blend of sweet and tart wrapped in warm spice flavor and tender pastry.

Mincemeat was historically a way to preserve meat 500 years ago in England — usually mutton or wild game — without having to salt or smoke. While conversing with a local man from England, he shared how his grandmother always made a densely packed fruit mince for the holidays. Meat pies packed with savory flavors are a regular dish all over Great Britain, and mince pies made primarily with fruit are still considered an essential accompaniment to holiday dinners.

Spices from the Orient came home with Crusaders to Europe; cinnamon, cloves, allspice (optional if you do not like nutmeg), and nutmeg. These spices were believed to be the gifts the Magi gave to the Christ Child. Historical accounts tell us that in honor of the birth of the Savior, the mince pie was made in oblong casings resembling a coffin or cradle, with a place for the Christ Child on top, which would be removed by the children, and the manger (pie) was eaten in celebration.[70] These pies were not very large, similar to today's pocket pies or muffin tin pastries. Today's pie is a remnant of a medieval tradition dating back to the Crusades. Tradition says it was good luck to eat one mince pie on each of the twelve days of Christmas, ending with Epiphany, the 6th of January.[71]

The spices from the Orient are rich in antimicrobial properties, hence their value in preserving meat through winter. The knowledge and efficacious use of these spices and herbs were part of a noblewoman's early training as it was her duty to ensure food stores lasted through the winter. Typically, the meat used in Tudor England and France was finely chopped or minced mutton giving this Christmas food its name. As time passed, fruit became the predominant ingredient; however, many parts of the Pacific Northwest still hold to the tradition of meat being in equal or greater parts to fruit.[72] Local fruits in the forests and valleys flavor mincemeat; huckleberry, currents, cranberries, crabapple, serviceberry, and salmonberry.[73] Wild game meat also plays a prominent role in mincemeat pie found in the West, along with beef and bison. The use of lamb or mutton would have been an affront to cattlemen in the west in the 1900s, and often elk and venison made up the staple meat for families, reserving valuable market animals for income.

In *Swan among the Indians: the life of James G. Swan, 1818-1900, unpublished diaries and journals*, by Lucile Saunders McDonald, Swan describes a Christmas dinner with a mincemeat pie using whale meat.

> "On December 25, 1861, three "Boston men" sat down to Christmas dinner in the trading post established four years earlier at the edge of the Makah Indian reservation, Washington Territory, U.S.A.
> Swan boiled the whale meat, and cut it finely, adding chopped apples and wild cranberries, raisins, currants, salt, nutmeg, cloves, allspice, cinnamon, and brown sugar. After packing it into a ten-gallon stone jar, he had added a quart of New England rum and sealed it for future use.
> The traditional holiday was a welcome break from the unloading and distribution of a shipment of goods promised to the Makah by the treaty they had signed in 1855. James Swan, a periodic resident in Neah Bay, had, in the absence of the trader, prepared a feast of roast goose and duck stew, presenting for dessert a mince pie made from whale meat."[74]

In the summer of 2023, a small book *The Good Housekeeper* (7th edition 1844) by Mrs. Sarah Hale, came into our collection; it contains my earliest obtained versions of mincemeat. This cookbook was so popular it sold over 2,000 copies in the first month in 1839. After reading through a handful of delicate pages, I can see why! On pages 85 and 86 of this almost 200-year-old book are captured the directions for *Mince Pies*, followed by a second version for *Rich Mince Meat*, a third for *Family Mince Pie*, and a fourth for *Plain Mince Pies*. All the recipes contain a combination of fruit, meat, and wine. Some use tongue, which will be included in our family holiday bowl of mincemeat henceforth.

A New Book of Cookery by Fannie Merritt Farmer (*1917*) contains a mince pie recipe that resembles the modern idea of mincemeat in many parts of North America today. Listed as a "mock mincemeat," this recipe contains a few surprises such as green tomatoes, mace, and black pepper in addition to the original three spices of antiquity and dried raisins and currants.[75, 76] Modern versions of mincemeat are crammed with processed sugar, artificial flavor, and hydrogenated trans fats or no fat at all. Additionally, store-bought versions lose many nutrients and flavors from traditional recipes. The holidays are especially problematic for those with diabetes; properly prepared homemade mincemeat pie can come to the rescue. The combination of fat and protein makes this a dish safer for many with blood sugar challenges to eat, providing portions are small, whole rather than dried fruit is used, and the cook went easy on the sweet. For several traditional mincemeat recipes, go to *Our Journey with Food Cookery Book,* pg 199 and 344.

> ***Principle 47:*** Exercise is king, nutrition is queen; put them together and you have a kingdom!" ~ Jack LaLanne

Food Sovereignty and Protein

Livestock farming systems provide multiple benefits to humans: protein-rich diets that contribute to food security, employment, and rural economies; capital, stock, and draught resiliency equal power in many developing countries and cultural landscapes worldwide. Despite these positive contributions to society, livestock is also at the center of many controversies regarding its environmental impacts, animal welfare, and health outcomes related to excessive meat consumption.[77]

Herbivores are found in a variety of ecosystems all over the world. Permanent pastures and meadows cover about 25% of global land and are highly diverse. This diversity results from thousands of years of natural selection, human-controlled breeding, migration, and trade. Because of the high diversity of domestic herbivore genetic resources, herders have been able to live in regions where no alternative for income generation exists. Meat and milk from domestic herbivores provide 16% and 8% of the global protein and kilocalorie consumption, respectively.[78] The role of herbivorous livestock in supporting the sustainability of the farming systems in which they are found is complex. In Sub-Saharan Africa (SSA), integrating livestock into farming systems is vital for sustainable agriculture. Recycling nutrients for crop production through animal manure is central to the dominant mixed crop-livestock systems. Sustainable agriculture has been widely advocated as the main practical pathway to address the challenge of meeting the food needs of the rapidly growing population.[79, 80]

"Less but better" is a pragmatic approach to tackling the sustainability challenges of meat consumption and production. A shared vision of livestock systems with improved sustainability across multiple indicators is needed to establish principles for decision-making and desired outcomes for everyone. A study conducted in the Netherlands in 2020 illustrated some of the growing challenges with *less but better* views on food. Within Dutch eating habits, optimization constraints required a shift from beef, cheese, butter, and snacks to plant-based foods, fish, and shellfish. The optimized solution resulted in a lack of food diversity and the (lacto-ovo) vegetarian and vegan-optimized diets were prone to nutritional inadequacies.[81] Unsurprisingly, resistance to removing deeply rooted cultural foods will continue to be a challenge for governments striving to present idealized dietary changes as a means to meeting targeted greenhouse gas emissions by 2050.[82, 83] A 2023 French study on income levels and food insecurity concluded that "study results underline the importance of considering individual dietary patterns and thinking at the whole diet level and not only considering specific food or food group impacts when designing educational tools or public policies to promote more sustainable diets."[84, 85]

As Western consumers reached for 'better' meat in the last decade, the local farm-to-table market grew, creating environmental sustainability, improved animal welfare, and better nutrition for consumers.[86, 87]

Food Sovereignty and Cultural Gastronomy

Many, including myself, are passionate about our right to food sovereignty. This topic, however, is not viewed with passion or even understanding from immigrants from other countries or all cultures. One example came from a group of students from Bulgaria, West Africa, Pacifica, and the Caribbean. The Bulgarian student kept hearing about the Mediterranean diet, but to them it was "just food" that they grew up with. The second student viewed their cultural food as largely unhealthy, as diabetes and heart disease had decimated their extended Hispanic family. And the West African student felt pressured by their family to eat foods that made them ill because they came from their home country. This illustrates differing perspectives on every aspect of the food conversation. For those whose only remaining tie to their ancestry (Basque and First Peoples) is food, they are passionate about the traditional integrity.
Equally, for those who embrace global cuisine without hesitation, the quality of the food or adventure of new foods may be of greater value.

My question about" what happens to cultural foods when government mandates pressure individuals to adopt a plant-based protein diet?" is about our right to use food as medicine, to be self-sufficient, have choice, and be independent. Hunger has been used to control individuals and cultures for centuries. When total control of food resides in the hands of a few versus everyone, the balance is skewed, and our health and that of future generations suffers. A cross-cultural study done in 2020 looked at how cultural foods were found to affect social identity in two Latin American countries, Argentina and Mexico. Similar findings for Spain, Portugal, Italy, African nations, and Asian cultures can be found when searching PubMed. These evidence-based validations of the gastronomy concept indicate the existence of a solid link to culture, food, and pleasure by eating and the sensory characteristics of foods and dishes.[88] Food sovereignty refers to people's right to healthy and culturally appropriate food produced through ecologically sound and sustainable methods and the ability/freedom to define their own food and agricultural systems.[89]

Mandates to reduce animal-based proteins are based on commercial/industrial food production, not on traditional herder/agrarian models.[90] Food sovereignty means individuals have the right to produce and consume traditional foods, and this is not limited to First Peoples, Indigenous, and Native populations. Food insecurity for cultures such as Māori and Pasifika peoples requires embracing food sovereignty for improved food security and health by strengthening existing networks to produce and distribute affordable and nutritious food.[91] Cultural gastronomy deeply defines individuals and currently mandated reductions, tariffs, and sanctions on producers are oversimplified and discriminatory to cultures that consume animal-based foods.[92, 93, 94]

---

1 Tagawa, R.; Watanabe, D.; Ito, K.; Ueda, K.; Nakayama, K.; Sanbongi, C.; Miyachi, M. Dose–response relationship between protein intake and muscle mass increase: A systematic review and meta-analysis of randomized controlled trials. Nutr. Rev. 2021, 79, 66–75.
2 Tao, L.; Xie, Z.; Huang, T. Dietary diversity and all-cause mortality among Chinese adults aged 65 or older: A community-based cohort study. Asia Pac. J. Clin. Nutr 2020, 29, 152–160.
3 Huang, W.-C.; Huang, Y.-C.; Lee, M.-S.; Chang, H.-Y.; Doong, J.-Y. Frailty Severity and Cognitive Impairment Associated with Dietary Diversity in Older Adults in Taiwan. Nutrients 2021, 13, 418.
4 Whitney, E.N. & Rolfes, S.R. (2015) Understanding Nutrition, 14th ed. Wadsworth Cengage Learning, Belmont, CA.
5 Protein and the Body (2021); https://extension.okstate.edu/fact-sheets/protein-and-the-body.html?Forwarded=pods.dasnr.okstate.edu/docushare/dsweb/Get/Document-2473/T-3163web.pdf
6 Loveday S. M. (2022). Protein digestion and absorption: the influence of food processing. Nutrition research reviews, 1–16. Advance online publication. https://doi.org/10.1017/S0954422422000245
7 Clark, S., & Mora García, M. B. (2017). A 100-Year Review: Advances in goat milk research. Journal of dairy science, 100(12), 10026–10044. https://doi.org/10.3168/jds.2017-13287
8 Gallier, S., Tolenaars, L., & Prosser, C. (2020). Whole Goat Milk as a Source of Fat and Milk Fat Globule Membrane in Infant Formula. Nutrients, 12(11), 3486. https://doi.org/10.3390/nu12113486
9 Thum, C., Wall, C., Day, L., Szeto, I. M. Y., Li, F., Yan, Y., & Barnett, M. P. G. (2022). Changes in Human Milk Fat Globule Composition Throughout Lactation: A Review. Frontiers in nutrition, 9, 835856. https://doi.org/10.3389/fnut.2022.835856
10 Lee, H., Padhi, E., Hasegawa, Y., Larke, J., Parenti, M., Wang, A., Hernell, O., Lönnerdal, B., & Slupsky, C. (2018). Compositional Dynamics of the Milk Fat Globule and Its Role in Infant Development. Frontiers in pediatrics, 6, 313. https://doi.org/10.3389/fped.2018.00313
11 Thum, C., Roy, N. C., Everett, D. W., & McNabb, W. C. (2023). Variation in milk fat globule size and composition: A source of bioactives for human health. Critical reviews in food science and nutrition, 63(1), 87–113. https://doi.org/10.1080/10408398.2021.1944049
12 Cholewa, J. M., Dardevet, D., Lima-Soares, F., de Araújo Pessôa, K., Oliveira, P. H., Dos Santos Pinho, J. R., Nicastro, H., Xia, Z., Cabido, C. E., & Zanchi, N. E. (2017). Dietary proteins and amino acids in the control of the muscle mass during immobilization and aging: role of the MPS response. Amino acids, 49(5), 811–820. https://doi.org/10.1007/s00726-017-2390-9
13 Sato, M., Ido, Y., Yoshimura, Y., & Mutai, H. (2019). Relationship of Malnutrition During Hospitalization With Functional Recovery and Postdischarge Destination in Elderly Stroke Patients. Journal of stroke and cerebrovascular diseases : the official journal of National Stroke Association, 28(7), 1866–1872. https://doi.org/10.1016/j.jstrokecerebrovasdis.2019.04.012
14 Ko, S. H., & Shin, Y. I. (2022). Nutritional Supplementation in Stroke Rehabilitation: A Narrative Review. Brain & NeuroRehabilitation, 15(1), e3. https://doi.org/10.12786/bn.2022.15.e3
15 Cruz-Jentoft, A. J., Dawson Hughes, B., Scott, D., Sanders, K. M., & Rizzoli, R. (2020). Nutritional strategies for maintaining muscle mass and strength from middle age to later life: A narrative review. Maturitas, 132, 57–64. https://doi.org/10.1016/j.maturitas.2019.11.007
16 Gielen, E., Beckwée, D., Delaere, A., De Breucker, S., Vandewoude, M., Bautmans, I., & Sarcopenia Guidelines Development Group of the Belgian Society of Gerontology and Geriatrics (BSGG) (2021). Nutritional interventions to improve muscle mass, muscle strength, and physical performance in older people: an umbrella review of systematic reviews and meta-analyses. Nutrition reviews, 79(2), 121–147. https://doi.org/10.1093/nutrit/nuaa011

Chapter 9 ~ Protein

17 Damluji, A. A., Alfaraidhy, M., AlHajri, N., Rohant, N. N., Kumar, M., Al Malouf, C., Bahrainy, S., Ji Kwak, M., Batchelor, W. B., Forman, D. E., Rich, M. W., Kirkpatrick, J., Krishnaswami, A., Alexander, K. P., Gerstenblith, G., Cawthon, P., deFilippi, C. R., & Goyal, P. (2023). Sarcopenia and Cardiovascular Diseases. Circulation, 147(20), 1534–1553. https://doi.org/10.1161/CIRCULATIONAHA.123.064071

18 Rogeri, P. S., Zanella, R., Jr, Martins, G. L., Garcia, M. D. A., Leite, G., Lugaresi, R., Gasparini, S. O., Sperandio, G. A., Ferreira, L. H. B., Souza-Junior, T. P., & Lancha, A. H., Jr (2021). Strategies to Prevent Sarcopenia in the Aging Process: Role of Protein Intake and Exercise. Nutrients, 14(1), 52. https://doi.org/10.3390/nu14010052

19 McKendry, J., Currier, B. S., Lim, C., Mcleod, J. C., Thomas, A. C. Q., & Phillips, S. M. (2020). Nutritional Supplements to Support Resistance Exercise in Countering the Sarcopenia of Aging. Nutrients, 12(7), 2057. https://doi.org/10.3390/nu12072057

20 Kim, D. W., & Song, S. H. (2023). Sarcopenia in chronic kidney disease: from bench to bedside. The Korean journal of internal medicine, 38(3), 303–321. https://doi.org/10.3904/kjim.2022.338

21 Zhao, J., Zhang, X., Liu, H., Brown, M. A., & Qiao, S. (2019). Dietary Protein and Gut Microbiota Composition and Function. Current protein & peptide science, 20(2), 145–154. https://doi.org/10.2174/1389203719666180514145437

22 De Angelis, M., Garruti, G., Minervini, F., Bonfrate, L., Portincasa, P., & Gobbetti, M. (2019). The Food-gut Human Axis: The Effects of Diet on Gut Microbiota and Metabolome. Current medicinal chemistry, 26(19), 3567–3583. https://doi.org/10.2174/0929867324666170428103848

23 Singh, P., Gollapalli, K., Mangiola, S., Schranner, D., Yusuf, M. A., Chamoli, M., Shi, S. L., Bastos, B. L., Nair, T., Riermeier, A., Vayndorf, E. M., Wu, J. Z., Nilakhe, A., Nguyen, C. Q., Muir, M., Kiflezghi, M. G., Foulger, A., Junker, A., Devine, J., . . . Yadav, V. K. (2023). Taurine deficiency as a driver of aging. Science. https://doi.org/abn9257

24 Neufingerl, N., & Eilander, A. (2021). Nutrient Intake and Status in Adults Consuming Plant-Based Diets Compared to Meat-Eaters: A Systematic Review. Nutrients, 14(1), 29. MDPI AG. Retrieved from http://dx.doi.org/10.3390/nu14010029

25 Rivera Del Rio, A., Boom, R. M., & Janssen, A. E. M. (2022). Effect of Fractionation and Processing Conditions on the Digestibility of Plant Proteins as Food Ingredients. Foods (Basel, Switzerland), 11(6), 870. https://doi.org/10.3390/foods11060870

26 Sá, A. G. A., Moreno, Y. M. F., & Carciofi, B. A. M. (2020). Food processing for the improvement of plant proteins digestibility. Critical reviews in food science and nutrition, 60(20), 3367–3386. https://doi.org/10.1080/10408398.2019.1688249

27 Alrosan, M., Tan, T. C., Mat Easa, A., Gammoh, S., & Alu'datt, M. H. (2022). Recent updates on lentil and quinoa protein-based dairy protein alternatives: Nutrition, technologies, and challenges. Food chemistry, 383, 132386. https://doi.org/10.1016/j.foodchem.2022.132386

28 Jamanca-Gonzales, N. C., Ocrospoma-Dueñas, R. W., Quintana-Salazar, N. B., Siche, R., & Silva-Paz, R. J. (2022). Influence of Preferments on the Physicochemical and Sensory Quality of Traditional Panettone. Foods (Basel, Switzerland), 11(17), 2566. https://doi.org/10.3390/foods11172566

29 Ketogenic Diet Shows Promising Results for All Dementia Stages: https://universityhealthnews.com/daily/memory/ketogenic-diet-shows-promising-results-for-all-dementia-stages/

30 Nutrition for the ageing brain: Towards evidence for an optimal diet: https://www.sciencedirect.com/science/article/pii/S1568163716301027

31 The Ketogenic Diet as a Treatment Paradigm for Diverse Neurological Disorders: https://www.ncbi.nlm.nih.gov/pmc/articles/PMC3321471/

32 The Neuroprotective Properties Of Calorie Restriction, The Ketogenic Diet, And Ketone Bodies: https://www.ncbi.nlm.nih.gov/pmc/articles/PMC2649682/

33 American Epilepsy Society (AES). "Adults and epilepsy diets: A novel therapy." ScienceDaily. ScienceDaily, 8 December 2014. www.sciencedaily.com/releases/2014/12/141208144152.htm.

34 American Academy of Neurology (AAN). "Low carb, high fat diets may reduce seizures in tough-to-treat epilepsy." ScienceDaily. ScienceDaily, 29 October 2014. www.sciencedaily.com/releases/2014/10/141029203747.htm.

35 Johns Hopkins Medicine. "Fasting may benefit patients with epilepsy." ScienceDaily. ScienceDaily, 6 December 2012. www.sciencedaily.com/releases/2012/12/121206203122.htm.

36 Michael V. Accardi, Bryan A. Daniels, Patricia M.G.E. Brown, Jean-Marc Fritschy, Shiva K. Tyagarajan, Derek Bowie. Mitochondrial reactive oxygen species regulate the strength of inhibitory GABA-mediated synaptic transmission. Nature Communications, 2014; 5 DOI: 10.1038/ncomms4168

37 Broekema, R., Tyszler, M., van 't Veer, P., Kok, F. J., Martin, A., Lluch, A., & Blonk, H. T. J. (2020). Future-proof and sustainable healthy diets based on current eating patterns in the Netherlands. The American journal of clinical nutrition, 112(5), 1338–1347. https://doi.org/10.1093/ajcn/nqaa217

38 University of Texas Medical Branch at Galveston. "Full serving of protein at each meal helps one achieve maximum muscle health." ScienceDaily. ScienceDaily, 20 May 2014. www.sciencedaily.com/releases/2014/05/140520133218.htm.

39 https://www.womensg.com/best-collagen-supplements/

40 https://www.loc.gov/collections/publications-of-the-law-library-of-congress/about-this-collection/

41 Cambridge World History of Food, Kenneth F. Kiple & Kriemhild Conee Ornelas [Cambridge University Press:Cambridge] 2000, Volume One (p. 490-1)

42 USDA Yearbook of Agriculture 1942 pg 645

43 (Tannerhill, 1988)
44 What's Cooking Uncle Sam, National Archives page 42
45 Joanna Kaluza, Agneta Åkesson, and Alicja Wolk. Processed and Unprocessed Red Meat Consumption and Risk of Heart Failure: A Prospective Study of Men. Circ Heart Fail., June 12 2014 DOI: 10.1161/CIRCHEARTFAILURE.113.000921
46 Raw Meat Products US Government: https://www.govinfo.gov/content/pkg/CFR-2012-title9-vol2/pdf/CFR-2012-title9-vol2-sec319-15.pdf
47 CULTURED MEAT – THE FOOD OF THE FUTURE? Publication of Merck KGaA, Darmstadt, Germany 2023 https://www.emdgroup.com/en/research/science-space/envisioning-tomorrow/scarcity-of-resources/cleanmeat.html
48 University of Nottingham. (2021, December 7). Stem cell study paves way for manufacturing cultured meat. ScienceDaily. Retrieved June 26, 2023 from www.sciencedaily.com/releases/2021/12/211207092449.htm
49 D'Alessandro AG, Maiorano G, Kowaliszyn B, et al. How the nutritional value and consumer acceptability of suckling lambs meat is affected by the maternal feeding system. Small Ruminant Research, Volume 106, Issues 2—3, August 2012, Pages 83-91.
50 Economic Research Service. Livestock and Meat Trade Data Lamb and mutton: Annual and cumulative year-to-date U.S. trade. U.S. Department of Agriculture, Washington, D.C. Available online at: http://www.ers.usda.gov/Data/MeatTrade/LambMuttonYearly.htm. 2011.
51 http://www.whfoods.com/genpage.php?tname=foodspice&dbid=117#references
52 https://ndb.nal.usda.gov/ndb/search
53 https://survivalexicon.files.wordpress.com/2014/09/various-pork-butcher-cuts.jpg
54 Journal of Food Composition and Analysis; Volume 9, Issue 3, September 1996, Pages 255-268
55 http://www.sciencedirect.com/science/article/pii/S0889157596900319
56 http://onlinelibrary.wiley.com/doi/10.1111/j.1467-3010.2010.01871.x/abstract
57 Harcombe Z. (2019). US dietary guidelines: is saturated fat a nutrient of concern?. British journal of sports medicine, 53(22), 1393–1396. https://doi.org/10.1136/bjsports-2018-099420
58 Heileson J. L. (2020). Dietary saturated fat and heart disease: a narrative review. Nutrition reviews, 78(6), 474–485. https://doi.org/10.1093/nutrit/nuz091
59 Szajewska, H., & Szajewski, T. (2016). Saturated Fat Controversy: Importance of Systematic Reviews and Meta-analyses. Critical reviews in food science and nutrition, 56(12), 1947–1951. https://doi.org/10.1080/10408398.2015.1018037
60 Oceana Canada discovers seafood mislabeling in four major cities. (2021) https://www.seafoodsource.com/news/food-safety-health/oceana-canada-discovers-seafood-mislabeling-in-four-major-cities
61 USDA Agricultural Marketing Services (2023) https://www.ams.usda.gov/grades-standards/fish-seafood
62 Why The U.S. Chills Its Eggs And Most Of The World Doesn't https://www.npr.org/sections/thesalt/2014/09/11/336330502/why-the-u-s-chills-its-eggs-and-most-of-the-world-doesnt
63 Most countries don't refrigerate their eggs — why do Americans? By Fiza Pirani The Atlanta Journal-Constitution
64 Clayton, Z. S., Scholar, K. R., Shelechi, M., Hernandez, L. M., Barber, A. M., Petrisko, Y. J., Hooshmand, S., & Kern, M. (2015). Influence of resistance training combined with daily consumption of an egg-based or bagel-based breakfast on risk factors for chronic diseases in healthy untrained individuals. Journal of the American College of Nutrition, 34(2), 113–119. https://doi.org/10.1080/07315724.2014.946622
65 Fernandez M. L. (2022). The Role of Eggs in Healthy Diets. The Journal of family practice, 71(6 Suppl), S71–S75. https://doi.org/10.12788/jfp.0408
66 Thomas, M. S., Puglisi, M., Malysheva, O., Caudill, M. A., Sholola, M., Cooperstone, J. L., & Fernandez, M. L. (2022). Eggs Improve Plasma Biomarkers in Patients with Metabolic Syndrome Following a Plant-Based Diet-A Randomized Crossover Study. Nutrients, 14(10), 2138. https://doi.org/10.3390/nu14102138
67 Missimer, A., Fernandez, M. L., DiMarco, D. M., Norris, G. H., Blesso, C. N., Murillo, A. G., Vergara-Jimenez, M., Lemos, B. S., Medina-Vera, I., Malysheva, O. V., & Caudill, M. A. (2018). Compared to an Oatmeal Breakfast, Two Eggs/Day Increased Plasma Carotenoids and Choline without Increasing Trimethyl Amine N-Oxide Concentrations. Journal of the American College of Nutrition, 37(2), 140–148. https://doi.org/10.1080/07315724.2017.1365026
68 Sun, C., Liu, J., Yang, N., & Xu, G. (2019). Egg quality and egg albumen property of domestic chicken, duck, goose, turkey, quail, and pigeon. Poultry science, 98(10), 4516–4521. https://doi.org/10.3382/ps/pez259
69 Quan, T. H., & Benjakul, S. (2019). Duck egg albumen: physicochemical and functional properties as affected by storage and processing. Journal of food science and technology, 56(3), 1104–1115. https://doi.org/10.1007/s13197-019-03669-x
70 The First American Cookbook: A Facsimile of "American Cookery," 1796 Paperback – Facsimile, October 1, 1984 by Amelia Simmons
71 British Food: A History- https://britishfoodhistory.com/2011/12/03/traditional-mincemeat/
72 European and American Cuisine by Gesine Lemcke: D. Appleton And Company 1895 pg 329
73 Pacific Northwest Foraging by Douglas Deur: Timber Press, 2014 pg 90, 149, 174, 184
74 Swan-Among the Indians, Life of James G. Swan by Lucile McDonald: Binford & Mort 1972 pg 99
75 A New Book of Cookery by Fannie Merritt Farmer: Boston Little Brown and Company 1917 pg 306

Chapter 9 ~ Protein

76 Wild Game Mincemeat Pie Recipe- http://www.montanaoutdoor.com/2013/09/grandma-myers-homemade-mincemeat-recipe-with-elk/

77 Dumont, B., Groot, J. C. J., & Tichit, M. (2018). Review: Make ruminants green again- how can sustainable intensification and agroecology converge for a better future?. Animal : an international journal of animal bioscience, 12(s2), s210–s219. https://doi.org/10.1017/S1751731118001350

78 Mottet, A., Teillard, F., Boettcher, P., De' Besi, G., & Besbes, B. (2018). Review: Domestic herbivores and food security: current contribution, trends and challenges for a sustainable development. Animal : an international journal of animal bioscience, 12(s2), s188–s198. https://doi.org/10.1017/S1751731118002215

79 Ayantunde, A. A., Duncan, A. J., van Wijk, M. T., & Thorne, P. (2018). Review: Role of herbivores in sustainable agriculture in Sub-Saharan Africa. Animal : an international journal of animal bioscience, 12(s2), s199–s209. https://doi.org/10.1017/S175173111800174X

80 Dumont, B., Groot, J. C. J., & Tichit, M. (2018). Review: Make ruminants green again- how can sustainable intensification and agroecology converge for a better future?. Animal : an international journal of animal bioscience, 12(s2), s210–s219. https://doi.org/10.1017/S1751731118001350

81 Heerschop, S. N., Kanellopoulos, A., Biesbroek, S., & van 't Veer, P. (2023). Shifting towards optimized healthy and sustainable Dutch diets: impact on protein quality. European journal of nutrition, 10.1007/s00394-023-03135-7. Advance online publication. https://doi.org/10.1007/s00394-023-03135-7

82 Reynolds, C. J., Horgan, G. W., Whybrow, S., & Macdiarmid, J. I. (2019). Healthy and sustainable diets that meet greenhouse gas emission reduction targets and are affordable for different income groups in the UK. Public health nutrition, 22(8), 1503–1517. https://doi.org/10.1017/S1368980018003774

83 Vieux, F., Perignon, M., Gazan, R., & Darmon, N. (2018). Dietary changes needed to improve diet sustainability: are they similar across Europe?. European journal of clinical nutrition, 72(7), 951–960. https://doi.org/10.1038/s41430-017-0080-z

84 Perignon, M., Vieux, F., Verger, E. O., Bricas, N., & Darmon, N. (2023). Dietary environmental impacts of French adults are poorly related to their income levels or food insecurity status. European journal of nutrition, 10.1007/s00394-023-03163-3. Advance online publication. https://doi.org/10.1007/s00394-023-03163-3

85 Annunziata, A., & Mariani, A. (2018). Consumer Perception of Sustainability Attributes in Organic and Local Food. Recent patents on food, nutrition & agriculture, 9(2), 87–96. https://doi.org/10.2174/2212798410666171215112058

86 Resare Sahlin K, Röös E, Gordon LJ. 'Less but better' meat is a sustainability message in need of clarity. Nat Food. 2020 Sep;1(9):520-522. doi: 10.1038/s43016-020-00140-5. PMID: 37128007.

87 Heerschop, S. N., Kanellopoulos, A., Biesbroek, S., & van 't Veer, P. (2023). Shifting towards optimized healthy and sustainable Dutch diets: impact on protein quality. European journal of nutrition, 10.1007/s00394-023-03135-7. Advance online publication. https://doi.org/10.1007/s00394-023-03135-7

88 Rojas-Rivas, E., Urbine, A., Zaragoza-Alonso, J., & Cuffia, F. (2021). Cross-cultural representations of gastronomy among consumers in two Latin American countries. Food research international (Ottawa, Ont.), 140, 109881. https://doi.org/10.1016/j.foodres.2020.109881

89 Ullah, N., Khan, J., Saeed, I., Zada, S., Xin, S., Kang, Z., & Hu, Y. (2022). Gastronomic Tourism and Tourist Motivation: Exploring Northern Areas of Pakistan. International journal of environmental research and public health, 19(13), 7734. https://doi.org/10.3390/ijerph19137734

90 Schiano, A. N., & Drake, M. A. (2021). Invited review: Sustainability: Different perspectives, inherent conflict. Journal of dairy science, 104(11), 11386–11400. https://doi.org/10.3168/jds.2021-20360

91 Akbar, H., Radclyffe, C. J. T., Santos, D., Mopio-Jane, M., & Gallegos, D. (2022). "Food Is Our Love Language": Using Talanoa to Conceptualize Food Security for the Māori and Pasifika Diaspora in South-East Queensland, Australia. Nutrients, 14(10), 2020. https://doi.org/10.3390/nu14102020

92 Merlino, V. M., Renna, M., Nery, J., Muresu, A., Ricci, A., Maggiolino, A., Celano, G., De Ruggieri, B., & Tarantola, M. (2022). Are Local Dairy Products Better? Using Principal Component Analysis to Investigate Consumers' Perception towards Quality, Sustainability, and Market Availability. Animals : an open access journal from MDPI, 12(11), 1421. https://doi.org/10.3390/ani12111421

93 Estradé, M., Alarcon Basurto, S. G., McCarter, A., Gittelsohn, J., Igusa, T., Zhu, S., Poirier, L., Gross, S., Pardilla, M., Rojo, M., Lombard, K., Haskie, H., Clark, V., Swartz, J., & Mui, Y. (2023). A Systems Approach to Identify Factors Influencing Participation in Two Tribally-Administered WIC Programs. Nutrients, 15(5), 1210. https://doi.org/10.3390/nu15051210

94 Rojas-Rivas, E., Urbine, A., Zaragoza-Alonso, J., & Cuffia, F. (2021). Cross-cultural representations of gastronomy among consumers in two Latin American countries. Food research international (Ottawa, Ont.), 140, 109881. https://doi.org/10.1016/j.foodres.2020.109881

> "The mineral world is a much more supple and mobile world than could be imagined by the science of the ancients. Vaguely analogous to the metamorphoses of living creatures, there occurs in the most solid rocks, as we now know, perpetual transformation of a mineral species."
>
> ~Pierre Teilhard de Chardin

Chapter Ten ~ *Minerals: the Foundation of Health*

Conversating about how vital minerals are for our health would take volumes and volumes. No sooner than we would finish the research, more will appear. So, I am selecting a few that have solid research supporting their benefits. The human body comprises five major minerals; calcium (Ca), phosphorus (P), potassium (K), sodium (Na), and magnesium (Mg), and 72 trace minerals. Approximately 4% of the body's mass comprises minerals. Minerals cannot be made in the body and must be obtained in our diet. Bacteria and fungi play an essential role in the weathering transformation of primary elements that release nutrients for their nutrition. An example of this is cobalt; through the processing by bacteria in the body, vitamin B_{12}, essential for our health, is formed.[1]

> ***Principle 48:*** Vital minerals cannot be made by the body; they must be obtained through diet.

Magnesium

Magnesium (Mg) has been called the most essential mineral for human beings and all living organisms. It is critical to the metabolic process of one-celled organisms and is the second most abundant mineral found in human cells. Magnesium is involved in all aspects of cell production and growth and is involved in more than 300 enzyme processes promoting life and health in plants and animals.

Currently, 17 minerals are considered essential for human life. As with most minerals, magnesium naturally combines with other elements. By combining with sulfur, magnesium makes Epsom salts. Magnesium combined with carbon makes magnesium carbonate, and it combines with calcium to make dolomite. Like calcium, magnesium is alkalizing, reducing acidosis (high acid).

Approximately 60% of the body's total magnesium is concentrated in the bones, 20% is in muscles, and 20% is in soft tissues and the liver. Magnesium works inside our tissue cells, producing vital ATP energy and triggering the production of the body's protein structures by building DNA.

> **What Does Magnesium Do?**
>
> - Magnesium is a cofactor, assisting enzymes in chemical reactions, including temperature regulation.
> - Magnesium transports energy.
> - Magnesium is necessary for the synthesis of protein.
> - Magnesium transports nerve signals.
> - Magnesium relaxes muscles.

A study released in 2018 reported that vitamin D couldn't be metabolized without sufficient magnesium levels, meaning vitamin D remains stored and inactive for up to 50% of Americans. In addition, vitamin D supplements can increase a person's calcium and phosphate levels even while they remain vitamin D deficient. People may suffer from vascular calcification if their magnesium levels aren't high enough to prevent complications.[2]

Calcium and magnesium are interrelated and antagonistic towards one another; neither can act without eliciting a reaction from the other. Enzymes that depend on enough intracellular magnesium will be detrimentally affected by small increases in cellular calcium. If too much calcium is present in the cellular tissue, cell division, growth, and intermediary metabolism are adversely affected. Magnesium causes calcium to dissolve in the body, enabling the blood to take it up and transport it. Suppose you are not receiving adequate amounts of magnesium and supplementing with calcium. In that case, calcium will build up and you may increase your risk factors for heart disease, muscle spasms, fibromyalgia, dental cavities, and kidney stones.

Magnesium and Immune Functions

Many of us may have had COVID or knew individuals who did. Researchers were baffled by why some individuals never caught COVID; by 2022, research scientists said it must be a gene mutation. While I am not opposed to studying genes and/or why and how they interplay with our health, genes are not the driving force for most health conditions humanity faces. The healthier an individual is through diet and lifestyle, the more resilience they have in combating viruses, bacteria, environmental, and lifestyle stressors. The answer to why some people contracted and even died from the COVID virus could come down to higher nutrition resiliency. Studies supporting this thought will be shared as we look deeper at these minerals. We looked at one study showing magnesium is critical for vitamin D utilization. How about magnesium's relationship to immune function? As it turns out, a study released in 2022 confirmed that magnesium deficiency is associated with various diseases, such as infections and cancer. Previous studies had shown that cancerous growths spread faster in the bodies of mice when the animals received a low-magnesium diet and that their defense against flu viruses was also impaired. The Department of Medicine at the University of Cambridge discovered that T-cells can eliminate abnormal or infected cells efficiently only in a magnesium-rich environment. Specifically, magnesium is essential for the function of a T cell surface protein called *Lymphocyte function-associated antigen 1* (LFA-1). LFA-1 acts as a docking site, which plays a crucial role in activating T cells.[3]

Magnesium and Kidney Health

For those who suffer from kidney disease, the options are few as the condition worsens to the point of dialysis or transplant being the only solutions. In my experience, the individual eventually knows far more about their condition than many providers they see for help. This is the case for Mausami (name changed to protect the individual), who came to the United States over 20 years ago and, after becoming a citizen, developed chronic kidney disease (CKD) not because she had diabetes but from NSAIDs use for inflammation. Since I have known Mausami, her condition has worsened, and as a south Asian, it is increasingly difficult to be approved for a kidney donation. However, she has continued to avidly research, looking for answers to how kidneys function in hopes of learning how to repair the damage. In 2021, Mausami found that researchers may have discovered the mechanisms involved in how kidneys control magnesium and calcium.

While investigating the underlying causes of a rare skin disorder, a Massachusetts General Hospital (MGH) researcher discovered an unknown mechanism in the kidneys that is important for regulating levels of magnesium and calcium in the blood. A genetic mutation causing the loss of KCTD1 results in defects in nephrons, the basic filtration units of the kidney; this little-studied gene is essential in the segments of the nephron involved in the regulation of reabsorption into the bloodstream of salt, magnesium, and calcium from filtered urine. Defects in nephrons resulting from KCTD1 loss cause abnormally low levels of magnesium (*hypomagnesemia*) and calcium (*hypocalcemia*) in the bloodstream. The abnormally low blood levels of calcium trigger the parathyroid hormone-producing glands in the neck to go into overdrive, a condition known as *secondary hyperparathyroidism*. The resulting high levels of parathyroid hormone led to a release of calcium from bones to counter the low calcium blood levels, eventually causing a loss of bone mass. Researchers found that KCTD1 acts in a part of the kidney known as the distal nephron to regulate the reabsorption of electrolytes from urine into the bloodstream and maintain balanced levels (homeostasis) of these electrolytes.[4]

Dementia and Magnesium

As the population ages, concerns regarding cognition increase for individuals and their families. The number of people diagnosed with dementia worldwide is expected to more than double from 57.4 million in 2019 to 152.8 million in 2050, placing a significant strain on health and social services and the global economy. It is often assumed dementia, once referred to as senility, is a forgone conclusion as individuals age. As I age and continue to dig deeper into nutrition, my own concerns over cognition have diminished. Why? Because there are many diet and lifestyle habits that are proving to be cognition-protective, even when the *APOE* gene for dementia and Alzheimer's is present. Changes in magnesium (Mg) metabolism have been reported with aging, including diminished Mg intake, impaired intestinal Mg absorption, and renal Mg wasting. Mild Mg deficits are generally asymptomatic and clinical signs are usually non-specific or absent. Asthenia, sleep disorders, hyperemotionality, and cognitive disorders are common in the elderly with mild Mg deficit and may often be confused with age-related symptoms. Chronic Mg deficits increase the production of free radicals, which have been implicated in development of several chronic age-related disorders.[5]

The growing body of research supports there is far more we can do with nutrition and lifestyle practices to abate cognition challenges, provided we are willing to do them. One study from 2023 on daily magnesium intake revealed that more magnesium in our daily diet leads to better brain health as we age. The study of more than 6,000 cognitively healthy participants in the United Kingdom aged 40-73 found people who consume more than 550 milligrams of magnesium each day have a brain age that is approximately one year younger by the time they reach 55 compared with someone with a normal magnesium intake of about 350 milligrams a day.

> The researchers say a higher magnesium intake in our diets from a younger age may safeguard against neurodegenerative diseases and cognitive decline by the time we reach our 40s. The neuroprotective effects of more dietary magnesium appear to benefit women more than men and more so in post-menopausal than pre-menopausal women, although this may be due to the anti-inflammatory effect of magnesium.[6]

Magnesium and Cancer

When battling cancer, often a host of drugs are given, and some cause severe constipation. A study done in 2023 showed that when patients with advanced cancer were given *magnesium-L-threonate*, (a novel magnesium compound) along with opioids, it performed better than standard constipation medications.[7] Magnesium has also been found to reduce the incidence of lung cancer and colon cancer as of 2021 when the Prospective Diet-wide Association study on calcium and magnesium-rich food confirmed an inverse relationship.[8, 9]

Health Challenges that Benefit from Optimum Magnesium Intake

All muscles, including the heart and blood vessels, are affected if magnesium is deficient. Calcium floods the smooth muscle cells causing spasms and constricted blood flow. This can lead to high blood pressure, arterial spasms, angina, and heart attack.

Magnesium absorption decreases rapidly when more than 200mg is consumed at once. It is, therefore, advisable to take magnesium supplements in divided doses during the day. Many of the therapeutic benefits associated with magnesium are optimized when magnesium is consumed as magnesium aspartate and combined with potassium aspartate. High dietary levels of phosphorus (found in soda) inhibit the body's absorption of magnesium. All processed foods and beverages are devoid of magnesium.

Poor digestion and low stomach acid can lead to magnesium deficiency, stress, advanced age, arthritis, diabetes, gallbladder disease, osteoporosis, asthma, and depression. Antacids are one of the most common over-the-counter drugs; heartburn and indigestion result from lousy eating choices. Taking acid reducers limits the amount of acid available for digesting essential minerals like magnesium. Calcium carbonate antacids deplete already deficient magnesium reserves, increasing the likelihood of insomnia, restless leg syndrome, and chronic health challenges.

Conditions that benefit from magnesium supplementation

Anxiety & panic attacks	Asthma	Blood clots
Bowel disease	Cystitis	Depression
Detoxification	Diabetes	Fatigue
Heart disease	Hypertension	Hypoglycemia
Insomnia	Kidney disease	Migraine
Musculoskeletal health	Nerve health	Gynecological health
Osteoporosis	Raynaud's syndrome	Tooth decay

What Kind of Magnesium

Supplemental magnesium should be taken at a different time than supplemental calcium, as calcium prevents magnesium absorption if consumed with magnesium.[10, 11]

Magnesium supplements are available in various forms, including:

magnesium citrate	magnesium glycinate	magnesium oxide	magnesium malate
magnesium chloride	magnesium sulphate	magnesium lactate	magnesium gluconate
magnesium aspartate	magnesium hydroxide	magnesium L-threonate	magnesium orotate

Magnesium glycinate is magnesium and glycine, an amino acid; people tend to tolerate magnesium glycine well, and it seems to cause minimal side effects. This means it may be a good option for people who require higher doses of this nutrient or who experience side effects when using other types of magnesium.

A 6-week study using supplementation with 400mg of magnesium as magnesium glycinate was effective at raising plasma magnesium readings in people who have had bariatric surgery (a comparison made pre-surgery to 6 weeks post-surgery). Magnesium oxide did not produce this effect in these same subjects albeit at a slightly lower dose.[12, 13]

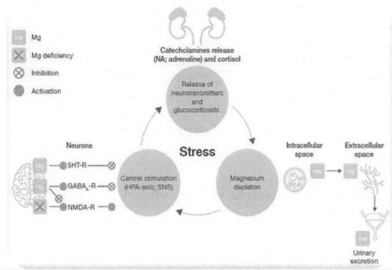

Pickering, G., Mazur, A., Trousselard, M., Bienkowski, P., Yaltsewa, N., Amessou, M., Noah, L., & Pouteau, E. (2020). Magnesium Status and Stress: The Vicious Circle Concept Revisited. Nutrients, 12(12), 3672. https://doi.org/10.3390/nu12123672

In physically fit young adults, supplementation for four weeks with 400mg of magnesium as magnesium glycinate, but not placebo, raised erythrocyte potassium content, a reflection of magnesium's role in the body's potassium retention and distribution. Magnesium supplementation also improved two measures of exercise performance (pre-supplementation vs. post-supplementation). Interestingly, plasma magnesium was not increased significantly, though this measure does not provide the most sensitive indicator of altered magnesium status.[14, 15, 16]

Calcium and Magnesium

Calcium and magnesium are present in the diet, and thus in the body, at levels much higher than trace minerals such as iron. Approximately 99% of the calcium and magnesium in the human body is located in the skeleton. For many years, women have been advised to increase their calcium intake substantially during pregnancy, and there has been concern that many pregnant women do not ingest enough calcium to maintain their skeletons while providing for fetal needs. Researchers have shown several changes in calcium metabolism associated with pregnancy that facilitate the transfer of calcium from the mother to the fetus while protecting calcium levels in maternal serum and bone. These include changes in calcium-regulating hormones, which affect intestinal absorption, renal reabsorption, and bone turnover of calcium.[17] However, much of the information on calcium and magnesium is well over 40 years old and repeated in new textbooks as if the story was done. This is why new research on calcium and the microbiome gets me excited! It means there is still far more to discover than what is assumed.

It was believed that magnesium overload (*hypomagnesium*) status promotes insulin resistance. A study released in 2019 followed by another in 2023 on the association between magnesium intake and metabolic controls showed the contrary. The studies revealed it was type 2 diabetes mellitus (T2DM) that exacerbates low serum magnesium levels and, in turn, worsens glycemic control of diabetes.[18, 19]

In 2022, researchers looked at the effects on medium-chain fatty acids and the gut microbiome when calcium and magnesium were supplemented into the diet for 12 weeks. The study results show a fascinating interrelationship between the minerals we ingest and the gut microbiome. Magnesium use significantly lowered plasma levels of sucrose, whereas calcium alone did not. The calcium and magnesium supplementation positively correlated with ketones and alterations in the microbiome diversity. At the end of the study, researchers found the calcium to magnesium ratio (2:3) enhanced production from microbial fermentation and increased circulating levels of medium-chain fatty acids.[20]

> ***Principle 49:*** Bacteria and fungi play an important role in the processing of elements (minerals) to allow release of their nutrients in the body.

Calcium

Calcium (Ca) is the most abundant mineral in the human body. While most of the body's calcium is sequestered in the skeleton, the free, hydrated Ca cation in solution is a key physiologic mediator in a host of metabolic and regulatory processes. (Calcium cations are very potent and versatile agents within a cell. Their divalent character makes them strong binders; hence, their physiological concentration must be strictly controlled.) Abnormalities in calcium concentration are frequent in patients receiving dialysis therapy. Most cases of hypo- and/or hypercalcemia are mild and asymptomatic. However, hypocalcemia can drive hyperparathyroidism and eventually lead to gland hypertrophy and independent functioning. Hypercalcemia can be associated with increased extraosseous calcium (Ca located outside the bones) and phosphate deposition leading to vascular calcification with attendant mortality and morbidity.[21]

Calcium is an essential integrative component of the human body and critical for human health. It has been well established that calcium intake is helpful in the prevention and treatment of osteoporosis, which has become one of the most serious public health problems worldwide. However, community-dwelling adults with and without osteoporosis are rarely concerned or even unaware of the potential side effects of high or inappropriate doses of calcium intake. Some recent studies have revealed that excessive calcium intake might increase the risks of cardiovascular diseases.[22] Osteoporosis and fragility fractures are associated with increased disability, morbidity, and mortality. It is known that an average calcium balance and a normal vitamin D status are essential for maintaining well-balanced bone metabolism. For many years, calcium and vitamin D have been crucial in preventing and treating osteoporosis.[23]

Most intervention studies have reported a positive effect of calcium and vitamin D supplementation on bone in patients with osteoporosis. But this therapeutic approach is hotly debated regarding the potential side effects on the cardiovascular (CV) system. A literature review found that postmenopausal women with osteoporosis were at an increased risk of experiencing cardiovascular events such as myocardial infarction. This increased CVD risk among postmenopausal women with osteoporosis has been linked to using calcium supplements.[24, 25]

A paper published in 2016 reviewed calcium intake and mortality from all causes, cancer, and cardiovascular disease. The findings from 132,823 participants in the Cancer Prevention Study II concluded that: "For women, total and supplemental calcium intakes are associated with lower mortality, whereas for men, supplemental calcium intake ≥1000mg/d may be associated with higher all-cause and CVD-specific mortality."[26]

By 2023, studies looking at the connection between calcium use and cardiovascular disease reported with a high level of confidence that elevated dietary calcium was associated with lower mortality risk from all-causes including cardiovascular disease (CVD) and cancer, and supplying sufficient dietary calcium intake between 1000 and 1200mg per day in people with hypertension may be considered cost-effective to decrease risk of premature death.[27]

Calcium and Cancer

Calcium is an essential intracellular messenger vital in controlling a broad range of cellular processes, including apoptosis, the programming built into healthy cells governing their normal lifespan.[28] Processes important in cancer progression, such as sustained cell growth, invasion of other organs, and resistance to cell death inducers, overlap with pathways regulated by calcium (Ca2+) signaling. Alterations to Ca2+ homeostasis and signaling are often deleterious and are associated with specific pathological states, including cancer. Altered Ca2+ transmission has been implicated in various processes fundamental for the uncontrolled proliferation and invasiveness of tumor cells and other processes necessary for cancer progression, such as developing resistance to cancer therapies.[29]

Is It Calcium or Dairy that Drives Some Cancers?

The consumption of cow's milk is a part of the rudimentary nutritional habits of Western industrialized countries. Recent epidemiological studies associate the intake of cow's milk with an increased risk of diseases. These studies confirm a correlation between cow's milk consumption and birthweight, body mass index, the onset of menarche (menstruation), linear growth during childhood, acne vulgaris, type 2 diabetes mellitus, prostate cancer, breast cancer, hepatocellular carcinoma, diffuse large B-cell lymphoma, neurodegenerative diseases, and all-cause mortality. Thus, long-term persistent consumption of cow's milk increases the risk of mTORC1-driven diseases of civilization.[30]

> mTORC1 is a highly conserved serine/threonine kinase that controls cell growth and metabolism in response to nutrients, growth factors, cellular energy, and stress.[31]

An Adventist Health Study released in 2023 found that men with a higher intake of dairy foods, but not taking non-dairy nondairy calcium, had a higher risk of prostate cancer than men with lower intakes. Associations were nonlinear, suggesting the greatest increases in risk at relatively low doses. A similar review of prospective cohort studies of women and breast cancer supported the association between cow's milk consumption and the risk of estrogen receptor-α-positive (ER+) BrCa. The researchers went on to state:

> "Milk is a complex biological fluid that increases systemic insulin-like growth factor 1 (IGF-1), insulin and estrogen signaling, and interacting hormonal promoters of BCa. Further potential oncogenic components of commercial milk include exosomal microRNAs (miR-148a-3p, miR-21-5p), bovine meat and milk factors, aflatoxin M1, bisphenol A, pesticides, and micro- and nanoplastics".[32]

Maybe something is missing in commercial milk? In my life of 60 years, commercial milk has increasingly moved farther away from the milk I had in my youth straight from the cow. I'm back to thinking about Dr. Bill Schindler's statement in his book, *Eat Like a Human*: *"It is not the food but how food is made."* According to the University of Minnesota, the U.S. is producing 60% more milk from 30% fewer cows than in 1967. Each cow produces over 2.5 times as much milk as 50 years ago. Honestly, the rest of the information on genetic innovations and 24-hour milking was disturbing, even for a ranch and farm kid like me.[33] Often sugar is added to commercial milk to cover the slightly "off" flavor resulting from stock feed or pasteurization. Also, remember I shared earlier that for every study proving a benefit, others show no effects or adverse effects. I think this may be the case with the relationships between milk, calcium, and cancer. When we look at raw milk consumed by many other cultures, research confirms bovine milk is a source of many valuable nutrients, including calcium, vitamin B, a significant amount of vitamin B_2, and the fat-soluble vitamins A, D and E. Malnutrition remains.[34, 35]

An abstract published in 2022 (declaring no conflict of interest or funding) stated:

> "Milk is an attractive product for fortification as it has a high nutritional density in a small volume and a relatively low price. Research shows the positive health effects of drinking milk and consuming dairy products. Even more health benefits can be obtained from consuming fortified dairy products. A literature review, current nutritional recommendations, medical recommendations, and an analysis of the market situation all recommend introducing milk enriched with minerals in combination with vitamins to the market. This concept corresponds to the current market demand and may supplement the missing and expected range of fortified milk and the correct number of recipients."[36]

The above statement leaves me puzzling even more over the link between dairy, calcium, and cancer. My instinct tells me that naturally occurring nutrients and cofactors are damaged during pasteurization, then the addition of synthetic vitamins and oxide minerals fail as substitutes for nature. Minerals consumed by a cow are chelated through plant photosynthesis, allowing for higher absorption, then the cow further binds the calcium for utilization by her calf. The complexity of nature providing nutrients versus human supplementing and livestock care may be at the root of the calcium link to cancer. An additional factor is how drastically bovine milk production has changed in the last 30 years.[37] Time and lots of research will hopefully answer my questions.

Who Will Shift the Paradigm?

Millennials and Generation Z are rapidly becoming the generations with the most significant purchasing power. Their dietary preferences, while different from previous generations, will also be driving industry and research in the future. These generations have been raised by parents who do not believe everything we hear or read. So, our children may be better described as skeptics. My son and great-niece, along with many in their age bracket (17-50) are the research generators, and they value experiences and personalization over cost. Will the trend to non-dairy continue? Long term, will these consumers reject or accept milk beverages and meat substitutes, or will they want the real products? Will research support real and natural over synthetic? Take the example of the beer industry. Large companies like Miller and Budweiser struggle as craft beer sales have skyrocketed, due mainly to the preferences of these two generations.

Supporting Resilient Immune Response

Much is unknown about the human virome, but researchers are seeing snippets of how nutrition and viruses interplay each year. The foundations of the emerging field were set throughout the decade by groups working in habitats as diverse as the pelagic region of the Sargasso Sea, hot springs in Yellowstone National Park, industrial-contaminated sediment from Seattle, human fecal samples, and soil. Viromics, or viral metagenomics, is a relatively new and burgeoning field of research that studies the complete collection of viruses forming part of the microbiota in any given niche. It has strong foundations rooted in more than a century of discoveries in virology and recent advances in molecular biology and sequencing technologies. Viruses are, in fact, much more than common parasites. They are by far the most dynamic and abundant entities on the planet and the greatest killers, as well as the most effective geo-transforming genetic engineers and resource recyclers, acting on all life strata in any habitat.[38]

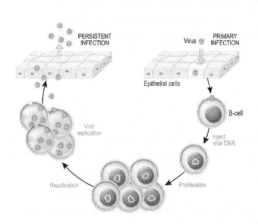

J Clin Invest. 2023;133(3):e163669. https://doi.org/10.1172/JCI163669.

The virome, which researchers believe makes up 6% of the human genome, comprises endogenous retroviruses, eukaryotic viruses, and bacteriophages, which are increasingly recognized as an essential part of the human microbiome. The state of the human virome is associated with type-1 diabetes (T1D), type-2 diabetes (T2D), inflammatory bowel disease (IBD), human immunodeficiency virus (HIV) infection, and cancer. Increasing evidence also supports trans-kingdom interactions of viruses with bacteria, small eukaryotes, and hosts in disease progression.[39]

The current hypothesis says that viruses have their favorite mineral when infecting a host. Epstein-Barr virus is associated with deficiencies in magnesium. A paper published in the *Journal of Clinical Investigation* in 2022 reported evidence of Epstein-Barr reactivation in long COVID individuals.[40]

The question is: Is the patient's low magnesium making them more susceptible to the virus, or is the deficiency also associated with the virus's need for magnesium? A review on the *Effects of Psychological and Environmental Stress on Micronutrient Concentrations* published in 2020 found that the bulk of evidence suggests stress can affect micronutrient concentrations (magnesium, zinc, calcium, iron, and niacin), often leading to micronutrient depletion.[41] I will not be surprised if researchers learn that opportunistic viruses crave and consume preferred minerals, like bacteria prefer specific nutrients. Furthermore, when these nutrients are not present in the diet for one, two, and three generations, a perfect storm for a pandemic could result.

In the early days of COVID, healthcare researchers looked at all the therapies available, especially in integrative/functional/holistic arenas. A research study released in 2021 looked at the role of vitamins and minerals as "preventive measures" to decrease morbidity and mortality in COVID patients. The scientists go on to say:

> "A balanced nutritional diet may play an essential role in maintaining general well-being by controlling chronic infectious diseases. A balanced diet including vitamins A, B, C, D, E, and K and micronutrients such as zinc, sodium, potassium, calcium, chloride, and phosphorus may benefit various infectious diseases."[42]

An exciting literature review statement released in the latter portion of 2021 on the vital role of micronutrients in preventing infection boldly stated:

> "The current evidence from the literature supports that zinc and vitamin C can potentially reduce the inflammatory response associated with SARS-CoV-2 while folate and vitamin D may have a role in antagonizing the entry of SARs-CoV-2 virus in host cells. Thus, further research should be conducted that could lead to the development of nutritional supplements involving natural and widely available compounds such as zinc, folate, vitamin C, and vitamin D. The latter could be an effective, safe, and inexpensive way to either prevent infection with SARS-CoV-2 and/or lessen the burden of COVID-19 disease."[43]

Several recent studies support the role of dysregulated magnesium homeostasis in COVID-19. A paper on NeuroCovid (the neurological aspects of COVID) showed some mechanisms were identified by which magnesium alterations contributed to SARS-CoV-2 affecting the nervous system in the context of infection.[44] A study released in 2023 looked at minerals and antioxidant micronutrient levels and clinical outcomes in older patients during COVID. Trace elements such as zinc, selenium, and copper modulate inflammation and immunity. Researchers tracked the levels of zinc, selenium, copper, vitamin A, β-carotene, and vitamin E measured in 94 patients within the first 15 days of hospitalization. A logistic regression analysis was conducted to test whether the levels of vitamins and minerals were independently associated with severity. In this cohort (average age of 78 years), <u>severe forms (46%) were</u>

associated with lower zinc (p = 0.012) and β-carotene (p < 0.001) concentrations. Results showed low plasma concentrations of zinc and vitamin A were associated with poor prognosis in older people hospitalized with COVID-19.[45]

> *Principle 50:* Minerals combine naturally with other elements; some act synergistically while some antagonize others.

Potassium: Do You Need It?

Over the years, I have had several elderly clients on low salt diets taking potassium supplements. This mineral became more of a personal focus as I entered menopause and looked into the role of potassium sensitivity in association with the hormone aldosterone produced in the adrenal glands; a delicate biological balance exists between the minerals sodium and potassium. When I ask clients about the foods they are eating to replace potassium, the answer is often bananas, which can be a problematic food for diabetics if they are not consuming adequate amounts of other fruits and vegetables to maintain healthy blood sugar and mineral balance.

Potassium is necessary for the proper function of the heart, kidneys, and other organs. It works in conjunction with sodium in the body. This mineral is easily obtainable from a diet rich in fruits, vegetables, and whole foods. A paper from 2021 called *Potassium* provided some additional context.

> "Potassium is an essential nutrient that performs a vital role in cellular functions, including maintaining fluid balance and osmolality of cells. The kidney maintains potassium balance, and the majority of ingested potassium is excreted in the urine. There is strong evidence of a negative association between dietary potassium and blood pressure and some evidence (much of it indirect) of negative associations between dietary potassium and cardiovascular disease (particularly stroke and coronary heart disease) and kidney disease (chronic renal failure and kidney stones)."[46]

Significant dietary sources of potassium include fruits and vegetables (including rice, potatoes, legumes, and whole grains), dairy products, and animal proteins. Many Americans do not eat a healthy diet, especially the elderly or chronically ill, and may be deficient in potassium. Low potassium is associated with a risk of high blood pressure, heart disease, stroke, arthritis, cancer, digestive disorders, and infertility.

In reviewing a paper on *Associations in Dietary Macroelements and Osteoarthritis* (OA), researchers found higher dietary magnesium and potassium were associated with fewer OA symptoms, higher quality of life, greater lower limb muscle strength, and fewer depressive symptoms but not with knee joint structures. More elevated dietary calcium and phosphorus were not associated with any OA-related outcomes, except that dietary phosphorus was associated with greater lower limb muscle strength.[47]

> **Potassium deficiencies are more common in people who:**
> - Use diuretics and birth control pills
> - Have physically demanding jobs
> - Are high-performance athletes
> - Have celiac, ulcerative colitis, IBS, or Crohn's disease
> - Have an eating disorder
> - Smoke
> - Abuse of alcohol or drugs

The Institute of Medicine recommends 4,700mg of potassium for the average adult. This number differs for endurance athletes, firefighters, marathon runners, and pregnant and breastfeeding women. These individuals need to carefully monitor their potassium and salt intake to prevent a condition known as hyponatremia. For information about this disorder, see Chapter 16.

The Downside of Potassium

Hyperkalemia (too much potassium in the bloodstream) is a frequent and sometimes life-threatening condition that may be associated with arrhythmias and cardiac dysfunction in patients with heart failure (HF). High potassium levels in HF represent both a direct risk for cardiovascular complications and an indirect biomarker of the severity of the underlying disease.[48] The kidneys play a crucial role in maintaining whole-body potassium homeostasis by controlling urinary potassium excretion. Older adults are not the only individuals who need to watch their potassium levels; children and athletes are also susceptible to high and low potassium (K) levels. Conversely, low urinary potassium excretion (as a proxy for insufficient dietary intake) is increasingly recognized as a risk factor for the progression of kidney disease.

Earlier, I said potassium exists in a delicate balance. There is a reciprocal relationship between potassium and the kidneys. The kidneys regulate potassium balance, but potassium also affects kidney function. The role of the kidneys in modifying the activity of sodium-chloride and potassium is an example of reciprocity. Activation of the sodium-chloride cotransporter reduces distal sodium delivery and potassium secretion and increases salt sensitivity. This mechanism helps explain the well-known relationship between dietary potassium and blood pressure. In children, blood pressure is related to dietary potassium but not to sodium intake.[49]

Since most ingested potassium is excreted through the kidneys, decreased renal function significantly increases serum potassium levels. In older individuals with impaired renal function, not only hyperkalemia but also hypokalemia (too little potassium in the bloodstream) are likely to develop due to anorexia, potassium loss by dialysis, and effects of various drugs. Abnormalities in potassium metabolism can cause lethal arrhythmia or sudden cardiac death.[50, 51]

The Unrecognized Prevalence of Primary Aldosteronism published in 2020 reported that the prevalence of primary aldosteronism (Conn's syndrome) is high and largely unrecognized. Beyond the categorical definition of primary aldosteronism (PA), an endocrine disorder in which your adrenal glands produce too much of the hormone aldosterone, there is a prevalent continuum of renin-independent aldosterone production that parallels the severity of hypertension. These findings redefine the primary aldosteronism syndrome and implicate it in the pathogenesis of "essential" hypertension.[52] Primary aldosteronism and milder pendent aldosteronism are highly prevalent yet vastly under-recognized in the general population.[53] Primary aldosteronism is the leading cause of curable endocrine hypertension and is associated with a higher risk of cardiovascular and metabolic insults than essential hypertension.[54]

In my area of North America, primary care providers often recommend potassium supplements and bananas to individuals with hypertension on diuretics, which drives me, well, bananas. Numerous other food sources contain a better ratio of electrolyte minerals without the risk of elevated blood sugars. Let's look at healthy foods that will help maintain your electrolyte balance without the risk of overdosing on potassium or elevating your blood sugars.

Balance is Critical

I routinely see elderly clients with dehydration. Some have ended up in the hospital for emergency rehydration. Many also have health conditions where supplemental potassium is contraindicated, such as kidney disease and congestive heart disease. All had low-to-normal sodium levels before the hospitalization, and several were told to take potassium supplements. Additionally, the clients or their family members often express concerns over memory loss or cognitive function. Confusion is a common symptom of dehydration and poor electrolyte balance.

Food Sources of Potassium

Almonds	Avocados	Bananas (high glycemic)
Beans (mung)	Beet greens	Broccoli
Cashews	Chard	Cod (canned)
Dates (high glycemic)	Figs (high glycemic)	Flounder
Kale	Kelp/dulse	Molasses
Parsley	Peanuts	Pistachios
Potatoes	Raisins (high glycemic)	Salmon
Sardines	Spinach	Tea (black and green)
Tomato paste	Watercress	

The FDA has determined that foods containing at least 350 milligrams of potassium can have the following label: "Diets containing foods that are good sources of potassium and low in sodium may reduce the risk of high blood pressure and stroke."

> **Risks Associated with Potassium**
>
> **Side effects:** Upset stomach. Some people have allergies to potassium supplements.
>
> **Interactions:** Potassium supplements may be unsafe if you take certain medicines for diabetes, high blood pressure, or heart disease.
>
> **Warnings:** People with kidney disease, diabetes, heart disease, Addison's disease, stomach ulcers, or other chronic health problems should never take potassium supplements without talking to a doctor first.
>
> **Overdose:** Signs of a potassium overdose include confusion, tingling sensation in the limbs, low blood pressure, irregular heartbeat, weakness, and coma.
> <u>Get emergency medical help immediately.</u>

Salt for Life

All types of salt — including table salt — originate from a sea or a salty body of water, but not all salts currently on the market come from the oceans in existence today. The media and Western mainstream medical establishment have derided salt for decades, claiming it leads to heart disease. In these reports, there was often no differentiation between refined table salt and other types of salt. The ability of sodium chloride – ordinary table salt – to suppress bitterness has been attributed by scientists to salt's popularity as a cooking ingredient worldwide, throughout human history. By quashing the perception of bitterness, salt allows other flavors, such as sweetness or umami, to come to the fore and truly shine. Sodium chloride is extremely effective at suppressing bitterness in coffee and all kinds of food.[55]

A little history

Historically, salt was a valuable commodity. Entire civilizations developed around the salt industry and trade. Salzburg, a city in Austria, is named after salt. Roman soldiers were paid in salt, leading to the expression," He's not worth his salt." The earliest known writings about salt occurred 5,000 years ago in China. Ancient Egyptians recorded salt production in paintings. In Sub-Saharan Africa in the 6th century, Moorish merchants regularly traded prized salt in equal amounts (by weight) for gold. There were salt trade routes worldwide, with the most popular one leading from Morocco south across the Sahara to Timbuktu. Later, in 1295, the explorer Marco Polo returned from his travels telling stories of the highly unique value of salt. <u>Note</u>: I didn't use Timbuktu puns – though I was tempted.

Sodium is the principal negatively charged ion in our cells, responsible for the conduction and regulation of electricity (energy); it is the body's primary electrolyte, with 60% of our total sodium stored in the fluids surrounding the cell and 10% stored inside the cell. Some clinicians believe salt is alkalizing, thus reducing acidosis. Dr. David Brownstein, MD, has found that many individuals with high blood pressure improve when they switch to unrefined salt. Water and salt are necessary for metabolism, detoxification, and hormone, immune, and nervous system function. An adult contains about 250 grams of salt, and a baby contains about 14 grams.

A connection between salt and hypertension was first discovered in 1904. Animal studies done over the next fifty years supported the hypothesis. However, no one looked at the amount of salt given to the animals and/or the form of salt consumed. A study from 2011 on *Low-Salt Diets* confirmed what I have long believed: A low-salt diet was significantly associated with higher homeostasis model assessment index independent of age, sex, blood pressure, body mass index, serum sodium and potassium, serum angiotensin II, plasma renin activity, serum and urine aldosterone, and urine epinephrine and norepinephrine. Additionally, a low-salt diet is associated with an increase in insulin resistance, and higher blood glucose levels might be expected in hypertensive or normotensive people with low-salt consumption compared to those with average or high-sodium consumption.[56, 57] In a 2011 study on low sodium that followed 3,681 participants for 7.9 years, researchers found that in this population-based cohort, systolic blood pressure, but not diastolic pressure, changes over time aligned with a change in sodium excretion. Still, this association did not translate into a higher risk of hypertension or CVD complications. Lower sodium excretion was associated with higher CVD mortality.[58]

Salt Insufficiency Symptoms

- People who crave salt are often found to be suffering from adrenal insufficiency.
- Sodium may alleviate constipation.
- Sodium sulfate may reduce diarrhea.
- Nausea, vomiting, and flatulence may occur due to sodium deficiency.
- Optimal (but not excessive) sodium levels are required for the correct function of the kidneys.
- Sodium deficiency may cause blurred vision.
- Optimal sodium levels are required for the correct function of the lymphatic system (sodium is a component of lymph).
- 30% of the body's sodium concentrates in the bones.
- Correct potassium-sodium balance is essential for the proper function of the muscles; shrinkage of the muscles can occur due to sodium deficiency. Sodium may facilitate proper muscle contraction. Muscle cramps may occur because of sodium deficiency.

Hypernatremia (Too much salt)

Symptoms of having too much sodium in your diet may include bloating, lethargy, dehydration, weakness, irritability, and muscle twitching. Hypernatremia occurs when there's an imbalance of sodium and water in your body. This condition is more common among:

Chapter 10 ~ Minerals the Foundation of Health

- Infants who have a low intake of breast milk or who are drinking formula that was not mixed properly
- Older adults
- People with diabetes or kidney problems
- Severe burn patients
- People who take diuretics
- Those who eat heavily processed food diets

Symptoms can include intense thirst, headache, confusion, irritability, restlessness, and drowsiness. If you think you may be experiencing hypernatremia, seek medical attention immediately.

Not All Salt is Good

Humankind, like animals, must have salt to survive. It is necessary for heart, thyroid, liver, brain, and stomach function. But the industrialized salt commonly used in the United States is very different from the salt mines in Asia and Europe. The type of salt used in commercial foods is not "health food." It is processed via chemicals used to clean and purify the salt from contaminants that strip out minerals. Salt isn't naturally white, nor does it flow smoothly; these characteristics result from chemical processing.

Some of the chemicals used in refining salt are sulfuric acid, chlorine, anti-caking agents like sodium ferrocyanide, ammonium citrate, aluminum silicates, and dextrose. Sea salt is a type of salt produced from the evaporation of seawater. The evaporation is accomplished by open-air solar evaporation or a quicker vacuum evaporation process. Some of the pricier sea salts available today often come from the slower sun-fueled evaporation method. Unrefined sea salt from companies like Celtic Sea Salt may contain over 80 key trace minerals. Key trace minerals are essential to health; they are the foundation of every biochemical response in the body. Standard table salt is simply straight sodium chloride, although it may have added iodine and the above-mentioned chemicals.

Celtic Sea Salt can help detoxify harmful chemicals from the body. Bromine is one such chemical found in processed foods and drinks like Mountain Dew. Bromine bumps iodine off cell receptor sites affecting healthy thyroid function. People who ingest bromine can feel dull and apathetic, have difficulty concentrating, and may have headaches, depression, and irritability. Bromine has also been linked to breast cancer. Salt competes with bromine in the kidneys for re-absorption. A low-salt diet allows for higher amounts of bromine to be absorbed.

For more information about salt, see page 78 in *Our Journey with Food Cookery Book*.

Iodine, The Forgotten Mineral

Iodine is a relatively rare element found primarily in seawater and seafood like kelp and fish (cod, sea bass, haddock, and perch). Seaweed is the most abundant source of iodine; these algae concentrate the iodine found in ocean water. Kelp, however, also concentrates significant quantities of contaminants and chemicals like perchlorate (rocket fuel), fluoride, and bromine. Every cell in the body utilizes iodine. The thyroid gland contains a higher concentration of iodine than any other organ in the body. Large amounts of iodine are also stored in the salivary glands, spinal fluid, gastric mucosa, breasts, ovaries, prostate, and the eyes.

Micronutrients play an essential role in the proper growth and development of the human body. Iodine deficiency affects healthy human functioning, contributing to the vicious cycle of malnutrition, low productivity, underdevelopment, and poverty. Micronutrient deficiency, especially iodine deficiency, is a public health problem affecting more than one-fourth of the global population.[59] In India, the entire population is prone to iodine-deficiency-disorder (IDDs) due to a deficiency of iodine in the soil of the sub-continent. Thus, both animal and plant food grown on the iodine-deficient soil are also iodine-deficient. IDDs encompass a wide spectrum of disability and disease which include goiter, cretinism, hypothyroidism, abortion, stillbirth, brain damage, learning disabilities, mental retardation, psychomotor defects, and hearing and speech impairment. Iodine deficiency is known to be the single largest cause of preventable brain damage.[60]

Iodine deficiency has been identified as a significant public health problem in 129 countries. Iodine deficiency can result in mental retardation, goiter, increased child and infant mortality, infertility, hypothyroidism, impaired immune function, fibrocystic breasts, and cancers of the thyroid, breast, prostate, endometrium, ovaries, and uterus. Iodine deficiency during pregnancy is a significant global public health issue and the leading preventable cause of neurodevelopmental impairments worldwide. The effects of severe iodine deficiency during pregnancy, including adverse obstetric outcomes and decreased child intelligence quotient, have been established.[61] The WHO has recognized that iodine deficiency is the world's most significant cause of preventable mental retardation.[62]

A Little History

Bernard Courtois discovered iodine in 1811 while making gunpowder. When he added sulfuric acid (made from seaweed) to this mixture, a purple vapor appeared (*iodes* is Greek for violet). Iodine was first used medically in 1824 by Jean-Baptiste Boussingault; he found that the iodine-rich water at silver mining sites prevented goiter. In the early 1900s, goiter was prevalent in the states bordering the Great Lakes. In 1924, a study in Michigan showed that 40% of school-age children had enlarged thyroid glands. Iodized salt was introduced to counter this, and by 1928, a 75% reduction in goiter was observed. The WHO actively promotes the use of iodized salt to prevent goiter.

Why Are We Low in Iodine?

You may think that iodized salt has eliminated deficiencies in the United States, but the data does not support this conclusion. Studies done by the National Health and Nutrition Examination Survey over the last 30 years show that iodine levels have dropped by over 50%. This occurs across all demographics, regardless of ethnicity, region, economic status, and race.

Refined salt does not provide the most bioavailable form of iodine. Foods such as bread can more efficiently raise serum iodine levels, but this changed in the 1980s when iodine was replaced by bromide in flour and baked goods and the population was encouraged to go on low-salt diets.

Bromide is in the halide family, and all halides (fluoride, chloride, bromide, iodine) compete for absorption and receptor sites. Bromide is a toxic substance with no therapeutic use in the human body. Perchlorate is a man-made material. Perchlorate contamination of water supplies is widespread and is another reason that iodine levels are dropping.

Individuals of northern European ancestry seem to be more prone to iodine deficiency. Iodine deficiency has re-emerged among pregnant cohorts in the UK. Thyroglobulin (Tg) is a protein produced uniquely by the thyroid gland, which appears to mount a U-shaped response to extremes of iodine status. Tg has been suggested as an alternative marker for chronic iodine deficiency, but Tg's value in pregnancy is low.[63]

A 2017 study provided insight into the iodine issue in Scandinavia.

> "Historically, iodine deficiency disorders such as goiter were common in Norway and Sweden but not Denmark. Different strategies have been used in Scandinavia to improve iodine nutrition. The major source of iodine is iodized salt in Sweden and milk and dairy products in Norway. In Denmark, drinking water, milk, dairy products and iodized salt used in the commercial production of bread are important sources of iodine. The current iodine status in Scandinavia is not optimal and action is ongoing to increase iodination in Denmark, where there is mild iodine deficiency in the general population. Data from all three countries indicate insufficient iodine nutrition during pregnancy and a need for data from children, adolescents, and young women."[64]

Over time farming practices changed in Europe and Scandinavia, and as each generation passed a generational deficiency resulted. In the past in the coastal areas of England, Wales, Ireland, Scotland, Scandinavia, and France, villagers, farmers, and landholders collected seaweed and spread it on the fields for fertilizer. This common practice added essential iodine back into the soil for the grain crops, which in turn fed the animals and the population.

A 2023 study from Norway looked at iodine concentrations in tap water, mineral water, and coffee. Overall, iodine concentrations in tap water were generally low; however, variations were observed for inland and coastal regions. A trend was seen for higher iodine concentrations in the coastal areas than inland regions. For Norway's average habitual iodine intake, tap water may not contribute significantly. One brand of mineral water could have a considerable impact on iodine intake. Coffee does not contribute substantially more to iodine intake than tap water unless the brew is added with milk or plant-based milk alternatives that contain iodine.[65]

Iodine Loading Test (Do only under qualified supervision)

This test assesses whole-body sufficiency for the essential element iodine. Ortho-iodo supplementation is the daily amount of the critical element iodine needed for whole-body adequacy. The test consists of ingesting four tablets of a solid dosage form of Lugol (Iodoral®) containing 50 mg of iodine/iodide.

Laboratories performing the iodine/iodide loading test that I trust are:
- Labrix Clinical Services Inc. in Oregon City, OR
- ZRT Lab in Portland, OR

> ***Principle 51:*** Micronutrients from minerals play an essential role in proper growth and development of the body throughout the entire human lifespan; from embryo to death.

Ferritin: Overlooked Biologically Available Iron

Serum ferritin was discovered in the 1930s and was developed as a clinical test in the 1970s. Many diseases are associated with iron overload or iron deficiency. Serum ferritin is widely used in diagnosing and monitoring these diseases.[66] Most of the time, the discovery of *hyperferritinemia* is by chance. Ferritin is a protein found inside cells that store iron until needed. A ferritin test indirectly measures the amount of iron in your blood. Ferritin is stored in the bone marrow, intestinal wall, liver, and spleen. You can have normal or even optimal serum iron and saturation levels and normal hemoglobin and hematocrit values and still have low ferritin.

The amount of ferritin in your blood (serum ferritin level) is directly related to the quantity of iron stored in your body.[67] The Linus Pauling Institute has stated that in addition to carrying oxygen, ferritin (iron) is an essential part of hundreds of proteins needed for energy, DNA synthesis, and antioxidant enzymes. Low ferritin is a potentially dangerous condition.

While iron stores and levels may be reflected in a standard CBC (complete blood count) or blood chemistry (electrolytes) panel, the client may have been without adequate iron for years by the time low ferritin levels are reflected.

In my office, we were often alerted that ferritin could be low in individuals with deficient vitamin D stores (<20 ng/dl). At other times, we checked individuals with hypothyroid conditions who still presented with a wide range of symptoms of low thyroid and digestive illness. These patients were checked automatically, as were peri-menopausal women with heavy periods.

Case Study 1: During my years of practice, hemochromatosis has been in my awareness due in large part to growing up around Irish immigrants. So, when a retired fisherman with a pleasant brogue came into the office with hepatitis C, I asked if he would share his story. As it turned out, he relocated to North America as a child, and in adulthood had been a commercial fisherman until an accident almost killed him. His leg was severely injured, and he developed a bone infection and required blood transfusions. A couple of years after his recovery, he came down with what he thought was the flu; it turned out he was diagnosed with hepatitis C. Widespread blood screening for hepatitis C began in 1992, and before 1992 the chance of contracting hepatitis C and other viral infections from donated blood was much more likely.

The first African American tennis star, Arthur Ashe, contracted AIDS following a blood transfusion during heart surgery in 1983.[68] Today individuals who have had or presently have/carry hepatitis C and AIDS are ineligible to donate blood or organs.

Now back to my story. My client shared his frustration over the frequent assumption he was/had been an IV drug user, and that is how he contracted hepatitis. My medical director agreed to run lab tests following our client review. My instinct told me the client was not lying and that something else was contributing. As it turned out, the client had hemochromatosis, which can result in liver cirrhosis. And this condition, combined with the history of bone infection and blood transfusions that led to hepatitis C, caused my client's liver to be on the verge of failure. For years providers had assumed my client was an alcoholic and drug user until he came to our office and learned he had an ancient iron storage condition that had gone untreated. Sadly, our client passed away before a liver transplant could be arranged.

Clinical findings and a few straightforward tests are generally used by biomedical healthcare providers to identify one of the four leading causes of elevated ferritin: alcoholism, inflammatory syndrome, cytolysis and metabolic syndrome. None of these causes is associated with a significant iron hepatic overload.[69] Following the event with the retired fisherman, our office requested serum ferritin levels on about one-third of our clients.

Case Study 2: Older clients may be told they are anemic based solely on their CBC panels, as was the case with one client in her 70s who had a family history of hemochromatosis. For years she had suffered from arthritic symptoms, for which her doctors recommended NSAIDs. Her doctor prescribed her iron supplements without knowing her family history or assuming it would not be an issue for her as a female. Instructed to improve her diet, she increased her iron-rich foods. During her appointment with me, I learned she grew up near my childhood home and was of Irish descent with two brothers who gave blood monthly. I asked if there was any particular reason her brothers donated blood? She replied their doctor said "they had too much iron" and needed to do it for their health. I asked whether she had ever been checked for hemochromatosis? She had not. On closer evaluation, her ferritin levels were 1,790 (the normal range is 12-500). This elevated level indicated that she could not convert iron into hemoglobin, and possibly had liver or kidney disease,[70] or a cardiac event caused the release of ferritin into the bloodstream. Our office referred the client to a specialist. When I saw her a few weeks later, she was doing better and had hope once more.

Case Study 3: Not everyone has high ferritin. Low ferritin levels can be caused by genetic conditions, celiac disease, anti-inflammatory medication use, or bacteria and viruses (they feed on iron). More of my clients have low ferritin and suffer needlessly for years before their labs reflect anemia. A peri-menopausal client with dysmenorrhea and an unknown genetic NSAIDs intolerance is a good example; she was frequently short of breath, tired, with rapid heart rate, frequent tendonitis, and muscle pain, was irritable, and would have a low-grade headache most days. Additionally, she had low vitamin D and elevated TSH (thyroid stimulating hormone) levels without deficiencies in free T3 or free T4. Her ferritin levels were at 9, almost low enough to finally register as anemic, which is generally about 5. The client was dedicated to getting well and dutifully consumed liver twice a week for three months, replaced her NSAIDs with Boswellia, and made other lifestyle modifications. By the six-month mark, her levels had improved and most of her symptoms were gone. The client knew to avoid NSAIDs and to be careful in using blood-thinning nutrients such as vitamin E and omega-3. The unfortunate aspect of her history was acute hypertension as the result of NSAIDs affecting her kidneys. We are happy to share that the client, after seven years of diet and lifestyle modifications and a very low dose of anti-hypertensive medication, has blood pressure within the normal range of 115/65.

Case Study 4: This client is a 45-year old female whose low iron levels had been overlooked by her primary care provider. Since her youth, she had suffered from weakness, heart palpitations, irritability, low-grade headaches, and mild restless leg symptoms. Antidepressants and pain medications were the solutions offered by her medical provider. Once the provider was alerted to the client's ferritin level being 5 (lab ranges can run between 15-500), they approved the dietary inclusion of a liquid iron and mineral supplement along with vitamin C. After six months, the client's levels had improved, and she no longer qualified for some of the once suggested medications.

Because ferritin levels are not revealed in a standard CBC lab test, low ferritin may be a widespread problem overlooked by providers.[71,72,73,74] Anemia is the most common form of micronutrient deficiency in India and affects almost 50-60% of preschool children and women. In contrast, vitamin A deficiency and iodine deficiency disorders (IDD) have improved over the years.[75] Conventional thinking is that iron levels are only low in menstruating women, cancer patients, and those with blood diseases. However, low ferritin can also reflect celiac disease or cancer for some, so in my opinion, the importance of ferritin and iron levels is being overlooked by many providers.

Low ferritin levels may increase the risk of fibromyalgia and restless legs syndrome (RLS); patients are often found to have significantly lower ferritin levels than healthy subjects.[76]

Low ferritin can be asymptomatic. It is a precursor to anemia, as revealed by labs (saturation and serum iron). Symptoms of anemia mimic hypothyroidism: depression, achiness, fatigue, weakness, increased heart rate, palpitations, loss of sex drive, hair loss, and foggy thinking. Patients may mistakenly believe they have heart problems or need more thyroid medication. Excessively low ferritin and low iron make it challenging to control thyroid and adrenal health problems.

Low iron levels slow the conversion of thyroid hormones T4 to T3. Biologically, insufficient iron levels may affect the first two or three steps of thyroid hormone synthesis by reducing the activity of the enzyme thyroid peroxidase, which is dependent on iron. Low iron levels can also increase circulating concentrations of TSH.

Iron is needed for the production of cortisol via the adrenal cortex. An iron-containing protein is present in high amounts in the adrenal cortex and is involved in corticosterone synthesis. Therefore, low iron can potentially lower cortisol levels, inducing adrenal fatigue.[77]

The World Health Organization estimates that as much as 80% of the world's population may be iron deficient. Many people in North America do not consume enough iron in their diet. Dietary iron comes in two chemical forms: heme and non-heme. Heme iron comes from flesh foods, primarily red meat. The iron from plant sources is non-heme and is roughly 10% bioavailable. Legumes, grains, and rice are plant sources of iron, but they contain phytic acid, which decreases iron absorption by as much as 50%.

Antacids, milk thistle, anti-inflammatory medications, black tea, and dairy products (including whey protein) can decrease ferritin levels and exacerbate malabsorption illnesses such as ulcerative colitis, IBS,

Crohn's disease, celiac disease, GI ulcers, and colon cancer. Low ferritin can also cause excessive blood loss after surgery and from menstruation.

Excessive stored iron (ferritin) was once believed to be a risk factor for cardiovascular diseases, including atherosclerosis and heart attack.[78, 79] More recently, researchers have shown serum ferritin levels become elevated due to (not as a precursor to) inflammatory processes that lead to cardiovascular diseases.[80, 81] In other words, the pre-existing cardiovascular disease most likely accounted for the high serum ferritin levels.[82] The *Integrative Medicine 5th ed.* and *Krause Food and the Nutrition Care Process 16th ed.* textbooks share that iron stored as ferritin is incapable of initiating free radical reactions. Ferritin, therefore, inhibits the ability of iron to cause some types of cardiovascular diseases.

> ***Principle 52:*** Ferritin, inhibits the ability of iron to cause some types of cardiovascular diseases.

Frequently Asked Question

I frequently hear clients ask, *"Why doesn't anyone tell you this? Why don't doctors look into this?"*

First, no one knows your body and health better than you do. Suppose you are exposed to information that empowers you to take back control of your health and do so. In that case, the job of your primary healthcare provider gets easier because you are doing your part by staying healthy, vibrant, and productive.

Secondly, many health challenges have the same symptoms. This is one of the reasons why knowing your family history is essential. Familial tendencies may give you a clue as to what is causing your fatigue, heart palpitations, dizziness, shortness of breath, or other symptoms associated with low ferritin. Low ferritin may also be a symptom of other health conditions like celiac disease, Crohn's disease, and thyroid dysfunction. The key is to ensure that a deficiency like low ferritin is not overlooked so that health can be efficiently managed.

What to do if ferritin is low? For your ferritin levels to read as low, a biologically iron-deficient state must occur over a prolonged period. When reviewing lab results (depending on the lab), ferritin ranges are 12-500 ng/mL or 15-400 ng/mL.[83, 84] The thyroid and adrenal glands work best when ferritin is between 80-110 ng/mL. Women will routinely complain of hair loss between 40-60 ng/mL and fatigue and lightheadedness between 20-40 ng/mL; 20 ng/mL and lower can manifest in heart arrhythmias, breathlessness, irritability, nerve pain, and restless leg symptoms. Note that all of these symptoms can occur within what the lab results deem an average range.

Food is Better than Supplements

The best food source of ferritin (iron) is liver, preferably pork. Liver has not been commonly consumed in the United States since the 1950s and 1960s. The cultural aversion to liver may account for the growing number of individuals with low iron and vitamins D and B_{12}.[85, 86, 87] Heme iron found in animal organs and muscle meat is the most bioavailable iron-bound form. Hydrochloric acid production diminishes as we age, affecting our ability to break phytic acid bonds and absorb iron, especially from plants and oxide-based supplements. It is found mainly in flesh foods such as lean red meat, lamb, buffalo, wild game, sockeye salmon, tuna, pork, and chicken legs. The next best sources of iron are molasses, amaranth, white beans, sesame and pumpkin seeds, pine nuts, cashews, pistachios, dandelion, cocoa, rice bran, spirulina, and cold-water kelp.

Many perimenopausal individuals take supplemental calcium to reduce the chance of osteoporosis and anti-inflammatory medications for osteoarthritis; both can interfere with ferritin. This and subpar nutritional intake could increase the likelihood of low ferritin in elderly individuals and those living with chronic illness. An early and accurate diagnosis of low ferritin may prevent accidental falls or medications and ultimately lead to a better quality of life.

Note: Phytates or phytic acid, most often found in plant-based foods like whole grains, cereals, soy, corn, nuts, and legumes, are proven to block the absorption of non-heme iron. Walnuts are especially high in phytates. Soak beans and lentils thoroughly (typically overnight) to eliminate phytic acid. Black, green and white tea, whey protein, and coffee can suppress ferritin production and conversion. Tea contains oxalates; oxalic acid compounds that impair the absorption of non-heme iron. Oxalate-rich foods, if not properly prepared, can also interfere with iron absorption. These foods include spinach, kale, beets, nuts, chocolate, wheat bran, rhubarb, and parsley. One cup of coffee can prevent iron absorption by up to 60%. Eggs can block iron absorption due to phosvitin, a protein compound that binds iron molecules together and prevents absorption. If an individual is anemic, they should avoid these foods until ferritin levels have improved. To learn more, go to the *Iron Disorders Institute*: https://irondisorders.org/diet/

> *Principle 53:* "It is not the food itself, but how the food is made."
> ~Dr. Bill Schindler

Zinc

The essentiality of zinc for humans was recognized in the early 1960s. Zinc is one of the most essential trace elements, and an important component of a balanced diet. Zinc is the second most abundant trace element after iron. The causes of zinc deficiency were published in multiple papers beginning in 1983 and have remained consistent in nutrition textbooks to the present. Deficiency-leading causes include malnutrition, alcoholism, malabsorption, extensive burns, chronic debilitating disorders, chronic renal diseases (following the use of certain drugs—such as penicillamine for Wilson's disease and diuretics in some cases), and genetic disorders such as acrodermatitis enteropathica and sickle cell disease. In pregnancy and during periods of growth, the requirement for zinc is increased.

Zinc is a growth factor. Its deficiency adversely affects development in many animal species and humans. Since zinc is needed for protein and DNA synthesis and for cell division, it is believed that the growth effect of zinc is related to its effect on protein synthesis. Zinc is required for the functions of over 2,000 enzymes. Thymopoeitin, a hormone needed for T cell maturation, has also been shown to be zinc-dependent. Zinc deficiency adversely affects T cell functions and chemotaxis (migration of cells toward attractive chemicals and away from repellents).

A paper published in 2023 on zinc and cardiovascular disease reported zinc is related to the molecular mechanisms of cardiovascular functions. Several clinical studies have reported the relationship between zinc levels and the onset and pathology of cardiovascular diseases.[88] Zinc transporters strictly control intracellular zinc localization. Zinc regulates the functions of various proteins and signal transduction pathways as a second messenger similar to calcium ions. Intracellular zinc dyshomeostasis is associated with impaired insulin synthesis, secretion and sensitivity, lipid metabolism, and vascular function.[89]

> **Manifestations** in severe cases of zinc deficiency include bullous pustular dermatitis, alopecia, diarrhea, emotional disorder, weight loss, intercurrent infections, and hypogonadism in males. It can be fatal if unrecognized and untreated.
>
> **Moderate deficiency** of zinc is characterized by growth retardation and delayed puberty in adolescents, hypogonadism in males, rough skin, poor appetite, mental lethargy, delayed wound healing, taste abnormalities, and abnormal dark adaptation.
>
> **Mild deficiency** of zinc observed are oligospermia, slight weight loss, and hyperammonemia.

Zinc deficiency is a major health problem worldwide. Zinc has antioxidant and immunomodulatory functions and plays important roles in the pathogenesis of various diseases. Causes of zinc deficiency can be nutritional, iatrogenic, genetic, or a result of diseases. Severe zinc deficiency results in symptoms like pustular dermatitis, alopecia, weight loss, diarrhea, infections secondary to immune dysfunction, hypogonadism, and problems in ulcer healing.[90]

After evaluating the client's nutritional status, appropriate nutritional supplements can correct the deficiency of various micronutrients in COVID-19 patients. Vitamin D, vitamin C, omega-3 fatty acids, zinc, and magnesium provide their synergistic support in enhancing immunity and, thus, maintaining homeostasis.[91] A 2023 study on nutritional deficiencies that predispose long-COVID reported:

> Multiple nutritional deficiencies (MND) confound studies designed to assess the role of a single nutrient in contributing to the initiation and progression of disease states. Despite the perception of many healthcare practitioners, up to 25% of Americans are deficient in five-or-more essential nutrients. Stress associated with the COVID-19 pandemic further increases the prevalence of deficiency states. Viral infections compete for crucial nutrients with immune cells. Viral replication and proliferation of immunocompetent cells critical to the host response require these essential nutrients, including zinc. Clinical studies have linked levels of more than 22 different dietary components to the likelihood of COVID-19 infection and the severity of the disease. People at higher risk of infection due to MND are also more likely to have long-term sequelae, known as long COVID.[92]

The World Health Organization names COVID a malnutrition-enhanced disease in a 2022 statement paper.

> We believe the evidence supports the need to consider COVID-19 as (also) a case of malnutrition-enhanced disease and disease-related malnutrition, with added risk for persons both with and without obesity. Similarities with many other disease conditions further support recommendations to implement standard nutritional screening and care in COVID-19 patients, and they underscore the relevance of appropriate nutritional and lifestyle prevention policies to limit infection risk and mitigate the negative health impact of acute pandemic bouts.[93]

These studies specifically mention zinc and many other nutrients listed in this book, re-affirming our premise that *food is medicine,* and nutrition is very important for resiliency in coping with stress and viral infections. In conjunction with new archaeological evidence from McMaster University in 2023, the results of these studies soundly debunk the myth of virus's effect on healthy and ill children and adults equally. Researchers examining the skeletal remains of nearly 400 Spanish Influenza victims from 1918 found that in 1918—just like in 2020—people exposed to environmental, social, or nutritional stressors beforehand were significantly more likely to succumb to a novel virus when it emerged.[94]

Benefits of Zinc[95]

- ✓ Zinc may stimulate the formation of bones; impaired bone growth in adolescents may occur due to (even minor) zinc deficiency.
- ✓ Fibromyalgia patients are often found to have low zinc levels. Lower zinc levels in fibromyalgia patients are associated with more tender points.
- ✓ Zinc facilitates wound healing and bone fractures.[96]
- ✓ Night muscle cramps may occur as a result of zinc deficiency.
- ✓ Zinc may improve muscle strength.
- ✓ Osteoporosis patients are often found to have low serum and bone zinc levels.
- ✓ Zinc may alleviate the symptoms of psoriatic and rheumatoid arthritis. Clinical studies have shown supplemental zinc may alleviate the joint swelling and morning stiffness associated with rheumatoid arthritis.
- ✓ Zinc may alleviate scleroderma.
- ✓ White specks on the fingernails or nails that split easily may occur due to zinc deficiency.

> ***Principle 54:*** Research is revealing that much can be done to avoid cognitive deterioration by eating a nutritious diet.

Zinc and Osteoarthritis

Osteoarthritis, especially in the knee, is a relatively common condition and a leading cause of disability. Other afflicted areas can include the shoulders or hips. Characterized by the destruction of cartilage tissue in joints, there is a lack of effective therapies because the underlying molecular causes have been unclear.

A study published on February 13, 2014, in the journal *Cell*, reveals that osteoarthritis-related tissue damage is caused by a molecular pathway involved in regulating and responding to zinc levels inside cartilage cells.

When the cartilage breaks down, the bones rub together, causing pain, swelling, and stiffness. This tissue destruction is caused by proteins called matrix-degrading enzymes produced by cartilage cells. The enzymes degrade the extracellular matrix, which is the structural support system surrounding and holding cells together. Because matrix-degrading enzymes require zinc to function, zinc levels inside cartilage cells may play a role in osteoarthritis.

The downsides of Zinc

- Zinc supplementation is necessary in cases of zinc deficiency, but high doses of zinc supplementation over a long time can result in copper deficiency or anemia.
- Zinc competes with copper and iron for the same receptor sites and may reduce magnesium and other minerals. It is best if this mineral is taken separately from other mineral supplements.
- Zinc may inhibit the absorption of tetracyclines.
- Excessive zinc intake may cause anemia.
- Excessive zinc intake may contribute to atherosclerosis.
- Large doses of zinc (>150mg per day) may reduce the body's production of HDL cholesterol. However, optimal zinc levels may enhance the production of HDL cholesterol.

How Much is Safe?

The optimal daily allowance (ODA) of zinc (for adults) is 15-50mg daily. The recommended therapeutic dosage of supplemental zinc for athletes is 30-60mg daily.

For the common cold, try an initial dose of 50mg of zinc followed by 25mg every two hours (using zinc lozenges or zinc tablets slowly dissolved in the mouth but not rapidly swallowed). The form of zinc should be zinc acetate or zinc gluconate.

The best food sources of zinc are oysters, beef, lamb, and liver. Unfortunately, the mineral zinc is tightly bound by phytic acid in plant foods making it hard to gain adequate amounts to correct deficiencies. I suggest supplementing with about 30mg of quality zinc from a reliable practitioner and incorporating zinc-rich foods into your diet.

1 Stabler SP (2020). "Vitamin B12". In BP Marriott, DF Birt, VA Stallings, AA Yates (eds.). Present Knowledge in Nutrition, Eleventh Edition. London: Academic Press (Elsevier). pp. 257–272. ISBN 978-0-323-66162-1.
2 American Osteopathic Association. (2018, February 26). Low magnesium levels make vitamin D ineffective: Up to 50 % of US population is magnesium deficient. ScienceDaily. Retrieved June 29, 2023 from www.sciencedaily.com/releases/2018/02/180226122548.htm
3 University of Basel. (2022, January 19). Magnesium is essential for the immune system, including in the fight against cancer. ScienceDaily. Retrieved June 29, 2023 from www.sciencedaily.com/releases/2022/01/220119121455.htm
4 Marneros A. G. (2021). Magnesium and Calcium Homeostasis Depend on KCTD1 Function in the Distal Nephron. Cell reports, 34(2), 108616. https://doi.org/10.1016/j.celrep.2020.108616
5 Barbagallo, M., Veronese, N., & Dominguez, L. J. (2021). Magnesium in Aging, Health and Diseases. Nutrients, 13(2), 463. https://doi.org/10.3390/nu13020463
6 Australian National University. (2023, March 23). A higher dose of magnesium each day keeps dementia at bay. ScienceDaily. Retrieved June 30, 2023 from www.sciencedaily.com/releases/2023/03/230323103415.htm
7 Wu, S., Jin, T., Ma, B., Ji, Y., Huang, X., Wang, P., Liu, X., Krylov, B. V., Liu, X., & Ma, K. (2023). Oral application of magnesium-L-threonate enhances analgesia and reduces the dosage of opioids needed in advanced cancer patients-A randomized, double-blind, placebo-controlled trial. Cancer medicine, 12(4), 4343–4351. https://doi.org/10.1002/cam4.4922
8 Dana, N., Karimi, R., Mansourian, M., Javanmard, S. H., Laher, I., & Vaseghi, G. (2021). Magnesium intake and lung cancer risk: A systematic review and meta-analysis. International journal for vitamin and nutrition research. Internationale Zeitschrift fur Vitamin- und Ernahrungsforschung. Journal international de vitaminologie et de nutrition, 91(5-6), 539–546. https://doi.org/10.1024/0300-9831/a000598
9 Papadimitriou, N., Bouras, E., van den Brandt, P. A., Muller, D. C., Papadopoulou, A., Heath, A. K., Critselis, E., Gunter, M. J., Vineis, P., Ferrari, P., Weiderpass, E., Boeing, H., Bastide, N., Merritt, M. A., Lopez, D. S., Bergmann, M. M., Perez-Cornago, A., Schulze, M., Skeie, G., Srour, B., ... Tsilidis, K. K. (2022). A Prospective Diet-Wide Association Study for Risk of Colorectal Cancer in EPIC. Clinical gastroenterology and hepatology : the official clinical practice journal of the American Gastroenterological Association, 20(4), 864–873.e13. https://doi.org/10.1016/j.cgh.2021.04.028
10 Ates, M., Kizildag, S., Yuksel, O., Hosgorler, F., Yuce, Z., Guvendi, G., Kandis, S., Karakilic, A., Koc, B., & Uysal, N. (2019). Dose-Dependent Absorption Profile of Different Magnesium Compounds. Biological trace element research, 192(2), 244–251. https://doi.org/10.1007/s12011-019-01663-0
11 Uysal, N., Kizildag, S., Yuce, Z., Guvendi, G., Kandis, S., Koc, B., Karakilic, A., Camsari, U. M., & Ates, M. (2019). Timeline (Bioavailability) of Magnesium Compounds in Hours: Which Magnesium Compound Works Best?. Biological trace element research, 187(1), 128–136. https://doi.org/10.1007/s12011-018-1351-9
12 Volume27, IssueS1, Experimental Biology 2013 Meeting Abstracts; (2013) Pg. lb291-lb291
13 Fiorentini, D., Cappadone, C., Farruggia, G., & Prata, C. (2021). Magnesium: Biochemistry, Nutrition, Detection, and Social Impact of Diseases Linked to Its Deficiency. Nutrients, 13(4), 1136. https://doi.org/10.3390/nu13041136
14 Pickering, G., Mazur, A., Trousselard, M., Bienkowski, P., Yaltsewa, N., Amessou, M., Noah, L., & Pouteau, E. (2020). Magnesium Status and Stress: The Vicious Circle Concept Revisited. Nutrients, 12(12), 3672. https://doi.org/10.3390/nu12123672
15 Zhang, Y., Xun, P., Wang, R., Mao, L., & He, K. (2017). Can Magnesium Enhance Exercise Performance?. Nutrients, 9(9), 946. https://doi.org/10.3390/nu9090946
16 Konopka, M. J., Zeegers, M. P., Solberg, P. A., Delhaije, L., Meeusen, R., Ruigrok, G., Rietjens, G., & Sperlich, B. (2022). Factors associated with high-level endurance performance: An expert consensus derived via the Delphi technique. PloS one, 17(12), e0279492. https://doi.org/10.1371/journal.pone.0279492
17 Nutrition During Pregnancy: Part I Weight Gain: Part II Nutrient Supplements. 16: Calcium, Vitamin D, and Magnesium 1990
18 Ozcaliskan Ilkay, H., Sahin, H., Tanriverdi, F., & Samur, G. (2019). Association Between Magnesium Status, Dietary Magnesium Intake, and Metabolic Control in Patients with Type 2 Diabetes Mellitus. Journal of the American College of Nutrition, 38(1), 31–39. https://doi.org/10.1080/07315724.2018.1476194
19 Kocyigit, E., Akturk, M., & Koksal, E. (2023). Relationships between serum and dietary magnesium, calcium, and metabolic parameters in women with type 2 diabetes mellitus. Clinical nutrition ESPEN, 54, 304–310. https://doi.org/10.1016/j.clnesp.2023.01.035
20 Fan, L., Zhu, X., Sun, S., Yu, C., Huang, X., Ness, R., Dugan, L. L., Shu, L., Seidner, D. L., Murff, H. J., Fodor, A. A., Azcarate-Peril, M. A., Shrubsole, M. J., & Dai, Q. (2022). Ca:Mg ratio, medium-chain fatty acids, and the gut microbiome. Clinical nutrition (Edinburgh, Scotland), 41(11), 2490–2499. https://doi.org/10.1016/j.clnu.2022.08.031
21 Morton, A. R., Garland, J. S., & Holden, R. M. (2010). Is the calcium correct? Measuring serum calcium in dialysis patients. Seminars in dialysis, 23(3), 283–289. https://doi.org/10.1111/j.1525-139X.2010.00735.x
22 Li, K., Wang, X. F., Li, D. Y., Chen, Y. C., Zhao, L. J., Liu, X. G., Guo, Y. F., Shen, J., Lin, X., Deng, J., Zhou, R., & Deng, H. W. (2018). The good, the bad, and the ugly of calcium supplementation: a review of calcium intake on human health. Clinical interventions in aging, 13, 2443–2452. https://doi.org/10.2147/CIA.S157523
23 Chiodini, I., & Bolland, M. J. (2018). Calcium supplementation in osteoporosis: useful or harmful?. European journal of endocrinology, 178(4), D13–D25. https://doi.org/10.1530/EJE-18-0113

24 Gilbert, Z. A., Muller, A., Leibowitz, J. A., & Kesselman, M. M. (2022). Osteoporosis Prevention and Treatment: The Risk of Comorbid Cardiovascular Events in Postmenopausal Women. Cureus, 14(4), e24117. https://doi.org/10.7759/cureus.24117

25 Muscogiuri, G., Barrea, L., Altieri, B., Di Somma, C., Bhattoa, H. P., Laudisio, D., Duval, G. T., Pugliese, G., Annweiler, C., Orio, F., Fakhouri, H., Savastano, S., & Colao, A. (2019). Calcium and Vitamin D Supplementation. Myths and Realities with Regard to Cardiovascular Risk. Current vascular pharmacology, 17(6), 610–617. https://doi.org/10.2174/1570161117666190408165805

26 Yang, B., Campbell, P. T., Gapstur, S. M., Jacobs, E. J., Bostick, R. M., Fedirko, V., Flanders, W. D., & McCullough, M. L. (2016). Calcium intake and mortality from all causes, cancer, and cardiovascular disease: the Cancer Prevention Study II Nutrition Cohort. The American journal of clinical nutrition, 103(3), 886–894. https://doi.org/10.3945/ajcn.115.117994

27 Lin, R., Feng, W., Yang, Y., Xu, J., Yang, H., Wu, J., Li, J., Qin, G., Yu, Y., & Chen, J. (2023). Association of dietary calcium with mortality from all causes, cardiovascular disease and cancer in people with hypertension. Journal of clinical hypertension (Greenwich, Conn.), 25(5), 480–488. https://doi.org/10.1111/jch.14657

28 Moon D. O. (2023). Calcium's Role in Orchestrating Cancer Apoptosis: Mitochondrial-Centric Perspective. International journal of molecular sciences, 24(10), 8982. https://doi.org/10.3390/ijms24108982

29 Patergnani, S., Danese, A., Bouhamida, E., Aguiari, G., Previati, M., Pinton, P., & Giorgi, C. (2020). Various Aspects of Calcium Signaling in the Regulation of Apoptosis, Autophagy, Cell Proliferation, and Cancer. International journal of molecular sciences, 21(21), 8323. https://doi.org/10.3390/ijms21218323

30 Melnik B. C. (2021). Lifetime Impact of Cow's Milk on Overactivation of mTORC1: From Fetal to Childhood Overgrowth, Acne, Diabetes, Cancers, and Neurodegeneration. Biomolecules, 11(3), 404. https://doi.org/10.3390/biom11030404

31 Hall M. N. (2008). mTOR-what does it do?. Transplantation proceedings, 40(10 Suppl), S5–S8. https://doi.org/10.1016/j.transproceed.2008.10.009

32 Melnik, B. C., John, S. M., Carrera-Bastos, P., Cordain, L., Leitzmann, C., Weiskirchen, R., & Schmitz, G. (2023). The Role of Cow's Milk Consumption in Breast Cancer Initiation and Progression. Current nutrition reports, 12(1), 122–140. https://doi.org/10.1007/s13668-023-00457-0

33 Britt, J.H., R.A. Cushman, C.D. Dechow, H. Dobson, P. Humblot, M.F. Hutjens, G.A. Jones, P.S. Ruegg, I.M. Sheldon, and J.S. Stevenson. "Invited Review: Learning from the Future—A Vision for Dairy Farms and Cows in 2067." Journal of Dairy Science 101, no. 5 (2018): 3722-741. doi:10.3168/jds.2017-14025.

34 Mak, T. N., Angeles-Agdeppa, I., Tassy, M., Capanzana, M. V., & Offord, E. A. (2020). Contribution of Milk Beverages to Nutrient Adequacy of Young Children and Preschool Children in the Philippines. Nutrients, 12(2), 392. https://doi.org/10.3390/nu12020392

35 Madrigal, C., Soto-Méndez, M. J., Hernández-Ruiz, Á., Ruiz-López, M. D., Samaniego-Vaesken, M. L., Partearroyo, T., Varela-Moreiras, G., & Gil, Á. (2022). Dietary Intake, Nutritional Adequacy, and Food Sources of Selected Antioxidant Minerals and Vitamins; and Their Relationship with Personal and Family Factors in Spanish Children Aged 1 to <10 Years: Results from the EsNuPI Study. Nutrients, 14(19), 4132. https://doi.org/10.3390/nu14194132

36 Woźniak, D., Cichy, W., Dobrzyńska, M., Przysławski, J., & Drzymała-Czyż, S. (2022). Reasonableness of Enriching Cow's Milk with Vitamins and Minerals. Foods (Basel, Switzerland), 11(8), 1079. https://doi.org/10.3390/foods11081079

37 Yan, M. J., Humphreys, J., & Holden, N. M. (2013). Life cycle assessment of milk production from commercial dairy farms: the influence of management tactics. Journal of dairy science, 96(7), 4112–4124. https://doi.org/10.3168/jds.2012-6139

38 García-López, R., Pérez-Brocal, V., & Moya, A. (2019). Beyond cells- The virome in the human holobiont. Microbial cell (Graz, Austria), 6(9), 373–396. https://doi.org/10.15698/mic2019.09.689

39 Santiago-Rodriguez, T. M., & Hollister, E. B. (2019). Human Virome and Disease: High-Throughput Sequencing for Virus Discovery, Identification of Phage-Bacteria Dysbiosis and Development of Therapeutic Approaches with Emphasis on the Human Gut. Viruses, 11(7), 656. https://doi.org/10.3390/v11070656

40 Published in Volume 133, Issue 3 on February 1, 2023, J Clin Invest. 2023;133(3):e163669. https://doi.org/10.1172/JCI163669.

41 Lopresti A. L. (2020). The Effects of Psychological and Environmental Stress on Micronutrient Concentrations in the Body: A Review of the Evidence. Advances in nutrition (Bethesda, Md.), 11(1), 103–112. https://doi.org/10.1093/advances/nmz082

42 Kumar, P., Kumar, M., Bedi, O., Gupta, M., Kumar, S., Jaiswal, G., Rahi, V., Yedke, N. G., Bijalwan, A., Sharma, S., & Jamwal, S. (2021). Role of vitamins and minerals as immunity boosters in COVID-19. Inflammopharmacology, 29(4), 1001–1016. https://doi.org/10.1007/s10787-021-00826-7

43 Pinnawala, N. U., Thrastardottir, T. O., & Constantinou, C. (2021). Keeping a Balance During the Pandemic: a Narrative Review on the Important Role of Micronutrients in Preventing Infection and Reducing Complications of COVID-19. Current nutrition reports, 10(3), 200–210. https://doi.org/10.1007/s13668-021-00356-2

44 Cenacchi, V., Maier, J. A., & Perini, M. P. (2022). A potential protective role of magnesium in neuroCOVID. A potential protective role of magnesium in neuroCOVID. Magnesium research, 35(1), 18–26. https://doi.org/10.1684/mrh.2022.0497

45 Lahaye, C., Parant, F., Haesebaert, J., Goldet, K., Bendim'red, L., Henaff, L., Saadatian-Elahi, M., Vanhems, P., Cuerq, C., Gilbert, T., Blond, E., Bost, M., & Bonnefoy, M. (2023). Minerals and Antioxidant Micronutrients Levels and Clinical Outcome in Older Patients Hospitalized for COVID-19 during the First Wave of the Pandemic. Nutrients, 15(6), 1516. https://doi.org/10.3390/nu15061516

46 McLean, R. M., & Wang, N. X. (2021). Potassium. Advances in food and nutrition research, 96, 89–121. https://doi.org/10.1016/bs.afnr.2021.02.013

47 Zhang, Y., Chen, T., Luo, P., Li, S., Zhu, J., Xue, S., Cao, P., Zhu, Z., Li, J., Wang, X., Wluka, A. E., Cicuttini, F., Ruan, G., & Ding, C. (2022). Associations of Dietary Macroelements with Knee Joint Structures, Symptoms, Quality of Life, and Comorbid Conditions in People with Symptomatic Knee Osteoarthritis. Nutrients, 14(17), 3576. https://doi.org/10.3390/nu14173576

48 Rakisheva, A., Marketou, M., Klimenko, A., Troyanova-Shchutskaia, T., & Vardas, P. (2020). Hyperkalemia in heart failure: Foe or friend?. Clinical cardiology, 43(7), 666–675. https://doi.org/10.1002/clc.23392

49 Wieërs, M. L. A. J., Mulder, J., Rotmans, J. I., & Hoorn, E. J. (2022). Potassium and the kidney: a reciprocal relationship with clinical relevance. Pediatric nephrology (Berlin, Germany), 37(10), 2245–2254. https://doi.org/10.1007/s00467-022-05494-5

50 Yamada, S., & Inaba, M. (2021). Potassium Metabolism and Management in Patients with CKD. Nutrients, 13(6), 1751. https://doi.org/10.3390/nu13061751

51 Yamada, S., & Inaba, M. (2021). Potassium Metabolism and Management in Patients with CKD. Nutrients, 13(6), 1751. https://doi.org/10.3390/nu13061751

52 Brown, J. M., Siddiqui, M., Calhoun, D. A., Carey, R. M., Hopkins, P. N., Williams, G. H., & Vaidya, A. (2020). The Unrecognized Prevalence of Primary Aldosteronism: A Cross-sectional Study. Annals of internal medicine, 173(1), 10–20. https://doi.org/10.7326/M20-0065

53 Hundemer, G. L., Kline, G. A., & Leung, A. A. (2021). How common is primary aldosteronism?. Current opinion in nephrology and hypertension, 30(3), 353–360. https://doi.org/10.1097/MNH.0000000000000702

54 Chang, Y. Y., Lee, B. C., Chen, Z. W., Tsai, C. H., Chang, C. C., Liao, C. W., Pan, C. T., Peng, K. Y., Chou, C. H., Lu, C. C., Wu, V. C., Hung, C. S., Lin, Y. H., & TAIPAI study group (2023). Cardiovascular and metabolic characters of KCNJ5 somatic mutations in primary aldosteronism. Frontiers in endocrinology, 14, 1061704. https://doi.org/10.3389/fendo.2023.1061704

55 https://doi.org/10.1073/pnas.77.3.168

56 Garg, R., Williams, G. H., Hurwitz, S., Brown, N. J., Hopkins, P. N., & Adler, G. K. (2011). Low-salt diet increases insulin resistance in healthy subjects. Metabolism: clinical and experimental, 60(7), 965–968. https://doi.org/10.1016/j.metabol.2010.09.005

57 Shen, Y., Shi, Y., Cui, J., He, H., & Ren, S. (2023). Effects of dietary salt intake restriction on blood glucose levels: a meta-analysis of crossover study. Nutrition research and practice, 17(3), 387–396. https://doi.org/10.4162/nrp.2023.17.3.387

58 Stolarz-Skrzypek, K., Kuznetsova, T., Thijs, L., Tikhonoff, V., Seidlerová, J., Richart, T., Jin, Y., Olszanecka, A., Malyutina, S., Casiglia, E., Filipovský, J., Kawecka-Jaszcz, K., Nikitin, Y., Staessen, J. A., & European Project on Genes in Hypertension (EPOGH) Investigators (2011). Fatal and nonfatal outcomes, incidence of hypertension, and blood pressure changes in relation to urinary sodium excretion. JAMA, 305(17), 1777–1785. https://doi.org/10.1001/jama.2011.574

59 Gonmei, Z., & Toteja, G. S. (2018). Micronutrient status of Indian population. The Indian journal of medical research, 148(5), 511–521. https://doi.org/10.4103/ijmr.IJMR_1768_18

60 Yadav, K., & Pandav, C. S. (2018). National Iodine Deficiency Disorders Control Programme: Current status & future strategy. The Indian journal of medical research, 148(5), 503–510. https://doi.org/10.4103/ijmr.IJMR_1717_18

61 Croce, L., Chiovato, L., Tonacchera, M., Petrosino, E., Tanda, M. L., Moleti, M., Magri, F., Olivieri, A., Pearce, E. N., & Rotondi, M. (2023). Iodine status and supplementation in pregnancy: an overview of the evidence provided by meta-analyses. Reviews in endocrine & metabolic disorders, 24(2), 241–250. https://doi.org/10.1007/s11154-022-09760-7

62 Chittimoju, S. B., & Pearce, E. N. (2019). Iodine Deficiency and Supplementation in Pregnancy. Clinical obstetrics and gynecology, 62(2), 330–338. https://doi.org/10.1097/GRF.0000000000000428

63 Mullan, K., McMullan, P., Kayes, L., McCance, D., Hunter, A., & Woodside, J. V. (2022). Thyroglobulin levels among iodine deficient pregnant women living in Northern Ireland. European journal of clinical nutrition, 76(11), 1542–1547. https://doi.org/10.1038/s41430-022-01144-z

64 Manousou, S., Dahl, L., Heinsbaek Thuesen, B., Hulthén, L., & Nyström Filipsson, H. (2017). Iodine deficiency and nutrition in Scandinavia. Minerva medica, 108(2), 147–158. https://doi.org/10.23736/S0026-4806.16.04849-7

65 Carlsen, M. H., Kielland, E., Markhus, M. W., & Dahl, L. (2023). Iodine concentration in tap water, mineral water, and coffee. Food & nutrition research, 67, 10.29219/fnr.v67.9517. https://doi.org/10.29219/fnr.v67.9517

66 Wang, W., Knovich, M. A., Coffman, L. G., Torti, F. M., & Torti, S. V. (2010). Serum ferritin: Past, present and future. Biochimica et biophysica acta, 1800(8), 760–769. https://doi.org/10.1016/j.bbagen.2010.03.011

67 www.nlm.nih.gov/medlineplus/ency/article/003490.htm

68 The rther Ashe Legacy at UCLA: https://arthurashe.ucla.edu/life-story/

69 Lorcerie, B., Audia, S., Samson, M., Millière, A., Falvo, N., Leguy-Seguin, V., Berthier, S., & Bonnotte, B. (2015). Démarche diagnostique devant une hyperferritinémie [Diagnosis of an increased serum level of ferritin]. La Revue de medecine interne, 36(8), 522–529. https://doi.org/10.1016/j.revmed.2014.12.007

70 Biomarkers for Assessing and Managing Iron Deficiency Anemia in Late-Stage Chronic Kidney Disease: Future Research Needs: Identification of Future Research Needs From Comparative Effectiveness Review No. 83 [Internet]. Chung M, Chan JA, Moorthy D, Hadar N, Ratichek SJ, Concannon TW, Lau J.Rockville (MD): Agency for Healthcare Research and Quality (US); 2013 Jan.PMID:23762920[PubMed]

71 http://www.nlm.nih.gov/medlineplus/ency/article/003490.htm

72 What Causes Low Ferritin? Mar 7, 2011 | By Sandi Busch

73 NIH/National Institute of Child Health and Human Development (NICHD) (2013, February 17). Lack of iron regulating protein contributes to high blood pressure of the lungs. ScienceDaily. Retrieved July 1, 2013, from http://www.sciencedaily.com /releases/2013/02/130217165414.htm

74 Imperial College London (2011, December 16). Low iron levels in blood raises blood clot risk, new research suggests. ScienceDaily. Retrieved July 1, 2013, from http://www.sciencedaily.com /releases/2011/12/111215095459.htm

75 Gonmei, Z., & Toteja, G. S. (2018). Micronutrient status of Indian population. The Indian journal of medical research, 148(5), 511–521. https://doi.org/10.4103/ijmr.IJMR_1768_18

76 In-Tele-Health © 2009 (from Hyperhealth Pro CD-ROM)

77 http://www.stopthethyroidmadness.com/ferritin/

78 Kadoglou, N. P. E., Biddulph, J. P., Rafnsson, S. B., Trivella, M., Nihoyannopoulos, P., & Demakakos, P. (2017). The association of ferritin with cardiovascular and all-cause mortality in community-dwellers: The English longitudinal study of ageing. PloS one, 12(6), e0178994. https://doi.org/10.1371/journal.pone.0178994

79 Salonen, J. U., et al. High stored iron levels associated with excess risk of myocardial infarction in western Finnish men. Circulation. 86(3):803-811, 1992.

80 Valero, N., Mosquera, J., Torres, M., Duran, A., Velastegui, M., Reyes, J., Fernandez, M., Fernandez, G., & Veliz, T. (2019). Increased serum ferritin and interleukin-18 levels in children with dengue. Brazilian journal of microbiology : [publication of the Brazilian Society for Microbiology], 50(3), 649–656. https://doi.org/10.1007/s42770-019-00105-2

81 Vanarsa, K., Ye, Y., Han, J., Xie, C., Mohan, C., & Wu, T. (2012). Inflammation associated anemia and ferritin as disease markers in SLE. Arthritis research & therapy, 14(4), R182. https://doi.org/10.1186/ar4012

82 Kunireddy, N., Jacob, R., Khan, S. A., Yadagiri, B., Sai Baba, K. S. S., Rajendra Vara Prasad, I., & Mohan, I. K. (2018). Hepcidin and Ferritin: Important Mediators in Inflammation Associated Anemia in Systemic Lupus Erythematosus Patients. Indian journal of clinical biochemistry : IJCB, 33(4), 406–413. https://doi.org/10.1007/s12291-017-0702-1

83 https://www.labcorp.com/wps/portal/patient/healthlibrary

84 https://www.labcorp.com/wps/portal/insurer/labcorpdifference

85 http://www.nlm.nih.gov/medlineplus/ency/article/002422.htm

86 Stanford University (2005, April 6). Undiagnosed Anemia Common With Chronic Illness.

87 [Guideline] American College of Obstetricians and Gynecologists (ACOG). Anemia in pregnancy. Jul 2008;[Full Text].

88 Hara, T., Yoshigai, E., Ohashi, T., & Fukada, T. (2023). Zinc in Cardiovascular Functions and Diseases: Epidemiology and Molecular Mechanisms for Therapeutic Development. International journal of molecular sciences, 24(8), 7152. https://doi.org/10.3390/ijms24087152

89 Tamura Y. (2021). The Role of Zinc Homeostasis in the Prevention of Diabetes Mellitus and Cardiovascular Diseases. Journal of atherosclerosis and thrombosis, 28(11), 1109–1122. https://doi.org/10.5551/jat.RV17057

90 Hawrysz, Z., & Woźniacka, A. (2023). Zinc: an undervalued microelement in research and treatment. Postepy dermatologii i alergologii, 40(2), 208–214. https://doi.org/10.5114/ada.2023.127639

91 Muthuvattur Pallath, M., Ahirwar, A. K., Chandra Tripathi, S., Asia, P., Sakarde, A., & Gopal, N. (2021). COVID-19 and nutritional deficiency: a review of existing knowledge. Hormone molecular biology and clinical investigation, 42(1), 77–85. https://doi.org/10.1515/hmbci-2020-0074

92 Schloss J. V. (2023). Nutritional deficiencies that may predispose to long COVID. Inflammopharmacology, 31(2), 573–583. https://doi.org/10.1007/s10787-023-01183-3

93 Barazzoni, R., Breda, J., Cuerda, C., Schneider, S., Deutz, N. E., Wickramasinghe, K., & COVID-19 Call Editorial Board (2022). COVID-19: Lessons on malnutrition, nutritional care and public health from the ESPEN-WHO Europe call for papers. Clinical nutrition (Edinburgh, Scotland), 41(12), 2858–2868. https://doi.org/10.1016/j.clnu.2022.07.033

94 Wissler, A., & DeWitte, S. N. (2023). Frailty and survival in the 1918 influenza pandemic. Proceedings of the National Academy of Sciences, 120(42), e2304545120. https://doi.org/10.1073/pnas.2304545120

95 Prasad A. S. (1985). Clinical manifestations of zinc deficiency. Annual review of nutrition, 5, 341–363. https://doi.org/10.1146/annurev.nu.05.070185.002013

96 Heintschel, M., & Heuberger, R. (2017). The Potential Role of Zinc Supplementation on Pressure Injury Healing in Older Adults: A Review of the Literature. Wounds : a compendium of clinical research and practice, 29(2), 56–61.

"I have always liked working in some scientific direction that nobody else is working in."

~ Linus Pauling

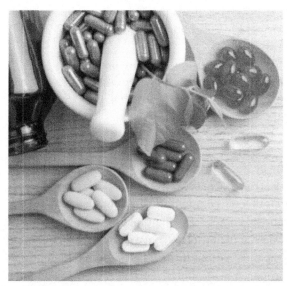

Chapter Eleven ~
Nutrients

In his book *Eat and Be Healthy*, published in 1919, Virgil MacMickle, MD, of Portland, Oregon, recognized how crucial nutrition was to health. He wrote that the "chemical substances of which the body is composed are very similar to those of the foods which nourish it. They are made up of the same chemical elements. The body can only get the materials from which it is made first from foods." There are 13 essential vitamins, of which four are fat-soluble; the remaining nine are water-soluble. The body also needs vitamin-like nutrients, such as choline and carnitine.

Food nutrient levels vary from area to area based on soil conditions, water, and temperature. While in an ideal world we should be able to gain all our nutrition from food, we may not be able to. Supplements are beneficial when obtained from high-quality sources; we refer to them as nutraceuticals recommended for anyone with a chronic illness or cancer. Hundreds of specialty nutraceuticals on the market are designed to deliver targeted antioxidants that are not easily attained from locally produced foods.[1] However, if individuals are unwilling to make healthy food choices, their health will continue to deteriorate. Supplements do not replace real food, but the average person can't eat enough "real food" to achieve optimum antioxidant intake if they are predisposed to a particular illness. In this case, nutraceuticals provide supplemental nutrients added into the diet of whole foods, filling the nutritional gaps and increasing total nutrient uptake.[2,3,4] The ideal management solution is a multifaceted support system consisting of nutrient-dense food, high-quality nutraceuticals, and healthcare practitioners willing to develop a holistic health and wellness plan.

> Fat-soluble vitamins are stored in the body's liver, fatty tissue, and muscles. The four fat-soluble vitamins are vitamins A, D, E, and K. These vitamins are absorbed more easily by the body in dietary fat. Water-soluble vitamins are not stored in the body. The nine water-soluble vitamins are vitamin C and all the B vitamins; any leftover or excess amounts of these leave the body through the urine. They must be consumed regularly to prevent shortages or deficiencies in the body. The exception is vitamin B12, which can be stored in the liver for many years.

Supplements: Vitamins, minerals, hormones, and herbal products are available over the counter at discount retail stores, mail-order companies, and vitamin shops. These products can contain synthetic ingredients such as fillers, binders, artificial colors, flavorings, and harmful chemicals like propylene glycol. Additionally, potency may be reduced or lacking due to improper storage and manufacturer formulation.

> **Nutraceutical** are vitamins, minerals, hormones, and herbal products that are certified organic and heavy metal-, gluten-, dairy-, soy- and contaminant-free. They are often referred to as "designer supplements."
>
> Nutraceuticals are utilized by the body comparably to whole foods, where optimum bioavailability can occur on the mitochondria level. High-quality nutraceuticals provide support without overburdening the digestive system with potential carcinogens.

The incredible potency of plants has been understood by healers for millenia, and the use of herbs for their medicinal effects predates modern pharmaceuticals. Herbs can contain anti-viral, antibacterial, antioxidant, anti-inflammatory, phytoestrogenic and adaptogenic compounds, vitamins, and minerals. They can be purchased from many high-quality nutraceutical companies. Additionally, fresh herbs are easy to grow in container gardens and some can be purchased in dry form from a company like Mountain Rose Herbs for making teas or tinctures. Tinctures are the most potent form of herbal supplementation. Herb Pharm and Gaia provide various quality herbals prepared in alcohol, glycerine, and pill form.

> ***Principle 55:*** Nutraceuticals and/or supplements do not replace REAL FOOD as nourishment. They are needed to fill nutritional gaps in daily nutrient intake.

Vitamin A

Vitamin A is an essential vitamin for the promotion of general growth, maintenance of visual function, regulation of differentiation of epithelial tissues, and embryonic development. Vitamin A is involved in immune function, cellular communication, growth and development, and male and female reproduction. Vitamin A supports cell growth and differentiation, playing a critical role in the normal formation and maintenance of the heart, lungs, eyes, and other organ tissues. It is also vital for maintaining healthy vision as an essential component of rhodopsin, the light-sensitive protein in the retina that responds to light entering the eye. In addition, it supports the normal differentiation and functioning of the conjunctival membranes and cornea.[5] Vitamin A is a fat-soluble vitamin obtained directly from animal sources or synthetized from β-carotene in plant sources. Vitamin A can be obtained from food, either as preformed vitamin A in animal products such as organ meats, fish, poultry eggs, and dairy products, or as provitamin A carotenoids, mainly β-carotene in plant products such as green leafy and yellow-colored vegetables and orange-colored fruit. The main provitamin A carotenoids in the human diet are β-carotene, alpha-carotene, and β-cryptoxanthin. Other carotenoids in food, such as lycopene, lutein, and zeaxanthin, are not converted to vitamin A and are referred to as non-provitamin A carotenoids.[6]

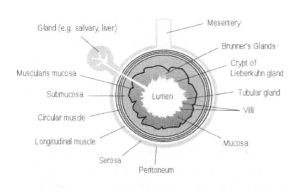

Exchange And Transport, Energy and Ecosystems page 16
Gut Wall by John Adds, Erica Larkcom and Ruth Miller.

Most of the body's Vitamin A is stored in the liver as retinyl esters. β-carotene is a provitamin, a precursor converted to retinol in the gut. Provitamin A carotenoids are converted to retinol after uptake into the lumen of the small intestine. Retinol is then oxidized to retinol and retinoic acid, the body's two primary active vitamin A metabolites. In first-world countries, the provitamin A carotenoids derived from plants provide <30% of daily vitamin A intake. Whereas preformed vitamin A derived from animal products provides >70% of daily vitamin A intake. In contrast, in developing countries, provitamin A carotenoids in vegetables and fruit provide >70% of daily vitamin A intake.[7, 8]

Either deficiency or excess of vitamin A can cause severe health consequences, especially involving the liver. Acute and chronic excess vitamin A is associated with liver damage and fibrosis, while hypovitaminosis (insufficient) A is associated with liver morphology and functional alterations.[9]

Producing, reporting, and interpreting vitamin A statistics present multiple challenges, mainly attributable to the systems of equivalence used to convert pro-vitamin A carotenoids into retinol equivalents and to the criteria used by institutions to set recommendations. Vitamin A adequacy ratios are lowest when the consumption unit is retinol activity equivalents (RAE) and the source of requirements is the U.S. Health and Medicine Division. When the consumption unit is defined as retinol equivalents (RE), adequacy ratios are higher; using those of the Food and Agriculture Organization and World Health Organization (FAO/WHO) rather than the European Food Safety Authority (EFSA) requirements.[10]

> According to the fifth edition of Integrative Medicine, in persons with vitamin A and iodine deficiency from malnutrition, hypothyroidism risk can be reduced with vitamin A supplementation. Vitamin A is involved with T4 manufacture and intracellular receptor formation for T3. In the United States, vitamin A deficiency is associated with alcohol intake and strict dietary restriction. It is recommended that vegetarians who avoid dairy and eggs consume a β-carotene rich diet and consult with their provider to ensure they can convert β-carotene to vitamin A.

A Little History

Three thousand five hundred years ago, the ancient Egyptians recognized that night blindness (caused by a lack of vitamin A) could be treated with particular foods. Native Alaskans used to eat the eyes of the fish and animals they hunted, believing they would keep the eyes of the hunter and his family healthy.

In 1913, attention turned to finding and isolating the vitamins themselves. The discovery of vitamin A is credited to a researcher named E. V. McCollum. He was curious to know why cows fed wheat did not thrive, became blind, and gave birth to dead calves while those fed yellow corn had no health problems. In rat experiments conducted at Yale University, Thomas Osborne and Lafayette Mendel showed that butter contained a growth-promoting factor necessary for development. Soon known as fat-soluble vitamin A, its chemical character was established in 1933 and then synthesized in 1947. Weston A. Price discovered the diets of healthy traditional peoples contained at least ten times as much vitamin A as the American diet of his day (1939). Weston A. Price's work revealed that vitamin A is one of several fat-soluble activators in animal fats and necessary for assimilating minerals into the diet.

More Than Just Your Eyes

Many have been led to believe that the best way to get vitamin A is via beta-carotene. While it is true that many vegetables are loaded with health-promoting carotenoids, not everyone can increase or correct a vitamin A deficiency with plant-based foods. Several factors could potentially interfere with converting carotenes in plant foods to vitamin A, such as being an infant or child, eating a low-fat diet, or having a condition like diabetes, low thyroid function, diarrhea, celiac disease, gluten sensitivity, or pancreatic disease.

Naturally occurring vitamin A is necessary for the prevention of anemia (due to vitamin A enhancing iron absorption), heart disease, blood clots, stroke, hemorrhoids, loss of appetite, celiac disease, colitis, Crohn's disease, heartburn, peptic ulcers, ulcerative colitis, deafness, tinnitus, urinary tract infections, macular degeneration, blurred vision, dry eye, and more.

The Merck Manual describes vitamin A toxicity: "Acute vitamin A poisoning can occur in children after taking a single dose of "synthetic" vitamin A in the range of 300,000 IU or a daily dosage of 60,000 IU for a few weeks. In adults, vitamin A toxicity has been reported in Arctic explorers who developed drowsiness, irritability, headaches, and vomiting, with subsequent skin peeling within a few hours of ingesting several million units of vitamin A from a polar bear or seal liver. Symptoms cleared up with discontinuation of the vitamin A-rich food. Vitamin A toxicity is much more frequent with megavitamin tablets containing synthetic vitamin A. Acute toxicity occurs at 100,000 IU synthetic vitamin A per day taken for many months."

Listed are approximate levels of vitamin A foods in IUs per 100 grams:

High-vitamin cod liver oil: 230,000
Regular cod liver oil: 100,000
Duck liver: 40,000
Beef liver: 35,000
Goose liver: 31,000
Liverwurst sausage (pork): 28,000
Lamb liver: 25,000

It should be noted that these amounts can vary according to how the animals are fed.

The U.S. Recommended Daily Allowance of vitamin A is currently 5,000 IU daily. From the work of Weston A. Price, we know the amount in primitive diets was about 50,000 IU per day. If you consume generous quantities of raw whole milk, cream, butter, and eggs from pastured animals; beef or duck liver several times per week; and one tablespoon of regular cod liver oil or ½ tablespoon of high-vitamin cod liver oil per day, you can come close to that. Some individuals may choose to supplement instead. If you do, find a reputable brand and know that top quality comes with a hefty price. If you like to eat liver, contact a local farmer who raises grass-fed animals.

> *Principle 56:* Modern humans cannot physically obtain sufficient nutrients from food alone. Supplements are required to attain properly balanced nutrition.

"B" to the Rescue

It seems like every day a client, student, or colleague mentions how tired they are, how their brains are not working, how they are under so much stress, and how their health seems to be slipping away. Some clients have a long history of chronic illness and nutritional deficiencies. Others are young; even adolescents are tired, listless and depressed.

How can a country with so many resources have so many sick citizens? Every day we consume thousands of calories — often calories without nutrients. Being healthy involves more than just consuming the right number of calories; it involves eating a complex and synergistic balance of nutrients. Have we ever been able to get everything we need from our food? Maybe, but my answer for today's modern humans is no; it is not physically possible to obtain enough nutrients from food without bursting from the mountain of food that would be required daily. But today, we can supplement. One example of when supplementation is beneficial: Prenatal low folic acid exposure has been linked to a higher risk of childhood asthma in countries that do not fortify the food supply with folic acid.[11]

Looking at the history of food and how it has affected the world's civilizations, we see some rather startling trends. Trends just as prevalent today as in the time of the Romans, Greeks, Mayans, and ancient India and China:
> - When a civilization can no longer feed its citizens, it crumbles.
> - When the land can no longer produce enough food to feed the populace, the populace migrates.
>   - ✓ When the food has no nutritional value, the populace becomes ill, cannibalism occurs, and the population/culture dies.

If these statements sounds harsh or extremist, I encourage you to read Reay Tannahill's book Food in History.

So what does this have to do with B vitamins? B vitamins were the first nutrients to be recognized as vital to health. Chinese physicians wrote about thiamine (B_1) in the early 7th century. First, the Japanese and later the Europeans learned that animals became ill when fed refined grains. Rarely are B vitamins found in food singularly; they are in complex groupings that reduces the likelihood of a single B vitamin resulting in a deficiency of those forms of B vitamins not being supplemented.

Thiamine (B₁) is a water-soluble B-complex vitamin. It was the first B vitamin to be identified and one of the first organic compounds to be recognized as a vitamin in the 1930s. It was through this discovery and naming of thiamine that the word vitamin from the Latin "vita" (life) and "amine" (nitrogen-containing compound) was coined. Its biologically active form, thiamine pyrophosphate (TPP), is a cofactor in macronutrient metabolism. In addition to its coenzyme roles, TPP plays a role in nerve structure, function, and brain metabolism. More advanced symptoms of B₁ deficiency include confabulation, memory loss, and/or psychosis, resulting in Wernicke's encephalopathy and/or Wernicke's Korsakoff syndrome.

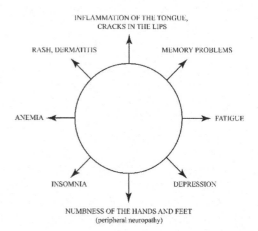

Risk factors include those with malnutrition due to one or more nutrition-related etiologies, such as decreased nutrient intake, increased nutrient losses, or impaired nutrient absorption. Clinical scenarios such as unexplained heart failure or lactic acidosis, renal failure with dialysis, alcoholism, starvation, hyperemesis gravidarum, or bariatric surgery may increase the risk for B₁ deficiency.

The critically ill require nutritional support and are at risk for B₁ deficiency, especially those given intravenous dextrose void of thiamine repletion. Thiamine's role as a potential therapeutic agent for diabetes, some inborn errors of metabolism, and neurodegenerative diseases is being explored.

A Little History
I find it fascinating that holistic providers have a long tradition of studying the actions of nutrients in the body, the importance of which the FDA, AMA, and pharmaceutical companies ignore or downplay in favor of designer drugs. The notion that the absence of particular substances in the diet could cause disease (e.g., beriberi) was revolutionary. Beriberi is a disease affecting the nerves and the heart, caused by a lack of B vitamins.

- **7th century:** First classical description of beriberi in a General Treatise on the Etiology and Symptoms of Diseases by Chao Yuan fang.[12]
- **1882:** Kanehiro Takaki, Navy Surgeon General, dramatically decreased the incidence of beriberi in the Japanese Navy by improving sailors 'diets.
- **1926:** Barend Jansen and Willem Donath isolated and crystallized a substance that cured polyneuritis in pigeons.[13]
- **1943:** Robert Runnels Williams, an American chemist known for being the first to chemically fully characterize and then synthesize thiamine, and Foltz carry out dietary studies documenting

widespread thiamine deficiency in the United States. Standards of identity for enriched flour are created by the U.S. Food and Nutrition Board, requiring that thiamin, niacin, riboflavin, and iron be added to white flour.

Thiamine (B$_1$) Functions

B$_1$ acts as a coenzyme in energy metabolism; it is an essential compound for several reactions in the breakdown of glucose to energy involved in nerve impulse conduction and muscle action and is required for pentose metabolism as a basis for nucleic acids formation.

Thiamine is found in small amounts in most foods. The best sources are dried brewer's yeast, meat flesh (especially pork, eel, and tuna), whole grain cereals and bread, nuts, dried legumes, and potatoes.

The thiamine-rich wheat bran is removed during the milling of wheat to produce white flour and during the polishing of brown rice to produce white rice. Consequently, synthetically enriched and fortified grain products are the standard fare today.

Absorption of B$_1$ occurs in the small intestine. Because thiamin has a high turnover rate and is not appreciably stored in the body, regular intake of B$_1$ is critical. The limited stores in the body are depleted within two weeks or less; clinical signs of deficiency begin shortly after. The heart, kidney, liver, and brain have the highest B$_1$ concentrations, followed by the leukocytes and red blood cells.

Other B vitamins, such as B$_6$, B$_{12}$, niacin, and pantothenic acid, support thiamine's action. Antioxidant vitamins, such as vitamins E and C protect thiamine by preventing oxidation.

Challenges with Absorption

- Foods such as coffee, tea, betel nuts (Southeast Asia), and some cereals act as antagonists to thiamin.

- Drugs that cause nausea and lack of appetite or increase intestinal function or urinary excretion decrease the availability of thiamine.

- Poisoning from arsenic or other heavy metals produces the neurological symptoms of thiamin deficiency.

- Marginal thiamine deficiency may manifest in vague symptoms such as fatigue, insomnia, irritability, lack of concentration, anorexia, abdominal discomfort, constipation, and loss of appetite.

- When there is insufficient B$_1$, the overall decrease in carbohydrate metabolism and its interconnection with amino acid metabolism has severe consequences.

Causes of Deficiency

- Alcohol-related disease
- Inadequate availability, storage and preparation of food

- Increased physiologic demand; during pregnancy and lactation, heavy physical exertion, fever, stress, or adolescent growth
- Inadequate nutrition
- High carbohydrate intake (milled or polished rice, sweets)
- Regular consumption of tea and coffee
- Regular consumption of raw fish or betel nuts
- Certain diseases (dysentery, diarrhea, cancer, nausea/vomiting, liver diseases, infections, malaria, AIDS, hyperthyroidism)
- Drugs (birth-control pills, neuroleptics, some cancer drugs)
- Long-term parenteral nutrition (highly concentrated dextrose infusions)

Riboflavin (B_2) is one of the most widely distributed water-soluble vitamins. B_2 can be isolated from milk, eggs, liver, plants, and urine. The term "flavin" originates from the Latin word "flavus," referring to the yellow color of this vitamin. The fluorescent riboflavin is a part of B-complex vitamins and is the cause of bright yellow urine after taking multivitamins or B-complexes.

As with all B vitamins, B_2 must be replaced daily from food sources. All processed foods have riboflavin listed on the label as do fortified flour and cereal foods. However, heat, light, and processing destroy B vitamins, so the nutritional value of processed foods is always questionable.

Riboflavin is an essential constituent of all living cells. However, there are very few foods that contain significant quantities. Yeast and liver have the highest concentrations but are not usually part of the standard American diet. The most common dietary sources are (organic) milk and dairy products, lean meat, eggs, and green leafy vegetables. Cereal grains are inferior sources of riboflavin. Animal sources of riboflavin are absorbed at the highest rate and are better than plant sources. In milk from cows, sheep, and goats, at least 90% of the riboflavin is in the "free" form, making it immediately available to the body. Because B_2 is degraded by light, up to 50% may be lost if foods are left out in sunlight or under UV light (85% within 2 hours).

Vitamin B_2 History

1879   Blyth isolates lactochrome; a water-soluble, yellow, fluorescent material from whey (the liquid remaining after milk has been curdled and strained).

1933   Kuhn and coworkers obtain a crystalline yellow pigment with growth-promoting properties from egg white and whey, which they identify as vitamin B_2.

1937   The *Council on Pharmacy and Chemistry* of the *American Medical Association* names the vitamin "riboflavin."

1941   Sebrell and coworkers demonstrate clinical signs of riboflavin deficiency in human feeding experiments.

Chapter 11 ~ Nutrients

> ***Principle 57:*** The vitamins we know today were identified and isolated in the 20th century from research investigating whether the absence of a particular substance in the diet could cause disease.

Functions of B$_2$

- Energy production
- Growth and reproduction
- Necessary to produce collagen
- Reduce urinary excretion of selenium
- Cofactor in production of superoxide dismutase
- Conversion of vitamin B$_6$ and folic acid into active coenzyme forms
- Antioxidant functions
- Growth of skin, hair, and nails
- Increases serum ferritin
- Lowers homocysteine levels

Vitamin B$_2$ deficiency affects many organs and tissues; most prominent are the effects on the skin, mucosa, and eyes. It can result from:

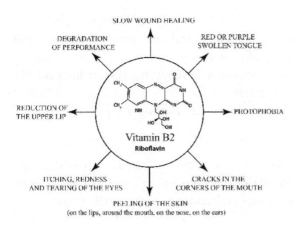

Chronic disorders (e.g., rheumatic fever, tuberculosis, subacute bacterial endocarditis, diabetes)

Intestinal malabsorption (e.g., Crohn's disease, sprue, lactose intolerance)

Regular medication use (tranquilizers, oral contraceptives, thyroid hormones, fiber-based laxatives, antibiotics)

Overt clinical symptoms of riboflavin deficiency are rarely seen in developed countries. However, subclinical deficiency is common. Riboflavin deficiency occurs in combination with deficiencies of other B-complex vitamins. Along with other B vitamins, low vitamin B$_2$ levels have been associated with increased homocysteine levels and impaired absorption of iron, zinc, and calcium.

Individuals at risk of deficiency are children from low socioeconomic backgrounds, older adults, chronic dieters, addicts, dairy-sensitive people, and vegans. Low riboflavin intake may be aggravated by chronic alcoholism and chronic stress; during pregnancy and lactation, riboflavin requirements increase.

With today's work practices, travel, and lifestyles, it can be tough to avoid manufactured foods. But this is one reason why taking additional supplements is so important — we could all benefit from a high-quality B-complex supplement daily.

Vitamin B₆: In 2009, the FDA announced it was taking synthetic B₆ off the market—not because of safety issues, but because it was so effective in treating diabetic-related conditions. Synthetic B₆ (pyridoxamine) has been proven to be very effective in treating neuropathy in diabetics. Because pyridoxamine is synthetically derived, it can be placed under patent; this very inexpensive and efficient nutrient is about to join the ranks of controlled substances with designer drug pricing.

Vitamin B₆ was discovered in the 1930s during the studies on pellagra, a deficiency disease caused by the absence of niacin. Humans and other primates depend on external sources to meet their vitamin B₆ requirements. Intestinal bacteria can synthesize negligible amounts of vitamin B₆.

B₆ Main Functions
Neurotransmitter synthesis	Red blood cell formation
Niacin formation	Down-regulation Homocysteine
Antibody production	
Steroid hormones binding inhibition	

Food Sources: Chicken and the livers of beef, pork, and veal are excellent sources of B₆ (pyridoxine). Good sources include fish (salmon, tuna, sardines, halibut, and herring), nuts (walnuts and peanuts), bread, corn, and whole-grain cereals. Generally, vegetables and fruits are relatively poor sources of vitamin B₆, although three plant foods contain considerable amounts of pyridoxine. They are lentils, courgettes (zucchini), and bananas.

Pasteurization causes milk to lose up to 20% of its vitamin B₆ content. B₆ is decomposed by oxidation and ultraviolet light in an alkaline environment. Because of this light sensitivity, vitamin B₆ will disappear (50% within a few hours) from milk in glass bottles exposed to the sun or bright fluorescent light. Alkalis, such as baking soda, also destroy pyridoxine. Freezing of vegetables causes a reduction of up to 25% while milling cereals leads to losses as high as 90%. Cooking may result in losses ranging from a few percent to nearly half the vitamin B₆ initially present.

B₆ requires riboflavin, zinc, and magnesium to fulfill its physiological function in humans. Women taking oral contraceptives have an increased requirement for B₆ (pyridoxine). More than 40 drugs interfere with vitamin B₆ absorption, potentially causing decreased availability and inadequate vitamin B₆ status.

B₆ Toxicity in the Scotch and Irish
Enzymopathy of polymorphism of B₆ is a genetic condition prevalent among people of Scottish and Irish descent; the enzyme that usually converts B₆ into its useful form is too big. This causes excessive B₆ to build up, even if no supplement form is taken.[14, 15] This condition is linked to neuropathy, Amyotrpic Lateral Sclerosis (ALS), and Multiple Sclerosis (MS). The restriction of all fortified grain products or B₆-rich foods would be indicated for individuals testing high in B₆ who are not using supplements.

- **Sideroblastic anemias** and pyridoxine-dependent abnormalities of metabolism: B₆ is an approved treatment for sideroblastic anemias and pyridoxine-dependent abnormalities of metabolism. In such cases, therapeutic doses of approximately 40-200 mg of vitamin B6 daily are indicated.

- **PMS** (premenstrual syndrome): Studies suggest that vitamin B_6 doses of up to 100 mg/day may help relieve the symptom complex of premenstrual syndrome.

- **Hyperemesis gravidarum**: Pyridoxine is often administered in doses of up to 40 mg/day to treat nausea and vomiting during pregnancy (hyperemesis gravidarum).

- **Depression**: B_6 is used to assist in relieving depression (especially in women taking oral contraceptives).

- **Carpal tunnel syndrome**: Pyridoxine has been shown to alleviate the symptoms of carpal tunnel syndrome. However, some studies report benefits while others do not.

- **Hyperhomocysteinemia/cardiovascular disease:** Elevated homocysteine levels in the blood are considered a risk factor for atherosclerotic disease. Several studies have shown vitamin B_6, vitamin B_{12}, and folic acid can lower critical homocysteine levels.[16]

- **Immune function**: The elderly are a group that suffers from impaired immune function. Adequate B_6 intake is essential, and it has been shown that the amount of vitamin B_6 required to improve the immune system is higher (2.4 mg/day for men; 1.9 mg/day for women) than the current RDA.[17]

- **Asthma:** Patients taking vitamin B_6 supplements may have fewer and less severe attacks of wheezing, coughing, and breathing difficulties.

- **Diabetes**: Current research suggests patients with diabetes mellitus or gestational diabetes experience an improvement in glucose tolerance when given vitamin B6 supplements.

- **Kidney stones:** Glyoxylate can be oxidized to oxalic acid, which may lead to calcium oxalate kidney stones. Pyridoxal phosphate is a cofactor for the degradation of glyoxylate to glycine. There is evidence that high doses of vitamin B_6 (>150 mg/day) help normalize oxalic acid metabolism to reduce the formation of kidney stones.[18]

- **"Chinese restaurant syndrome"**: People who are sensitive to glutamate, often used in the preparation of Asiatic dishes, can react with a headache, tachycardia (accelerated heart rate), and nausea. Fifty to 100 mg of pyridoxine can be of therapeutic value.

- **Autism**: Total vitamin B_6 is abnormally high in autism, consistent with previous reports of an impaired pyridoxal kinase for the conversion of pyridoxine and pyridoxal to PLP. This may explain the many published studies of benefits of high-dose vitamin B_6 supplementation in some children and adults with autism.[19]

Vitamin B_{12} (cyanocobalamin) is an injectable nutrient for those with anemia. Vitamin B_{12} is the largest and most complex of the vitamin's molecules; the term "vitamin B_{12}" encompasses a particular molecular group of human cobalt-containing corrinoid biological activity.[20] It is the only known metabolite to contain cobalt, which gives this water-soluble vitamin its red color.

The body's ability to absorb dietary vitamin B_{12} declines with the progression of the aging process (supplements of 500-1,000 mcg daily are recommended to counteract impaired absorption in persons over the age of 60).

Alexander R. Todd, at the University of Cambridge was awarded the Nobel Prize in Medicine for discovering the lifesaving properties of Vitamin B_{12} in 1957. Dorothy Hodgkin (1910-1994) was only the third woman to be awarded a Nobel Prize (1964) for working out the molecular structure of vitamin B_{12}. They had found that eating large amounts of raw liver containing high doses of Vitamin B_{12} could save the lives of previously incurable patients diagnosed with pernicious anemia. This finding saves 10,000 lives a year in the U.S. alone! Vitamin B_{12} was isolated from a liver extract in 1948, and its structure was elucidated seven years later.[21]

1948	West shows that injections of vitamin B_{12} dramatically benefit patients with pernicious anemia.
1955	Synthesis of vitamin B_{12} from cultures of certain bacteria/fungi.

B_{12} Functions

Essential growth factor
Reduces atherosclerosis and heart attack risks
Protects from after-effects of ischemic stroke
Prevents damage to chromosomes
Prevents neural tube defects in pregnancy

Creation of blood cells and nerve sheaths
Treatment for hepatitis C
Regeneration of folic acid
Prevents cataracts

Coenzyme-function in the intermediary metabolism, especially in cells of the nervous tissue, bone marrow, and gastrointestinal tract[22]

Dietary Sources

Vitamin B_{12} is produced exclusively by microbial synthesis in the digestive tract of animals. Animal protein products are the best source of vitamin B_{12} in the human diet, particularly organ meats (liver, kidney). Other sources are fish, eggs, and dairy products. Foods of plant origin contain no vitamin B_{12} beyond that derived from microbial contamination. Vitamin B_{12} from food sources is bound to proteins and is only released by an adequate concentration of hydrochloric acid in the stomach. B_{12} content is found in the kidneys, heart, spleen, and brain in the human body. B_{12} plasma levels peak at 8-12 hours after ingestion. Sublingual forms of B_{12} (methylcobalamin) have high absorption rates equal to an injectable form. Absorption of B_{12} is impaired by alcohol, certain drugs, and vitamin B_6 (pyridoxine) deficiency.

Chapter 11 ~ Nutrients

Supplementation may be necessary if:

Celiac disease	Crohn's disease	Chronic fatigue syndrome
Liver medications	Anti-gout medication	Antibiotics
Anticonvulsants		
Potassium chloride medications		Oral contraceptives

Anti-diabetics drugs: metformin and phenformin Chemotherapy treatment
27% of people afflicted with chronic noise-induced hearing loss exhibit B_{12} deficiency
47% of tinnitus patients exhibit vitamin B_{12} deficiency
Stomach antacid medication: proton pump inhibitors, H2 receptor antagonists
Nitrous oxide (anesthetic) interferes with B_{12} metabolism

Vitamin B_{12} deficiency occurs over several years and is most evident in vegetarians and vegans. Others with impaired digestion also have a reduced ability to absorb cobalamin via the intestine and develop a deficiency state more rapidly.

Methylcobalamin: An active endogenous coenzyme form of Vitamin B_{12} that transfers a methyl group from an inactive form of folic acid to homocysteine, forming methionine. Methylcobalamin accounts for approximately 70% of blood plasma vitamin B_{12} reserves. Clinical trials have shown that supplemental methylcobalamin is substantially superior to other vitamin B_{12} supplements in terms of its ability to enhance human health. The liver converts approximately 1% of the cyanocobalamin form of vitamin B_{12} to methylcobalamin.

Cyanocobalamin: A complex of cyanide and cobalamin, is the most commonly found form of vitamin B_{12} supplements. It must be converted to an active coenzyme form within the body to exert therapeutic effects. It is not as effective as methylcobalamin. Most supplemental cyanocobalamin is converted within the intestines to adenosylcobalamin.

Niacin is a member of the water-soluble B vitamin complex. The amino acid tryptophan can be converted to nicotinic acid in humans. Nicotinic acid is a specific form of vitamin B_3. Nicotinic acid supplements are manufactured by oxidizing nicotine (this is not a cause for alarm as nicotinic acid is not associated with any toxic effects of nicotine). Nicotinic acid was isolated in 1867, and in 1937 it was demonstrated that this substance cures the disease pellagra, which is characterized by skin changes, severe nerve dysfunction, mental symptoms, and diarrhea. The name niacin is derived from "nicotinic acid" and "vitamin."

Niacin is mainly involved in reactions that generate tissue energy by the biochemical degradation of carbohydrates, fats, and proteins; B_3 functions in reductive biosynthesis, such as synthesizing fatty acids and cholesterol.

Niacin Benefits
Niacin improves blood circulation and helps prevent hypertension, atherosclerosis, abnormal blood clotting, and stroke by lowering elevated fibrinogen levels in the bloodstream. Niacin may prevent heart attacks and reduce the recurrence rate for second heart attacks by 30%. It may also alleviate Raynaud's

disease by improving blood circulation to the hands and feet. B_3 is beneficial for the treatment of age-related macular degeneration (ARMD).

Nicotinic acid may inhibit the ability of candida glabrata to cause urinary tract infections (by inhibiting the ability of candida glabrata to adhere to the epithelial cells of the urinary tract).

Niacin may reduce the mortality rate of cancer patients and help prevent some forms of cancer. It may decrease the recurrence rate of bladder cancer in people treated with gamma rays in radiation therapy and may help prevent endometrial cancer.

Dietary Sources

Nicotinamide and nicotinic acid occur widely in nature. Nicotinic acid is more prevalent in plants, and nicotinamide is more common in animals. Yeast, liver, poultry, lean meats, nuts, and legumes contain niacin; milk and green leafy vegetables provide lesser amounts. In cereal products, especially corn and wheat, nicotinic acid is bound to individual chemical components and thus is not bioavailable. Specific cultural food processing practices, such as treating maize with lime water in the traditional preparation of tortillas in Mexico and Central America, increases the bioavailability of nicotinic acid.

Tryptophan contributes as much as two-thirds of the niacin activity required by adults in typical diets. Important food sources of tryptophan are meat, milk, and eggs. There is no evidence that niacin from foods causes adverse effects.

Deficiency: Copper deficiency can inhibit the conversion of tryptophan to niacin. The drug penicillamine has been demonstrated to inhibit the tryptophan-to-niacin pathway in humans. This may be due in part to the copper-chelating effect of penicillamine. The pathway from tryptophan to niacin is sensitive to various nutritional alterations. Inadequate iron, riboflavin, or vitamin B_6 status reduces the synthesis of niacin from tryptophan. Other drugs interacting with niacin metabolism may also lead to niacin deficiency: tranquilizers (diazepam) and anticonvulsants (phenytoin, phenobarbital).

Moderate Deficiency Symptoms

Insomnia	Weight and strength loss
Soreness of the tongue and mouth	Indigestion
Abdominal Pain	Vertigo
Numbness	Mental symptoms: nervousness, apprehension, poor concentration,
Headaches	confusion, forgetfulness
Loss of appetite	
Burning sensations in various parts of the body	

Severe Deficiency

Pellagra	Diarrhea	Dementia	Headaches
Stomatitis	Fatigue	Depression	Apathy
Bright red tongue	Rash when exposed to sunlight		

Pharmacological doses of nicotinic acid (but not nicotinamide) exceeding 300 mg daily have been associated with various side effects, including nausea, diarrhea, and temporary skin flushing. Doses exceeding 2.5 grams daily have been associated with hepatotoxicity, glucose intolerance, hyperglycemia, elevated blood uric acid levels, heartburn, nausea, and headaches. Severe jaundice may occur, even with doses as low as 750 mg per day and may eventually lead to irreversible liver damage. Doses of 1.5-5 grams per day of nicotinic acid have been associated with blurred vision and other eye problems.

I believe niacin should be taken with or as part of a B-complex program and at the recommended lower levels. As with all supplements, **more is not better**; they should be just one part of a healthy diet.

Vitamin D: We often hear information about the merits of vitamin D. Along with this information comes an astounding amount of myth, misunderstanding, and confusion.

In the 1920s and 1930s, researcher Dr. Weston A. Price discovered Factor X in dairy foods and fish oils. He found that butter made from spring milk was richer, darker in color, and higher in nutrients. Dr. Price learned that individuals with diets high in Factor X were far less susceptible to cavities, tuberculosis, and chronic health issues. Later, Factor X was renamed vitamins D and A. Physiologically, each of us should be capable of producing upwards of 20,000 IU of vitamin D from 15 to 20 minutes of sun exposure to the skin without sunscreen. Sadly, this is often not the case, and current research indicates vitamin D deficiency in much of the world's population.

The epidermal layer of human skin synthesizes vitamin D when exposed to UV radiation. In the presence of sunlight, a form of vitamin D_3 called cholecalciferol is synthesized from a derivative of the steroid cholesterol in the skin. The liver converts cholecalciferol to calcidiol, which is then converted to calcitriol (the active chemical form of the vitamin) in the kidneys. Vitamin D can regulate the expression of hundreds of genes involved in skeletal and other biological functions.[23] We know that vitamin D is essential for bone health, but that is just the tip of the iceberg. Research shows that vitamin D not only prevents bone loss, but according to John Jacob Cannell, MD, founder of the non-profit Vitamin D Council (now the Vitamin D Society), "Research indicates vitamin D deficiency plays a role in causing 17 varieties of cancer as well as heart disease, stroke, hypertension, autoimmune diseases, diabetes, depression, chronic pain, osteoarthritis, osteoporosis, muscle weakness, muscle wasting, congenital disabilities, and periodontal disease."

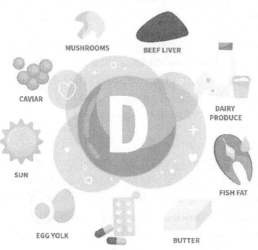

Research shows there is a world of difference between the synthetic vitamin D analogs D_2 and D_3 (cholecalciferol). From a holistic health viewpoint, toxicity occurs whenever we place a synthetic into our bodies. Natural forms of vitamin D_3 derived from lanolin are safe and efficient at higher levels. The current RDA standards for vitamin D are pitifully low, at 200 to 600 IU. Healthy vitamin D blood levels, between 50-80 ng/ml, are demonstrated by fewer than 5% of Americans.[24]

For many years, physicians believed vitamin D was toxic when given in doses over 400 IU for prolonged periods. The Vitamin D Council, one of the largest research bodies on vitamin D_3, has found children through individuals in their 20s should be consuming 2,000 IU of vitamin D_3 daily—not vitamin D_2, which is toxic to the liver. Adults 20 years and older should be consuming 5,000+ IU daily for optimal health. The elderly, homebound, or chronically ill are at the highest risk for vitamin D_3 deficiency. Many individuals with blood levels of vitamin D_3 lower than 32 ng/ml often respond best to injectable vitamin D_3 therapy.

> ***Principle 58:*** Although there is a world wide epidemic of vitamin D deficiency, Western medicine promotes management through pharmaceuticals rather that nutritional supplements.

In 2006, Mary L. Hagood, MS, FNP-C, and I began testing vitamin D levels in our clients. What we found in our small clinical study supported information from the Vitamin D Council and Ellie Campbell, DO, in North Carolina. The following is a sampling of the information we gathered.

Clinical Study: From 2006 to 2015, we saw 580 white men and women with an average age of 41. These individuals worked in various professions, and those who worked outside had levels just as low as those who were elderly, homebound, or living with chronic illness. Of these 580 clients, we had five participants who were within the optimal range on their 25-hydroxy D_3 test (LabCorp serum range 32-100 ng/dl; optimal range 65 ng/dl). These were all women over 60 who had been supplementing with 5,000 IU of vitamin D_3 daily for more than ten years.

Our sampling included 149 men and 431 women; 345 participants needed or used bio-identical hormones for thyroid and sex hormone replacement. Twenty-nine female participants had abnormal thermographic breast scans and were on an estrogen-free diet, using supplemental iodine and natural progesterone to lower breast cancer risk. Of these, 398 participants participated in injectable vitamin D_3 supplementation administered monthly by study supervisor Mary L. Hagood, MS, FNP-C. The D_3 dosage was compounded at 100,000 IU (2.5 mg) intramuscular injection (IM), combined with 5,000 IU (625 mcg) and 45 mcg vitamin K_2 orally daily. The total daily dosage averaged 8,333 IU daily.

Methodology: Blood tests were done on the study participants at four-month intervals to determine optimal dosage. Clients 'calcium, potassium, and magnesium levels were monitored. Vitamin K_2 was added to the custom-compounded injectable vitamin D_3 (in olive oil) protocol to protect kidneys from spilling excess calcium into the urine. Additionally, vitamin A (7,500 mcg RAE) and magnesium (500 mg) were added to the study protocol to improve the bioavailability of vitamin D to cell receptor sites.

Client Case Review 1: When lab values were reviewed, we found our lowest 25-hydroxy level was 5 ng/dl in an 84-year-old male World War II veteran who had undergone a quadruple bypass cardiac surgery eight years earlier. Vitamin D levels reached 32 ng/dl at 12 months, and IM vitamin D_3 injections were stopped, at which point the client was placed on 5,000 IU oral only and retested in 60 days. His levels had decreased to 15 ng/dl. His oral dosage was adjusted to 10,000 IU with K_2. At the 24-month follow-up, the client was living independently and feeling good. His levels were within low normal lab value range.

Client Case Review 2: The next lowest level was 9 ng/dl in a 47-year-old female of English ancestry who was a professional landscaper and worked outside an average of 300 days a year. The client could not reach a desirable vitamin D level on 5,000 IU following the IM 8-month time frame. She continued with IM vitamin D_3 for 24 additional months. A genetic test revealed she carried the gene SNIP which affected vitamin D storage. According to researchers, this occurs in roughly 5% of the Northern European female population[25]. Her daughter, with a severe bipolar condition, also tested low for vitamin D_3 and carried the FLG mutation.

Client Case Review 3 and 4: The next two lowest levels were 9.5 ng/dl; one was a male in his mid-fifties with brittle type 1 diabetes, and the second was his wife and caregiver, who suffered from severe depression and anxiety. All symptoms of deficiency improved for these two participants in 6 months.

NOTE: These four individuals required additional vitamin D_3 at higher doses for 12-24 months than we recommended for the remainder of our client study base, and their current levels are still lower than optimum.

Client Case Review 5: A very active mother and wife had a level of 12 ng/dl; a third-generation Irish-American with very fair skin, blue eyes, and dark hair. She was teetering on the edge of metabolic syndrome and type 2 diabetes. Her vitamin D levels remained below the optimal range on the 5,000 IU oral vitamin D daily regimen. This client could not participate in the injectable vitamin D program; accordingly, in order to reach optimal vitamin D lab values, she could potentially require 5,000 IU orally for ten years to reach the 32 ng/dl goal on lab tests. This low vitamin D deficiency history places the client in the twofold increase bracket for deficiency-related illness complications in menopause.

Client Case Review 6: A woman and mother of twins who was morbidly obese, weighing 426 pounds, and about to have gastric bypass surgery. Her lower spine was very painful, and the response from her primary care providers was to tell her to lose weight. Upon testing, her vitamin D_3 levels were 17 ng/dl. On average, this client consumed 1,000 calories daily, was active at home, and worked full-time. She had a family history of obesity and rickets (a vitamin D deficiency disease of children characterized by insufficient bone calcification).

Conclusions: The clients with the lowest values of vitamin D were all of Northern European descent. All participants resided in Oregon, with 50 having relocated from other states within five years of the study. In the 29 women with abnormal breast scans or breast cancer, vitamin D levels were found to be very low in addition to having low levels of progesterone.

<u>Vitamin D injections are controversial: High levels of vitamin D (>5,000 IU) are not recommended unless supervised by a provider who can monitor nutrient intake and labs.</u>

By administering vitamin D_3 shots, clinicians can, in essence, fill the "empty reserves" of clients as well as their "primary fuel tank" of available vitamin D without involving the kidneys and liver. Many clients found a marked increase in energy and a reduction in pain and depression within 72 hours of their first shot. This therapy was done in a four-to-eight-shot series based on the client's repeated 25-hydroxy blood test at months four, eight and twelve.

> NOTE: As of 2019, compounding pharmacists 'ability to provide customized injectable formulas, similar to the one used in this study, was blocked by the FDA.

Northern European Ancestry

There is a correlation between individuals of Northern European descent and low vitamin D levels. Many of these individuals are prone to digestive disorders such as irritable bowel syndrome (IBS), ulcerative colitis (IBD), gluten sensitivity, and thyroid problems. The reason for this may possibly be the digestive system's inability to manufacture healthy levels of vitamin D. Clinical research supports administration of injectable vitamin D_3 for individuals with low D_3 blood levels, which is determined by the health practitioner requesting a 25-hydroxy blood test.

Oral or sublingual supplements may be adequate for other individuals to restore healthy levels. The use of cod liver oil is not advised for those with low levels as it could prove potentially toxic due to concurrent high vitamin A levels at the doses necessary to reach optimal D_3 blood levels. It is best to test your blood levels before beginning vitamin D therapies. This can be done through ZRT, Lab Corp, or Life Extension Labs, as there have been calibration issues with other labs.[26]

Cardiovascular Health and Vitamin D

The vitamin D receptor is expressed in cells throughout the vascular system; many of these also express 1α-hydroxylase and are therefore able to convert 25-hydroxyvitamin D (25(OH)D) to calcitriol, the active form of Vitamin D. Calcitriol reduces inflammation, regulates the renin-angiotensin-aldosterone system, and inhibits proliferation of vascular smooth muscle. A study published in June 2008 showed that men with low vitamin D levels suffer 2.42 times more heart attacks. If every American optimized their vitamin D levels, the number of deaths prevented would be 92,500 per year. According to the latest studies, the burden of CVD could be reduced by population-wide correction of low vitamin D status. Men with higher vitamin D levels had a 142% reduction in heart attacks.[27, 28] The *American Heart Association* estimated that the annual cost of health care services, medications, and lost productivity related to heart attacks was over $156 billion.[29]

At the American Heart Association's 49th *Annual Conference on Cardiovascular Disease Epidemiology and Prevention*, Jared P. Reis, PhD, and his team of researchers at Johns Hopkins Bloomberg School of Public Health in Baltimore announced their findings of a study of 3,577 adolescents 12-19 years old (51% boys). "We showed strong associations between low levels of vitamin D and a higher risk of high blood pressure, hyperglycemia, and metabolic syndrome among adolescents, confirming the results of studies among adults," Dr. Reis said. Children and teenagers with the lowest levels of vitamin D were 2.36 times more likely to have hypertension, 2.54 times more liable to have high blood sugar, and about four times more susceptible to metabolic syndrome—a group of cardiovascular disease and diabetes risk factors that includes an increased waist circumference, high blood pressure, elevated triglycerides, low levels of high-density lipoprotein (HDL or "good") cholesterol, and high fasting glucose levels.

There is a worldwide epidemic of vitamin D insufficiency, and the U.S. mainstream medical community is promoting illness management with high-cost pharmaceuticals instead of cost-effective nutritional supplements. Banning junk foods from schools and replacing vitamin D-robbing fluorescent lighting with skylights, LED, or full spectrum lights could be a far better use of resources. If every American achieved optimal vitamin D levels, a minimum savings of $84 billion in healthcare costs could be realized. If we add up all the money saved by promoting wellness care through nutrition and lifestyle changes to the $84 billion, the U.S. would not have a healthcare crisis.

Currently, Medicare has discontinued coverage of vitamin D₃ 25-hydroxy blood testing as part of an effort to curb escalating medical costs that are bankrupting the Medicare system. Wouldn't it be better to look at more cost-effective therapies, real wellness management, improved food quality, and reduce the use of unnecessary and low-efficacy medications? Consider this historical tidbit: When Traditional Chinese Medicine was practiced thousands of years ago, you paid the doctor to keep you well. If you became ill, the doctor provided your care for free until the condition resolved, after which you went back to regular payments for health maintenance. It seems obvious that the motivation for the physician was pretty high to restore you to health! I believe this model is one we could all benefit from.

Immune Function and Vitamin D
Vitamin D supplementation is linked to improved outcomes from respiratory virus infection, and the COVID-19 pandemic renewed the interest in understanding the potential role of vitamin D in protecting the lungs from viral infections. A research paper released in 2022 confirmed that vitamin D deficiency enhanced disease severity, while vitamin D sufficiency/supplementation reduced inflammation following infections with H1N1 influenza and SARS-CoV-2.[30]

> Vitamin D is a steroid hormone with potent immune-modulating properties. It has been shown to stimulate innate immunity and induce immune tolerance. Extensive research efforts have shown that vitamin D deficiency may be related to the development of autoimmune diseases. Vitamin D deficiency has been observed in patients with rheumatoid arthritis (RA) and is inversely associated with disease activity. Moreover, vitamin D deficiency may be implicated in the pathogenesis of the disease. Vitamin D deficiency has also been observed in patients with systemic lupus erythematosus (SLE). It is inversely related to disease activity and renal involvement. Vitamin D levels have been studied in patients with Sjogren's syndrome, and vitamin D deficiency may be related to neuropathy and the development of lymphoma in the context of Sjogren's syndrome. Vitamin D deficiency has been observed in ankylosing spondylitis, psoriatic arthritis (PsA), and idiopathic inflammatory myopathies. Vitamin D deficiency has also been observed in systemic sclerosis. Vitamin D deficiency may be implicated in the pathogenesis of autoimmunity, and it may be administered to prevent autoimmune disease and reduce pain in the context of autoimmune rheumatic disorders.[31]

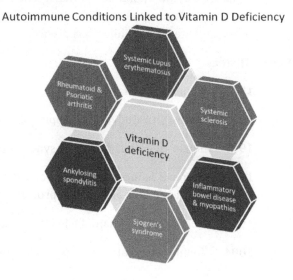

Autoimmune Conditions Linked to Vitamin D Deficiency

Vitamin E: It seems that every year we hear news reports claiming nutritional supplements are a waste of money — especially vitamin E. Major media companies appear to take delight in telling only part of the story, usually the part that looks the worst. The volume of information they don't tell you is the part that may save your life, however. Vitamin E is an essential nutrient discovered in the 1920's, but many of the physiological functions of vitamin E, including its antioxidative effects, have been studied for more than a 100 years.

Originally discovered as a dietary factor essential for reproduction in rats, research has revealed many more important properties of this molecule, such as the scavenging of reactive oxygen and nitrogen species with consequent prevention of oxidative damage associated with many diseases or the modulation of signal transduction and gene expression in antioxidant and non-antioxidant manners.[32] Despite its antioxidant function, dietary vitamin E requirements in humans are limited only to alpha-tocopherol because the other forms of vitamin E are poorly recognized by the hepatic alpha-tocopherol transfer protein (TTP), and they are not converted to alpha-tocopherol by humans.[33]

Depletion of vitamin E tissue stores takes a very long time; no overt clinical deficiency symptoms have been noted in otherwise healthy adults. Symptoms of vitamin E deficiency are seen in patients with fat malabsorption syndromes or liver disease, in individuals with genetic defects affecting the α-tocopherol transfer protein, and in newborn infants, particularly premature infants.

> Vitamin E is all of the following eight compounds: alpha, beta, gamma, and delta-tocopherol and alpha, beta, gamma, and delta-tocotrienol. Alpha-tocopherol is the only compound of the eight known to meet human dietary needs. All of the vitamin E forms are absorbed in the small intestine, and then the liver metabolizes only alpha-tocopherol. The liver then removes and excretes the remaining vitamin E forms.
>
> Vitamin E deficiency is extremely rare in humans as it is unlikely caused by a diet consisting of low vitamin E. Rather, it tends to be caused by irregularities in dietary fat absorption or metabolism. Vitamin E may have a role in reducing atherosclerosis and lowering rates of ischemic heart disease.[34]

A Little History

1922 Vitamin E is discovered

1936 Researchers studying α-tocopherol isolates its pure form from wheat germ oil

1977 Human vitamin E deficiency syndromes are described

1980 Vitamin E reduces carcinogenic oxidative products of unsaturated fatty acids and is a significant lipid-soluble antioxidant protecting cell membranes

1990 Effectiveness of vitamin E in inhibiting LDL (low-density lipoprotein) oxidation is shown

2004 Vitamin E regulates gene expression in the liver

Dietary Sources

Vegetable oils, nuts, whole grains, and wheat germ are the primary dietary sources of vitamin E. Other sources are seeds and green leafy vegetables. The vitamin E content of vegetables, fruits, dairy products, fish, and meat is relatively small.

Vitamin E is absorbed with lipids in the small intestine, depending on adequate pancreatic function and biliary secretion. Vitamin E is found in most human body tissues. The adipose tissue, liver, and muscles have the highest vitamin E content. The pool of available vitamin E in the plasma, liver, kidneys, and spleen turns over rapidly, whereas the turnover of adipose tissue content is slow.

Vitamin E is thought to play a role in preventing heart disease and stroke due to its effects on a number of steps in the development of atherosclerosis (e.g., inhibition of LDL oxidation, inhibition of smooth muscle cell proliferation, inhibition of platelet adhesion, aggregation, and platelet release reaction). Recent studies suggest vitamin E enhances immunity in the elderly and that supplementation with vitamin E lowers the risk of contracting an upper respiratory tract infection, particularly the common cold.

Researchers are investigating the role of vitamin E in protecting against pollutants and lowering the risk of cancer and cataracts. Vitamin E and vitamin C may protect the body from oxidative stress caused by extreme sports (e.g., ultramarathon running). Currently under investigation is the role of vitamin E supplementation in treating Alzheimer's and ALS.

An extensive study done in 2018 reported in humans that vitamin E's effects on the natural incidence of infectious diseases have been determined in several studies. Vitamin E has been shown to enhance immune responses in animal and human models and to confer protection against several infectious diseases. Suggested mechanisms involved with these changes are the reduction of PGE2 production by the inhibition of COX2 activity mediated through decreasing NO production, the improvement of effective immune synapse formation in naive T cells and the initiation of T cell activation signals, and the modulation of Th1/Th2 balance. Higher NK activity and changes in dendritic function, such as lower IL-12 production and migration, were observed with vitamin E.[35]

> "The 2014 study showed drastically different health effects of vitamin E depending on its form. The form of vitamin E called gamma-tocopherol in the ubiquitous soybean, corn, and canola oils is associated with decreased lung function in humans, the study reports. The other form of vitamin E, alpha tocopherol, which is found in olive and sunflower oils, does the opposite. It is associated with better lung function."
>
> "Considering the rate of affected people we found in this study, there could be 4.5 million individuals in the U.S. with reduced lung function as a result of their high gamma-tocopherol consumption," said senior author Joan Cook-Mills, an associate professor of medicine in allergy/immunology at Northwestern University Feinberg School of Medicine. This is the first study to show that gamma-tocopherol is associated with worse lung function."[36]

Different forms of vitamin E exert differential effects on immune cells. Cell-specific effects of vitamin E provide valuable evidence regarding the immunomodulatory mechanisms of vitamin E, but the interplay between immune cells should not be ignored, because interactions between immune cells are critical in the regulation of immune function. When selecting a vitamin E supplement, be sure to buy a complete blend of alpha, beta, delta, and gamma tocopherols. They should be extracted from natural sources and come from an extremely reputable company. Adding vitamin E to a wholesome natural diet will help you to take control of your health.

Vitamin K is a fat-soluble vitamin. It has received far less attention from the media and public than its more famous "cousins" A, D, and E. Vitamin K contains several subtypes which all contain the fundamental 2-methyl-1,4-naphthoquinone ring structure also termed menadione; vitamins K_1, K_2, K_3, K_4 and K_5, with K_1 and K_2 being the two major subtypes, (vitamin K_3 is a synthetic form). Vitamin K_1 and K_2 are both fat soluble allowing them to enter cells without transmembrane transport proteins, while K_3 is water soluble. It has been hypothesized that vitamin K_2 is just as significant in effect as K_1, owing to the differing structure of these subtypes. In particular, vitamin K_2 has been shown to have a considerable effect on calcium metabolism.

Over the last 25 years, research has given a new and expanded view of vitamin K due to the potentially crucial role of vitamin K_2 in calcium metabolism. A deficit can disrupt many mechanisms, resulting in an array of different issues, such as broken bones, stiff arteries, and poor fertility. It is now known to be essential for bone and brain health and help prevent atherosclerosis and calcified arterial plaque. A 2021 study on medical benefits of K_2 affirmed the earlier conclusion that vitamin K_2 had a positive impact on osteoporosis, cardiovascular disease, parathyroid disorders, cerebral palsy, and sperm motility.[37, 38, 39]

A Little History
Vitamin K_2 was first discovered by Henrik Dam in 1935. Through experimenting with dietary regimens of chickens and interchanging various dietary sources, Dam isolated this compound and named it after the German word for coagulation. The chickens showed a decrease in hemorrhages when given dietary regimens containing the vitamin, and this was the defining moment that sparked further research into vitamin K.

Vitamer or Vitamin

Each vitamin not only differs from the others through their function but also in how they are metabolized in the body. For example, vitamin D can be synthesized through the interaction of ultraviolet B rays activating 7-dehydrocholesterol (7-DHC), which is present in the skin. The precursor to this active form of vitamin D is termed the vitamer, defined as a molecular analogue of its given vitamin. This feature of inter-changeability from their active and inactive forms is common amongst vitamins.

Vitamin K_2 Benefits
Vitamin K_2 plays a vital role in ensuring that calcium stays in the bones—maintaining adequate bone mineral density—and out of the arteries. It is an essential cofactor for a chemical process known as carboxylation, which enables calcium-regulating proteins to perform their functions. Vitamin K_2 protects against excess bone resorption by turning off excess osteoclast activity, and it supports the critical role of new bone formation by enabling osteocalcin to pull calcium from the blood and layer it onto the bone. Vitamin K_2 has proven to be as effective as prescription drugs in reducing the incidence of bone fractures.[40]

A Japanese study in postmenopausal women compared the effect of K_2 with the drug Didronel® on the incidence of vertebral (spine) fracture. Women taking K_2 at a dose of 45 mg daily experienced a fracture rate of 8.0% compared with 8.7% for those taking the drug therapy. Furthermore, women taking K_2 and the drug experienced only a 3.8% fracture rate. In a placebo group that received neither K_2 nor drug therapy, nearly 21% of women suffered bone fractures.[41]

The Nurses 'Health Study followed 72,000 women for ten years and found women whose vitamin K intakes were in the lowest quintile (1/5) had a 30% higher risk of hip fracture than women with vitamin K intakes in the higher four quintiles.[42]

The Framingham Heart Study, a seven-year study of more than 888 older men and women, found men and women with dietary vitamin K intakes in the highest quartile (1/4) had a 65% lower risk of hip fracture than those with dietary vitamin K intakes in the lowest quartile (approximately 254 mcg vs. 56 mcg of vitamin K). Vitamin K may confer anti-aging effects throughout the body by preventing pathological tissue calcification. Higher vitamin K intake has been associated with reduced all-cause mortality.

Vitamin K shows promise in preventing and treating numerous cancers, including prostate cancer. (Under a doctor's supervision, vitamin K can help stabilize blood indicators of coagulation in Coumadin® users while conferring other health benefits). Published reports have shown that vitamin K in combination therapy improved the efficacy of clinical drugs by promoting apoptosis and cell cycle arrest and overcoming drug resistance by inhibiting P-glycoprotein.[43] The newly (2022) discovered functions of vitamin K in cancer cells, including activation of the steroid and xenobiotic receptor (SXR) and regulation of oxidative stress, apoptosis, and autophagy, is expanding the use of vitamin K.[44]

Vitamin K and Kidney Health

Chronic kidney disease (CKD) is commonly associated with vitamin K deficiency. Some of the serious complications of CKD are represented by cardiovascular disease (CVD) and skeletal fragility with an increased risk of morbidity and mortality. Poor vitamin K status seems to have a key role in the progression of CKD, but also in the onset and advance of both bone and cardiovascular complications.[45] Researchers are looking at how vitamin K can improve outcomes for kidney transplant recipients and organ health. Currently, the research supports that vitamin K reduces transplant complications and can be an effective therapy.[46]

Vitamin K_2 and Heart Health

In 2004, a ground-breaking seven-year study of 4,800 subjects (the Rotterdam Study) linked K_2 intake with a reduced risk of coronary heart disease (CHD). Researchers set out to compare the effects of vitamin K_1 and K_2 on arterial health. The results indicated that 62% of the women had coronary calcification. Subjects with the highest vitamin K2 intakes experienced a 20% reduction in the calcification of the arteries. According to the researchers, "This study shows high dietary vitamin K_2 intake is associated with reduced coronary calcification. Adequate vitamin K_2 intakes could, therefore, be important in preventing cardiovascular disease." Those with higher levels of vitamin K_2 in their diets experienced lower death rates from heart disease and less calcium deposition in the aorta compared with subjects with minimal K_2 intake; K_1 did not confer this benefit. The researchers concluded, "Our findings suggest a protective effect of K_2 intake against CHD, which could be mediated by inhibiting arterial calcification. Adequate intake of K_2 may contribute to CHD prevention."[47]

K₂ for Adolescents, a study of 766 otherwise healthy adolescents, showed that those who consumed the least vitamin K_1—found in spinach, cabbage, iceberg lettuce and olive oil—were at 3.3 times greater risk for an unhealthy enlargement of the primary pumping chamber of their heart.[48]

Dietary Sources

Vitamin K_1 is predominantly found in green leafy vegetables, such as spinach, cabbage and kale, and absorption is increased in the presence of butter or oils.[49] Sources of vitamin K_2 differ with the variation of their menaquinone lengths. MK-4 is found in animal products, such as chicken meat, beef, and salmon. The richest source of MK-7 comes from bacterially fermented food, such as natto, a traditional soybean dish commonly found in Japan. The production of natto is challenging due to the specific measurements required for the beans and the complex fermentation process.[50] Other food sources rich in vitamin K_2 include egg yolks, hard cheeses, cottage cheese, butter, and sauerkraut. As plants produce both vitamins K_1 and K_2, they are both commonly found in the intestinal tract due to the presence of fermenting bacteria. Bacteria such as *Escherichia coli* can manufacture vitamin K_2; however, they only produce the menaquinones MK-7 to MK-11: *Bacilus Subtilis*. Vitamin K_1 is the main constituent of vitamin K consumed in a Western diet, accounting for 75–90%, with the remainder owing to K_2.

Vitamin C and Orthomolecular Nutrition

Linus Pauling (1901-1994), famous for research on vitamin C and the orthomolecular nutrition approach, was born In Portland, Oregon. He won scholarships to Oregon State University and worked long hours as a laborer to support himself while he earned his Bachelor of Science degree. He earned a PhD in chemistry at the California Institute of Technology, where he taught and carried out his research for the next 33 years.[51, 52]

Linus Pauling circ. 1930's at the California Institute of Technology in Pasadena. Oregon Historical Society

Linus Pauling and Ewan Cameron, MD, authored *Vitamin C and the Common Cold* in 1970, *How to Live Longer and Feel Better* in 1986, and *Cancer and Vitamin C* in 1993. Dr. Pauling's view of vitamin C is at odds with most in the scientific community; this research launched the *Orthomolecular Nutrition* approach of mega-dosing with nutrients for heart disease and cancer.[53, 54]

Vitamin C, also known as L-ascorbic acid, is a water-soluble vitamin. Unlike most mammals and other animals, humans do not synthesize vitamin C and must obtain it from the diet. Vitamin C is an essential cofactor in numerous enzymatic reactions (e.g., in the biosynthesis of collagen, carnitine, and neuropeptides and gene expression regulation). It is also a potent antioxidant.[55]

Vitamin C supports epithelial barrier function against pathogens and promotes the oxidant scavenging activity of the skin, thereby potentially protecting against environmental oxidative stress. Vitamin C accumulates in phagocytic cells, such as neutrophils, and can enhance chemotaxis, phagocytosis, generation of reactive oxygen species, and ultimately microbial killing. It is also needed for apoptosis and clearance of the spent neutrophils from sites of infection by macrophages, thereby decreasing necrosis/NETosis and potential tissue damage.[56, 57]

It All Started with Scurvy and Limes

In modern times, scurvy is viewed as a rare condition; however, it continues to present even within highly developed nations due to malnutrition and unbalanced diets. According to trials by the *National Health and Nutrition Examination Survey*, the prevalence of vitamin C deficiency within the United States has reduced from 13% in 1988-1994 to 7.1% in 2003-2004.[58] Additionally, alcohol and tobacco intake both impair ascorbic acid absorption, leading to a higher risk of scurvy. Published research on *Early Scurvy in the Modern Era* in 2023 supported that vitamin C is implicated in fatty acid regulation, immune function, neurotransmitter generation, prostaglandin metabolism, and nitric oxide synthesis. The paper outlined how scurvy can lead to serious functional breakdowns of health.[59]

> "Therefore, severe cases of scurvy may result in serious systemic functional deficits and, in untreated cases, even sudden death. Dermatologic findings associated with clinical scurvy include follicular hyperkeratosis, perifollicular hemorrhage, hair coiling (corkscrew hairs [CH]), and petechia. Mucosal findings include ecchymosis and gingivitis with recidivism and atrophy."[60]

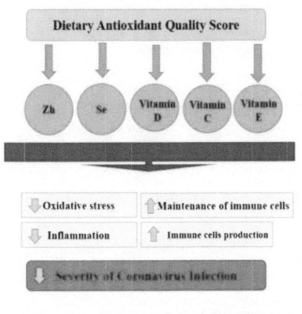

Shahbaz, U., Fatima, N., Basharat, S., Bibi, A., Yu, X., Hussain, M. I., & Nasrullah, M. (2022). Role of vitamin C in preventing of COVID-19 infection, progression and severity. AIMS microbiology, 8(1), 108–124. https://doi.org/10.3934/microbiol.2022010

Scurvy is a disease resulting from a lack of vitamin C (ascorbic acid). Early deficiency symptoms include weakness, fatigue, and sore arms and legs. Without treatment, decreased red blood cells, gum disease, changes to hair, and bleeding from the skin may occur.

Vitamin C and COVID

The use of vitamin C IV for improved recovery from COVID began appearing in PubMed in 2020. By 2022, multiple papers discussed the merits of vitamin C for strengthening the immune system and reducing long COVID complications. Multiple lines of evidence in the literature associate vitamin C with antioxidant, anti-inflammatory, anticoagulant, and immunomodulatory actions. According to many studies, pneumonia and sepsis patients had poor ascorbic acid status and high oxidative stress. Pneumonia patients who get vitamin C may have less severe symptoms and a shorter course of the illness. COVID-19 management in China and the United States exhibited remarkable results when using a high percentage of intravenous vitamins C with patients. The conclusion abstract states: "Patients with hypovitaminosis C or severe respiratory illnesses, such as COVID-19, may benefit from taking vitamin C due to its good safety profile, simplicity of use, and potential for rapid production scaling."[61]

Cancer there is mounting evidence indicating that vitamin C has the potential to be a potent anti-cancer agent when administered intravenously and in high doses (high-dose IVC). Early-phase clinical trials have confirmed the safety and efficacy of IVC in eradicating tumor cells of various cancer types.[62] Research from 2019 looked at how vitamin C can target three vulnerabilities that many cancer cells share: redox imbalance, epigenetic reprogramming, and oxygen-sensing regulation.[63]

The most frequent cancer in women is breast cancer, which is a major cause of death. Research from 2020 on breast cancer looked at how IV high-dose vitamin C was an excellent complement to pharmacological therapies. Trials of intravenous injection of vitamin C at high doses to enhance the antitumor activity of drugs and/or decrease their side effects has shown significant results.[64]

The Linus Pauling Institute at Oregon State University published the following statement on vitamin C IV therapy for cancer: "Current evidence of the efficacy of intravenous vitamin C in cancer patients is limited to observational studies, uncontrolled interventions, and case reports. There is a need for large, longer-duration phase II clinical trials that test the efficacy of intravenous vitamin C in cancer progression and overall survival."[65, 66]

Foods high in vitamin C are tomatoes, potatoes, chili, kale, snow peas, cherries, kiwi, peppers, strawberries, broccoli, papaya, limes, oranges, tangerines, grapefruit, and lemons.

> ***Principle 59:*** "When a civilization can no longer feed its citizens, it crumbles."
>
> ~Reay Tannahill

---

[1] Arulselvan, P., Fard, M. T., Tan, W. S., Gothai, S., Fakurazi, S., Norhaizan, M. E., & Kumar, S. S. (2016). Role of Antioxidants and Natural Products in Inflammation. Oxidative medicine and cellular longevity, 2016, 5276130. https://doi.org/10.1155/2016/5276130

[2] Sosa Henríquez, M., & Gómez de Tejada Romero, M. J. (2020). Cholecalciferol or Calcifediol in the Management of Vitamin D Deficiency. Nutrients, 12(6), 1617. https://doi.org/10.3390/nu12061617

[3] Khutami, C., Sumiwi, S. A., Khairul Ikram, N. K., & Muchtaridi, M. (2022). The Effects of Antioxidants from Natural Products on Obesity, Dyslipidemia, Diabetes and Their Molecular Signaling Mechanism. International journal of molecular sciences, 23(4), 2056. https://doi.org/10.3390/ijms23042056

[4] Chidambaram, S. B., Bhat, A., Mahalakshmi, A. M., Ray, B., Tuladhar, S., Sushmitha, B. S., Saravanan, B., Thamilarasan, M., Thenmozhi, A. J., Essa, M. M., Guillemin, G. J., & Qoronfleh, M. W. (2020). Protein Nutrition in Autism. Advances in neurobiology, 24, 573–586. https://doi.org/10.1007/978-3-030-30402-7_20

Chapter 11 ~ Nutrients

5 Carazo A, Macakova K, Matousova K, Krcmova LK, Protti M, Mladenka P. Vitamin A update: Forms, sources, kinetics, detection, function, deficiency, therapeutic use and toxicity. Nutrients 2021;13:1703.

6 Blaner WS. Vitamin A and Provitamin A Carotenoids. In: Marriott BP, Birt DF, Stallings VA, Yates AA, eds. Present Knowledge in Nutrition. 11th ed. Cambridge, Massachusetts: Wiley-Blackwell; 2020:73-91.

7 USDA Food Surveys Research Group (2020): https://www.ars.usda.gov/northeast-area/beltsville-md-bhnrc/beltsville-human-nutrition-research-center/food-surveys-research-group/

8 Melse-Boonstra A, Vossenaar M, van Loo-Bouwman CA, Kraemer K, de Pee S, West KP, Russell RM, Solomons NW. Dietary vitamin A intake recommendations revisited: global confusion requires alignment of the units of conversion and expression. Public Health Nutr. 2017 Aug;20(11):1903-1906. doi: 10.1017/S1368980017000477. Epub 2017 Mar 22. PMID: 28327209; PMCID: PMC10261660.

9 Chen G, Weiskirchen S, Weiskirchen R. Vitamin A: too good to be bad? Front Pharmacol. 2023 May 22;14:1186336. doi: 10.3389/fphar.2023.1186336. PMID: 37284305; PMCID: PMC10239981.

10 Moltedo A, Álvarez-Sánchez C, Grande F, Charrondiere UR. The complexity of producing and interpreting dietary vitamin A statistics. J Food Compost Anal. 2021 Jul;100:103926. doi: 10.1016/j.jfca.2021.103926. PMID: 34219918; PMCID: PMC8140404.

11 Trivedi, M. K., Sharma, S., Rifas-Shiman, S. L., Camargo, C. A., Jr, Weiss, S. T., Oken, E., Gillman, M. W., Gold, D. R., DeMeo, D. L., & Litonjua, A. A. (2018). Folic Acid in Pregnancy and Childhood Asthma: A US Cohort. Clinical pediatrics, 57(4), 421–427. https://doi.org/10.1177/0009922817729482

12 Liang Y, Salim AM, Wu W, Kilgore PE. Chao Yuanfang: Imperial Physician of the Sui Dynasty and an Early Pertussis Observer? Open Forum Infect Dis. 2016 Jan 29;3(1):ofw017. doi: 10.1093/ofid/ofw017. PMID: 26977422; PMCID: PMC4786867.

13 Carpenter KJ. The discovery of thiamin. Ann Nutr Metab. 2012;61(3):219-23. doi: 10.1159/000343109. Epub 2012 Nov 26. PMID: 23183292.

14 http://www.ncbi.nlm.nih.gov/pubmed/20056620

15 Cancer Epidemiol Biomarkers Prev. 2010 Jan;19(1):28-38. doi: 10.1158/1055-9965.EPI-08-1096.

16 Stanger, O., Herrmann, W., Pietrzik, K., Fowler, B., Geisel, J., Dierkes, J., & Weger, M. (2004). Clinical use and rational management of homocysteine, folic acid, and B vitamins in cardiovascular and thrombotic diseases. Zeitschrift fur Kardiologie, 93(6), 439–453. https://doi.org/10.1007/s00392-004-0075-3

17 Maggini, S., Pierre, A., & Calder, P. C. (2018). Immune Function and Micronutrient Requirements Change over the Life Course. Nutrients, 10(10), 1531. https://doi.org/10.3390/nu10101531

18 Karr, T., Guptha, L., Bell, K., Thenell, J (2023) Literature Review ~ Oxalates: Dietary Oxalates and Kidney Inflammation, page 87 Our Journey with Food

19 Adams, J. B., George, F., & Audhya, T. (2006). Abnormally high plasma levels of vitamin B6 in children with autism not taking supplements compared to controls not taking supplements. Journal of alternative and complementary medicine (New York, N.Y.), 12(1), 59–63. https://doi.org/10.1089/acm.2006.12.59

20 If my Vitamin B12 levels are above normal, is that OK? (n.d.). Retrieved from https://answers.yahoo.com/question/index?qid=20110224122408AAZugEJ_br

21 "The Nobel Prize and the Discovery of Vitamins". www.nobelprize.org. Archived from the original on 2018-01-16. Retrieved 2018-02-15.

22 Walpar Healthcare | Products- Healthcare. (n.d.). Retrieved from http://www.walpar.in/(S(e1pcm4ih5j155h45t5e1xnvd))/ayurvedic.html_br

23 Vitamin D (2014) Oregon State University; Linus Pauling Institute: https://oregonstate.edu/

24 Vitamin D Fact Sheet for Consumers, NIH: https://ods.od.nih.gov/factsheets/VitaminD-Consumer/

25 Thyssen, J. P., & Elias, P. M. (2017). It Remains Unknown Whether Filaggrin Gene Mutations Evolved to Increase Cutaneous Synthesis of Vitamin D. Genome biology and evolution, 9(4), 900–901. https://doi.org/10.1093/gbe/evx049

26 Zittermann, A., Trummer, C., Theiler-Schwetz, V., & Pilz, S. (2023). Long-term supplementation with 3200 to 4000 IU of vitamin D daily and adverse events: a systematic review and meta-analysis of randomized controlled trials. European journal of nutrition, 62(4), 1833–1844. https://doi.org/10.1007/s00394-023-03124-w

27 Ang Zhou and others, Non-linear Mendelian randomization analyses support a role for vitamin D deficiency in cardiovascular disease risk, European Heart Journal, Volume 43, Issue 18, 7 May 2022, Pages 1731–1739, https://doi.org/10.1093/eurheartj/ehab809

28 Sutherland, J. P., Zhou, A., & Hyppönen, E. (2022). Vitamin D Deficiency Increases Mortality Risk in the UK Biobank : A Nonlinear Mendelian Randomization Study. Annals of internal medicine, 175(11), 1552–1559. https://doi.org/10.7326/M21-3324

29 . (FoodBev.com | News | Coffee breaks are good for us. (n.d.). Retrieved from http://www.foodbev.com/news/coffee-breaks-are-good-for-us_br)

30 Arora, J., Patel, D. R., Nicol, M. J., Field, C. J., Restori, K. H., Wang, J., Froelich, N. E., Katkere, B., Terwilliger, J. A., Weaver, V., Luley, E., Kelly, K., Kirimanjeswara, G. S., Sutton, T. C., & Cantorna, M. T. (2022). Vitamin D and the Ability to Produce 1,25(OH)2D Are Critical for Protection from Viral Infection of the Lungs. Nutrients, 14(15), 3061. https://doi.org/10.3390/nu14153061

31 Athanassiou, L., Kostoglou-Athanassiou, I., Koutsilieris, M., & Shoenfeld, Y. (2023). Vitamin D and Autoimmune Rheumatic Diseases. Biomolecules, 13(4), 709. https://doi.org/10.3390/biom13040709

32 Mustacich, D. J., Bruno, R. S., & Traber, M. G. (2007). Vitamin E. Vitamins and hormones, 76, 1–21. https://doi.org/10.1016/S0083-6729(07)76001-6

33 Nakatomi, T., Itaya-Takahashi, M., Horikoshi, Y., Shimizu, N., Parida, I. S., Jutanom, M., Eitsuka, T., Tanaka, Y., Zingg, J. M., Matsura, T., & Nakagawa, K. (2023). The difference in the cellular uptake of tocopherol and tocotrienol is influenced by their affinities to albumin. Scientific reports, 13(1), 7392. https://doi.org/10.1038/s41598-023-34584-z

34 Kemnic, T. R., & Coleman, M. (2022). Vitamin E Deficiency. In StatPearls. StatPearls Publishing.

35 Lee, G. Y., & Han, S. N. (2018). The Role of Vitamin E in Immunity. Nutrients, 10(11), 1614. https://doi.org/10.3390/nu10111614

36 Northwestern University. (2014, May 20). Vitamin E in canola, other oils hurts lungs. ScienceDaily. Retrieved July 25, 2023 from www.sciencedaily.com/releases/2014/05/140520220424.htm

37 Khalil, Z., Alam, B., Akbari, A. R., & Sharma, H. (2021). The Medical Benefits of Vitamin K2 on Calcium-Related Disorders. Nutrients, 13(2), 691. https://doi.org/10.3390/nu13020691

38 Cai, H., Cao, X., Qin, D., Liu, Y., Liu, Y., Hua, J., & Peng, S. (2022). Gut microbiota supports male reproduction via nutrition, immunity, and signaling. Frontiers in microbiology, 13, 977574. https://doi.org/10.3389/fmicb.2022.977574

39 Wang, Y., & Xie, Z. (2022). Exploring the role of gut microbiome in male reproduction. Andrology, 10(3), 441–450. https://doi.org/10.1111/andr.13143

40 Myneni, V. D., & Mezey, E. (2017). Regulation of bone remodeling by vitamin K2. Oral diseases, 23(8), 1021–1028. https://doi.org/10.1111/odi.12624

41 Capozzi, A., Scambia, G., & Lello, S. (2020). Calcium, vitamin D, vitamin K2, and magnesium supplementation and skeletal health. Maturitas, 140, 55–63. https://doi.org/10.1016/j.maturitas.2020.05.020

42 Feskanich, D., Weber, P., Willett, W. C., Rockett, H., Booth, S. L., & Colditz, G. A. (1999). Vitamin K intake and hip fractures in women: a prospective study. The American journal of clinical nutrition, 69(1), 74–79. https://doi.org/10.1093/ajcn/69.1.74

43 Gul, S., Maqbool, M. F., Maryam, A., Khan, M., Shakir, H. A., Irfan, M., Ara, C., Li, Y., & Ma, T. (2022). Vitamin K: A novel cancer chemosensitizer. Biotechnology and applied biochemistry, 69(6), 2641–2657. https://doi.org/10.1002/bab.2312

44 Welsh, J., Bak, M. J., & Narvaez, C. J. (2022). New insights into vitamin K biology with relevance to cancer. Trends in molecular medicine, 28(10), 864–881. https://doi.org/10.1016/j.molmed.2022.07.002

45 Bellone, F., Cinquegrani, M., Nicotera, R., Carullo, N., Casarella, A., Presta, P., Andreucci, M., Squadrito, G., Mandraffino, G., Prunestì, M., Vocca, C., De Sarro, G., Bolignano, D., & Coppolino, G. (2022). Role of Vitamin K in Chronic Kidney Disease: A Focus on Bone and Cardiovascular Health. International journal of molecular sciences, 23(9), 5282. https://doi.org/10.3390/ijms23095282

46 Fusaro, M., Cosmai, L., Evenepoel, P., Nickolas, T. L., Cheung, A. M., Aghi, A., Tripepi, G., Plebani, M., Iervasi, G., Vettor, R., Zaninotto, M., Ravera, M., Foramitti, M., Giannini, S., Sella, S., & Gallieni, M. (2020). Vitamin K and Kidney Transplantation. Nutrients, 12(9), 2717. https://doi.org/10.3390/nu12092717

47 www.reuters.com/article/2015/02/19/idUSnMKW7j9M2a+1c4+MKW20150219

48 Medical College of Georgia at Augusta University. "Low consumption of vitamin K by adolescents associated with unhealthy enlargement of the heart's major pumping chamber." ScienceDaily. ScienceDaily, 2 October 2017. www.sciencedaily.com/releases/2017/10/171002105224.htm.

49 Halder, M., Petsophonsakul, P., Akbulut, A. C., Pavlic, A., Bohan, F., Anderson, E., Maresz, K., Kramann, R., & Schurgers, L. (2019). Vitamin K: Double Bonds beyond Coagulation Insights into Differences between Vitamin K1 and K2 in Health and Disease. International journal of molecular sciences, 20(4), 896. https://doi.org/10.3390/ijms20040896

50 Kubo, Y., Rooney, A. P., Tsukakoshi, Y., Nakagawa, R., Hasegawa, H., & Kimura, K. (2011). Phylogenetic analysis of Bacillus subtilis strains applicable to natto (fermented soybean) production. Applied and environmental microbiology, 77(18), 6463–6469. https://doi.org/10.1128/AEM.00448-11

51 http://www.achievement.org/achiever/linus-pauling/

52 http://lpi.oregonstate.edu/about/linus-pauling-biography

53 http://orthomolecular.org/history/index.shtml

54 Bland J. S. (2019). Linus Pauling (1901-1994). Integrative medicine (Encinitas, Calif.), 18(3), 50–51.

55 Peeling, P., Sim, M., & McKay, A. K. A. (2023). Considerations for the Consumption of Vitamin and Mineral Supplements in Athlete Populations. Sports medicine (Auckland, N.Z.), 10.1007/s40279-023-01875-4. Advance online publication. https://doi.org/10.1007/s40279-023-01875-4

56 Carr, A. C., & Maggini, S. (2017). Vitamin C and Immune Function. Nutrients, 9(11), 1211. https://doi.org/10.3390/nu9111211

57 Kuhn, S. O., Meissner, K., Mayes, L. M., & Bartels, K. (2018). Vitamin C in sepsis. Current opinion in anaesthesiology, 31(1), 55–60. https://doi.org/10.1097/ACO.0000000000000549

58 Schleicher R.L., Carroll M.D., Ford E.S., Lacher D.A. Serum vitamin C and the prevalence of vitamin C deficiency in the United States: 2003-2004 national Health and nutrition examination Survey (NHANES) Am J Clin Nutr. 2009;90(5):1252–1263. doi: 10.3945/ajcn.2008.27016.

59 Hanania, H., Maheshwari, K., Dunn, C., & Rosen, T. (2023). Early scurvy in the modern era: A case series. JAAD case reports, 38, 130–135. https://doi.org/10.1016/j.jdcr.2023.06.030

60 Olmedo J.M., Yiannias J.A., Windgassen E.B., Gornet M.K. Scurvy: a disease almost forgotten. Int J Dermatol. 2006;45(8):909–913. doi: 10.1111/j.1365-4632.2006.02844.x.

61 Shahbaz, U., Fatima, N., Basharat, S., Bibi, A., Yu, X., Hussain, M. I., & Nasrullah, M. (2022). Role of vitamin C in preventing of COVID-19 infection, progression and severity. AIMS microbiology, 8(1), 108–124. https://doi.org/10.3934/microbiol.2022010

62 Böttger, F., Vallés-Martí, A., Cahn, L., & Jimenez, C. R. (2021). High-dose intravenous vitamin C, a promising multi-targeting agent in the treatment of cancer. Journal of experimental & clinical cancer research : CR, 40(1), 343. https://doi.org/10.1186/s13046-021-02134-y

63 Ngo, B., Van Riper, J. M., Cantley, L. C., & Yun, J. (2019). Targeting cancer vulnerabilities with high-dose vitamin C. Nature reviews. Cancer, 19(5), 271–282. https://doi.org/10.1038/s41568-019-0135-7

64 Codini M. (2020). Why Vitamin C Could Be an Excellent Complementary Remedy to Conventional Therapies for Breast Cancer. International journal of molecular sciences, 21(21), 8397. https://doi.org/10.3390/ijms21218397

65 Chambers, S. T., Storer, M., Scott-Thomas, A., Slow, S., Williman, J., Epton, M., Murdoch, D. R., Metcalf, S., Carr, A., Isenman, H., & Maze, M. (2023). Adjunctive intravenous then oral vitamin C for moderate and severe community-acquired pneumonia in hospitalized adults: feasibility of randomized controlled trial. Scientific reports, 13(1), 11879. https://doi.org/10.1038/s41598-023-37934-z

66 Wen, C., Li, Y., Hu, Q., Liu, H., Xu, X., & Lü, M. (2023). IV Vitamin C in Sepsis: A Latest Systematic Review and Meta-Analysis. International journal of clinical practice, 2023, 6733465. https://doi.org/10.1155/2023/6733465

Our Journey with Food

"Why do we believe *Food is Medicine*? The *Why* involves countless nutrients, first and foremost found in foods. The *How* involves the use of *Herbs* – without herbs and their inseparable role in gastronomy; it is impossible to fully understand *Food as Medicine*."

~ Tammera J. Karr PhD, BCHN®

Chapter Twelve ~ *Herbs to Nourish & Support*

From the dawn of time, herbs have been part of human gastronomy; this includes cultural healing practices and ceremonies. Research in anthropology and archaeology in the 21st century clearly shows the use of herbs by archaic peoples. Ethnobotanists can track Indians of the Americas 'migratory pathways by locating selective plant-cultivated areas. You or I may be hiking in the forest or along a river and find a choice patch of miners lettuce or wild garlic. The Northwest area blackcaps, strawberries, and elderberry all lend medicinal compounds, in addition to other fruits. The tansy ragwort and wild carrot seeds and leaves provide contraceptive chemicals. Besides being used as chewing gum by ancient travelers, tree resin's anti-inflammatory benefit yields itself to wound healing.

I have reached for a plant as my medicine for most of my life, even as a child. In no way does this affinity with herbs make me an herbalist – I am a casual dabbler, like many others who enjoy herbs in cooking, use their oils for body care, and hold respect for their ancient use in healing. Not far from my home giant Ponderosa pines with distinctive scars soar high into the air – they are medicine trees. In times past the bark was carefully cut so the tree would run sap for *Kalapuya, Klamath, Modoc* and *Yahooskin* peoples. The sap was collected and served as an antiseptic, astringent, anti-inflammatory, and antibacterial medicine. The soft sap from pine trees was chewed straight off the tree like gum for sore throats and colds by those who knew its properties. Throughout the world, resin or sap from plants can be found in traditional healing formularies. Over 40 years ago, my husband introduced me to sap for treating wounds. His family kept a little brown glass jar with white fir sap in the first aid kit. When a nasty cut needs to be glued together or has a little infection, out comes the tree sap. Even on our pets, especially cats prone to abscesses, benefit from sap as it reduces inflammation and draws out the infection, healing the wound efficiently and safely.

Humans are not alone in the selective use of plants for healing. I was always fascinated when my horse - Nibbles McGee - would carefully nip off a spiky-green teasel top and roll it in his mouth to his back teeth to eat. Or he would grab a mouthful of tender horsetail (*Equisetum* is a "living fossil") along the trail edge by

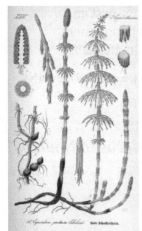

the lake, swallow it down, then act like he was filled with energy. These plants have anti-inflammatory, diuretic, antibacterial, antimicrobial, coagulant, demulcent, and astringent properties. Horsetail is rich in silica, potassium, malic acid, and a number of flavonoids.[1]

Teasel has a history of medical use in Europe, where teasel roots and leaves are widely used as a tincture. Herbal sources list teasel as an effective analgesic for muscle and joint pain, with antibacterial, antiviral, and diuretic properties (to name only a few). Currently, teasel root is most known for treating Lyme disease and is traditionally used in Chinese medicine for structural repair of bones and connective tissue. Researchers in 2014 found that teasel root helps build bone mass and treat porous bones.[2]

Our cat and dog have their herbal preferences, too – cat nip, parsley, and green grass to soothe tummies.

Culinary and Decorative Herbs

A pot of rosemary and basil may grace the dabbler's steps, or hyssop and lavender clumps adorn the yard edge. Our yard has sage, marjoram, thyme, lovage, mint, bee balm, and many other herbs in the flower bed jungle, all for the wild honeybees. A great or small assortment of dried herbs and spices usually clutter a kitchen cupboard or shelf. The volume of culinary herbs listed in *Our Journey with Food Cookery Book* spills out of their dedicated space weaving their way throughout every recipe. The efficacy of oregano and garlic as antivirals kept them close at hand in our home during the darkest days of the COVID-19 pandemic of 2020.[3, 4, 5]

Not all herbs are green and leafy, but they all provide chemicals with varying degrees of safety. Often, the most toxic substances to pests also carry the greatest healing properties. Research on garlic published on PubMed (2020) confirmed what millions of Spanish and Italian grandmothers knew – *"Eat it; it is good for you."* Pre-clinical data showed that garlic and its active organosulfur compounds (OSCs) have potential antiviral activity against different pathogenic viruses affecting humans, animals, and plants through blocking viral entry into host cells; inhibiting viral RNA polymerase, reverse transcriptase, DNA synthesis and immediate-early gene 1(IEG1) transcription; as well as via downregulating the extracellular-signal-regulated kinase (ERK)/mitogen-activated protein kinase (MAPK) signaling pathway. Clinical studies further demonstrated a prophylactic effect of garlic in preventing widespread viral infections in humans by enhancing the immune response.[6]

The Chinese herb Lianhuaqingwen *(forsythia honeysuckle)* in 2021 was effective in treating COVID-19. It caught my attention when the researchers wrote, "TCM exerts its effects through multiple targets and multiple pathways, and LH capsules are not an exception."[7] Another traditional Chinese herb, Lianhua Qingwen, also has been found to exert a remarkable anti-COVID-19 effect and is being reviewed and researched.[8]

Chapter 12 ~ Herbs to Nourish & Support

Herbs Are Not Straightforward

I suspect one of the most significant challenges bioscience-based Western medicine has with herbs is the commonly accepted "cause and effect" view through Galilean-Baconian reductionist science, which is insufficient to explain and/or predict their results. Plants are complicated, fickle, and independent – just like humans can be. They contain all the powers of invading armies, plagues, climate change, bullies, and starvation within their sphere of influence. Surviving in nature requires adaptability, which is why a scientist from the 18th century still influences how physicists and biologists explore natural processes today. Johann Wolfgang von Goethe (1749–1832) spent his long life pursuing a living science of the natural world. Goethean science lends itself to biology, especially the world of plants.[9] The current Goethean revival strives to study the internal ecology of plants and animals, elucidating how structures and functions interrelate in forming a specific natural life form as a whole. Researchers can then investigate the whole organism as part of the larger web of life. This interdisciplinary approach integrates natural history, anatomy, physiology, behavior, development, genetics, and evolution.[10]

This Western approach, supporting the wisdom of First Peoples, Traditional Chinese Medicine, and Ayurveda practices, allows us to see the *evidence-informed* use of herbs when there doesn't seem to be a "logical" answer for why they work. If only anecdotal and historical evidence supports their use, then it is just a matter of "*eat it because it is good for you.*"[11,12]

> ***Principle 60:*** Many present-day medications originated as herbal formulas.

Boswellia serrata

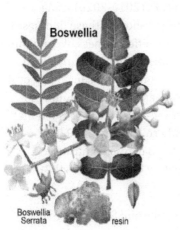
Boswellia Serrata   resin

Boswellia, also called Indian Frankincense, is an extract of the gummy oleoresin derived from beneath the bark of the Boswellia serrata tree, which is native to India, the Middle East, and Northern Africa. The resin is rich in triterpenic acids and has been used for centuries in traditional Ayurvedic health practices to treat inflammatory conditions. More recently, Boswellia serrata extracts have been marketed as helpful in arthritis, colitis, and asthma. Extracts of Boswellia serrata have not been linked to serum aminotransferase elevations during treatment or to cause clinically apparent acute liver injury.[13]

Boswellia serrata is native to the mountainous regions of the Middle East and is related to the tree that yields the frankincense referenced in the Bible. Its trunk is slashed to permit the flow of a resinous gum, also known as guggulu and locally called *shallaki* (Sanskrit). After collection, the resin is cured in specialized bamboo baskets before being broken into pieces and graded according to color and shape. Boswellia serrata has a delightful, exotic scent when burned as incense alone or combined with other resins.

The gum oleoresin consists of essential oils, gum, and terpenoids. The terpenoid portion contains the boswellic acids that are the active constituents in Boswellia. The resinous part of Boswellia serrata possesses monoterpenes, diterpenes, triterpenes, tetracyclic triterpenic acids: β-boswellic acid, acetyl-β-boswellic acid, 11-keto-β-boswellic acid, and acetyl-11-keto-β-boswellic acid responsible for inhibition of pro-inflammatory enzymes. Of these four boswellic acids, acetyl-11-keto-β-boswellic acid is the most potent inhibitor of 5-lipoxygenase, an enzyme responsible for inflammation. Boswellia is as efficient and, in many cases, better than drugs like phenylbutazone and other anti-inflammatory medications. Boswellia serrata gum resin is widely used in Ayurvedic formulations for treating asthma and arthritis.[14]

Boswellia was found to have neuroprotective and anti-neuroinflammatory activity in 2023.[15] For individuals with osteoarthritis in the knee, two studies released in 2023 found the use of a topical oily solution containing enriched extract of boswellic acids and an oral formula (Aflapin®) could decrease pain severity and improve the function in patients with knee OA without complications associated with typical orally administered medications.[16, 17]

So before you pop another Advil® or Aleve® for the pain in your back, consider your options. Increase your consumption of mineral water which helps improve kidney function. Reduce inflammatory foods, including polyunsaturated oils, and try Boswellia for pain relief. This herb has no known side effects and is also safe for dogs.[18, 19]

Turmeric

For years, curry lovers have sworn by the anti-inflammatory properties of turmeric, but its active compound, curcumin, has long frustrated scientists hoping to validate these claims. A review of clinical trials over ten years (2010-2020) using curcumin on different types of cancer showed these findings: 16 out of 21 clinical trials supported the effectiveness of curcumin or turmeric on chronic myeloid leukemia, multiple myeloma, prostate, colorectal and pancreatic cancer as well as cancer therapy-related complications, including oral mucositis and radiation dermatitis. The other five clinical trials related to the efficacy of curcumin or turmeric in relieving the side effects of cancer chemotherapy and radiotherapy. The data confirmed that curcumin has the potential for cancer prevention and intervention.[20] A study released in 2019 by Washington State University developed a drug delivery system with the refined extract of turmeric – curcumin, that successfully inhibited bone cancer cells while promoting healthy bone cell growth.[21]

Cognition
Turmeric (*Curcuma longa*) or Indian saffron has been used for centuries in India and Southeast Asia.[22] Turmeric, which is used widely in cooking, comes from the plant rhizome and is partially attributed with the reduced rate of cognitive decline conditions. In these areas, the prevalence of Alzheimer's disease and various cancers are much lower than they are in the United States and other Western countries. In 2020, researchers from the University of South Australia, McMaster University in Canada, and Texas A&M University showed in animal experiments that nanoparticles containing curcumin not only prevent cognitive deterioration but also reverse neural damage. This finding paves the way for clinical

development trials for Alzheimer's disease.[23] Curcumin's natural anti-inflammatory and antioxidant properties may reduce both oxidative damage and pathological changes that could lead to brain abnormalities. More precisely, curcumin has been shown to decrease the incidence of harmful plaques by slowing the deposition of the beta-amyloid precursor protein (APP) within the brain. In January 2018, the *American Journal of Geriatric Psychiatry* published a study of 40 individuals between the ages of 50 and 90. The people who took curcumin experienced significant improvements in their memory and attention abilities, while the subjects who received a placebo did not. In memory tests, the people taking curcumin improved by 28% over the 18 months. Those taking curcumin also had mild improvements in mood, and their brain PET scans showed significantly fewer amyloid and tau signals in the amygdala and hypothalamus than those who took placebos.[24]

Antiviral Effects
According to a study from 2020, curcumin has been shown to inhibit the replication of some types of viruses, including dengue virus, hepatitis B, and Zika virus. The compound has also been found to have several significant biological effects, including anti-tumor, anti-inflammatory and antibacterial activities.[25]

An animal study evaluated curcumin's effects on allergic airway inflammation and hyper-responsiveness. According to the *American Academy of Allergy, Asthma, and Immunology*, 34.1 million Americans have been diagnosed with asthma during their lifetime, and the academy estimates that the number of Americans with asthma will increase by >100 million by 2025. The study authors stated that in mice, "Curcumin attenuates the development of allergic airway inflammation and hyper-responsiveness, possibly through inhibition of NF-kappaB activation in the asthmatic lung tissue. Our results indicate that curcumin may attenuate asthma development by inhibiting NF-kappaB activation."

Common Uses of Curcumin

Abrasions/cuts	Aches and pains	Cancer prevention
Candida/yeast infection	Cholesterol control	Concentration/memory
Eye care/vision	Gout	Heart tonics
Lupus	Osteoarthritis	Rheumatoid arthritis
Smoking cessation		

Properties

Anti-inflammatory	Analgesic	Antibacterial
Cardiac tonic	Hepatic	COX-2 inhibitor
Antifungal constituents	Volatile oils (terpene, curcumin)	Starch
Albumen (30%)	Coloring (due to curcumin)	Potassium

Spices have been an integral part of human diets and commerce for millennia. Spices, in addition to giving color and taste to foods, are essential nutraceuticals. Recently, more scientists are recognizing the link between health and nutrition, which has strengthened their importance in the food sector and sparked the interest of researchers, especially the curcumin component found in turmeric.

Turmeric is a perennial plant native to India and cultivated in China, Bengal, and Java for its rhizomes. Several other species of the *curcuma* genus grow wild in the forests of Southern Asia, including in India, Indonesia, Indochina, and in some Pacific Islands such as Hawaii. Turmeric is a mild aromatic stimulant used to manufacture curry powders and mustards. It is in the same family as ginger, cardamom, and zedoary. For more than a millennium, Eastern and Pacific Island cultures have used turmeric for culinary and medicinal purposes.

> A nutraceutical product can be defined as a substance that has a physiological benefit or provides protection against chronic diseases. The term nutraceutical is a hybrid term derived from the union of "nutrition" and "pharmaceutical." The list of studied nutraceuticals is constantly changing and reflects ongoing market developments, research, and consumer interest. The curcumin in turmeric has been found to be effective against breast cancer, osteoporosis, gluten sensitivity, Alzheimer's disease, skin conditions, and arthritis.[26]

Scientific literature supports this widely used spice's potent properties. However, curcumin cannot be readily absorbed from dietary sources and does not produce adequate, sustained blood levels for optimal impact. Use in combination with black pepper or dried ginger to help activate turmeric, or choose supplements that include them. For individuals with digestive challenges, IBS, Crohn's, and celiac disease, fresh turmeric containing natural buffering compounds is gentler on the stomach and intestines than more concentrated supplements.

I encourage you to use turmeric in cooking for salad dressings, soups, rice dishes, or sauces, as this is one of the most traditional ways of utilizing this herb. The book *The Blue Zones* shows that the cultures with the most centenarians commonly use turmeric liberally in their diets. One interesting way is via goat milk.[27, 28] For those who are unable or do not like hot and spicy food, take heart. There are herbs available to you also that are effective in improving metabolism and blood sugars. Many of them are perfect for tossing into warming broths or stews.

Pain Relievers

Herbs and spices like Boswellia and turmeric are increasingly well known for their ability to reduce inflammation. However, they may take longer to demonstrate effects, and the quantity needed is higher than once-daily prescription medication. In my work with rheumatoid arthritis clients, using Boswellia with prescribed medications allowed clients nonaddictive adjunct options for pain management with fewer side effects. Other clients were highly sensitive to NSAIDs, and Boswellia was an effective non-prescriptive herb they could use for headaches and muscle and joint pain. In addition to Boswellia and turmeric, there are countless herbs or nutraceuticals that reduce inflammation. When combined with acupuncture, trigger point and massage therapies, and dietary adjustments, the need for potentially dangerous NSAIDs, steroids, or invasive surgery is reduced.[29, 30, 31]

NSAIDs: A Cautionary Tale
Millions of Americans routinely take over-the-counter medications known as NSAIDs (nonsteroidal anti-inflammatory drugs), namely:

- Ibuprofen (e.g., brand names Advil®, Motrin®, Nuprin®)
- Naproxen (e.g., brand names Aleve®, Naprosyn®)
- COX-2 inhibitors (e.g., brand name Celebrex®)

NSAIDs comprise a large class of drugs used to reduce inflammation and relieve pain. In addition to aspirin, there are currently several non-prescription (over-the-counter) NSAIDs and prescription brands of NSAIDs. These medications do not come with a red warning label which would alert the consumer to the potential dangers.[32, 33]

NSAIDs are known to damage kidney and liver function in some individuals. On April 9, 2014, physician news site Medscape posted that NSAIDs are linked to higher atrial fibrillation risk.

> "Taking nonsteroidal anti-inflammatory (NSAID) drugs appears to be associated with an increased risk for atrial fibrillation (AF), even after adjustment for ventricular end-diastolic dimension, known to be increased with NSAID use," a new study confirms.
>
> "Researchers found that patients using NSAIDs for 2-4 weeks had a 76% higher risk of developing AF than those who hadn't taken these pain medications."
>
> "The underlying mechanism connecting NSAID use with AF isn't clear and 'deserves further attention,'" the authors conclude. AF, a common arrhythmia in older adults, is associated with stroke, heart failure, increased mortality, and reduced life expectancy. NSAID use has also been related to myocardial infarction, stroke, and heart failure. "Other recent studies have suggested that NSAID use may increase the risk for AF," the researchers note.[34]

Millions of people use these medications regularly. I use them myself occasionally, but I always increase my water consumption when taking them to reduce potential kidney damage.

If you have a history of heart problems or kidney disease, please speak with a knowledgeable pharmacist and your healthcare provider before taking NSAIDs.

> ***Principle 61:*** Herbs provide beneficial chemicals for health, but adequate knowledge is needed for safe use.

Herbs That Support Metabolism

Some herbs and foods viewed historically as beneficial during the winter months help keep the dangers of a downregulated metabolism in check. Herbs most commonly thought of as heat-generating and metabolism-boosting are garlic, ginger, cayenne, turmeric, and tea. Although plant extracts are no longer a significant aspect of medical care practiced in Western populations, it is still prevalent in large numbers of the world's population, particularly in Asia and Europe.

Many plant-based compounds appear to exert an anti-aging effect; the most effective being flavonoids, terpenoids, saponins, and polysaccharides, which include astragaloside, ginkgolide, ginsenoside, and gypenoside. These are covered explicitly in a 2020 review.[35] Their effects as anti-aging factors, improvers of cognitive impairments, and reducers of cardiovascular risks are described, as well as the molecular mechanisms underlying the effects mentioned above and their potential safety. Telomere and telomerase,

PPAR-α, GLUTs, FOXO1, and caspase-3, bcl-2, along with SIRT1/AMPK, PI3K/Akt, NF-κB, and insulin/insulin-like growth factor-1 pathways appear to be their preferential targets. Moreover, their ability to work as antioxidants improves the resistance to DNA damage. When we are inactive, our metabolism shifts to a slower speed, designed to conserve resources necessary for survival. This down-regulation affects our thyroid, a gland that governs body temperature and plays a role in blood pressure and circulation.[36] The metabolic pathways leading to disturbances in lipid, carbohydrate, and hormonal metabolism commonly result in sleep disorders and changes in mental health parameters, plus causes of oxidative stress and inflammation. These conditions consistently lead to severe diseases in individuals with diabetes, fatty degeneration of internal organs, infertility, atherosclerosis, cardiovascular diseases, dysbiosis, and cancer. A 2021 study on lifestyle and herbal nutraceutical approaches for polycystic ovarian syndrome found the condition was largely modifiable through lifestyle changes, diet patterns, proper selection of nutrients, pharmacological and natural supplementation in herbs, and physical activity.[37]

Tea derived from the plant *Camellia sinesis* can be classified as green, oolong, or black depending on its level of fermentation. Green tea has been shown to reduce cholesterol and fasting blood glucose levels in the general population. Tea (*Camellia sinensis*) has been consumed for centuries as traditional medicine for various diseases, including diabetes. Purple tea is a natural mutant of *Camellia sinensis*, grown in China and Kenya and is rich in anthocyanins and ellagitannins.[38] Additionally, small trials suggest there may be specific benefits to the diabetic population.[39] The scientific interest in the medicinal properties of Kombucha beverages, a carbonated drink with live microorganisms, has increased. A study done in 2023 suggested that the fermented extracts of green tea, coffee, and Reishi exert significant antioxidant effects, although they were lower compared to the unfermented extracts. The unfermented green tea extract exhibited the highest scavenging activity (87.46%) and the highest preservation of β-carotene (92.41%).[40] Diabetes is one of the fastest-growing chronic illnesses in America, and winter may be the tipping point for many who become sedentary due to worsening weather.

Rosemary (*Rosmarinus officinalis L.*) is a medicinal plant native to the Mediterranean region and cultivated worldwide. Besides the therapeutic purpose, it is commonly used as a condiment and food preservative. *R. officinalis L.* is constituted by bioactive molecules, the phytocompounds responsible for implementing several pharmacological activities, such as anti-inflammatory, antioxidant, antimicrobial, antiproliferative, anti-tumor; and protective, inhibitory, and attenuating activities. Plus, it helps normalize blood sugar levels naturally. It also promotes weight loss, a double boon for many people with diabetes who struggle with weight issues. Research conducted in Jordan to study the effects of rosemary on lipid profile in diabetic rats proved that rosemary has no significant influence on normal rats' serum glucose levels and lipid profile. However, when rosemary extract was administered to diabetic rats for four weeks, their blood sugar levels were reduced by 20%, cholesterol levels by 22%, triglyceride levels by 24%, and LDL by 27%, while HDL increased by 18%.[41, 42]

Oregano species are rich sources of phytochemicals such as phenolic compounds like rosmarinic acid, salvianolic acid, and luteolin. A study on oregano as an antidiabetic agent in 2022 showed that the antidiabetic pharmacological reports of oregano phenolic compounds are mainly in vitro reports.[43] However, oregano historically is considered one of the best herbs to lower blood sugar levels.[44] A Mexican study on *Inhibition of Advanced Glycation End-Product Formation by Origanum majorana L. In Vitro and Streptozotocin-Induced Diabetic Rats* revealed that oregano alleviated oxidative stress under diabetic

Chapter 12 ~ Herbs to Nourish & Support

conditions through the inhibition of lipid peroxidation. Oregano may also prevent and delay the onset of renal damage.[45, 46, 47]

Sage has been used in traditional medicine for centuries as one of the essential herbs to reduce blood sugar. According to the *Journal of Nutrition,* sage can have Metformin-like effects. A word of warning – taking high doses of sage and diabetes medications might cause your blood sugar to go too low, a condition called hypoglycemia. Monitor your blood sugar carefully.[48]

Marjoram, a lesser-known herb that lowers blood sugar, is high in polyphenols and aids in stabilizing blood glucose levels. A 2012 *Journal of Evidence-Based Alternative and Complementary Medicine* study found that marjoram reduced the formation of advanced glycation end (AGE) products. AGE is responsible for many of the complications associated with diabetes, like damage to arteries and eyes.[49] Sprinkle marjoram on your dinner to help add variety in flavor or use it as a substitute for oregano.

Fennel, traditionally, has been used to treat cough/cold, fever, cuts, stomach aches, nausea, flatulence, diarrhea, constipation, insomnia, arthritis, conjunctivitis, and colic in children and to increase breast milk production.[50, 51] A 2021 review found evidence for fennel improving menopausal symptoms.[52] In a study from 2022 on the traditional Chinese nursing care use of fennel, it was found to improve epigastric pain, enhance quality of life, and increase patient satisfaction.[53]

Fenugreek is used for medicinal purposes in various traditions. Some studies have demonstrated that the seeds of this plant may have an anti-diabetic effect by lowering fasting blood sugar levels and improving glucose tolerance.[54, 55] Results from a 2020 paper on clinical trials suggest that fenugreek extract supplement affects serum total testosterone levels in males.[56] A 2020 study on the lipid-lowering effects of fenugreek reported that fenugreek supplementation significantly improved lipid profile (LDL, TG, TC, and HDL). It could be considered an effective lipid-lowering medicinal plant.[57] This was followed by a 2022 study on combining fenugreek and berberine. The combination of berberine and fenugreek seed can improve cardio-metabolic status in patients with diabetes and support the herbs' anti-diabetic and anti-inflammatory role in enhancing the quality of life.[58]

> ***Principle 62:*** Herbs work best in combination with other herbs or plant substances. Many function as "adaptogens," which have no treatment corollary in Western medicine.

Edema and High Blood Pressure: Dandelion to the Rescue

I have known for many years dandelion was good for water retention, kidneys, and liver health. What I did not think about was its benefit to those with high blood pressure, diabetes, and Raynaud, a painful circulatory system syndrome. A paper from 2022 looked at the *European Society of Cardiology* recommendations for a prophylactic strategy, including a varied diet rich in fruits, vegetables, and medicinal plants; all of which are sources of natural compounds with antiplatelet, anticoagulant or antioxidant activities, such as phenolic compounds. Dandelion is one such plant with multidirectional health-promoting effects and a rich source of secondary metabolites, including phenolic compounds (*Taraxacum officinale*).[59] The whole herb may alleviate some symptoms related to GI immuno-

inflammatory issues based on the abundant anti-inflammatory and anti-oxide active substances. Dandelion root could be a nontoxic and effective anticancer alternative owing to its abundant terpenoids and polysaccharides.[60]

Dandelion may be the most efficacious natural treatment available to those with high blood pressure and edema, especially when combined with celery seed. Dandelion herb, revered since earlier times, is one of the most sought-after herbs available that grow wild just about anywhere. Until modern times, this wild green was harvested and fed to young and old alike. For those who are *Outdoor Life* readers, you may remember Patrick MacManus's stories about wild gobo and dandelions. Almost all the plant parts, leaves, flower tops, and roots, can be used for culinary purposes or as a curative remedy for specific medical conditions.[61]

What is so nutritious about this weed?
Its leaves contain carotene-β, carotene-α, lutein, cryptoxanthin, and zeaxanthin. Zeaxanthin has photo-filtering functions and protects the retina from UV rays; perfect for those worried about cataracts and macular degeneration.

Dandelion is a source of potassium, calcium, manganese, iron, and magnesium. Potassium is an essential component of cells and body fluids, which helps regulate heart rate and blood pressure. Iron is essential for red blood cell production. The body uses manganese as a cofactor for the antioxidant enzyme superoxide dismutase. Studies in Russia and Eastern Europe by Gerasimova, Racz, Vogel, and Marei (Hobbs 1985) indicate dandelion is rich in the micronutrients copper, cobalt, zinc, boron, molybdenum, and vitamin D.

The vitamins found in dandelion include folic acid, riboflavin, pyridoxine, niacin, and vitamins E and C. Vitamin C is a powerful natural antioxidant used by your body for various functions. Dandelion greens provide 58% of the daily recommended levels of vitamin C. Dandelion may be the most abundant natural source of vitamin K, proven to be beneficial in preventing osteoporosis. It also has an established role in treating Alzheimer's disease by limiting neuronal damage in the brain.

The diuretic properties of the leaves once prompted the French to give the plant the nickname "piss-le-lit," which means the same thing as its former English nickname "bed-wetter." A potassium-rich food like dandelion, in adequate quantities and particularly in balance with magnesium, helps keep blood pressure down and reduces the risks of strokes. Dandelions as fresh food, herb, tincture, or tea can provide these necessary minerals. While dandelion acts as an effective diuretic, it does not drain the body of essential potassium – it is potassium-rich.[62]

According to the University of Maryland Medical Center, dandelion leaves may treat conditions affecting the liver, kidneys, and gallbladder characterized by fluid retention. Dandelion had a diverse range of therapeutic uses in bygone days, but today's herbalists mainly use it as an appetite stimulant and digestive aid. Some research suggests that it may play a role in improving immune system function and promoting gastrointestinal health.[63, 64]

Dandelion leaves may alleviate the symptoms of arthritis. The root may relieve rheumatism, ailments of the kidneys, the severity of hepatitis (primarily due to its inulin content), gallstones (due to its ability to facilitate the flow of bile), constipation, colitis, enhance liver function, improve blood sugar levels, reduce general inflammation, inhibit the growth of breast cancer cells, and improve blood circulation for those with Raynaud's.[65, 66, 67]

Celery - A Gentle and Effective Herb

I have regularly recommended celery seed tea to individuals with edema and hypertension for several years. This common household herb has impressive benefits for clients with mild hypertension when they use one teaspoon of celery seed to make a cup of tea twice daily. Celery seed tea is perfect in the evenings as it is calming.[68]

The antihypertensive effects of celery seed extract (*Apium graveolens*) with the active ingredient 3-n-butylphthalide were studied in 2022 as a drug supplement for treating hypertension. This study was a randomized, triple-blind, placebo-controlled, cross-over clinical trial. Fifty-two patients were divided into two groups (celery and placebo) and completed the two-step clinical trial. The results were promising and indicated the therapeutic effects of celery seed extract as a supplement in managing hypertension.[69]

An impressive study was released in 2023 on the cognitive effects of celery. Celery could decrease  symptoms of depression, such as sadness, crying, loss of energy, insomnia, irritability, fatigue, loss of interest in sex, and feelings of punishment. The mean reduction in blood pressure parameters was also significant during celery therapy.[70] A paper on the *Beneficial Effects of Celery*, released in 2019, further convinced me of its efficacy. According to various studies, among natural compounds, celery is one of the most essential sources of phytochemicals such as phenolic acids, flavones, flavonols, and antioxidants such as vitamin C, beta-carotene (pro-vitamin A), and manganese. These antioxidants have a role in decreasing oxidative damage. The phytochemicals in celery reduce the activity of pro-inflammatory cytokines and prevent inflammation. Also, flavonoids in celery suppress cardiovascular inflammation. Oxidative stress and inflammation in the bloodstream are the main risk factors for cardiovascular disease, especially atherosclerosis. Celery phthalides lead to expanding smooth muscle in the blood vessels and lower blood pressure.[71]

The commonly overlooked health benefits of celery include it being a healthy source of fiber, about 1.6 grams per cup of raw celery. Minerals are also present, especially in organic and locally grown versions. Celery is rich in essential minerals, including iron, zinc, magnesium, calcium, selenium, and potassium.

Celery seeds contain about 20 anti-inflammatory agents, which can help alleviate pain and discomfort from gout and arthritis.[72] The anti-inflammatory properties in celery seeds can help reduce muscle spasms and cramps, which is especially useful for athletes and women who suffer from menstrual pains.[73] Celery is related to parsley and fennel, another herb known for calming the digestive system. Celery seed has been used as medicine for thousands of years in the Eastern world. During ancient times, Indian Ayurvedic medicine used celery seed to treat colds, flu, water retention, poor digestion, different types of arthritis, and certain liver and spleen diseases.

Caution:
Celery seed renders some medications useless or magnifies their effect. Some of the medicines that you should not take when consuming celery seed include:
- Lithium; celery seed increases levels of this medication.
- Levothyroxine, other thyroid medications.
- Diuretic medications; celery seeds can increase their effects, which may cause dehydration.
- Celery seed should not be taken with aspirin, warfarin, and other blood-thinning medications. This herb contains blood-thinning components, which can heighten the risk of bleeding.

Yarrow

The biological activities of yarrow were reported in PubMed in 2008. The genus *Achillea* comprises about 140 perennial herbs native to the northern hemisphere. Traditional indications for their use include digestive problems, liver and gallbladder conditions, menstrual irregularities, cramps, fever, and wound healing. The European Medicines Agency (EMA) is responsible for compiling and assessing scientific data on herbal substances, preparations and combinations. The EMA approves its internal use for loss of appetite and dyspeptic ailments (gastric catarrh, spastic discomfort) and externally as a sitz bath or as a compress with skin inflammation, slow-healing wounds, and bacterial or fungal infections.[74] Pharmacological studies have become intensive in the last decades, although human clinical investigations are still rare. Recent findings have confirmed several traditional uses; the largest  number of data was accumulated for antioxidant and anti-inflammatory effects. There are positive results on analgesic, anti-ulcer, choleretic, hepatoprotective, and wound healing activities. Initial reports on other interesting therapeutical areas, such as antihypertensive, anti-diabetic, antitumor, and antispermatogenic activities, need confirmation. Yarrow can also be used as an insect repellent.[75, 76, 77, 78]

Hawthorn

Hawthorn (*Crataegus monogyna Jacq.*) is a wild edible fruit tree of the genus *Crataegus*, one of the most interesting genera of the *Rosaceae* family. The pharmaceutical, phytochemical, functional, and therapeutic properties of *C. monogyna* are based on numerous valuable secondary metabolites, including flavonoids, vitamin C, glycoside, anthocyanin, saponin, tannin, and antioxidants.[79, 80]

A 2022 study found that consuming hawthorn preparations has been chiefly associated with  pharmacological benefits for cardiovascular diseases, including congestive heart failure and angina pectoris. Treatment with hawthorn extracts can be related to improvements in the complex pathogenesis of various hepatic and cardiovascular disorders. In this regard, the recent review described that the presence of hawthorn extracts ameliorated hepatic injury, lipid accumulation, inflammation, fibrosis, and cancer in an abundance of experimental models. Hawthorn extracts might have these promising activities, mainly by enhancing the hepatic antioxidant system. In addition, several mechanisms, including AMP-activated protein kinase (AMPK) signaling and apoptosis, are responsible for the role of hawthorn extracts in repairing the dysfunction of injured hepatocytes.[81, 82]

Hawthorn is a tall-growing shrub with white flowers, red berries, and large vicious thorns. Approximately 280 species have been primarily cultivated in East Asia, North America, and Europe. Some believe the thorns were used to weave the crown Christ wore at the crucifixion.[83]

"The use of hawthorn dates back to Dioscorides. Native Americans, Europeans, and Chinese people have long used the hawthorn shrub, including its fruit, leaves, and flowers as a remedy for health problems."[84] The plant gained widespread popularity in European and American herbal medicine only toward the end of the 19th century. Hawthorn preparations remain popular in Europe and have gained some acceptance in the U.S. Hawthorn has been used over the centuries to prevent and treat arrhythmias, heart attack, hypertension, congestive heart disease, stroke, colitis, and diarrhea and to improve oxygen utilization in the heart muscle.

Traditional herbalists report that the protective effects of hawthorn berries, flowers, and leaves are achieved after long-term use. It usually takes one to two months before the effects of hawthorn become noticeable. It can be safely used for long periods without the risk of toxicity or side effects.

Hawthorn fruit can be eaten as food. The fruits are also canned and processed into jam, candy, and drinks. According to Monica Shaw, haws (the berry) "should be picked late in the season (October and November are ideal), when they are as ripe as possible. Although hawthorn berries come off the tree easily, they often bring lots of stems that should be removed before cooking—a slightly time-consuming process. On their own, haw berries aren't anything exciting—they're mostly pip and taste a bit like a dry, under-ripe apple. They need to be cooked to get anything useful out of them."[85, 86, 87]

Note: Hawthorn can interfere with many types of blood pressure medications. Consult a knowledgeable herbalist and let your integrative cardiologist or doctor know you are using hawthorn.

> ***Principle 63:*** Herbal use is gaining popularity in mainstream medicine, largely due to research studies providing evidence of their effectiveness and safety.

Powerful Compound OPC

A natural compound, oligomeric proanthocyanidins (OPC), is a group of potent antioxidant compounds commonly found in grape seed extract. Oligomeric proanthocyanidin complexes are naturally occurring plant metabolites widely available in fruits, vegetables, nuts, seeds, flowers, and bark. OPCs are primarily known for their antioxidant activity. However, these compounds have also demonstrated antibacterial, antiviral, anticarcinogenic, anti-inflammatory, anti-allergic, and vasodilatory actions. In addition, they have been found to inhibit lipid peroxidation, platelet aggregation, capillary permeability and fragility, and to affect enzyme systems, including phospholipase A2, cyclooxygenase, and lipoxygenase.[88] Anthocyanins are water-soluble flavonoids responsible for red, violet, and blue colors in fruits, vegetables, and grains.[89] Anthocyanins also play significant roles in plant propagation, ecophysiology, and plant defense mechanisms.[90] Anthocyanin possesses anticancer activities for various types of cancer, such as breast, liver, lung, prostate, and thyroid cancer. A paper from 2023 reported that cyanidin also optimizes the chemotherapeutic targets, which are cancer cells less responsive to chemotherapy. Cancer is considered the most widely spread disease, and cyanidin, from its natural origin, provides an essential role in treating cancer by approaching various mechanistic pathways.[91, 92]

"The term *proanthocyanidins* is derived as follows: pro = before, anthocyanins = red, referring to their colorless property and ability to be transformed into (red) anthocyanins."[93]

OPCs are highly beneficial in preventing and reversing atherosclerosis by inhibiting the histidine decarboxylase enzyme, which catalyzes the excessive conversion of histidine to histamine pathway that is usually observed in atherosclerosis patients and by inhibiting the oxidation of LDL cholesterol. Additionally, OPC inhibits some aspects of the aging process by enhancing the body's collagen renewal and inhibiting excessive cross-linking. Research has shown that OPCs help heal and prevent gastric ulcers by inhibiting the excessive production of histamine within the gastric mucosa by the histidine decarboxylase enzyme.[94] OPCs also benefit the eyes, brain, and skin. OPCs are found in high levels in some "superfoods."

OPCs found in hawthorn, Concord grapes, and other plants are vital heart and circulatory system nutrients. Once again, modern science is validating what historical herbalists learned via observation and oral tradition; that hawthorn improves the structural integrity of collagen and lowers serum cholesterol.

Immune Support

When we catch a cold due to poor eating habits, stress, long hours, and overindulging, we have worn down our immune systems. This may be one of the reasons so many folks come down with colds following the holiday season. Most of us need to rest and drink lots of fluids.

Medicinal plants represent rich sources of traditional medicines, and numerous currently used medications are either directly or indirectly derived from plants. Every traditional culture possesses a vast pharmacopeia of herbs to help the body fight off foreign invaders. This natural pharmacy has been relegated to the realm of "quacks and oddballs" over the last five decades and replaced with popular

Chapter 12 ~ Herbs to Nourish & Support

designer drugs. But the side effects of these drugs can open up a Pandora's box of health challenges. They also, for the most part, do not cure but merely suppress symptoms. Herbs can help build natural resistance through nutrients, vitamins, phytochemicals, tannins, and many ingredients that we are not even aware of yet.

Viruses do not become resistant to herbs as they do to commonly prescribed medications, many of which are intended for bacterial infections. Herbs strengthen the immune system without killing the beneficial flora in the digestive system. Remember that 85% of your immune system is in your digestive tract. Overuse of antibiotics can lead to side effects from drug-resistant microbes.

My herb of choice for allergies, colds, and congestion is mullein. I am fortunate this herb grows wild on our property along with yarrow. I save the heavy hitter of horehound for more serious lung congestion.

Great Mullein (*Verbascum thapsus L.*), or common mullein, is a medicinal herb indigenous to northern Africa, western and central Asia, and Europe. Mullein was brought to the Americas and to Australia by immigrants. It has been used as a medicine for lung, skin, and throat disorders and has a long history of therapeutic importance, particularly as an astringent and calming agent. Presently, the dried leaves, flowers, various plant extracts, and flower oil are used in several formulations within Indian traditional medicine. An extract taken from the roots is useful in minimizing toothache and relieves stiffness and seizures. *V. thapsus* contains a wide variety of phytoconstituents, such as flavonoids, iridoid, phenylethanoid and phenylpropanoid glycosides, saponins, vitamin C, and minerals. The most valuable constituents are coumarin and hesperidin, which possess healing properties.[95] A 2022 review concluded with the following statement: "Emerging literature based on experimental studies on *V. thapsus* demonstrates various biological and pharmacological properties, including antiviral, antioxidant, analgesic, sedative, anti-inflammatory, hypnotic, antibacterial, antifungal, as well as anticancer activities."[96]

V. sinuatum, commonly known as the scallop-leaved mullein or the wavyleaf mullein, contains bioactive compounds that have several biological activities. These include antioxidant, anticancer, cardiovascular, antimicrobial, antidiabetic, and neuroprotective activities that may be increased by encapsulation since the bioactive compounds extracted from *V. sinuatum* present good potential as functional food ingredients.[97]

Mullein has long been used in herbal medicine, especially in remedies that soothe the respiratory tract.[98] Traditional therapies involve the use of mullein flowers and leaves. In test-tube research, mullein has been found to fight flu-causing viruses.[99]

Horehound

I have a small herb garden in my yard; it consists of those herbs that thrive on abuse. One such herb is horehound. Some of you may be old enough to remember horehound candy drops; others may remember a nasty syrup that you were given as children for chest colds or coughs. I have a recollection of a grandfather who carried horehound drops in his pocket. I thought they were the "cat's meow" as a three-year-old; proof that little kids will believe most anything you tell them.

Horehound is a garden mint with green and white leaves and a distinctively bitter taste. It is native to Asia and Europe but is naturalized in North America. The name may suggest a breed of dog, but that is misleading. "Hore-" does mean hoary (gray or white) in Old English, but "-hound" is not canine; it is merely an old name for the herb. The generic name *Marrubium* is the name by which the Romans knew the herb, and *vulgare* means common.[100, 101] Although the herb grows in a wide range of climates, the best quality is produced in the desert heat. Its primary use has been as an expectorant and is a common ingredient in cough medicines. *Marrubium vulgare* (horehound) and *Prunus serotina* (wild cherry) have been traditionally used to treat inflammatory-related symptoms such as cold, fever, and sore throat. Both horehound and wild cherry extracts cause suppression of cell growth as well as induction of apoptosis. The extracts of horehound leaves and wild cherry bark exhibit anti-inflammatory and anti-proliferative activity in human colorectal cancer cells.[102]

Horehound contains a variety of nutrients that are needed for the immune system to work. Examples include B-complex vitamins, iron, potassium, and vitamins A, C, and E. Horehound primarily acts on your lungs. The late herbalist and naturopath Dr. William Mitchell Jr. noted that horehound is a respiratory stimulant, expectorant, and cough suppressant. It reduces the mucus thickness in your lungs and your bronchial tubes, making it easier to expel the mucus. According to the University of Michigan Health System, because of horehound's ability to loosen bronchial secretions and help expel mucus, this herb may be especially useful in treating bronchitis.

Researchers looked earnestly at herbs such as horehound during the early days of COVID-19; a 2022 study looked at the benefits of use to reduce the compounding complications from the virus. COVID-19 infection can cause lingering complications, even in people with a mild course of the disease. The most dangerous complications seem to be neurological ailments, such as anxiety, depression, mixed anxiety-depressive (MAD) syndromes, and irreversible dementia. These conditions can negatively affect respiratory, circulatory, and heart function. The possibility of reducing post-COVID-19 with phytotherapy is helpful in all of these conditions. Clinical trials confirm the benefits of phytotherapy in lowering the associated neurological, respiratory, and cardiovascular complications, which can affect the functioning of the nervous system.[103]

Natural health care practitioners and some medical doctors prescribe this herbal remedy for a broad range of health problems. The University of Michigan Health System states horehound may be useful for increasing poor appetite, treating coughs, and reducing indigestion by aiding the gallbladder in its function. Other conditions that horehound may help include sinus inflammation, hay fever symptoms, and abdominal swelling. Horehound is also known to increase immune system activity.[104] Horehound has been used to make lozenge candies that are believed to help heal sore throats, improve appetite, and relieve intestinal gas.[105] Horehound is also recorded as one of the "bitter herbs" eaten at Passover.

Horehound is used to make cough medicines for people whose upper respiratory symptoms are caused by acid reflux. The *marubiinic acid* in the herb stimulates the release of phlegm. It stimulates the release of gastric acids so digestion is completed more efficiently and nighttime gastric reflux is minimized. This compound is also mildly analgesic, relieving pain caused by a cough or indigestion.

Caution:
Horehound is useless unless it tastes terrible or at least bitter. The bitter taste activates a reflex action that helps normalize breathing and digestion, and the herb's beneficial effects are not realized if it is combined with too much sugar or another sweetener. Large doses of horehound are contraindicated (not recommended) because it may cause irregular heart rhythms – a condition known as arrhythmia. Do not take horehound if pregnant because it can stimulate uterine contractions. Also, avoid horehound if you have gastritis or peptic ulcer disease, as it can boost the production of stomach acid.[106]

Oregon Grape

For those who live in the Pacific Northwest, especially in the mountainous areas, we are familiar with the holly-like shrub with yellow blossoms and purple berries clusters – Oregon grape (*Mahonia aquifolium*) or also known as mountain grape and holly-leaved barberry. As the name might indicate, it is also the state flower for Oregon.

Berberine is a quaternary ammonia compound found in many botanical products, including goldenseal, barberry, and Oregon grape, which is used for its purported antioxidant and antimicrobial properties for a host of conditions, including obesity, diabetes, hyperlipidemia, heart failure, H. pylori infection, and colonic adenoma prevention. Berberine has not been linked to serum aminotransferase elevations during therapy nor to clinically apparent liver injury.[107] Preliminary clinical evidence suggests the ability of berberine to reduce endothelial inflammation improving vascular health, even in patients already affected by cardiovascular diseases.[108] The golden yellow stems and roots, rich in berberine and equal to turmeric, are where the medicinal qualities are highest and the portion most commonly harvested by wildcrafters and herbalists. The root is traditionally prepared in one of two methods - either steeping the root to create a tea or using the root to make a tincture.

This prickly shrub has a long history as a medicinal plant and food source in Indians of North American. Oregon grapes have been used for skin ailments, herpes, acne, hepatitis, upper respiratory congestion, STIs, arthritis, fever, gallbladder conditions, and liver and eye ailments. According to WebMD, Oregon grape is used for stomach ulcers, gastroesophageal reflux disease (GERD), and stomach upset as a bitter tonic to treat infections and cleanse the bowels.[109, 110]

Oregon grape root is renowned among herbalists for its ability to stimulate liver function, improve bile flow, and for blood cleansing. It contains many alkaloids, and because of this – it has a very bitter taste – Oregon grape root can take some getting used to if taken straight. Taste aside, the positive benefits of these alkaloids far outweigh the brief discomfort and bitter taste. In China, where Oregon grape root is substituted for the herb coptis, studies have shown one of the alkaloids the plant contains, berbamine, can help strengthen bone marrow and assist chemotherapy and radiation patients in their recovery; not bad for a little shrub grown in the Pacific Northwest.

According to traditional and modern herbal sources, the bitterness of Oregon grape also has a positive effect on the digestive tract. This herb has a sedative effect on the smooth muscles lining the digestive tract and stimulates the flow of bile, which loosens waste in the gut and helps prevent constipation, stomach cramps, diverticulosis, hemorrhoids, gallbladder disease, and irritable bowel syndrome.[111, 112, 113]

Native American healers will use the stem of the tall Oregon grape over the root of the dwarf variety. When berberine content is checked with a chromatograph, we see the wisdom of this practice. The stem contains a slightly higher berberine level and is less labor-intensive to prepare. With dwarf plants, digging, washing, and pealing are involved with the preparation of the herb. The use of stems from the tall Oregon grapes allows for one plant to provide decades of berberine collection without killing the plant.

While the medicinal qualities of the berries do not match that of the bark, they do, however, make a wonderful jelly. The berries are used to make jelly, wine, and juice. However, Oregon grape berries are quite tart, and blending them with sweeter salal and huckleberries is customary. Deep blue berries are usually ripe from July to September. In the same way that fine wine carries complex flavors, Oregon grape is earthy and rich with undertones of cherry, raspberry, and lemon. This wild food makes purple grape jelly pale in comparison. We always look forward to cornbread from a cast-iron skillet slathered with Kerrygold butter and a generous dollop of Oregon grape jelly.

Note to reader: The herbs contained in this chapter are only a fraction of what has been used throughout human history as medicine. Additional information on culinary herbs is contained in the Culinary Herbs & Spices section of *Our Journey with Food Cookery Book,* pages 67-80 and *Empty Plate: Food~Sustainability~Mindfulness,* page 50.

> ***Principle 64:*** Herbs strengthen the immune system; pathogens do not develop resistance to them, and they do not damage beneficial gut flora.

---

1 Sureshkumar, J., Jenipher, C., Sriramavaratharajan, V., Gurav, S. S., Gandhi, G. R., Ravichandran, K., & Ayyanar, M. (2023). Genus Equisetum L: Taxonomy, toxicology, phytochemistry and pharmacology. Journal of ethnopharmacology, 314, 116630. https://doi.org/10.1016/j.jep.2023.116630

2 Chen, F. P., Chang, C. M., Hwang, S. J., Chen, Y. C., & Chen, F. J. (2014). Chinese herbal prescriptions for osteoarthritis in Taiwan: analysis of National Health Insurance dataset. BMC complementary and alternative medicine, 14, 91. https://doi.org/10.1186/1472-6882-14-91

3 Gilling, D. H., Kitajima, M., Torrey, J. R., & Bright, K. R. (2014). Antiviral efficacy and mechanisms of action of oregano essential oil and its primary component carvacrol against murine norovirus. Journal of applied microbiology, 116(5), 1149–1163. https://doi.org/10.1111/jam.12453

4 Sharifi-Rad, M., Varoni, E. M., Iriti, M., Martorell, M., Setzer, W. N., Del Mar Contreras, M., Salehi, B., Soltani-Nejad, A., Rajabi, S., Tajbakhsh, M., & Sharifi-Rad, J. (2018). Carvacrol and human health: A comprehensive review. Phytotherapy research : PTR, 32(9), 1675–1687. https://doi.org/10.1002/ptr.6103

5 Zhang, Y., Liu, X., Ruan, J., Zhuang, X., Zhang, X., & Li, Z. (2020). Phytochemicals of garlic: Promising candidates for cancer therapy. Biomedicine & pharmacotherapy = Biomedecine & pharmacotherapie, 123, 109730. https://doi.org/10.1016/j.biopha.2019.109730

6 Rouf, R., Uddin, S. J., Sarker, D. K., Islam, M. T., Ali, E. S., Shilpi, J. A., Nahar, L., Tiralongo, E., & Sarker, S. D. (2020). Antiviral potential of garlic (Allium sativum) and its organosulfur compounds: A systematic update of pre-clinical and clinical data. Trends in food science & technology, 104, 219–234. https://doi.org/10.1016/j.tifs.2020.08.006

7 Liang, C., Hui, N., Liu, Y., Qiao, G., Li, J., Tian, L., Ju, X., Jia, M., Liu, H., Cao, W., Yu, P., Li, H., & Ren, X. (2021). Insights into forsythia honeysuckle (Lianhuaqingwen) capsules: A Chinese herbal medicine repurposed for COVID-19 pandemic. Phytomedicine plus : international journal of phytotherapy and phytopharmacology, 1(2), 100027. https://doi.org/10.1016/j.phyplu.2021.100027

8 Chen, Y., Zhang, C., Wang, N., & Feng, Y. (2023). Deciphering suppressive effects of Lianhua Qingwen Capsule on COVID-19 and synergistic effects of its major botanical drug pairs. Chinese journal of natural medicines, 21(5), 383–400. https://doi.org/10.1016/S1875-5364(23)60455-8

9 Whitelegg M. (2003). Goethean science: an alternative approach. Journal of alternative and complementary medicine (New York, N.Y.), 9(2), 311–320. https://doi.org/10.1089/10755530360623428

10 Niemeyer, K., Bell, I. R., & Koithan, M. (2013). Traditional Knowledge of Western Herbal Medicine and Complex Systems Science. Journal of herbal medicine, 3(3), 112–119. https://doi.org/10.1016/j.hermed.2013.03.001

11 Kellogg, J. J., Paine, M. F., McCune, J. S., Oberlies, N. H., & Cech, N. B. (2019). Selection and characterization of botanical natural products for research studies: a NaPDI center recommended approach. Natural product reports, 36(8), 1196–1221. https://doi.org/10.1039/c8np00065d

12 Sharma, H., & Keith Wallace, R. (2020). Ayurveda and Epigenetics. Medicina (Kaunas, Lithuania), 56(12), 687. https://doi.org/10.3390/medicina56120687

13 Boswellia Serrata. (2020). In LiverTox: Clinical and Research Information on Drug-Induced Liver Injury. National Institute of Diabetes and Digestive and Kidney Diseases.

14 Siddiqui M. Z. (2011). Boswellia serrata, a potential antiinflammatory agent: an overview. Indian journal of pharmaceutical sciences, 73(3), 255–261. https://doi.org/10.4103/0250-474X.93507

15 Mirshafiei, M., Yazdi, A., & Beheshti, S. (2023). Neuroprotective and anti-neuroinflammatory activity of frankincense in bile duct ligaion-induced hepatic encephalopathy. Iranian journal of basic medical sciences, 26(8), 966–971. https://doi.org/10.22038/IJBMS.2023.68775.14991

16 Mohsenzadeh, A., Karimifar, M., Soltani, R., & Hajhashemi, V. (2023). Evaluation of the effectiveness of topical oily solution containing frankincense extract in the treatment of knee osteoarthritis: a randomized, double-blind, placebo-controlled clinical trial. BMC research notes, 16(1), 28. https://doi.org/10.1186/s13104-023-06291-5

17 Karlapudi, V., Sunkara, K. B., Konda, P. R., Sarma, K. V., & Rokkam, M. P. (2023). Efficacy and Safety of Aflapin®, a Novel Boswellia Serrata Extract, in the Treatment of Osteoarthritis of the Knee: A Short-Term 30-Day Randomized, Double-Blind, Placebo-Controlled Clinical Study. Journal of the American Nutrition Association, 42(2), 159–168. https://doi.org/10.1080/07315724.2021.2014370

18 Italiano, G., Raimondo, M., Giannetti, G., & Gargiulo, A. (2020). Benefits of a Food Supplement Containing Boswellia serrata and Bromelain for Improving the Quality of Life in Patients with Osteoarthritis: A Pilot Study. Journal of alternative and complementary medicine (New York, N.Y.), 26(2), 123–129. https://doi.org/10.1089/acm.2019.0258

19 Zapata, A., & Fernández-Parra, R. (2023). Management of Osteoarthritis and Joint Support Using Feed Supplements: A Scoping Review of Undenatured Type II Collagen and Boswellia serrata. Animals : an open access journal from MDPI, 13(5), 870. https://doi.org/10.3390/ani13050870

20 Karaboga Arslan, A. K., Uzunhisarcıklı, E., Yerer, M. B., & Bishayee, A. (2022). The golden spice curcumin in cancer: A perspective on finalized clinical trials during the last 10 years. Journal of cancer research and therapeutics, 18(1), 19–26. https://doi.org/10.4103/jcrt.JCRT_1017_20

21 Washington State University. (2019, June 20). Timed release of turmeric stops cancer cell growth. ScienceDaily. Retrieved July 26, 2023 from www.sciencedaily.com/releases/2019/06/190620121404.htm

22 Sharma H. (2016). Ayurveda: Science of life, genetics, and epigenetics. Ayu, 37(2), 87–91. https://doi.org/10.4103/ayu.AYU_220_16

23 University of South Australia. (2020, March 5). Curcumin is the spice of life when delivered via tiny nanoparticles: Treatment for Alzheimer's and genital herpes. ScienceDaily. Retrieved July 26, 2023 from www.sciencedaily.com/releases/2020/03/200305132144.htm

24 University of California- Los Angeles. "Curcumin improves memory and mood: Twice-daily supplements boosted cognitive power over 18 months." ScienceDaily. ScienceDaily, 23 January 2018. www.sciencedaily.com/releases/2018/01/180123101908.htm.

25 Microbiology Society. (2020, July 17). Turmeric could have antiviral properties. ScienceDaily. Retrieved July 26, 2023 from www.sciencedaily.com/releases/2020/07/200717120154.htm

26 Hay, E., Lucariello, A., Contieri, M., Esposito, T., De Luca, A., Guerra, G., & Perna, A. (2019). Therapeutic effects of turmeric in several diseases: An overview. Chemico-biological interactions, 310, 108729. https://doi.org/10.1016/j.cbi.2019.108729

27 Flis, Z., & Molik, E. (2021). Importance of Bioactive Substances in Sheep's Milk in Human Health. International journal of molecular sciences, 22(9), 4364. https://doi.org/10.3390/ijms22094364
28 Gatzias, I. S., Karabagias, I. K., Kontakos, S. P., Kontominas, M. G., & Badeka, A. V. (2018). Characterization and differentiation of sheep's milk from Greek breeds based on physicochemical parameters, fatty acid composition and volatile profile. Journal of the science of food and agriculture, 98(10), 3935–3942. https://doi.org/10.1002/jsfa.8914
29 MacPherson, H., Vertosick, E. A., Foster, N. E., Lewith, G., Linde, K., Sherman, K. J., Witt, C. M., Vickers, A. J., & Acupuncture Trialists' Collaboration (2017). The persistence of the effects of acupuncture after a course of treatment: a meta-analysis of patients with chronic pain. Pain, 158(5), 784–793. https://doi.org/10.1097/j.pain.0000000000000747
30 Vickers, A. J., Vertosick, E. A., Lewith, G., MacPherson, H., Foster, N. E., Sherman, K. J., Irnich, D., Witt, C. M., Linde, K., & Acupuncture Trialists' Collaboration (2018). Acupuncture for Chronic Pain: Update of an Individual Patient Data Meta-Analysis. The journal of pain, 19(5), 455–474. https://doi.org/10.1016/j.jpain.2017.11.005
31 Hübner, J., Keinki, C., & Büntzel, J. (2023). Komplementäre und alternative Medizin – eine Option bei chronischen Schmerzpatienten? [Complementary and alternative medicine-An option for chronic pain patients?]. Schmerz (Berlin, Germany), 37(3), 215–227. https://doi.org/10.1007/s00482-023-00719-4
32 Yeh, C. H., Chang, W. L., Chan, P. C., Mou, C. H., Chang, K. S., Hsu, C. Y., Tsay, S. L., Tsai, M. T., Hsu, M. H., & Sung, F. C. (2021). Women With Osteoarthritis Are at Increased Risk of Ischemic Stroke: A Population-Based Cohort Study. Journal of epidemiology, 31(12), 628–634. https://doi.org/10.2188/jea.JE20200042
33 Ying, D., Gianfrancesco, M. A., Trupin, L., Yazdany, J., Greidinger, E. L., & Schmajuk, G. (2020). Increased Risk of Ischemic Stroke in Systemic Sclerosis: A National Cohort Study of US Veterans. The Journal of rheumatology, 47(1), 82–88. https://doi.org/10.3899/jrheum.181311
34 Krijthe BP, Heeringa J, Hofman A, et alNon-steroidal anti-inflammatory drugs and the risk of atrial fibrillation: a population-based follow-up studyBMJ Open 2014;4:e004059. doi: 10.1136/bmjopen-2013-004059
35 Phu, H. T., Thuan, D. T. B., Nguyen, T. H. D., Posadino, A. M., Eid, A. H., & Pintus, G. (2020). Herbal Medicine for Slowing Aging and Aging-associated Conditions: Efficacy, Mechanisms and Safety. Current vascular pharmacology, 18(4), 369–393. https://doi.org/10.2174/1570161117666190715121939
36 Phu, H. T., Thuan, D. T. B., Nguyen, T. H. D., Posadino, A. M., Eid, A. H., & Pintus, G. (2020). Herbal Medicine for Slowing Aging and Aging-associated Conditions: Efficacy, Mechanisms and Safety. Current vascular pharmacology, 18(4), 369–393. https://doi.org/10.2174/1570161117666190715121939
37 Szczuko, M., Kikut, J., Szczuko, U., Szydłowska, I., Nawrocka-Rutkowska, J., Ziętek, M., Verbanac, D., & Saso, L. (2021). Nutrition Strategy and Life Style in Polycystic Ovary Syndrome-Narrative Review. Nutrients, 13(7), 2452. https://doi.org/10.3390/nu13072452
38 Tolmie, M., Bester, M. J., Serem, J. C., Nell, M., & Apostolides, Z. (2023). The potential antidiabetic properties of green and purple tea [Camellia sinensis (L.) O Kuntze], purple tea ellagitannins, and urolithins. Journal of ethnopharmacology, 309, 116377. https://doi.org/10.1016/j.jep.2023.116377
39 Zhao, T., Li, C., Wang, S., & Song, X. (2022). Green Tea (Camellia sinensis): A Review of Its Phytochemistry, Pharmacology, and Toxicology. Molecules (Basel, Switzerland), 27(12), 3909. https://doi.org/10.3390/molecules27123909
40 Pavlović, M. O., Stajić, M., Gašić, U., Duletić-Laušević, S., & Ćilerdžić, J. (2023). The chemical profiling and assessment of antioxidative, antidiabetic and antineurodegenerative potential of Kombucha fermented Camellia sinensis, Coffea arabica and Ganoderma lucidum extracts. Food & function, 14(1), 262–276. https://doi.org/10.1039/d2fo02979k
41 de Oliveira, J. R., Camargo, S. E. A., & de Oliveira, L. D. (2019). Rosmarinus officinalis L. (rosemary) as therapeutic and prophylactic agent. Journal of biomedical science, 26(1), 5. https://doi.org/10.1186/s12929-019-0499-8
42 Allegra, A., Tonacci, A., Pioggia, G., Musolino, C., & Gangemi, S. (2020). Anticancer Activity of Rosmarinus officinalis L.: Mechanisms of Action and Therapeutic Potentials. Nutrients, 12(6), 1739. https://doi.org/10.3390/nu12061739
43 Gutiérrez-Grijalva, E. P., Leyva-López, N., Vazquez-Olivo, G., & Heredia, J. B. (2022). Oregano as a potential source of antidiabetic agents. Journal of food biochemistry, 46(12), e14388. https://doi.org/10.1111/jfbc.14388
44 Odeyemi, S., & Bradley, G. (2018). Medicinal Plants Used for the Traditional Management of Diabetes in the Eastern Cape, South Africa: Pharmacology and Toxicology. Molecules (Basel, Switzerland), 23(11), 2759. https://doi.org/10.3390/molecules23112759
45 Perez Gutierrez R. M. (2012). Inhibition of Advanced Glycation End-Product Formation by Origanum majorana L. In Vitro and in Streptozotocin-Induced Diabetic Rats. Evidence-based complementary and alternative medicine : eCAM, 2012, 598638. https://doi.org/10.1155/2012/598638
46 Mammari, N., Albert, Q., Devocelle, M., Kenda, M., Kočevar Glavač, N., Sollner Dolenc, M., Mercolini, L., Tóth, J., Milan, N., Czigle, S., Varbanov, M., & On Behalf Of The Oemonom (2023). Natural Products for the Prevention and Treatment of Common Cold and Viral Respiratory Infections. Pharmaceuticals (Basel, Switzerland), 16(5), 662. https://doi.org/10.3390/ph16050662
47 Hacioglu, M., Oyardi, O., & Kirinti, A. (2021). Oregano essential oil inhibits Candida spp. biofilms. Zeitschrift fur Naturforschung. C, Journal of biosciences, 76(11-12), 443–450. https://doi.org/10.1515/znc-2021-0002
48 Takamura, T., Misu, H., Yamashita, T., & Kaneko, S. (2008). SAGE application in the study of diabetes. Current pharmaceutical biotechnology, 9(5), 392–399. https://doi.org/10.2174/138920108785915184

49 Granado, M., González-Hedström, D., Amor, S., Fajardo-Vidal, A., Villalva, M., de la Fuente-Fernández, M., Tejera-Muñoz, A., Jaime, L., Santoyo, S., & García-Villalón, A. L. (2022). Marjoram extract prevents ischemia reperfusion-induced myocardial damage and exerts anti-contractile effects in aorta segments of male wistar rats. Journal of ethnopharmacology, 282, 114660. https://doi.org/10.1016/j.jep.2021.114660

50 Foeniculum vulgare Mill: A Review of Its Botany, Phytochemistry, Pharmacology, Contemporary Application, and Toxicology; Biomed Res Int. 2014; 2014: 842674. Published online 2014 Aug 3. doi: 10.1155/2014/842674

51 Fennel. (2023). In Drugs and Lactation Database (LactMed®). National Institute of Child Health and Human Development.

52 Lee, H. W., Ang, L., Kim, E., & Lee, M. S. (2021). Fennel (Foeniculum vulgare Miller) for the management of menopausal women's health: A systematic review and meta-analysis. Complementary therapies in clinical practice, 43, 101360. https://doi.org/10.1016/j.ctcp.2021.101360

53 Zhang, Y. Y., Wang, S. T., Long, X. H., Wei, L. H., Pang, C., Guan, Q., & Li, Q. Y. (2022). Traditional Chinese Nursing Using Fennel With Coarse Salt for Ironing and Umbilical Moxibustion for Epigastric Pain With Spleen-stomach Vacuity Cold. Alternative therapies in health and medicine, 28(7), 88–94.

54 Shabil, M., Bushi, G., Bodige, P. K., Maradi, P. S., Patra, B. P., Padhi, B. K., & Khubchandani, J. (2023). Effect of Fenugreek on Hyperglycemia: A Systematic Review and Meta-Analysis. Medicina (Kaunas, Lithuania), 59(2), 248. https://doi.org/10.3390/medicina59020248

55 Correia, A. G. D. S., Alencar, M. B., Dos Santos, A. N., da Paixão, D. C. B., Sandes, F. L. F., Andrade, B., Castro, Y., & de Andrade, J. S. (2023). Effect of saffron and fenugreek on lowering blood glucose: A systematic review with meta-analysis. Phytotherapy research : PTR, 37(5), 2092–2101. https://doi.org/10.1002/ptr.7817

56 Mansoori, A., Hosseini, S., Zilaee, M., Hormoznejad, R., & Fathi, M. (2020). Effect of fenugreek extract supplement on testosterone levels in male: A meta-analysis of clinical trials. Phytotherapy research : PTR, 34(7), 1550–1555. https://doi.org/10.1002/ptr.6627

57 Heshmat-Ghahdarijani, K., Mashayekhiasl, N., Amerizadeh, A., Teimouri Jervekani, Z., & Sadeghi, M. (2020). Effect of fenugreek consumption on serum lipid profile: A systematic review and meta-analysis. Phytotherapy research : PTR, 34(9), 2230–2245. https://doi.org/10.1002/ptr.6690

58 Nematollahi, S., Pishdad, G. R., Zakerkish, M., Namjoyan, F., Ahmadi Angali, K., & Borazjani, F. (2022). The effect of berberine and fenugreek seed co-supplementation on inflammatory factor, lipid and glycemic profile in patients with type 2 diabetes mellitus: a double-blind controlled randomized clinical trial. Diabetology & metabolic syndrome, 14(1), 120. https://doi.org/10.1186/s13098-022-00888-9

59 Olas B. (2022). New Perspectives on the Effect of Dandelion, Its Food Products and Other Preparations on the Cardiovascular System and Its Diseases. Nutrients, 14(7), 1350. https://doi.org/10.3390/nu14071350

60 Li, Y., Chen, Y., & Sun-Waterhouse, D. (2022). The potential of dandelion in the fight against gastrointestinal diseases: A review. Journal of ethnopharmacology, 293, 115272. https://doi.org/10.1016/j.jep.2022.115272

61 http://www.nutrition-and-you.com/dandelion-herb.html

62 Chen, P., Chen, Y., Yan, Z. Q., Ding, S. Y., Liu, H. P., Tu, J. Q., & Zhang, X. W. (2022). Protective Effect of the Polysaccharides from Taraxacum mongolicum Leaf by Modulating the p53 Signaling Pathway in H22 Tumor-Bearing Mice. Foods (Basel, Switzerland), 11(21), 3340. https://doi.org/10.3390/foods11213340

63 http://www.herbcompanion.com/herbal-living/the-health-benefits-of-dandelions.aspx

64 Li, P., Shen, J., Wang, Z., Liu, S., Liu, Q., Li, Y., He, C., & Xiao, P. (2021). Genus Paeonia: A comprehensive review on traditional uses, phytochemistry, pharmacological activities, clinical application, and toxicology. Journal of ethnopharmacology, 269, 113708. https://doi.org/10.1016/j.jep.2020.113708

65 In-Tele-Health © 2009 (from Hyperhealth Pro CD-ROM)

66 Chen, P., Ding, S., Yan, Z., Liu, H., Tu, J., Chen, Y., & Zhang, X. (2022). Structural Characteristic and In-Vitro Anticancer Activities of Dandelion Leaf Polysaccharides from Pressurized Hot Water Extraction. Nutrients, 15(1), 80. https://doi.org/10.3390/nu15010080

67 http://www.leaflady.org/health_benefits_of_dandelions.htm

68 Mosby's Handbook of Herbs and Natural Supplements, 3rd edition by Linda Skidmore-Roth pp 256-260

69 Shayani Rad, M., Moohebati, M., & Mohajeri, S. A. (2022). Effect of celery (Apium graveolens) seed extract on hypertension: A randomized, triple-blind, placebo-controlled, cross-over, clinical trial. Phytotherapy research : PTR, 36(7), 2889–2907. https://doi.org/10.1002/ptr.7469

70 Shayani Rad, M., Moohebati, M., & Mohajeri, S. A. (2023). Beneficial effects of celery seed extract (Apium graveolens), as a supplement, on anxiety and depression in hypertensive patients: a randomized clinical trial. Inflammopharmacology, 31(1), 395–410. https://doi.org/10.1007/s10787-022-01083-y

71 Hedayati, N., Bemani Naeini, M., Mohammadinejad, A., & Mohajeri, S. A. (2019). Beneficial effects of celery (Apium graveolens) on metabolic syndrome: A review of the existing evidences. Phytotherapy research : PTR, 33(12), 3040–3053. https://doi.org/10.1002/ptr.6492

72 Pioneer Thinking- http://pioneerthinking.com/natural-gout-pain-relief-with-celery-seeds

73 Healthy Living – Herbs- https://healthyliving-herbs.co.za/celery/

74. Yarrow flower, Achillea millefolium L., flos 2020: https://www.ema.europa.eu/en/documents/herbal-summary/yarrow-flower-summary-public_en.pdf
75. Albahri, G., Badran, A., Hijazi, A., Daou, A., Baydoun, E., Nasser, M., & Merah, O. (2023). The Therapeutic Wound Healing Bioactivities of Various Medicinal Plants. Life (Basel, Switzerland), 13(2), 317. https://doi.org/10.3390/life13020317
76. Isopencu, G. O., Covaliu-Mierlă, C. I., & Deleanu, I. M. (2023). From Plants to Wound Dressing and Transdermal Delivery of Bioactive Compounds. Plants (Basel, Switzerland), 12(14), 2661. https://doi.org/10.3390/plants12142661
77. Mouhid, L., Gómez de Cedrón, M., García-Carrascosa, E., Reglero, G., Fornari, T., & Ramírez de Molina, A. (2019). Yarrow supercritical extract exerts antitumoral properties by targeting lipid metabolism in pancreatic cancer. PloS one, 14(3), e0214294. https://doi.org/10.1371/journal.pone.0214294
78. Mouhid, L., Gómez de Cedrón, M., Quijada-Freire, A., Fernández-Marcos, P. J., Reglero, G., Fornari, T., & Ramírez de Molina, A. (2019). Yarrow Supercritical Extract Ameliorates the Metabolic Stress in a Model of Obesity Induced by High-Fat Diet. Nutrients, 12(1), 72. https://doi.org/10.3390/nu12010072
79. Martinelli, F., Perrone, A., Yousefi, S., Papini, A., Castiglione, S., Guarino, F., Cicatelli, A., Aelaei, M., Arad, N., Gholami, M., & Salami, S. A. (2021). Botanical, Phytochemical, Anti-Microbial and Pharmacological Characteristics of Hawthorn (Crataegus monogyna Jacq.), Rosaceae. Molecules (Basel, Switzerland), 26(23), 7266. https://doi.org/10.3390/molecules26237266
80. Shaito, A., Thuan, D. T. B., Phu, H. T., Nguyen, T. H. D., Hasan, H., Halabi, S., Abdelhady, S., Nasrallah, G. K., Eid, A. H., & Pintus, G. (2020). Herbal Medicine for Cardiovascular Diseases: Efficacy, Mechanisms, and Safety. Frontiers in pharmacology, 11, 422. https://doi.org/10.3389/fphar.2020.00422
81. Kim, E., Jang, E., & Lee, J. H. (2022). Potential Roles and Key Mechanisms of Hawthorn Extract against Various Liver Diseases. Nutrients, 14(4), 867. https://doi.org/10.3390/nu14040867
82. Sun, Y. S., Wang, Z. W., Gao, Z., Zhao, W., Thakur, K., Zhong, Q., & Wei, Z. J. (2022). Proanthocyanidin oligomers extract from hawthorn mediates cell cycle arrest, apoptosis, and lysosome vacuolation on HCT116 cells. Current research in food science, 5, 904–917. https://doi.org/10.1016/j.crfs.2022.05.009
83. Natural-Medicinal-Herbs.com/herbs/hawthorn.htm, 2015
84. webmd.com/vitamins-and-supplements/hawthorn-uses-and-risks, 2015
85. www.antiagingdoctor.co.za
86. www.sensitivefoods.com/opcgeneraloverview.html
87. www.greatbritishchefs.com
88. de la Iglesia, R., Milagro, F. I., Campión, J., Boqué, N., & Martínez, J. A. (2010). Healthy properties of proanthocyanidins. BioFactors (Oxford, England), 36(3), 159–168. https://doi.org/10.1002/biof.79
89. Francavilla, A., & Joye, I. J. (2020). Anthocyanins in Whole Grain Cereals and Their Potential Effect on Health. Nutrients, 12(10), 2922. https://doi.org/10.3390/nu12102922
90. Alappat, B., & Alappat, J. (2020). Anthocyanin Pigments: Beyond Aesthetics. Molecules (Basel, Switzerland), 25(23), 5500. https://doi.org/10.3390/molecules25235500
91. Safdar, M. A., Aslam, R. M. N., Shakeel, A., Shiza, Waqar, M., Jmail, A., Mehmood, M. H., & Gul, H. (2023). Cyanidin as potential anticancer agent targeting various proliferative pathways. Chemical biology & drug design, 101(2), 438–452. https://doi.org/10.1111/cbdd.14173
92. Franco-San Sebastián, D., Alaniz-Monreal, S., Rabadán-Chávez, G., Vázquez-Manjarrez, N., Hernández-Ortega, M., & Gutiérrez-Salmeán, G. (2023). Anthocyanins: Potential Therapeutic Approaches towards Obesity and Diabetes Mellitus Type 2. Molecules (Basel, Switzerland), 28(3), 1237. https://doi.org/10.3390/molecules28031237
93. General Health Benefits of OPC Pycnogenol Super AntiOxidant ... (n.d.). Retrieved from http://www.allergydiets.com/opcgeneraloverview.html_br
94. Fine A. M. (2000). Oligomeric proanthocyanidin complexes: history, structure, and phytopharmaceutical applications. Alternative medicine review : a journal of clinical therapeutic, 5(2), 144–151.
95. Mahdavi, S., Amiradalat, M., Babashpour, M., Sheikhlooei, H., & Miransari, M. (2020). The Antioxidant, Anticarcinogenic and Antimicrobial Properties of Verbascum thapsus L. Medicinal chemistry (Shariqah (United Arab Emirates)), 16(7), 991–995. https://doi.org/10.2174/1573406415666190828155951
96. Gupta, A., Atkinson, A. N., Pandey, A. K., & Bishayee, A. (2022). Health-promoting and disease-mitigating potential of Verbascum thapsus L. (common mullein): A review. Phytotherapy research : PTR, 36(4), 1507–1522. https://doi.org/10.1002/ptr.7393
97. Donn, P., Barciela, P., Perez-Vazquez, A., Cassani, L., Simal-Gandara, J., & Prieto, M. A. (2023). Bioactive Compounds of Verbascum sinuatum L.: Health Benefits and Potential as New Ingredients for Industrial Applications. Biomolecules, 13(3), 427. https://doi.org/10.3390/biom13030427
98. https://www.herb-pharm.com/products/product-detail/mullein-blend
99. Garcia-Oliveira, P., Carreira-Casais, A., Pereira, E., Dias, M. I., Pereira, C., Calhelha, R. C., Stojković, D., Sokovic, M., Simal-Gandara, J., Prieto, M. A., Caleja, C., & Barros, L. (2022). From Tradition to Health: Chemical and Bioactive Characterization of Five Traditional Plants. Molecules (Basel, Switzerland), 27(19), 6495. https://doi.org/10.3390/molecules27196495

Chapter 12 ~ Herbs to Nourish & Support

100 Milani, F., Bottoni, M., Bardelli, L., Colombo, L., Colombo, P. S., Bruschi, P., Giuliani, C., & Fico, G. (2023). Remnants from the Past: From an 18th Century Manuscript to 21st Century Ethnobotany in Valle Imagna (Bergamo, Italy). Plants (Basel, Switzerland), 12(14), 2748. https://doi.org/10.3390/plants12142748

101 http://www.herbcompanion.com/Herb-Profiles/HERB-To-KNOW-Horehound.aspx#ixzz20v65NGEf

102 Yamaguchi, K., Liggett, J. L., Kim, N. C., & Baek, S. J. (2006). Anti-proliferative effect of horehound leaf and wild cherry bark extracts on human colorectal cancer cells. Oncology reports, 15(1), 275–281.

103 Nawrot, J., Gornowicz-Porowska, J., Budzianowski, J., Nowak, G., Schroeder, G., & Kurczewska, J. (2022). Medicinal Herbs in the Relief of Neurological, Cardiovascular, and Respiratory Symptoms after COVID-19 Infection A Literature Review. Cells, 11(12), 1897. https://doi.org/10.3390/cells11121897

104 http://www.livestrong.com/article/368945-what-are-the-benefits-of-the-horehound-herb/#ixzz20v3d5Uls

105 http://www.livestrong.com/article/368945-what-are-the-benefits-of-the-horehound-herb/#ixzz20v2MeWC7

106 http://www.mountainroseherbs.com/learn/horehound.php

107 Berberine. (2020). In LiverTox: Clinical and Research Information on Drug-Induced Liver Injury. National Institute of Diabetes and Digestive and Kidney Diseases.

108 Cicero, A. F., & Baggioni, A. (2016). Berberine and Its Role in Chronic Disease. Advances in experimental medicine and biology, 928, 27–45. https://doi.org/10.1007/978-3-319-41334-1_2

109 Cardiovascular Effects of Berberine: A Review of the Literature, Journal of Restorative Medicine, Volume 6, Number 1, 6 December 2017, pp. 37-45(9); https://restorativemedicine.org/journal/cardiovascular-effects-berberine/?utm_source=AARM&utm_campaign=4f788e0112-EMAIL_CAMPAIGN_2018_01_26&utm_medium=email&utm_term=0_5b926a06ea-4f788e0112-71776041

110 https://www.mountainroseherbs.com/learn/oregon_graperoot.php

111 Mosby's Handbook of Herbs & Natural Supplements 3rd edition by Linda Skidmore-Roth pp789-793

112 Pacific Northwest Foraging by Douglas Deur, Timber Press pp 38-39, 147-148

113 Plants of the Pacific Northwest Coast by Pojar and Mackinnon, Lone Pine Press pp 95

> "Food safety oversight is largely, but not exclusively, divided between two agencies, the FDA and the USDA. The USDA mostly oversees meat and poultry; the FDA mostly handles everything else, including pet food and animal feed. Although this division of responsibility means that the FDA is responsible for 80% of the food supply, it only gets 20% of the federal budget for this purpose. In contrast, the USDA gets 80% of the budget for 20% of the foods. This uneven distribution is the result of a little history and a lot of politics."
>
> ~ Marion Nestle, *Pet Food Politics*: *The Chihuahua in the Coal Mine*

Chapter Thirteen ~
When Food Becomes the Enemy

In 2015, when I first wrote a newspaper article on food becoming the enemy, it was inspired by clients with debilitating chronic digestive system conditions. These illnesses are Crohn's, celiac, ulcerative colitis, IBS, eating disorders and complications of gastric bypass. In 2023, these conditions are still in my thoughts, but no longer carrying the specter of *food as the enemy* – today, *pathogens* are unseen, smelled, or tasted enemies, in my opinion. I'm going out on a limb, but not a flimsy one when I say there is compelling research supporting pathogens as the root cause of autoimmune and inflammatory digestive diseases.[1, 2]

The Centers for Disease Control in the United States lists on their website the following:

- the CDC estimates that each year, 48 million people get sick from a foodborne illness,
- 128,000 are hospitalized, and 3,000 die

The compelling documentary *Poisoned: The Dirty Truth About Your Food* (2023) brought to my attention how regulatory agencies and food-producing sectors are *slowly and reluctantly* seeking solutions to food-borne pathogens in the United States. However, the methods used by food manufacturers and approved by the USDA and FDA may result in even further damage to human health through toxic chemicals, antibacterials and biotechnology. We will look more at *Forever Chemicals* in Chapter 14.

Foodborne Pathogens

The World Health Organization, on their website, lists the following as "key facts."[3]

- Food safety, nutrition and food security are inextricably linked.
- An estimated 600 million – almost 1 in 10 people in the world – fall ill after eating contaminated food and 420 000 die yearly, resulting in the loss of 33 million healthy life years (DALYs).
- In low- and middle-income countries, US$ 110 billion is lost yearly in productivity and medical expenses resulting from unsafe food.
- Children under five carry 40% of the foodborne disease burden, with 125,000 deaths yearly.

Salmonella, Campylobacter, and enterohaemorrhagic *Escherichia coli* are the most common foodborne pathogens.

- Foods involved in outbreaks of *salmonellosis* include eggs, poultry and other products of animal origin.
- *Campylobacter* is mainly caused by raw milk, raw or undercooked poultry and drinking water.
- Enterohaemorrhagic *Escherichia coli* is associated with unpasteurized milk, undercooked meat and contaminated fresh fruits and vegetables.
- *Listeria* infections can lead to miscarriage in pregnant women or death of newborn babies. Although disease occurrence is relatively low, Listeria's severe and sometimes fatal health consequences, particularly among infants, children, and the elderly, count them among the most severe foodborne infections. Listeria is found in unpasteurized dairy products and various ready-to-eat foods and can grow at refrigeration temperatures.
- *Vibrio cholerae* can infect people through contaminated water or food. Rice, vegetables, millet gruel and various types of seafood have been implicated in cholera outbreaks.

Following the *Jack in the Box* fatal food-born pathogen outbreak (*E. coli O157:H7*) in *1992-1993* and the subsequent policy changes enacted by the *2010-2011 FDA Food Safety Modernization Act*; the incidence of *E. coli* contaminated ground beef has dropped to almost zero. In the United States, the most significant pathogen contamination concern, according to the CDC website in 2023, is bagged salads, strawberries, Romain lettuce, containers of chopped mixed melon, whole cantaloupe melon, spinach, peanuts, and raw almonds. Whole and cut-up chicken is the leading source of *Salmonella* contamination from meat.

- *Salmonella* can cause salmonellosis and, typhoid fever and paratyphoid fever.
- *Botulism* is most often caused by *Clostridium botulinum*.
- Some other germs that cause foodborne illness include Cryptosporidium, Cyclospora, hepatitis A virus, Shigella, and Yersinia.

A study review from 2016 states: "Foodborne pathogens, mostly bacteria and fungi, but also some viruses, prions and protozoa, contaminate food during production and processing, and during storage and transport before consuming. These microorganisms can secrete different components, including toxins, into the extracellular environment during their growth. Other harmful substances can also be liberated and can contaminate food after disintegration of food pathogens. Some bacterial and fungal toxins can be resistant to inactivation and can survive harsh treatment during food processing." [4]

The contamination of fresh produce by pathogenic Enterobacteriaceae strains remains a major challenge and is responsible for frequent foodborne disease outbreaks. The use of antibiotics has proved an effective treatment, but the increase in occurrences of antibiotic resistance is becoming a health challenge. A 2022 study on *Incidence of Drug-Resistant Enterobacteriaceae Strains in Organic and Conventional Watermelons Grown in Tennessee* found the following:

> "Watermelons used for this study were cultivated at the Tennessee State University Certified Organic Farm, Nashville. At harvest, nine fruits were selected from among fruits lying on plastic mulch and nine from fruits lying on the soil of both organic and conventional plots. These were placed in sterile sample bags for microbial analysis. Seventeen *Enterobacteriaceae* strains were isolated and identified. Isolates were susceptible to gentamycin, ciprofloxacin, and chloramphenicol, but were resistant to cefoxitin. *Citrobacter freundii* showed a 14.3% resistance to Streptomycin. *Pantoea spp.* and *Providencia rettigeri* showed 50% and 100% resistance to tetracycline. Findings from this study confirm the presence of antibiotic-resistant *Enterobacteriaceae* strains on organic watermelons in Nashville, TN." [5]

Contamination in Nuts and Alternative Milk Products

According to a study from 2018, "Nuts and grains can be contaminated with foodborne pathogens at any stage during production, processing, storage, and distribution. Focusing on preharvest contamination, the various potential sources of contamination include soil, animal intrusion, contaminated harvesting equipment, harvest and preharvest handling, storage conditions, and others. The low water activity of nuts and grains prevents the growth of most foodborne pathogens on their surfaces. The long-term survival of bacterial foodborne pathogens (Salmonella, Escherichia coli O157:H7, and Listeria monocytogenes) on dry foods has been documented in the literature for different nut types." [6]

The growing use of milk alternatives also comes with foodborne illness risks. When researchers in 2021 analyzed 138 extracts from almonds, cashews, and soya beans, 31% contained multiple pathogens. The findings of this study suggest that milk alternatives, though considered healthy, may be a reservoir of multidrug-resistant opportunist pathogens. [7]

Adding some perspective

For most of my life, I have been involved with food from the ground up, in one way or another. As a child, it was fowl, lamb, swine, cattle and the meat, eggs and fresh milk they provided. As a teen, it was 4-H and more poultry production, and as an adult, gardening and food preservation filled our pantry shelves. Those who were mentors or teachers always shared words of caution on the dangers of botulism, salmonella and the importance of food safety. Don't eat the deviled eggs or potato salad at the potluck, watch out for undercooked meats, and wash your hands. While this was all important, it also had roots in the 1950s and 1960s sterilizing everything campaigns that lead to extremism. In 1987, the U.S. Food and Drug Administration (FDA) outlawed interstate raw milk sales. It established the *Pasteurized Milk*

Ordinance (PMO) after years of study, public testimony, and a petition from a citizen health group led by Ralph Nader. The agency determined unpasteurized milk too hazardous for a warning label since the risks were unrelated to misuse. Only an outright ban could protect public health, a federal judge ruled. For decades the US government firmly maintained that only pasteurization—the process of heating milk to over 161 degrees Fahrenheit to kill pathogens, including Campylobacter, E. coli, and Salmonella—makes milk safe for human consumption.

As with all trends, the pendulum swings to and fro. By 2000, raw milk was returned for consumer use in some areas of the United States. In areas where raw milk was illegal to sell, individuals located underground sources or purchased shares in a milk cow. A decade later, farmer's markets and farm-to-table became popular. Then, government agencies began cracking down again on availability in California and Pennsylvania. Even with media coverage and increased raids on raw milk sellers, by 2019, raw milk production was seen as the salvation of traditional small-farm dairy despite being hotly contested. By 2023, patio gardens, garden by the square foot and buy organic and chemical-free campaign trends were sweeping through large and small communities. Farmer's markets are popular avenues for acquiring a wide range of locally produced foods, including goat and bovine raw dairy. Raw milk is used for fermented artisanal cheese, yogurt, and kiefer, and raw milk production has once more come out into local whole food and coop markets.

Based on evidence-based-scientific, the Weston Price Foundation "believes that raw milk is an important component of a healthy diet. To assist its members and the public in obtaining raw milk, the Foundation publishes a list of farms that produce it because this information is not otherwise readily and comprehensively available to consumers. Listing a farm does not imply endorsement by the Foundation. Individuals who purchase raw milk and other natural foods for themselves and their families need to "know their farmer" because they are responsible for ensuring that they are getting safe and healthy products."[8]

Buy local, buy organic became a grassroots movement in 2007. By 2023, most of the contaminated food does not come from local vendors, markets, or producers – it is from mega organic companies owned by General Mills, Cargill, Pepsi, Coke and Bayer/Monsanto. With wholesale large production, quality control and pride in the product diminish. Local farmers wouldn't dream of using confined industrial animal effluent runoff for watering and fertilizing their crops – because they know better than most that the conditions in intensive stockyards are a breeding ground for pathogens. In the 1930s, my great-grandfather and his sons were awarded the water works contract for Jerome, Shoshone and Gooding counties in Idaho. As a child visiting, there was never a concern over water quality. Then, in 2017, I saw a marked increase in industrial dairy farms moving into the area, followed by warnings of dangerous water contamination from animal runoff. It isn't just the contaminated water; the air is almost unbreathable some days. There is NO WAY I would buy or serve milk or butter made in the Jerome Creamery, where my grandmother worked in the 1960s. <u>Sick animals equal sick soil and food crops</u>; it isn't rocket science to see the connection between pathogens spread from animal to lettuce when intensive livestock pens are right next to food crops and the irrigation water is runoff from the dairy feedlot.

More on the Microbiome

> "Kids who play in dirt face exposure to germs and parasites that can help reduce risks of suffering certain allergies and illnesses later in life. Researchers say that early microbial exposures help our bodies learn how to regulate inflammation."[9]
>
> July 2017 ~Northwestern University.

In 2010, using data from a long-running study in Cebu, Philippines, Thom McDade and fellow Northwestern anthropologist Chris Kuzawa published the first-ever research showing that babies surrounded by germs grow up to have lower levels of inflammation in later life. Inflammation is a frequent indicator of trouble at our body's cellular level. Studies like McDade and Kuzawa's link inflammation to increased risk for various diseases, from asthma to dementia. Exposure to germs, especially in early life, educates our immune system and helps it regulate inflammation more effectively.

> "The developing immune system is similar to the brain," McDade says. "No one questions that a baby needs exposure to language to drive the neurological processes that underlie the development of speech. The immune system is similar; its development is driven by environmental exposure. In this case, the key exposures are microbial. Without those exposures, it doesn't work quite right."[10]

> In 2021, studies were published on children in rural areas having greater microbiome diversity. A study published in 2020 on the *Gut Microbiome in Children from Indigenous and Urban Communities* concluded: "The depletion of microbial diversity can be associated with a broad range of inflammatory diseases, such as allergies, asthma, inflammatory bowel disease, obesity, and associated non-communicable diseases. Gut microbiota is also driven by other factors contrasting the two communities explored, such as sanitation, social behavior, climate, type of birth, breastfeeding, parental care, etc. We are just beginning to describe and understand the microbiota in traditional populations worldwide, introducing new perspectives regarding what constitutes a "good" microbiome for human health."

> ***Principle 65:*** To be healthy, humans need clean food, water, air, natural light, and a safe living environment.

Bread is not the "Staff of Life"

Clients don't generally want to accept that they may have a health challenge that could mean giving up bread, pasta, baked goods, and pizza. Many of us believe bread to be the staff of life. After all, the ancient Egyptians, Greeks, and Romans cultivated wheat. My great Aunt Amy's bread would have been made with local hard winter wheat, milk, yeast, sorghum, or white sugar from beets. Her biscuits and hot cakes would have come from the same flour tin. In the early 20th century wheat sensitivities were known and nursing texts contained dietary guidelines, in the 1940s-1980s, celiac disease was known but not commonly discussed in texts. In my cookbooks and nursing texts from the 19th and early 20th centuries, foods for the patient with digestive disorders from wheat were far ahead of us today, in their understanding of food sensitivities resulting in digestive illnesses.

The incidence of celiac disease has increased an average of 7.5% per year over the past five decades, with the incidence highest in females and children.

In the spring of 2010, I was introduced to Tom O'Bryan, DC, CCN, DACBN, and his compelling information on gluten sensitivity. I also poured through mountains of medical journal research supporting gluten as a leading cause of inflammation, cognitive decline and autoimmune illnesses. The information I learned has been invaluable, but is also complex and an emotional subject for many.

If I had known, then...

Donna (1951-2011), Tammera and Dwain (1952-2012) in 1964

In the late 1970s, my older sister was diagnosed with Type 1 diabetes. This surprised her and our mother because there was no family history of diabetes, and my sister was in her late twenties. Wasn't type 1 diabetes a childhood condition? As it turns out, autoimmune diseases such as type 1 diabetes can be activated when individuals are under intense stress, such as the death of a child, end of a marriage or an Epstein-bar virus infection. For my sister, this was very much the case.

"A unique finding from this study is that the seven autoimmune disorders: SLE, multiple sclerosis, rheumatoid arthritis, juvenile idiopathic arthritis, inflammatory bowel disease, celiac disease, and type 1 diabetes, share a common set of abnormal transcription factors – and each is affected by the Epstein-bar (EBNA2) protein".[11]

Similar EBNA2-anchored associations exist in multiple sclerosis, rheumatoid arthritis (RA), inflammatory bowel disease, type 1 diabetes (T1D), juvenile idiopathic arthritis, Hashimoto's thyroiditis (HT), and celiac disease.[12] Viruses are opportunistic during heightened moments of stress when the immune system is at its lowest, which can result in multiple autoimmune conditions manifesting.

In my sister's case, by the time she was 35 years old, she had three autoimmune conditions (RA, HT, T1D), impacting her ability to work and fully participate in life.[13] By 2009, I had learned individuals with autoimmune diseases benefit from a gluten-free diet. Unfortunately, my sister had developed neuropathy affecting

WHAT ARE THE LONG-TERM EFFECTS OF UNTREATED CELIAC DISEASE?

Celiac disease can develop at any age after people start consuming gluten. Left untreated, celiac disease can lead to additional serious health problems, including:

- → Delayed puberty
- → Early onset osteoporosis or osteopenia
- → Heart disease
- → Hyposplenism
- → Infertility and miscarriage
- → Iron deficiency anemia
- → Lactose intolerance
- → Liver failure
- → Malnutrition
- → Neurological symptoms, including attention-deficit/hyperactivity disorder (ADHD), headaches, lack of muscle coordination and seizures
- → Short stature
- → Small intestine cancer and non-Hodgkin lymphoma

Compared to the general population, celiac disease tends to be more common in people who have:

- → A family member with celiac disease or dermatitis herpetiformis (itchy, blistering skin disease)
- → IgA deficiency
- → Liver disease
- → Microscopic colitis
- → Sjogren's syndrome

https://celiac.org/main/wp-content/uploads/2022/05/General-Brochure-2022.pdf

the vagus nerve, which controls the digestive system.[14] Food was almost impossible for her to eat. And when she could, she was unwilling to give up the pleasures of fresh bread or pasta. The connection between gluten and autoimmune conditions was not fully understood in the 1980s – and if we had known then, dietary changes could have added to quality longevity for Donna.

Undiagnosed Celiac Disease

The prevalence of undiagnosed celiac disease dramatically increased in the US in the early 21st century, with an estimated 80% of people undiagnosed celiac disease in 2009.[15] CD clinical presentations can vary widely, and each manifestation has its characteristics.[16] Gluten proteins are immunological triggers for inflammation, resulting in mucosal lesions in celiac disease (CD) patients. Adherence to a strict gluten-free diet (GFD) is currently the only effective treatment for CD.[17]

A 2023 study on mucosal recovery in celiac patients confirmed the opinion of Dr. O'Bryan and others working with celiac clients. The paper titled *Predictors of slow responsiveness and partial mucosal recovery in adult patients with Celiac Disease* looked at 102 patients. Two-thirds were females, with a median age of 39 years. The initial biopsy analysis showed different stages of villous atrophy (VA) in 79 (77.4%) cases, while 23 (22.5%) subjects showed mild enteropathy. After at least 12 months of a gluten-free diet, 26 (25.5%) patients had persistent VA despite good or excellent adherence to a gluten-free diet. Younger patients (< 35 yrs) who showed severe mucosal damage and had increased anti-gliadin antibody levels were at risk for failure to recover mucosal.[18]

- 30-40% of the general population carries the two genes associated with celiac disease.[19]
- 3% of individuals with celiac-associated genes develop celiac disease.[20]

> ***Principle 66:*** *The incidence of gluten sensitivity is increasing in the United States. It is a hereditary condition that is a delayed allergic reaction to proteins found in many cereal grains.*

What is gluten and what foods contain it?

The proteins found in grains within the wheat family have toxic effects on the brain and body. Celiac disease, also called non-tropical sprue and gluten-sensitive enteropathy, is a hereditary condition in which a person has a delayed allergic reaction to gluten (a protein that causes the dough to be sticky) found in cereals such as oats, wheat, barley, and rye.

Gluten is a dietary protein, a mixture of two proteins (the prolamine *gliadin* and the dietary protein *glutenin*) found in some cereal grains. The gliadin content of gluten is responsible for most of the toxic effects of gluten.

Gliadin is a type of prolamine—one of 35 found in wheat. These proteins create inflammation and gut permeability; as gluten proteins wear away the fine brushes called villi, the immune system sends out armies called leukocytes to drive away invaders. Over time, the immune system's response to gluten erodes cells and tissues in the digestive tract, brain, liver, bones, pancreas, heart, and thyroid glands. The gut wall begins, allowing partially digested foods to enter the bloodstream.

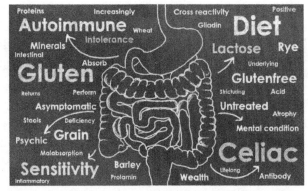

It is not unusual for clients with wheat and gluten sensitivities to become sensitive to the whole grass family, including corn, oat, and rice, over time. The grass family has over 19 polypeptides that can affect individuals with Leaky Gut and celiac disease.[21, 22] This is why individuals with wheat and gluten sensitivities, including celiac, need to rotate grains and use care with pseudo-grains.[23]

Here is a short list of the most common gluten-containing food ingredients:

Barley, bulgur, cereal binding, couscous, durum, einkorn, emmer, filler, farro, Graham flour, Kamut, malt, malt extract, malt flavoring, malt syrup, oat bran, oats, oat syrup, rye, semolina, spelt, triticale, wheat, wheat bran, wheat germ, wheat starch, hydrolyzed plant or vegetable protein (HPP/HVP), seasonings, flavorings, turkeys (may be injected with gluten for moistness or have gravy packets), starch, modified food starch, dextrin and maltodextrin.

Gluten can be found in thousands of everyday items, including shampoo, gum, chocolate milk, fruit fillings, commercial soups, beer, lunch meats, syrups, soy sauce, ketchup, barbeque sauce, ice cream, non-dairy creamer and potato chips.

Why can someone be on a strict gluten-free diet and continue to have problems? This is a question I have been asked many times. The answer to this involves two areas.

    a. Often, clients are on medications to slow transit time, reduce inflammation, or suppress the immune system. They may also be on any number of other medicines. All or part of these medications and nutritional support supplements are common sources of micro-contamination of gluten. Gluten is a common filler in medications, vitamins, and mineral supplements.

    Additionally, body care products, including toothpaste, can contain trace amounts of gluten. Based on the individual, the levels of gluten that can trigger them may be well below the guidelines. (As one of the criteria for using the claim "gluten-free," the FDA set a limit of less than 20 ppm (parts per million) for the unavoidable presence of gluten in foods that carry this label.)[24] This was the case for two of my clients, who had to call companies for information regularly due to micro traces of gluten resulting in hospitalization. Contrary to what some clinicians and the FDA. This statement from the FDA is deeply concerning: "Most people with celiac disease can tolerate foods with very small amounts of gluten."

    b. Many clinicians and resources for celiac do not cover information on the importance of nutritional supplements for gut health and repair. If too frequently, it is a foregone conclusion by providers that if a celiac client continues to have challenges and worsens, it is because they have cheated on their diet. The reality is that key nutrients must be replaced for remission and healing. While this approach will not cure celiac or other auto-immune diseases, it facilitates long-term remission and quality of life, reducing risks of serious secondary conditions.

Note: Gluten and lactose are the most common fillers for medications

Rest, Recover, and Restore your digestive system

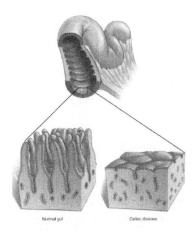

https://www.mayoclinic.org/-/media/kcms/gbs/patient-consumer/images/2013/08/26/10/49/ds00319_im04515_mcdc7_celiac_diseasethu_jpg.jpg

Merely going gluten-free will not be enough to repair the damage done to the small intestine's villi. A study from 2011 revealed that once damaged by gluten, the small intestine develops a host of harmful bacteria such as streptococcus, *neisseria, veillonella, gemellia, actinomyces, rothia*, and *haemophillus*.[25, 26] Additionally, researchers have found over 35 sequences of new bacteria in gluten-sensitive patients' biopsies. Some feel these mutations or new bacteria result from genetically modified grains and the herbicides their cells have interfaced with. Resting the digestive system from processed and industrial food-like substances and giving the microbiome time to reset is key to healing.

Green Smoothy: Swap one meal or snack for a green juice or smoothy made from low oxalate foods, which provides vital nutrients, sugars and anti-inflammatory compounds. The polyphenols, fibers and nutrients in smoothies boost the severely damaged microbiome.

Bone Broths: Bone broths contain amino acids, essential fats, vitamins, trace minerals, and collagen. All of these are necessary for GI health and support the microbiome.

Intermittent Fasting: Another way to rest your digestive system is to employ intermittent fasting, but don't go over-the-top crazy with fasting.

Limit Foods: Processed meat, dairy products, processed seed oil, all grains, carbonated sodas, alcohol, beans and lentils are hard to digest and should be avoided as much as possible during the healing process.

Vitamin D plays a protective role in the gastrointestinal tract. Researchers say, "Vitamin D protects the gut barrier by regulating tight junction proteins." Tight junctions allow for nutrients from food to enter the bloodstream and feed the rest of the body.[27]

B Complex: Another essential vitamin lacking in people with celiac disease is Vitamin B_{12}. Research suggests that 41% of celiac disease patients have a Vitamin B_{12} deficiency.[28]

Probiotics: There are several quality probiotic products specially formulated for celiac clients. The use of probiotics to repopulate a damaged gut, especially if someone has celiac disease, gluten sensitivity, autoimmune disease, or any chronic condition, is necessary for the microbiome to gain resiliency.

Omega-3 fatty acid supplement or Omega 9 from evening primrose or borage oil.[29] Fish oil is widely associated with lower levels of inflammation. However, a growing number of individuals do not do the conversion from Omega 3 to non-essential Omegas efficiently. This can result in increased inflammation.[30] If you have challenges with quality fish oil (increased bruising, rapid heart rate, indigestion, body ach), use a non-essential fatty acid product from borage or evening primrose instead. [31,32]

Antioxidants: There is a wide selection of quality antioxidants that reduce inflammation and support the microbiome. I prefer clients to include foods high in these compounds over a supplement.

Zinc: The Mayo Clinic researchers also found that nearly 60% of newly diagnosed celiac disease patients were zinc deficient. Zinc came back into awareness during COVID-19 due to its role in supporting the immune system and healing. [33]

L Glutamine: Gastrointestinal mucosa is lined with multifunctional, rapidly proliferating epithelial cells. They form a primary interface between luminal contents and the interstitial tissue. These cells depend on both luminal and systemic sources for their nutrition and are affected by intra and extra-luminal nutrient intake. During an average lifetime, 60 tons of food pass through the gastrointestinal tract, posing a continuous threat to the integrity of the gastrointestinal tract and the whole body. Oral Glutamine supplementation supports gastrointestinal mucosal growth and prevents mucosal and villous atrophy. [34, 35]

Celiac Disease

Gluten sensitivity is relatively common in Ireland, Northern Europe, and Italy. Gluten intolerance has a hereditary component; 1 in 3 Americans of Northern European descent may have gluten sensitivity. This devastating autoimmune condition is regularly featured in the *Journal of American Medicine*, the *American Journal of Hematology* and the *New England Journal of Medicine*.

In a 2003 study published in the *Wake Forest University School of Medicine's Pediatric Gastroenterology and Nutrition*, 1,200 individuals were studied. The conclusion states, "Celiac disease is not rare in the United States and may be as common as in Europe."

An increased rate of malignancies (cancer) is associated with celiac disease. The rates decline to normal levels after five years on a gluten-free therapeutic diet. The earlier the diagnosis and the sooner a patient can commence a gluten-free diet, the fewer autoimmune-type diseases the patient will acquire.

A 2004 study from the *Maribor General Hospital Department of Pediatrics* reported, "The prevalence of celiac disease among first-degree relatives (children) is much higher than that in the general population. Most of these patients have an atypical form of the disease and would, therefore, be overlooked without an

WHAT IS CELIAC DISEASE?

Celiac disease is a genetic autoimmune disorder in which the ingestion of gluten leads to serious damage in the small intestine. Gluten is a combination of proteins found in wheat, barley, rye, and triticale. Celiac disease is estimated to affect 1 in 100 people worldwide. The majority of Americans are undiagnosed and at risk for long-term health complications.

Celiac disease is hereditary, meaning that it runs in families. People with a first-degree relative with celiac disease (parent, child, sibling) have a 1 in 10 risk of developing celiac disease themselves.

1 in 100 — 1 IN 100 WORLDWIDE HAVE CELIAC DISEASE

active search. Malignancy may be the first manifestation of subclinical (silent) celiac disease." A retrospective study of Mayo Clinic data found that 44% of screened first-degree relatives had celiac disease. Of those patients, 94% had symptoms that were not classic or had no symptoms at all.[36]

According to the *Division of Gastroenterology, Department of Internal Medicine, American University of Beirut,* "The prevalence of celiac disease in Middle Eastern and North African countries among low-risk populations is like that of Western countries but is higher in high-risk populations such as those with type 1 diabetes. Clinical presentations regarding gastrointestinal, hematologic, skeletal and liver manifestations are similar between both populations except for a high prevalence of short stature in some Middle Eastern and North African countries." Among adults with type 1 diabetes, celiac disease is ten times more prevalent than in the general population. It is widespread in children with type 1 diabetes. [37]

In 2010, the *Department of Neurology, Päijät-Häme Central Hospital* in Lahti, Finland, reported on a study involving "381 elderly persons positive for gluten antibodies and confirmed a celiac diagnosis. Rheumatoid arthritis and depression were found significantly more often in the subjects with positive tests than in control subjects. The significance remained even when known celiac disease cases were excluded.

> ***Principle 67:*** The brain is the body's "central computer" controlling all chemical responses, and it lives on sugar. 6% of the glucose converted from food goes to support brain functioning.

DO YOU HAVE CELIAC DISEASE?

Common symptoms in adults include, but are not limited to:

- Abdominal pain
- Bloating and gas
- Cognitive impairment
- Constipation
- Diarrhea
- Depression and anxiety
- Fatigue
- Headaches or migraines
- Iron-deficiency anemia
- Itchy, blistery skin rash (dermatitis herpetiformis)
- Joint pain
- Missed periods
- Mouth ulcers and canker sores
- Nausea and vomiting
- Osteoporosis and osteomalacia
- Peripheral neuropathy
- Reduced functioning of the spleen (hyposplenism)
- Weight loss

DOES YOUR CHILD HAVE CELIAC DISEASE?

Common symptoms in children include, but are not limited to:

- Abdominal bloating and pain
- Anxiety and depression
- Attention-deficit/hyperactivity disorder (ADHD) and learning disabilities
- Chronic diarrhea
- Constipation
- Damage to tooth enamel
- Delayed puberty
- Failure to thrive
- Fatigue
- Gas
- Headaches
- Iron-deficiency anemia
- Irritability
- Nausea and vomiting
- Pale, foul-smelling stools
- Seizures and lack of muscle coordination
- Short stature
- Weight loss

https://celiac.org/main/wp-content/uploads/2022/05/General-Brochure-2022.pdf

Paradigm Shift – Food is My Friend

Whenever we are told to stop eating certain foods, our automatic response is to resist because we are being asked to deprive ourselves. Our necks stiffen, and we dig in our heels, insistent that the problem isn't a food or lifestyle choice.

Eliminating potentially harmful foods like wheat, corn, and soy should not be a matter of deprivation and denial; instead, this is an opportunity to embrace traditional and life-building foods rather than genetically modified and commercialized versions.

Bread and baked goods can be made from alternative grains, and there are many creative ways to go gluten-free. Instead of a sandwich, try cheese slices with fruit and rice crackers or steak strips with gluten-free macaroni salad, tabouli, or fresh veggies—snack on hummus and organic non-GMO corn chips. Soups, chilies, and stews are always an excellent choice, and many cold soups are very satisfying in the warmer months.

Fermented Beverages for those Gluten Sensitive.

Beer, wine, and fermented drinks have been enjoyed for thousands of years. They were first created to address contaminated water supplies. Unpasteurized versions contain

Fleischmann's Yeast ad Ladies Home Journal October 1920

friendly bacteria that aid in digestion. There are many good beers made from rice and sorghum available. Wine and hard liquors are gluten-free.

The earliest consumption of fermented drinks dates to neolithic African tribesmen who sought out the liquid from tree hollows where honeybee hives had been flooded from the seasonal rain. Beers, wines, and distilled spirits allowed for a safe and efficient water treatment, protecting people from E. coli, Giardia, and dysentery. The alcohol content of these early beverages was lower than many of today's augmented blends, where grain alcohol is used to bring alcohol levels up so that young wines, beers, and spirits can be sold sooner. Gluten-Free fermented beers and ales may be safe for some to use, however low gluten products are still not an option for individuals with celiac.

> ***Principle 68*** : Make the time to enjoy your food, feel gratitude, and savor the flavor; dump the guilt, anxiety and fear associated with food. These "feelings" are as destructive as toxic chemicals.

Oats to the Rescue

Oats (*avena sativa*), whether rolled or steel cut, are considered a whole grain because all three parts of the grain are present and preserved during the milling process. The seed portion of the oat plant (the groat), rolled, quick-cook, instant, oat flour and oat bran all come from the grass (*Gramineae*) family.

Oats were one of the earliest cultivated grains, believed to have originated in Eurasia and consumed in China before 7000 B.C. The ancient Greeks were the first documented people to have made porridge from oats. The English considered oats an inferior grain, while Ireland and Scotland considered it a staple and used it in many forms for baking and porridge. The British Quakers (thus the name Quaker Oats®) brought oats to America in the 1600s for cultivation.

Nutrient-packed oats contain vitamin E, B vitamins, calcium, magnesium, potassium, copper, zinc, iron, manganese, phytochemicals, and soluble and insoluble fibers. All these nutrients in their combined natural state led to many health benefits.

Oats contain proteins called *avenin* and *gliadin*. Research is showing that non-contaminated oats may be safe for many celiac patients. An article by the Irish gastroenterologist William Dickey in the European Journal of Gastroenterology and Hepatology supports the idea that most people with celiac disease can tolerate pure oats and that only in rare cases do pure oats elicit an adverse reaction. Dickey notes that contamination of commercially viable oats is the cause of most negative reactions in people with celiac disease.

A study in Spain measured wheat and barley contamination levels of oats from Europe, the United States, and Canada. Results showed that 25 of the 134 samples contained no detectable gluten contamination levels. The other 109 samples showed wheat, barley and/or rye contamination. The results also showed that contamination levels vary among oats from the same source.[38]

Most concern about oats stems from mills that process oats and handle gluten-containing grains, creating a substantial risk for cross-contact. Oats without a gluten-free label are not considered safe for those with celiac disease.

Specialty gluten-free oats are grown, harvested, and processed to keep them away from other grains and the high risk of gluten contact, and are widely accepted as safe for those with celiac disease.

Avenin Sensitivity

Even though oats are naturally gluten-free, a small portion of people with celiac disease still react to them. Research suggests that a protein in oats called *avenin* can trigger a similar response to gluten, though it is considered a separate sensitivity. The symptoms can be like those with celiac disease, but the intestines have no damage.

Oat milks is a popular alternative to traditional dairy milks. They are made by soaking oats in water, blending them, and then straining the liquid. Whether or not oat milk is gluten-free depends on the oats used to make it. Read the food label to ensure it's marked gluten-free before drinking oat milk.[39]

However, if you have an avenin sensitivity, you should not eat oats; avoid oat milk, too. Researchers know of just three confirmed cases of active celiac disease flaring up in adults after ingesting oats, which indicates that intolerance to oats may be rare. Clinical monitoring of celiac disease patients who eat oats is still recommended, as damage may result even if no symptoms appear.

What if it isn't Gluten?

It is currently estimated that one-third of Americans are going gluten-free. But what if, for those with non-celiac gluten sensitivity (NCGS), it isn't the gluten driving up inflammation markers but something else? What if it's the Nightshade family or Sugar? The reasons why some respond favorably to gluten-free programs while others do not are still not fully understood.

Fructans may be one factor. This group belongs to a diverse family of carbohydrates that are notorious for being difficult to digest. A failure to absorb these compounds into the blood may draw excess water into the digestive tract and agitate its resident bacteria. Wheat proteins known as amylase-trypsin inhibitors stimulate immune cells to release inflammatory cytokines that overexcite the immune system. Wheat is one of the foods that are high in fructans.[40]

A gluten-free or wheat-free diet will not necessarily solve the inflammatory puzzle because these carbohydrates are found in many foods—not just grains. One of the types of dietary fiber high in fructans is inulin. Inulin, in its refined form, is found in a broad range of food products including refined wheat flour, sugar, and oils. Inulin is a starchy substance found in a wide variety of fruits, vegetables, grains, and herbs, including wheat, rye, barley, spelt, kamut, brown rice, onions, bananas, leeks, artichoke, beets and asparagus.

The type of inulin that is used for medicine is most obtained by soaking chicory roots in hot water. Inulin is used for high blood fats, including cholesterol and triglycerides, and for weight loss and constipation. It is used as a food additive to improve taste and in gluten-free foods to improve texture. Could this be why some individuals on a gluten-free diet experience no improvement in symptoms? Researchers are finding a higher number of individuals exhibiting carbohydrate digestion failure; for example, up to 40% of people with Crohn's disease do not absorb carbohydrates properly.[41]

A study released in 2014 reported that intake of sugar-sweetened soda is associated with an increased risk of rheumatoid arthritis (RA) in women. The Centers for Disease Control and Prevention (CDC) estimate that 1.5 million American adults have RA; 2.5 times more women are affected than men. The subjects from the Nurses' Health Study (1980-2008) and the Nurses' Health Study II (1991-2009) completed a food frequency questionnaire regarding sugar-sweetened soda consumption (including regular cola, caffeine-free cola, and other sugar-sweetened carbonated soda) at the beginning of the study and every four years during the follow-up period. Researchers found that women who consumed one or more servings of sugar-sweetened soda daily had a highly significant (63%) increased risk of developing seropositive RA compared to those who drank none or less than one serving per month. When the researchers evaluated the subjects who had onset of RA after age 55, they found that the association was even more significant, with a 164% increased risk of developing seropositive RA.[42]

<u>Consider</u> the source of the sweetener and its highly refined fructose content as a contributing factor. If you do not digest carbohydrates well, you may need to eliminate high-fructan foods and supplement with digestive enzymes. Even if gluten is not the issue, wheat still may be an inflammation trigger.

List of high fructose foods and low fructose alternatives that may be effective during the "elimination phase."

Category	Low fructose alternatives	High fructose foods
Fruits	Avocado, cranberries, lime, lemon cantaloupe, pineapple, strawberries, mandarin orange, bananas.	All fruits not on the allowed list, especially juices, dried fruits (such as prunes, raisins or dates) and fruits canned in juice or syrup.
Vegetables	Bamboo shoots, beets, bok choy, carrots, celery, chives, green pepper, kale, parsnip, plum tomato, radish, rhubarb, spinach, sweet potato, turnip greens, white potato, winter squash. Allowed vegetables that are more likely to give you gas: Brussels sprouts, cabbage, cauliflower, lettuce.	Artichoke, asparagus, broccoli, chutney, leeks, mushrooms, okra, onions, peas, red pepper, shallots, tomato paste, tomato products (canned tomatoes, ketchup).
Grains and Cereals	Buckwheat flour, corn chips, cornmeal, corn tortillas, gluten-free breads, crackers and pastas without added HFCS, grits, oatmeal, popcorn without HFCS, quinoa, rice, rye breads without added HFCS, soba noodles and all other flours made from allowed grains.	Foods with wheat as a major ingredient (wheat bread, pasta, couscous), grains with added dried fruit, grains with added HFCS.
Meats	Plain unprocessed meats of any type (beef, chicken, fish, eggs, etc.) Legumes, tofu (note that these tend to be more gas-forming and may need to be avoided), nut butters that do not contain HFCS.	Marinated or processed meats containing restricted ingredients.
Dairy Products	Milk, cheese, yogurt, soy milk, rice milk, almond milk without added HFCS.	Any product with HFCS. Be especially careful with yogurts and flavored milks.

Type 2 Diabetes: possibly the most preventable illness

I remember when Dr. C. Everett Koop (1916-2013) became Surgeon General for the United States in 1981. I was 18, newly married and could vote for the first time. Everything was new and exciting, so when Dr. Koop, an esteemed pediatrician, stood at the podium in his dress blues and stated that type 2 diabetes was a preventable pandemic with diet and lifestyle changes, I believed him. Dr. Koop did not seem worried about what the food industry thought about his dietary recommendations. He was dedicated to using his office as an authoritative platform to educate the nation on health promotion, disease prevention and emerging health threats.[43]

The 1980s were the age of food additives, artificial sweeteners, colors, and preservatives. Plastic soon replaced waxed paper and cardboard. The cookies, breads, chips, snack crackers and frozen foods were not all that great in flavor or texture, but boy, could they last forever. Boxes of diet cookies with no pat or zero-calorie sodas were top sellers. Soon, Twinkies were regaled as lasting forever and placed in time capsules. Between the chemicals, refined sugar, flour, and hydrogenated oils; the bacteria and fungi that led to spoilage didn't have a chance.

In 1964, the first shipment of Pop-Tarts sold out in just two weeks." Kellogg's issued the above advert explaining its "Oops!" and soon the Pop-Tarts were back on shelves again. Since 1967, Kellogg has released 30 flavors of Pop-Tarts.

By 2023, type 2 diabetes is so prevalent; that it is assumed by many that they will "get it" like a cold or flu bug as they get older. The truth is that type 2 diabetes is still one of the most preventable illnesses. However, you will have difficulty finding such statements on the CDC or NIH websites. According to the CDC: More than 37 million Americans have diabetes (about 1 in 10), and approximately 90-95% have type 2 diabetes. Type 2 diabetes most often develops in people over age 45, but more and more children, teens, and young adults are also developing it.[44]

Type 2 diabetes is unique primarily to industrialized countries and is directly caused by diet and lifestyle. Family histories of type 2 diabetes indicate the MTHFR gene interferes with methylation nutrients that help prevent metabolic conditions. Before we knew much about deactivating bad genes with diet and nutrients; conversations with clients would go much like this – "My grandfather or mother had diabetes, so I guess I'll get it also." I would ask the client; "How old was your family member when they were diagnosed with diabetes?" "Oh, they were in their late seventies."

My mother came from southern stock. Cornbread soaked in sweet milk or buttermilk was a favorite. The problem was her blood sugars would go through the roof because her bloodstream could not process the sugar formed. As a female in her late 30s and early 40s, these sugar surges increased depression and drove cravings for alcohol. In the case of my sister with type 1 diabetes, her blood sugar challenges were the opposite: her blood sugars would drop to low – glucose gel was generally at hand to bring her blood sugars up, and as she got older, three saltine crackers would elevate her glucose levels faster than glucose tabs or gel which she would refuse to take at times (it doesn't taste great and is sticky and hard to swallow) — good to know if you are traveling with a person with type 1 diabetes.

As we age, our cells can become more resistant to insulin and sugars.[45] As a client visual tool for cell receptor sites, I use a Tupperware® toy for toddlers that is a ball with multiple shapes that enter the ball through corresponding holes (pictured at the right). I explain the ball represents our cells in the blood stream and body; each shape represents glucose, neurotransmitters (serotonin), the hormones; insulin, progesterone, testosterone and the estrogens E_1, E_2 and E_3 — necessary for cellular health. Each hormone has a matching opening that only it will fit into.

Now, lay a piece of clear plastic wrap loosely around the ball's surface, this represents what happens when we have too much of the estrogen hormones or glucose from sugar in our blood stream. What happens when you try to place a shape in its slot, becomes apparent to clients as they recognize the plastic wrap interferes with the shape entering the ball or even stops it altogether.

Elevations in estrogen in the modern world can result from normal metabolic changes, birth control, cancer drugs and environmental toxins from plastic, petroleum, herbicides, and pesticides. We will look more at Forever Chemicals in the next chapter. Life changes due to andropause (men), perimenopause or menopause, referred to most often as *Metabolic Syndrome* is a leading factor of type 2 diabetes.[46] Hormone changes also are a result of plastics and pesticide/herbicide exposure.[47] This can be the case for Vietnam Veterans exposed to Agent Orange and later military personnel and families exposed to mold, heavy metals and contaminated base housing water.[48, 49] The plastic wrap (estrogens, insulin) interferes with the cells receiving the right chemicals and replaces them with xenoestrogens. Xenoestrogens are synthetic industrial chemicals that imitate estrogen. They can alter the activities of estrogen receptors and send false signals, disrupting the normal estrogen response, changing physiological functions, and promoting diseases, including cancer.[50]

These hormones and neurotransmitters interact with the microbiome, efficiently protecting the body when clean foods, water and lifestyle modification are embraced.[51] In the modern age of the 21st century, it is surprising how much movement is no longer part of the average daily routine. Movement is necessary for metabolism, hormones, elimination and detoxification.

Processed foods sold globally are rapidly absorbed into the bloodstream, generally lower in fiber and higher in refined salt, sugar, oils and carbohydrates. According to Michael Moss, author of *Salt, Sugar, Fat*: the food industry knows how to manipulate our sense of taste to stimulate cravings, leading to higher and higher calorie consumption. Oh, and processed food sales. With this awareness, we understand how type 2 diabetes is no longer a condition of aging, but a leading cause of health challenges in younger individuals and children worldwide.

> Type 2 diabetes is the most common form of diabetes, meaning the body doesn't use insulin properly. More than 95% of people with diabetes have type 2 diabetes.[52]

It was previously thought all insulin producing cells were lost within a few years of developing type 1 diabetes. However, research led by the University of Exeter Medical School, funded by *Diabetes UK* and published in *Diabetologia* (the journal of the European Association for the Study of Diabetes), shows that around three-quarters of patients with the condition possess a small number of beta cells that are not only producing insulin but are producing it in response to food in the same way as someone without the condition.[53] This understanding can help type 1 diabetics adjust their injectable insulin better and reduce the risks associated with brittle diabetes.

> Type 1 diabetes occurs when the body's immune system destroys most of the cells that make insulin, the substance that enables glucose in the blood to access the body's cells.

60% of the glucose converted from our food goes straight to feed the brain; the rest is used for rapid energy or put into fat storage.[54] The foods we eat and drink directly and profoundly affect our brain; the brain is the central computer that controls the rest of the body's chemical responses.

What To Do?

It may not be reasonable to expect everyone to give up their favorite restaurant. Still, if Americans are going to get healthy, it will not be because of a new health care bill, drug, or insurance company. It will be because of the proactive, holistic diet and lifestyle choices outlined throughout this book.

1. Eat locally grown meat and eggs—organic or home-raised. Consume three to five ounces of protein per meal or about 30 grams daily. Look at the palm of your hand—that is about how much meat you need per meal.

2. Start your meal with raw or steamed vegetables and a tablespoon of vinegar—no potatoes, and iceberg lettuce doesn't count. The darker the greens, the better for your liver and eyes. Raw carrots and snap peas make great snacks, but if cooked, they are prone to elevated blood sugars in some individuals. Many foods considered low glycemic affect individuals differently. One may have perfect sugars with tomatoes, while another can have elevated sugars. The era of bio-individual diets considers this.

3. Cooking with olive oil, unrefined coconut oil, organic butter and Ghee, walnut oil and macadamia nut oil makes blood sugars more stable. The additional health benefits of these oils protect nerves from damage.

A 2014 study by researchers at the Harvard School of Public Health found that those who improved their diet quality index scores by 10% over four years (by eating more whole grains, fruits and vegetables, and less sweetened beverages and saturated fats, for example) reduced their risk for type 2 diabetes by about 20%, compared to those who made no changes to their diets.[55, 56]

> *Principle 69*: Diabetes and heart disease go hand-in-hand.

Fasting & Diabetes

Fasting is often overlooked as a method of preventing chronic diseases such as diabetes. The Mediterranean diet and Blue Zones® note that fasting, as practiced in various cultures, can help prevent diabetes and heart disease.

At the Intermountain Heart Institute at Intermountain Medical Center in Murray, Utah, researchers noticed that after 10 -12 hours of fasting, the body scavenges for other energy sources to sustain itself. The body pulls LDL (bad) cholesterol from the fat cells and uses it for energy.

> "Fasting has the potential to become an important diabetes intervention," says Benjamin Horne, Ph.D., director of cardiovascular and genetic epidemiology at the Intermountain Medical Center Heart Institute and lead researcher on the study. "Though we've studied fasting and its health benefits for years, we didn't know why fasting could provide the health benefits we observed related to the risk of diabetes." [57]

This is the first evidence of a natural intervention triggering stem cell-based regeneration of an organ or system. It shows that cycles of prolonged fasting not only protect against immune system damage— a significant side effect of chemotherapy—but also induce immune system regeneration, shifting stem cells from a dormant state to a state of self-renewal.[58]

This evidence continues to support the religious traditions like fasting benefit the body, mind, and soul.

Supplements

- ✓ **Chromium** and vanadium are found to be deficient in people with diabetes. They play a significant role in blood sugar regulation and uptake into the cells.
- ✓ **Selenium** is an antioxidant and necessary for healthy cell formation.
- ✓ **Vitamin C** is a must of 2000 mg daily for protecting cells, blood sugar regulation and heart health. Remember, heart disease and diabetes go hand in hand. Avoid the ascorbic acid form of vitamin C, as it is manufactured primarily in China and is heavily contaminated with heavy metals.
- ✓ **B-complex** vitamins are a daily requirement. It is crucial to protect the brain and nervous system from damage. B vitamins play a vital role in keeping the entire body healthy.
- ✓ **Antioxidants** from OPC (*Oligomeric Proanthocyanidins*) and resveratrol.[59]
- ✓ **Probiotics** for healthy gut bacteria are the superstars in correcting, maintaining, and balancing digestive health when it comes to the breakdown of carbohydrates. Our blood sugars are profoundly affected when digestion is slow, sluggish, or overactive. These beneficial bacteria are proving to be our health's best friends.
- ✓ **Gymnema** help to stabilize sugar cravings. However, it should be used with supervision due to its effectiveness in lowering blood sugars may require medication adjustments. *MediHerb* product.[60]

Weightlifting and Movement

Mild weightlifting and strength-building exercises should be done thrice weekly to maintain bone health, circulation, brain health and balance. People who live in neighborhoods that are conducive to walking experience a substantially lower rate of obesity and diabetes than those who live in more auto-dependent communities, according to a pair of studies.[61]

Specifically, the studies found that people living in areas with greater "walkability" saw, on average, a 13% lower development of diabetes incidence over ten years than those less walkable.[62] For many individuals, physical therapy is the best place to start. Therapists will help you establish a workout program appropriate for your abilities. They can help you stay motivated and keep you from having injuries that would cut short your efforts.

My last recommendation involves sleep. Kathleen and I wrote about the healing powers of quality sleep in *Empty Plate: Food, Sustainability, Mindfulness.* If you have sleep apnea, I encourage you to be faithful in using a C-pap breathing machine.[63] This alone may bring your blood sugars down to healthier levels.[64, 65]

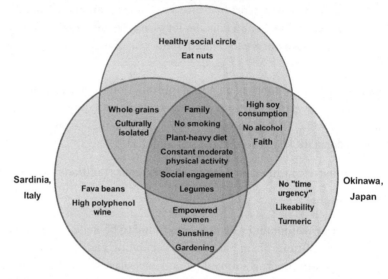

https://upload.wikimedia.org/wikipedia/commons/9/98/3_blue_zones_venn_diagram.svg

Principle 70: Fasting has the potential to become an important health intervention.

---

1 Martinović, T., Andjelković, U., Gajdošik, M. Š., Rešetar, D., & Josić, D. (2016). Foodborne pathogens and their toxins. Journal of proteomics, 147, 226–235. https://doi.org/10.1016/j.jprot.2016.04.029

2 Zhang L, Liu F, Xue J, Lee SA, Liu L and Riordan SM (2022) Bacterial Species Associated With Human Inflammatory Bowel Disease and Their Pathogenic Mechanisms. Front. Microbiol. 13:801892. doi: 10.3389/fmicb.2022.801892

3 Food Safety: https://www.who.int/news-room/fact-sheets/detail/food-safety

4 Aladhadh M. (2023). A Review of Modern Methods for the Detection of Foodborne Pathogens. Microorganisms, 11(5), 1111. https://doi.org/10.3390/microorganisms11051111

Chapter 13 ~ When Food Becomes the Enemy

5 Akaeze, O., Kilonzo-Nthenge, A., Nandwani, D., Mafiz, A., Nzomo, M., & Aniume, T. (2022). Incidence of Drug-Resistant Enterobacteriaceae Strains in Organic and Conventional Watermelons Grown in Tennessee. Foods (Basel, Switzerland), 11(21), 3316. https://doi.org/10.3390/foods11213316

6 Brar, P. K., & Danyluk, M. D. (2018). Nuts and Grains: Microbiology and Preharvest Contamination Risks. Microbiology spectrum, 6(2), 10.1128/microbiolspec.PFS-0023-2018. https://doi.org/10.1128/microbiolspec.PFS-0023-2018

7 Mukuna, W., Mafiz, A., Pokharel, B., Tobenna, A., & Kilonzo-Nthenge, A. (2021). Antibiotic Resistant Enterobacteriaceae in Milk Alternatives. Foods (Basel, Switzerland), 10(12), 3070. https://doi.org/10.3390/foods10123070

8 A Campaign for Real Milk, a project of the Weston A. Price Foundation: https://www.realmilk.com/raw-milk-finder/

9 McDade Thomas W., Rutherford Julienne, Adair Linda and Kuzawa Christopher W. 2010 Early origins of inflammation: microbial exposures in infancy predict lower levels of C-reactive protein in adulthoodProc. R. Soc. B.2771129–1137 http://doi.org/10.1098/rspb.2009.1795

10 Playing in the Dirt As Kids Makes Later Life Chronic Disease Less Likely. https://neurosciencenews.com/germs-dirt-kids-inflammation-7117/

11 Harley JB, Chen X, Pujato M, et al. Transcription factors operate across disease loci, with EBNA2 implicated in autoimmunity. Nat Genet. 2018; Ahead of print. Available at: www.ncbi.nlm.nih.gov/pubmed/29662164. Accessed April 18, 2018.

12 Harley, J. B., Chen, X., Pujato, M., Miller, D., Maddox, A., Forney, C., Magnusen, A. F., Lynch, A., Chetal, K., Yukawa, M., Barski, A., Salomonis, N., Kaufman, K. M., Kottyan, L. C., & Weirauch, M. T. (2018). Transcription factors operate across disease loci, with EBNA2 implicated in autoimmunity. Nature genetics, 50(5), 699–707. https://doi.org/10.1038/s41588-018-0102-3

13 Torfs, C. P., King, M. C., Huey, B., Malmgren, J., & Grumet, F. C. (1986). Genetic interrelationship between insulin-dependent diabetes mellitus, the autoimmune thyroid diseases, and rheumatoid arthritis. American journal of human genetics, 38(2), 170–187.

14 Breit, S., Kupferberg, A., Rogler, G., & Hasler, G. (2018). Vagus Nerve as Modulator of the Brain-Gut Axis in Psychiatric and Inflammatory Disorders. Frontiers in psychiatry, 9, 44. https://doi.org/10.3389/fpsyt.2018.00044

15 https://celiac.org/main/wp-content/uploads/2020/02/Incidence_of_Celiac_Disease_Is_Increasing_Over.99422.pdf

16 Mędza, A., & Szlagatys-Sidorkiewicz, A. (2023). Nutritional Status and Metabolism in Celiac Disease: Narrative Review. Journal of clinical medicine, 12(15), 5107. https://doi.org/10.3390/jcm12155107

17 Rostami-Nejad, M., Asri, N., Olfatifar, M., Khorsand, B., Houri, H., & Rostami, K. (2023). Systematic Review and Dose-Response Meta-Analysis on the Relationship between Different Gluten Doses and Risk of Coeliac Disease Relapse. Nutrients, 15(6), 1390. https://doi.org/10.3390/nu15061390

18 Nemteanu, R., Danciu, M., Clim, A., Girleanu, I., Ciortescu, I., Gheorghe, L., Trifan, A., & Plesa, A. (2023). Predictors of slow responsiveness and partial mucosal recovery in adult patients with celiac disease. Gastroenterology and hepatology from bed to bench, 16(2), 194–202. https://doi.org/10.22037/ghfbb.v16i2.2734

19 Sciurti, M., Fornaroli, F., Gaiani, F., Bonaguri, C., Leandro, G., Di Mario, F., & De' Angelis, G. L. (2018). Genetic susceptibilty and celiac disease: what role do HLA haplotypes play?. Acta bio-medica : Atenei Parmensis, 89(9-S), 17–21. https://doi.org/10.23750/abm.v89i9-S.7953

20 Sciurti, M., Fornaroli, F., Gaiani, F., Bonaguri, C., Leandro, G., Di Mario, F., & De' Angelis, G. L. (2018). Genetic susceptibilty and celiac disease: what role do HLA haplotypes play?. Acta bio-medica : Atenei Parmensis, 89(9-S), 17–21. https://doi.org/10.23750/abm.v89i9-S.7953

21 Odintsova, T. I., Slezina, M. P., & Istomina, E. A. (2020). Defensins of Grasses: A Systematic Review. Biomolecules, 10(7), 1029. https://doi.org/10.3390/biom10071029

22 Burkhardt, J. G., Chapa-Rodriguez, A., & Bahna, S. L. (2018). Gluten sensitivities and the allergist: Threshing the grain from the husks. Allergy, 73(7), 1359–1368. https://doi.org/10.1111/all.13354

23 Cabanillas B. (2020). Gluten-related disorders: Celiac disease, wheat allergy, and nonceliac gluten sensitivity. Critical reviews in food science and nutrition, 60(15), 2606–2621. https://doi.org/10.1080/10408398.2019.1651689

24 'Gluten-Free' Means What It Says (2020): https://www.fda.gov/consumers/consumer-updates/gluten-free-means-what-it-says

25 Zamakhchari, M., Wei, G., Dewhirst, F., Lee, J., Schuppan, D., Oppenheim, F. G., & Helmerhorst, E. J. (2011). Identification of Rothia Bacteria as Gluten-Degrading Natural Colonizers of the Upper Gastro-Intestinal Tract. PLOS ONE, 6(9), e24455. https://doi.org/10.1371/journal.pone.0024455

26 van den Bogert, B., Meijerink, M., Zoetendal, E. G., Wells, J. M., & Kleerebezem, M. (2014). Immunomodulatory properties of Streptococcus and Veillonella isolates from the human small intestine microbiota. PloS one, 9(12), e114277. https://doi.org/10.1371/journal.pone.0114277

27 Gubatan, J., & Moss, A. C. (2018). Vitamin D in inflammatory bowel disease: more than just a supplement. Current opinion in gastroenterology, 34(4), 217–225. https://doi.org/10.1097/MOG.0000000000000449

28 Pirzadeh, S. A., Amiriani, T., Besharat, S., Norouzi, A., Mirkarimi, H., Shokouhifar, N., Roshandel, G., & Sharifi, A. (2023). Assessment of iron status and iron deficiency anemia in patients with celiac, a single center experience. Gastroenterology and hepatology from bed to bench, 16(2), 217–221. https://doi.org/10.22037/ghfbb.v16i2.2728

29 Casas-Cardoso, L., Mantell, C., Obregón, S., Cejudo-Bastante, C., Alonso-Moraga, Á., de la Ossa, E. J. M., & de Haro-Bailón, A. (2021). Health-Promoting Properties of Borage Seed Oil Fractionated by Supercritical Carbon Dioxide Extraction. Foods (Basel, Switzerland), 10(10), 2471. https://doi.org/10.3390/foods10102471

30 Farag, M. A., & Gad, M. Z. (2022). Omega-9 fatty acids: potential roles in inflammation and cancer management. Journal, genetic engineering & biotechnology, 20(1), 48. https://doi.org/10.1186/s43141-022-00329-0

31 Tasset-Cuevas, I., Fernández-Bedmar, Z., Lozano-Baena, M. D., Campos-Sánchez, J., de Haro-Bailón, A., Muñoz-Serrano, A., & Alonso-Moraga, A. (2013). Protective effect of borage seed oil and gamma linolenic acid on DNA: in vivo and in vitro studies. PloS one, 8(2), e56986. https://doi.org/10.1371/journal.pone.0056986

32 Santos, H. O., Price, J. C., & Bueno, A. A. (2020). Beyond Fish Oil Supplementation: The Effects of Alternative Plant Sources of Omega-3 Polyunsaturated Fatty Acids upon Lipid Indexes and Cardiometabolic Biomarkers-An Overview. Nutrients, 12(10), 3159. https://doi.org/10.3390/nu12103159

33 Bledsoe, A. C., King, K. S., Larson, J. J., Snyder, M., Absah, I., Choung, R. S., & Murray, J. A. (2019). Micronutrient Deficiencies Are Common in Contemporary Celiac Disease Despite Lack of Overt Malabsorption Symptoms. Mayo Clinic Proceedings, 94(7), 1253-1260. https://doi.org/10.1016/j.mayocp.2018.11.036

34 Rao, R., & Samak, G. (2012). Role of Glutamine in Protection of Intestinal Epithelial Tight Junctions. Journal of epithelial biology & pharmacology, 5(Suppl 1-M7), 47–54. https://doi.org/10.2174/1875044301205010047

35 Aleman, R. S., Paz, D., Cedillos, R., Tabora, M., Olson, D. W., & Aryana, K. (2023). Attributes of Culture Bacteria as Influenced by Ingredients That Help Treat Leaky Gut. Microorganisms, 11(4), 893. https://doi.org/10.3390/microorganisms11040893

36 https://newsnetwork.mayoclinic.org/discussion/mayo-clinic-study-calls-for-screening-of-family-members-of-celiac-disease-patients/

37 Eland, I., Klieverik, L., Mansour, A. A., & Al-Toma, A. (2022). Gluten-Free Diet in Co-Existent Celiac Disease and Type 1 Diabetes Mellitus: Is It Detrimental or Beneficial to Glycemic Control, Vascular Complications, and Quality of Life?. Nutrients, 15(1), 199. https://doi.org/10.3390/nu15010199

38 European Journal of Gastroenterology and Hepatology 20: 492–493; 494–495; 545–554.

39 A small subset of those with celiac disease react to the protein in oat, study confirms (2023): https://www.beyondceliac.org/research-news/a-small-subset-of-those-with-celiac-disease-react-to-the-protein-in-oat-study-confirms/

40 Liu, J., Chey, W. D., Haller, E., & Eswaran, S. (2020). Low-FODMAP Diet for Irritable Bowel Syndrome: What We Know and What We Have Yet to Learn. Annual review of medicine, 71, 303–314. https://doi.org/10.1146/annurev-med-050218-013625

41 Vedantam, S., Graff, E., Khakoo, N. S., Khakoo, N. S., & Pearlman, M. (2023). Food as Medicine: How to Influence the Microbiome and Improve Symptoms in Patients with Irritable Bowel Syndrome. Current gastroenterology reports, 25(3), 52–60. https://doi.org/10.1007/s11894-023-00861-0

42 Hu Y, et al. Am J Clin Nutr. 2014 Jul 16. [Epub ahead of print.

43 The C. Everett Koop Papers (retrieved 2023): https://profiles.nlm.nih.gov/spotlight/qq/feature/biographical

44 Centers for Disease Control (retrieved 2023): https://www.cdc.gov/diabetes/basics/type2.html

45 Galicia-Garcia, U., Benito-Vicente, A., Jebari, S., Larrea-Sebal, A., Siddiqi, H., Uribe, K. B., Ostolaza, H., & Martín, C. (2020). Pathophysiology of Type 2 Diabetes Mellitus. International journal of molecular sciences, 21(17), 6275. https://doi.org/10.3390/ijms21176275

46 Gorodeski Baskin, R., & Alfakara, D. (2023). Root Cause for Metabolic Syndrome and Type 2 Diabetes: Can Lifestyle and Nutrition Be the Answer for Remission. Endocrinology and metabolism clinics of North America, 52(1), 13–25. https://doi.org/10.1016/j.ecl.2022.10.007

47 Xu, Y., Jakobsson, K., Harari, F., Andersson, E. M., & Li, Y. (2023). Exposure to high levels of PFAS through drinking water is associated with increased risk of type 2 diabetes-findings from a register-based study in Ronneby, Sweden. Environmental research, 225, 115525. https://doi.org/10.1016/j.envres.2023.115525

48 National Academies of Sciences, Engineering, and Medicine, Health and Medicine Division, Board on Population Health and Public Health Practice, & Committee to Review the Health Effects in Vietnam Veterans of Exposure to Herbicides (Eleventh Biennial Update). (2018). Veterans and Agent Orange: Update 11 (2018). National Academies Press (US).

49 Xu, Y., Jakobsson, K., Harari, F., Andersson, E. M., & Li, Y. (2023). Exposure to high levels of PFAS through drinking water is associated with increased risk of type 2 diabetes-findings from a register-based study in Ronneby, Sweden. Environmental research, 225, 115525. https://doi.org/10.1016/j.envres.2023.115525

50 Wang X, Ha D, Yoshitake R, Chan YS, Sadava D, Chen S. Exploring the Biological Activity and Mechanism of Xenoestrogens and Phytoestrogens in Cancers: Emerging Methods and Concepts. Int J Mol Sci. 2021 Aug 16;22(16):8798. doi: 10.3390/ijms22168798. PMID: 34445499; PMCID: PMC8395949.

51 Gurung, M., Li, Z., You, H., Rodrigues, R., Jump, D. B., Morgun, A., & Shulzhenko, N. (2020). Role of gut microbiota in type 2 diabetes pathophysiology. EBioMedicine, 51, 102590. https://doi.org/10.1016/j.ebiom.2019.11.051

52 World Health Organization (2023): https://www.who.int/news-room/fact-sheets/detail/diabetes

53 Diabetologia. "Insulin 'still produced' in most people with type 1 diabetes." ScienceDaily. ScienceDaily, 9 October 2013. www.sciencedaily.com/releases/2013/10/131009213816.htm.

Chapter 13 ~ When Food Becomes the Enemy

54 Zhang, S., Lachance, B. B., Mattson, M. P., & Jia, X. (2021). Glucose metabolic crosstalk and regulation in brain function and diseases. Progress in neurobiology, 204, 102089. https://doi.org/10.1016/j.pneurobio.2021.102089

55 American Diabetes Association. "Improving diet quality reduces risk for type 2 diabetes." ScienceDaily. ScienceDaily, 14 June 2014. www.sciencedaily.com/releases/2014/06/140614150313.htm.

56 Wayne State University Division of Research. "Grape skin extract may soon be answer to treating diabetes." ScienceDaily. ScienceDaily, 9 May 2014. www.sciencedaily.com/releases/2014/05/140509110201.htm.

57 Intermountain Medical Center. "Fasting reduces cholesterol levels in prediabetic people over extended period of time, new research finds." ScienceDaily. ScienceDaily, 14 June 2014. www.sciencedaily.com/releases/2014/06/140614150142.htm.

58 Cell Stem Cell, ISSN: 1934-5909, Vol: 18, Issue: 2, Page: 291-292 Publication Year 2016. https://plu.mx/plum/a/?doi=10.1016/j.stem.2016.01.018

59 Ngamsamer, C., Sirivarasai, J., & Sutjarit, N. (2022). The Benefits of Anthocyanins against Obesity-Induced Inflammation. Biomolecules, 12(6), 852. https://doi.org/10.3390/biom12060852

60 Standard Process Fundamentals – MediHerb (800)292-6699

61 Lang, I. M., Antonakos, C. L., Judd, S. E., & Colabianchi, N. (2022). A longitudinal examination of objective neighborhood walkability, body mass index, and waist circumference: the REasons for Geographic And Racial Differences in Stroke study. The international journal of behavioral nutrition and physical activity, 19(1), 17. https://doi.org/10.1186/s12966-022-01247-7

62 Kowaleski-Jones, L., Zick, C., Smith, K. R., Brown, B., Hanson, H., & Fan, J. (2017). Walkable neighborhoods and obesity: Evaluating effects with a propensity score approach. SSM- population health, 6, 9–15. https://doi.org/10.1016/j.ssmph.2017.11.005

63 Bener, A., Al-Hamaq, A. O. A. A., Agan, A. F., Öztürk, M., & Ömer, A. (2020). Sleeping disturbances and predictor risk factors among type 2 diabetic mellitus patients. Annals of African medicine, 19(4), 230–236. https://doi.org/10.4103/aam.aam_51_19

64 Lee, S. W. H., Ng, K. Y., & Chin, W. K. (2017). The impact of sleep amount and sleep quality on glycemic control in type 2 diabetes: A systematic review and meta-analysis. Sleep medicine reviews, 31, 91–101. https://doi.org/10.1016/j.smrv.2016.02.001

65 Alamer, W. M., Qutub, R. M., Alsaloumi, E. A., Natto, N. K., Alshehri, R. M., & Khafagy, A. (2022). Prevalence of Sleep Disorders Among Patients With Type 2 Diabetes Mellitus in Makkah City: A Cross-Sectional Study. Cureus, 14(12), e33088. https://doi.org/10.7759/cureus.33088

Our Journey with Food

Chapter 14 ~Forever Chemicals

> Now the Lord can make you tumble
> Lord can make you turn
> The Lord can make you overflow
> But the Lord can't make you burn
>
> Burn on, big river, burn on
> Burn on, big river, burn on
>
> ~ Randy Newman, "Burn On"

Nov. 3rd, 1952. Fireman on railroad bridge apply water to tugboat 'Arizona' amidst flames from the burning Cuyahoga River. Original United Press photo caption reported that "fire started in an oil slick on the river, swept docks at the Great Lakes Towing Co., destroying three tugs, three buildings and the ship repair yards." (photo mistakenly used by Time magazine as 1969 fire).

Chapter Fourteen ~ Forever Chemicals
The Excitotoxins & PFAS

As a kid, TV made an impression on me, like millions of others. The commercials were entertaining and left indelible images in our minds. In 1971, I remember the "Give a Hoot and Don't Pollute" Woodsy the Owl slogan and the "Crying Indian" TV commercials. In the 1980s, Woodsy was removed from commercials and from kids 'goody bags at USDA Forest Service offices due to the spotted owl controversy. In 2023, the Keep America Beautiful "Crying Indian" commercial with Iron Eyes Cody was retired and listed as inappropriate (with mixed feelings from family members) by the National Congress of American Indians.[1] Awareness – and meaningful action do not always go hand-in-hand. In this chapter, we will examine the "forever chemicals" polyfluoroalkyl substance (PFAS) or fluoropolymers, neurotoxins, and water contamination.

https://pophistorydig.com/wp-content/uploads/2014/05/Roberts-Cartoon-320.jpg

The unmitigated pollution of the 1960s to 1980s was devastating to soil, water, and air for millions of U.S. and Canadian residents. Watching the Cuyahoga River in Cleveland burn in 1969 was incomprehensible, yet it had burned 9 times between 1868 and 1952! In truth, the Cuyahoga

River had been a sewer for Cleveland and industrial companies along its banks for 100 years; locals took little notice.

Then Rachel Carson's book *Silent Spring* was published, and an oil spill of 3 million gallons entered the Pacific Ocean at Santa Barbara, California, all within the same time frame. Suddenly, people's televisions and newspapers featured images of oil-slicked birds and dead dolphins. Interviews with Ms. Carson highlighted the insecticide DDT as the cause of the plummeting wild bird population and graphic images of crushed bald eagle eggs in nests. The power of media reporting outraged and shocked citizens into action to clean up beaches and lobby oil companies. In 1972, Congress overrode Nixon's veto to pass the Clean Water Act, which created national water quality standards.[2] This little walk through history may be fascinating, but what does this have to do with food, nutrition, and health?

> "Medicine aims to prevent disease plus prolong life; the idea of medicine is to eliminate the needs of a physician."
>
> ~ William Mayo

To have health, we must have food, water, light, and air to live.[3] Each year, the world leaders gather to talk about pollution, yet piles of plastic float on the oceans; nanoplastics burrow into the soil and drift into the air. Odorless and colorless chemicals glide through our water, air, and earth, entering fruits, vegetables, legumes, grains, livestock, wild game, and human bodies. As Kathleen and I shared in *Empty Plate: Food~Sustainability~Mindfulness* and in Chapter 13, which looked at pathogens, chemicals are driving a multitude of chronic and life-threatening illnesses in the year 2023, indiscriminate of age or gender.

> ***Principle 71***: Chemical contamination is EVERYWHERE on the planet. The presence of chemicals in all of the above-listed requirements for life is making us sick and threatening lives with chronic and deadly illnesses.

Water, Water Everywhere but None to Drink

In April 2014, Flint, Michigan, changed their municipal water supply source from the Detroit-influenced Lake Huron to the Flint River, causing water distribution pipes to corrode and leach lead and other contaminants into municipal drinking water. The lead-tainted water crisis in Flint showed us that safe, potable tap water is not a given in the United States. In 2018, five additional cities (Detroit, Modesto, Dallas, and Morovis and Coamo in Puerto Rico) joined Flint in the headlines. By 2020, the list had grown to 12 cities with Pittsburg, Milwaukee, Newark, Washington, DC, Brady, TX, and Baltimore joining Charleston, W. Virginia; Dos Palos, California; Newburg, NY; and Miami, Florida, resulting in roughly 2 billion people not having reliable sources of clean water.[4] Access to safe drinking water reflects inequalities based on income, age, sex, and ethnicity. A study from the Environmental Working Group (EWG) revealed in 2021 that the drinking water of most Americans contains "forever chemicals." These

Chapter 14 ~Forever Chemicals

compounds may take hundreds or even thousands of years to break down in the environment. Scientifically known as *perfluoroalkyl* and *polyfluoroalkyl* substances (PFAS), they persist in the human body, potentially causing health problems.

Of the more than 9,000 known PFAS compounds, 600 are currently used in the U.S. in countless products, including firefighting foam, cookware, cosmetics, carpet treatments, food packaging, and dental floss. By 2023, Washington and California had banned PFAS chemicals in food packaging.[5] Scientists call PFAS "forever chemicals" because their chemistry keeps them from breaking down under typical environmental conditions. "One of the unique features of PFAS compounds is the carbon-fluorine bond," explains David Andrews, a senior scientist at the watchdog Environmental Working Group.

Lead poisoning has a far greater impact on global health than previously thought, potentially contributing to over five million deaths a year and posing a similar threat to air pollution. Lead pollution has been shown to cause severe health problems, particularly heart disease and young children's brain development.[6] People are still exposed to the potent neurotoxin via drinking water, food, soil, cookware, fertilizers, vaccines, cosmetics, lead–acid car batteries, and other such sources.[7] Lead has been associated with anemia, hypertension, loss of appetite, colic, kidney damage, and cataracts, and activates hyaluronidase (an endogenous enzyme that facilitates the growth of cancer cells).[8,9] Chronic exposures to heavy metals may lead to breast cancer, endometriosis, endometrial cancer, menstrual disorders, and spontaneous abortions, as well as pre-term deliveries and stillbirths. The impact of environmental exposure to heavy metals on female fertility is, therefore, a well-known fact.[10]

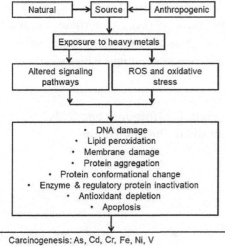

Haidar, Z., Fatema, K., Shoily, S. S., & Sajib, A. A. (2023). Disease-associated metabolic pathways affected by heavy metals and metalloid. Toxicology reports, 10, 554–570.
https://doi.org/10.1016/j.toxrep.2023.04.010

The association of heavy metals with chronic, age-related metabolic disorders has gained much interest in 2023. The underlying molecular mechanisms are often complex and incompletely understood. In a 2023 review, researchers summarize the currently known disease-associated metabolic and signaling pathways that are altered following different heavy metals and metalloids exposure. The focus of the study was to explore how affected pathways are associated with chronic multifactorial diseases, including diabetes, cardiovascular diseases, cancer, neurodegeneration, inflammation, and allergic responses upon exposure to arsenic (As), cadmium (Cd), chromium (Cr), iron (Fe), mercury (Hg), nickel (Ni), and vanadium (V). Research is ongoing.[11]

Lead (Pb) is a natural and toxic heavy metal that can be chelated and reduced by various foods, herbs, and minerals. Lead has been part of human life from the beginning of recorded history. For centuries, toxic lead has been used in traditional and herbal medicine to activate immune responses as well as being a contaminant from manufacturing in highly contaminated areas.[12, 13, 14] Floride (F), another toxic natural mineral, is believed to enhance lead absorption, which is especially problematic for individuals unknowingly drinking-contaminated water and using fluoride dental products. A study done in 1994 found the average American daily intake of lead was 200-400mg. A 2022 study found that water and beverages were significant dietary sources of Pb (31% of the total daily intake).[15, 16, 17]

No Place to Hide

Researchers have confirmed that chemical contamination has reached the most inaccessible areas of the earth. (Note: Some reported toxic elements may naturally occur in the sampled environment.) Scientists have reported finding traces of plastic and hazardous chemicals in Antarctica. Seven of eight tested sea-surface water samples contained one microplastic element per liter of water. An additional nine samples collected with a mantra trawl ocean skimming net showed microplastics in two samples. Seven out of nine snow samples showed traces of toxic chemicals.[18]

Mt. Everest contains the highest altitude chemical contamination on land. Meltwater and snow samples from Everest's Khumbu Glacier were analyzed for "forever chemicals" (PFAS) in 2021. Testing for 14 PFAS compounds, perfluorooctanesulfonic acid (PFOS), perfluorooctanoic acid (PFOA), and perfluorohexanoic acid (PFHxA), were found in Mt. Everest snow and meltwater. The highest concentrations found were 26.14 ng/L and 10.34 ng/L PFOS at Base Camp and Camp 2, respectively, suggesting a widespread presence on the mountain.[19]

> ***Principle 72***: Almost all drinking water in the U.S. contains "forever chemicals," so named because they do not break down naturally in the environment.

The Last Straw

I clearly remember festive colored spiraled paper straws and snazzy bendy plastic ones in my childhood. These bendy straws were a game changer for children and ill and infirmed individuals who had challenges drinking from a glass or cup – all before YETI® and Hydro Flask® sippy cups for young and old. The earliest use of straws dates to the Sumerians of Mesopotamia who used straws to drink beer that they brewed in large vats, which were too heavy to lift and pass around.[20] Marvin Stone, an American, filed a patent for drinking straws made of manila paper in 1888. Stone created the prototype for his paper straw by spiraling a strip of paper around a pencil, gluing the paper together and removing the pencil. Joseph Friedman created the world's first bendable straw in 1937.

In 2019, California announced a ban on plastic straws in restaurants unless specifically requested by the customer. Starbucks announced plans to phase out plastic straws by 2020 in favor of plastic sippy cups and compostable straws. I'm confused – *straws are the danger and plastic cups are not?* What about the

Chapter 14 ~Forever Chemicals

thousands of disposable shopping bags, containers, and products on the market? Are they not a problem? Paper and other plant-based drinking straws replacing plastic straws in commercial settings is a political response to activists' demands to reduce plastic pollution.

Yet as the last straw (figuratively) rolls by, forever chemicals and industrial toxins are pervasive in drinking water and food supplies, affecting the health of multiple generations. Are the alternatives safer? Researchers in 2021 and 2023 looked at this question. The water-resistant properties of many plant-based straws are attributed to the use of PFAS during the manufacturing process. In a 2021 study, 43 brands of straws (5 plastic, 29 paper, 9 other plant-based) were analyzed for 53 semi-volatile PFAS using ultra-high-performance liquid chromatography-tandem mass spectrometry. While the plastic straws had no measurable PFAS, 21 PFAS were detected in the paper and other plant-based straws.[21] A fully biodegradable straw formed by stereocomplexation of poly (lactic acid) (SC-PLA) was being evaluated in 2023.[22]

Smoke and Mirrors

> *Principle 73*: American military personnel and their families suffer the consequences of exposure to a myriad of dangerous substances.

I have a nephew who is a submariner in the Navy, students who are either veterans or spouses of active military personnel, clients who served in World War II and the Korean, Vietnam, and Gulf Wars, and co-workers who are veterans or spouses representing all branches of military service. These individuals have, at one time or another, shared information on what military life is like. By 2020, gone were the stories of foreign postings. In their place were stories of toxic mold, heavy metals, chemical exposure, undrinkable water, and bans on local fruits. Captain Soup, as his customers and fellow Apache helicopter pilots know Bryan, confirmed what I had heard from my students in the spring of 2023 at the National Association of Nutrition Professionals (NANP) HEALCon event. Bryan had been stationed on the East Coast when we first met but had been reassigned to Fort Lewis in Washington state to participate in a heavy metal and mold detox program for the active military. The unsafe water at Pearl Harbor or toxic effects of mold in base housing are not limited to the active military personnel. They also have a lasting impact on families who live and are exposed for decades to forever chemicals and toxins.

In the summer of 2023, I met Joe, a retired Air Force veteran. Joe candidly shared how he had seen jet fuel and spilled chemicals regularly fire-hosed off pavement into runoff drains. "Most of the guys I served with are fighting cancer, have passed away from cancer, or have dementia," Joe said." We will never see the Air Force or government admit to the chemicals being the cause of our health problems. They will just wait until none of us are left."

Also in 2023, the journal *JAMA Neurology* published a study on the risk of Parkinson's disease (PD) being 70% higher in Camp Lejeune veterans than those stationed at U.S. Marine Corps bases on the opposite side of the country in California. The study included over 300,000 service members stationed at Camp Lejeune for at least three months between 1975 and 1985. An increased risk of PD has been associated with exposure to the solvent trichloroethylene (TCE). Millions of people in the U.S. and worldwide are exposed to TCE in air, food, and water. Even veterans not diagnosed with Parkinson's disease still had a "significantly higher" risk for early signs and symptoms, the researchers reported in the study.[23]

> "Superior doctors prevent disease. Mediocre doctors treat the disease before it is evident. Inferior doctors treat the full-blown disease."
> ~Huang Dee Nai-Chang

How Food is Prepared Matters

A team from the University of Nebraska-Lincoln ran experiments using baby food containers made from polypropylene and polyethylene, both approved as safe to use by the regulators at the FDA. After three minutes of being heated in a 1,000-watt microwave, various liquids put inside the containers were analyzed for microplastics and nanoplastics. Particle numbers varied, but the researchers estimated that 4.22 million microplastic and 2.11 billion nanoplastic particles (from 1 square centimeter of plastic) were released during three minutes of microwave heating.

Microwaving water or dairy products inside polypropylene or polyethylene products delivers the highest

relative concentrations of plastic. Particles were also released when food and drinks were refrigerated and stored at room temperature, though concentrations were not as high. Studies have shown that nanoplastics can potentially harm the intestine and critical biological processes, but just how is unclear.[24]

When old and young rodents drank microscopic fragments of plastic suspended in their water over three weeks in a 2020 a study by researchers at the University of Rhode Island, traces of the pollutants had accumulated in every organ of the tiny mammals' bodies, including the brain. Ingesting these microplastics was also accompanied by behavioral changes akin to dementia in humans, as well as changes to immune markers in the liver and brain. Scientists have found microplastics hiding in human intestines, circulating in our bloodstream, gathering deep in the lungs, as well as in breast milk and seeping through the placenta to fetuses in utero. The fact that the pollutants were detected outside the digestive system suggests they are undergoing systemic circulation.[25] In 2021, toxicologists warned that future studies urgently need to address what these pollutants do to our health, especially since exposure is now impossible to avoid.

Polystyrene Microplastics Exacerbate Inflammation in High-Fat Diet-Induced Obesity

Findings suggest that polystyrene microplastics (PS-MPs) significantly contribute to systemic inflammation in high-fat diet-induced obesity by activating peripheral and central inflammatory immune cells. Obesity rates, even despite stable caloric intake, have continued to rise. There is a growing link between obesity and exposure to environmental pollutants, including MPs. A comprehensive investigation utilizing silicon, in vitro, and in vivo approaches to explore the brain distribution and physiological effects of MPs was conducted in 2023. Molecular docking simulations assessed the binding affinity of three plastic polymers (ethylene, propylene, and styrene) to immune cells (macrophages, CD4+, and CD8+ lymphocytes). The results revealed that styrene exhibited the highest binding affinity for macrophages.[26]

A 2023 study on airborne micro- and nanoplastics found they are widely spread and pose a risk to human health. The third polymer plastic most commonly produced and present in atmospheric fallout is polystyrene (PS). Airborne micro- and nanoplastics are derived from a variety of sources, including synthetic fibers, waste disposal products, incinerators, agricultural practices, and road traffic. In particular, tire wear and brake pad wear particles are mixtures of metal and microplastics. It has been estimated that in ambient air around 4% and 11% of the respirable (fine) and inhalable (coarse) particulate matter are formed by micro- and nanoplastics derived from only tires and brakes.

Indoor exposure to airborne micro- and nanoplastics is highly relevant, considering time spent in indoor environments (on average 70–90% of our lifetimes) and sources of these pollutants (synthetic textile fibers, polyester fleece/fibers, upholstery and furnishing objects or building materials). Significant DNA damage and mitochondrial impairment were observed after exposure. The enhancement of effects due to environmental aging processes highlights the true potential impact on human health of these airborne pollutants.[27]

What can you or your clients do? In the case of airborne and water contaminants, consider converting to natural fibers for home and personal use and employing high-quality water and air filters for those who can afford them. Exercise away from roadways. Other options can include increasing natural heavy metal chelators available in organic produce, affordable charcoal-based water filters to remove some of the larger contaminants of lead, chlorine, and fluoride, regularly changing heat and ventilation filters, and adding house plants as natural air purifiers (provided the soil is not filled with mold spores). Keep areas prone to dampness well-ventilated and seal sheetrock to reduce mold development. Buy foods in bulk to reduce plastic packaging and store foods in glass. Use only clear glass in microwaves and for food storage. For more suggestions, read *Empty Plate: Food~Sustainability~Mindfulness*.

> ***Principle 74***: Exposure to microplastics causes significant cellular (DNA/mitochondria) damage in every living organism on Earth.

Neurotoxins in Food

Individuals may religiously work out, take supplements, and eat an organic plant-based diet but feel like they are losing their edge. This may be due to neurotoxins in foods labeled organic and natural. These ingredients often cause severe reactions such as migraines, insomnia, asthma, depression, anxiety, aggression, chronic fatigue, and even amyotrophic lateral sclerosis (ALS). Some researchers hypothesize neurotoxin food additives may be responsible for the growing number of children diagnosed with ADHD and autism.[28]

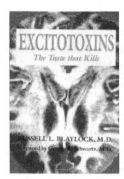 Noted researcher and neurosurgeon Russell L. Blaylock, MD (1945),[29] published *Excitotoxins: The Taste that Kills* in 1996. In 2023, he continues to research and educate on the chemicals being added to food that are damaging a critical part of the brain that controls hormones, leading to endocrine problems. They are called *excitotoxins* and include artificial colors (FD&C), sodium nitrite and nitrate, butylated hydroxytohicne (BHT), saccharin, monosodium glutamate (MSG), aspartame, caffeine, propylene glycol (food grade antifreeze), sulfites (sodium bisulfite), sulfur dioxide, brominated vegetable oil (BVO), and bisphenol A (BPA invented in the 1960s).[30] Bisphenol A (BPA) is a ubiquitous environmental xenobiotic impacting millions worldwide. BPA has long been proposed to promote ovarian carcinogenesis.[31] Other forms of bisphenol include AF, BPA, BPB, BPF, BADGE, and BFDGE.

A study from 2022 showed meat and meat products are a significant source of contamination by chemical hazards, including bisphenol A. BPA is well-known for its endocrine-disrupting properties, which may cause potential toxicological effects on reproductive, nervous, and immune systems. Dietary consumption is the main route of BPA exposure.[32, 33]

> Bisphenol A is found mainly in plastics labeled with the recycling codes 3 or 7. Bisphenol A is used in the production of polycarbonate plastic and in the coating inside food and beverage cans. Bisphenol A exposure happens mainly through the digestion of food and liquids stored in or heated in plastic materials. Bisphenol A exerts estrogenic activity and is considered an endocrine disruptor. [34]

Monosodium glutamate (MSG), in its many forms, is the best-known neurotoxin and is present in yeast extract, maltodextrin, carrageenan, hydrolyzed vegetable protein, dough conditioners, seasonings, flavoring powders, bouillon, and spices. MSG is a natural substance and has been used in Asian cooking for a century as a flavor enhancer, and therefore can be listed as a "natural flavoring or additive" on labels. Intake of glutamate can be derived from its natural occurrence as a constituent of proteins, from the presence of free glutamate in certain fermented foods, and from adding glutamic acid and glutamates to foods as flavor-enhancing additives.[35] Glutamate is a non-essential amino acid that plays a key role in nitrogen homeostasis. The dietary exposure to glutamate in adults is extensive due to its ubiquitous presence in foods under three forms: bound to proteins, naturally free, and in free form as an additive. Glutamate naturally included in proteins is the major source of dietary glutamate, thus it plays a role in nitrogen homeostasis.[36]

During World War II, American food manufacturers began using MSG to improve the unappetizing taste of C-rations (C stands for *combat)* for military troops to ensure adequate calorie intake. Originally isolated from seaweed, MSG in the 21st century is made by fermenting corn, potatoes, and rice. MSG is naturally present in dried shiitake mushrooms (1,1,060 mg), walnuts, beetroot, wakame, soybean (soy sauce contains > 50% MSG), tomatoes, peas, grape juice, anchovies, and Parmesan cheese. These whole foods have built-in protection in the form of antioxidants to offset the damage from the naturally occurring glutamates.[37]

Adulteration refers to the deliberate addition of a compound usually not present in food. These compounds are known as food additives or food adulterants. Monosodium glutamate is one of the most common food additives. Several studies have revealed that MSG is toxic to fetal development/fetus, children, adolescents, and adults. Physiological complications associated with MSG toxicity are hypertension, obesity, gastrointestinal tract troubles, and impairment of the function of the brain and the nervous, reproductive, and endocrine systems.[38]

Glutamate is the brain's most abundant free amino acid and is at the crossroads between multiple metabolic pathways. Considering this, it was a surprise to discover that glutamate has excitatory effects on nerve cells and can excite cells to their death in a process now referred to as "excitotoxicity." This effect is due to glutamate receptors present on the surface of brain cells. Powerful uptake systems (glutamate transporters) prevent excessive activation of these receptors by continuously removing glutamate from the extracellular fluid in the brain. Further, the blood–brain barrier shields the brain from glutamate in the blood. The highest concentrations of glutamate are found in synaptic vesicles in nerve terminals, from which exocytosis can release it. Glutamate is the major excitatory neurotransmitter in the mammalian central nervous system.[39]

Due to rapid absorption, MSG causes excessive stimulation of N-methyl-D-aspartate (NMDA) receptors more readily than other excitotoxins. The glutamic acid component of MSG is comprised of both the D-glutamic acid and the L-glutamic acid forms. The D-glutamic acid component is believed to be the form of glutamic acid responsible for the associated toxicity. Studies indicate that approximately 30% of people experience over-stimulation of NMDA receptors due to MSG consumption.[40, 41]

When hydrolyzed, as in soy protein isolates, glutamate is released. Findings of a longitudinal study on vegetarians who consumed a significant amount of soy products showed they had the highest incidence of dementia and brain atrophy.[42] This is one area where research can be confusing; for every study saying soy is good, others counter that it is bad. The greatest research challenge involves confounding factors that have little to do with food and more to do with stress and lifestyle.

> The definition of "natural flavor" under the Code of Federal Regulations is "the essential oil, oleoresin, essence or extractive, protein hydrolysate, distillate, or any product of roasting, heating, or enzymolysis, which contains the flavoring constituents derived from a spice, fruit or fruit juice, vegetable or vegetable juice, edible yeast, herb, bark, bud, root, leaf or similar plant material, meat, seafood, poultry, eggs, dairy products, or fermentation products thereof, whose significant function in food is flavoring rather than nutritional (21CFR101.22)."[43]

A 2022, study linked fast food consumption with a higher risk of depression.[44] The 2023 study *Ultra-Processed Food Consumption* (UPF) *and Depressive Symptoms in a Mediterranean Cohort* found that current evidence demonstrates a substantial association with an increased risk of metabolic disorders, a positive association between UPF consumption, and the likelihood of having depressive symptoms in younger Italian individuals. Given the consistency of the findings after adjustment for diet quality, further studies are needed to understand whether non-nutritional factors may play a role in human neurobiology.[45, 46]

Many infant and toddler foods contain caseinate hydrolyzed protein, soy extracts, and broth; all are significant glutamate sources.[47] In 2017, a European Food Safety Authority (EFSA) opinion on using glutamate and its salts as food additives led to an Acceptable Daily Intake (ADI) of 30 mg/kg body weight/day. Then, in 2021, an EFSA statement presented a proposal for harmonizing the establishment of Health-Based Guidance Values for nutrients that are also regulated substances (including food additives).[48]

Aspartame (APM) (NutraSweet®, Equal®) was discovered by James M. Schlatter in 1965. Being 180-200 times sweeter than sucrose, its intake was expected to reduce obesity rates in developing countries and help those struggling with diabetes. Aspartame is mainly used as a sweetener for soft drinks, confectionery, and medicines. Despite its widespread use, its safety remains controversial and has been reported to be responsible for neurological and behavioral disturbances in people.[49] Upon ingestion, aspartame is hydrolyzed in the gut and provides the metabolites of the essential amino acid phenylalanine (50%), aspartic acid (40%), and methanol (10%). Altered brain neurochemical compositions [such as dopamine (DA), norepinephrine (NE), and serotonin (5-HT)] have long been a concern in observed neurophysiological symptoms, such as headaches, memory loss, mood changes, as well as depression, in aspartame consumers. Aspartame might act as a chemical stressor through increasing plasma cortisol levels. Aspartame consumption was also found to alter gut microbiota.[50] The researchers found that when life-span exposure to APM begins during fetal development, its carcinogenic effects increase.[51] A 2006 study demonstrated that APM use caused the following, primarily in females:[52]

> incidence of malignant tumors
> incidence of lymphomas-leukemias
> incidence of transitional cell carcinomas of the renal pelvis and ureter in females
> incidence of malignant schwannomas of the peripheral nerves

Brominated vegetable oil (BVO) has been approved by the U.S. Food and Drug Administration on an interim basis as a food additive. Animal studies have raised concerns about potential toxicities from consuming BVO, primarily in swine and Sprague Dawley rats. A toxicology study in 2022 found statistically significant increases in the incidence of thyroid follicular cell hypertrophy in the two highest BVO dose groups of males and the high-dose group of females. An increase in serum thyroid stimulating hormone (TSH) was observed in the high-dose group for both sexes, as well as a decrease in serum T4 in the high-dose males. A clear dose response was observed in di- and tetra-bromostearic acid levels in the heart, liver, and inguinal fat. The data from the study expands upon previous observations in rats and pigs that oral exposure to BVO is associated with increased tissue levels of inorganic and organic bromine, and that the thyroid is a potential target organ of toxicity.[53] BVO displaces iodine, a necessary mineral for thyroid function also used by breasts and prostates in maintaining healthy tissue. BVO is found in Mountain Dew®, Fanta Orange®, and processed foods; it is used as a flame retardant in plastics and is banned in Europe and Japan.

Chapter 14 ~Forever Chemicals

Nutrition-Based Detoxification Tools

As many as 84,000 commercial and industrial chemicals are now used in the United States; hundreds more are introduced weekly. It is important to remember that chemicals used in food packaging and commercial foods as flavor enhancers and preservatives were not part of the human diet before 1980.

> "In reality, we don't know how many chemicals are currently in commerce in the United States because updating the inventory wasn't designed to answer that question. Instead, it was designed to inform us about chemicals that are produced at higher volumes."[54]
>
> ~Lynn R. Goldman, Dean of the George Washington University School of Public Health and former Assistant Administrator for Toxic Substances at the U.S. Environmental Protection Agency (EPA)

The lack of information available on the effects of these substances on human health at chronic low-dose exposure is very concerning. Food manufacturing companies are not required to provide long-term research on the impact of these chemicals. Furthermore, the effect of exposure to multiple substances simultaneously, which is the norm, is virtually unknown. A study by the Agency for Toxic Substances and Disease Registry (ATSDR) states:

> "When examining the components of 15 combinations and how they may interact, they predicted that 41% of them would have additive effects, 20% would have synergistic effects, but for 24% they did not have the minimum information necessary to predict the effects. It has been estimated that at current funding levels, it would take 1,000 years to document adequately the health effects of the chemicals commonly encountered in commerce and industry."[55]

The Centers for Disease Control (CDC) published data on the levels of selected persistent organic pollutants (POPs), "a category of toxins which includes dioxins, phthalates, PDBEs, PCBs, etc.—and found that among a representative sample of the U.S. population, some toxins were present in essentially every individual over the age of 12. An analysis of National Health And Nutrition Examination Study (NHANES) data found up to a 38-fold adjusted increase in risk for diabetes prevalence in those with the highest levels," and increased risk has also been documented for cardiovascular disease, insulin resistance, impaired neurological development, learning and attention deficit disorders, endometriosis, and deficiencies in the hypothalamic-pituitary-thyroid axis. In a nutshell, all the chemicals we are exposed to daily are making us sick.

A variety of physiologic mechanisms cause damage. Most toxins increase oxidative stress by poisoning enzymes, directly damaging DNA or cellular membranes, and acting as endocrine disruptors. For example, the toxic metal cadmium increases oxidative damage by causing the formation of free radicals and by directly poisoning several enzymes that reduce oxidative stress, including catalase, glutathione reductase, and the most abundant cellular antioxidant, glutathione.

Most detoxification programs focus exclusively on the liver, but the role of the GI tract is crucial in the body's normal detoxification processes, because the greatest portion of the toxic load on the liver comes from the bowel. To efficiently eliminate toxins, the body undergoes a series of processes that must occur sequentially. While detoxifying, it is essential to support the body with adequate levels of vitamins, minerals, amino acids, phytochemicals, and dietary fiber.

Nutrients to repair damaged intestinal lining and regulate the elimination of toxins:

- **L-glutamine**: A primary amino acid source for intestinal cells, glutamine has been shown to regulate intercellular junction integrity.
- **Probiotics** are the greatest factor in determining intestinal integrity is the health of the microbial flora.
- **N-acetyl glucosamine** (NAG) provides a substrate for the repair of gut tissues.
- **Zinc** deficiency has been shown to disrupt cell formation, alter membrane permeability, impair immune function, and cause intestinal ulceration.
- **Antioxidants** (vitamin C, vitamin E, beta-carotene, grape seed extract, and milk thistle extract) protect the GI tract from oxidant damage and help with hepatic detoxification of compounds associated with intestinal dysfunction.
- **Quercetin**, critical to intestinal integrity, acts through several mechanisms.
- Highly digestible **protein** and low-allergy water-soluble **fiber** are known to restore intestinal health and aid in eliminating chemicals.
- **N-acetyl cysteine** increases the urinary excretion of toxic metals in proportion to body burden, especially mercury. It has been shown to increase hepatic glutathione, assisting in the detoxification of acetaminophen.

  - **Chlorella** has been proven to reduce the absorption of specific toxins in the GI tract, dioxins, and the reabsorption of stored dioxins. Supplementation with chlorella has been shown to reduce the maternal transfer of dioxins in breast milk.
  - **Milk thistle** is a powerful hepatoprotective agent and a potent antioxidant against environmental toxins.
  - **Broccoli** supports several Phase 2 metabolic pathways and has been shown to reduce harmful estrogens, reducing breast, prostate, and cervical cancer risk.
  - **Lipoic acid** is a heavy metal chelator and restores glutathione levels.
- **Green tea** has been shown to protect the liver from alcohol.

Molds and Environmental Allergens

Fungi represent one of the most diverse and abundant eukaryotes on earth. Many fungi live in harmony with humans, rarely causing diseases. Possible fungi-related health effects generally include infections (mycosis), allergic reactions, or toxic effects. Some individuals are highly sensitive to fungus in the forms of both mushrooms and mold. While molds' induction of allergic immune responses is generally acknowledged, other direct health effects like the toxic mold syndrome are controversial. Recent observations indicate particular importance of mold/mycotoxin exposure in individuals with pre-existing dysregulation of the immune system due to exacerbation of underlying pathophysiology, including allergic and non-allergic chronic inflammatory diseases, autoimmune disorders, and even human immunodeficiency virus (HIV) disease progression.[56]

Significant exposure to mycotoxins has also been found in developed countries, even in highly controlled infant food products.[57] Harmful effects caused by mycotoxins include acute poisoning after consumption of high dosages, which may even result in death. Carcinogenic aflatoxins (AF), as the most prominent example, can cause irreversible liver damage.[58] Furthermore, adverse effects on many internal organs have been reported. The respiratory system is the first point of contact during inhalation of mold spores and mycotoxins. Mycotoxins like AF have been shown in vivo to slow down basal and stimulate respiratory ciliary beat frequency, potentially increasing pathogenesis and infection by impaired clearance.[59]

It is estimated that more than five billion people are exposed to mycotoxins daily by unknown pathways and consuming contaminated foods daily.[60] *Mycotoxicosis* occurs when a mycotoxin leads to acute or chronic toxicity involving hepatotoxicity, cytotoxicity, teratogenicity, neurotoxicity, mutation, and carcinogenicity. Mycotoxins inhibit DNA and RNA synthesis by interacting with nucleic acids at cellular levels.[61, 62]

The most prevalent mycotoxins found in food commodities are aflatoxins and ochratoxins produced by Aspergillus species, ochratoxins and patulin produced by Penicillium, as well as fumonisins, deoxynivalenol, and zearalenone produced by Fusarium species. Worldwide, fumonisins, patulin, aflatoxins, and ochratoxins, among others, are responsible for numerous acute and chronic diseases in people and domestic animals.[63]

Emerging health effects of residents of mold-infested housing can only be clarified if mycotoxin research in residential settings is as consequently performed as mycotoxin exposure studies via the food chain have been over the past decades. Attempts should be made to correlate indoor mycotoxin exposures with adverse health impairments of occupants of infested buildings. Additionally, houses without mold infestation should be included as controls in future studies. For this purpose, human indoor exposure biomarkers might be helpful, as they are used extensively for mycotoxin exposure by food intake.[64]

Health issues of residents of mold-infested housing are reported regularly. Toxic mold syndrome is a complex of symptoms including various vague characteristics like cognitive impairment, emotional disturbance, respiratory complaints, and muscle aches. It is thought to be a direct effect of indoor "black mold" and its mycotoxins.[65] Prolonged black mold toxicity combined with asthma and other health factors played a pivotal role in the death of my former medical oversight professional partner, Mary Hagood, FNP, in 2023.

The incidence of inflammatory bowel diseases (IBD) is increasing in Western and developing countries and is linked with mycotoxin contamination in food. IBD is a multifactorial disorder involving complex interactions between genetic, immune, and environmental factors, such as exposure to food contaminants. Previously, IBD had been classified as an autoimmune disease, but new research has shown instead that an immune barrier defect causes inflammation.[66, 67]

The following symptoms of mold exposure have been reported by persons within a mold-contaminated environment (on and off) for an extended period of time. Symptoms become more severe and longer lasting, directly proportional to the exposure time.

Constant headaches	Nosebleeds	Constant fatigue
Breathing disorders	Coughing blood or black phlegm	Skin rash
Diarrhea	Vomiting	Loss of appetite
Memory loss, short-term	Weight loss	Hair loss
Open sores on the skin	Chronic bronchitis	Ear infections and pain
Pain in joints and muscles	Nausea	Chronic sinus infections
Neurological and nervous disorders		Sexual dysfunction
Swollen glands in the neck and armpit		Sudden asthma attacks or breathing disorders

Severe reactions may occur among workers exposed to large amounts of mold in occupational settings, such as farmers working around moldy hay or in greenhouses. Severe reactions may include fever and shortness of breath. Immunocompromised persons and people with chronic lung diseases like COPD are at increased risk for opportunistic infections and may develop fungal lung infections.[68]

In 2004, the Institute of Medicine (IOM) found there was sufficient evidence to link indoor exposure to mold with upper respiratory tract symptoms, coughing, and wheezing in otherwise healthy people, with asthma symptoms in people with asthma, and with hypersensitivity pneumonitis in individuals susceptible to that immune-mediated condition. The IOM also found limited or suggestive evidence linking indoor mold exposure to respiratory illness in otherwise healthy children.

These facts seem reason enough to eat immune-supporting foods like onion, garlic, oregano, basil, and rosemary while limiting the consumption of the many toxic foods found in the modern American diet.[69,70]

Airborne Allergies

Approximately 38% of the population of Western nations experience allergies. Mild allergies like hay fever are highly prevalent in humans and cause allergic conjunctivitis, itchiness, and a runny nose. Hay fever involves nose inflammation due to an allergic reaction to wind-borne pollens, grasses, or weeds. Hay fever is caused primarily by antigens that initiate an allergic response. Some antigens that can initiate hay fever include house dust, animal hair/dander, dust mites, fungus spores, feathers, powders, pesticides, and tree and grass pollen.

> "An allergy is a disorder of the immune system often called *atopy*. Allergic reactions occur to normally harmless environmental substances known as allergens; these reactions are acquired, predictable, and rapid. Strictly, allergy is one of the four forms of hypersensitivity and is called *type I* (or *immediate*) hypersensitivity. It is characterized by excessive activation of certain white blood cells called *mast cells* and *basophils* by a type of antibody known as IgE, resulting in an extreme inflammatory response. Common

Chapter 14 ~Forever Chemicals

allergic reactions include eczema, hives, hay fever, asthma, food allergies, and reactions to the venom of stinging insects such as wasps and bees."[71]

Allergy Tips and Tools

Not everyone can safely take over-the-counter antihistamines due to high blood pressure, drug interactions or sensitivities to the chemicals they contain. If you are one of these individuals or you choose to avoid drug use for other reasons, here are some suggestions for reducing hay fever naturally:

- **Bee pollen** has been used for centuries in China for seasonal allergies. It dries up the nasal cavity and slows or stops that annoying post-nasal drip that leads to the nagging coughing, sore throat, and drippy nose. Clinically, I have found pollen does not have to come from local sources to work.

- **Chinese herbs**: For years, I have managed most of my allergy symptoms with Chinese herb teas.

- **Bioflavonoid complex by Perque®**: Quercetin acts like a natural Singulair (Singular); the combined benefits of this product benefit blood pressure, circulation, and heart health, and it's combination of bioflavonoids work as a mast cell inhibitor.

- **OPC** or grape seed extract: All the antioxidants, including vitamins C and E, significantly reduce inflammation. As we have seen, allergies are a form of inflammation, and they respond well to antioxidants.

- **Silver** (Colloidal or Ionic) 500-10,000 ppm. A 50% solution of saline to 50% silver used as a nasal spray reduces infection and inflammation associated with environmental allergens (based on authors clinical use).

The history of silver in medicine is long. Antibiotic resistance in bacteria is a major problem worldwide that costs 55 billion USD annually for extended hospitalization, resource utilization, and additional treatment expenditures in the United States. The increase of antibiotic resistance in bacteria has become a major concern for successful diagnosis and treatment of infectious diseases. Over the past few decades, significant progress has been achieved on the development of nanotechnology-based medicines for combating multidrug resistance in microorganisms. Among this, silver nanoparticles (AgNPs) hold great promise in addressing this challenge due to their broad-spectrum and robust antimicrobial properties.[72, 73, 74]

The benefits of using these natural protocols far outweigh the minor inconvenience of taking nutraceuticals several times daily to reduce allergies, helping the body regain balance and health.

> ***Principle 75***: Specific nutrients and herbs can help repair damage and eliminate toxins caused by chemicals.

1. Native American advocacy group to retire 'Crying Indian' anti-pollution ad (2023), NBC News: https://www.nbcnews.com/news/us-news/native-advocacy-group-retire-crying-indian-anti-pollution-ad-rcna72398
2. Blakemore, E, The Shocking River Fire That Fueled the Creation of the EPA (2020) History.com: https://www.history.com/news/epa-earth-day-cleveland-cuyahoga-river-fire-clean-water-act
3. Karr, T. Our Journey with Food Online Education Course (2021): yourwholenutrition.com
4. Bendix, A., INSIDER (2020) 12 cities with the worst tap water in the US: https://www.businessinsider.com/cities-worst-tap-water-us-2019-3
5. Washington State Legislature (2022): Prohibition on the manufacture, sale, or distribution of certain food packaging—Safer alternatives assessment by department of ecology—Publication of findings—Report to legislature—Prohibition effective date contingent on findings. https://app.leg.wa.gov/rcw/default.aspx?cite=70A.222.070
6. Machoń-Grecka, A., Dobrakowski, M., Kasperczyk, A., Birkner, E., & Kasperczyk, S. (2022). Angiogenesis and lead (Pb): is there a connection?. Drug and chemical toxicology, 45(2), 589–593. https://doi.org/10.1080/01480545.2020.1734607
7. Global health burden and cost of lead exposure in children and adults: a health impact and economic modelling analysis Crossref DOI link: https://doi.org/10.1016/S2542-5196(23)00166-3
8. Dean, W. Role of heavy metals in disease and aging. Vitamin Research News. 17(4), 2003.
9. Apostoli, P., et al. [Lead and cardiopathy.] Med Lav. 95(2):124-132, 2004.
10. Dutta, S., Gorain, B., Choudhury, H., Roychoudhury, S., & Sengupta, P. (2022). Environmental and occupational exposure of metals and female reproductive health. Environmental science and pollution research international, 29(41), 62067–62092. https://doi.org/10.1007/s11356-021-16581-9
11. Haidar, Z., Fatema, K., Shoily, S. S., & Sajib, A. A. (2023). Disease-associated metabolic pathways affected by heavy metals and metalloid. Toxicology reports, 10, 554–570. https://doi.org/10.1016/j.toxrep.2023.04.010
12. Abdulla, N. M., Adam, B., Blair, I., & Oulhaj, A. (2019). Heavy metal content of herbal health supplement products in Dubai- UAE: a cross-sectional study. BMC complementary and alternative medicine, 19(1), 276. https://doi.org/10.1186/s12906-019-2693-3
13. Jairoun, A. A., Shahwan, M., & Zyoud, S. H. (2020). Heavy Metal contamination of Dietary Supplements products available in the UAE markets and the associated risk. Scientific reports, 10(1), 18824. https://doi.org/10.1038/s41598-020-76000-w
14. Brodziak-Dopierała, B., Fischer, A., Chrzanowska, M., & Ahnert, B. (2023). Mercury Exposure from the Consumption of Dietary Supplements Containing Vegetable, Cod Liver, and Shark Liver Oils. International journal of environmental research and public health, 20(3), 2129. https://doi.org/10.3390/ijerph20032129
15. Pirkle, J. L., et al. The decline in blood lead levels in the United States. The National Health and Nutrition Examination Surveys (NHANES). JAMA. 272(4):284-291, 1994.
16. Xiao, M., Li, D., Wang, X., Zhang, J., Wang, X., & Gao, J. (2023). Serum levels of lead are associated with venous thromboembolism: a retrospective study based on the NHANES database (1999 to 2018). Journal of thoracic disease, 15(8), 4426–4433. https://doi.org/10.21037/jtd-23-1071
17. Koch, W., Czop, M., Iłowiecka, K., Nawrocka, A., & Wiącek, D. (2022). Dietary Intake of Toxic Heavy Metals with Major Groups of Food Products-Results of Analytical Determinations. Nutrients, 14(8), 1626. https://doi.org/10.3390/nu14081626
18. NIELD, D. ENVIORMENT (2018) It's Official, Plastic Pollution Has Now Reached Our Last Unspoilt Wilderness: https://www.sciencealert.com/plastic-pollution-reaches-last-unspoilt-wilderness-antarctica
19. Miner, K. R., Clifford, H., Taruscio, T., Potocki, M., Solomon, G., Ritari, M., Napper, I. E., Gajurel, A. P., & Mayewski, P. A. (2021). Deposition of PFAS 'forever chemicals' on Mt. Everest. The Science of the total environment, 759, 144421. https://doi.org/10.1016/j.scitotenv.2020.144421
20. Drinking straw. (2023, September 1). In Wikipedia. https://en.wikipedia.org/wiki/Drinking_straw
21. Timshina, A., Aristizabal-Henao, J. J., Da Silva, B. F., & Bowden, J. A. (2021). The last straw: Characterization of per- and polyfluoroalkyl substances in commercially-available plant-based drinking straws. Chemosphere, 277, 130238. https://doi.org/10.1016/j.chemosphere.2021.130238
22. Li, R., Feng, Y., Gong, R. H., & Soutis, C. (2023). A Biodegradable Stereo-Complexed Poly (Lactic Acid) Drinking Straw of High Heat Resistance and Performance. Materials (Basel, Switzerland), 16(6), 2438. https://doi.org/10.3390/ma16062438
23. Goldman SM, Weaver FM, Stroupe KT, et al. Risk of Parkinson Disease Among Service Members at Marine Corps Base Camp Lejeune. JAMA Neurol. 2023;80(7):673–681. doi:10.1001/jamaneurol.2023.1168
24. Kazi Albab Hussain, Svetlana Romanova, Ilhami Okur, Dong Zhang, Jesse Kuebler, Xi Huang, Bing Wang, Lucia Fernandez-Ballester, Yongfeng Lu, Mathias Schubert, and Yusong Li Environmental Science & Technology 2023 57 (26), 9782-9792 DOI: 10.1021/acs.est.3c01942
25. Campanale, C., Massarelli, C., Savino, I., Locaputo, V., & Uricchio, V. F. (2020). A Detailed Review Study on Potential Effects of Microplastics and Additives of Concern on Human Health. International journal of environmental research and public health, 17(4), 1212. https://doi.org/10.3390/ijerph17041212
26. Lee, A. G., Kang, S., Yoon, H. J., Im, S., Oh, S. J., & Pak, Y. K. (2023). Polystyrene Microplastics Exacerbate Systemic Inflammation in High-Fat Diet-Induced Obesity. International journal of molecular sciences, 24(15), 12421. https://doi.org/10.3390/ijms241512421

Chapter 14 ~Forever Chemicals

27 Laganà, A., Visalli, G., Facciolà, A., Celesti, C., Iannazzo, D., & Di Pietro, A. (2023). Uptake of Breathable Nano- and Micro-Sized Polystyrene Particles: Comparison of Virgin and Oxidised nPS/mPS in Human Alveolar Cells. Toxics, 11(8), 686. https://doi.org/10.3390/toxics11080686

28 Welshons, W. V., Nagel, S. C., & vom Saal, F. S. (2006). Large effects from small exposures. III. Endocrine mechanisms mediating effects of bisphenol A at levels of human exposure. Endocrinology, 147(6 Suppl), S56–S69. https://doi.org/10.1210/en.2005-1159

29 https://totalityofevidence.com/dr-russell-blaylock/

30 http://www.mayoclinic.org/healthy-living/nutrition-and-healthy-eating/expert-answers/bpa/faq-20058331

31 Lam, S. S. N., Shi, Z., Ip, C. K. M., Wong, C. K. C., & Wong, A. S. T. (2023). Environmental-relevant bisphenol A exposure promotes ovarian cancer stemness by regulating microRNA biogenesis. Journal of cellular and molecular medicine, 27(18), 2792–2803. https://doi.org/10.1111/jcmm.17920

32 Wang, X., Nag, R., Brunton, N. P., Siddique, M. A. B., Harrison, S. M., Monahan, F. J., & Cummins, E. (2022). Human health risk assessment of bisphenol A (BPA) through meat products. Environmental research, 213, 113734. https://doi.org/10.1016/j.envres.2022.113734

33 Wang, X., Nag, R., Brunton, N. P., Siddique, M. A. B., Harrison, S. M., Monahan, F. J., & Cummins, E. (2023). Risk assessment of bisphenol A (BPA) in Irish meat and meat products. The Science of the total environment, 881, 163496. https://doi.org/10.1016/j.scitotenv.2023.163496

34 Konieczna, A., Rutkowska, A., & Rachoń, D. (2015). Health risk of exposure to Bisphenol A (BPA). Roczniki Panstwowego Zakladu Higieny, 66(1), 5–11.

35 Tennant D. R. (2018). Review of Glutamate Intake from Both Food Additive and Non-Additive Sources in the European Union. Annals of nutrition & metabolism, 73 Suppl 5, 21–28. https://doi.org/10.1159/000494778

36 Loï, C., & Cynober, L. (2022). Glutamate: A Safe Nutrient, Not Just a Simple Additive. Annals of nutrition & metabolism, 78(3), 133–146. https://doi.org/10.1159/000522482

37 WebMD, High Glutamate Foods (2022) https://www.webmd.com/diet/high-glutamate-foods

38 Chakraborty S. P. (2019). Patho-physiological and toxicological aspects of monosodium glutamate. Toxicology mechanisms and methods, 29(6), 389–396. https://doi.org/10.1080/15376516.2018.1528649

39 Zhou, Y., & Danbolt, N. C. (2014). Glutamate as a neurotransmitter in the healthy brain. Journal of neural transmission (Vienna, Austria : 1996), 121(8), 799–817. https://doi.org/10.1007/s00702-014-1180-8

40 Olney J. W. (1994). Excitotoxins in foods. Neurotoxicology, 15(3), 535–544.

41 Kraal, A. Z., Arvanitis, N. R., Jaeger, A. P., & Ellingrod, V. L. (2020). Could Dietary Glutamate Play a Role in Psychiatric Distress?. Neuropsychobiology, 79(1), 13–19. https://doi.org/10.1159/000496294

42 Hogervorst, E., Kassam, S., Kridawati, A., Soni, M., Xin, X., Shifu, X., & Rahardjo, T. B. (2017). Nutrition research in cognitive impairment/dementia, with a focus on soya and folate. The Proceedings of the Nutrition Society, 76(4), 437–442. https://doi.org/10.1017/S0029665117000404

43 https://fdasimplified.com/fda-is-finally-addressing-requests-for-a-definition-of-natural/

44 Lane, M. M., Gamage, E., Travica, N., Dissanayaka, T., Ashtree, D. N., Gauci, S., Lotfaliany, M., O'Neil, A., Jacka, F. N., & Marx, W. (2022). Ultra-Processed Food Consumption and Mental Health: A Systematic Review and Meta-Analysis of Observational Studies. Nutrients, 14(13), 2568. https://doi.org/10.3390/nu14132568

45 Godos, J., Bonaccio, M., Al-Qahtani, W. H., Marx, W., Lane, M. M., Leggio, G. M., & Grosso, G. (2023). Ultra-Processed Food Consumption and Depressive Symptoms in a Mediterranean Cohort. Nutrients, 15(3), 504. https://doi.org/10.3390/nu15030504

46 Lee, S., & Choi, M. (2023). Ultra-Processed Food Intakes Are Associated with Depression in the General Population: The Korea National Health and Nutrition Examination Survey. Nutrients, 15(9), 2169. https://doi.org/10.3390/nu15092169

47 Zhou, Y., Sui, H., Wang, Y., Yong, L., Zhang, L., Liang, J., Zhou, J., Xu, L., Zhong, Y., Chen, J., & Song, Y. (2023). Dietary Exposure to Glutamates of 2- to 5-Year-Old Toddlers in China Using the Duplicate Diet Method. Foods (Basel, Switzerland), 12(9), 1898. https://doi.org/10.3390/foods12091898

48 Roberts, A., Lynch, B., & Rietjens, I. M. C. M. (2018). Risk Assessment Paradigm for Glutamate. Annals of nutrition & metabolism, 73 Suppl 5(Suppl 5), 53–64. https://doi.org/10.1159/000494783

49 Czarnecka, K., Pilarz, A., Rogut, A., Maj, P., Szymańska, J., Olejnik, Ł., & Szymański, P. (2021). Aspartame-True or False? Narrative Review of Safety Analysis of General Use in Products. Nutrients, 13(6), 1957. https://doi.org/10.3390/nu13061957

50 Choudhary, A. K., & Lee, Y. Y. (2018). The debate over neurotransmitter interaction in aspartame usage. Journal of clinical neuroscience : official journal of the Neurosurgical Society of Australasia, 56, 7–15. https://doi.org/10.1016/j.jocn.2018.06.043

51 Soffritti, M., et al. Life-span exposure to low doses of aspartame beginning during prenatal life increases cancer effects in rats. Environ Health Perspect. 115(9):1293-1297, 2007.

52 Belpoggi, F., et al. Results of long-term carcinogenicity bioassay on Sprague-Dawley rats exposed to aspartame administered in feed. Ann N Y Acad Sci. 1076:559-577, 2006.

53 Woodling, K. A., Chitranshi, P., Jacob, C. C., Loukotková, L., Von Tungeln, L. S., Olson, G. R., Patton, R. E., Francke, S., Mog, S. R., Felton, R. P., Beland, F. A., Zang, Y., & Gamboa da Costa, G. (2022). Toxicological evaluation of brominated vegetable oil in Sprague Dawley rats.

Food and chemical toxicology : an international journal published for the British Industrial Biological Research Association, 165, 113137. https://doi.org/10.1016/j.fct.2022.113137

54 Roundtable on Environmental Health Sciences, Research, and Medicine; Board on Population Health and Public Health Practice; Institute of Medicine. Washington (DC): National Academies Press (US); 2014 Oct 2.

55 Tracking chemical exposures and human health. Environ Health Prospect. 2003;111(7): A374-375

56 Kraft, S., Buchenauer, L., & Polte, T. (2021). Mold, Mycotoxins and a Dysregulated Immune System: A Combination of Concern? International Journal of Molecular Sciences, 22(22). https://doi.org/10.3390/ijms222212269

57 Vin K., Riviere G., Leconte S., Cravedi J.P., Fremy J.M., Oswald I.P., Roudot A.C., Vasseur P., Jean J., Hulin M., et al. Dietary exposure to mycotoxins in the French infant total diet study. Food Chem. Toxicol. 2020;140:111301. doi: 10.1016/j.fct.2020.111301.

58 Franco L.T., Ismail A., Amjad A., Oliveira C.A.F.D. Occurrence of toxigenic fungi and mycotoxins in workplaces and human biomonitoring of mycotoxins in exposed workers: A systematic review. Toxin Rev. 2020:1–16. doi: 10.1080/15569543.2020.1795685.

59 WHO Mycotoxins. [(accessed on 9 August 2021)]. Available online: https://www.who.int/news-room/fact-sheets/detail/mycotoxins

60 Khodaei, D., Javanmardi, F., and Khaneghah, A. M. (2021). The global overview of the occurrence of mycotoxins in cereals: a three-year survey. Curr. Opin. Food Sci. 39, 36–42. doi: 10.1016/j.cofs.2020.12.012

61 Smith, C. A., Woloshuk, C. P., Robertson, D., and Payne, G. A. (2007). Silencing of the aflatoxin gene cluster in a diploid strain of Aspergillus flavus is suppressed by ectopic aflR expression. Genetics 176, 2077–2086. doi: 10.1534/genetics.107.073460

62 Pandey, A. K., Samota, M. K., Kumar, A., Silva, A. S., & Dubey, N. K. (2023). Fungal mycotoxins in food commodities: Present status and future concerns. Frontiers in Sustainable Food Systems, 7, 1162595. https://doi.org/10.3389/fsufs.2023.1162595

63 Pandey, A. K., Samota, M. K., Kumar, A., Silva, A. S., & Dubey, N. K. (2023). Fungal mycotoxins in food commodities: Present status and future concerns. Frontiers in Sustainable Food Systems, 7, 1162595. https://doi.org/10.3389/fsufs.2023.1162595

64 Lindemann, V., Schleiner, T., Maier, U., Fels, H., Cramer, B., & Humpf, U. (2022). Analysis of mold and mycotoxins in naturally infested indoor building materials. Mycotoxin Research, 38(3), 205-220. https://doi.org/10.1007/s12550-022-00461-3

65 Rudert A., Portnoy J. Mold allergy: Is it real and what do we do about it? Expert Rev. Clin. Immunol. 2017;13:823–835. doi: 10.1080/1744666X.2017.1324298.

66 Stange E.F., Schroeder B.O. Microbiota and mucosal defense in IBD: An update. Expert Rev. Gastroenterol. Hepatol. 2019;13:963–976. doi: 10.1080/17474124.2019.1671822.

67 Payros D., Menard S., Laffitte J., Neves M., Tremblay-Franco M., Luo S., Fouche E., Snini S.P., Theodorou V., Pinton P., et al. The food contaminant, deoxynivalenol, modulates the Thelper/Treg balance and increases inflammatory bowel diseases. Arch. Toxicol. 2020;94:3173–3184. doi: 10.1007/s00204-020-02817-z.

68 Mold Symptoms.Org- Developed For the Public's Better Understanding of The Dangers Of Fungal Contamination and Infections

69 http://www.cdc.gov/mold/stachy.htm

70 http://www.biosignlabs.com/Symptoms_Mold_Sickness.html

71 Merck Manual Professional Version, Overview of allergic and atopic disorders (2022): https://www.merckmanuals.com/professional/immunology-allergic-disorders/allergic,-autoimmune,-and-other-hypersensitivity-disorders/overview-of-allergic-and-atopic-disorders

72 Tang S, Zheng J. Antibacterial Activity of Silver Nanoparticles: Structural Effects. Adv Healthc Mater. 2018 Jul;7(13):e1701503. doi: 10.1002/adhm.201701503. Epub 2018 May 29. PMID: 29808627.

73 Medici S, Peana M, Nurchi VM, Zoroddu MA. Medical Uses of Silver: History, Myths, and Scientific Evidence. J Med Chem. 2019 Jul 11;62(13):5923-5943. doi: 10.1021/acs.jmedchem.8b01439. Epub 2019 Feb 21. PMID: 30735392.

74 Kaiser KG, Delattre V, Frost VJ, Buck GW, Phu JV, Fernandez TG, Pavel IE. Nanosilver: An Old Antibacterial Agent with Great Promise in the Fight against Antibiotic Resistance. Antibiotics (Basel). 2023 Jul 31;12(8):1264. doi: 10.3390/antibiotics12081264. PMID: 37627684; PMCID: PMC10451389.

> "If there is magic on this planet, it is contained in water."
>
> ~ Loren Eiseley

Chapter Fifteen ~ *Hydration*

By Kathleen Bell, RN, MSN, CNM, AHN-BC, WHCNP (ret)

As food has shaped human evolution, so too has water. Water is essential for all life on Earth. Without enough water, our physical and cognitive functions decline. Without water, we die within a matter of days. In this way, humans are more dependent on water than many other mammals.

Water is the first and most important nutrient for every cell in the human body. Water is the primary building material for all cell components; literally all our cells are full of water, fully two-thirds of the body's water is intracellular. Every metabolic function in the body depends on it. Your body can live weeks without food; death will occur in 2-4 days without consuming water.[1,2]

In contrast with other mammals whose bodies evolved to become suited to available water in the environments they inhabit — from desert mice and camels in the desert to chimpanzees in the jungle — humans throughout history have drastically engineered their environments to ensure access to water. Take the historic Roman city of Caesarea in modern-day Israel. Back when it was built more than 2,000 years ago, the region did not have enough naturally occurring freshwater to sustain a city. Because of its geographic importance to their colonial rule, the Romans built a series of aqueducts to transport water from springs as far away as approximately 10 miles (16 kilometers). This arrangement provided up to 50,000 people with about 38 gallons (145 liters) of daily water per capita.[3]

Most of the human body is composed of water. The actual percentage of body composition will vary with gender and age. About 60% of an adult male's body is water, however, fat tissues do not contain as many fluids as leaner tissues such as muscles or skin. In most female bodies, fat comprises a higher percentage than in men of similar age, and women's bodies are closer to 50% water. Infants' and children's bodies are comprised of much more fluid than adults; a newborn's body is roughly 78% water, and by 12 months of age that amount has decreased to 65%.[4] In contrast, older adults begin to lose body fluid composition due to changes in metabolism and macronutrient oxidation.[5]

Dr. H. H. Mitchell and other physiologists at the University of Illinois first did actual composition estimates of human bodies in the 1940s; these numbers are still pertinent today. According to Dr. Mitchell's team, the heart and brain are composed of 73% water, with the lungs tipping the scales at 83%. Skin (the body's largest organ) weighs in at 64%, topped by muscles and kidneys, which are tied at 79% water composition; even bones are not completely solid, containing 31% water.[6]

Despite adaptive changes in biological development over the ages, healthy humans regulate daily water balance remarkably well, even with exposure to stressors in hydration status. When ancient humans had to chase down their animal food sources on foot, water loss equivalent to 10% of the hunter's body mass — about 5 hours with no drinking — was considered the physiological limit of a hunt for large prey. Even today, serious medical complications can result from this amount of water loss.[7]

Sweat glands are a crucial part of our evolutionary story. Mammals have three types of sweat glands: apocrine, sebaceous, and eccrine. The eccrine glands mobilize the water and electrolytes inside cells to produce sweat. Humans have more eccrine sweat glands than any other primate. A recent study by Daniel Aldea and his colleagues at the University of Pennsylvania found that repeated mutations of a gene called *Engrailed 1* may have led to this abundance of eccrine sweat glands.[8] In relatively dry environments, similar to the ones early hominins evolved in, the evaporation of sweat cools the skin and the blood within the blood vessels which, in turn, cools the body's core temperature.

Water and sodium balances in the body are tightly regulated and monitored by the brain. Few studies have explored the relationship between water and salt intake; whether sodium intake compared with different levels of fluid intake leads to changes in hydration status remains unknown.[9]

What does water do for you?

The figure illustrates a few of water's many functions in the body. Water is critically needed by the brain to maintain normal cognition, manufacture hormones and neurotransmitters, and balance internal body temperature. Water makes cerebrospinal fluid, which acts as a shock absorber for the brain and spinal cord. Water helps form saliva, initiating digestion, and it serves to keep all mucosal membranes moist. In the lungs, water's surface tension keeps delicate air sacs (*alveoli*) open so respiration can take place. Lungs also metabolize certain substances (like alcohol and anesthetics) and assist in regulating body temperature. In the stomach, water creates enzymes that convert food to nutritional components that will be absorbed in the intestines for survival and growth. Joints remain healthy when lubricated by synovial fluid, which is built from water. Drinking water keeps the skin healthy.

 Lubrication

 Temperature regulation

 Helps convert food into energy

 Participates in the process of digestion

 Good skin

Sweat is formed by the skin to aid in temperature regulation and to dispose of toxins. Water is necessary for healthy blood supply and circulation; both cellular and liquid components of the blood depend on adequate hydration, and it is vital for fluid and electrolyte balance. The bloodstream delivers nutrients, oxygen, and medications all over the body allowing its trillions of cells to grow, reproduce, and survive in harmony with one another.

Chapter 15 ~ Hydration

The bowels need water to move solid waste, and the kidneys depend on water to filter the blood and flush liquid waste from the body.

> ***Principle 76***: Water is the most important nutrient and the major component of a human body.

Properties of Water

The substance we know on Earth as water appears to be unique in our galaxy – and its existence is completely responsible for any and every form of life on our planet. Water's qualities and properties are what make it so miraculous and so important to the survival of living organisms.

First, water is a solvent, allowing many substances to dissolve into it – more than any other liquid. This property makes it possible for plants, animals, and humans to ingest and utilize valuable nutrients, minerals, and chemicals needed for basic biologic functioning. Second, its "stickiness" – also known as surface tension – plays a part in coating membranes and in transporting dissolved materials all throughout the body tissues. Many necessary body processes, digestion and elimination among them, depend on water's ability to absorb and transport nutrients into and waste out of cells, and out of our bodies.[10]

Two other properties, adhesion and cohesion, affect how water works in every living organism. In cohesion, water is attracted to water; adhesion occurs when water is attracted to other substances or materials.[11] These two properties are involved in a critical biological process called capillary action which takes place in plants, animals, and humans.

Water Requirements

Almost everyone has heard the common 8 X 8 "rule of thumb" about drinking 8 glasses containing 8 ounces of water daily. And if you are actually doing that, you are probably doing well! But better science is available to help us figure out what we need. In order to ensure optimal hydration, it is proposed that optimal total water intake should approach 2.5 to 3.5 liters per day to allow for the daily excretion of 2-3 liters of dilute (< 500 mOsm kg-1) urine. Simple urinary markers of hydration such as urine color or void frequency, may be used to monitor and adjust fluid intake.[12]

Water requirements are usually stated per 24-hour period and vary depending on age, gender, environment (including geographical location and altitude), and health status. As a rule of thumb, a healthy adult male who lives neither in the desert nor at high altitude needs about 3 liters (3.2 quarts)/day, and an adult female of the same age and location needs about 1 liter less = 2.2 liters (2.3 quarts)/24-hour period. Importantly, all of this water doesn't need to be consumed as liquids, as many foods contain a significant amount of water.

Daily water requirements for infants and children are calculated with a formula using age in days/months/years and body weight. Many other factors need to be considered in this population besides those already mentioned for adults: prematurity, dehydration/rehydration, nasogastric or enteral feeding, metabolic issues, failure to thrive, gastrointestinal issues, etc. Dehydration is a real danger in small humans; specialized pediatric medical attention is always advised to rebalance fluid and electrolytes.

Many children and young adults between the ages of 10 and 20 in the U.S. are currently obese and showing suboptimal hydration, as 60% fail to meet the U.S. Dietary Reference Intakes for water. Studies have shown a significant inverse association between hydration status and body composition in children.[13] Although low water intake has been associated with adverse health outcomes, available literature indicates that most children do not meet the water intake guidelines and are underhydrated based on elevated hydration biomarkers.[14, 15]

Dr. Rosinger, a biologist at Pennsylvania State University, studies the evolution of human needs for survival. "Even under favorable conditions, with food and water readily available, people generally do not recover all of their water losses from heavy exercise for at least 24 hours. And so, we must be careful to strike a balance in how we lose and replenish the water in our bodies. Our dietary flexibility is perhaps our best defense against dehydration. In the U.S., around 20% of the water people ingest comes from food, yet my work among Tsimané (in Africa) found that foods, including fruits, contribute up to 50% of their total water intake. Adults in Japan, who typically drink less water than adults in the U.S., also get around half their water from the foods they eat. Other populations employ different dietary strategies to meet their water needs. Daasanach pastoralists in northern Kenya consume a great deal of milk, which is 87% water. They also chew on water-laden roots."[16, 17]

Debate continues over whether or not individuals with low total water intake are in a chronic fluid deficit.[18] Research findings suggest that dehydration may be associated with suppressed immune function in generally healthy middle-to-older aged community-dwelling adults.[19] Core body temperature (CBT) shows a diurnal rhythm, and the nocturnal decrease in CBT is blunted in older people.[20]

One in three individuals worldwide (2.2 billion people) lacks access to safe drinking water. Water intake requirements largely reflect water turnover, the water used by the body each day.[21] In 2005, U.S. water intake recommendations were based on analyses of Nutrition Health and Examination Surveys (NHANES) III data that examined whether hydration classification varied by water intake and estimated the median water intake associated with hydration in persons aged 19-30.[22]

> ***Principle 77***: Water requirements vary throughout the life cycle depending on gender, age, physical activity, environment, and health status.

A 2018 study published in the journal *Nutrients* recommends these daily amounts of water intake by age and gender.

Infants 0-6 months	700 ml/day	Females 14 years - adult	2.3L/day
Infants 6-12 months	800ml/day	Males 14 years - adult	3.3L/day
Kids 4-8 years	1.7L/day	Pregnancy	3L/day
Girls 9-13 years	2.1L/day	Lactating females	3.8L/day
Boys 9-13 years	2.4L/day		

Healthline.com suggests an easy formula to estimate daily water requirements for an adult who does not live in the desert or at altitude. Divide your weight in pounds by half, this is how many ounces of water per day you need. Example: Half of 135 pounds is 67.5, and 67.5 oz = 2 liters.[23]

The Importance of Fluids for Elimination

The circulatory and urinary systems serve the extremely important functions of maintaining fluid balance in the body. Blood vessels in the circulatory system carry blood to and from the heart with every heartbeat; both the pressure and volume of blood in the body are affected by hydration status. The urinary system is a complex of organs. Kidneys govern the entire process, connecting to the bladder via the ureters, which channel urine into the bladder so that it may be excreted from the body via the urethra.

Most of us pay little attention to urination unless something goes wrong, but it is one of the body's most important functions. Living every day, we are exposed to a multitude of toxins — in the food we eat, the air we breathe, the water we drink, the clothing we wear, the personal care products we use (shampoo, cosmetics, medications), and our home environments (furniture, carpeting, bedding, and cleaning products). Elimination of toxins daily is necessary to keep us alive and well. Body processes to get rid of toxins include urination, bowel movements, sweat, and tears. The main function of the large intestine (colon) is to recycle nutrients and water back into our bodies and to eliminate all waste products. Sweating releases PCBs (a family of man-made chemicals known as chlorinated hydrocarbons) along with phthalates, bisphenols, and other toxic compounds such as alcohol metabolites. It can be an even more efficient form of elimination than urination. Of course, *the best way to support all these important functions is to hydrate adequately* each and every day.

If toxins cannot be properly excreted, they accumulate in the body causing many (seemingly unrelated) problems, such as weight gain, fatigue, headaches, skin disorders, digestive issues, and frequent colds/flu/infections. More toxic build-up leads to more serious consequences like autoimmune diseases and cancer.

Balance is Key

Good health is always related to balance. Our hydration needs change by the year, month, week, day, and hour depending on our general health status, weight and body mass (BMI), the weather/ambient humidity, and the altitude where we are breathing. Understanding the body's water requirements is related to the concept of intake and output, best explained as attempting to equalize the amount of water consumed with the amount that the body is losing via urination, sweating, digestion, and respiration. During a medical assessment, after monitoring vital signs — temperature, heart rate, and respiration — measurement of intake and output is the next critical indicator of health status.

The best way to assess hydration status is to monitor urine output. This can easily be done in infants and toddlers who are not potty-trained by counting wet diapers. After the first week of a term newborn's life, the baby is well hydrated if they have at least 6 wet diapers/day, with no more than 8 hours between wet diapers. For both children and adults, looking at the color of the urine is also important to determine hydration status. Adequate hydration results in urine that is pale yellow and clear. Any color darker than straw-colored indicates some degree of dehydration.[24] **<u>NOTE</u>**: Multivitamin use can turn urine a very bright yellow, but the color is not darker. Dark urine means the kidneys have highly concentrated it; in the hospital setting urine concentration is measured by testing the specific gravity (USG). It is advisable to push oral fluids and seek medical attention if an individual's urine is amber or light brown and/or if the urine is bloody, cloudy, or foul-smelling.[25]

Feeling **thirsty is a late sign** of inadequate hydration. The sensation of thirst evolved in the brains of prehistoric humans who could not be certain that the water they were drinking was safe, and it does not 'kick in 'until we are past the point of dehydration. By the time you feel thirsty you have already stressed your body and your urinary system. I have been a hiker for decades and have learned to do what the military often teaches soldiers who are about to march for long distances, "Drink at least a quart of water before you take the first step." During pregnancy, water requirements increase with gestational age. Insufficient water intake causes dehydration, which may adversely affect maternal health and birth outcomes. Breastfeeding mothers, whose water requirements

Colors of Urine

 Pink /red-tinged: Menstrual or post-partum blood, eating beets or other red foods/red or dyed beverages, bleeding from a health issue (STI, urinary tract infection, kidney stone, etc.). See a healthcare practitioner.

Clear and colorless: May be overhydrated.

Cloudy: Possible dehydration, more probably indicates a urinary tract infection. See a healthcare practitioner.

Pale yellow: Hydrated.

Bright yellow: Hydrated. Vitamins will often increase the color intensity, but not deepen/darken the color.

 Medium yellow to darker gold (straw-colored): Hydration needed, may need to include electrolytes. Also could indicate medications and/or vitamins, coffee.

 Dark gold to light brown (amber): Dehydrated, needs fluid and electrolyte replacement. Also could indicate medications or other health conditions.

are elevated to ensure adequate milk production, especially need to avoid thirst. La Leche League's tried and true advice to avoid dehydration is for the lactating mother, regardless of thirst, to always have a glass of fluid herself as the baby is nursing; in other words, "drink when the baby drinks." Older adults should be particularly aware of dehydration's varied signs and symptoms, as the sense of thirst can disappear with advancing age. The sensation of thirst is one of the body's three main physiologic mechanisms to prevent dehydration. The other two involve methods of fluid conservation: hormonal signals to the kidneys to hold on to/concentrate the urine as well as producing less, and osmotic transfer of water cells to areas of the body that need it most to continue proper functioning.

> *Principle 78*: Adequate hydration requires a balance between water intake and output. Thirst is not a reliable indicator of hydration status.

Dangers of Dehydration

<u>**Encourage oral fluids and seek medical attention if you notice any of these signs or symptoms in yourself or your companions, as IV fluids may be needed to restore fluid and electrolyte balance in the body.**</u>

Persons at increased risk for dehydration include infants and children, pregnant and lactating women, adults aged 65+yrs, and those with conditions such as diabetes and chronic kidney disease. Gastrointestinal disturbances and illnesses that cause vomiting and diarrhea can result in dehydration, sometimes within a few hours, especially in babies, children, and older adults. Fever also contributes to dehydration in these special populations.[26]

When the body is dehydrated, vital electrolytes needed to perform essential functions cannot travel. Electrolytes are minerals that carry an electrical charge: sodium, potassium, chloride, magnesium, phosphate, calcium. Concentration gradients exist to highly regulate their presence within the body's cells, a process which insufficient fluids can disrupt. Critical electrolyte balances within cells, body fluids, and tissues facilitate effective water transport, nutrient distribution, acid/base balance, heart rhythm and function, proper operation of muscles and the nervous system, and waste removal.[27]

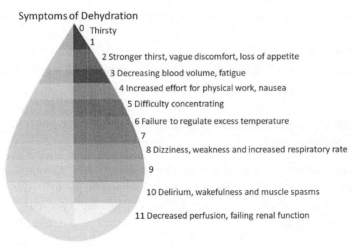

Let's take a closer look at just one of the electrolytes listed above: potassium. Potassium's main role in the body is to maintain normal fluid levels *inside* our cells, while sodium - its counterpart - maintains normal fluid levels *outside* the cells. Potassium helps muscles (like the heart) to contract, regulates the nervous system, and supports normal blood pressure. Normal blood potassium levels range from 3.6 – 5.2 millimoles/liter, not a very wide range! Even a small fraction lower or higher than this narrow window of safety for blood potassium levels can be dangerous, requiring immediate medical treatment.

In senior citizens, even mild dehydration can result in decreased blood pressure, leading to fainting and falls, low blood oxygen levels, or hypovolemic shock – all potentially life-threatening conditions. Left untreated, dehydration can lead to serious medical conditions and even death.

> ***Principle 79***: Dehydration can kill.

Achieving Hydration Goals

Besides drinking plain water, flavored and coconut waters, fruit/vegetable juices, smoothies/shakes, milk, tea, and coffee also count in your fluid intake. Research as recent as 2020 indicates that whole or skim milk might be a better choice for hydration after exercise, because subjects were able to retain fluids for a longer period after ingestion.[28] Be cautioned that some beverages act as a diuretic, causing your body to lose water via more frequent urination. These include coffee, tea, sodas, and alcoholic beverages.[29]

Many foods have a high-water content to help you maintain good hydration. My favorite food on a long hike is grapes; they are sweet and juicy, giving me a burst of energy as well as making me feel like I have had something to drink. Other examples of water-laden foods are melons, berries, citrus and many other fruits, cucumbers, lettuce, celery, and leafy greens.

A few well-tested techniques to boost your daily water intake

- Carry a re-usable water bottle and refill it throughout the day. Set mini goals of drinking at least one or two containers per day by splitting the day into increments and making water your first beverage choice whenever possible.
- Try drinking your water between meals ICE COLD or add a slice of your favorite fruit to the container.
- Drink at least two 8 oz glasses of water before and after exercise. If walking/biking/running or engaging in any form of sustained exertion (dancing, hiking, climbing, etc.) drink small amounts of water at regular intervals to avoid thirst.

Remember: <u>Thirst is a late signal from your body that more water is needed.</u> If you drink before, during, and after exercising you may not feel thirsty, which is good.

- Take all oral medications with 8 oz of plain water for adults, 4-6 oz for children under 13 years.
- Drink 8 to 16 oz of water (warm, hot, or room temperature but not iced) when you get up in the morning and the same quantity 15-30 minutes before every meal. This is an ancient Ayurvedic practice that will be explained later in this chapter.

Too much of a good thing

Although rare, it is possible to drink too much water. Usually, if your body is healthy and you drink more fluids than your requirements, your kidneys increase urine production until the proper balance is achieved. Heart and kidney function needs to be normal to accomplish this, however. Individuals who have chronic conditions such as diabetes, chronic kidney disease, or congestive heart failure can develop a condition called hyponatremia (water intoxication). This happens when the amount of water in your system overwhelms your kidneys, and they can't keep up with a normal filtration rate. The sodium content of your blood becomes dangerously diluted, which causes cells to swell. Elite, high-level athletes may experience hyponatremia if they don't replace their electrolytes along with water after exercising.

Electrolyte Replacement and Gatorade®

The most common way to deplete electrolytes is by sweating. Sodium and chloride are the electrolytes lost in the highest concentrations in sweat, along with lower amounts of potassium and magnesium. In some cases, especially in very hot temperatures, athletes can lose up to 3 ounces of electrolytes during a game, race, or an especially long workout (>2 hours).

In 1965, James Robert Cade, MD (1927-2007) and a team of researchers at the University of Florida College of Medicine were investigating why their football players did not urinate after practice or playing a game in the Florida heat and humidity. The wisdom of the day discouraged replenishing fluids after sweating; such thinking may have been explained by fear of hyponatremia. Dr. Cade was a nephrologist who studied the physiology of exercise and was aware of the electrolytes lost by sweating. He most certainly understood that the University of Florida football players, the Gators, lost so much fluid and so many electrolytes during strenuous exertion that their kidneys went into fluid conservation mode and did not form urine for many hours. Dr. Cade and his team developed a drink containing salts and sugars which could be absorbed even more quickly than plain water, which later was produced and marketed as Gatorade. He also worked on other drinks for protein replacement.

Up until now, there has been no "gold standard" test to assess dehydration outside a medical setting. An interesting 2020 European study on water-induced thermogenesis (WUT) investigated the relationships between urine color, specific gravity (USG), osmolality (UOSM), thirst level, and body mass loss (BML). Measurements of these markers were taken for three days on 22 females and 21 males to establish baseline levels of normal (euhydration), followed by seven days of testing markers for predetermined dehydration thresholds. The WUT criteria were defined as >1% BML, urine color >5, and thirst level >5; these markers can be measured outside a hospital setting and do not require bloodwork or specialized equipment. In the study the other markers were summed up when each variable met each defined threshold.[30]

Results showed that when three markers indicated dehydration levels, UOSM and USG were greater than euhydrated cut points. When two markers indicated dehydration levels, USG was higher than the euhydrated cut point. Additionally, UOSM and USG were significantly lower when zero or one marker indicated dehydration levels. Thus, the WUT criteria are a useful tool to assess hydration status. Athletes, coaches, sports scientists, and medical professionals can use this strategy in field settings to optimize athletes 'performance and health without consuming money and time.[31]

Unmitigated vomiting and diarrhea can also cause electrolyte imbalance; these conditions can develop quickly in infants, children, and the elderly. However, treatment or prevention with oral Gatorade or other "sports drinks" is not recommended for these individuals. The concentrations of salts and sugars in Gatorade may be too high for very young or older kidneys to tolerate. Pedialyte® may be a better choice for replacement in these special populations.

Of course, long before Gatorade's invention, people who lived in hot climates or did strenuous physical work had figured out that they needed to replace the body fluids and salts that had been "sweated out" every day. There are numerous effective recipes for homemade remedies for dehydration. One of these is mentioned in *Our Journey with Food Cookery Book* on page 270; a beverage called switchel. This became a popular drink in the late 1600s in what were then the American colonies. By the 19th century switchel had become a traditional drink for hard-working farm crews in the fields. Switchel is a fermented drink made of water mixed with raw apple cider vinegar, honey or brown sugar, and seasoned with ginger. An Ayurvedic recipe for your own electrolyte-balancing sports drink that is easy to make at home is to add fresh lime juice, a pinch of rock (or black) salt, and maple syrup to taste to one quart of water. Adjust the ingredients to your preference and keep the beverage refrigerated. Black salt is a healthy food choice available in Indian and Asian markets. Because of its high trace mineral content, it smells like sulfur, and the taste is inimitable.

Eastern Wisdom: Water's Relationship to Digestion

According to expert Ayurvedic consultant Simon Chokoisky, drinking water does more for your body than replacing lost fluids. It also boosts metabolism and energy levels by optimizing nutrient assimilation. Drinking warm (room temperature) water promotes blood circulation in the stomach, allowing for better food absorption and increased detoxification of harmful substances. Drinking 8 to 16 oz of water first thing in the morning and the same amount 15-30 minutes before every meal ensures your stomach lining's bicarbonate layer is fully buffered and hydrated, signaling the production of hydrochloric acid (HCl). This digestive acid kills bacteria and breaks down food in the stomach. A dehydrated (dry) stomach doesn't produce optimal amounts of HCl, which can lead to indigestion and other issues further down along the gastrointestinal tract.

More water intake, and increasing stomach HCl, can also lead to fat loss. As reported in the *Journal of Clinical Diagnostic Research*, drinking 16 oz of water 30 minutes before eating breakfast, lunch, and dinner burned fat and resulted in significant changes in body composition in a study group of 50 overweight girls. Not only did they lose weight, but the shape of their bodies changed significantly – all from drinking water!

An important study conducted between 2009 and 2012 used a nationally representative sample of 9,528 adults ages 18 to 64 years from the National Health and Nutrition Examination Survey (NHANES). The primary outcome of interest was body mass index (BMI), categorized as obese (BMI ≥30) or not (BMI

<30). Individuals with urine osmolality values of 800 mOsm/kg or greater were considered to be inadequately hydrated. Nearly 51% (50.8%) were women, 64.5% were non-Hispanic white, and the mean age was 41 years. Mean urine osmolality was 631.4 mOsm/kg; fully 32.6% of the sample was inadequately hydrated. In adjusted models, adults who were inadequately hydrated had higher BMIs and higher odds of being obese compared with hydrated adults. This relationship had not previously been shown on a population level and suggests that water, an essential nutrient, may deserve greater focus in weight management research and clinical strategies.[32]

Before meals, add a few drops of lime juice and salt to a small slice of fresh ginger root, chew, and swallow to stimulate good digestion. Ayurveda also recommends taking the herb *trikatu* — a combination of ginger, long-pepper and black pepper — with room-temperature water before meals to avoid indigestion. Another practice is to sip hot water every 15-30 minutes throughout the day; lemon/lemon juice can be added if desired. Lemon water has numerous health benefits. It supports digestion and the immune system; contains natural antioxidants, vitamins and minerals; and stimulates peristalsis. This regimen is best during the cooler months of fall, winter, and spring, as it may be too heating for the body during summer.

Do you remember the *pH* scale of acidity from high school chemistry? The scale ranges from 0-14, with 7 being considered neutral. Measuring below 7, a substance is considered acidic; above 7 the substance is called alkaline. Ayurveda teaches to avoid drinking water during and after meals. The *pH* of HCl is about 2, and water is around 7, so water actually works against digestion with a full stomach. The Ayurvedic rule of thumb is that "water on an empty stomach boosts digestion, on a full stomach water bogs it down." It makes good chemical sense. If you need something to wash down your food, try sipping hot tea or wine. This may take some getting used to, but if you have followed the above tips, you should not feel thirsty during meals.

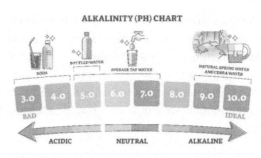

For a hydrating treat at the end of a meal (instead of dessert) you could try drinking *takram*, a slightly astringent mixture that helps digest and assimilate the food you have just eaten. According to Ayurveda (which means *science of life* in Sanskrit) meals should end with astringency rather than sweetness. To make takram, combine a cup of buttermilk with a cup of water and add ½ teaspoon roasted cumin powder and black salt to taste. Stir/shake well or mix in a blender.

Lastly, Ayurveda teaches that cold water dampens digestion, so save iced water/beverages for drinking at other times than meals. Colder beverages can be especially good during exercise/workouts, as some fitness gurus say it forces the body to spend extra calories warming them up to body temperature. By learning to drink enough water you will probably feel less need to drink coffee, sodas, or alcohol – improving your general health status.

Other Substances in Water

Alkaline water is a new trend being marketed as beneficial for your body. The human body has a baseline normal *pH* of 7.4 and "regular" water's *pH* is around 7. Most alkaline water brands have a *pH* >8, achieved by ionization and contain added minerals (calcium, potassium, magnesium, silica). The water is purified by various techniques like filtration and reverse osmosis, removing fluoride and chlorine, and adding electrolytes (mostly sodium bicarbonate). Very little scientific evidence supports the benefit of drinking these expensive products. Of note: Healthy functioning lungs, liver, and kidneys maintain the body's normal *pH*. Drinking a manufactured water product to achieve/restore this balance seems unnecessary and could carry potential risks, especially in persons with abnormal kidney function.

The U.S. Environmental Protection Agency (EPA) estimates that *1.5 trillion* gallons of pollutants leak into the ground each year! The biggest contamination culprits in the water supply are lead, radon, and nitrates (from agricultural fertilizers). More than 700 different kinds of chemicals have been identified in tap water; however, standard testing is commonly done for fewer than 200 of these, and the health significance of many chemicals in very low concentrations (measured as parts per trillion) is often unknown.

Much controversy continues to exist about chlorination of public water supplies. As more bacteria gain resistance to commonly used substances to exterminate them (both chemicals and pharmaceuticals), the level of chlorine needed to purify water will rise. Many years of study have associated chlorine use with elevated risks for cancers. Options for removing chlorine from household water range from hand-held charcoal filter pitchers to whole-house filtration systems. For more detailed information about substances that contaminate our drinking water, please see *Empty Plate: Food~Sustainability~Mindfulness,* Chapters 1 and 2.

Bottled water has gained worldwide popularity in the last few decades. Bottled water may not actually be any better than local tap water, so it is important to do your research if you are going to buy water. If you drink tap water, find out where it originates, how it is processed, what additives it contains, and ask your local water department for an analysis. If you drink well water, you can have a sample tested for pollutants and bacterial content.

Water from plastic containers contributes to the omnipresence of microplastics in the environment today, now being found literally everywhere on earth in locations as diverse as Antarctica to the Mariana Trench in the ocean to human fetuses in utero. Defined as plastic pieces <5 millimeters in size, microplastic particles are virtually everywhere on earth and have been found in human lungs, blood, and fetal tissues. Even smaller nanoplastics are particles < 1 micrometer in length. Every day we eat these particles, breathe them into our lungs, and drink them. Twenty years ago, marine biologists began announcing their presence in the ocean, but only recently have scientists focused on the microplastics in our food and drinking water. Although plastics have many different compositions, some contain chemicals known to interfere with hormone production (endocrine disruptors). Microplastics can enter drinking water at its source, during treatment and distribution, or (in bottled water) from packaging. Microplastics enter a fetus via the maternal placental circulation, and babies can also ingest the particles in breast milk. Plastic feeding bottles and toys increase exposure in toddlers and children.

Chapter 15 ~ Hydration

The good news? Current research shows that microplastics seem unable to penetrate the skin – so exposure during bathing may be minimal. Several countries (not the U.S.) have banned the use of microbeads in personal care products. But there are no policies or regulations anywhere in the world right now that address the continued issues of concentrations of microplastics found in our drinking water and in foods, and few monitoring efforts exist. California has recently approved the world's first requirements for testing microplastics in drinking water sources; mandatory testing is scheduled to begin over the next several years.

The Element of Water

Water is one of the building blocks of nature. The ancient Eastern wisdom traditions of Traditional Chinese Medicine and Ayurveda tell us that everything in the known universe is made up of five basic elements: **Space** (potential), **Earth** (solids), **Air** (movement), **Fire** (transformation), and **Water** (protection). The words in parentheses are an Ayurvedic interpretation of the Sanskrit words for each of these basic elements. These five elements are present in all human bodies, and our good health is influenced by choices made which enhance the needed balance among them. The holistic system of health and healing known as Ayurveda defines disease as *the absence of vibrant health* while the Western medical model's definition of health is defined as *the absence of disease*. The classic Sanskrit "prescription" for healthy living is made up of four phrases. Two of these phrases deal with the body's processes of hydration and digestion. The first one addresses systemic/constitutional balance and a strong digestive "fire" (called *agni* in Sanskrit). The second addresses balance among all the body's tissue needs regarding hydration and elimination.[33]

In the book *Whole Detox*, Dr. Deanna Minich refers to our body's ability to balance the element of water as "*flow*." In her comprehensive and integrative program of recommendations for healthy living, eating, and drinking, she assigns the element of water with an awesome additional responsibility of creative energy, associating it with the second energy center (chakra) in the body which governs reproduction. *Flow* energy enables us to create newness of life — which does not only mean babies! When we are in the *flow*, we easily take in and let go of food, water, and life experiences. Entering into this fluid and balanced state of being is the gateway to improved physical and emotional health, artistic and scientific creativity, and to novel thinking needed to innovate new ideas and solve problems by creating new solutions. The flow also influences our emotions, relationships, and partnerships.[34]

Mindful Choices

For many people worldwide, the food and water consumed daily are not always a matter of personal choice. If you are among the fortunate ones who can choose what you drink to stay well hydrated, you must pay attention to what you are ingesting with every sip. Mindful consumption of clean and

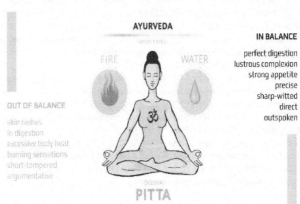

357

healthful drinks will serve you well over the long term; indeed, changing your habits and "cleaning up" your fluids may be one of the keys to the proverbial "fountain of youth." Nutrition research is finding that maintaining good hydration throughout life is a key factor in decreasing age-related illnesses such as cardiovascular disease, lung and liver conditions, and cognitive decline.[35, 36]

---

1 Johnson, J., & Luo, E. MD, Medical reviewer. (May 4, 2019) How Long Can You Live Without Water? https;//www.Medicalnewstoday.com

2 Popkin, B. M., D'Anci, K. E., & Rosenberg, I. H. (2010). Water, hydration, and health. Nutrition reviews, 68(8), 439–458. https://doi.org/10.1111/j.1753-4887.2010.00304.x

3 Rosinger, A. (2021) Human Evolution Led to an Extream Thirst for Water; Scientific America: https://www.scientificamerican.com/article/human-evolution-led-to-an-extreme-thirst-for-water/

4 USGS (5/22/2019) The Water in You; Water and the Human Body www.usgs.gov/special-topic/Water-science-school/science/water-you-water-and-human-body

5 St. Onge, M. & Gallagher, D. (2010) Body Composition Changes with Aging: The Cause or Result of Alterations in Metabolic Rate and Macronutrient oxidation. Nutrition, pp.152-155. doi:10.1016/j.nut.2009.07.004 PMCID: PMC2880224 NIHMSID: NIHMS 201762 PMID: 20004080

6 Journal of Biological Chemistry, v. 158, issue 3, pp.625-637.

7 https://onlinelibrary.wiley.com/doi/abs/10.1111/j.1753-4887.2005.tb00152.x

8 Aldea, D., & Kamberov, Y. G. (2022). En1 sweat we trust: How the evolution of an Engrailed 1 enhancer made humans the sweatiest ape. Temperature (Austin, Tex.), 9(4), 303–305. https://doi.org/10.1080/23328940.2021.2019548

9 Zhang, J., Zhang, N., Liu, S., Du, S., & Ma, G. (2022). Young Adults with Higher Salt Intake Have Inferior Hydration Status: A Cross-Sectional Study. Nutrients, 14(2), 287. https://doi.org/10.3390/nu14020287

10 Sheibani, E., & Mohammadi, A. (2018). The impacts of water compositions on sensory properties of foods and beverages cannot be underestimated. Food research international (Ottawa, Ont.), 108, 101–110. https://doi.org/10.1016/j.foodres.2018.03.024

11 Mallamace, F., Mallamace, D., Chen, S. H., Lanzafame, P., & Papanikolaou, G. (2021). Hydrophilic and Hydrophobic Effects on the Structure and Themodynamic Properties of Confined Water: Water in Solutions. International journal of molecular sciences, 22(14), 7547. https://doi.org/10.3390/ijms22147547

12 Perrier, E. T., Armstrong, L. E., Bottin, J. H., Clark, W. F., Dolci, A., Guelinckx, I., Iroz, A., Kavouras, S. A., Lang, F., Lieberman, H. R., Melander, O., Morin, C., Seksek, I., Stookey, J. D., Tack, I., Vanhaecke, T., Vecchio, M., & Péronnet, F. (2021). Hydration for health hypothesis: a narrative review of supporting evidence. European journal of nutrition, 60(3), 1167–1180. https://doi.org/10.1007/s00394-020-02296-z

13 Clayton, P., Trak-Fellermeier, M. A., Macchi, A., Galván, R., Bursac, Z., Huffman-Ercanli, F., Liuzzi, J., & Palacios, C. (2023). The association between hydration status and body composition in healthy children and adolescents. Journal of pediatric endocrinology & metabolism : JPEM, 36(5), 470–477. https://doi.org/10.1515/jpem-2022-0462

14 Suh, H., & Kavouras, S. A. (2019). Water intake and hydration state in children. European journal of nutrition, 58(2), 475–496. https://doi.org/10.1007/s00394-018-1869-9

15 Zhang, N., Zhang, F., Chen, S., Han, F., Lin, G., Zhai, Y., He, H., Zhang, J., & Ma, G. (2020). Associations between hydration state and pregnancy complications, maternal-infant outcomes: protocol of a prospective observational cohort study. BMC pregnancy and childbirth, 20(1), 82. https://doi.org/10.1186/s12884-020-2765-x

16 Scientific America Article citation earlier

Chapter 15 ~ Hydration

17 Pontzer, H., Yamada, Y., Sagayama, H., Ainslie, P. N., Andersen, L. F., Anderson, L. J., Arab, L., Baddou, I., Bedu-Addo, K., Blaak, E. E., Blanc, S., Bonomi, A. G., Bouten, C. V. C., Bovet, P., Buchowski, M. S., Butte, N. F., Camps, S. G., Close, G. L., Cooper, J. A., Cooper, R., ... IAEA DLW Database Consortium (2021). Daily energy expenditure through the human life course. Science (New York, N.Y.), 373(6556), 808–812. https://doi.org/10.1126/science.abe5017

18 Caldwell, A. R., Rosa-Caldwell, M. E., Keeter, C., Johnson, E. C., Péronnet, F., & Ganio, M. S. (2020). Effects of a 14-Day Hydration Intervention on Individuals with Habitually Low Fluid Intake. Annals of nutrition & metabolism, 76 Suppl 1, 67–68. https://doi.org/10.1159/000515375

19 Davis, K. M., Rosinger, A. Y., & Murdock, K. W. (2023). Ex vivo LPS-stimulated cytokine production is associated with hydration status in community-dwelling middle-to-older-aged adults. European journal of nutrition, 62(4), 1681–1690. https://doi.org/10.1007/s00394-023-03105-z

20 Seol, J., Kokudo, C., Park, I., Zhang, S., Yajima, K., Okura, T., & Tokuyama, K. (2023). Energy metabolism and thermoregulation during sleep in young and old females. Scientific reports, 13(1), 10416. https://doi.org/10.1038/s41598-023-37407-3

21 Yamada, Y., Zhang, X., Henderson, M. E. T., Sagayama, H., Pontzer, H., Watanabe, D., Yoshida, T., Kimura, M., Ainslie, P. N., Andersen, L. F., Anderson, L. J., Arab, L., Baddou, I., Bedu-Addo, K., Blaak, E. E., Blanc, S., Bonomi, A. G., Bouten, C. V. C., Bovet, P., Buchowski, M. S., ... International Atomic Energy Agency (IAEA) Doubly Labeled Water (DLW) Database Consortium§ (2022). Variation in human water turnover associated with environmental and lifestyle factors. Science (New York, N.Y.), 378(6622), 909–915. https://doi.org/10.1126/science.abm8668

22 Stookey J. D. (2019). Analysis of 2009-2012 Nutrition Health and Examination Survey (NHANES) Data to Estimate the Median Water Intake Associated with Meeting Hydration Criteria for Individuals Aged 12-80 in the US Population. Nutrients, 11(3), 657. https://doi.org/10.3390/nu11030657

23 Chang, T., Ravi, N., Plegue, M. A., Sonneville, K. R., & Davis, M. M. (2016). Inadequate Hydration, BMI, and Obesity Among US Adults: NHANES 2009-2012. Annals of family medicine, 14(4), 320–324. https://doi.org/10.1370/afm.1951

24 Nishi, S. K., Babio, N., Paz-Graniel, I., Serra-Majem, L., Vioque, J., Fitó, M., Corella, D., Pintó, X., Bueno-Cavanillas, A., Tur, J. A., Diez-Ricote, L., Martinez, J. A., Gómez-Martínez, C., González-Botella, A., Castañer, O., Alvarez-Sala, A., Montesdeoca-Mendoza, C., Fanlo-Maresma, M., Cano-Ibáñez, N., Bouzas, C., ... Salas-Salvadó, J. (2023). Water intake, hydration status and 2-year changes in cognitive performance: a prospective cohort study. BMC medicine, 21(1), 82. https://doi.org/10.1186/s12916-023-02771-4

25 Sekiguchi, Y., Benjamin, C. L., Butler, C. R., Morrissey, M. C., Filep, E. M., Stearns, R. L., & Casa, D. J. (2020). The Relationship between %BML, Urine Color, Thirst Level and Urine Indices of Hydration Status. Annals of nutrition & metabolism, 76 Suppl 1, 65–66. https://doi.org/10.1159/000515217

26 Hooper, L., Abdelhamid, A., Attreed, N. J., Campbell, W. W., Channell, A. M., Chassagne, P., Culp, K. R., Fletcher, S. J., Fortes, M. B., Fuller, N., Gaspar, P. M., Gilbert, D. J., Heathcote, A. C., Kafri, M. W., Kajii, F., Lindner, G., Mack, G. W., Mentes, J. C., Merlani, P., Needham, R. A., ... Hunter, P. (2015). Clinical symptoms, signs and tests for identification of impending and current water-loss dehydration in older people. The Cochrane database of systematic reviews, 2015(4), CD009647. https://doi.org/10.1002/14651858.CD009647.pub2

27 Fortes, M. B., Owen, J. A., Raymond-Barker, P., Bishop, C., Elghenzai, S., Oliver, S. J., & Walsh, N. P. (2015). Is this elderly patient dehydrated? Diagnostic accuracy of hydration assessment using physical signs, urine, and saliva markers. Journal of the American Medical Directors Association, 16(3), 221–228. https://doi.org/10.1016/j.jamda.2014.09.012

28 Berry, C. W., Wolf, S. T., Murray, B., & Kenney, W. L. (2020). Hydration Efficacy of a Milk Permeate-Based Oral Hydration Solution. Nutrients, 12(5), 1502. https://doi.org/10.3390/nu12051502

29 Seal, A. D., Bardis, C. N., Gavrieli, A., Grigorakis, P., Adams, J. D., Arnaoutis, G., Yannakoulia, M., & Kavouras, S. A. (2017). Coffee with High but Not Low Caffeine Content Augments Fluid and Electrolyte Excretion at Rest. Frontiers in nutrition, 4, 40. https://doi.org/10.3389/fnut.2017.00040

30 Patil. D.Y. (2013) "Effect of Water-Induced Thermogenesis on Body Weight, Body Mass Index, and Body composition of Overweight Subjects". Journal of Clinical and Diagnostic Research, 7, No. 9, 1894-1896. doi: 10.7860/JCDR/2013/5862.3344

31 Sekiguchi, Y., Benjamin, C. L., Butler, C. R., Morrissey, M. C., Filep, E. M., Stearns, R. L., & Casa, D. J. (2020). The Relationship between %BML, Urine Color, Thirst Level and Urine Indices of Hydration Status. Annals of nutrition & metabolism, 76 Suppl 1, 65–66. https://doi.org/10.1159/000515217

32 Chang, T., Ravi, N., Plegue, M. A., Sonneville, K. R., & Davis, M. M. (2016). Inadequate Hydration, BMI, and Obesity Among US Adults: NHANES 2009-2012. Annals of family medicine, 14(4), 320–324. https://doi.org/10.1370/afm.1951

33 Mahdihassan S. (1986). Salvaging the ancient doctrine of cosmology as contribution to modern science. The American journal of Chinese medicine, 14(1-2), 11–16. https://doi.org/10.1142/S0192415X8600003X

34 Zhang Y. (2021). Introduction of human anatomy before modern China: The preface of anatomical education in mainland China. Anatomical record (Hoboken, N.J. : 2007), 304(11), 2632–2640. https://doi.org/10.1002/ar.24759

35 Melnyk, B. M., Kelly, S. A., Stephens, J., Dhakal, K., McGovern, C., Tucker, S., Hoying, J., McRae, K., Ault, S., Spurlock, E., & Bird, S. B. (2020). Interventions to Improve Mental Health, Well-Being, Physical Health, and Lifestyle Behaviors in Physicians and Nurses: A Systematic Review. American journal of health promotion : AJHP, 34(8), 929–941. https://doi.org/10.1177/0890117120920451

36 Zagórska-Dziok, M., Ziemlewska, A., Bujak, T., Nizioł-Łukaszewska, Z., & Hordyjewicz-Baran, Z. (2021). Cosmetic and Dermatological Properties of Selected Ayurvedic Plant Extracts. Molecules (Basel, Switzerland), 26(3), 614. https://doi.org/10.3390/molecules26030614

> "Wine is a living liquid containing no preservatives. Its life cycle comprises youth, maturity, old age, and death. When not treated with reasonable respect, it will sicken and die."
>
> – Julia Child

Chapter Sixteen ~
Alcohol

Photo courtesy of Independence Heritage Museum

Most cultures imbibe at least one traditional alcoholic beverage. Alcohol was reserved for special occasions like baptisms, weddings, bar mitzvahs, and funerals. During the holiday season, it is typical for beer, wine, and spirits to be given as gifts.

Early alcoholic beverages contained no herbicides, pesticides, or GMO grains; however, they sometimes carried high levels of heavy metals. Ancient Roman wine had lead from the piping and cooking vessels.

The information following the opposing view from current science may illustrate why it has been so difficult for 75% of my clients to give up the occasional beer or nightly glass of wine.

Controversy: Who's Right, Who's Wrong?

Some researchers suggested that drinking small amounts of alcohol helps prevent conditions such as diabetes, ischemic heart disease (IHD), dementia, and cognitive decline. Still, none of the seminal review studies reported a "safest level" of alcohol consumption. Another primary concern about alcohol intake is that its health implications that occur through the mechanisms of other diseases, especially cancers, are likely to be underreported. Such consumption, for instance, is associated with 18% of suicides, 18% of interpersonal conflicts and violence, 27% of road accidents, 13% of epilepsy cases, 48% of liver cirrhosis cases, 26% of oral cancer cases, 20% of tuberculosis (TB) cases, 11% of colon cancer cases, 5% of breast cancer cases, and 7% of hypertension (HTN) and heart disease cases worldwide, as indicated by the World Health Organization (WHO).[1]

Alcoholic-dilated cardiomyopathy (ACM) is the most prevalent form of ethanol-induced heart damage. Ethanol induces ACM in a dose-dependent manner, independent of nutrition, vitamin, or electrolyte disturbances. At a high dose (more than 60 g/day for men and 40 g/day for women) and chronic consumption (usually more than ten years), ethanol increases the atherosclerosis process with coronary, cerebral, and peripheral vascular involvement, increases arterial hypertension, and causes progressive myocardial damage (ACM) as well as induction of arrhythmias. The effect of a low dose of alcohol consumption on the cardiovascular system has also been extensively evaluated with evidence of a dual effect; beneficial for coronary artery disease at low doses but reversing to a damaging impact at moderate to high doses.[2] Study findings from 2023 demonstrate a significant correlation between alcohol consumption and an increased risk of sexual dysfunction in women.[3]

> ***Principle 80***: Alcoholic beverages/substances have been a part of human life since the Stone Age and are woven into the social fabric of civilization.

Beer

Late Stone Age beer jugs found by an archeologist established that deliberately fermented beverages existed at least as early as 10,000 BC. It has been suggested that beer may have preceded bread as a dietary staple. The invention of bread and beer has been heralded as vital to the development of civilization.

In every culture, from hunter-gatherers to nation-states, alcoholic beverages are often an important part of social events. Drinking plays a significant role in social interaction—some believe mainly because of alcohol's neurological effects.

Fermentation is the process whereby microorganisms are utilized to produce alcoholic beverages such as wine, beer, and cider. Fermentation is also employed in the leavening of bread, for preservation, and to create lactic acid in sour foods such as sauerkraut, dry sausages, kimchi, pickles (vinegar), and yogurt. Fermented foods protect and maintain healthy bacteria in the digestive tract. Fermentation was an essential preservation tool before refrigeration and canning, and in areas where ice is unavailable.

Beer is one of the world's oldest prepared beverages, possibly dating back to early Neolithic or 9500 BC when cereal was first farmed, as recorded in the written history of ancient Egypt and Mesopotamia.

The earliest known chemical evidence of beer dates to circa 3500–3100 BC and comes from the site of Godin Tepe in the Zagros Mountains of western Iran. A prayer to the goddess Ninkasi, known as *The Hymn to Ninkasi*, served as both a prayer and a method of remembering the recipe for beer in a culture with few literate people. The Ebla tablets, discovered in 1974 in Syria and dating back to 2500 BC, reveal that the city produced a range of beers, including one named Ebla, after the city. A beer made from rice, which, unlike sake, was prepared for fermentation by malting, was made in China around 7000 BC.

> "Beer was spread through Europe by Germanic and Celtic tribes as far back as 3000 BC, and it was mainly brewed on a domestic scale. The product that the early Europeans drank might not be recognized as beer by most people today. Alongside the basic starch source, the early European beers might contain fruits, honey, numerous plants, spices, and other substances such as narcotic herbs. They did not contain hops, as that

was a later addition first mentioned in Europe around 822 by a Carolingian Abbot and again in 1067 by Abbess Hildegard of Bingen."[4]

In 1516, William IV, Duke of Bavaria, adopted the *Reinheitsgebot* (purity law), perhaps the oldest food-quality regulation still in use. According to this law, beer's only ingredients are water, hops, and barley malt. Beer produced before the Industrial Revolution continued to be made and sold domestically, although by the 7th century AD beer was also being produced and sold by European monasteries. During the Industrial Revolution, the production of beer moved from artisanal manufacture to industrial manufacture, and domestic manufacture ceased by the end of the 19th century.

Today, the brewing industry is a global business consisting of several dominant multinational companies and thousands of smaller producers ranging from brewpubs to regional breweries. The Pacific Northwest is famous for its microbrews and has received national and international recognition for its specialty beers. In 2006, more than 133 billion liters (35 billion gallons) of beer were sold, earning total global revenues of $294.5 billion.

Practically all hops in the U.S. are grown in the Willamette Valley of Oregon and the Yakama Valley in Washington.

Photo courtesy of Independence Heritage Museum. Circ 1960

In a study published in 2018 on a group of compounds derived from hops, researchers at Oregon State University and Oregon Health & Science University suggest that hops can improve cognitive function and insulin resistance in people with metabolic syndrome. The research focused on xanthohumol (XN), a prenylated flavonoid from hops, and two hydrogenated derivatives: DXN and TXN.

Earlier research had suggested XN could be an effective treatment for metabolic syndrome; the problem is that it transforms into 8-prenylnaringenin, or 8-PN, an estrogenic metabolite. Estrogens are the female sex hormones.

> "We were always criticized about potential side effects because 8-PN is one of the most potent phytoestrogens known in nature, and that's not good news," said Fred Stevens, professor of pharmaceutical sciences in the OSU College of Pharmacy and a principal investigator at Oregon State's Linus Pauling Institute. "If someone took XN over longer periods, it could potentially lead to estrogenic side effects."[5]

Those include endometriosis and breast cancer; most types of breast cancer are sensitive to estrogen, meaning estrogen helps tumors grow.

That's good news for the estimated 35% of the U.S. adult population with metabolic syndrome. A patient is considered to have metabolic syndrome if they have at least two conditions: abdominal obesity, high blood pressure, high blood sugar, low levels of "good" cholesterol, and high levels of triglycerides.

A diet high in refined saturated fat results in chronic low-grade inflammation in the body that, in turn, leads to the development of metabolic syndrome, a severe condition associated with cognitive dysfunction and dementia, as well as being a significant risk factor for cardiovascular disease and type 2 diabetes.

Benefits with beer

Moderate consumption of alcohol (4 ounces of spirits, 6-8 ounces of beer and wine) is associated with a decreased risk of cardiac disease, stroke, and cognitive decline. The long-term effects of alcohol abuse, however, include the risk of developing alcoholism and alcoholic liver disease. Anyone with elevated liver enzymes or hepatitis C should avoid all alcohol.

Brewer's yeast is a rich source of nutrients used in beer fermentation. Beer can contain significant nutrients, including magnesium, selenium, potassium, phosphorus, biotin, and B vitamins. Beer is sometimes referred to as "liquid bread." Filtered beer may contain fewer nutrients.

A 2005 Japanese study found that low-alcohol beer may possess potent anti-cancer properties. Another study found that non-alcoholic beer provides the cardiovascular benefits associated with moderate consumption of alcoholic beverages; however, research suggests the primary health benefits of alcoholic beverages are due to alcohol.

During the 2018 Winter Olympics, nonalcoholic beer drew attention as athletes used this calorie-dense beverage to help recover following competition. These nonalcoholic athletic recovery beers mainly emerged from Bavaria. In 2011, David Nieman and the University of Munich's Johannes Scherr investigated the effects of beer, which contains around 50 phenols, on athletes whose intense physical activity can compromise their immune activity. When marathon runners were instructed to drink 1.5 liters of nonalcoholic beer a day, their risk of upper respiratory infection was reduced. The activity of white blood cells, a good indicator of inflammation, was lowered by 20%.

However, phenols aren't the only health benefits of beer — and not just any brew can be called a sports beer. For example, regular alcoholic beer is a diuretic, and urinating more dehydrates athletes, says biologist Mauricio Sepulveda of Chile's Pontifical Catholic University. It also can disrupt crucial protein synthesis, says Ben Desbrow with Griffith University in Southeast Queensland, Australia.[6]

The key, of course, is moderation. Beer can be calorie-dense and estrogenic, so watch out for the dreaded "beer belly."

AppleJack / Cider

When the Romans arrived in England in 55 BC, they were reported to have found the local Kentish villagers drinking a delicious cider-like beverage made from apples. According to ancient records, the Romans and their leader, Julius Caesar, embraced the pleasant pursuit enthusiastically. How long the locals had been making this apple drink before the arrival of the Romans is a mystery. By the beginning of the 9th century, European cider drinking was well established.

Historical information on drinkfocus.com reports, "After the Norman Conquest of 1066, cider consumption became widespread in England, and orchards were established specifically to produce cider apples. During medieval times, cider-making was an important industry. Monasteries sold vast quantities of their strong, spiced cider to the public. Farm laborers received a cider allowance as part of their wages, which increased during haymaking. English cider-making probably peaked around the mid-17th century when almost every farm had its own cider orchard and press."

Early English settlers introduced cider to America by bringing with them seeds for cultivating cider apples. During the colonial period, grains did not thrive well and were costly to import. On the other hand, apple orchards were plentiful, making apples cheap and readily obtainable. The early American Puritans forbade alcoholic beverages; however, apple cider was not prohibited as it was made from fruit and not grain. Safer than water and more accessible and cheaper to produce than beer or wine, cider was typically the day's first drink.

Cider was fermented from apple juice in the colonial period and up to the middle of the 19th century. During that time, it was the most popular and vital beverage in America. Cider consumption increased steadily during the 18th century due in part to the efforts of the legendary Johnny Appleseed, who planted many apple trees in the Midwest. Cider regained popularity during the 20th century, but demand was mainly for the mass-produced variety. Only in recent years has traditional cider-making finally triumphed.

Water of Life

The Gaelic *usquebaugh*, meaning "water of life," phonetically became "usky" and then "whiskey" in English. Scotland has internationally protected the term "Scotch;" to be labeled as Scotch, it must be produced in Scotland. Scots spell the drink whisky, without the 'e.' Whisky has thousands of compounds that impact taste; *guaiacol* gives the drink its smoky flavor. Guaiacol gets trapped by ethanol molecule clusters, but if it is diluted to about 25% with water, the ethanol and the guaiacol rise to the surface, to an area the researchers call the top of the liquid. And now you know why a splash of water is added to even the best of Irish whiskeys, Scotch, and bourbons.[7]

"Eight bolls of malt to Friar John Cor wherewith to make aqua vitae." This entry appeared in the Exchequer Rolls in 1494 and seems to be the earliest documented record of distilling in Scotland.

"Scotland's great Renaissance king, James IV (1488-1513), was fond of "ardent spirits." When the king visited Dundee in 1506, a payment to the local barber for a supply of aqua vitae for the king's pleasure was recorded. In 1505, the Guild of Barber Surgeons in Edinburgh was granted a monopoly over the manufacture of aqua vitae—a fact that reflects the spirit's perceived medicinal properties and the medicinal talents of the barbers."[8]

In early 2010, three crates of Mackinlay's Rare Old Highland Malt Whiskey were found under the floor of John Shackleton's 1908 Nimrod expedition shelter in Antarctica. The original recipe for this particular breed of Scotch has been lost, and master blenders worldwide are waiting with great anticipation for the opportunity to sniff this Scotch. Authorities in New Zealand's Antarctic Museum in Christchurch plan to extract small samples for analysis, and then the bottles will be returned to Antarctica for posterity.

Legend says St. Patrick introduced distilling to Ireland in the 5th century, and it is believed Patrick acquired the knowledge in Spain and France. The distilling process was initially applied to perfume, then to wine, and finally adapted to fermented mashes of cereals in countries where grapes were not plentiful.

The spirit was universally termed aqua vitae ("water of life") and was commonly made in monasteries. It was chiefly used for medicinal purposes, being prescribed for preserving health, prolonging life, and for relieving colic, palsy, and even smallpox.

The art of distilling is believed to have been brought to Europe by Irish missionary monks. The secrets also traveled with the Dalriadic Scots when they arrived in Kintyre, Scotland, around 500 AD—the knowledge of distilling spread through monastery communities. The oldest licensed whiskey distillery in the world, Bushmills, lies in Northern Ireland and received its license from Jacob VI in 1608.[9]

Sine Metu, meaning "without fear," appears on every bottle of Jameson whiskey. This has been Jameson's motto since the founding of the Dublin Distillery in 1780. John Jameson set new standards for the distillation of whiskey. Discovering that certain strains of barley made better whiskey than others, he persuaded local farmers to grow the desired grains by providing them with seed each spring. By 1820, John Jameson & Sons had become Ireland's second-largest distilling company.

As a youngster, I remember the first taste of whiskey, which was in a hot toddy with lemon and honey, when I had a bad chest cold. Over the years, this home remedy has been used in our household. This is a far better option than over-the-counter cold medications, loaded with sugar, artificial sweeteners, and colorings.

A Tot If You Please

Rum was not commonly available until after 1650, when it was imported from the Caribbean. The rum cost dropped after the colonists began importing molasses and cane sugar and distilling it themselves. By 1657, a rum distillery was operating in Boston. It was highly successful, and within a generation rum production became colonial New England's largest and most prosperous industry. Almost every important town, from Massachusetts to the Carolinas, had a rum distillery to meet the local demand, which had increased dramatically. Rum was often enjoyed in mixed drinks, including flip. This was a favorite winter beverage made of rum and beer sweetened with sugar and warmed by plunging a red-hot fireplace poker into the serving mug.

Shaken, Not Stirred

During the 17th century, Franciscus Sylvius (or Franz de la Boe), a professor of medicine at the University of Leyden, distilled spirits from grain. This spirit was generally flavored with juniper berries. The resulting beverage was known as *junever*, the Dutch word for juniper. The French changed the name to *genievre*, which the English changed to "Geneva" and then modified to "gin."

Initially used for medicinal purposes, gin was not often consumed socially. However, in 1690, England passed "An Act for Encouraging of the Distillation of Brandy and Spirits from Corn." Within four years, the annual production of spirits, mostly gin, reached nearly one million gallons.

Chapter 16 ~ Alcohol

South Of the Border

Tequila is distilled from the sap of the agave plant indigenous to Mexico, not the mescal cactus, as many believe. This clear peppery liquor was traditionally used as a dietary aid, consumed following a heavy meal to stimulate digestion. Many still drink tequila and rich Tex-Mexican food loaded with fat and cheese. The Jaime family in Arandes, Jalisco, Mexico, has been growing "all natural" Weber Blue Agave for the tequila industry for over 100 years. No pesticides, chemical weed control, hormonal fertilizers, or chemicals are used to grow or speed the distillation process of Oregon's only family-owned tequila.

If you like to drink alcoholic beverages, make sure they come from reputable distilleries and are made from pure ingredients. Ask if the drink contains grain alcohol. If it is, try one made with grain less likely to be a GMO product or contaminated with herbicides.

> "Drink is in itself a good creature of God, and to be received with thankfulness, but the abuse of drink is from Satan; the wine is from God, but the drunkard is from the Devil."
> ~Rev. Increase Mather
> Sermon on drunkenness (d.1723)

Protestant leaders such as Luther and Calvin, the Anglican Church, and even the Puritans did not differ substantially from the teachings of the Catholic Church when it came to alcohol. They believed alcohol was a gift from God and created to be used in moderation for pleasure, enjoyment, and health; drunkenness was regarded as a sin.

Fruit of the Vine

Wine is the second oldest of the developed fermented beverages. According to an ancient Persian fable, the wine was the accidental discovery of a princess seeking to end her life with what she thought was poison. Instead, she experienced the elixir's intoxicating effects, releasing her from the anxieties of royal court life.

Experts agree wine probably dates to 6000 BC Mesopotamia, where wild grape vines grew. The drink was savored by royalty and priests, while commoners drank beer, mead, and ale. The ancient Egyptians were the first culture to document the process of winemaking.

Winemaking made its way to Greece, where it permeated all aspects of society: literature, mythology, medicine, leisure, and religion. The Romans took vine clippings from Greece back to Italy, and centers of viticulture soon developed in France, Germany, Italy, Spain, Portugal, and the rest of Europe.[10]

367

From the Bible to ancient legends, tales of intoxication by ingesting fermented grapes abound. In addition, fossilized vines prove that the earliest humans recognized the pleasures of this tantalizing liquid.

> "Good wine is a necessity of life for me."
> – Thomas Jefferson

> ***Principle 81***: Results of medical research on alcohol use are conflicting and confusing. Moderate intake shows some health benefits, but no "safe" level of consumption has been established. Tee-totally is the only guaranteed health strategy.

From Honey to Happy Mead

The history of mead dates back 20,000 to 40,000 years and originates on the African continent. In Africa, during the dry season, wild bees would nest in tree hollows; during the wet season, the hollows would fill with water. Water, honey, osmotolerant yeast, time, and *voila*—mead is born. As successive waves of people left Africa, they took with them some knowledge of mead and mead-making. Not until the time of Louis Pasteur, in the mid-1800s, did man become aware of yeast as the life form responsible for fermentation.

Honey was prized throughout history; it was often available only to royalty. With time, the tradition of mead was only sustained in the monasteries of Europe.[11,12]

Ancient Irish manuscripts reveal bees were sacred animals, and they were brought to the country from Wales in the 5th century by Saint Modomnóc. The tradition of Blessing the Bees has returned to Ireland with fall festivals dedicated to the event.

> "At one point, nearly every house in Ireland would have had access to a beehive, as it would have been the only source of a sweetener, and wax would have been used for candles. It's the first time I've heard it done in modern Ireland. There's a lot of folklore attached to the bees, so it's nice to keep that going," said Tidy Towns' committee member Gerard Meaney.

Eventually, mead-making spread throughout Europe, India, and China. But mead-making died out as people became urbanized. However, mead resurged in popularity in the 21st century, and individuals are once more making traditional mead as well as flavor-blended vintages.

In medieval times, Christmas was quite a pagan celebration. Foods were heavily spiced if the lord of the manor was wealthy enough to purchase clove, cardamom, cinnamon, and ginger from travelers and tradesmen. The lady of the manor would combine these herbs with meats as a preservative and with wine or mead to improve digestion and prevent food poisoning.

Chapter 16 ~ Alcohol

> ***Principle 82***: Prolonged consumption of alcohol leads to a physiological state of "tolerance," increasing the risks of overuse, abuse, and addiction.

Bottom line: Traditional use of alcohol is very much a part of human history. The likelihood that we will cease to imbibe is doubtful. Women and men alike use alcohol in mating rituals, religion, and sports. Alcohol lowers inhibitions and relaxes. It also drives hot flashes, blood sugar surges, cardiovascular risks, hypertension, chronic kidney disease, depression, and insomnia. Alcohol strips the body of vitamin C, the B vitamins, and trace minerals resulting in malnourishment when used to excess with a poor diet.

Any time a food, no matter how traditional, is over-consumed or made with inferior ingredients, health is damaged. As a child of an alcoholic and sibling of one who died from alcoholism, the cost family members pay for an individual's overindulgence and addiction is life-altering. Two out of three adults of alcoholics will generally become addicts or alcoholics. The remaining one may have lifelong challenges with abuse, depression, and failed relationships. The challenges families and individuals face do not end with an empty bottle.

---

1 Iranpour, A., & Nakhaee, N. (2019). A Review of Alcohol-Related Harms: A Recent Update. Addiction & health, 11(2), 129–137. https://doi.org/10.22122/ahj.v11i2.225

2 Fernández-Solà J. (2020). The Effects of Ethanol on the Heart: Alcoholic Cardiomyopathy. Nutrients, 12(2), 572. https://doi.org/10.3390/nu12020572

3 Salari, N., Hasheminezhad, R., Almasi, A., Hemmati, M., Shohaimi, S., Akbari, H., & Mohammadi, M. (2023). The risk of sexual dysfunction associated with alcohol consumption in women: a systematic review and meta-analysis. BMC women's health, 23(1), 213. https://doi.org/10.1186/s12905-023-02400-5

4 This section similar to here: http://www.thegreatestbeers.com/katcef/beer-101/history-of-beer/

5 Oregon State University. "Compounds derived from hops show promise for metabolic syndrome patients." ScienceDaily. ScienceDaily, 5 February 2018. www.sciencedaily.com/releases/2018/02/180205092935.htm

6 Olympians Are Using Nonalcoholic Beer As Recovery Drinks. Here's The Science by Ian Graber-Stiehl; NPR February 2018 NPR

7 Karlsson, B. C. G., & Friedman, R. (2017). Dilution of whisky- the molecular perspective. Scientific Reports, 7(6489). https://doi.org/10.1038/s41598-017-06423-5

8 whiskyman.com

9 Scotch! The Story of Whisky, Presenter David Hayman; BBC Two, 2016

10 http://www.winepros.org/wine101/history.htm

11 Levi-Strauss C.: From honey to ashes (1966)

12 Enright M. J.: Lady with a mead cup, Four courts press (1996)

> "I believe preconception planning is one of the most impressive commitments you can make to your own and your future children's well-being. One of the single most important things you will ever do for your children, that will affect them each and every day of their whole lives, is to be healthy when they are conceived."
>
> ~Kathleen Bell, RN, MSN, CNM, AHN-BC®, WHCNP

Chapter Seventeen ~
Preconception Nourishment

By Kathleen Bell RN, MSN, CNM, AHN-BC, WHCNP (ret)

If you have stayed on *Our Journey with Food* this far, by now it is clear that the importance of good nutrition throughout the life cycle is irrefutable. Additionally, the significance of adequately balanced food and fluid intake during the decades of fertility in most humans 'lives cannot be exaggerated. During my professional nursing career spanning 50 years, research has continued to accumulate linking the merits of healthy nutrition to fertility in both men and women, as well as to normal pregnancy outcomes.

Examining the effects of preconception and prenatal nutrition on a fetus encompasses the health histories of both the mother and father. The parents 'genetic makeup has been determined by individual heredity and the environments in which they were each conceived and developed as children, as well as continuing personal choices regarding lifestyle during fertile adulthood. Dietary patterns and cultural practices adopted as children lead to chronic conditions later in life, such as metabolic syndrome, obesity, diabetes, and cardiovascular disease, all of which have potential effects on fertility.

Conception

The forty-week period required for gestation of a full-term human infant is longer than that of most large mammals on our planet, and it sets the stage for the health of future generations. The only source of nourishment for the fetus is the mother; the developing fetus depends completely on her nutritional status before and during pregnancy for all of its needs: vitamins, minerals, immune properties, and energy-rich macronutrients for growth and development. This "perfect parasite" relationship begins at the moment of conception, and throughout all its stages of growth the developing human(s) continue to take all that is necessary at the expense of their "host." When I was in practice as a Certified Nurse-Midwife and Women's Healthcare Nurse Practitioner, I used to tell my clients that their bodies would give "everything they ate and drank *first* to the baby" and the "leftovers" would be for nourishing themselves. And if they didn't eat/drink something - calcium, for example – their bodies would supply it to the fetus from their own physical makeup. Pioneer midwives used to say that women "lost a tooth for every child," because women's bodies are designed to make the best babies possible and will send necessary nutrients derived from their own teeth and bones for fetal development.

Even before the fertilized ovum (called a *zygote*) implants within the mother's prepared uterine lining, a process that can take up to 12 days, all conditions must be optimal for a pregnancy to take hold. A woman is only able to conceive during a few days in each menstrual cycle. The quality of the ovum, along with both the quality and quantity of available sperm for fertilization are the direct results of the genetic and nutritional status of both parents. Conception involves a complex series of endocrine events, the result of which is healthy sperm penetrating and fertilizing a healthy ovum within 24 hours of ovulation. Once fertilized, the rapidly changing zygote has no guarantee of reaching the embryo stage of development (2-8 weeks after fertilization), which precedes the fetal stage that lasts from 8 weeks until birth.[1] It is estimated that between 41% and 70% fail, depending on the timing and sensitivity of the pregnancy test being used. And the rate of miscarriage in the U.S. is 25%, an event which very commonly happens before the woman is aware she has conceived.[2]

> ***Principle 83***: Healthful nutrition is linked to fertility in both males and females of all animal species, including humans.

Fetal Origin of Disease

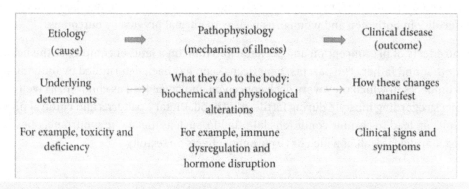

Genuis, S. J., & Genuis, R. A. (2015). Preconception Care: A New Standard of Care within Maternal Health Services. BioMed Research International, 2016. https://doi.org/10.1155/2016/6150976

The concept known as the fetal origin of disease posits that the quality and quantity of nourishment available to the developing zygote, then to the fetus, then to the infant and child, and finally during adulthood emerges as one explanation for diseases that manifest along the lifespan.[3] For example, a meta-analysis done in 2018 showed that high doses of folic acid supplementation in the first trimester of pregnancy increased the risk of asthma in the children of those women. Based on the analysis of dose-response done on the data, a dose of <58 micrograms of folic acid per day in pregnancy was advised to prevent birth defects, especially neural tube defects.[4]

Currently, more than 60% of reproductive-age women in the U.S. are overweight, and 35% of them are obese (BMI >30). These staggering figures represent a 70% increase in pre-pregnancy obesity. Incidence of childhood obesity and early-onset metabolic syndrome have risen in parallel. Studies done on large populations of women from the U.S. and Europe demonstrate that maternal obesity, maternal high-fat diets, and infants born who are large for gestational age (LGA) have deleterious effects on the neurodevelopment of fetal, infant, and children's brains. Maternal obesity and LGA increases the odds of cognitive deficits, decreased IQ, and intellectual disabilities; autism spectrum disorders; attention deficit and hyperactivity disorders; and cerebral palsy in children.[5]

A study on mice out of the Robinson Institute at the University of Adelaide, Australia, found that seminal fluid and its interaction with the female reproductive tract can have a significant effect on the offspring's health.

> "We've discovered that it's not just the sperm, but the entire composition of the seminal fluid which has an important role to play in establishing the offspring's future health, and this is most notably seen in male offspring," lead researcher and Director of the Robinson Institute, Professor Sarah Robertson said.[6]

Adopting Healthy Behaviors

Adopting healthy behaviors is the first step people wishing to conceive can take to get ready for the healthiest pregnancy possible. A series of three papers in the British medical journal *Lancet* emphasizes that women can do more to improve their BMI and nutritional status before pregnancy, because the risks during pregnancy and birth to both mother and fetus are increased and poorer birth outcomes can be avoided. Importantly, the recommended behaviors listed below *apply to both men and women,* with only the last one specifically focused on females. These recommendations are echoed by the U.S. CDC for those contemplating conception within the next three to 12 months.[7,8]

1. Achieve a healthy weight (BMI 18.5 – 25.9) by adopting and maintaining a well-balanced diet.
2. Incorporate at least 30 minutes of physical activity into a normal daily routine.
3. Quit all use of alcohol, tobacco, and non-essential drugs. Take only necessary physician-prescribed medications.
4. Decrease caffeine consumption to <200mg/day.
5. Follow proper medical management for chronic diseases.
6. Screen for sexually transmitted infections and treat appropriately.
7. Lower your stress levels (meditation, yoga, support groups, work/life balance).
8. Use effective contraception *every time* to prevent unintended pregnancy. Discontinue when ready to conceive.
9. Work on having a safe and healthy relationship, without intimate partner violence.
10. If pregnancy is desired within the next 12 months, women should take prenatal vitamins daily containing the recommended amount of folic acid (folate or vitamin B_9) to prevent neural tube defects (NTD): 400 micrograms. Adequate amounts of this critical nutrient before conception and very early in pregnancy greatly reduce the risk of NTD.[8]

> ***Principle 84***: Nourishment available during preconception and gestation affects the health of progeny for their entire lifespan.

Unintended Pregnancy and Preterm Birth

Not all pregnancies are planned events. The CDC reports that unintended pregnancies have fallen from a rate of greater than 50% in 2008 to around 45% since 2011. Although the rate of unintended pregnancy has fallen in the U.S. over the past two decades, teens aged 15-19 have a 75% unintended pregnancy rate, and rates per 1,000 women in this country are highest among young women ages 18–24 (physiologically the most fertile years of a woman's life).

According to CDC data, many women with unintended pregnancy live on incomes that are <100% of the federal poverty level, are not high school graduates, are Black or African American, and are cohabiting but not married. These facts put both the women and their fetuses at the highest possible risk for poor outcomes. Adequate prenatal care is not obtained by >21% of Black women and >26.8% of Native American and Alaskan women in the United States. Pre-existing maternal conditions such as hypertension and diabetes – both related to poor nutrition and obesity – contribute to the high rate of preterm births (PTB). Nutritional deficiencies can also result in PTB (before 37 weeks gestation). Black and Native American women are 62% more likely to have PTB, and their babies are *twice as likely to die* as compared to White women.[8]

In 2021, one in 10 infants born in the U.S. were preterm. In fact, during my 70+ years, the rate of PTB has continued its staggering increase in this country, rising 4% between 2020 and 2021 alone to the highest recorded rate since 2007 and earning the United States a D+ grade on the *March of Dimes* annual report card in 2022.[9] This makes the U.S. one of the most dangerous developed nations in the world for childbirth safety.

The COVID pandemic created its own mini baby boom and exacerbated the struggle for parents to access adequate prenatal care from healthcare providers and hospitals.

> 'This year's report sheds new light on the devastating consequences of the pandemic for moms and babies in our country," says Stacey D. Stewart, President and CEO of the March of Dimes. "More babies are being born too sick and too soon, which can lead to lifelong health problems. Pregnant women with COVID have a 40% higher risk of PTB, and we know more women are starting their pregnancies with chronic health conditions, which can further increase their risk of complications. It's clear that we are at a critical moment in our country."[9]

> ***Principle 85***: Optimal nutrition decreases risks for both mother and fetus during pregnancy, as well as improving birth outcomes for the neonate.

The Microbiome in Pregnancy

Previous chapters in this book have explained the functions of the intestinal microbiome: nutrient metabolism, enhancement of the immune system, protection against pathogens, and maintaining the integrity of each individual's own microbial "community." During pregnancy, bacterial components can be transferred to the fetus along with nutrients and metabolites via the maternal blood supply in the placenta. Each one of us is made up of a unique and complex ecosystem of human cells and microorganisms all existing together. Current research is still trying to determine the proportion of these varied microbes that exist in and on us in comparison to our human cells. There are literally thousands of different species of bacteria, viruses, fungi, and other microbes co-existing within us, all of which contain their own genetic material. Estimates from the *Human Microbiome Project* say that there exists within each of us "several hundred times more genetic material within our microbes than there is carried in our human genes."[10] That fact is so astonishing that it is worth reading again: *We are made up of several hundred times more microbial DNA than human DNA!*

In the past, it had been believed that the fetus was in a sterile container while in utero and that "normal flora" did not take up residence in and on the baby until after it was born and began to feed. We now know differently. Researchers from Budapest stated in 2021, "The fetus is not sterile or immunologically naïve but interacts with the maternal immune system through the effects of environmental stimuli through the mother."[11] Bacteria is bound to be present within the placenta, as it is not a completely sterile environment, either.

All this to say that it is important for persons planning a pregnancy to pay attention to protecting the beneficial microbes in their microbiome by discontinuing drug and substance use, eating a wholesome balanced diet, maintaining adequate hydration and other nourishing behaviors such as stress management, and keeping their immediate environment and relationships positive and safe. Please see our recent collaborative book, *Empty Plate: Food~Sustainability~Mindfulness,* for more information about expanding the concept of nourishment as not being restricted to dietary intake.

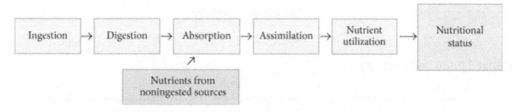

Genuis, S. J., & Genuis, R. A. (2015). Preconception Care: A New Standard of Care within Maternal Health Services. BioMed Research International, 2016. https://doi.org/10.1155/2016/6150976

Fertility

Most people assume that they are capable of reproducing any time after puberty. Without medical or surgical intervention, fertile females remain so until the decade of their 50s when menopause occurs. Males experience decreasing fertility with age but can remain capable of siring children into their 80s. Census data gathered before the COVID pandemic shows sexual fertility trends in the U.S. as being relatively stable from 1990-2019 as compared to previous decades, but the U.S. has been experiencing an overall drop in fertility rates for U.S. women ages 15-44 since the 1960s.

In her book, *Baby Maker*, nutritionist Barbara Rodgers draws some very interesting correlations between falling fertility rates and milestones in the U.S. food industry that implicate nutritional deficiencies as contributing factors. First, let's look at the numbers.

Among women, the rates of fertility vary widely according to age: 20-24 years has decreased to 43%, while ages 35-39 increased to 67%. In 1990, there were 70.77 births per 1,000 women aged 15-44 years. By 2019, the number of births for that same age group was 58.21 per 1,000. This gradual decline masks a concerning trend in the fertility rates of younger women, which fell substantially. In 1990 there were 116.4 births per 1,000 women aged 20-24 years; in 2019 the rate was 66.59 per 1,000 for that age group, a decline of 42.79%. During the same period fertility rates for older women rose. In 1990, there were 31.5 births per 1,000 women ages 35-39; in 2019 the number was 52.72 per 1,000 women in that age group, an increase of 67.35%, which was not enough to offset the general downward trend of fewer births per year. The result is a shift in the median maternal age at first birth from 27 years in 1990 to 30 years in 2019.[12]

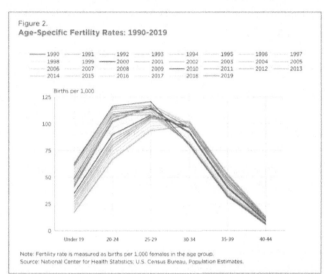

Figure 2. Age-Specific Fertility Rates: 1990-2019

> ***Principle 86***: Fertility rates in the U.S. began a steady decline in the 1960s that continues today.

Industrialized Food and Fertility

The following changes in the industrialized food system of the U.S. are mentioned in *Baby Maker* as correlated with declining rates of fertility:

- The use of shortening and vegetable oils high in omega-6 fats skyrocketed in the 1950s as replacements for higher-quality saturated fats that are high in omega-3 (like butter). Hydrogenation is a process that makes the concentrations of trans fats in these products very high. Research has shown that consuming trans fats increases the risk of infertility by 70%.[13] Because of their many recognized dangers, the U.S. FDA has banned the use of trans fats in food manufacturing, but this was not done until the year 2018. Of note: the rise of obesity in the U.S. began in the mid-1970s and directly correlates to issuance of USDA guidelines for a low-fat diet.

- Around 1930, per capita consumption of sugar surged to 85 lbs per year (38,555 g). Today the U.S. continues to consume more sugar than any other country in the world. According to the American Heart Association, Americans consume more than 17 teaspoons of sugar per day (or 71 g), which is nearly double what we should be eating.
- Consumption of sodas, fruit juices, and processed and 'fast foods 'has increased sharply since the 1970s. These sugar sources are directly related to increased BMI and incidence of diabetes.
- Daily calorie intake went up by 20% between 1970 and 2010.
- Between 1954 and 1960, the FDA enacted regulations allowing the use of additives to foods, including coloring and pesticides.[14] These molecules, known as excitotoxins and endocrine disruptors, affect blood sugar levels and increase production of free radicals that lead to inflammation. Hormone disruption affects fertility.
- The use of prescription medications rose dramatically in the 1950s with the development of many new products. The effects of medications on both male and female fertility are numerous. There is evidence that discontinuing medications (including antibiotics) for a number of conditions can improve semen quality, with consequent improvement in rates of conception.[15]

Infertility: A Growing Global Crisis

The WHO's definition of infertility states: "Infertility is a disease of the male or female reproductive system defined by the failure to achieve a pregnancy after 12 months or more of regular unprotected sexual intercourse."[16] When I was a teenager in the 1960s, oral contraceptives were brand new and difficult to obtain, and the prevailing wisdom about achieving pregnancy was "all it takes is once." (Considering the fertility tables earlier in this chapter, that sentiment wasn't too far from wrong at the time.) Though that may still be the case today for some couples, the "one and done" scenario definitely is not true for the majority of the U.S. childbearing population today. Millions of couples are affected by some degree of decreased fertility, with the physiologic causes of infertility being shared almost equally among males and females. A staggering 1 in 6 adults across the globe experience infertility, or nearly 20% of the population, according to data from the World Health Organization. Both female and male fertility rates have fallen drastically over the past few decades. Stemming from diverse factors, such as hormonal imbalances, lifestyle patterns, and increased parental age, infertility has become a growing global public health crisis threatening sustainable population levels.[17]

For most contemporary couples getting pregnant takes planning, careful timing, and a lot of patience. About one third of fertile women with fertile partners will conceive within 3-6 months, so it is important to be patient and not to declare yourself or your partner "infertile" too soon. A study done 20 years ago by the National Institute of Environmental Health Sciences found that the majority of women up to age 39, whose male partner was under 40 years old, who did not become pregnant after the first year of "trying" were successful at achieving pregnancy within the second year without any medical reproductive assistance.[18]

While it is beyond the scope of this chapter to examine all possible causes of infertility, it is important to understand that many of them are related to phenomena in the body that are affected by diet. For example, endometriosis, a common cause for female infertility, is under investigation as a chronic inflammatory condition with possible gut involvement. Amenorrhea has already been mentioned as being related to poor nutrition, and polycystic ovarian syndrome (PCOS) is one of the hallmark components of metabolic syndrome, with insulin resistance often caused by a diet high in sugar and carbohydrates. Causes of male infertility also involve obesity, metabolic syndrome, and chronic inflammation – all health conditions that are related to diet.

Antioxidants

Oxidative stress (OS) can affect all components of the female reproductive cycle, whether that is ovulation, preparing the uterine lining for implantation, menstruation, fertilization, and/or development and implantation of the zygote in the uterus. The menstrual cycle is regulated by the physiological concentration of reactive forms of oxygen and nitrogen as signal molecules that trigger and regulate the length of individual phases of the menstrual cycle. A 2023 research review states:

> "It has been suggested that the decline in female fertility is modulated by pathological OS that triggers many disorders of female reproduction, which could lead to gynecological diseases and to infertility. Therefore, antioxidants are crucial for proper female reproductive function. Antioxidants can directly scavenge radicals and act as a cofactor of highly valuable enzymes of cell differentiation and development or enhance the activity of antioxidant enzymes. Compensation for low levels of antioxidants through their supplementation can improve fertility. This review considers the role of selected vitamins, flavonoids, peptides, and trace elements with antioxidant effects in female reproduction mechanisms."[19]

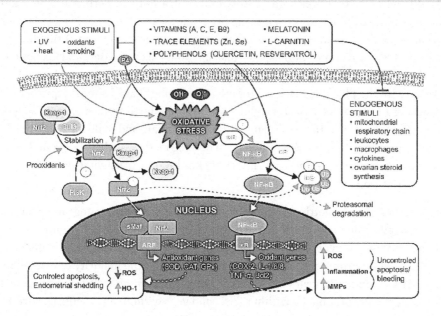

Vašková, J., Klepcová, Z., Špaková, I., Urdzík, P., Štofilová, J., Bertková, I., Kľoc, M., & Rabajdová, M. (2023). The Importance of Natural Antioxidants in Female Reproduction. Antioxidants, 12(4), 907. https://doi.org/10.3390/antiox12040907

Epigenetics

Young couples today should be aware of the genetic influence of what their parents and grandparents ate in decades past on their present fertility status. If you are a prospective parent and your parents were undernourished or ate too much sugar and processed foods, abused alcohol and/or tobacco and other drugs, or were plagued by obesity and related chronic diseases, these issues have been passed on to your genes. It behooves prospective parents to investigate their family dietary histories in order to develop nutritional strategies to "turn on" the genes that encourage fertility.

The area of research that studies exactly how nutrition affects how our genes express either health or disease is called *nutrigenomics* and is directly related to the concept of *epigenetics*, which means how our environment and lifestyle choices influence changes in gene expression. Research in these fields keeps accumulating to show that nourishing food sources, as well as environmental and lifestyle factors, play a significant role in the body's ability to maintain good health – of which fertility is a part – along with the ability to resist disease and heal from conditions that were previously believed to be normal functions of aging.

For example, genetic testing can reveal that a parent has the MTHFR (methylenetetrahydrofolate reductase) gene *variant*. The MTHFR gene provides "instructions" for your body to make the MTHFR protein, specifically needed to process folate. Folate is necessary to build new DNA, as well as for metabolizing dietary proteins. A gene *variant* is a change in the usual DNA sequence of proteins. In this case, at the 677th position on the MTHFR gene, the normally expected nucleopeptide base is a "C," but "T" is substituted by the information contained in a *variant* gene.

Each person carries 2 copies of the MTHFR gene, one inherited from their mother and the other from their father. There are 3 possible combinations for the set of genes responsible for making MTHFR. These combinations are called *genotypes*:

- 🐍 *MTHFR* 677 CC (two copies of C, one copy from each parent);
- 🐍 *MTHFR* 677 CT (one copy of C from one parent, one copy of T from the other parent); or
- 🐍 *MTHFR* 677 TT (two copies of T, one copy from each parent).[20]

Another common gene variant is the MTHFR A1298C variant, occurring at the 1,298th position on the MTHFR gene. In this position on the MTHFR gene, the expected nucleopeptide base "A" is replaced by "C" as the gene variant. There is not enough evidence to show that the MTHFR A1298C variant *alone* significantly affects how the body processes folate.[20]

The number of people who have each of these genotypes will vary from population to population. Although this research is fairly recent, you might have read or heard that taking folic acid is not safe if you have one or two copies of the MTHFR C677T variant. <u>This is not true</u>. Even if you have one or two copies of the MTHFR C677T variant, your body can safely and effectively process all different types of folate, including folic acid. Importantly, folic acid is the only type of folate shown to help prevent neural tube defects (severe birth defects of the brain or spine). The two most important factors that determine whether you have enough folate in your blood to help prevent a neural tube defect are:[21]

1. The amount of folic acid you consume each day from organic and fortified foods and from vitamins/supplements containing folic acid.
2. The length of time folic acid is consumed before becoming pregnant.

> ***Principle 87***: Nutrigenomics and epigenetics research data is accumulating to support the interplay of good nutrition and environmental and lifestyle factors on fertility.

Preparing for Pregnancy

Before pregnancy, women need a nutritious diet to establish sufficient reserves for the greatly increased physiologic demands on the body that accompany pregnancy. Mechanically inclined readers can think about this behavior as being similar to "priming the pump." A healthy, nutritionally balanced diet is illustrated by the *Mediterranean Diet Pyramid towards Sustainability: Focus on Environmental Concerns* in Chapter 3 of this book, page 49.

It takes at least 60,000 "extra" calories to build one new human. A mother's energy (caloric) needs increase by 50% in a singleton pregnancy, and nutritional requirements are increased even more with twins, triplets, etc. All nutrients eaten by the pregnant woman go first to the developing fetus(es) with the balance remaining used by the mother's body. If she is not consuming sufficient calories, her own body's reserves will be called into play. However, metabolic rate also increases during pregnancy - an average of 15% in a singleton pregnancy - but this amount varies widely, especially in the third trimester.[22]

No simple formula exists to establish exact caloric requirements that apply to every woman during pregnancy, but what does universally apply is the need for high-quality nutrients to support adequate fetal growth and normal development, while sparing critical components in a woman's body: bones, teeth, organs, and metabolic functions. Pre-pregnant weight directly influences the baby's birth weight. An underweight mother will more likely deliver a smaller baby, regardless of gestational age, even though her actual weight gain during pregnancy may have been within the amount recommended. An overweight or obese mother puts herself at greater risk of developing gestational diabetes (which carries its own increased risk of type 2 diabetes later in her lifetime), hypertension, and delivering a very large newborn. If you are planning a pregnancy, it is a good idea to talk with your primary care physician or maternity healthcare provider about weight/height ratios, calculate your BMI with an ideal weight, and to try to achieve that weight before pregnancy. In obstetrical and midwifery circles, ideal BMI to begin a pregnancy is 18.5- 24.9.[23, 24]

Chapter 17 ~ Preconception Nourishment

NOTE: To calculate your BMI go to www.nhlbi.nih.gov/health/education/lose_wt/bmitools.htm
Causes of underweight (BMI<18.5) can include:

- Very restrictive diet or an eating disorder. Most adult women need to consume about 2000 kcal/day. If you become pregnant with an eating disorder, you will be considered at higher risk for miscarriage and IUGR (intrauterine growth restriction) and need special management. The fetus is at risk for gastroschisis, low birth weight, and preterm birth.
- Excessive exercise. Calories are a measure of energy. If energy expended consistently exceeds energy intake, it is difficult to impossible to gain weight.
- Disease: hyperthyroidism, intestinal parasites, etc.
- Severe mental/emotional stress leads to appetite suppression.
- Decreased food availability due to few financial resources. WIC, local food banks, and charities can help with access to a better food supply.
- Underweight females are often anovulatory (infertile) and/or have irregular menstrual cycles and amenorrhea (absence of periods).

Overweight is defined as BMI 25-29.5; BMI>30 constitutes obesity. Bringing your BMI down by even one or two points can make a real difference in the risks of pregnancy for the woman and in the infant's outcome. Once a woman becomes pregnant, weight loss is not recommended, so it is preferable to accomplish beforehand. When planning a pregnancy and wanting to lose weight, following a program like Weight Watchers or the Whole30 diet is a good idea in order to avoid nutritional deficiencies if/when pregnancy occurs. Exercise for both men and women is recommended by every professional group out there to help with weight loss. Increase physical activity: walk/jog/swim/dance/bike, etc., for 30 minutes per day or a total of 150-300 minutes per week to achieve weight goals.

For Men Only

Men should aspire to attain a normal BMI if planning parenthood. Obesity in men has been shown to affect the quality of sperm. Obese men have lower testosterone levels, which are directly related to sperm count, viability, and motility. Smoking can also affect these same markers of sperm quality as well as contributing to erectile dysfunction; stopping tobacco use reverses the ill effects. The same foods that promote fertility in women work for men; a diet high in fruits, vegetables, whole grains and high quality proteins like nuts, eggs, and fish increases semen and sperm quality. Diets high in processed foods, meats, caffeine, saturated and trans fats, and alcohol lead to lower quality semen. Alcohol consumption should not exceed 3-4 oz per day.

Sexually transmitted infections (STI) are often asymptomatic in males. Chlamydia, gonorrhea, and syphilis are curable with antibiotics but can lead to decreased fertility if untreated. Syphilis and HIV can be transmitted from a pregnant woman to the fetus. These serious infections can result in miscarriage, birth defects, or an infant born with disease. Testing for sickle cell anemia or thalassemia is recommended if you or your family of origin is from Africa, the Caribbean, Middle East, Mediterranean, India, Pakistan, South or Southeast Asia.

Other things to do to increase male fertility:

- ✓ Avoid hot baths or showers; testicles are outside the body to decrease their temperature.
- ✓ Avoid saunas or jacuzzis for the same reason.
- ✓ Don't work with your laptop or tablet directly on your lap for long periods of time.
- ✓ Avoid prolonged sitting or bicycling.
- ✓ Wear loose-fitting underwear and trouser styles.[25]

For decades, Dr. Sarah Robertson has researched semen's important role in conception and the establishment of healthy pregnancy, going beyond sperm's count and dynamics.

> "It's clear to us now that the seminal fluid produces signals that the embryo absolutely needs for the best possible start to life. Assisted reproductive techniques, as good as they are today, cannot currently replicate such complexity. Therefore, it's helpful if we can find other ways to encourage couples to take care of their reproductive health, including men as well as women," Robertson added.[26]

Building a Healthy Foundation

We live in a world of strategies and action plans. It may seem quite "businesslike" to actually create a health plan and strategize before a planned pregnancy; the very idea may even tarnish the romance and wonder of conception for some people. In my (admittedly biased) view as a nurse-midwife, however, I believe preconception planning is one of the most impressive commitments you can make to your own and your future children's well-being. One of the single most important things you will ever do for your children, that will affect them each and every day of their whole lives, is to be healthy when they are conceived. Another is to maintain good health throughout the length of a normal pregnancy. I cannot imagine a greater gift than to pass along a genetic predisposition for good health.

Optimizing your health will result in improved fertility. This statement feels so basic that it may leave you wondering why it is necessary. If you were a racehorse breeder or worked with dairy farmers to improve milk production/quality or a veterinarian consulting on breeding expensive show dogs, or if you were a researcher in a lab setting that raises animals, you would be very familiar with exactly the conditions needed and specific foods that your animals required to be fertile, become pregnant, and produce top-quality offspring. Hundreds of thousands of dollars are spent in the U.S. each year to achieve prize-winning results in all of these areas. Hmmm, have you ever thought about why we do not loudly preach the need for similar goals and disciplinary regimes to our current childbearing generations? Doesn't it seem a bit ludicrous for our human "breeders" to carelessly choose a diet of industrially created foods and beverages, or to drive through fast food chains more times than cooking fresh whole foods for dinner and still expect to be abundantly fertile at any given time/age and to be able to deliver prize-winning healthy, normal term babies who will grow into healthy normally developing children and long-living vital adults?

None of us can control all of the millions of incredibly complex processes that are continually at work in our amazing human bodies. But there are many areas we can control by making mindful choices. One of those areas is our diet, and science continues to demonstrate that our genes respond to what we eat. More

Chapter 17 ~ Preconception Nourishment

than gaining/losing weight — or maybe getting rid of heartburn — changing what we eat and drink alters our genetic codes in the present and for the future, even affecting later generations.[27] The primary goal of the work that Dr. Karr and I continue to do together is to convince people that *what we eat can minimize or resolve many, if not most, health problems* without the need for pharmaceuticals or medical/surgical interventions. Educating ourselves and others about recognizing and changing our engrained dietary habits can help us figure out what steps we can take to overcome inherited and biological predispositions and weaknesses.

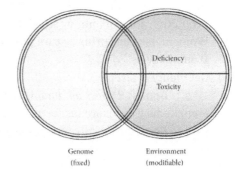

Genuis, S. J., & Genuis, R. A. (2015). Preconception Care: A New Standard of Care within Maternal Health Services. BioMed Research International, 2016. https://doi.org/10.1155/2016/6150976

If you are hoping to be a parent, your goals should be to deliver high quality nourishment to all of your body's cells in order to boost fertility. You can do this by paying close attention to your diet and to what kind of things you should avoid. If your diet consists of too much "junk food," the molecules that will circulate in your body will be toxic, creating chaos where order is needed. Cellular communication will be interrupted or non-existent, the GI tract will be inflamed and unable to properly absorb nutrients, dysfunction will rule internal filtration and detoxification processes, the immune system will be impaired — the list goes on and on of problems that can contribute to infertility.

TO DO and NOT TO DO List to Enhance Fertility: GOALS

1. Review and adopt the healthy behaviors listed at the beginning of this chapter.
2. Eliminate inflammatory and toxic foods (sugar, yeast, gluten, soy, and non-organic dairy) as well as processed and "fast" foods. Develop the habit of reading food labels, avoiding GMO.
    a. Set a **daily goal** of <20% of your food intake as this category.
3. Buy and cook fresh organic whole foods; eggs, butter from grass-fed cows, LOTS of veggies with a special focus on greens and legumes, organic fish and seafood. Include organ meats if they agree with your palate.
    a. **Goal**: 90% of your food intake is organically sourced.
4. Drink filtered or purified water.
    a. **Goal**: Half your body weight (in ounces) daily.
5. Keep your stress levels as low as possible. Adopt practices like meditation, yoga/breathwork, time in nature, or seek counseling or hypnosis as more intensive therapy to mediate your body's endocrine responses to stress.
    a. **Goal**: Minimum of 10 minutes/day, 5-7 days/week.
6. Women: Take high-quality whole food-based prenatal vitamins daily. DO NOT EXCEED recommended dosages. Consider probiotics and/or other supplements as recommended by a qualified nutritional healthcare provider.
7. Men: Take a high-quality whole food-based multivitamin/supplement daily. Include vitamins C, E, A, D, K, the Bs, and zinc (related to testosterone levels). Consider supplements with carnitine,

selenium, ALA (alpha-lipoic acid) and coenzyme Q10 as antioxidants required for optimal fertility.[28]
8. Always check with your primary care physician to discuss the need for additional medications, probiotics, antioxidants, or supplements.
9. Women: Ask your primary care physician to check CBC, electrolytes, folate, ferritin, and vitamins D and K levels.
10. Get plenty of sleep.
    a. **Goal:** *7-8 hours minimum/day.*
11. Men: Reduce exposure to electromagnetic fields.
    a. **Goal:** *Do not carry cell phone in front trouser pocket.*[29]

Back to the Future

These statements from the abstract of an article published by *Biomed Research International* in 2016 emphasize the importance of choices made by prospective parents before and during pregnancy.

Emerging research suggests that many pediatric afflictions have origins in the vulnerable phase of fetal development. Prenatal factors including deficiency of various nutrients and exposure to assorted toxins are major etiological determinants of myriad obstetrical complications, pediatric chronic diseases, and perhaps some genetic mutations. With recent recognition that modifiable environmental determinants, rather than genetic predestination, are the etiological source of most chronic illness, modification of environmental factors prior to conception offers the possibility of precluding various mental and physical health conditions. Environmental and lifestyle modification through informed patient choice is possible, but evidence confirms that, with little to no training in clinical nutrition, toxicology, or environmental exposures, most clinicians are ill-equipped to counsel patients about this important area. With the totality of available scientific evidence that now exists on the potential to modify disease-causing gestational determinants, failure to take necessary precautionary action may render members of the medical community collectively and individually culpable for preventable illness in children. We advocate for environmental health education of maternity health professionals and the widespread adoption and implementation of preconception care. This will necessitate the translation of emerging knowledge from recent research literature to health professionals, to reproductive-aged women, and to society at large.[29]

Chapter 17 ~ Preconception Nourishment

1 Mahan, K., & Raymond, J. (Editors) (2017) Food and the Nutrition Process, 14th Ed. Elsevier
2 Kwak- Kim, J., et al. (2010) Immunological Modes of Pregnancy Loss. American Journal of Reproductive Immunology, 63:6
3 Monk, C., et al. (2013) Research review: Maternal prenatal distress and poor nutrition – mutually influencing risk factors affecting infant neurocognitive development. Journal of Child Psychiatry, 54:115.
4 Trivedi, Sharma, et al. (2018) Folic Acid In Pregnancy and Childhood Asthma: A U.S. Cohort. Clinical Pediatrics, 57(4), 4210427. https://doi.org/10.1177/000922817729482
5 Edlow, A. & Mattei, L. (2016). Maternal Obesity and the Fetal Brain. Contemporary OBGYN, June, pp.16 – 22. www.contemporaryobgyn.net/obesity-fetal-brain
6 Bromfield J, Schjenken J, Chin P, Care A, Jasper M, Robertson S. (2014) Maternal tract factors contribute to paternal seminal fluid impact on metabolic phenotype in offspring. Proceedings of the National Academy of Sciences.
7 https://www.thelancet.com/pdfs/journals/lancet/PIIS 140-7378(18), pp.3011-3018
8 https://www.cdc.gov/preconceptioncare/planning.html
9 www.marchofdimes.com
10 National Institutes of Health, (2012). NIH Human Microbiome Project Defines Normal Bacterial Makeup of the Body. https://www.nih.gov/news/health/june2012/nhgri-13.htm.
11 Fülöp, V., Demeter, J., & Cseh, Á. (2021). A praenatalis és postnatalis mikrobiom jelentősége és hatásai a korai egyedfejlődés időszakában és az intervenciós kezelés lehetőségei [Significance and effects of prenatal and postnatal microbiome in the period of early individual development and options for interventional treatment]. Orvosi hetilap, 162(19), 731–740. https://doi.org/10.1556/650.2021.32082
12 Morse, A. (2022) Stable Fertility Rates Mask Distinct Variations by Age. U.S Census Bureau. www.census.gov
13 Gunnars, K. (2017) 11 Graphs That Show Everything That is Wrong With the Modern Diet. Healthline http://www.healthline.com/nutrition/11-graphs-that-show-what-wrong-with-modern-diet
14 Rodgers. B. (2018). Baby Maker. PostHill Press: NY-Nashville
15 Gaffney, A. (2014). How Many Drugs Has FDA Approved in its Entire History? New Paper Explains, Regulatory Affairs Professional Society. https://www.raps.org/regulatory-focus%E2%84%A2/news-article/2014/10/how-many-drugs-has-fda-approved-in-its-entire-history-new-paper-explains.
16 www.who.int
17 1 in 6 people globally affected by infertility:WHO (2023): https://www.who.int/news/item/04-04-2023-1-in-6-people-globally-affected-by-infertility
18 NIEHS. (2002) Don't Turn to Assisted Reproduction Too Quickly Warn US Experts
https://www.niehs.nih.gov/news/newsroom/releases/2002/july03/index/cfm
19 Vaskova, J., et al. (2016). The Importance of Natural Antioxidants in Female Reproduction, National Center for Biotechnology Information. https://www.ncbi.nlm.nih.gov/pmc/articles/PMC10135990
https://www.mdpi.com/2076-3921/12/4/907?fbclid=IwAR2sSofC3uJK4PpAyDjumTLqInrb3Rh3qzS8CKPluMAnaz4J0336-t1taz4
20 https://www.cdc.gov/ncbdd/folicacid/mthfrgene-and-folic-acid.html
21 van der Put NMJ, Gabreëls F, Stevens EMB, et al. A second common mutation in the methylenetetrahydrofolate reductase gene: An additional risk factor for neural tube defects? Am J Hum Genet. 1998;62(5):1044-1051.
22 Crider KS, Yang TP, Berry RJ, Bailey LB. Folate and DNA methylation: A review of molecular mechanisms and the evidence for folate's role. Adv Nutr. 2012;3(1):21-38.
23 Stanford Medicine Children's Health, Nutrition Before Pregnancy: https://www.standfordchildrens.org/en/topic/default?
24 www.tommy's.org/pregnancy-information/planningapg/are-you-ready-to-conceive.htm
25 MacDonald, S. & Mayes. (2017) Midwifery. Edinburgh: Ballire Tindall Elsevier
26 Robertson SA, Prins JR, Sharkey DJ, Moldenhauer LM. Seminal fluid and the generation of regulatory T cells for embryo implantation. Am J Reprod Immunol. 2013;69(4):315–30. [PubMed] [Google Scholar]
27 Brower, J. (2017). A Crash Course in Epigenetics, Part 1: An Intro to Epigenetics. Bitesize Bio. https://bitesizebio.com/8807/.
28 Murray. M. & Pizzorno, J. (2014) The Encyclopedia of Healing Foods. London: Simon and Schuster.
29 Genuis SJ, Gengis RA. (2016) Preconception Care: A New Standard of Care Within Maternal Health Services, Biomed Res Int.   doi: 10.1155/2016/6150976. Epub 2016 May. PMID: 27314031
PMCid : 4903143

Our Journey with Food

Chapter Eighteen ~ Research: A Literature Review

Redefining Nourishment: Expanding the definition of Nourishment to include lifestyle and environmental sources beyond diet.

By Bell, Kathleen, RN, MSN, CNM, AHN-BC™, Karr, Tammera, PhD, BCHN®, CDSP™, CNW®
Published in the Acupuncture and Integrative Medicine Newspaper Pacific College of Natural Health Spring 2023

Introduction

This literature review aims to expand the limitations of the common scientific definition of *Nourishment* into a broader holistic understanding of health. These questions were addressed: Is *Nourishment* limited to nutrients extracted through digestion? Or does *Nourishment* include components from an individual's environment, culture, beliefs, social connections, surrounding wavelengths, and calories? This review shows that food alone is insufficient to generate or sustain vibrant health and well-being.[1] Holistic health and well-being are outcomes of constant interaction between and among many dimensions of human life. The authors reviewed more than 750 scientific papers and historical texts related to well-being, health, diet, culture, anthropology, archeology, natural sciences, microbiome, and philosophy, then developed a set of six essential ingredients that comprise an expanded definition of *Nourishment*. Goethean [2,3] and Quantum science [4,5] recognize the effects of and relation between multiple influences that nourish the whole person, promoting health from conception to the end of life. By redefining the concept of *Nourishment*, the reviewers intend to illuminate the deficiencies remaining within the confines of a reductionist paradigm and to highlight possibilities available in the quantum era for persons to develop and regenerate health.

For purposes of this review, the following definitions have been selected by the authors:

Belief

A state or habit of mind in which confidence is placed in the reality of some person, thing, or phenomenon, especially when based on an examination of evidence.[6] Beliefs are the initiator for biochemical responses in the body that release neurotransmitters, hormones, and other chemical mediators resulting in health and a sense of well-being. Health is defined as being well or free from disease, being in good overall condition of body/mind/spirit, thriving, hearty, robust, and fit.[7] Well-being is a positive outcome that is meaningful for both individuals and society.[8,9]

Wavelength

Wavelength is the distance between successive crests of a wave, especially points in a sound wave or electromagnetic wave.[10] Wavelengths depend on the medium (water, air, vacuum) through which they travel—examples of waves: sound, light, water, and periodic electrical signals via conductor.

Diet (Gastronomy)

Nutrition derived through diet[11] refers to the process of obtaining and consuming food and drink daily, which is necessary for health and growth, along with the mental and physical circumstances connected to eating. Diet influences biochemical responses through macro and micro ingredients that feed the microbiome and human cell energy.[12] Nutrition's inclusive definition is *gastronomy*,[13] the art or science of good eating, custom, or style. Gastronomy is inseparable from history, culture, and tradition and strongly contributes to social identity.[14]

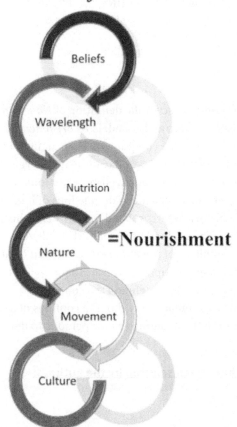

Elements of Nourishment = Nourishment

These six elements of nourishment are supported by *Quantum* and *Goethean* science's concepts of interrelationship between mind/body/spirit, while acknowledging and connecting with *Reductionistic* science's definitions of diet and health.

© Tammera J. Karr & Kathleen Bell 2022

Nature

The collective phenomena of the physical world, including plants, animals, fungi, the landscape, and other features and products of the earth, as opposed to human creations.[15] Being outside in the natural world produces a myriad of biochemical responses, such as activating neurotransmitters, endorphins, and immune reactions, including killer T-cells.[16]

Movement

A body or object is said to be moving if it changes its position with respect to its immediate environment.[17] Movement is necessary for adequate circulation and balanced neurotransmitter function in the human body; without movement, failure to thrive and death result.[18]

Culture

Social definition: Customs, arts, social institutions, and achievements of a particular group of people.[19, 20] Biological definition: Conditions suitable for the growth and sustainability of living organisms.[21]

The Literature Review

Beliefs

The authors agree with the works of Drs. Bruce Lipton, Candace Pert,[22] and Deepak Chopra, which support the theory that each of the approximately 50 trillion human body cells has its own innate intelligence. Research by Dr. Bruce Lipton and others demonstrates that individuals with some form of belief system recover more readily from illness and retain a greater social connection, leading to healthy longevity.[23, 24] In her international study of cancer patients who fully recover, Dr. Kelly Turner found strong spiritual beliefs to be one of nine essential elements in the 'formula' for healing.[25]

Beliefs are the initiator for biochemical responses that release neurotransmitters and hormones that affect digestion, behavior, sleep, and immune responses.[26] The complex chemical signaling pathways between the human brain and body are made possible by healthy physiologic functioning of the central nervous system and bloodstream, which can be regarded as an "information superhighway."[27] Unless each particular cell receives information regarding its activity/lifespan and is kept informed about the activities of trillions of other cells, there can be no organization of the body into functional systems.[28, 29]

Dr. Candace Pert's groundbreaking studies in the late 20th century mapped neuropeptides and their receptors throughout the brain and body, paving the way for the emergence of a new paradigm.[30] This new paradigm views the human being as a singular entity, which she and Dr. Deepak Chopra refer to as the *bodymind*. The *bodymind* is a holistic entity encompassing the physical body, psyche, and a level of reality and humanity referred to as spirit or consciousness. The chemistry of beliefs, or *Molecules of Emotion*, acts as an integral communication network in continual and elegant conversation throughout the *bodymind*. Dr. Pert proposed, "Your body is your subconscious mind." [31]

How a person sees themselves in the present makes a real and measurable difference in what their body will be like tomorrow. Caroline Myss, who began her career as a medical intuitive working with Harvard-trained neurosurgeon Dr. C. Norman Shealy, learned *what drains the spirit drains the body and what drains the body drains the spirit*.[32] In the 1980s, Dr. Ellen Langer, the first woman psychologist to be tenured at Harvard University, performed a famous *time-capsule* experiment on aging men that demonstrated statistically significant changes in multiple physiologic outcome measures: grip strength, dexterity, flexibility, posture, and even eyesight. The researchers replicated the findings again in 2019.[33] The primary intervention involved in this experiment was directing the beliefs of the men to change their perspectives (minds) about their actual ages, which led to measurable physical changes in their bodies. In addition, sixty-three % of the subjects in the time-capsule group scored higher on an intelligence test as compared with forty-four % of the control group.[34]

A study from 2007 looked at the relationship between exercise and health moderated by one's mindset in 84 females. The results support the hypothesis that exercise affects health in part or whole by mindset.[35, 36] Cancer patients in a 2019 study reported "a better sense of controlling health" and "improved overall health and feeling better" when employing complementary therapies, including movement, diet, cultural practices and lifestyle.[37]

Wavelengths

Made up of light (*Biophotons*)[38, 39] and sound,[40] wavelengths are elemental organizational forces of the universe.[41] Exposure to biophotons, sound vibrations, and color transforms human biochemical responses.[42] In his comprehensive study of the biological effects of sunlight, Dr. Michael Holick delineates many health benefits, the most well-known of which is the manufacture of vitamin D and its relationship to the use of calcium in the body. Sunlight exposure is the primary source of vitamin D for humans, as very few foods naturally contain vitamin D.[43] People have a feeling of well-being when exposed to sunlight because ultraviolet A and B wavelengths lead to increased expression and production of beta-endorphins.[44] For women of childbearing age, vitamin D and calcium insufficiencies were found to increase associated risks of bacterial infections[45] and cardiovascular disease[46] in a series of systematic reviews and meta-analyses published in 2022. Sunlight deprivation is associated with depression, and seasonal exposure variations dramatically influence cardiovascular events and mortality, such as stroke, heart attack, and autoimmune and infectious diseases.[47]

According to Dr. John Ott, 98% of the sun's energy enters the body thru the eyes—regulating brain chemistry and circadian rhythms that control appetite, energy, mood, sleep, libido, and many more functions. Light also affects muscle movements, enzyme reactions, food digestion, fat burning, and energy storage. Dr. Ott and Dr. Fritz Albert Popp, International Institute of Biophysics, agree that light is a nutrient much like food, publishing this statement on the Ott website, "We can now say emphatically that the function of our entire metabolic system depends on light."[48] Research published in 2019 indicates long-term memory may be stored in biophotons through the light-conductive protein molecule tubulin.[49, 50]

The understanding of how color can affect health is called color psychology. Without being aware of color's effect on health, individuals may miss out on ways to improve responses and reactions within their surroundings.[51] Dr. Deanna Minich, a leading expert in color and food, published a literature review in 2019. "My study of colorful carotenoids and phytonutrients in graduate school had shown me that there is an important *color connection* in nutrition science ... I began to realize that color, nutrition, and life issues were intertwined ... I started to see correlations rather distinctly."[52, 53]

Sounds of all kinds surround humans; the human ear can only hear some sounds, and many are outside the conscious hearing range.[54] Humans and other living creatures perceive sounds as mechanical waves of pressure, which are measured - similar to light waves – in frequencies. Sounds are characterized by regular fluctuations in vibration, as differentiated from noises containing irregular fluctuations. Sound vibrations have been shown to change body chemistry, altering the hypothalamic–pituitary–thyroid axis (HPTA), which governs stress responses.[55, 56]

Music impacts humans more than any other human-made sound. Researchers believe simple music predated speech and played a vital role in human development.[57] Music plays a central role in the U.S. food and restaurant industries, affecting marketing strategies, shopping behavior, and eating environments. "Music has been used for thousands of years in healing ceremonies and as a digestive aid; each country across the world has traditional music to connect the threads of life and lift the spirit."[58]

Gastronomy and Nutrition

Nutrition refers to assimilating and incorporating substances necessary for health, growth, and the mental and physical circumstances connected to ingestion. Nutrients are absorbed and digested, providing components[59] of biochemical responses that feed the microbiome(s)[60] and fuel human cellular development and energy. Elements contained within vegetables, fruits, fungi, and herbs provide volatile compounds and color[61] to stimulate the brain, activate the immune system, and nourish the microbiome.[62] In their natural state, these energy sources create an array of synergistic responses within DNA. These chemical activators stimulate and down-regulate DNA receptors associated with multiple sought-after health traits: reducing cancer,[63] heart disease,[64] allergies, and autoimmune conditions.[65] A 2017 breast cancer research study revealed the importance of natural food sources of phytochemicals with anti-oncogenic properties on multiple cancer-related biological pathways and breast cancer prevention.[66] These same naturally occurring food sources improved cognitive function, physical performance, and increased fertility.[67, 68]

The enduring effects of nutrition have also been demonstrated on fetuses as related to their future health. A 2020 study of pregnant women by Kings College faculty illustrates how the mother's diet and lifestyle during pregnancy directly affect their children's future development of cardiovascular disease.[69]

Epidemiological research done in 2019 by Srour and Kesser-Guyot reported a significant association between eating whole, unprocessed, or minimally processed foods and lower risks of all reported diseases.[70] Research on chronic pain from 2021, done on veterans with Gulf War Illness (GWI) placed on a low glutamate diet, produced a measurable reduction of symptoms from chemical toxins.[71]

Gastronomy is the primary vehicle for foods that provide *Nourishment*. UNESCO describes gastronomy as one of the most universal cultural and creative contributors to social identity and an inherent carrier of tangible and intangible heritage.[72] Gastronomy represents the cultural knowledge of preparing foods for the highest nutritional value.[73] Traditional understandings of nutrition in Asian culture are documented in texts dating back over 6000 years.[74] Ayurveda, known as the oldest comprehensive medical system in the world, contains extensive nutrition that emphasizes the body/mind/spirit relationship with foods as a whole.[75] Traditional Asian understandings of nutrition come from Taoism, which underlines the individual and their foods' specific properties to support health and longevity.[76] All forms of eastern nutrition utilize harvesting and preparation methods to enhance nutrient compounds while reducing or removing naturally occurring toxins. Research on chronic illness among native/first peoples/aboriginals supports that returning to traditional foods reduces chronic diseases and increases lifespan.[77] Worldwide traditional diets are higher in nutrient diversity; research on the Mediterranean and Nordic diets illustrate that traditional foods beyond those of Asian and Native Peoples provide health and longevity benefits.[78]

Nature and Environment

Within the past decade, the body of evidence associating time spent in natural surroundings with improvements in health, wellness, and longevity has grown from a few dozen studies to hundreds.[79] Nature is very much a form of Nourishment, feeding human biochemistry in various ways that affect physical, mental, and spiritual satisfaction. "Being in Nature, or even viewing scenes of nature, reduces feelings of anger, fear, and stress along with their associated neurochemicals while increasing pleasant feelings and their many beneficial biochemical responses in the body."[80, 81] Exposure to nature contributes to physical and spiritual well-being by reducing blood pressure, heart rate, muscle tension and the production of stress-related hormones.[82, 83] It may even be associated with reduced mortality, according to scientists Stamatakis and Mitchell.[84, 85]

Many plants and trees secrete organic compounds called phytoncides into the surrounding air. These chemicals were studied in 2008 by Japanese researchers for their beneficial health effects on cancer expression in women. On a three-day, two-night forest bathing trip, participants' daily activity level and NK (natural killer) cells significantly increased in blood and urine samples along with perforin, granulysin, and granzymesa/b-expressing cells, while the concentrations of adrenaline, noradrenaline, and T-cells decreased. Additionally, the positive effects of the trip were found to last at least seven days after the end of the trip. Serial studies done since 2004 on the effect of forest environments on human health have been conducted in Japan, leading to the formation of the new interdisciplinary science (integrative medicine, environmental medicine, and preventive medicine) of Forest Medicine.[86]

A 2017 study published in *The Lancet Planetary Health* suggests that people residing in "green" neighborhoods live longer than those in urban settings.[87] Transdisciplinary researchers from Drexel University have investigated how nature relatedness—simply feeling connected with the natural world, benefits dietary diversity and fruit and vegetable intake in a study published in the *American Journal of Health Promotion*.[88] "Nature relatedness has been associated with better cognitive, psychological, and physical health and greater levels of environmental stewardship. Our findings extend this list of benefits to include dietary intake," says Brandy-Joe Milliron, PhD, an associate professor in Drexel's College of Nursing and Health Professions and lead author of the publication. "We found people with higher nature relatedness were more likely to report healthful dietary intake, including greater dietary variety and higher fruit and vegetable consumption."[89] Research on mental health conditions related to the strict indoor isolation mandated by the Japanese government during the COVID-19 pandemic reveals that outdoor exposure and views of green space and natural surroundings make a measurable difference in reported levels of depression, anxiety, and loneliness.[90]

Children are highly sensitive to environments and especially need to spend time outside in green spaces. A study published by the *American Academy of Ophthalmology* reported that chances of developing myopia (near-sightedness) were reduced by 2% for every hour a child spends outside in the garden, yard, or park. The leading conclusion was that increased exposure led to higher vitamin D levels, significantly improving their sight.[91] According to another study, children with Attention Deficit and Hyperactivity Disorder were able to concentrate better after taking a walk in a park than after a walk through an urban area.[92] In 2014, researchers at the University of Colorado demonstrated that time spent in green spaces outdoors had immediately measurable effects on children's stress levels, which were reduced overall when outdoor playtime was a part of their daily routines.[93] The first nature-based clinic in the U.S. to be associated with a major hospital is located at the University of California San Fransisco's Benif Children's Hospital. The clinic collaborates with the East Bay Regional Park District in a program called 'Stay Healthy in Nature Every Day,' with participating doctors offering nature outings for families. In June 2018, the clinic began billing insurance companies for patient visits that included time in Nature as part of the treatment plan.[94]

Movement

Human bodies are designed to move and remain in a state of constant change and activity, even when "at rest." Movement is one of the most basic functions of the human body, and severe health problems/disorders result from immobility,[95] even for a fetus in utero. At any age, inactivity is often more to blame than other health factors when ability declines.[96] A recent British Journal of Sports Medicine study highlights the synergistic effects of a good diet and regular exercise. The cohort study assessed data from almost 350,000 Australian participants over 11 years regarding relationships between physical exercise, diet quality, and all-cause mortality. Over that time, 13,569 people died: 2,650 from cardiovascular disease (CVD) and 4,522 from adipose-related cancers (CA). Vigorous physical activity lowered the risk for all causes of mortality.[97, 98] Diet quality was not found to be statistically significant for all-cause mortality or CVD deaths, but a high-quality diet was associated with decreased risk of adipose-related Ca mortality. People who ate a high-quality diet, including at least 4.5 cups of vegetables and fruits a day, and had regular physical activity, had the most significant reductions in risk of death. Physical activity, including walking, was associated with benefits, but a vigorous activity that led to sweating was especially protective against CVD risk, even for 10 to 75 minutes per week.[99]

The American Heart Association states that stroke is the 5th most common cause of death in the U.S. and a leading cause of long-term disability.[100] Tai chi (similar to Qigong) is an intervention used in Traditional Chinese Medicine (TCM). Both practices involve controlled movements and breathing techniques, although Tai chi is usually done while standing. These practices are powerful mind-body integrative skills meant to train the individual to regulate body/breath/mind to bring about the optimum state for healing and maintain healthy functioning.[101]

A recent study was conducted at two traditional Chinese medicine hospitals in Kunming, China. Researchers recruited 160 adults (average age of 63; 81 men and 79 women) who had suffered their first-ever ischemic stroke within six months of joining the study and retained their use of at least one arm. Among the study participants, half were randomly assigned to a sitting Tai chi program, and the other half were part of the control group that practiced a standard stroke rehabilitation exercise program (hospital-recommended upper limb movements). Sixty-nine people in the sitting Tai chi group and 65 people in the control group completed the 12-week program and 4-week follow-up.[102] The findings were as follows:

> Those in the sitting Tai chi group had better hand and arm function and sitting balance control compared to those in the standard stroke rehabilitation group.
>
> The participants in the sitting Tai chi group had significant reductions in symptoms of depression, better shoulder range of motion, and showed significant improvements in activities of daily living and quality of life compared with the control group.
>
> More than half the people in the Tai chi group continued to practice after the 12-week intervention. Improvement in outcome measures continued during the 4-week follow-up period for the Tai chi group.

One of the limitations of the study is that it was conducted at only two centers. In addition, the Chinese centers' physicians and health care professionals are trained in TCM and are supportive of its principles, so the results may not be generalizable to stroke survivors who receive rehabilitation care at other hospitals.[103]

Culture

Throughout the entirety of this paper, cultural aspects have been present within each segment. Research has illustrated the wavelengths of sounds forming spoken language and the taste of foods are introduced via the mother to a fetus in the womb.[104] Elements of *Nourishment* enter the body through multiple cutural pathways. Gathering a community around traditional feasts or ceremonies involving song and color benefits individuals' mental well-being, immunity, and longevity. Research supports reduced stress response, improved immunity and longevity through time spent in cultural activities. Aspects of cultural foods, environment, and lifestyle often determine the development and resiliency of an individual's microbiome.[105, 106] The individual's culture affects a diverse diet of nutrient-rich foods,[107] community support, and a place of purpose. In contrast, a lifestyle devoid of the multiple elements of *Nourishment* for the body, mind, and spirit–one of isolation and disconnection from the larger world, can result in an overall increase in morbidity and mortality.[108] Anthropologists Margaret Mead and Franz Boas affirmed the vital role of culture in human survival in the early 20th century.[109, 110] These pioneers of science challenged how individuals and their culture were viewed, then and now.[111, 112] The question of how a supportive culture, ancient or modern, brings *Nourishment* to an individual is yet to be fully researched or understood.

> *"Listen: there was once a king sitting on his throne. Around Him stood great and wonderfully beautiful columns ornamented with ivory, bearing the banners of the king with great honor. Then it pleased the king to raise a small feather from the ground, and he commanded it to fly. The feather flew, not because of anything in itself but because the air bore it along. Thus am I, a feather on the breath of God."*
>
> ~Hildegard of Bingen 1098-1179

Conclusion

This review shows that food alone is insufficient to generate or sustain vibrant health and well-being. If it is true that nutrition involves more than simply eating a "good diet," it is also true that defining *Nourishment* is highly dependent upon the paradigm through which it is viewed– reductionist or holistic. [113] East Asian, Ayurvedic, and Indigenous[114] cultures have deeply rooted beliefs, practices and gastronomy supporting body, mind, and spirit *Nourishment*.[115] Much of the scientific community in the Western world continues to make choices based on the limitations of the science of the past. The authors believe this review demonstrates ample scientific evidence and rationale to change the way we think, practice and operate beyond our former paradigms.

Embrace the Nourishment (NEW) Paradigm

- Making conscious decisions to eat healthy foods.
- Keep our bodies moving.
- Spend time in nature and with our chosen communities.
- Limit the ingestion of disruptive or harmful substances.
- And becoming aware of the power of our beliefs.
- These all constitute *Nourishment* for bodies, minds, and spirits — resulting in well-being that supports thriving health.

---

1 Epigenetics: How You Can Change Your Genes And Change Your Life: https://reset.me/story/epigenetics-how-you-can-change-your-genes-and-change-your-life/
2 Johann Wolfgang von Goethe (1749–1832): https://www.britannica.com/biography/Johann-Wolfgang-von-Goethe
3 Alicia Landman-Reiner, Complementing reductionism: Goethean science part 1: Qualities and wholeness, EXPLORE, Volume 17, Issue 4, 2021, Pages 360-365, ISSN 1550-8307: https://www.sciencedirect.com/science/article/pii/S1550830720300987
4 A century of quantum mechanics questions the fundamental nature of reality; https://www.sciencenews.org/article/quantum-theory-history-reality-uncertainty-physics
5 The Challenge Of A Unified Theory Of Information https://www.sciencedirect.com/topics/computer-science/reductionist-approach
6 Belief; Definition From The American Heritage® Dictionary of the English Language, 5th Edition; https://www.merriam-webster.com/dictionary/belief
7 Health; Definition From The American Heritage® Dictionary of the English Language, 5th Edition; https://www.merriam-webster.com/dictionary/health
8 Anand, Paul. 2016. Happiness, well-being and human development. New York.
9 Well-Being Concepts: https://www.cdc.gov/hrqol/wellbeing.htm
10 Wavelength; Definition From The American Heritage® Dictionary of the English Language, 5th Edition: https://www.merriam-webster.com/dictionary/wavelength
11 Diet; Definition from The Merriam-Webster Dictionary; https://www.merriam-webster.com/dictionary/diet
12 Assimilation Definition Cambridge Dictionary: https://dictionary.cambridge.org/us/dictionary/english/assimilation
13 Gastronomy; Definition from The Merriam-Webster Dictionary; https://www.merriam-webster.com/dictionary/gastronomy
14 The United Nations Educational, Scientific and Cultural Organization (UNESCO) recognized foods, typical dishes, and food systems as a World Heritage Site, UCCN (Creative Cities Network) project was created. https://www.unesco.org/en
15 Biology Online Definition of Nature: https://www.biologyonline.com/dictionary/nature
16 Karr,T., Bell, K. (2020) Empty Plate: Food Sustainability, Mindfulness, chapter 5, pg. 267-280, 287-294; Summerland; UT
17 Merriam-Webster Dictionary Definition, Movement: https://www.merriam-webster.com/dictionary/movement
18 Lu, T. W., & Chang, C. F. (2012). Biomechanics of human movement and its clinical applications. The Kaohsiung journal of medical sciences, 28(2 Suppl), S13–S25. https://doi.org/10.1016/j.kjms.2011.08.004
19 Culture: Definition from Merriam Webster Dictionary: https://www.merriam-webster.com/dictionary/culture
20 Karr,T., Bell, K. (2020) Empty Plate: Food Sustainability, Mindfulness, chapter 3, pg. 234-236, Summerland; UT
21 Eriksson O (2018) What is biological cultural heritage and why should we care about it? An example from Swedish rural landscapes and forests. Nature Conservation 28: 1-32. https://doi.org/10.3897/natureconservation.28.25067

22 Foss L. The necessary subjectivity of bodymind medicine: Candace Pert's molecules of emotions. Adv Mind Body Med. 1999 Spring;15(2):122-34. doi: 10.1054/ambm.1999.0161. PMID: 10367495.
23 Pert, C. (1999) Molecules of Emotion: The Science Behind Mind/Body Medicine, Simon and Schuster.
24 Lipton, B. (2016) The Biology Of Belief 10th Anniversary Edition: Unleashing The Power Of Consciousness, Matter & Miracles. Hay House.
25 Turner, K. (2015) Radical Remission: Surviving Cancer Against All Odds. HarperOne
26 Sen, H. E., Colucci, L., & Browne, D. T. (2022). Keeping the Faith: Religion, Positive Coping, and Mental Health of Caregivers During COVID-19. Frontiers in psychology, 12, 805019. https://doi.org/10.3389/fpsyg.2021.805019
27 Koenig H. G. (2012). Religion, spirituality, and health: the research and clinical implications. ISRN psychiatry, 2012, 278730. https://doi.org/10.5402/2012/278730
28 Chopra, D. (2018). The Healing Self. Harmony Books: New York.
29 Dispenza, J. (2015). You Are the Placebo: Making Your Mind Matter. Hay House: USA
30 Pert, C. (1999). Molecules of Emotion: The Science Behind Mind/Body Medicine, Simon and Schuster.
31 Brower V. Mind-body research moves towards the mainstream. EMBO Rep. 2006 Apr;7(4):358-61. doi: 10.1038/sj.embor.7400671. PMID: 16585935; PMCID: PMC1456909.
32 Myss. C (1998). The Creation of Health: The Emotional, Psychological, and Spiritual Responses That Promote Health and Healing, Harmony Book
33 Pagnini, F., Cavalera, C., Volpato, E., Comazzi, B., Vailati Riboni, F., Valota, C., Bercovitz, K., Molinari, E., Banfi, P., Phillips, D., & Langer, E. (2019). Ageing as a mindset: a study protocol to rejuvenate older adults with a counterclockwise psychological intervention. BMJ open, 9(7), e030411. https://doi.org/10.1136/bmjopen-2019-030411
34 Pagnini, F., Cavalera, C., Volpato, E., Comazzi, B., Vailati Riboni, F., Valota, C., Bercovitz, K., Molinari, E., Banfi, P., Phillips, D., & Langer, E. (2019). Ageing as a mindset: a study protocol to rejuvenate older adults with a counterclockwise psychological intervention. BMJ open, 9(7), e030411.
35 Crum, A. J., & Langer, E. J. (2007). Mind-set matters: exercise and the placebo effect. Psychological science, 18(2), 165–171. https://doi.org/10.1111/j.1467-9280.2007.01867.x
36 Bangsbo, J., Blackwell, J., Boraxbekk, C. J., Caserotti, P., Dela, F., Evans, A. B., Jespersen, A. P., Gliemann, L., Kramer, A. F., Lundbye-Jensen, J., Mortensen, E. L., Lassen, A. J., Gow, A. J., Harridge, S. D. R., Hellsten, Y., Kjaer, M., Kujala, U. M., Rhodes, R. E., Pike, E. C. J., Skinner, T., … Viña, J. (2019). Copenhagen Consensus statement 2019: physical activity and ageing. British journal of sports medicine, 53(14), 856–858. https://doi.org/10.1136/bjsports-2018-100451
37 Rhee TG, Pawloski PA, Parsons HM. Health-related quality of life among US adults with cancer: Potential roles of complementary and alternative medicine for health promotion and well-being. Psychooncology. 2019 Apr;28(4):896-902. doi: 10.1002/pon.5039. Epub 2019 Mar 13. PMID: 30803097; PMCID: PMC670539
38 Cohen S, Popp FA. Biophoton emission of human body. Indian J Exp Biol. 2003 May;41(5):440-5. PMID: 15244265.
39 Wijk RV, Wijk EP. An introduction to human biophoton emission. Forsch Komplementarmed Klass Naturheilkd. 2005 Apr;12(2):77-83. doi: 10.1159/000083763. PMID: 15947465.
40 Frontiers. (2017, June 20). The story of music is the story of humans: Where did music come from? Recent article discusses how music arose and developed. ScienceDaily. Retrieved January 19, 2023 from www.sciencedaily.com/releases/2017/06/170620093153.htm
41 Who was Hans Jenny: http://www.janmeinema.com/cymatics/who_was_hans_jenny.html
42 Fritz-Albert Popp – Publications: https://www.liquisearch.com/fritz-albert_popp/publications
43 Bulut, Serdar, et al. "The Relationship between Symptom Severity and Low Vitamin D Levels in Patients with Schizophrenia." PLoS One, vol. 11, no. 10, Public Library of Science, Oct. 2016, p. e0165284.
44 Holick MF. Biological Effects of Sunlight, Ultraviolet Radiation, Visible Light, Infrared Radiation and Vitamin D for Health. Anticancer Res. 2016 Mar;36(3):1345-56. PMID: 26977036.
45 Ma, L., Zhang, Z., Li, L., Zhang, L., Lin, Z., & Qin, H. (2022). Vitamin D deficiency increases the risk of bacterial vaginosis during pregnancy: Evidence from a meta-analysis based on observational studies. Frontiers in nutrition, 9, 1016592. https://doi.org/10.3389/fnut.2022.1016592
46 University of Edinburgh. (2013, May 7). Sunshine could benefit health and prolong life, study suggests. ScienceDaily. Retrieved January 25, 2023 from www.sciencedaily.com/releases/2013/05/130507195807.htm
47 Karr,T., Bell, K. (2020) Empty Plate: Food Sustainability, Mindfulness, chapter 3, pg. 215-230; Summerland; UT
48 Cohen, S., & Popp, F. A. (2003). Biophoton emission of human body. Indian journal of experimental biology, 41(5), 440–445: https://pubmed.ncbi.nlm.nih.gov/15244265/
49 Binarová P, Tuszynski J. Tubulin: Structure, Functions and Roles in Disease. Cells. 2019 Oct 22;8(10):1294. doi: 10.3390/cells8101294. PMID: 31652491; PMCID: PMC6829893.
50 Janke, C., Magiera, M.M. The tubulin code and its role in controlling microtubule properties and functions. Nat Rev Mol Cell Biol 21, 307–326 (2020). https://doi.org/10.1038/s41580-020-0214-3
51 Karr,T., Bell, K. (2020) Empty Plate: Food Sustainability, Mindfulness, chapter 3, pg. 227, Summerland; UT

Chapter 18 ~ Redefining Nourishment, A Literature Review

52 Minich. D. (2019). A Review of the Science of Colorful, Plant-Based Food and Practical Strategies for Eating the Rainbow. Journal of Nutrition and Metabolism, page numbers needed. https://www.Hindawi.Com/Journals/Inme/2019/2125070/

53 Minich, D. (2018). The Rainbow Diet Conari Press, Miami, FL pg. Xiii

54 City College of New York. (2019, March 8). Music captivates listeners and synchronizes their brainwaves. ScienceDaily. Retrieved January 25, 2023 from www.sciencedaily.com/releases/2019/03/190308133358.htm

55 University of Turku. (2020, December 28). Music-induced emotions can be predicted from brain scans. ScienceDaily. Retrieved January 25, 2023 from www.sciencedaily.com/releases/2020/12/201228101801.htm

56 Karr,T., Bell, K. (2020) Empty Plate: Food Sustainability, Mindfulness, chapter 4, pg. 245, 257, Summerland; UT

57 Frontiers. (2017, June 20). The story of music is the story of humans: Where did music come from? Recent article discusses how music arose and developed. ScienceDaily. Retrieved January 25, 2023 from www.sciencedaily.com/releases/2017/06/170620093153.htm

58 Karr,T., Bell, K. (2020) Empty Plate: Food Sustainability, Mindfulness, chapter 4, pg. 239, Summerland; UT

59 Thompson, H. J., Levitt, J. O., McGinley, J. N., Chandler, P., Guenther, P. M., Huybrechts, I., & Playdon, M. C. (2021). Measuring Dietary Botanical Diversity as a Proxy for Phytochemical Exposure. Nutrients, 13(4), 1295. https://doi.org/10.3390/nu13041295

60 Carolina, M., C., E., Guyonnet, D., Desjardins, Y., & Roy, D. (2021). Polyphenol-Mediated Gut Microbiota Modulation: Toward Prebiotics and Further. Frontiers in Nutrition, 8. https://doi.org/10.3389/fnut.2021.689456.

61 Minich D. M. (2019). A Review of the Science of Colorful, Plant-Based Food and Practical Strategies for "Eating the Rainbow". Journal of nutrition and metabolism, 2019, 2125070. https://doi.org/10.1155/2019/2125070

62 Thompson HJ, Levitt JO, McGinley JN, Chandler P, Guenther PM, Huybrechts I, Playdon MC. Measuring Dietary Botanical Diversity as a Proxy for Phytochemical Exposure. Nutrients. 2021 Apr 14;13(4):1295. doi: 10.3390/nu13041295. PMID: 33919845; PMCID: PMC8070776.

63 Koklesova L, Liskova A, Samec M, Qaradakhi T, Zulli A, Smejkal K, Kajo K, Jakubikova J, Behzadi P, Pec M, Zubor P, Biringer K, Kwon TK, Büsselberg D, Sarria GR, Giordano FA, Golubnitschaja O, Kubatka P. Genoprotective activities of plant natural substances in cancer and chemopreventive strategies in the context of 3P medicine. EPMA J. 2020 May 29;11(2):261-287. doi: 10.1007/s13167-020-00210-5. PMID: 32547652; PMCID: PMC7272522.

64 Houston M, Minich D, Sinatra ST, Kahn JK, Guarneri M. Recent Science and Clinical Application of Nutrition to Coronary Heart Disease. J Am Coll Nutr. 2018 Mar-Apr;37(3):169-187. doi: 10.1080/07315724.2017.1381053. Epub 2018 Jan 9. PMID: 29313752.

65 Gondivkar, S. M., Gadbail, A. R., Gondivkar, R. S., Sarode, S. C., Sarode, G. S., Patil, S., & Awan, K. H. (2019). Nutrition and oral health. Disease-a-month : DM, 65(6), 147–154. https://doi.org/10.1016/j.disamonth.2018.09.009

66 Kapinova A, Stefanicka P, Kubatka P, Zubor P, Uramova S, Kello M, Mojzis J, Blahutova D, Qaradakhi T, Zulli A, Caprnda M, Danko J, Lasabova Z, Busselberg D, Kruzliak P. Are plant-based functional foods better choice against cancer than single phytochemicals? A critical review of current breast cancer research. Biomed Pharmacother. 2017 Dec;96:1465-1477. doi: 10.1016/j.biopha.2017.11.134. Epub 2017 Dec 1. PMID: 29198744.

67 Coelho-Júnior HJ, Trichopoulou A, Panza F. Cross-sectional and longitudinal associations between adherence to Mediterranean diet with physical performance and cognitive function in older adults: A systematic review and meta-analysis. Ageing Res Rev. 2021 Sep;70:101395. doi:

68 Chavarro JE, Rich-Edwards JW, Rosner BA, Willett WC. Diet and lifestyle in the prevention of ovulatory disorder infertility. Obstet Gynecol. 2007 Nov;110(5):1050-8. doi: 10.1097/01.AOG.0000287293.25465.e1. PMID: 17978119.

69 King's College London. (2020, September 11). Healthy diet and exercise during pregnancy could lead to healthier children. ScienceDaily. Retrieved October 10, 2020 from www.sciencedaily.com/releases/2020/09/200911110804.htm

70 BMJ. (2019, May 29). New evidence links ultra-processed foods with a range of health risks: Policies that limit ultra-processed food intake are urgently needed, say researchers. ScienceDaily. Retrieved January 25, 2023 from www.sciencedaily.com/releases/2019/05/190529221040.htm

71 Murray, S. L., Baron, M., & Baraniuk, J. N. (2021). Effect of the low glutamate diet on inflammatory cytokines in veterans with Gulf War Illness (GWI): A pilot study. Life sciences, 280, 119637. https://doi.org/10.1016/j.lfs.2021.119637

72 UNESCO Universal Declaration on Cultural Diversity: https://en.unesco.org/about-us/legal-affairs/unesco-universal-declaration-cultural-diversity

73 Neithammer, C (2020) A Desert Feast; Celebrating Tuson's Culinary Heritage, University of Arizona Press

74 Ni, M., McNease, C (2012). The Tao of Nutrition third edition, Tao of Wellness Press, CA, USA

75 Shi, Y., Zhang, C., & Li, X. (2021). Traditional medicine in India. Journal of Traditional Chinese Medical Sciences, 8, S51-S55. https://doi.org/10.1016/j.jtcms.2020.06.007

76 Zhao, X., Tan, X., Shi, H., & Xia, D. (2021). Nutrition and traditional Chinese medicine (TCM): a system's theoretical perspective. European journal of clinical nutrition, 75(2), 267–273. https://doi.org/10.1038/s41430-020-00737-w

77 Dipayan Sarkar, Jacob Walker-Swaney, Kalidas Shetty, Food Diversity and Indigenous Food Systems to Combat Diet-Linked Chronic Diseases, Current Developments in Nutrition, Volume 4, Issue Supplement_1, January 2020, Pages 3–11, https://doi.org/10.1093/cdn/nzz099

78 Galbete, C., Kröger, J., Jannasch, F., Iqbal, K., Schwingshackl, L., Schwedhelm, C., Weikert, C., Boeing, H., & Schulze, M. B. (2018). Nordic diet, Mediterranean diet, and the risk of chronic diseases: the EPIC-Potsdam study. BMC medicine, 16(1), 99. https://doi.org/10.1186/s12916-018-1082-y

79 Orioli, R., Antonucci, C., Scortichini, M., Cerza, F., Marando, F., Ancona, C., Manes, F., Davoli, M., Michelozzi, P., Forastiere, F., & Cesaroni, G. (2019). Exposure to Residential Greenness as a Predictor of Cause-Specific Mortality and Stroke Incidence in the Rome Longitudinal Study. Environmental health perspectives, 127(2), 27002. https://doi.org/10.1289/EHP2854

80 Tomasso, L. P., & Chen, J. T. (2022). Toward a Theory of Nature Experience and Health. Ecopsychology, 14(4), 282–297. https://doi.org/10.1089/eco.2022.0005

81 Karr,T., Bell, K. (2020) Empty Plate: Food Sustainability, Mindfulness, chapter 5, pg. 270, Summerland; UT

82 Andersen, L.; Corazon, S.S.; Stigsdotter, U.K. Nature Exposure and Its Effects on Immune System Functioning: A Systematic Review. Int. J. Environ. Res. Public Health 2021, 18, 1416. https://doi.org/10.3390/ijerph18041416

83 James, P., Hart, J. E., Banay, R. F., & Laden, F. (2016). Exposure to Greenness and Mortality in a Nationwide Prospective Cohort Study of Women. Environmental health perspectives, 124(9), 1344–1352. https://doi.org/10.1289/ehp.1510363

84 Frumkin, H., Bratman, G. N., Breslow, S. J., Cochran, B., Kahn, P. H., Jr Lawler, J. J., Levin, P. S., Tandon, P. S., Varanasi, U., Wolf, K. L., & Wood, S. A. (2017). Nature Contact and Human Health: A Research Agenda. Environmental health perspectives, 125(7), 075001. https://doi.org/10.1289/EHP1663

85 Karr,T., Bell, K. (2020) Empty Plate: Food Sustainability, Mindfulness, chapter 5, pg 305, 309, Summerland; UT

86 Li Q. Effects of forest environment (Shinrin-yoku/Forest bathing) on health promotion and disease prevention-the Establishment of "Forest Medicine". Environ Health Prev Med. 2022;27:43. doi: 10.1265/ehpm.22-00160. PMID: 36328581; PMCID: PMC9665958.

87 What Are The Benefits Of Sunlight? By Rachel Nall, RN, BSN,CCRN, 2019: Https://Www.Healthline.Com/Health/Depression/Benefits-Sunlight

88 Drexel University. (2022, April 25). Being in nature: Good for mind, body and nutrition. ScienceDaily. Retrieved January 25, 2023 from www.sciencedaily.com/releases/2022/04/220425135943.htm

89 Being in Nature: Good for Mind, Body and Nutrition- Drexel University. https://drexel.edu/news/archive/2022/April/Being-in-Nature-Good-for-Mind-Body-and-Nutrition

90 Soga M, Evans MJ, Tsuchiya K, Fukano Y. A room with a green view: the importance of nearby nature for mental health during the COVID-19 pandemic. Ecol Appl. 2021 Mar;31(2):e2248. doi: 10.1002/eap.2248. Epub 2020 Nov 17. Erratum in: Ecol Appl. 2021 Oct;31(7):e02434. PMID: 33205530; PMCID: PMC7744839.

91 Zhang, L., Wang, W., Dong, X., Zhao, L., Peng, J., & Wang, R. (2020). Association between time spent outdoors and myopia among junior high school students: A 3-wave panel study in China. Medicine, 99(50), e23462. https://doi.org/10.1097/MD.0000000000023462

92 Karr,T., Bell, K. (2020) Empty Plate: Food Sustainability, Mindfulness, chapter 5, pg 308, Summerland; UT

93 Max Planck Institute for Human Development. (2021, July 15). Spending time outdoors has positive effect on our brains. ScienceDaily. Retrieved January 23, 2023 from www.sciencedaily.com/releases/2021/07/210715103025.htm

94 Karr,T., Bell, K. (2020) Empty Plate: Food Sustainability, Mindfulness, pg. 300, Summerland; UT

95 Master, H., Annis, J., Huang, S. et al. Association of step counts over time with the risk of chronic disease in the All of Us Research Program. Nat Med 28, 2301–2308 (2022). https://doi.org/10.1038/s41591-022-02012-w

96 Hillman, C. H., Pontifex, M. B., Raine, L. B., Castelli, D. M., Hall, E. E., & Kramer, A. F. (2009). The effect of acute treadmill walking on cognitive control and academic achievement in preadolescent children. Neuroscience, 159(3), 1044–1054. https://doi.org/10.1016/j.neuroscience.2009.01.057

97 Faulkner, J. A., Larkin, L. M., Claflin, D. R., & Brooks, S. V. (2007). Age-related changes in the structure and function of skeletal muscles. Clinical and experimental pharmacology & physiology, 34(11), 1091–1096. https://doi.org/10.1111/j.1440-1681.2007.04752.x

98 Ding D, Van Buskirk J, Nguyen B, et al. Physical activity, diet quality and all-cause cardiovascular disease and cancer mortality: a prospective study of 346 627 UK Biobank participants British Journal of Sports Medicine 2022;56:1148-1156.

99 Real-Life Benefits of Exercise and Physical Activity: https://www.nia.nih.gov/health/real-life-benefits-exercise-and-physical-activity

100 "Ireland : Medtronic Receives FDA Clearance for Riptide(TM) Aspiration System." MENA Report, Albawaba (London) Ltd., Jan. 2018.

101 Karr,T., Bell, K. (2020) Empty Plate: Food Sustainability, Mindfulness, chapter 3, pg. 215-230, Summerland; UT

102 Sitting Tai Chi exercises improved recovery outcomes for older stroke .... https://newsroom.heart.org/news/sitting-tai-chi-exercises-improved-recovery-outcomes-for-older-stroke-survivors

103 American Heart Association. (2022, April 7). Sitting Tai Chi exercises improved recovery outcomes for older stroke survivors. ScienceDaily. Retrieved January 25, 2023 from www.sciencedaily.com/releases/2022/04/220407101026.htm

104 Aston University. (2022, September 22). Babies react to taste and smell in the womb: Direct evidence that babies react differently to various smells and tastes while in the womb. ScienceDaily. Retrieved January 25, 2023 from www.sciencedaily.com/releases/2022/09/220922103255.htm

105 Park, K. Y., Jeong, J. K., Lee, Y. E., & Daily, J. W., 3rd (2014). Health benefits of kimchi (Korean fermented vegetables) as a probiotic food. Journal of medicinal food, 17(1), 6–20. https://doi.org/10.1089/jmf.2013.3083

Chapter 18 ~ Redefining Nourishment, A Literature Review

106 Lin, T. L., Lu, C. C., Lai, W. F., Wu, T. S., Lu, J. J., Chen, Y. M., Tzeng, C. M., Liu, H. T., Wei, H., & Lai, H. C. (2021). Role of gut microbiota in identification of novel TCM-derived active metabolites. Protein & cell, 12(5), 394–410. https://doi.org/10.1007/s13238-020-00784-w

107 Carr, A. C., & Rowe, S. (2020). Factors Affecting Vitamin C Status and Prevalence of Deficiency: A Global Health Perspective. Nutrients, 12(7), 1963. https://doi.org/10.3390/nu12071963

108 Robertson, S. (2019) What are the effects of total isolation? An expert explains. University of Central Lancashire. Retrived Febuary 02, 2023. https://theconversation.com/what-are-the-effects-of-total-isolation-an-expert-explains-109091

109 Mead, M. (1928). Coming of Age in Samoa: A Psychological Study of Primitive Youth for Western Civilisation, Mariner Books

110 Darnell, R. (2021) Who was Franz Boas and why should we read him today? Western University. https://www.routledge.com/blog/article/who-was-franz-boas-and-why-should-we-read-him-today

111 Hernandez LM, Blazer DG, editors. (2006) Genes, Behavior, and the Social Environment: Moving Beyond the Nature/Nurture Debate. National Acadamy Press

112 How culture influences health beliefs. EuroMed Information. https://www.euromedinfo.eu/how-culture-influences-health-beliefs.html/

113 Hickie IB, Scott EM, Cross SP, Iorfino F, Davenport TA, Guastella AJ, Naismith SL, Carpenter JS, Rohleder C, Crouse JJ, Hermens DF, Koethe D, Markus Leweke F, Tickell AM, Sawrikar V, Scott J. Right care, first time: a highly personalised and measurement-based care model to manage youth mental health. Med J Aust. 2019 Nov;211 Suppl 9:S3-S46. doi: 10.5694/mja2.50383. PMID: 31679171.

114 Johnson PJ, Jou J, Rockwood TH, Upchurch DM. Perceived Benefits of Using Complementary and Alternative Medicine by Race/Ethnicity Among Midlife and Older Adults in the United States. J Aging Health. 2019 Sep;31(8):1376-1397. doi: 10.1177/0898264318780023. Epub 2018 Jun 14. PMID: 29900809; PMCID: PMC8048740.

115 Griffiths V. Eastern and Western paradigms: the holistic nature of traditional Chinese medicine. Aust J Holist Nurs. 1999 Oct;6(2):35-8. PMID: 11898209.

Our Journey with Food

> "Nutrition starts in the shopping cart, so it is all about the food. Change the food fads and nutrition habits not your diet."
>
> ~ Leena & Soneil Guptha

Chapter Nineteen ~ Nutrition for Our Golden Years - An Opinion

Soneil Guptha MD FACC FESC FCCP FICA MFPM GFMD

Dr. Leena Guptha with her father Timir Mitra (90 years young)

The importance of nutrition is one essential matter which remains on our back burner, starting as a newborn to gradually progressing to the twilight years of life and its end. As a newborn, hunger prompts our "cry," and the nipple feeds the nutritious milk that the mother produces. Gradually, it dries out and the pediatricians or family elders/peers start their version of nutritious feeding. If the baby is well-rounded, the baby is considered "healthy." But a "chubby" baby may not be fed nutritious food or formula.[1] Very soon, the baby migrates towards food cravings and soon the family/parents gravitate to comfort food, which can quickly translate to fast food either cooked at home or in fast food merchant kitchens. After that, a "habit" can develop, reinforced by "life on a treadmill," and with a few inebriations of "enriched soda," life sails towards the "pot of gold at the end of the rainbow," commonly labeled as our perception of "security-stability." Lifestyle changes are unhealthy diet, stress, and increased nicotine dependency, alcohol, or abuse of medicines or narcotics, as shown in the figure below.[2]

Furthermore, this lulls our brain to think "all is well," and the focus or interest in food habits or well-being is on the back burner to be visited later in life. The "health is wealth" mantra is forgotten and replaced with "wealth is wealth" and "power is wealth" as a mantra of life. Soon we realize that our skin is "scaly," bones are "fragile," the gut is "leaky," muscles are "weak," the brain is "foggy," and the motivation to make and eat "nutritious" food is "not inspiring."[3, 4, 5] In addition, we thank the heavens that "all is well," or so we think again—no attention to nutrition. No, nope, never.

It is humbly suggested that……ALL IS NOT WELL. Though the food was/is/will be available, the diet or food habits and fads are NOT nutritious. Our eating habits mostly lack attention to a nutritious and balanced diet. We have a theoretical orientation and conceptual framework, but translation to daily routine that health promotes well-being is a forgotten mission. For this reason, we say, "Nutrition begins in the shopping cart."

According to Dana DeSilva, "Good nutrition across life span prevent diseases, and it is never too late to make improvements to support healthy aging."[6]

So let's begin with how a food shopping cart should look that is predestined to be labeled as a "HOLISTICALLY HEALING FOOD CART for a BALANCED and NUTRITIOUS DIET for the Golden Years."

To start, we must first accept the concept of a BALANCED NUTRITION CART which is an extension or reconstruction of a balanced diet. A balanced diet is pictorially described below.

Figure 1: Factors that influence lifestyle. Source: Farhud DD. Impact of Lifestyle on Health. Iran J Public Health. 2015 Nov;44(11):1442-4. PMID: 26744700; PMCID: PMC4703222

The images demonstrate a plethora of ideas and represent great considerations. Still, we ask the following questions to understand the concept of nutrition with special reference to age and aging.

1. Do we know if a balanced diet and balanced nutrition are the same?

2. Do we know how to translate this concept for nutrition and diet to the shopping cart?

3. Do we understand and accept that nutrition needs adjusting to meet the changing body physiology with age and/or different health needs/ailments?

Principle 88: Unfortunately, attention to healthy food habits in relationship to general well-being does not usually occur until later in life.

Are a Balanced Diet and Balanced Nutrition the Same?

A **balanced diet** includes carbohydrates, proteins, and fats with vitamins and minerals from fruits and vegetables and avoids excessive intake of a particular ingredient (refined ingredients such as sugar, flour, and oils, and foods such as freezer dinners, deli and processed meats). **Balanced nutrition** focuses on the above food categories + fiber and antioxidants and addresses the special needs of certain health conditions or specific nutritional needs as we age.

Chapter 19 ~ Nutrition for Our Golden Years

The goal of both may be the same; ensuring adequate and appropriate foods and nutrients in what we eat. What is different is the conscious decision of our body and health needs in relation to our age, gender, activity level, health needs, and, including to some extent, personal preferences.

- ▲ A balanced diet commonly dictates certain percentages of the macronutrients (fats, proteins, and carbohydrates with fruits and vegetables).
- ▲ Balanced nutrition is a cognizant selection of food (macronutrients, micronutrients; vitamins and minerals; portion control, and variety.
- ▲ Individualized nutritional needs based on age, gender, activity level, and health.

> *Principle 89:* A one-size fits all approach is not the name of the game when it comes to balanced individual food and nutrient needs.

The following are some common factors to keep in mind for changing body needs during the aging process.

1. **Calorie intake:** With age, metabolism tends to slow down, which means older adults may require fewer calories to maintain a healthy weight. However, the exact caloric needs vary depending on factors such as activity level, muscle mass, and overall health. Consulting with a healthcare professional or a Board Certified Holistic Nutritionist (BCHN®) can help determine the appropriate calorie intake.

2. **Hydration:** Older adults usually have a reduced sense of thirst, making them more prone to dehydration. It's important to ensure an adequate fluid intake throughout the day, primarily through water, herbal teas, and other hydrating beverages throughout the day. However, specific fluid requirements may vary based on an individual's health conditions, so it's best to consult a healthcare professional.

3. **Nutrient density:** Aging, bodies require the same or even higher levels of nutrients, despite a decrease in caloric intake. Choosing nutrient-dense foods, such as fruits, vegetables, whole grains, and lean proteins, can help meet these nutritional needs without excess calories.

4. **Protein intake:** Older adults have increased protein requirements to support muscle maintenance and repair, but for those over the age of 71, protein consumption usually becomes less and less.[6] Including protein-rich foods such as lean meats, poultry, fish, eggs, legumes, and dairy products in the diet can help meet these needs. However, those with kidney problems should consult a healthcare professional for personalized guidance on protein intake.

5. **Calcium and vitamin D:** Adequate calcium and vitamin D intake is crucial for maintaining bone health, which becomes increasingly important with age. Dairy products, leafy greens, fortified plant-based milk alternatives, and exposure to sunlight are good sources of calcium and vitamin D.

6. **Fiber:** Consuming adequate dietary fiber can help prevent constipation, promote digestive health, and regulate blood sugar and cholesterol levels. Whole grains, fruits, vegetables, legumes, and nuts are excellent sources of fiber. They support digestive health and regulate blood sugar and cholesterol levels.

7. **Processed foods and added sugars:** It's important to minimize the intake of processed foods, which are often high in unhealthy fats, added sugars, and sodium. These can contribute to weight gain, inflammation, and the development of chronic diseases. Instead, focus on whole, unprocessed foods whenever possible.

A **balanced nutrition cart** can thus look as follows.

Macronutrients:

✓ **Carbohydrates:** Includes whole grains, fruits, vegetables, and legumes (green beans) as sources of complex carbohydrates (like sweet potato).

✓ **Proteins:** Includes lean meats, poultry, fish, eggs, dairy (milk, cheese, yogurt) products, legumes (beans, chickpeas soya, edamame), and plant-based protein (tofu and tempeh).

✓ **Fats:** Includes sources such as nuts, seeds, avocados, olive oil, and fatty fish like salmon.

Micronutrients:

✓ **Vitamins:** Available through fruits, vegetables, whole grains, and fortified foods. Obtain a range such as vitamins A, C, D, E, and B-vitamins, especially B$_{12}$; ones ability to absorb vitamins reduces with age and may require supplementation with the consent of a healthcare provider.

✓ **Minerals:** Include minerals like calcium, iron, magnesium, potassium, and zinc through foods such as dairy products, leafy greens, nuts, seeds, and lean meat.

At the time of serving, conscious attention to the following will go a long way toward establishing healthy and nutritious eating habits:

- **Portion Control:** Paying attention to portion sizes to avoid excessive calorie intake and maintain a healthy weight. Balancing calorie intake with energy expenditure is important for overall health.

- **Variety and moderation:** Including a wide range of foods from different food groups to ensure diverse nutrient intake. Eliminating or minimizing the consumption of processed foods, added sugars, unhealthy fats, and sodium is very important.

Chapter 19 ~ Nutrition for Our Golden Years

How to translate this concept of balanced nutritional food to my shopping cart?

Thoughtful "choices" is the name of the game. Thinking starts with weekly meal planning and creating a shopping list for balanced meals. For example, reach for a rainbow of colored fruits and vegetables that are fresh rather than prepackaged; include grains for fiber (quinoa, brown rice, whole wheat bread, or pasta are better than refined grain products); add proteins that are lean and skinless and inclusive of a combination of beans, legumes, and eggs to provide vital amino acids; fats from sources like olive oil, avocados, nuts, and seeds (these choices provide healthy essential fatty acids); limit sugary beverages and processed foods focusing instead on coconut water, kefir, almond milk, green or herbal teas - cold or hot - that not only quench thirst but limits the intake of salt and sugar. One good habit is to stick to the periphery (outer aisles); while not foolproof in markets, it is still where the freshest food is stacked. Reading labels helps with good decision-making and helps result in a shopping cart full of nutritious food individualized to the person/family and needs of our health and body.

> ***Principle 90:*** Nutritional requirements change throughout the lifespan, and recommendations must be adjusted to meet specific individual needs.

How to adjust nutrition to meet the changing body physiology with age and/or different health needs/ailments?

Changes in **physiology, psychology, and social environments** are significant as age advances, and so are nutritional needs. Body composition, nutrition absorption, and changing metabolism are key elements of aging. Muscle mass needs maintenance, bone density needs attention, the immune system needs boosting, and cognitive abilities must continue. Hence, strategies to promote a nutritious diet are paramount for overall vitality and continued quality of life. The above cart should be able to give nutrition despite changing body metabolism or needs. Keep in mind, calcium, fiber, protein, and vitamin B, especially B_{12}, to prevent malnutrition is an excellent start to keep an eye on our nutrition state. This becomes vital in chronic ailments like diabetes, hypertension, and gastrointestinal upsets, including medication interactions.

Dr. Soneil Guptha takes pride in the meals he prepares for his family.

An altered metabolic state can and does affect **hunger/appetite or taste**, so a conscious and tailored dietary management of food habits and eating patterns is vital. For example, increasing nutrients and better hydration may be necessary as thirst decreases or urinary issues hamper the overall intake of fluids. Remember, filling the cart with nutritious food is the start of the journey to a dietary/eating habit that gets this nutrition into the body and developing habits to fulfill the dictum of "Health is wealth."

Once the cart is home, some coaching and trial and error experience or experimentation may **augment cooking, eating habits, and nutrition**. Individual and group sessions can be helpful for coaching on the balanced cooking of nutritious meals.

Other possible adjustments are listed below but are not limited to these alone.
- Consistent mealtimes
- Portions assessment
- Regular mealtime with supplements augmenting overall nutrition
- Social opportunities with meals to promote and nurture healthy nutritional eating habits, especially with communal dining and cooking groups
- Experimenting with different textures and flavors to assist in chewing abilities, tastes, and textures that are enjoyable and acceptable/appealing to older adults

Healthcare professionals must put equal weight on **compliance to medication** and **compliance with food** along with gentle exercise and hydration, and key prohibitions with the medications and/or interactions of the medicines and/or the side effects of the pharmacological agents as they may have a negative influence on nutrition.

Some of the **other challenges** include (but are not limited to) reduced ability to chew,[7] loss of or decreased appetite, changes in tastes and flavor preferences, medical conditions affecting changing dietary needs, and the overall increases in **cost of goods**, including food. There is no panacea for these. Each situation requires individual assessment and improvisation of the delivery of nutrition.

Disabilities - physical, mental, cognitive, or in any combination- are individual challenges. Family members, friends, caregivers, volunteers, or those hired in assisted living residential homes need training in such holistic nutrition to help reduce older adults from withering away or remaining in a consistent starvation or unwanted intermittent fasting state, where the body mechanisms move to survival mode and become malnourished.

In summary, critical to the attention of health and well-being with age and aging, nutritious habits start with understanding the challenges of aging and implementing food buying, storage, and cooking strategies that can help overcome any nutrition-related hurdle as we wheel the shopping cart. Education and support to the aging and their caregivers can enhance nutritional status and quality of life and help older adults thrive with age and aging.

Ideal Nutritious Shopping Cart for Someone with No Specific Dietary Need or Confounding Illness
✓ A rainbow of vegetables and greens, a variety of nuts and seeds, olive oil.
✓ Proteins such as eggs, fish, beans, lentils, skinless lean meat.
✓ Carbohydrates such as sweet potato, brown rice, whole wheat pasta.

Chapter 19 ~ Nutrition for Our Golden Years

- ✓ When preparing meals, keep an eye on balancing calories versus calories expended (a negative balance to lose weight; otherwise, a balance reflecting input = output).
- ✓ For diets that support specific health conditions, consult with a healthcare provider or qualified nutrition practitioner for guidance about meal and shopping cart planning to ensure appropriate nutrition requirements are met.

The following are sample nutrition schedules that can be used and improvised from the start of the journey from a nutrition-rich shopping cart to a nutritious body.

Eat Daily	Fats	Protein	Eat weekly	Eat monthly**
Legumes Beans Peas Garbanzo bean Soya bean Pinto bean Kidney bean (*Jaggery - see Our Journey with Food Cookery Book, page 40)** High fructose foods)	Ghee Olive oil Nuts Seeds	Poultry Lean meat Salmon Oily fish Eggs	Maple syrup Jaggery* Honey	Apricots Apples Pears Cherries Mangoes Watermelon Dates Sultanas Chutneys
Greens Chard Spinach Kale Cabbage Leaf lettuce **Vegetables** Broccoli Summer squash Carrots Egg plant **Fruits** Berries Honeydew melon Cantaloupe Bananas Citrus			**Grains** Oat Wild rice Brown rice Buckwheat Quinoa Ancient grains (rye, winter wheat, barley, spelt) Pasta	**Starches** Winter squash Sweet potato Red and purple potato Corn
Herbs Green Onion Shallots Rosemary **Drinks** Herb tea (green preferably) Milk Yogurt or buttermilk			Onion Garlic	Ginger Turmeric

> ***Principle 91:*** Independent older adults may benefit from health coaching to achieve nutrition goals. Others may benefit from community meal service programs.

Resources to Help Older Adults Eat Healthy

According to Dana DeSilva, Nutrition Advisor for the Office of Disease Prevention and Health Promotion (ODPHP):[8, 9, 10]

> *There are several government resources that health professionals can use to support older individuals in accessing and achieving a healthy dietary pattern.*
> - *Congregate Nutrition Services provides meals for people ages 60 and older and their spouses in senior centers, schools, and churches.*
> - *Supplemental Nutrition Assistance Program (SNAP) provides temporary benefits to help with food purchases for people with limited incomes.*
> - *Commodity Supplemental Food Program (CSFP) distributes monthly packages of nutritious foods from the U.S. Department of Agriculture.*
> - *Home-Delivered Nutrition Services provides home-delivered meals for older adults who have trouble leaving home or have certain health conditions.*
> - *Child and Adult Care Food Program provides reimbursements for nutritious meals and snacks to older adults enrolled in daycare facilities.*
>
> *Choosing healthy foods and actively using nutrition resources can help people make every bite count, no matter their age. For more information about these resources for older adults, check out [Nutrition Programs for Seniors from Nutrition.gov](#).*[6]

Understanding Our Older Family Members

Family/Client History by Tammera Karr, PhD, BCHN®

H. Jean Fallon-Hunnecutt
Oregon Coast 2002
(1939-2022)

Life is ever-changing and with it are surprises and challenges. We can't always plan for the unknown, as hard as we might try.

Over the years, my aunt and I had communicated primarily by phone several times a month. We engaged in lively conversations on politics, the Constitution, and life. Aunt Jean was a lifelong learner and never one to watch the world pass by; she married in her 40s and retired in her early 70s. Jean was never far from a musical instrument; she played bass guitar and learned the fiddle in her 60s. She and her husband, Paul, had always been independent. They owned their home and vehicles, had good insurance and savings, and had a comfortable retirement income.

Chapter 19 ~ Nutrition for Our Golden Years

Jean never liked to cook, and Paul was a picky eater, preferring diner and buffet meals. Their freezer and cupboards were filled with processed foods. Vegetables and fruit were canned and sweetened. Dental health was poor, even from a young age for Jean.[11, 12] As an AB blood type, she would have thrived on fish and vegetables. Instead, it was fast food.[13] As a child in southern Idaho, Jean came down with scarlet fever. As a teen and adult, Jean had increasing challenges with the cold and developed Raynaud's.[14, 15, 16]

Jean's husband had a history of being bright and somewhat of a schemer and dreamer – there was always a plan to make lots of money. Paul retired from the U.S. Air Force in the late 1970s and became a house contractor and real-estate agent; his dream was to make it big in music, so nights and weekends found him jamming at local bars. During the Vietnam War, Paul loaded and unloaded Agent Orange from aircraft in the Philippines, and it would take decades before the military acknowledged the role of Agent Orange in countless health problems, including type 2 diabetes and heart disease. A traumatic event when his wife shot him in the chest in his 40s added to the growing health challenges. Paul was the son of a poor sharecropper in Missouri, and the recollection of being hungry or going without food manifested into glutenous eating when he aged, worsening his health. By the time he was in his 70s, Paul had had three open heart surgeries and developed skin rashes, vision problems, congestive heart failure, and diabetes. By his mid-80s, Paul had had two more heart attacks and was weak, barely able to walk or stay awake, but he was still driving himself and dreaming of making it big in Nashville. Paul was diagnosed with Alzheimer's disease and placed on Aricept®. Aricept (donepezil hydrochloride) is a cholinesterase inhibitor used to treat mild to moderate dementia caused by Alzheimer's disease.[17] The next thing we knew, Paul became excessive in his purchases and planned to become a cattle rancher and hay farmer in a neighboring county in Arkansas. Paul began telling everyone that his wife Jean had Alzheimer's and couldn't make any banking or contractual agreements.

> ***Principle 92:*** Healthcare providers must be attentive to interactions between drugs, their side effects, and foods as well as medication compliance, as these can have negative effects on nutritional status in elders.

Every day, Paul would tell Jean she had Alzheimer's, just like her mother, and needed to be put in a home. Additionally, he forced Jean to change her will and medical power of attorney. Paul's behavior concerned her so much that, in secret, she retained a lawyer to draw up medical power of attorney forms designating me as her guardian.

In 2015, Paul emptied the bank accounts, cashed in CDs, mortgaged the house, and took out loans without Jean's consent or, at times, knowledge. If she tried to reason with or challenge him, he responded with threats, including divorcing and leaving her with nothing. This was no idle threat; he had done so in the past with ex-wives. His mind didn't grasp the whole idea of getting older and being chronically ill; he had things to do with his life, and he wouldn't tolerate doing them anyway but his way. Jean now expressed fear and anger in her weekly phone calls.

In the fall of 2015, the stress put Jean in the hospital with diverticulosis. After a week in the hospital on IV antibiotics, her fear and anxiety overtook her mind, and increased memory problems became more

H. Jean Christmas 2016

apparent. When Jean went into the hospital, she weighed 160 pounds and was 5'7". After Jean was released, food became her enemy; she was terrified of eating. She had been told not to eat nuts, seeds, or high fiber, and no one followed up with a wellness check. By the time Jean was relocated to California in the early part of 2016, Jean weighed 98 pounds.

No one had considered how Jean's diet, scarlet fever, and Reynaud's would affect brain circulation as she aged. To what extent, the family would not fully know until the summer of 2016 when Jean was diagnosed with mild to moderate memory impairment due to microvascular ischemia. With the diagnosis of dementia, like Alzheimer's disease, Paul's questionable judgment and ability to care for himself and Jean became the source of traumatic times for those who cared for them. The family began to pay more attention, and their life came under scrutiny – the "interference" placed Paul at odds with everyone involved.

By spring 2018, Jean was in mental limbo, not knowing any of the individuals around her, what city or state she was in; the date and time of day were equally lost to her. When she was with me, her meals were loaded with brain-supporting foods, and she went for supervised walks and enjoyed TV in the evenings. When with her conservator, they did their best to provide healthy food. I mailed meal replacement powders, vitamins, and brain support nutrients. She would get up in the middle of the night, walk around the house, and open doors. Jean now required 24-hour supervision and was largely unable to communicate.

H. Jean left and sister Linda right at Crater Lake NP 2018

Soon, Jean was in a care home, which ended supplements and special diets. This was when her family learned insurance did not cover many things, including her care. The care home cost came out of what funds Jean had from her pension. When Jean needed to change residences due to the first one closing, the price had to be negotiated to leave $50 a month for medication copay. By the fall of 2018, Jean could no longer converse with family members and was uncertain who they were. She just knew they were family. Her voice, once strong, was now so faint it was difficult to hear. Incontinence and the inability to feed herself followed after she was told her baby sister Linda had passed away.

Paul had abandoned Jean in a hotel in Sacramento, California, in 2017 to "live his life." This initiated Adult Protective Services becoming involved with Jean's care and court hearings appointing a conservator. Paul returned to central California in the spring of 2019 from North Carolina, where he had lived with a stepdaughter, and obtained a driver's license (California had revoked his license in 2017). Paul had learned Jean's sister had left an inheritance. He bought a new car, moved into a hotel, and registered as an Uber driver (frightening). Now, he wanted his wife back and accused Jean's conservator of elder abuse and fraud. A long and ugly custody case ensued between Paul and his youngest daughter, who had been appointed conservator.

Paul passed in 2020, just weeks short of his 92 birthday. Jean's conservator faced new challenges in dealing with the Veteran's Administration and the State of California regarding Jean's widow's benefits.

Chapter 19 ~ Nutrition for Our Golden Years

The stress was so great that the conservator notified the family they could no longer be responsible for Jean. With the shambles and tatters of Jean's life, the family sought counsel from social workers and trusted nurse practitioners. The family knew Jean's resources were gone; they all lived in different states and were elderly or working full-time with limited resources to travel to California. They decided Jean would get better care with the county advocating as her financial conservator. The court appointed me as her medical guardian. I got Jean on hospice right away; this helped ensure she was being seen weekly by a nurse, personal care items (diapers and bed pads) were provided, and her decline was monitored. Due to COVID, it was impossible to see Aunt Jean in person for two years; she passed away in her care home just short of her 83rd birthday in 2022.

Everything Jean had saved and invested in during her working years to ensure her financial security for the Golden Years was gone, and she was at the mercy of strangers and government advocates. Jean's worst fear was developing dementia; stress, poor diet, the wrong medication, lack of sleep, and anxiety would lead to the demise of her mind far more than family history.

In one of my last conversations with my beloved aunt, when she was cognizant, she looked me in the eye, took my hand and said, "Tell my story so others can learn from it."

> ***Principle 93:*** Food choices carry consequences over time; both good and bad are amplified and magnified with aging.

Before You say Yes

Not everyone is well suited to being a caregiver, and often, those who are caregivers burn out or collapse from the "stress" of always being vigilant to the needs of their charge. It is the same regardless of the health challenge. When dealing with older adults, I hear clients say," If they are going to act like a child, then I'm going to treat them like one." But older adults are not children. New parents go through changes with their infants; there is an adjustment period of getting to know each other, growth, development, and establishment of a routine; then, as time passes, a balance – a new normal settles in.

Establishing a new routine and balance isn't easy for our older loved ones. They have their own idea of what is to happen, normal, and often firmly resist interference in what is still their life.

Unlike children, our parents or older charges have lived independently, functioning, and in control for a lifetime. They have moved and shaken businesses, politics, industry, and community – shaping our world. For them, losing independence is heartbreaking, frustrating, and depressing. The realization they are in the final portion of their journey through life makes for frustration, anger, fear, and confusion.

As their bodies fail to answer their commands, their minds rebel – you see, they mentally do not feel like an "old man or woman." I distinctly remember my mother-in-law saying, "*It makes me so damn mad, my brain isn't any different than when I was in my forties, but my body has betrayed me.*"

When older family members move in with family or a care home, they have given up a big chunk of themselves to have help and a safety net. They balk at "your rules" just like any average adult would do, and while some may thrive on being "cared for" like a child, others begin to resist and respond with anger. Frustration over the loss of independence creates confrontation and stress for everyone. The older family members have to change their schedule to suit whomever they are living with, and this is not easy. Years or decades of habits may conflict with what the caregiver feels is correct.

Equally, the caregiver has their privacy, independence, work schedule, and life altered. Often, the caregiver is a family member in their early 50s planning for retirement and all the things they have always wanted to do, or they are at the peak of their career and soon feel overwhelmed by the addition of care responsibilities. These responsibilities often come together with those already involving college-age children.

Memories are fickle when it comes to the reality of the time. We do not have the same history as the older generations; we may know the stories or history, but we did not live it like our parents or older charges did. We do not carry the baggage that goes along with the history of an adult that is uniquely theirs. My Aunt Linda told us, *"Your memories are not the memories of those you are caring for. If they are not correct by your recollection, it is ok; you can still enjoy them."*

Most seniors do not require three full meals daily but small snacks and two dinners. For those who are diabetic or concerned about memory challenges, selecting low glycemic foods and following a paleo/ketogenic diet plan reduces inflammation and erratic blood sugar spikes. Don't overlook the need for healthy fat; the diet should contain 15% saturated fats from real butter, animal and plant sources, with the remaining 15% coming from avocados, olives, nuts, seeds, and fish. Fat is crucial to blood sugar regulation and maintaining weight for an elder who has borderline sarcopenia. Both fat and protein play critical roles in the utilization of neurotransmitters necessary for cognition and memory.

As daytime temperatures increase, pay close attention to water consumption and sodium. Low sodium levels and dehydration are common causes of memory loss and confusion. The standard of care is to restrict water for those with low sodium. However, this may be counter-productive and should be discussed with healthcare providers to be sure it is the best option for your senior and their health.

Minimizing inflammation is a huge part of dietary concerns for elderly family members. While meat and potatoes may be the foods they want most, they can also cause increased pain for them. Gout is caused by sugar, processed flour, red meat, and some fish like salmon, which are high in purines. Here is when tart cherries come to the rescue for many. Cherries are highly beneficial for those with inflammatory illnesses.[18,19] Currently, there is great interest in studying the treatment of obesity with food-derived bioactive compounds, which have low toxicity and no severe adverse events compared with pharmacotherapeutic agents. Foods rich in anthocyanins include tart cherries, red raspberries, black soybeans, blueberries, sweet cherries, strawberries, and Queen Garnet plums. These anthocyanin-rich foods have been evaluated in cell culture, animal, and clinical studies and found to be beneficial for health, reducing inflammatory markers.[20]

Chapter 19 ~ Nutrition for Our Golden Years

A Caution on Microplastics and Heavy Metals

Let's not forget the importance of storage and eating dishware. In *Empty Plate: Food~Sustainability~Mindfulness,* pages 116-117, Kathleen and I looked at heavy metal toxicity with vintage dishware and inferior cookware. There is a growing body of research on microplastics and the dangers to human cognitive health.[21] People aged 80 and above cannot detoxify environmental contaminants efficiently and may have different toxic metal risk profiles. In 2023, individuals reheating or cooking their meals in inferior plastic ware and cookware may be worsening their health. A 2021 study looked at heavy metal concentrations and cognition in older individuals. A total of 932 younger elderly, 643 octogenarians, 540 nonagenarians, and 386 centenarians were included in the cross-sectional *Healthy Aging and Biomarkers Cohort Study* in 2017-2018. Blood or urine biological substrates were collected from each participant to determine toxic and essential metals concentrations by inductively coupled plasma mass spectrometry. Higher biomarker concentrations in men for toxic metals (41.2 μg/L vs. 34.4 μg/L for blood lead, 1.56 μg/L vs. 1.19 μg/L for blood mercury) and lower concentrations of essential metals (0.48 μg/L vs 0.58 μg/L for blood molybdenum, 10.0 μg/L vs 11.1 μg/L for blood manganese) were found. Blood lead and urine cadmium levels tended to increase with age ($P < 0.001$), blood cobalt, molybdenum, and manganese increased with age, and blood selenium decreased with age, while the prevalence of selenium deficiency was extremely low in centenarians.[22]

Research from 2023 indicates that microplastics are linked to inflammation in the human brain. Researchers found significantly increased activation of immune and neurodegeneration-related human-derived microglial cells at the proteome level pathways.[23] Many older individuals may heat their meals in the microwave, but just like baby formula heated in a plastic bottle in a microwave, meals heated in plastic containers or on plastic dishware can increase in nano-plastic particle residue.[24] For more on this topic, refer to Chapter 14 in this book titled *Forever Chemicals*.

Older people are at nutritional risk due to multiple physiological, social, psychological, and economic factors.[25] Elderly persons have a higher incidence of chronic diseases and associated intake of medications that may affect nutrient utilization. Social and economic conditions can adversely affect dietary choices and eating patterns.[26] According to a study on *The Role of Nutrition in Alzheimer's Disease* conducted in 2021, preventive intervention gives the best results if introduced before the first symptoms of dementia, around the age of 50. This is when the nutritional status, number of synapses, cognition, and neuropathological changes in the nervous system compensate for each other, increasing the chances of staying healthy for a longer period.[27] It has been proven that dietary habits, which lead to the development of cardiovascular and metabolic diseases, significantly increase the risk of dementia.

On the other hand, a Mediterranean diet rich in antioxidants, fiber, and omega-3 polyunsaturated fatty acids may have a protective effect on the neurodegenerative process. Physiological functions naturally decline with age, which may influence absorption and metabolism. Loneliness and reluctance to eat may complicate an already marginal situation.[28]

Foods that Fuel and Heal the Brain

In many respects, my mother-in-law, Libby, is responsible for the books I have written. Libby was a Renaissance woman of sorts. She loved jazz, could play the cello and organ, and could type with perfect accuracy faster than the wind. She had been influenced by an aunt who ran a Kansas newspaper, another in San Fransisco who was a professional photographer, and she loved her husband and son with every fiber of her being. In contrast, Libby cooked everything from scratch, gardened, and canned fruits, vegetables, game meat, and wild-caught fish. The trips to fast food joints happen once or twice a year. The bulk of her adult life was spent in nature with her husband. Even after she retired from working for a newspaper at 83, she continued to travel and enjoy music, books, and real food. An avid follower of Adelle Davis, Libby faithfully took the best quality vitamins she could obtain from midlife until her passing.[29, 30]

Elizabeth (Libby) Karr 1918-2013

When I came into the picture, it took some work to win her acceptance. We worked on many projects over the years, and she was the first to have a computer in her home so she could type and edit the information I gave to clients.

At 90, Libby did two back-to-back cruises with her son and family. She would walk the promenade deck each day, enjoying the ocean air. Even in her nineties, she had good bone health and minimal macular degeneration with no cataracts.[31] Movement was a part of her daily routine until she was 91; after that she limited herself to light housework and savoring the adventures and romance of the books piled by her chair. Leaving the house and walking on uneven surfaces created anxiety by the time she reached 92.

Libby incorporated the following into her life from when she became pregnant in 1954. These changes may be why she lived a relatively illness-free life well into her 90s. She had one medication for hypothyroidism.

> Regular exercise, quitting smoking, drinking in moderation, watching your weight, and eating plenty of fruits and vegetables are all simple things that make a massive difference to your biological age. There's a roughly 15-year difference in life expectancy between someone who does four of these five things and someone who does none.[32]

Libby always cooked us hamburgers when we came; they tasted much better than mine, even when using the same ingredients. She took pride in making this simple meal for us. As time passed and she decided it was time to move in with us, food became essential for me to communicate that I cared about her.[33] Libby was very private; her feelings, thoughts, and personal history were rarely shared. Libby never turned away a plate of food carried into her. Each day before leaving for work, I would put soup into the small Crockpot® to warm for her; the pot was always clean and waiting for the next day when I returned. I took care to make sure she not only had adequate calories from wholesome foods but that it also looked and tasted good. Occasionally, I would include a special dark chocolate side or even a reminiscent of her youth, a gin and tonic.

Libby taught me it was okay to eat two meals a day. As she moved into her late eighties, the three meals daily were no longer satisfying or necessary. A cup of good organic coffee and a bowl of soup was often the start of her day.[34] Dinner was her favorite; salmon, free-range chicken, beef or wild game meat, vegetables, rice, quinoa, or homemade biscuits or bread.[35] I was told this accounted for her mental sharpness and health until days before her passing. She ate well, slept in comfort, and passed in her bed at home.[36]

Don't get me wrong, Libby was not always easy to get along with; she resented her loss of independence and her body failing while her mind still felt 40. She could be nasty at times, but she was also generous. We have since learned that her life lessons were invaluable as we took responsibility for other family members after her passing in 2013.

The following is a sample of the foods Libby consumed from her 50s through her 90s. Science came later.

Probiotics

Recent observations suggest a bidirectional communication between the gut microbiota and the brain via immune, circulatory, and neural pathways, termed the gut-brain axis (GBA). Alterations in gut microbiota composition, an increased number of pathobionts and a decreased number of symbionts, termed gut dysbiosis or microbial intestinal dysbiosis, play a prominent role in the pathogenesis of central nervous system (CNS)-related disorders. Clinical reports confirm that GI symptoms often precede neurological symptoms several years before developing neurodegenerative diseases (NDDs).[37] Researchers in 2023 looked deeper into the connection between gut-brain health and the increased incidence of Alzheimer's disease (AD). Microbial dysbiosis has been identified as a significant factor in the onset and progression of AD. An imbalance in gut microbiota affects central nervous system (CNS) functions through the gut-brain axis and involves inflammatory, immune, neuroendocrine, and metabolic pathways. An altered gut microbiome is known to affect the gut and blood-brain barrier permeability, resulting in an imbalance in levels of neurotransmitters and neuroactive peptides/factors. Restoration of levels of beneficial microorganisms in the gut has demonstrated promising effects in AD in pre-clinical and clinical studies.[38, 39]

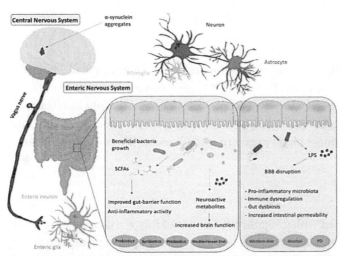

Alfonsetti, M., & Castelli, V. (2022). Are We What We Eat? Impact of Diet on the Gut–Brain Axis in Parkinson's Disease. Nutrients, 14(2). https://doi.org/10.3390/nu14020380

Multiple studies also revealed the gut microbiome's involvement in enhancing the degree of many neurological disorders, including neurodegenerative diseases. It was widely observed that there were distinct microbiome profiles and dysbiosis within patients who have Alzheimer's disease, Parkinson's disease, amyotrophic lateral sclerosis, and multiple sclerosis.[40, 41] The exact relationship between neurodegenerative diseases and gut microbiota remains unclear. Gut microbiome restoration through probiotics, synbiotics (mixtures of helpful probiotics for gut health), prebiotics (non-digestible fibers that help these bacteria grow), or other dietary mean that synergistically work together in your digestive tract could potentially slow Parkinson's disease. A recent review discussed the influence of diet on the bidirectional communication between gut and brain, thus supporting the hypothesis that this disorder could begin in the gut.[42, 43]

Salmon

There's a reason fish is called brain food, says Lauri Wright, PhD, RD, LD, Assistant Professor of Nutrition at the University of South Florida and a spokesperson for the Academy of Nutrition and Dietetics. "Several studies have shown that a diet containing generous amounts of omega-3 fatty acids leads to decreased rates of dementia and improved memory recall," she says. Researchers at the Rush University Medical Center in Chicago followed more than 6,000 people for four years to see how diet affected their memory. The frequent fish eaters (at least once a week) had a 12% slower memory decline than those who did not eat fish. The fish eaters also saw a 60% reduction in the risk of developing Alzheimer's disease. Wright suggests three four-ounce servings weekly of omega-3-rich fatty fish like salmon, mackerel, herring, and sardines.

Dark Skinned Fruits

"Berry fruits and vegetables contain compounds essential for optimal function and resisting decline with aging," says Robert Krikorian, PhD, who leads the Cognitive Aging Program at the College of Medicine at the University of Cincinnati. One of his studies found that those who drank blueberry juice every day for two months significantly improved their performance on learning and memory tests. In another study, he found similar results with Concord grape juice. Additional studies from 2023 support the inclusion of antioxidant-rich fruits in the diet of older adults.[44]

Beets

Not only are beets super-trendy these days, they are also loaded with nitrates. Great — but what are nitrates? "Nitrates are a form of nitric oxide, which is a natural compound involved in vascular dilation (associated with blood pressure lowering)," explains Dr. Krikorian. Nitrates increase blood flow and oxygen to the brain, thus improving mental performance. Beets contain high concentrations of nitrate, which can be converted into nitric oxide (NO) after consumption. NO has various functions in the human body, including a vasodilatory effect, which reduces blood pressure, and increases oxygen and nutrient delivery to multiple organs.[45]

Eat Greens

Leafy greens contain antioxidants and are loaded with a significant amount of folate, a general term used to describe the many forms of vitamin B. Studies support that folate-rich foods improve memory by decreasing inflammation and improving blood flow to the brain. Folic acid (vitamin B_9) has also been proven to lower homocysteine levels, an amino acid linked to a higher risk of heart disease. In a 2019 study published in *Clinical Epigenetics*, inadequate dietary intake of vitamin B_{12} was significantly associated with accelerated cognitive decline in the prospective analysis. In contrast, adequate folate, vitamin B$_6$, and vitamin B$_{12}$ intake were significantly associated with better cognitive reserve.[46] A cross-sectional study evaluated the relationship between cognitive ability and folic acid, B vitamins, vitamin D and co-enzyme Q10 (CoQ10) supplementation. The sample consisted of 892 adults aged >50 who were assessed for their cognitive status from July 2019 to January 2022 in the Shanghai Sixth People's Hospital Affiliated with Shanghai Jiao Tong University School of Medicine (China). The study findings confirmed a lower prevalence of cognitive impairment in those with higher folic acid, B vitamins, vitamin D, and CoQ10 levels.[47]

Coffee and Tea

Can't remember where you put your phone? (Oh, that's right, it's in your hand!) Have a cup — or three — of Joe. Several bioactive compounds, such as polyphenols and caffeine, implicate coffee as a potential nutritional therapeutic in aging. Moderate coffee consumption (three to five cups a day) in humans significantly decreases the risk of developing certain chronic diseases.[48] Studies from 2016 and 2023 used MRI imaging of the brains of high coffee consumers in a population-based study. They found a complex association between coffee consumption, brain structure, and cognition. Higher coffee consumption was cross-sectionally associated with a lower occurrence of lacunar infarcts and better executive function, but also with smaller hippocampal volume and worse memory function.[49, 50]

Increasing evidence suggests that regular coffee, tea, and dark chocolate consumption can promote brain health and reduce the risk of age-related neurodegenerative disorders. One class of phytochemicals present in relatively high amounts in coffee, tea, and cacao are *methylxanthines*. Among such methylxanthines, caffeine has been the most widely studied and has clear effects on neuronal network activity, promoting sustained cognitive performance and possibly protecting neurons against dysfunction and death.[51] A 2021 study found coffee consumption and total dietary caffeine intake were associated with better cognitive functioning as measured by various neuropsychological tests in a Mediterranean cohort of elderly individuals.[52] The beneficial effects of coffee on cognitive function are attributed to the reorganization of functional connectivity toward more efficient network properties.[53]

Dark Chocolate

Chocolate is a rich source of antioxidant and anti-inflammatory flavonoids and dietary minerals with the potential to benefit bone health.[54] However, other chocolate constituents, such as cocoa butter, sugar, and methylxanthines, may be detrimental to bone. Human studies investigated the role of chocolate consumption on serum bone markers and bone mineral density (BMD) in 2019. Studies showed postmenopausal women had no bone effects at moderate chocolate intakes, whereas adolescents consuming chocolate had greater longitudinal bone growth. Based on flavonoid and mineral content, unsweetened cocoa powder appeared to be the best option, followed by dark chocolate with higher cocoa content to support and preserve bone health. Determining dietary recommendations for chocolate consumption relative to bone health is vital because of the growing popularity of chocolate, particularly dark chocolate, and an expected increase in consumption owing to suggestions of health benefits against various degenerative diseases.[55] A 2013 study found that older adults (73 years old, on average) who drank two cups of cocoa (not instant *Swiss Miss*® but a bitter lower sugar research version) every day for a month had improved blood flow to the brain and performed better on memory tests. I suggest a small piece from a bar of dark chocolate with at least 70% cocoa; a good source of flavonoids and antioxidants linked to brain health daily.

Saffron

By 2018, several randomized, controlled clinical trials had been conducted to evaluate the efficacy of another plant, saffron (Crocus sativus), in treating mild to moderate depression. According to the current data, saffron has a significant effect on the severity of depression.[56] The effects of saffron were again reviewed in 2020 and included looking at anxiety and C-reactive protein. Twenty-one trials were included in this meta-analysis. Consumption of saffron resulted in a significant reduction in Beck Depression Inventory (BDI) scores (11 studies with 12 effect size) (WMD: -4.86; 95 % CI: -6.58, -3.14), Beck Anxiety Inventory (BAI) (5 studies) (WMD: -5.29; 95 % CI: -8.27, -2.31), and Pittsburgh Sleep Quality Index (PSQI) scores (three studies with four effect size) (WMD: -2.22; 95 % CI: -2.73, -1.72).[57] In 2021, saffron was also found to significantly improve blood pressure and inflammatory biomarkers.[58, 59] By 2022, additional reviews and studies looked at this ancient Indian and Mediterranean herb for liver, renal, and diabetic function. At this time, the findings are very encouraging overall.[60, 61, 62]

Chronic stress and high levels of glucocorticoids produce functional and structural changes in the brain, especially in the hippocampus. This important limbic system structure is crucial in cognitive functions, including learning and memory. Alzheimer's disease (AD) is a chronic neurodegenerative disease that usually starts slowly and worsens over time. Indeed, cognitive dysfunction, neuronal atrophy, and synaptic loss are associated with AD and chronic stress. Recent preclinical and clinical studies have highlighted a possible link between chronic stress, cognitive decline, and AD development. A study released in 2020 concluded with the following: "Human studies demonstrated that saffron and its main constitutive crocin are effective against chronic stress-induced cognitive dysfunction and oxidative stress and slowed cognitive decline in AD. The inhibitory actions on acetylcholinesterase activity, aggregation of beta-amyloid protein into amyloid plaques and tau protein into neurofibrillary tangles, and also the antioxidant, anti-inflammatory, and the promotion of synaptic plasticity effects are among the possible mechanisms to explain the neuroprotective effects of saffron."[63]

It is astounding that this herb from the crocus flower could be so powerful! When we look at the low incidence of diabetes and heart disease in the Indian population, it is clear to see how traditional cultural foods and the herbs used have protected them for centuries from these devastating conditions – all too common in the aging population of the modern world.

Rosemary

In folk medicine, rosemary has been used as an antispasmodic and a mild analgesic to cure intercostal neuralgia, headaches, migraines, insomnia, emotional upset, and depression.[64] Different investigations have highlighted rosemary's neuropharmacological properties as their main topics. Rosemary has significant antimicrobial, anti-inflammatory, antioxidant, anti-apoptotic, anti-tumorigenic, antinociceptive, and neuroprotective properties.

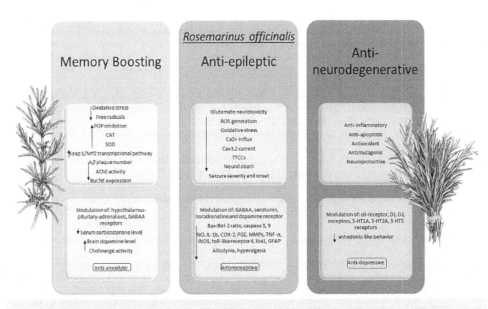

Rahbardar, M. G., & Hosseinzadeh, H. (2020). Therapeutic effects of rosemary (Rosmarinus officinalis L.) and its active constituents on nervous system disorders. Iranian Journal of Basic Medical Sciences, 23(9), 1100-1112. https://doi.org/10.22038/ijbms.2020.45269.10541

Conclusion

The digestive systems of older individuals have undergone decades of abuse from toxins in the environment, lifestyle choices, and medications. Everything from salivation to elimination no longer functions as it once did, making their biological responses delicate. The elderly client is best served on an individual basis and with caution. Mega-dosing with supplements, high protein isolate meal replacements, and medium chain triglycerides (coconut oil) can lead to digestive distress and worsening of health in older clients. In my experience, going slow and gently nets greater positive outcomes than aggressive nutrient replacement strategies which can affect stomach acid, gallbladder and pancreas function. Older individuals' health status should be re-evaluated regularly and adjusted for age-related changes.

The quality of life is directly affected when proactive lifestyle changes are incorporated; this continues to be true even later in life. These sometimes intangible factors increase an individual's capability for independence, as well as lowering risks for depression and anxiety in older individuals. A holistic approach to elder care is preferable to maintain quality of life versus what often transpires in nursing homes and the debilitating financial burden on individuals and families.

---

1 Kouwenhoven SMP, Muts J, Finken MJJ, Goudoever JBV. Low-Protein Infant Formula and Obesity Risk. Nutrients. 2022 Jun 30;14(13):2728. doi: 10.3390/nu14132728. PMID: 35807908; PMCID: PMC9268498

2 Farhud DD. Impact of Lifestyle on Health. Iran J Public Health. 2015 Nov;44(11):1442-4. PMID: 26744700; PMCID: PMC4703222.

3 Muñoz, M., Robinson, K., & Shibli-Rahhal, A. (2020). Bone Health and Osteoporosis Prevention and Treatment. Clinical obstetrics and gynecology, 63(4), 770–787. https://doi.org/10.1097/GRF.0000000000000572

4 Rorteau, J., Chevalier, F. P., Fromy, B., & Lamartine, J. (2020). Vieillissement et intégrité de la peau- De la biologie cutanée aux stratégies anti-âge [Functional integrity of aging skin, from cutaneous biology to anti-aging strategies]. Medecine sciences : M/S, 36(12), 1155–1162. https://doi.org/10.1051/medsci/2020223

5 Ahmadi, S., Wang, S., Nagpal, R., Wang, B., Jain, S., Razazan, A., Mishra, S. P., Zhu, X., Wang, Z., Kavanagh, K., & Yadav, H. (2020). A human-origin probiotic cocktail ameliorates aging-related leaky gut and inflammation via modulating the microbiota/taurine/tight junction axis. JCI insight, 5(9), e132055. https://doi.org/10.1172/jci.insight.132055

6 DeSilva D (2021) Nutrition as We Age: Healthy Eating with the Dietary Guidelines. https://health.gov/news/202107/nutrition-we-age-healthy-eating-dietary-guidelines

7 Azzolino, D., Damanti, S., Bertagnoli, L., Lucchi, T., & Cesari, M. (2019). Sarcopenia and swallowing disorders in older people. Aging clinical and experimental research, 31(6), 799–805. https://doi.org/10.1007/s40520-019-01128-3

8 Behavioral Nutrition (2020): https://behavioralnutrition.org/aging-and-nutrition/

9 Leitão C, Mignano A, Estrela M, Fardilha M, Figueiras A, Roque F, Herdeiro MT. The Effect of Nutrition on Aging-A Systematic Review Focusing on Aging-Related Biomarkers. Nutrients. 2022 Jan 27;14(3):554. doi:10.3390/nu14030554. PMID: 35276919; PMCID: PMC8838212.

10 Food for thought: the role of Nutrition in healthy aging. https://www.agingresearch.org/video/food-for-thought-the-role-of-nutrition-in-healthy-aging/

11 Sureda, A., Daglia, M., Argüelles Castilla, S., Sanadgol, N., Fazel Nabavi, S., Khan, H., Belwal, T., Jeandet, P., Marchese, A., Pistollato, F., Forbes-Hernandez, T., Battino, M., Berindan-Neagoe, I., D'Onofrio, G., & Nabavi, S. M. (2020). Oral microbiota and Alzheimer's disease: Do all roads lead to Rome?. Pharmacological research, 151, 104582. https://doi.org/10.1016/j.phrs.2019.104582

12 Li, Y. C., Liu, Y., Chen, F., Chu, M., & Chen, X. C. (2022). Sichuan da xue xue bao. Yi xue ban = Journal of Sichuan University. Medical science edition, 53(2), 194–200. https://doi.org/10.12182/20220360304

13 Vasan, S. K., Rostgaard, K., Ullum, H., Melbye, M., Hjalgrim, H., & Edgren, G. (2015). ABO Blood Group and Dementia Risk--A Scandinavian Record-Linkage Study. PloS one, 10(6), e0129115. https://doi.org/10.1371/journal.pone.0129115

14 Scarlet fever. (2016). Nursing standard (Royal College of Nursing (Great Britain) : 1987), 30(35), 17. https://doi.org/10.7748/ns.30.35.17.s20

15 Patterson, M. J. (1996). Streptococcus. In S. Baron (Ed.), Medical Microbiology. (4th ed.). University of Texas Medical Branch at Galveston.

16 Herrick, A. L., & Wigley, F. M. (2020). Raynaud's phenomenon. Best practice & research. Clinical rheumatology, 34(1), 101474. https://doi.org/10.1016/j.berh.2019.101474

17 Greaves, D., Psaltis, P. J., Davis, D. H. J., Ross, T. J., Ghezzi, E. S., Lampit, A., Smith, A. E., & Keage, H. A. D. (2020). Risk Factors for Delirium and Cognitive Decline Following Coronary Artery Bypass Grafting Surgery: A Systematic Review and Meta-Analysis. Journal of the American Heart Association, 9(22), e017275. https://doi.org/10.1161/JAHA.120.017275

18 Markovics, A., Biró, A., Kun-Nemes, A., Fazekas, M. É., Rácz, A. A., Paholcsek, M., Lukács, J., Stündl, L., & Remenyik, J. (2020). Effect of Anthocyanin-Rich Extract of Sour Cherry for Hyperglycemia-Induced Inflammatory Response and Impaired Endothelium-Dependent Vasodilation. Nutrients, 12(11), 3373. https://doi.org/10.3390/nu12113373

19 Biro, A., Markovich, A., Homoki, J. R., Szőllősi, E., Hegedűs, C., Tarapcsák, S., Lukács, J., Stündl, L., & Remenyik, J. (2019). Anthocyanin-Rich Sour Cherry Extract Attenuates the Lipopolysaccharide-Induced Endothelial Inflammatory Response. Molecules (Basel, Switzerland), 24(19), 3427. https://doi.org/10.3390/molecules24193427

20 Ngamsamer, C., Sirivarasai, J., & Sutjarit, N. (2022). The Benefits of Anthocyanins against Obesity-Induced Inflammation. Biomolecules, 12(6), 852. https://doi.org/10.3390/biom12060852

21 Gerardo, B., Cabral Pinto, M., Nogueira, J., Pinto, P., Almeida, A., Pinto, E., Marinho-Reis, P., Diniz, L., Moreira, P. I., Simões, M. R., & Freitas, S. (2020). Associations between Trace Elements and Cognitive Decline: An Exploratory 5-Year Follow-Up Study of an Elderly Cohort. International journal of environmental research and public health, 17(17), 6051. https://doi.org/10.3390/ijerph17176051

22 Lv, Y., Wei, Y., Zhou, J., Xue, K., Guo, Y., Liu, Y., Ju, A., Wu, B., Zhao, F., Chen, C., Xiong, J., Li, C., Gu, H., Cao, Z., Ji, J. S., & Shi, X. (2021). Human biomonitoring of toxic and essential metals in younger elderly, octogenarians, nonagenarians and centenarians: Analysis of the Healthy Ageing and Biomarkers Cohort Study (HABCS) in China. Environment international, 156, 106717. https://doi.org/10.1016/j.envint.2021.106717

23 Kim, H., Ashim, J., Park, S., Kim, W., Ji, S., Lee, S., Jung, Y., Jeong, S. W., Lee, S., Kim, H., Lee, Y., Kwon, M. K., Hwang, J., Shin, J. M., Lee, S., Yu, W., Park, J., & Choi, S. (2023). A preliminary study about the potential risks of the UV-weathered microplastic: The proteome-level changes in the brain in response to polystyrene derived weathered microplastics. Environmental Research, 233, 116411. https://doi.org/10.1016/j.envres.2023.116411

24 Dunzhu Li, Yunhong Shi, Luming Yang, Liwen Xiao, Daniel K. Kehoe, Yurii K. Gun'ko, John J. Boland, Jing Jing Wang. Microplastic release from the degradation of polypropylene feeding bottles during infant formula preparation. Nature Food, 2020; DOI: 10.1038/s43016-020-00171-y

Chapter 19 ~ Nutrition for Our Golden Years

25. Miller, V. M., Jayachandran, M., Barnes, J. N., Mielke, M. M., Kantarci, K., & Rocca, W. A. (2020). Risk factors of neurovascular ageing in women. Journal of neuroendocrinology, 32(1), e12777. https://doi.org/10.1111/jne.12777

26. Śliwińska, S., & Jeziorek, M. (2021). The role of nutrition in Alzheimer's disease. Roczniki Panstwowego Zakladu Higieny, 72(1), 29–39. https://doi.org/10.32394/rpzh.2021.0154

27. Śliwińska, S., & Jeziorek, M. (2021). The role of nutrition in Alzheimer's disease. Roczniki Panstwowego Zakladu Higieny, 72(1), 29–39. https://doi.org/10.32394/rpzh.2021.0154

28. Hoogendijk, E. O., Smit, A. P., van Dam, C., Schuster, N. A., de Breij, S., Holwerda, T. J., Huisman, M., Dent, E., & Andrew, M. K. (2020). Frailty Combined with Loneliness or Social Isolation: An Elevated Risk for Mortality in Later Life. Journal of the American Geriatrics Society, 68(11), 2587–2593. https://doi.org/10.1111/jgs.16716

29. Adelle Davis Remembered: The Mother of Nutrition (2017): https://www.wholefoodsmagazine.com/blogs/1-wholefoods-magazine/post/13638-adelle-davis-remembered-the-mother-of-nutrition

30. Eating habits have a substantial effect on health, not only because of consumed foods and nutrients, but also because of the regularity of meals: Stalling, I., Albrecht, B. M., Foettinger, L., Recke, C., & Bammann, K. (2022). Meal Patterns of Older Adults: Results from the OUTDOOR ACTIVE Study. Nutrients, 14(14), 2784. https://doi.org/10.3390/nu14142784

31. Association between Visual Impairment and Nutritional Risk among Older Adults with Diabetes: A Population-Based Cross-Sectional Study: Yang, E., & Lee, K. H. (2023). Association between Visual Impairment and Nutritional Risk among Older Adults with Diabetes: A Population-Based Cross-Sectional Study. Journal of Korean Academy of Nursing, 53(2), 167–176. https://doi.org/10.4040/jkan.22141

32. Your body can be younger than you are – here's how to understand (and improve) your 'biological age' (2023): https://theconversation.com/your-body-can-be-younger-than-you-are-heres-how-to-understand-and-improve-your-biological-age-211061

33. Diet and nutritional status of elderly people depending on their place of residence: Bogacka, A., Heberlej, A., Usarek, A., & Okoniewska, J. (2019). Diet and nutritional status of elderly people depending on their place of residence. Roczniki Panstwowego Zakladu Higieny, 70(2), 185–193. https://doi.org/10.32394/rpzh.2019.0069

34. Fasting and health benefits: Paoli, A., Tinsley, G., Bianco, A., & Moro, T. (2019). The Influence of Meal Frequency and Timing on Health in Humans: The Role of Fasting. Nutrients, 11(4), 719. https://doi.org/10.3390/nu11040719

35. Nutritional Status and Nutritional Treatment Are Related to Outcomes and Mortality in Older Adults with Hip Fracture: Malafarina, V., Reginster, J. Y., Cabrerizo, S., Bruyère, O., Kanis, J. A., Martinez, J. A., & Zulet, M. A. (2018). Nutrients, 10(5), 555. https://doi.org/10.3390/nu10050555

36. Presbyphagia: Dysphagia in the elderly: Feng, H. Y., Zhang, P. P., & Wang, X. W. (2023). Presbyphagia: Dysphagia in the elderly. World journal of clinical cases, 11(11), 2363–2373. https://doi.org/10.12998/wjcc.v11.i11.2363

37. Chidambaram, S. B., Essa, M. M., Rathipriya, A. G., Bishir, M., Ray, B., Mahalakshmi, A. M., Tousif, A. H., Sakharkar, M. K., Kashyap, R. S., Friedland, R. P., & Monaghan, T. M. (2022). Gut dysbiosis, defective autophagy and altered immune responses in neurodegenerative diseases: Tales of a vicious cycle. Pharmacology & therapeutics, 231, 107988. https://doi.org/10.1016/j.pharmthera.2021.107988

38. Thakkar, A., Vora, A., Kaur, G., & Akhtar, J. (2023). Dysbiosis and Alzheimer's disease: role of probiotics, prebiotics and synbiotics. Naunyn-Schmiedeberg's archives of pharmacology, 10.1007/s00210-023-02554-x. Advance online publication. https://doi.org/10.1007/s00210-023-02554-x

39. Wang, Q., Luo, Y., Ray Chaudhuri, K., Reynolds, R., Tan, E. K., & Pettersson, S. (2021). The role of gut dysbiosis in Parkinson's disease: mechanistic insights and therapeutic options. Brain : a journal of neurology, 144(9), 2571–2593. https://doi.org/10.1093/brain/awab156

40. Sasmita A. O. (2019). Modification of the gut microbiome to combat neurodegeneration. Reviews in the neurosciences, 30(8), 795–805. https://doi.org/10.1515/revneuro-2019-0005

41. Cryan, J. F., O'Riordan, K. J., Sandhu, K., Peterson, V., & Dinan, T. G. (2020). The gut microbiome in neurological disorders. The Lancet. Neurology, 19(2), 179–194. https://doi.org/10.1016/S1474-4422(19)30356-4

42. Alfonsetti, M., Castelli, V., & d'Angelo, M. (2022). Are We What We Eat? Impact of Diet on the Gut-Brain Axis in Parkinson's Disease. Nutrients, 14(2), 380. https://doi.org/10.3390/nu14020380

43. Zhu, X., Li, B., Lou, P., Dai, T., Chen, Y., Zhuge, A., Yuan, Y., & Li, L. (2021). The Relationship Between the Gut Microbiome and Neurodegenerative Diseases. Neuroscience bulletin, 37(10), 1510–1522. https://doi.org/10.1007/s12264-021-00730-8

44. Keller, J. E., Taylor, M. K., Smith, A. N., Littrell, J., Spaeth, K., Boeckman, C. R., Burns, J. M., & Sullivan, D. K. (2022). Correlation of Skin Carotenoid Content with 3-Day Dietary Intake in Community Dwelling Older Adults. Journal of food composition and analysis : an official publication of the United Nations University, International Network of Food Data Systems, 105, 104243. https://doi.org/10.1016/j.jfca.2021.104243

45. Zamani, H., de Joode, M. E. J. R., Hossein, I. J., Henckens, N. F. T., Guggeis, M. A., Berends, J. E., de Kok, T. M. C. M., & van Breda, S. G. J. (2021). The benefits and risks of beetroot juice consumption: a systematic review. Critical reviews in food science and nutrition, 61(5), 788–804. https://doi.org/10.1080/10408398.2020.1746629

46. An, Y., Feng, L., Zhang, X., Wang, Y., Wang, Y., Tao, L., Qin, Z., & Xiao, R. (2019). Dietary intakes and biomarker patterns of folate, vitamin B6, and vitamin B12 can be associated with cognitive impairment by hypermethylation of redox-related genes NUDT15 and TXNRD1. Clinical epigenetics, 11(1), 139. https://doi.org/10.1186/s13148-019-0741-y

47 Jiang, X., Guo, Y., Cui, L., Huang, L., Guo, Q., & Huang, G. (2023). Study of Diet Habits and Cognitive Function in the Chinese Middle-Aged and Elderly Population: The Association between Folic Acid, B Vitamins, Vitamin D, Coenzyme Q10 Supplementation and Cognitive Ability. Nutrients, 15(5), 1243. https://doi.org/10.3390/nu15051243

48 Shukitt-Hale, B., Miller, M. G., Chu, Y. F., Lyle, B. J., & Joseph, J. A. (2013). Coffee, but not caffeine, has positive effects on cognition and psychomotor behavior in aging. Age (Dordrecht, Netherlands), 35(6), 2183–2192. https://doi.org/10.1007/s11357-012-9509-4

49 Araújo, L. F., Mirza, S. S., Bos, D., Niessen, W. J., Barreto, S. M., van der Lugt, A., Vernooij, M. W., Hofman, A., Tiemeier, H., & Ikram, M. A. (2016). Association of Coffee Consumption with MRI Markers and Cognitive Function: A Population-Based Study. Journal of Alzheimer's disease : JAD, 53(2), 451–461. https://doi.org/10.3233/JAD-160116

50 Mayer, C., Nägele, F. L., Petersen, M., Schell, M., Aarabi, G., Beikler, T., Borof, K., Frey, B. M., Nikorowitsch, J., Senftinger, J., Walther, C., Wenzel, J. P., Zyriax, B. C., Cheng, B., & Thomalla, G. (2023). Association between Coffee Consumption and Brain MRI Parameters in the Hamburg City Health Study. Nutrients, 15(3), 674. https://doi.org/10.3390/nu15030674

51 Camandola, S., Plick, N., & Mattson, M. P. (2019). Impact of Coffee and Cacao Purine Metabolites on Neuroplasticity and Neurodegenerative Disease. Neurochemical research, 44(1), 214–227. https://doi.org/10.1007/s11064-018-2492-0

52 Paz-Graniel, I., Babio, N., Becerra-Tomás, N., Toledo, E., Camacho-Barcia, L., Corella, D., Castañer-Niño, O., Romaguera, D., Vioque, J., Alonso-Gómez, Á. M., Wärnberg, J., Martínez, J. A., Serra-Majem, L., Estruch, R., Tinahones, F. J., Fernandez-Aranda, F., Lapetra, J., Pintó, X., Tur, J. A., García-Rios, A., … PREDIMED-Plus Investigators (2021). Association between coffee consumption and total dietary caffeine intake with cognitive functioning: cross-sectional assessment in an elderly Mediterranean population. European journal of nutrition, 60(5), 2381–2396. https://doi.org/10.1007/s00394-020-02415-w

53 Kim, H., Kang, S. H., Kim, S. H., Kim, S. H., Hwang, J., Kim, J. G., Han, K., & Kim, J. B. (2021). Drinking coffee enhances neurocognitive function by reorganizing brain functional connectivity. Scientific reports, 11(1), 14381. https://doi.org/10.1038/s41598-021-93849-7

54 Montagna, M. T., Diella, G., Triggiano, F., Caponio, G. R., De Giglio, O., Caggiano, G., Di Ciaula, A., & Portincasa, P. (2019). Chocolate, "Food of the Gods": History, Science, and Human Health. International journal of environmental research and public health, 16(24), 4960. https://doi.org/10.3390/ijerph16244960

55 Seem, S. A., Yuan, Y. V., & Tou, J. C. (2019). Chocolate and chocolate constituents influence bone health and osteoporosis risk. Nutrition (Burbank, Los Angeles County, Calif.), 65, 74–84. https://doi.org/10.1016/j.nut.2019.02.011

56 Tóth, B., Hegyi, P., Lantos, T., Szakács, Z., Kerémi, B., Varga, G., Tenk, J., Pétervári, E., Balaskó, M., Rumbus, Z., Rakonczay, Z., Bálint, E. R., Kiss, T., & Csupor, D. (2019). The Efficacy of Saffron in the Treatment of Mild to Moderate Depression: A Meta-analysis. Planta medica, 85(1), 24–31. https://doi.org/10.1055/a-0660-9565

57 Ghaderi, A., Asbaghi, O., Reiner, Ž., Kolahdooz, F., Amirani, E., Mirzaei, H., Banafshe, H. R., Maleki Dana, P., & Asemi, Z. (2020). The effects of saffron (Crocus sativus L.) on mental health parameters and C-reactive protein: A meta-analysis of randomized clinical trials. Complementary therapies in medicine, 48, 102250. https://doi.org/10.1016/j.ctim.2019.102250

58 Ghaderi, A., Asbaghi, O., Reiner, Ž., Kolahdooz, F., Amirani, E., Mirzaei, H., Banafshe, H. R., Maleki Dana, P., & Asemi, Z. (2020). The effects of saffron (Crocus sativus L.) on mental health parameters and C-reactive protein: A meta-analysis of randomized clinical trials. Complementary therapies in medicine, 48, 102250. https://doi.org/10.1016/j.ctim.2019.102250

59 Asbaghi, O., Sadeghian, M., Sadeghi, O., Rigi, S., Tan, S. C., Shokri, A., & Mousavi, S. M. (2021). Effects of saffron (Crocus sativus L.) supplementation on inflammatory biomarkers: A systematic review and meta-analysis. Phytotherapy research : PTR, 35(1), 20–32. https://doi.org/10.1002/ptr.6748

60 Norouzy, A., Ghodrat, S., Bahrami, L. S., Feizy, Z., & Arabi, S. M. (2022). The effects of saffron supplementation on the measures of renal function indicators: a systematic review and meta-analysis. International urology and nephrology, 54(9), 2215–2226. https://doi.org/10.1007/s11255-022-03127-2

61 Mousavi, S. M., Mokhtari, P., Asbaghi, O., Rigi, S., Persad, E., Jayedi, A., Rezvani, H., Mahamat-Saleh, Y., & Sadeghi, O. (2022). Does saffron supplementation have favorable effects on liver function indicators? A systematic review and meta-analysis of randomized controlled trials. Critical reviews in food science and nutrition, 62(23), 6315–6327. https://doi.org/10.1080/10408398.2021.1900059

62 Asbaghi, O., Soltani, S., Norouzi, N., Milajerdi, A., Choobkar, S., & Asemi, Z. (2019). The effect of saffron supplementation on blood glucose and lipid profile: A systematic review and meta-analysis of randomized controlled trials. Complementary therapies in medicine, 47, 102158. https://doi.org/10.1016/j.ctim.2019.07.017

63 Saeedi, M., & Rashidy-Pour, A. (2021). Association between chronic stress and Alzheimer's disease: Therapeutic effects of Saffron. Biomedicine & pharmacotherapy = Biomedecine & pharmacotherapie, 133, 110995. https://doi.org/10.1016/j.biopha.2020.110995

64 Ahmed, H. M., & Babakir-Mina, M. (2020). Investigation of rosemary herbal extracts (Rosmarinus officinalis) and their potential effects on immunity. Phytotherapy research : PTR, 34(8), 1829–1837. https://doi.org/10.1002/ptr.6648

> "Our cells carry the memories of our ancestors: those memories influence the foods we like, the sounds that comfort, our adaptability to stress, illnesses that may occur and more still not fully understood ~ At the heart of the whole thing is nutrition and our lifestyle that equally influences our cells. This interrelationship is why we are all unique."
>
> ~ Tammera Karr, PhD, BCHN®

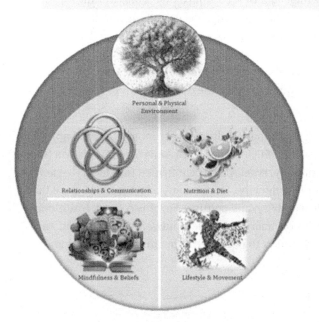

Chapter Twenty ~

The <u>NEW</u> Paradigm for Building Better Health

Science and technology in the 21st century have catapulted us into a brave new world containing nutrigenomics, DNA/RNA activators, and a new conversation on bio-individuality health options. Most people are unclear about what any or all of this means for them and their health. So, let's look at a little bit of history.

Mark Kurlansky, author of *Food of a Younger Land*, chronicles the work of the Federal Writers Project and the mountain of copy that would have made up *What America Eats*, a project suspended with the start of World War II. When the Great Depression hit in 1929, the food of North America was vastly different than it is today. In this era, each region of the United States had distinctive gastronomy traditions. The Manhattan tomato-based clam chowder versus the milk and cream versions of New England and the West Coast is one of countless such examples. Gastronomy in North America included traditional foods from the many peoples of the American Indian cultures, African-American, Creole, Cajun, Gullah, and Southern. The rich Hispanic Tex-Mex, Californian, and Cuban dishes instill warmth and a sense of celebration. Each gastronomy tradition displayed the cultures of individuals from all over the world. The immigrants who became Americans possessed centuries of cellular memory of foods from their homelands, and these foods, wild-foraged herbs, and fermented beverages contained the bacteria and minerals found in the soil of their original countries and of its air and water; the same unique minerals that made up the bone, blood, and tissue cells of generation upon generation of people.

When World War II began, the military sought a homogenous diet that could be mass-produced for soldiers to ensure adequate calories and nutrition. They hit upon the (then) Midwestern diet, bland by comparison and easy to replicate. This era also began *scientific* nutrition as we think of it today. Adopting the Midwestern dietary model brought about a national homogenous food model and formed the foundation of today's industrialized foods franchises that pretty much all taste alike. These foods contain none of the regional flavors that had been distinctive to the water, soil, and bacteria influences from personal gardens, saltwater bays, fresh water rivers, family dairies, recipes written by generations of cooks in home kitchens used for centuries to feed populations.

Bio-individuality

There is no one perfect way of eating that works for everybody; this concept is called bio-individuality. Each person has particular needs for their health according to age, constitution, gender, size, lifestyle, and ancestry. When discussing bio-individuality, we are talking about all the ancestral, environmental, and cultural influences surrounding a person. In Chapter 18, we looked at various aspects of nourishment and redefined how we think about nourishment and its role in human health. Research is learning more about the influence of life events during our grandparents 'and parents 'lives that subsequently affect the development of stress adaptation and response in later generations.[1]

In the previous pages of this book, we detailed nutrients found in cultural gastronomy. Each chapter has been followed by research that demonstrates greater than 40% of the North American population (mainly European ancestry) carries the MFTHR gene. Additionally, research has confirmed that lifestyle choices, not our genes, are the most significant driving factor of longevity. Gastronomy encompasses more than food; it also represents beliefs, environment, physical activity, and culture. For this reason, traditional foods nourish us on deeper levels than simple calories or macro- and micronutrients. Recognized and utilized on a cellular level, traditional foods affect our ability to build better health – health that is resilient.

> Here are some examples:
>
> Individuals of Japanese heritage will most likely thrive on a Japanese-type diet high in rice, sea vegetables, fermented sauces, buckwheat, and fish.
>
> If your heritage is from one of the many provinces of India, your digestive system will probably do well with ghee, dairy, basmati rice, cooked beans, and curry.
>
> Traditional African communities had abundant beans, grains, animal protein, sweet potatoes, and green vegetables. Dairy was not easily accessible or easy to store in hot regions and, therefore, not a part of the traditional diet, which may be why some individuals of African descent are lactose intolerant.

So, when we consider ancestral nutrition deficiencies and stressors, combined with the stress of a 21st century lifestyle, the choices an individual selects daily can make the difference between *peak performance*, poor health, and the loss of cognitive abilities and independence. For example, my maternal family originated from Scotland and Ireland (Scotch-Irish). My ancestors fled war, famine and religious persecution to Denmark where they later sailed from to North America in the late 1600s.

These individuals' diets changed almost entirely upon reaching North Carolina. Gone were the centuries-old soil augmentation with mineral-rich seaweed and animal husbandry practices of grazing cattle and sheep with mineral-rich sieges and browse (brambles, leaves, herbs, weeds). Now, new foods, bacteria, fungi, and environments became the influencers of health.[2] Corn replaced wheat, barley, and rye but not many individuals learned about the necessity of nixtamalizing the corn to increase B vitamin availability; this new dietary staple provided calories but little nutrition. Potatoes replaced turnips, wild asparagus, and collard greens, increasing the calorie content again, with a loss of vital food-sourced methylators.

Four generations of the Armer family May 1957. This family carries the MTHFR gene, which increases the risk for dementia, Alzheimer's disease, hypertension, macular degeneration, type 1 diabetes, rheumatoid arthritis, and alcohol addiction. All pictured are diseased.

As each generation moved farther from traditional foods and the influence of the former environment, deficiencies in key nutrients (methylators) increased. With increased deficiencies, cell receptor sites for chronic diseases were activated, as those for health maintenance closed down. By my grandmother's generation, the MFTHR gene fully influenced her family's health, driving Hashimoto's thyroiditis, depression, alcoholism, heart disease, hypertension, cognitive decline, and autoimmune conditions.[3] Although my grandfather grew a garden, my grandmother had little affinity for cooking; foods were overcooked and devoid of many healing herbs and vegetables. As my mother's generation grew into adults, highly processed foods in their diets increased, along with alcohol and tobacco use (viewed as stylish or chic in the 1940s-70s). And in my generation (born in the 1960s), chronic illnesses, dementia, depression, type 2 diabetes, alcohol addiction, and cardiovascular disease claimed all but myself, one aunt, and a cousin (not counting children in the fifth and sixth generations).[4] A study released in 2019 found that Raynaud's disease increases in individuals with elevated homocysteine from the MTHFR gene mutation (thinking back to my Aunt Jean).[5] As my Aunt (80s), cousin and I (60s) age, health challenges are increasing with each decade. Two individuals pictured above reached their mid-90s, which gives me hope that I can equal them by utilizing my knowledge of nutrients and foods as medicine. Research cited in earlier chapters has shown that life expectancy increases for individuals who make lifestyle changes (including the use of nutrients) by their fifth decade of life. More hope springs forth.

> The term *epigenetics* can be outlined as the meiotically/mitotically heritable alterations in gene expression related to environmental factors without changes to the sequence of bases in the DNA.[6] Epigenetic mechanisms, known for their ability to regulate gene transcription and genomic stability, are key players for maintaining normal cell growth, development, and differentiation.

"While many observational studies have identified diet-gene-health interactions, few studies have effectively used this type of information to develop personalized diets," says Patrick Wilson, PhD, RD, an assistant professor in Old Dominion University's Human Movement Sciences department.[7] "Some studies are now showing that a person's genotype partly dictates whether they respond favorably to caffeine ingestion," Wilson says. He points to a 2015 study published in the *Scandinavian Journal of Medicine and Science in Sports* that found different outcomes during a time trial depending on a single gene called CYP1A2. One group did better by rinsing and swallowing the caffeine.[8]

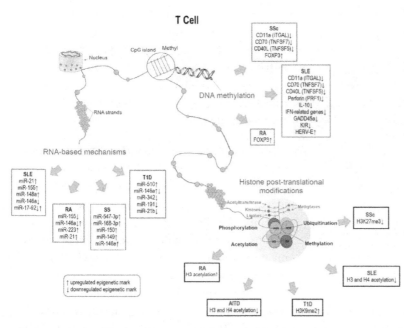

Schematic representation of key epigenetic mechanisms (DNA methylation, histone post-translational modifications, and RNA-based mechanism) involved in the pathogenesis of autoimmune diseases, including SLE, RA, SSc, SS, AITD, and T1D.

Newer research from 2019 at the Max Planck Institute of Immunobiology and Epigenetics in Freiburg, Germany, shows robust evidence that not only the inherited DNA itself but also the inherited epigenetic instructions contribute to regulating gene expression in the offspring.[9]

We are more than the sum of our genes. Epigenetic mechanisms modulated by environmental cues such as diet, disease, or lifestyle significantly regulate DNA activity by switching genes on and off. However, it has been long debated whether epigenetic modifications accumulated throughout life can cross the border of generations and be inherited by children or grandchildren.[10]

Since I was a teenager, I have chosen vitamins, minerals, and flavorful natural foods. Each day, my husband and I remind ourselves of the importance of our choices to move, eat and sleep well, maintain family connections, and nurture our beliefs. While I was writing this edition, my husband turned 68; he is physically active, continues to do rigorous work, and shares his knowledge and experience with those in their 20s and 30s. In a nutshell, each of us has the opportunity to make the most out of our health through the nourishment we provide the mind, body, and spirit.

> **Principle 94 :** "The whole is greater than the sum of the parts."
> ~ Aristotle, Book VIII, 1045a.8-10

The MTHFR Gene

At least 8,425 research articles exist about Methylenetetrahydrofolate Reductase (MTHFR), a key regulatory enzyme in folate and homocysteine metabolism. A total of 34 rare but deleterious mutations in

MTHFR, as well as a total of nine common variants (polymorphisms), have been reported.[11] Individuals can get personalized diets from organizations like Julie Matthews 'BioIndividual Nutrition Institute[12] and GeneFood[13] if they do not employ a holistic nutritionist specializing in genetic programs. Keep in mind that the evidence for using this information to guide eating and lifestyle behavior makes dieters more successful is still-inconclusive.

A study of more than 1,000 Europeans found that personalizing diets helped people adopt healthier behaviors. But the level of personalization needed was surprising. Asking about food preferences was as successful as considering people's health biomarkers and genes.

When reviewing information on illnesses or conditions associated with the MTHFR gene, you will find a laundry list of common health challenges, such as cardiovascular disease, pulmonary embolisms, addictions, bed wetting, fibromyalgia, miscarriages, schizophrenia, severe depression, cancer, and autism, to name a few.

According to the researchers at 23andMe.com, people need to be cautious about believing claims about the MTHFR gene and chronic illnesses. "Based on the existing data, scientists at 23andMe have concluded that people should not interpret their genotypes at the common MTHFR variants as affecting their health. For a connection between a genetic variant and a health condition to be considered real and clinically meaningful, well-run scientific studies need to show convincing and consistent evidence for that association."[14, 15, 16]

Closed Head Traumatic Brain Injury (TBI)

Bonnie McCarroll a champion rodeo performer and bronc rider, is most remembered for her death at the Pendleton Round-up in Pendleton, Oregon September 1929.

This fatal accident where McCarrol broke her neck during the fall, resulted in women being barred from rodeo events deemed to dangerous for women for seven decades.

All of us know someone affected by cognitive impairment. Alzheimer's disease and Parkinson's disease seem synonymous with the ever-growing aging population in America today. However, these sufferers are not the only ones who have cognitive challenges. Individuals with closed head trauma also experience cognitive decline. Other individuals with a family disease history or who possess the apolipoprotein (ApoE4) gene can choose to be proactive and change to a brain-supportive diet and lifestyle. All the ApoE proteins have the same normal function. They carrying fat, cholesterol, and vitamins throughout the body, including into the brain. While ApoE2 is protective and ApoE3 appears to have no effect, a mutation in ApoE4 is a well-established genetic risk factor for late-onset Alzheimer's disease.[17] The unfortunate part of having this knowledge is the accompanying belief that nothing can be done to prevent cognitive decline.

In our book *Empty Plate: Food, Sustainability, Mindfulness*, we look at foods for TBI, and lifestyle changes that are showing great promise in aiding veterans, athletes and others recover cognitive balance or function.[18]

Evidence-based guidelines on traumatic brain injured (TBI) military personnel from 2011[19] stated: "The body of research to support clinical practice guidelines specific to the nutrition care of TBI patients is extremely limited." Recommendations are: "Evidence-based nutrition guidelines specific for severe TBI should be updated. These guidelines should address unique nutritional concerns of severe TBI when different from general critical-illness nutrition guidelines...In addition, current guidelines to manage mild and moderate TBI should include recommendations for nutritional interventions." Wow, it appears to me that nutrition care for military patients with TBI is pretty limited in allopathic systems.

Interestingly, the same book covers the benefits of a ketogenic diet for individuals with TBI and says:[20] "The ketogenic diet has been further shown to be neuroprotective in animal models of several central nervous system (CNS) disorders, including Alzheimer's disease, Parkinson's disease, hypoxia, glutamate toxicity, ischemia, and traumatic brain injury (TBI)."

More than any other disease, severe cognitive impairments can potentially unravel families. They drag on for years, and cognitive decline illnesses are not "lethal" in the ordinary sense. People with TBI and Alzheimer's disease can lead long lives, the latter portion of which can get very difficult for everyone involved. There is an entire body of literature devoted to studying the effects of Alzheimer's disease on families and caregivers and dedicated to discovering practical methods for mitigating the damage done, which is not as commonly studied relating to other diseases.

Most other diseases affect what scientists consider to be peripheral tissues. Heart disease is about the heart. Kidney disease affects the kidneys. Cancer can strike anywhere, usually in an organ or bone, but most diseases leave our personhood intact. We are still ourselves, even when we are riddled with tumors or on dialysis. However, with the cognitive decline of Alzheimer's disease, dementia, and Parkinson's disease, we essentially disappear. We lose who we are, where we live, how old we are, and the names of family and friends – past and present. People define themselves by their intellect; our superior human mind is what sets us apart from the rest of the animal kingdom. When that goes, what is left?

Here's what research is showing makes the difference.[21, 22, 23, 24, 25, 26]

- To reduce hyperinsulinemia, eliminate all simple carbs and follow a low-glycemic, low-grain (especially refined grains) diet.
- Observe a 12-hour eating window and 12-hour fast each day, including at least three hours before bed.
- Stress reduction (yoga, meditation, whatever works for the individual).
- Get 8 hours of sleep each night (with melatonin if required).
- Do 30-60 minutes of exercise 4-6 days per week.
- Get regular brain stimulation (exercises, games, crossword puzzles).
- Supplement to optimize homocysteine, vitamin B12, and C-reactive protein levels.
    - Take vitamin D and vitamin K2.
    - Quality DHA (an omega-3 fatty acid found in fish) to support synaptic health.
    - Optimize mitochondrial function with co-enzyme Q10, zinc, selenium, other nutrients.
    - Use medium-chain triglycerides (coconut oil, MCT oil).

- Moreover, one of the most critical factors is improving gut health (prebiotics and probiotics).
- Eat antioxidant-rich foods and spices (blueberries, turmeric).
- Optimize hormone balance (monitor thyroid panel, cortisol, pregnenolone, progesterone, estrogen, and testosterone levels).

Why Cancer Doesn't Worry Me

Nutritional genomics has a growing role in the treatment of diseases and illnesses, along with promoting wellness through clinical research.[27] One area that caught my attention was using individualized nutrition for breast cancer. Clinically, I have seen how dietary and lifestyle changes can make a remarkable difference for clients with breast cancer. A 2020 study states nutritional interventions constitute crucial and empowering strategies, and offer an unprecedented opportunity for developing personalized diets in women at risk of developing breast cancer.[28] In my clinical experience with those diagnosed with hormone-responsive breast cancer or prostate cancer (in men) — the sooner the individual makes and owns positive changes in their lifestyle, the better the outcome for themselves and those they love. This does not mean they will have a miraculous healing or no longer face challenges. I have witnessed a return of hope, which positively impacts brain chemistry and natural killer cell action. When an individual personally selects and takes charge of the aspects of their lifestyle that are meaningful to them, a sense of control, connection, activity, restorative sleep, and perspective return. Their belief system allows them to focus on what they value. A belief system is not exclusively religion; it can encompass family, the environment, or leaving a legacy for children, all of which provide a purpose (reason to live, a goal to strive for). The empowering aspect of this action and change takes the power away from the specter of cancer. In *Empty Plate: Food~Sustainability~Mindfulness*, the sister book in the *Our Journey with Food* trilogy, Kathleen Bell discusses how tools such as reiki, meditation, HeartMath®, and holistic nursing aid in helping clients shift their attention to healing versus disease management.[29]

HeartMath® helps to improve heart rate variability (HRV). When you go to the doctor, they usually measure your heart rate (pulse), but not HRV. HRV is used as a measure of a person's overall fitness, well-being, and adaptability to stressful situations. HRV is governed by the autonomic nervous system (ANS), which is the part of the nervous system that regulates functions like breathing, digestion, and heart rate.[30] Mastering breathing techniques such as those used in yoga and meditation practices gives a measure of conscious control to functions like heart rate and blood pressure that are usually thought to be autonomic.

Chronic Autoimmune Conditions and Efficacy of Diet Changes

When health coaches tailor different lifestyle choices to various individuals, we are looking at a *new paradigm* in wellness; where the individual model is "actually me!" (as my husband says), and not an approximation or generalization based on a large demographic classification. OK, here is something I say to clients," You are not your cholesterol, weight, age, gender, or ethnicity – YOU are YOU, and what is normal for you may not fit into the accepted 'normal' range."

Clinical observation and research literature support the significant impact nutrigenetics/nutrigenomics or *nutritional genomics* have on modifying and preventing noncommunicable diseases. Remember Dr. C. Everette Koop in the 1980s? How about what we have learned from the *Blue Zones* research? The North American population has had the information to make positive health changes for decades (or even centuries). Now, it is a matter of finding the personal motivator – the 'why 'that makes the individual and lasting difference. This is not accomplished without challenges, but it is not an insurmountable task, especially with the aid of a Peak Performance coach. Dr. Leena Guptha will take us through the personal coaching steps that are part of the *2B Well Peak Performance* model in Chapter 21.

Rheumatoid arthritis (RA) is another condition that I research. RA is a chronic autoimmune disease that presents as a systemic immune-inflammatory response in genetically vulnerable individuals exposed to environmental triggers, including diet.[31] This debilitating disease is present in my family genetics and contributed to a shortened life expectancy for my sister. According to a 2021 study, diet and food components are critical environmental factors that interact with the genome, transcriptome, proteome, metabolome and microbiota. This life-long interplay defines the health and disease state of the individual.[32, 33, 34] A 2020 review confirmed that:

> Rheumatoid arthritis (RA) is a chronic systemic autoimmune disease that affects synovial joints, leading to inflammation, joint destruction, loss of function, and disability. Although recent pharmaceutical advances have improved the treatment of RA, patients with RA often inquire about dietary interventions to improve RA symptoms, as they perceive rapid changes in their symptoms after consumption of certain foods. There is evidence that some ingredients have pro- or anti-inflammatory effects. In addition, recent literature has shown a link between diet and microbiome changes. Both diet and the gut microbiome are linked to circulating metabolites that may modulate inflammation.[35]

Autoimmune diseases, of which there are many, are currently improving in clients utilizing the Wahls Protocol without expensive genetic testing. It is vital to remember that nutritional genomics is an emerging area of research; it may be decades before there is any real value to the information. It could be nothing more than an affirmation of past gastronomy knowledge and integrative nutrition practices around eating foods that make our DNA sing.[36]

Blood Type: Controversy or Untapped Tool?

Before gene studies, however, an equally helpful dataset known as blood type was being developed and used by Peter D'Adamo, ND. Dr. D'Adamo points to research showing that bacteria share the same ABO markers as humans. According to D'Adamo, "This results from the fact many microbes possess ABO 'blood types 'of their own. It is perhaps useful in understanding that the ABO blood group antigens are not unique to humans. They are relatively simple sugars that are not abundantly found in nature.

"A bacteria, for example, possessed an antigen on its surface that mimics the blood group A antigen and would have a much easier time infecting a person who was group A since that bacteria would more likely be considered 'self 'to the immune system. Also, microbes may adhere to the tissues of one ABO group in preference to another by possessing specialized adhesion molecules for that particular blood group."[37, 38]

Blood type science is not quite as old as many may believe. While the ABO blood groups were developed around 20 million years ago,[39] our understanding of how people with each of these distinct blood types are unique as individuals is much newer. It wasn't until World War II that advances in research on blood types began.[40]

A Little History

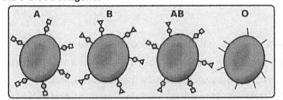

Associations between blood type and disease have been studied since the early 1900s, when Karl Landsteiner — an Austrian-born American biologist, physician and immunologist — determined that antibodies and antigens are inherited. In the 1950s, the chemical identification of the carbohydrate structure of surface antigens led to the understanding of biosynthetic pathways. The blood type is defined by oligosaccharide structures specific to the antigens. Thus, blood group antigens are secondary gene products, while the primary gene products are various glycosyltransferase enzymes that attach the sugar molecules to the oligosaccharide chain.

ABO blood antigens: • The A and B antigens are determined by which terminal sugar is expressed on a precursor oligosaccharide chain, the H antigen. • The FUT1 gene encodes a fucosyltransferase responsible for the assembly of the H-antigen on RBC. • The expression of A or B or both is determined by the ABO gene, which has three alleles that encode the glycosyltransferases responsible for the assembly of the A or B antigen and leaves the H precursor unmodified. • These antigens are expressed throughout the body and can be anchored in cell membranes by proteins or lipids or can be secreted.

Arnolds, K. L., Martin, C. G., & Lozupone, C. A. (2020). Blood type and the microbiome- untangling a complex relationship with lessons from pathogens. Current Opinion in Microbiology, 56, 59. https://doi.org/10.1016/j.mib.2020.06.008

Landsteiner classified human blood into the four well-known types through a series of experiments. The "type" actually refers to the presence of a particular antigen sticking up from the surface of a red blood cell. An antigen elicits a response from an immune cell called an antibody. Antibodies latch onto foreign substances that enter the body, such as bacteria and viruses, and clump them together for removal by other components of the immune system. A study from 2023 found that blood cells varied among patients with Brucella bloodstream infection. The main symptoms of the patients were fever (94.81%), and 72.70% were complicated with liver injury. The highest proportion of liver injury was 93.33% in patients with blood group A, and 52.38% in blood group O.[41]

Our blood groups are not a hit-or-miss act of random genetics without any real purpose. Instead, the ABO blood groups are a set of different solutions to a host of environmental variables, such as diet and infection, which ensure the survival of the human race. Looking at the distribution of blood groups today, we can see the threads of our evolutionary history. In the United States, O is the most common blood group, A is second, followed by B and AB. The breakdown in Great Britain is very similar to that in the United States. In Germany, there are slightly more A than O types. In Japan and China, those with type A, O and B are relatively evenly split, with AB increased over that found in European populations.[42, 43]

After Landsteiner determined the pattern of the ABO blood groupings, he realized blood types are inherited, and blood typing became one of the first ways to test paternity. Later, researchers learned a single gene governs ABO blood types. People who are type AB inherit an A gene from one parent and a B gene from the other.[44] Over the last hundred years, scientists have also discovered that the ABO blood group is just one of more than 35 human blood groups.[45] According to the International Society of Blood Transfusion, 341 blood group antigens are collected in 35 blood group systems.[46]

Blood Type and COVID

In 2020, a study looked for associations between blood type and COVID–19 infection. Researchers reviewed observational healthcare data on 14,112 individuals tested for SARS-CoV-2 with known blood type in the New York Presbyterian (NYP) hospital system. There was a slightly increased infection prevalence among non-O types. Compared with type O, the risk of intubation decreased among those with A and increased among AB and B types. In contrast, the risk of death was increased for type AB and dropped for types A and B. Researchers estimate Rh-negative blood type to have a protective effect for all three outcomes. "Our results add to the growing body of evidence suggesting blood type may play a role in COVID-19."[47, 48]

There is no doubt that genetic factors of the host play a role in susceptibility to infectious diseases. An association between ABO blood groups and SARS-CoV-2 infection, as well as the severity of COVID-19, was suggested relatively early during the pandemic and gained enormously high public interest. While inconclusive and controversial, researchers in 2022 did find evidence supporting an association between the ABO blood groups and the risk of contracting SARS-CoV-2.[49, 50]

Blood Type and Dementia

Research has revealed people with blood type AB may be more likely to develop memory loss in later years than people with other blood types, according to a study published in the September 10, 2014, online issue of *Neurology*, the medical journal of the American Academy of Neurology.[51] AB is the least common blood type, found in about 7% of the U.S. population. The study found people with AB blood were 82% more likely to develop cognitive and memory problems that lead to dementia than those with other blood types.

Previous studies have shown people with type O blood have a lower risk of heart disease and stroke, factors which can increase the risk of memory loss and dementia. These findings were from a more extensive study (*Reasons for Geographic and Racial Differences in Stroke* or REGARDS study) of more than 30,000 people followed for an average of 3.4 years.[52] Researchers also examined blood levels of Factor VIII, a protein that helps blood clot; high levels of Factor VIII are related to a higher risk of cognitive impairment and dementia. People in this study with higher levels of Factor VIII were 24% more likely to develop thinking and memory problems than individuals with lower protein levels. People with AB blood had a higher average level of Factor VIII than other blood types. Additionally, people in this study with the rarest blood type (AB) also had the highest increase in heart disease risk, at 23%. Those with type B had an 11% increased risk, and those with type A had a 5% increased risk. About 43% of Americans have type O blood.[53, 54]

One of the best parts about using blood type information is that once a client knows their blood type, bioindividual recommendations for foods can be made without further testing, which saves the client and practitioner time and money.[55]

Regardless of blood type, I always come back to the influence of culture on health. This has been illustrated in the *Blue Zones* studies. Unfortunately, the number of individuals who continue utilizing the cultural practices that led to their own unique formation is decreasing, and with them, the knowledge that led to their vitality. Working one-on-one with clients for years, bio-individuality is something I've always known to be true. I sincerely believe no one way of eating will work for everyone. Yet, Western medicine and science are constantly searching for the magic bullet – the *one perfect way* of eating that will solve all of humanity's problems. Our diet encompasses too many varied elements responsible for nourishing health to be limited to any set-in-stone restrictive food model. Once again, when we look at history, we can find gems of wisdom to guide our understanding.

Cultural and Ancient Medicine

Before the rise of Greek civilization, the Persian medical scholars were writing textbooks.[56] Almost all these ancient works are gone, but three copies remain of one of the rarest manuscripts written in old Persian (Farsi Dari). The oldest is in the Bodleian Library of Oxford, UK, which is dated 478 AH/1085 CE; the second in the Fateh Library in Istanbul, Turkey (written in 520 AH/1128 CE); and the third manuscript in the Malek Library in Tehran, Iran.[57] In 1879, the scholar of oriental studies, Charles Rieu (1820-1902), mentioned the *Hedayat al-Motaallemin fi-Tebb* (the Students' Guide in Medicine) written by Abubakr Rabi-ibn Ahmad Akhawayni Bukhari in his *Catalogue of the Persian Medical Manuscripts of the British Museum*.

- A section of Hedayat al-Motaallemin is devoted to the beneficial effects of exercise and sports for young men and girls, including traditional physical games.
- In the section on *sarsam* (meningitis), he describes the clinical findings of fever, headache, and loss of consciousness. He mentions its cause as inflammation of the covering of the brain (meninges).

▲ The word *pormiz* for diabetes mellitus is a compound Persian word consisting of por- meaning *poly* and *miz*- for urination, which indicates polyuria in diabetic patients.[58]

Persian physician-philosopher Abu Bakr Mohammad Ibn Zakariya al-Razi, known in the West as Rhazes, was born in 865 AD in Rey, near Tehran. A musician during his youth, he became an alchemist. He discovered alcohol and sulfuric acid. He classified substances as plants, organic, and inorganic. At age 30, he undertook the study of medicine. He was a prolific writer with more than 184 texts in medicine attributed to him, with 40 still currently available. Among them are *Kitab al-Mansoori, Kitab al-Hawi* and *Kitab al-Judari wa al-Hasabah*. The latter is the first scientific description for recognizing and differentiating smallpox and measles.

The *Bulletin of the World Health Organization* in May 1970 pays tribute to Razi by stating, "His writings on smallpox and measles show originality and accuracy, and his essay on infectious diseases was the first scientific treatise on the subject." Razi established qualifications and ethical standards for the practice of medicine. Zakariya Razi was not only one of the most important Persian physician-philosophers of his era, but for centuries, his writings became fundamental teaching texts in European medical schools.[59]

> **Principle 95**: "Medicine is the art of maintaining a healthy body and once it has been disturbed by illness, to return it again to health."
>
> ~ Hedayat al-Motaallemin

> Persian food culture emphasizes the balance in the consumption of the two kinds. Different people have different tastes, of course, and they tilt towards one of the two kinds. However, to maintain a healthy and happy body, the balance of the two regimes is of paramount importance.
>
> Iranian traditional medicine emphasizes the nature of ancient Iranian foods in the treatment of a variety of diseases. The doctor considers the nature of the person, the nature of the food he or she eats, and the nature of the disease, and then prescribes a diet to mitigate or possibly cure the disease.
>
> From Ancient Persian Foods Up to Today by Ghazale Fallahi 2020:
> https://goirantours.com/from-ancient-persian-foods-up-to-todays/

Purposeful Movement for Vitality

Using your muscles helps protect your bones, and individuals who use their bodies to be physically active have higher longevity rates. Queen Elizabeth II, former U.S. President Jimmy Carter, and former First Lady Rosalynn Carter are perfect examples. For decades, they were walking, riding horses, swinging hammers, and building homes for those less fortunate. A strong sense of purpose and belief system have also played a role in these individuals all living well into their 90s – more important than wealth, power, or access to modern healthcare. Former President Carter turned 99 in the fall of 2023, making him the longest-living president in history. Queen Elizabeth II represented the longest-living monarch; both individuals had marriages lasting seven decades. Have their lives been perfect or without challenge? No, but each day they faced the challenges and made choices that contributed to their longevity. The Carters are still holding hands as they enter their "final chapter" together at home in Plains, Georgia.

The two-year FINGER trial involved people aged 60-77 living in Finland with risk factors for memory disorders. The trial showed that lifestyle and dietary changes affect cognition and brain health. The study participants were divided into two groups: one was given regular lifestyle counseling and the other enhanced lifestyle counseling. Enhanced counseling involved nutrition counseling, physical and cognitive exercises, and support in managing the risk of cardiovascular diseases.

> "Many people worry that genetic risk factors for dementia may thwart potential benefits from healthy lifestyle changes. We were very happy to see that this was not the case in our intervention, which was started early, before the onset of substantial cognitive impairment," says Adjunct Professor Alina Solomon, the study's lead author. [60]

Nutrition and Sleep

Sleep may be elusive for both caregivers and older family members. Changes in environment can increase insomnia, pain, listlessness, confusion, and short tempers. When sleep is in short supply, cognitive functions decline; words may escape you, and forgetfulness and spaciness may be your daily or weekly companions. Along with this may come headaches, increased blood pressure, and cravings for sugar, salt, and alcohol; all ways of self-medicating to relax. The downside is that consuming food, just like drugs, never actually provides all the hoped-for relief.

There is research available today showing the benefits of *L-theanine* for the support of sleep architecture. L-theanine comes from green tea; theanine is a constituent believed to counterbalance the stimulatory effects of the caffeine content in tea. Theanine comprises approximately 1% to 2% of the dry weight of tea leaves; theanine is also present in *Xerocomus badius* (a type of mushroom).

L-theanine lowers blood pressure in hypertension patients, prevents ischemic stroke, and minimizes memory impairment after stroke. Theanine increases alertness and is used in the prevention and treatment of Alzheimer's disease and various subgroups of dementia; L-theanine helps treat anxiety due to its ability to generate relaxing alpha waves in the brain and increase attention span.

Rhodiola rosea contains phenylpropanoids, believed to enhance cognitive function and have a calming effect. In addition, it contains antioxidant compounds that help prevent diseases such as cancer and heart disease. It is also shown to improve glycogen production and increase endurance, all beneficial during physical activity. Studies on students and physicians demonstrate the herb's ability to reduce stress and fatigue. Additionally, research has shown that the herb slows the breakdown of the neurotransmitter acetylcholine, which is linked to memory.[61, 62] These effects are in sharp contrast to drugs for aiding sleep, which typically cause sleep disorders, digestive upset, sexual dysfunction, and a variety of mood disorders.[63, 64, 65]

Exercises to Build Mobility and Strength

According to the Mayo Clinic, "Starting an exercise program can help you avoid falls and keep your bones from weakening. For postmenopausal women, regular physical activity can increase muscle strength, improve balance, make you better able to carry out daily tasks and activities, maintain or improve your posture, relieve or decrease pain, and improve your sense of well-being."[66]

Current studies show inactive older women with osteoporosis can regain 15% of bone mass by engaging in mild weight-lifting exercise three days a week. Bone support medications have an efficacy of 6%. Research from 2018 confirmed physical exercise is an effective means to stimulate bone osteogenesis in osteoporotic women. One type in particular emerged as beneficial; weight-bearing aerobic exercises, such as walking, stair climbing, jogging, and tai chi. Walking alone did not appear to improve bone mass; however, it can limit its progressive loss.[67] According to the literature, bone loss in a postmenopausal woman increases with age with a loss of 0.6%, 1.1%, and 2.1% per year for individuals ages 60-69, 70-79, and > 80 respectively.[68] More precisely, the loss is 1.5% per year for the spine and 1.1% to 1.4% for the femoral neck in the first 4-5 years.[69]

Strength training exercises, especially those for the back: Strength training includes using free weights, weight machines, resistance bands, or water exercises to strengthen the muscles and bones in your arms and upper spine. Strength training can also work directly on your bones to slow mineral loss.

Weight-bearing aerobic activities: Weight-bearing aerobic activities involve aerobic exercise on your feet, with your bones supporting your weight. Examples include walking, dancing, low-impact aerobics, elliptical training machines, stair climbing, and gardening. These types of exercises work directly on the bones in your legs, hips, and lower spine to slow mineral loss.

Flexibility exercises: Moving your joints through their full range of motion helps you maintain good balance and prevent muscle injury. Increased flexibility can also help improve your posture. When your joints are stiff, abdominal and chest muscles become tight, pulling you forward and giving you a stooped stance.

Stability and balance exercises: Fall prevention is important for people who have osteoporosis. Stability and balance exercises help your muscles work together in a way that helps keep you more stable and less likely to fall. Exercises such as standing on one leg or movement-based exercises such as tai chi can improve your stability and balance.

Exercises that Exacerbate Osteoporosis

If you have osteoporosis, don't do high-impact exercises such as jumping, running, or jogging. These activities increase compression in your spine and lower extremities and can lead to fractures in weakened bones. Choose exercises with slow, controlled movements.

Also, avoid exercises where you bend forward and twist your waist, such as touching your toes or doing sit-ups. These movements put pressure on the bones in your spine, increasing your risk of compression fractures. Other activities requiring you to bend or twist forcefully at the waist are golf, tennis, bowling, and some yoga poses.

So get out and get moving—and drag a friend, dog, or loved one along with you!

Although the important contribution of nutrition and physical activity to people's health is known, it is equally well known that there are many barriers to adherence to healthy habits (i.e., those of an organizational, economic, and/or psychological nature) experienced by the general population, as well as by people with noncommunicable diseases. Knowledge of these barriers seems essential to implementing the activities and strategies needed to overcome them. A paper published in the journal *Nutrients* in 2023 provides recommendations on how to help clients overcome challenges.[70]

Build Your Team

I hope you enjoy a great relationship with your medical provider. If you don't, you should consider why that is and what you are willing to do about it. You are paying for a service — customer service, respect, and cooperation should be expected.

Your health is like an old-fashioned wagon wheel. You are the inner hub, your health is the outer rim, and each of the spokes that support you are your healthcare providers. They are a collection of individuals and modalities that help you stay well. They should be willing to work together and respect the others' roles; no single spoke can hold the wheel together. This team can include family nurse practitioners, compounding pharmacists, massage therapists, chiropractors, acupuncturists, herbalists, biofeedback specialists, osteopaths, environmental dentists, ophthalmologists, and nutritionists.

Join Us in a
Nourished
Energized
Wellness
Lifestyle
Paradigm

Being Proactive

Retirees are often preyed upon by the health industry. They are subjected to sales pitches for everything from erectile dysfunction to age spots. Please be aware of this and get a second opinion before buying the latest panacea promising instant health. My clients often come in with bags and boxes of supplements. Most of them are outdated, of poor quality, and redundant. More is not always better, and it is important to be just as careful about what supplements you take as you are about prescription medications.

If you need assistance choosing supplements, ask a pharmacist, medical practitioner, or natural healthcare provider with training in nutritional and/or herbal therapy. Don't just take the advice of a sales representative unless you know they can be trusted. Regarding nutraceuticals, please keep-it-simple, using high quality and food-based products. Vitamin and mineral synthetics are not ideal; neither are products loaded with chemical additives like propylene glycol (food-grade antifreeze). As much as I like Costco®, I do not recommend most of their supplements because of the "other ingredients" listed on their labels: artificial colors, flavors, chemicals, fillers, binders, preservatives, and who knows what else?

Eat real food. I can't stress this enough. With costs increasing due to inflation and fuel taxes, cutting out processed foods is even more worthwhile. Additives, flavorings, glitzy packaging, and questionable health claims often falsely lure you into purchasing synthetic foods that are bad for your wallet and your health.

Advertisers are skilled at manipulating consumers to buy; there is an entire body of scientific research on the art of making the sale. Instead, choose fresh and organic foods, preferably from local farmers. Cook extra servings and keep leftovers in the refrigerator and freezer. When a consumer's food budget goes to supporting mega-corporations, it does nothing to help foster local agriculture in our communities.

Keep copies of your medical records. Recently, a medical practitioner told me they had to close their office doors for a day due to power outages; it wasn't due to lighting but because they could not access the patients' medical records that are now commonly stored on Internet cloud servers. By having a hard copy of your records you will know when/if they have been altered and can have them available for copying when changing providers or seeing specialists. These records are yours; you have paid for them and have a right and responsibility to access them. This practice also ensures that medications, histories, and personal information are accurate.

Grow a garden, even if it is only a container garden of fresh herbs. This helps lower costs and allows you to take control of your food supply. It also helps to be in touch with Mother Nature. My husband told me that when working with explosives, the handlers reach down and touch the soil to discharge accumulated static charge built up from clothing friction and the air. Our ancestors made contact with the earth daily; it seems like a good idea.

Finally, spend time doing things you love, and laugh every day, even at yourself.

M. A., works in her extensive garden each day, ferments her foods and in active in volunteer for organizations. in her 8th decade enjoying a single independent life.

In a 1990 interview, renowned chef Julia Child said, "Everybody is overreacting. If fear of food continues, it will be the death of gastronomy in the United States. Fortunately, the French don't suffer from the same hysteria we do. We should enjoy food and have fun. It is one of the simplest and nicest pleasures in life."

The 4 Roadblocks to Health

Before moving into the next chapter about wellness coaching tools from 2B Well, here are some final thoughts.

It can be easy for a wellness coach, nutritionist, or healthcare provider to rattle off information, often overwhelming clients and leaving them confused. We don't do this intentionally, but in an attempt to provide meaningful information as much and as fast as our time with a client allows. For this reason, we are concluding the third edition of *Our Journey with Food* with wellness coaching tools from 2B Well program developer Dr. Leena Guptha. With her information, you will be better equipped to take care of your health and sidestep the *4-C* trap.

Chapter 20 ~ The New Paradigm for Building Better Health

Psychologically, there are four roadblocking factors (the 4-Cs) that play into the effectiveness of natural health protocols and the overall outcome:

1. ***Complacency***. As individuals begin to feel better or their symptoms resolve, they become less compliant or stop the nutritional program they are on, whether it is a liquid supplement, intravenous therapy, or a tailored nutrient delivery program.
2. ***Carelessness***. The clients forget why they take the nutraceuticals, stretch, or walk daily. I have seen clients repeatedly sabotage their success by second-guessing their natural health practitioner and adding more supplements from retailers.
3. ***Confusion***. It is common for clients to forget the information relayed by a practitioner before the client makes it across the parking lot. Recommendations need to be given in a form that clients can read and understand again and again; a hand-written note often results in noncompliance.
4. ***Cost***. For whatever reason, individuals can justify the purchase of fingernail extensions, beer, alcohol, video games, cigarettes, pet care, and junk food. Still, they fail to see the cost-benefit and importance of cleaning up their diet, buying organic foods, and using quality nutraceuticals.

---

1 Karr, T., Bell, K. (2020) Empty Plate: Food, Sustainability, Mindfulness; ISBN:978-1-7329072-3-2

2 Su Y, Liu L, Deng Q, Lü Z, Wang Z, He Z, Wang T. Epigenetic architecture of Pseudotaxus chienii: Revealing the synergistic effects of climate and soil variables. Ecol Evol. 2023 Sep 10;13(9):e10511. doi: 10.1002/ece3.10511. PMID: 37701023; PMCID: PMC10493196.

3 Kotanidou EP, Kosvyra A, Mouzaki K, Giza S, Tsinopoulou VR, Serbis A, Chouvarda I, Galli-Tsinopoulou A. Methylation haplotypes of the insulin gene promoter in children and adolescents with type 1 diabetes: Can a dimensionality reduction approach predict the disease? Exp Ther Med. 2023 Aug 8;26(4):461. doi: 10.3892/etm.2023.12160. PMID: 37664671; PMCID: PMC10469396.

4 Yuan B, Sun X, Xu Z, Pu M, Yuan Y, Zhang Z. Influence of genetic polymorphisms in homocysteine and lipid metabolism systems on antidepressant drug response. BMC Psychiatry. 2020 Aug 14;20(1):408. doi: 10.1186/s12888-020-02798-4. PMID: 32795354; PMCID: PMC7427977.

5 Yalçın KS, Koşar A. The frequency of Raynaud's phenomenon in patients with methylenetetrahydrofolate reductase gene mutation and hyperhomocysteinemia. Turk J Med Sci. 2019 Oct 24;49(5):1444-1449. doi: 10.3906/sag-1903-206. PMID: 31651110; PMCID: PMC7018243.

6 Bird A. Perceptions of epigenetics. Nature. 2007 May 24;447(7143):396-8. doi: 10.1038/nature05913. PMID: 17522671.

7 Are Diets Based on DNA the Next Big Thing? http://www.triathlete.com/2017/12/nutrition/diets-based-dna-next-big-thing_309371#dfkOiYMJmxPgzltw.99

8 https://www.npr.org/sections/thesalt/2018/01/22/579003429/personalized-diets-can-your-genes-really-tell-you-what-to-eat

9 Mazzone, R., Zwergel, C., Artico, M. et al. The emerging role of epigenetics in human autoimmune disorders. Clin Epigenet 11, 34 (2019). https://doi.org/10.1186/s13148-019-0632-2

10 Lacal, I., & Ventura, R. (2018). Epigenetic Inheritance: Concepts, Mechanisms and Perspectives. Frontiers in Molecular Neuroscience, 11, 389508. https://doi.org/10.3389/fnmol.2018.00292

11 Raghubeer S, Matsha TE. Methylenetetrahydrofolate (MTHFR), the One-Carbon Cycle, and Cardiovascular Risks. Nutrients. 2021 Dec 20;13(12):4562. doi: 10.3390/nu13124562. PMID: 34960114; PMCID: PMC8703276.

12 http://bioindividualnutrition.com/methylation-diet-mthfr/

13 https://www.mygenefood.com/custom-nutrition-plan/

14 https://blog.23andme.com/health-traits/our-take-on-the-mthfr-gene/
15 Hickey SE et al. (2013). "ACMG Practice Guideline: lack of evidence for MTHFR polymorphism testing." Genet Med. 15(2):153-6. http://www.ncbi.nlm.nih.gov/pubmed/23288205
16 American College of Obstetricians and Gynecologists Women's Health Care Physicians. (2013). "ACOG Practice Bulletin No. 138: Inherited thrombophilias in pregnancy." Obstet Gynecol. 122(3):706-17. http://www.ncbi.nlm.nih.gov/pubmed/23963422
17 https://medicalxpress.com/news/2016-08-scientists-reveal-people-apoe4-gene.html
18 Karr, T., Bell, K. Empty Plate: Food, Sustainability, Mindfulness (2020), pg 184-185, 272-275; ISBN:978-1-7329072-3-2
19 Nutrition and Traumatic Brain Injury: Improving Acute and Subacute Health Outcomes in Military Personnel. https://www.ncbi.nlm.nih.gov/books/NBK209309/
20 Nutrition and Traumatic Brain Injury: Improving Acute and Subacute Health Outcomes in Military Personnel. https://www.ncbi.nlm.nih.gov/books/NBK209323/
21 https://www.ncbi.nlm.nih.gov/pubmed/27294343
22 http://www.telegraph.co.uk/science/2017/11/07/dementia-now-britains-biggest-killer-overtaking-heart-disease/
23 https://www.sciencedaily.com/releases/2017/09/170907112408.htm
24 https://www.sciencedaily.com/releases/2015/03/150330112227.htm
25 https://www.ncbi.nlm.nih.gov/pubmed/25324467
26 https://www.ncbi.nlm.nih.gov/pubmed/29022278
27 Marcum J. A. (2020). Nutrigenetics/Nutrigenomics, Personalized Nutrition, and Precision Healthcare. Current nutrition reports, 9(4), 338–345. https://doi.org/10.1007/s13668-020-00327-z
28 Sellami, M., & Bragazzi, N. L. (2020). Nutrigenomics and Breast Cancer: State-of-Art, Future Perspectives and Insights for Prevention. Nutrients, 12(2), 512. https://doi.org/10.3390/nu12020512
29 Bogdon, K. (2023) Sleepless Nights After Mastectomy: Understanding and Overcoming Insomnia: https://ourhealingroots.net/blog/author/Katrina%20Bogdon,%20ND
30 Bogdon, K. (2022) HeartMath and Cancer: https://ourhealingroots.net/blog/heartmath-breast-cancer
31 Cassotta, M., Forbes-Hernandez, T. Y., Cianciosi, D., Elexpuru Zabaleta, M., Sumalla Cano, S., Dominguez, I., Bullon, B., Regolo, L., Alvarez-Suarez, J. M., Giampieri, F., & Battino, M. (2021). Nutrition and Rheumatoid Arthritis in the 'Omics' Era. Nutrients, 13(3), 763. https://doi.org/10.3390/nu13030763
32 Guagnano, M. T., D'Angelo, C., Caniglia, D., Di Giovanni, P., Celletti, E., Sabatini, E., Speranza, L., Bucci, M., Cipollone, F., & Paganelli, R. (2021). Improvement of Inflammation and Pain after Three Months' Exclusion Diet in Rheumatoid Arthritis Patients. Nutrients, 13(10), 3535. https://doi.org/10.3390/nu13103535
33 Papandreou, P., Gioxari, A., Daskalou, E., Grammatikopoulou, M. G., Skouroliakou, M., & Bogdanos, D. P. (2023). Mediterranean Diet and Physical Activity Nudges versus Usual Care in Women with Rheumatoid Arthritis: Results from the MADEIRA Randomized Controlled Trial. Nutrients, 15(3), 676. https://doi.org/10.3390/nu15030676
34 Cassotta, M., Forbes-Hernandez, T. Y., Cianciosi, D., Elexpuru Zabaleta, M., Sumalla Cano, S., Dominguez, I., Bullon, B., Regolo, L., Alvarez-Suarez, J. M., Giampieri, F., & Battino, M. (2021). Nutrition and Rheumatoid Arthritis in the 'Omics' Era. Nutrients, 13(3), 763. https://doi.org/10.3390/nu13030763
35 Bustamante, M. F., Agustín-Perez, M., Cedola, F., Coras, R., Narasimhan, R., Golshan, S., & Guma, M. (2020). Design of an anti-inflammatory diet (ITIS diet) for patients with rheumatoid arthritis. Contemporary clinical trials communications, 17, 100524. https://doi.org/10.1016/j.conctc.2020.100524
36 Koromina, M., Konstantinidou, V., Georgaka, M., Innocenti, F., & Patrinos, G. P. (2020). Nutrigenetics and nutrigenomics: ready for clinical use or still a way to go?. Personalized medicine, 17(3), 171–173. https://doi.org/10.2217/pme-2020-0007
37 Jorgensen G. Human genetics and infectious diseases. MMW Munch Med Wochenschr. 1981 Sep 25;123(39):1447-52.
38 Lopera-Maya EA, Kurilshikov A, van der Graaf A, Hu S, Andreu-Sánchez S, Chen L, Vila AV, Gacesa R, Sinha T, Collij V, Klaassen MAY, Bolte LA, Gois MFB, Neerincx PBT, Swertz MA; LifeLines Cohort Study; Harmsen HJM, Wijmenga C, Fu J, Weersma RK, Zhernakova A, Sanna S. Effect of host genetics on the gut microbiome in 7,738 participants of the Dutch Microbiome Project. Nat Genet. 2022 Feb;54(2):143-151. doi: 10.1038/s41588-021-00992-y. Epub 2022 Feb 3. Erratum in: Nat Genet. 2022 Sep;54(9):1448. PMID: 35115690.
39 The ABO blood group is a trans-species polymorphism in primates. http://www.pnas.org/content/109/45/18493
40 History of Blood Transfusions by the American Red Cross. https://www.redcrossblood.org/learn-about-blood/blood-transfusions/history-blood-transfusions
41 Su L, Cao Y, Liu Y, Zhang J, Zhang G. Analysis of Clinical Characteristics and Blood Cell in Adult Patients with Brucella Bloodstream Infection of Different Blood Groups. Indian J Hematol Blood Transfus. 2023 Jul;39(3):429-434. doi: 10.1007/s12288-022-01617-y. Epub 2022 Dec 13. PMID: 37304470; PMCID: PMC10247920.
42 Cavalli-Sforza, L. L., Menozzi, P., & Piazza, A. The History and Geography of Human Genes (Princeton: Princeton University Press, 1994)
43 Tills D, Teesdale P, Mourant AE. Blood groups of the Irish. Ann Hum Biol 1977 Jan;4(1):23-4
44 https://www.smithsonianmag.com/science-nature/the-mystery-of-human-blood-types-86993838/#rdKKTV8eJARYqsAx.99
45 Blood Groups and Red Cell Antigens. https://www.ncbi.nlm.nih.gov/books/NBK2264/

46 Czerwiński M. Grupy krwi-minusy i plusy. Czy antygeny grupowe krwi chronią nas przed chorobami zakaźnymi? [Blood groups-minuses and pluses. Do the blood group antigens protect us from infectious diseases?]. Postepy Hig Med Dosw (Online). 2015 Jun 25;69:703-22. Polish. doi: 10.5604/17322693.1158795. PMID: 26206987.

47 Zietz M, Zucker J, Tatonetti NP. Associations between blood type and COVID-19 infection, intubation, and death. Nat Commun. 2020 Nov 13;11(1):5761. doi: 10.1038/s41467-020-19623-x. PMID: 33188185; PMCID: PMC7666188.

48 Shokri P, Golmohammadi S, Noori M, Nejadghaderi SA, Carson-Chahhoud K, Safiri S. The relationship between blood groups and risk of infection with SARS-CoV-2 or development of severe outcomes: A review. Rev Med Virol. 2022 Jan;32(1):e2247. doi: 10.1002/rmv.2247. Epub 2021 May 14. PMID: 34997677; PMCID: PMC8209917.

49 Bullerdiek J, Reisinger E, Rommel B, Dotzauer A. ABO blood groups and the risk of SARS-CoV-2 infection. Protoplasma. 2022 Nov;259(6):1381-1395. doi: 10.1007/s00709-022-01754-1. Epub 2022 Apr 1. PMID: 35364749; PMCID: PMC8973646.

50 Pereira E, Felipe S, de Freitas R, Araújo V, Soares P, Ribeiro J, Henrique Dos Santos L, Alves JO, Canabrava N, van Tilburg M, Guedes MI, Ceccatto V. ABO blood group and link to COVID-19: A comprehensive review of the reported associations and their possible underlying mechanisms. Microb Pathog. 2022 Aug;169:105658. doi: 10.1016/j.micpath.2022.105658. Epub 2022 Jun 25. PMID: 35764188; PMCID: PMC9233352.

51 https://www.eurekalert.org/pub_releases/2014-09/aaon-cyb091014.php

52 The REasons for Geographic And Racial Differences in Stroke (REGARDS) Study and the National Institute of Neurological Disorders and Stroke (NINDS). https://www.ncbi.nlm.nih.gov/pubmed/16556882

53 Can your blood type affect your memory?
American Academy of Neurology- Public Release: 10-Sep-2014. https://www.eurekalert.org/pub_releases/2012-08/aha-btm080912.php

54 Blood type may influence heart disease risk
American Heart Association- Public Release: 14-Aug-2012. https://www.eurekalert.org/pub_releases/2012-08/aha-btm080912.php

55 Wang J, García-Bailo B, Nielsen DE, El-Sohemy A. ABO genotype, 'blood-type' diet and cardiometabolic risk factors. PLoS One. 2014 Jan 15;9(1):e84749. doi: 10.1371/journal.pone.0084749. PMID: 24454746; PMCID: PMC3893150.

56 Stephan, A. In Search of One of the World's Oldest Religions (2013): https://www.getty.edu/news/in-search-of-one-of-the-worlds-oldest-religions/

57 Nayernouri T, Azizi M. History of medicine in iran the oldest known medical treatise in the persian language. Middle East J Dig Dis. 2011 Mar;3(1):74-8. PMID: 25197537; PMCID: PMC4154935.

58 Akhawayni Bukhari A. Hedayat al-Motaallemin fi Tebb. [In Persian]. Edited by J.Matini, Mashhad University Press, Mashhad, 1965:505,246-7,797,327.

59 Modanlou HD. A tribute to Zakariya Razi (865- 925 AD), an Iranian pioneer scholar. Arch Iran Med. 2008 Nov;11(6):673-7. PMID: 18976043.

60 University of Eastern Finland. "Lifestyle changes prevent cognitive decline even in genetically susceptible individuals." ScienceDaily. ScienceDaily, 25 January 2018. www.sciencedaily.com/releases/2018/01/180125101309.htm.

61 https://www.alzheimers.net/2013-11-14/rhodiola-rosea-for-alzheimers/

62 http://alzheimers-review.blogspot.com/2012/05/rhodiola-rosea-and-alzheimers.html

63 http://www.safealternativemedicine.co.uk/rhodiolaroseaandanti-aging.html

64 http://www.evolutionhealth.com/supplements/Rhodiola_Rosea.pdf

65 University of California- Los Angeles. "Curcumin improves memory and mood: Twice-daily supplements boosted cognitive power over 18 months." ScienceDaily. ScienceDaily, 23 January 2018. www.sciencedaily.com/releases/2018/01/180123101908.htm.

66 Caprara G. Mediterranean-Type Dietary Pattern and Physical Activity: The Winning Combination to Counteract the Rising Burden of Non-Communicable Diseases (NCDs). Nutrients. 2021 Jan 28;13(2):429. doi: 10.3390/nu13020429. PMID: 33525638; PMCID: PMC7910909.

67 Benedetti, M. G., Furlini, G., Zati, A., & Mauro, G. L. (2018). The Effectiveness of Physical Exercise on Bone Density in Osteoporotic Patients. BioMed Research International, 2018. https://doi.org/10.1155/2018/4840531

68 Gómez-Cabello A., Ara I., González-Agüero A., Casajús J. A., Vicente-Rodríguez G. Effects of training on bone mass in older adults: a systematic review. Sports Medicine. 2012;42(4):301–325. doi: 10.2165/11597670-000000000-00000.

69 Bae S, Lee S, Park H, Ju Y, Min SK, Cho J, Kim H, Ha YC, Rhee Y, Kim YP, Kim C. Position Statement: Exercise Guidelines for Osteoporosis Management and Fall Prevention in Osteoporosis Patients. J Bone Metab. 2023 May;30(2):149-165. doi: 10.11005/jbm.2023.30.2.149. Epub 2023 May 31. PMID: 37449348; PMCID: PMC10345999.

70 Cavallo M, Morgana G, Dozzani I, Gatti A, Vandoni M, Pippi R, Pucci V, Vaudo G, Fanelli CG. Unraveling Barriers to a Healthy Lifestyle: Understanding Barriers to Diet and Physical Activity in Patients with Chronic Non-Communicable Diseases. Nutrients. 2023 Aug 5;15(15):3473. doi: 10.3390/nu15153473. PMID: 37571410; PMCID: PMC10421422.

Chapter 21 ~ Maximizing Wellness and Longevity

> "Your health and wellness is utmost in our minds"
>
> ~Rita Mitra

Chapter Twenty-One ~
Maximizing Wellness and Longevity Tools to develop your Personal Peak Performance Plan (P4) for life

By Leana Susan Guptha, ND, DO, MS, MBA, PhD

Introduction

In a 2022 survey, the American Psychological Association (APA) found around three-quarters of adults (76%) reported they experienced health impacts due to stress in the prior month, including headache (38%), fatigue (35%), feeling nervous or anxious (34%), and/or feeling depressed or sad (33%). In the same article the APA reported seven in 10 adults (72%) have experienced additional health impacts due to stress, including feeling overwhelmed (33%), experiencing changes in sleeping habits (32%), and/or worrying constantly (30%).

This chapter guides you on a self-empowering journey to combat stressors utilizing simple exercises to prioritize your goals and live life by design, Dr. Leena Guptha developed and refers to throughout this chapter as 2B Well.

Inspiration Behind Wellness and Longevity: 2B Well

Dr. Leena is driven to support clients, students, and all humans by reflecting the principle of "Discover Your Potential." Leena loves working with individuals and groups on positive mindset, affirmations, and maximizing their human potential 2B Well and serves as Chief Empowerment Officer of 2BWell.solutions.com, 2BWell-Edu.com and Chief Learning Officer of www.TrioCoachingAcademy.com. But how did this lifetime journey of coaching and educating others 2B Well emerge?

Back to the Future

As a child, I wanted to be an engineer building bridges. At age 7, my mother, Rita, was diagnosed with an aggressive form of Systemic Lupus Erythematosus (SLE) and offered a prognosis at the age 33 to only live until 40. As a child, I dedicated the next 4 years to reading about auto-immune disease at local libraries, and by age 11 embarked, with my mother, on a pursuit of identifying the best natural therapies for my mother's condition and support for improved quality of life and longevity. When I was 17, my mother had exceeded her prognosis and could navigate the allopathic/bio-medical treatment together with a "farm-acy" of natural therapeutics and practitioners. In some ways, coaching my mother was the beginning of my personal education in therapies that added years to her life: osteopathic medicine, naturopathic medicine, acupuncture, hypnotherapy and more. I have sense gained degrees in these modalities and have continued to practice each for a 25-year period. In 2015, my integrative therapy practice became one devoted to health and human performance coaching, or as my students know it – *Personal Peak Performance*.

Mission and Vision

As a lifelong learner, educator and physician my mission and vision have been inspired by my mother. Over the decades my mission has changed little; *"To educate and inspire a global community as to the value of personal peak performance health and happiness through innovative solutions or 2B Well for life"*. Similarly, the vision is to "live in a world where bio-medical and integrative therapies are offered with equal availability to all; where healthcare focuses on balancing mind, body and spirit, utilizing the best of all medicines, interventions, and modern-day technologies through evidence-inspired practice."

Living in San Diego, CA, it is easy and vital for *peak performance* to include "time in nature." I resonate with, water-based activities, time spent with family and friends at the lake, and a variety of artistic hobbies — all independently and collectively support my "personal peak performance" bringing balance of body, spirit and mind. I, like you make choices in lifestyle, practice, and teaching to honor those we love. For me it is a deep love for my mother's spirit and the desire to disseminate her philosophy, spirituality, and resilience that fuels my energy for wellness coaching. (Rita lived 30 years beyond her medical prognosis to the age of 70). My pursuit, though initiated through my journey with mother, has equally made it possible for a loving and devoted husband, colleagues, and friends — all of whom knew Rita, to accept her and what seemed, in the earlier decades, her radical approach to whole health. In the 21st century the science and evidence are ever increasing to support her/our choices 2B Well.

PART 1: Coaching Process and Principles; Considerations to Coach Yourself 2B Well

Coach Thyself: A Quick Look at What is Coaching
Before we get too deep into what it is going to make 2B Well your own priority for crafting a life of personal peak performance — whether giving yourself permission to heal or combating a challenging goal or life transformation — let's take a look at the role of a coach to set the stage for *coaching you*.

Chapter 21 ~ Maximizing Wellness and Longevity

Coaching can be defined in various ways at 2B Well.[1] The essence of coaching serves to:

- facilitate **positive change** through the Goals, Reality, Options, and Way Forward (GROW) Model,[2]
- support you at every level to **become who you want to be** through building awareness, integrating positive affirmations, guided imagery/flow to deepening the learning and forward the action, and
- **unlock your potential to maximize your peak performance** in area(s) you choose through the Wheel of Wellness and Longevity; from wellbeing, business, career, sports, and/or so much more.

What is a Health Coach?

This is both a term and a profession that has emerged in recent decades. Much like a sports coach who can provide motivation, encouragement, guidance, and support, a health coach can help you navigate your journey toward sustainable lifestyle changes. The health coach partners with you to prioritize goals for whole health, which can include the eight domains we will discuss later in the Wheel of Wellness and Longevity. Though some coaches may be trained in a range of healthcare field(s), for the most part health coaches are not expert in specific dis-ease areas; they do not diagnose or treat. Instead, they are trained in *core coaching competencies*.[3] Health coaches enable you to be in the driver's seat of your life with the coach by your side; together setting the GPS and traversing the countryside to achieve your best life. This is your "personal peak performance."

In many cases, a seasoned practitioner or clinician becomes a "health coach" without formal coach training by intuitively placing the patient or client in the position of the lead actor in the movie version of their life or the main author of the book of their life. The patient or client is no longer the "patient" or the subject of other's decision making in isolation, but rather empowered to proactively address one or several areas of wellness and longevity, leading towards self-actualization.

Whether you are the coach or *coachee* (recipient of coaching or coaching self), there are some principles that help define context and the road map to maximize your potential. Our 2B Well coaching practices focus on supporting the self-discovery journey to living your healthy, happy lifestyle to create wellbeing. This solution-based coaching approach to personal peak performance encourages YOU to:

- balance and integrate your physical, mental, emotional, and spiritual well-being,
- establish respectful, co-operative relations with others and the environment,
- make health and human performance-orientated lifestyle choices to bring dream goals to reality,
- actively participate in YOUR health decisions to create and maintain health and happiness.

Let's explore the five areas of coaching - *Personalization, Connection, Challenge, Experience* and *Facilitator*.

Principle 1 - Personalization

In this area, we use the eight domains represented in the Wheel of Wellness and Longevity as a starting point to build your personalized peak performance plan (P4). We view the individual as a whole person and recognize that the human being is comprised of and affected by the physical, mental, emotional, spiritual, environmental, genetic, and social. As such, planning and goal personalization is key to ensuring that your personal peak performance plan (P4) is ideally suited to your unique nature.

Principles 2 - Connection

This area supports accountability. We work to identify and connect any factors of imbalance. These may appear in the Wheel of Wellness and Longevity assessment and can be mental, physical, emotional, spiritual, environmental or lifestyle related. Time is spent in discovery of these elements to identify your needs, prioritize goals, and promote connectedness with self and others. Connection also relates to motivation, flow, longevity and how you determine your measures of success, as well as who is part of your accountability team to help you get there.

Principles 3 - Challenge

Challenge yourself to think or rethink how you approach your Wheel of Wellness and Longevity priorities and the outcomes of your GROW Model assessment. This area challenges you beyond your current reality in mind/body activities, whether with affirmations, guided imagery, breath work, optimizing athletic performance, or simply challenging you to think differently on your approach to personal and professional development, nutrition, movement, sleep, environment or other domains of your wheel. From being a professional athlete to learning a new skill, from creativity to innovation," challenge" supports you during your journey to reach your personal peak as defined by you. (We will refer you back to this model throughout this chapter.)

Principle 4 - Experience

We acknowledge that the body has the ability to create, maintain, and restore peak health and happiness by boosting the inherent vital force present within the human frame. Experiencing your goal- focused activities: whether breath work, meditation, positive affirmation, self-care, physical activities, or nutritional choices, can support your personal peak performance plan. In addition, utilizing learnings from prior experiences and identifying what is needed to create an optimal, sustainable experience to support your wellbeing is a way to help choose lifestyle experiences.

Chapter 21 ~ Maximizing Wellness and Longevity

Principle 5 - Facilitator

This final area enables you to coach yourself, optimizing peak performance, health, and happiness. To go beyond these initial steps, you may choose to work directly with (or pursue certification) an International Coach Federation (ICF) trained coach who can play an important role in helping you to move forward with action, deepen the learning, and guide and encourage you to take responsibility for your lifestyle goals, all while working in partnership. Your coach can offer inspiration, understanding and resources. Like all good facilitators, you or your guide will be committed to an ongoing personal, professional and spiritual development. At the end of this chapter, we will we share resources for 2B Well coach training if you are seeking to elevate life beyond the bounds of this text.

The 2B Well Wheel of Wellness and Longevity

The GROW Model is best explained with a graphic; viewed earlier. The word GROW is an acronym for Goals, Reality, Options and Will (or Way Forward) used in business and coaching to help individuals or groups develop realistic, achievable goals and define how success is measured.

The Wheel of Wellness and Longevity to the left was created explicitly for this book and chapter to represent the relationship between mind, body, and spirit, and to identify a roadmap based on the client's current life (reality) for understanding whole health as being greater than the sum of its parts. It was designed to enable you to focus and prioritize current areas as they relate to whole health in developing a plan (P4) for current and future goals.

PART 2: The Wheel of Wellness and Longevity

The 2B Well Wheel of Wellness and Longevity has been created to:

- ✓ Recognize the relationship of mind, body, and spirit,
- ✓ Identify a roadmap based on current situations (reality),
- ✓ Understand whole health as greater than the sum of its parts,
- ✓ Enable the reader to focus and prioritize current areas related to whole health, and
- ✓ Develop a personalized personal peak performance plan (P4) for current and future goals.

Each domain of the Wheel includes a case vignette drawn from 6 years of primary care, 19 years of integrative health, and the last 7 years of a coaching practice; comprising over 9,000+ patient/client consultations before focusing on wellness as a way of life.

Let's first explore each category within the Wheel of Wellness and Longevity, and then assess how smooth or bumpy might be your personal wheel?

Purpose and Mindset: In this area, we explore your personal vision or mission. Positive affirmation can be used to capture goals and rewards. You may consider mindfulness, guided imagery, and breath work to support positive mindset. By first identifying your desired health and life vision, other categories in the Wheel of Wellness and Longevity can then be prioritized as areas for immediate work, for short-term attention, or for defining your long-term vision and purpose.

An excerpt from the serenity prayer by Reinhold Niebuhr speaks about being positive and realistic: *Grant me the serenity to accept the things I cannot change, the courage to change the things I can, and the wisdom to know the difference.*

Case Vignette: A teenager was seeking 2B a competitive swimmer. During her spare time, she trained consistently and often placed among the top three. Through the process of visualizing each phase of the race, in particular the turn at the end of each lap and mindfully swimming in the "flow" or "zone," she could program the subconscious mind to successfully achieve a state championship medal. Purpose and mindset positively reinforced her reality to *not hide away from the negative* but rather bolster up the positive in mind and body.

Personal and Professional Development: This category brings focus to assessing where you are now personally and professionally, where you wish to be, and any changes you may seek in life or career goals. It serves as a reflection of your lifestyle choices, work demands, financial wellness, and life balance– prompting an envisioned future for your current path to consider what needed to manifest self-actualization.

In life we may focus on professional goals from early college days to retirement, and that may leave the personal development goals a distant second. The opposite may be true, too; that we are personally well-developed but lacking in defining or achieving professional goals. Whether personal or professional, there may be goals not yet realised to achieved. As you read on, think about how important this area is to you for your Wheel assessment. Can you have both? Hold both? Be satisfied with both? Seek balance in both? Or is your current focus one over the other?

Case Vignette: A senior executive of a once multi-million-dollar company was close to bankruptcy some years ago. The daily anxiety and pressure spread through the business, and there was a general malaise amongst the staff. Coaching of self and staff contributed to a focus on *work-balance in life* and greater creativity in management. Later, the cultural shift led to a transition from a barely surviving enterprise to a thriving stable business. The rebirth included company leadership and staff embracing both internal and external personal and professional development 2B healthy in business and life.

Chapter 21 ~ Maximizing Wellness and Longevity

Gastronomy and Nutrition: Lindlahr's words (way back in Chapter 1), "you are what you eat," relate to this domain. Many chapters in this book emphasize that nutrition starts in the shopping cart. It serves as a reflection that by addressing healthy choices, food related behaviors, challenges, obstacles, and outcomes, all will come together in developing your optimal healthy self. Motivation, accountability, and measures of success feature here, too, in crafting your personalized peak performance plan (P4).

We can struggle with making healthful choices at times. Although nutrition starts in the shopping cart, sometimes it is easier to opt for fast food, snacking, and high carbohydrate satisfaction (feeling full) rather than making the effort to mindfully plan and prepare meals. An exploration into what might make the process engaging and fun rather than a chore to be completed can support nutrition. Engaging others in positive reinforcement may be key to a positive tipping point toward heathy, delicious nutrition.

Case Vignette: Prior to re-entering the work force, a health conscious homemaker was well organized with meal planning and took pride in healthy nutrition. As she returned to work, nutrition was more than a distant second. Convenience meals became the norm rather than the exception, and frustration set in. Through working the GROW model, Options and the Way Forward became useful strategies. This woman used a white board through the week to note ingredients of interest, meal preferences, and healthy treats. She designated Sunday as the shopping day and make food prep an activity with her partner. In just a few short weeks, they were *enjoying healthy meals together that were fun and engaging*, creating a lifestyle habit that both could look forward to.

Movement: Movement is life. Here we consider movement through the day as well as planned exercise. The goal is to make exercise fun, exciting, and manageable to help keep you on track with developing or maintaining posture, strength, endurance, mobility, and/or the resilience you desire. If you are an avid athlete, then over-training and recovery may be considerations, too. If you are more sedentary, spending much of the day sitting at a desk or even standing at a new-fangled ergonomic up and down table, then movement may be both the challenge and the solution to boost vitality.

Case Vignette: As this is the domain where my Wheel has the deepest dent, I choose to share my challenges and solutions. I've invested in premium gym equipment (rarely seen but housed in the basement), an array of gym memberships, a personal trainer and more. All start with great gusto and fade within a weeks or months. I know and agree that "movement is life" and have learned that *positive reinforcement and an enjoyable environment* are key for me. I joined Pilates and found inspiration from the owner and all the instructors (coaches if you will) to be motivating, inspiring, and enjoyable. Later I moved closer to an area with El Capitan on one side and Lake Jennings on the other after many similar fails of integrating walking into my life. I now look forward to walking the scenic surroundings and cooling down in aqua aerobics class with friends two to three times a week. *Finally,* movement is part of my daily life. What changes can facilitate your key to success in this domain?

Restorative Sleep and Breath: Sleep is like gas to our car. It fuels us each day. Sleep hygiene, environment, patterns, waking refreshed, alert, and ready to start a new day are all components of sleep quality. Restorative breathing through the day or at night (use of mouth taping, tongue guard or a c-pap for sleep apnea) can support keeping your mind clear, alert, and refreshed in the day (like refilling the gas tank) and sending a message to your body when it is time to sleep.

Case Vignette: This case is about a teacher who slept or remained in bed 8+ hours a night yet awoke fatigued with an alarm and found the demands of teaching to be an added drain. A sleep study offered little insight into the issue, and various physicians found no pathological reason for the fatigue. As a last resort the teacher became open to changes. Over time, the teacher addressed the pillow, mattress, sleep hygiene, started using alpha wave music, positive affirmations, aromatherapy, guided imagery, and *eliminated both nighttime TV and snacking in bed.* Over several months their quality of sleep improved, and they began to reconnect with the reasons they became a teacher, engaged in committees at school, and became an advocate of work-life balance for other teachers.

Note: Once the sleep component was addressed, this led to changes in other areas of the Wellness Wheel, and the primary goal became positive lifestyle change.

Time in Nature and the Environment: Our physical environment and the experience of nature, whether forest bathing, mindfully experiencing the sandy beach, enjoying cool mountain breezes, rain on your face, reading a book by the pool, the early morning dew on grass against your toes, or simply appreciating the wonders of nature from bright sunrises to soothing sunsets — can positively impact your mindset, emotions, spirit, and capacity for creativity and productivity.

Sometimes the specific goal may not be one of exploring/appreciating nature or changing your internal/external environment. There may be more pressing measurable goal areas, and a break outside in nature may be just what the doctor ordered.

Case Vignette: This case is of a physician working 60-70 hours a week and on call one to two weekends a month who reported being disconnected with self and others. Although the original goal was not time in nature, *a walk-in nature starting with a few minutes* grew into an hour, and eventually it became a sacred rejuvenating time away from both the hustle and bustle of practice and the fear of burnout. The hourly walks grew into an activity with colleagues, and eventual it became a Saturday community event at the practice, too. The simple act of *enjoying the outside with self and others* became a transformational step in appreciating how a seemingly small and simple goal could free the mind and invigorate the spirit.

Relationships: The myriad of relationships, from family to work, can directly impact our mind-body-sprit health. There can be relationships that fill your energy reservoir or drain your tank causing your internal resiliency engine to run dry or overheat. Relationships that serve you well can be nurtured and finessed. Those that no longer serve a purpose may be deserving of a re-evaluation as to where that relationship falls in creating your P4 health plan.

Our lives are filled with relationships at work and with family, friends, neighbors, mentors, teachers, and some who may unofficially be our coach. However, it should be underscored that a coach is **not** a substitute for a licensed mental health or relationship professional. If this domain has a need or a goal beyond self-care, then the reader may need to consult a specifically trained healthcare professional whose scope of practice is to diagnose and treat accordingly.

Case Vignette: I'm reminded of the case of a parent and child, where exchanges faded from full conversations to curt verbal exchanges between the two following a move. At the time of coaching, these exchanges were reduced to cursory gestures across the kitchen island. During the coaching through other more tangible or measurable goals, the parent began to appreciate the use of powerful questions and active listening; *listening to understand rather than respond.* After just two instances of asking open-ended exploratory questions (e.g., What did you learn today? How are you feeling about the test?), a dialogue opened, and the bridge was rebuilt. The parent could not believe that simply by creating space to listen and not responding to topics around packed lunches, dinner, and homework, the exchanges improved. The parent was so overwhelmed with joy after employing a more open-ended, less judgmental "coach-like" dialogue, they cried while recounting how the act of actively listening changed the relationship and created more energy in the home and a more positive mindset for both.

Culture and Community: Assessing your culture and community can help to identify how you are meeting your desires in this area as part of the richness in your life and where more focus and attention may bring you closer to a sense of wholeness, wellbeing, or self-satisfaction. For our purposes here we have merged the two categories into one though the goal setting and affirmation process can be applied to either or both.

Case Vignette: Sometimes all that is needed is to evoke awareness of a domain (in this case the lack of community) and the ball starts moving in that direction. This librarian gradually became more isolated in the home and lost sight of where to find a community or how to engage with it. As a result of exploring the GROW model, she joined a card group. It took a couple of months before this activity became part of her reality. Through the group, she met a partner. Two years later they married, and the deep-seated loneliness she described was resolved. Sometimes simply having the confidence or a supporter to help you engage with others in your community can *open doors to being part of something greater than self* and reaping fulfilling rewards. This client did not continue with coaching but stayed in touch with life updates as all she needed was a booster to get her engine started.

PART 3: Your Personal Peak Performance Plan (P4) = Optimal Self

Now that you have had an opportunity to consider the Wheel of Wellness and Longevity domains, let's start building your plan for your optimal self. First, we start with a summary of peak performance which seeks to dispel the notion that "peak performance" is a term used by athletes; peak performance is for everyone. The steps that follow will lead you through a process to develop your own peak performance plan (P4).

What is Personal Peak Performance?

When some people hear the words *personal*, *peak*, or *performance*, they might think," Oh, but I'm not an athlete." In this context we are not specifically speaking of sports. We are speaking of better health for a better life. Whether you are wheelchair bound, have chronic pain, an auto-immune challenge, are a professional runner, a million-dollar producer, a CEO, or are simply striving to embrace a positive mindset and live your best life path, reaching your personal peak performance can be as simple as focusing on the next step/goal for a healthier happier you. Reaching your personal peak performance may involve committing to healthy food choices, enjoying movement or regular exercise, improving sleep hygiene for restorative sleep, getting out of a wheelchair unassisted, time in nature forest bathing, or simply adding breath work to clear your mind, energize your body, or uplift your spirit.

The process in this chapter takes you on a journey of self-care, whether your role is as a practitioner, student, or other, to maximize your wellness and live a more balanced life.

Step 1: Define Your Personal Health Vision

Your health vision is personal to you. It can range from one to several paragraphs. How much detail you wish to envision for your health is your choice. You can choose to create a health vision for each domain on the Wheel of Wellness and Longevity or simply focus on a single priority area. Your health vision captures your desired end state, optimizes the inherent potential within you, and maximizes how you desire to be in health and life.

Questions to consider:

- If you had a magic wand, what would your health look like?
- If there were no obstacles, how would you see yourself and your life?
- Which areas on the Wheel of Wellness and Longevity are most important to you?

ACTION: You can place your answers/personal health vision in the P4 section on page 464.

Step 2: Create Your Vision Statement

The vision statement is aimed at looking forward. It condenses the personal health vision and captures goals in your priority life areas and deepest aspirations.

Example - Here is an example of a vision statement for writing this chapter and book: "My vision is that each reader becomes a strong and transformational participant in their self-care who lives their personal peak performance plan, develops their optimal self, and serves as an active ambassador in transforming the landscape of wellness for all".

Example - Personal health vision statement: "I see myself feeling healthy with clarity of mind, physically energized, sleeping well, and enjoying an active community life in my neighborhood and at the local elementary school."

Example - Personal health vision statement: "My ideal health vision is waking up after restful sleep each day with a sense of purpose and boundless energy, creating healthy meals for myself and my family, and feeling a sense of contentment in work and play."

ACTION: You can place your vision statement in the P4 section on page 464.

Step 3: Create Your Mission Statement

Your mission statement is a concise statement of your person peak performance strategy that aligns with your vision statement. The mission statement defines your day-to-day activities and can define your purpose and primary focus in areas for health.

Questions to consider:
What actions do you need to take to reach your goal?
How will you hold yourself accountable?
What is the reward for achieving the mission?

Example - Here is an example of a mission statement for writing this chapter and book: "To provide knowledge, tools, motivation, and coaching to help you develop your personal peak performance plan that takes you to a phase of learning, growth, and challenge."

Example – Exercise mission statement:" To develop a regular cycling schedule, exercising a total of three hours a week with the local cycle club, and enjoying both the social community interaction and feel fit."

Example – Professional development mission statement:" To focus attention on career progression through networking, training in business, increasing a customer base, and feeling a sense of professional satisfaction."

ACTION: You can place your mission statement in the P4 section on page 464.

Step 4: Wheel of Wellness and Longevity – Where you are now? Where do you wish 2B?

When you assign a rating of 1 through 10 (10 being your highest personal peak performance) in the circle, you can quickly see how smooth or bumpy your Wheel may be and it can help you prioritize areas of focus. *Bear in mind you may have an area with a lower rating that is simply not a priority at this time in life and addressing the area could be a future priority.* These ratings are for you to use as a tool for prioritizing

Our Journey with Food

now and anytime in the future. The intent is not to reach a 10 in each area, rather to determine at any given time where you wish to concentrate your efforts for optimal wellbeing.

To complete the exercise, rate each area 1-10.
ACTION: You can place your current scores for the eight domains in the P4 section on page 464.

Area	Satisfaction Ratings, Priorities and Goals Questions to consider for where you are now.	Where do you want 2B?
Relationships	1 2 3 4 5 6 7 8 9 10 Who is in your inner circle of friends? Who is in your inner circle inner circle family? How do you feel about your outer circle and acquaintances?	1 2 3 4 5 6 7 8 9 10 What would make this rating a 10? What changes would you like to make? What needs to happen to make the change?
Purpose & Mindset	1 2 3 4 5 6 7 8 9 10 How much is your life driven by purpose? When do you embrace positive mindset? What is your level of resilience?	1 2 3 4 5 6 7 8 9 10 What would make this rating a 10? What changes would you like to make? What needs to happen to make the change?
Personal & Professional Development	1 2 3 4 5 6 7 8 9 10 What are your personal development goals (met/ongoing/unknown)? What are your professional development goals (met/ongoing/unknown)? What is the potential to explore new domains?	1 2 3 4 5 6 7 8 9 10 What would make this rating a 10? What changes would you like to make? What needs to happen to make the change?
Nutrition	1 2 3 4 5 6 7 8 9 10 What's in your shopping cart? How often to you run to fast food? How about your nutrition-based food plan?	1 2 3 4 5 6 7 8 9 10 What would make this rating a 10? What changes would you like to make? What needs to happen to make the change?
Movement	1 2 3 4 5 6 7 8 9 10 How active or sedentary are you daily? What is your movement/exercise program? Where is there room for positive change?	1 2 3 4 5 6 7 8 9 10 What would make this rating a 10? What changes would you like to make? What needs to happen to make the change?

Restorative Sleep & Breath	1 2 3 4 5 6 7 8 9 10 How happy are you with your sleep hygiene and quality of sleep? What's your morning attitude? Raring to go? Reluctant to leave that cozy bed? How is your breathing (full deep breaths, upper chest breathing, mindful breathing, breath work)?	1 2 3 4 5 6 7 8 9 10 What would make this rating a 10? What changes would you like to make? What needs to happen to make the change?
Time in nature & environment	1 2 3 4 5 6 7 8 9 10 When do you spend time in nature? How happy are you with your internal environment? How satisfied are you with your external environment?	1 2 3 4 5 6 7 8 9 10 What would make this rating a 10? What changes would you like to make? What needs to happen to make the change?
Culture	1 2 3 4 5 6 7 8 9 10 How impactful is culture to your sense of wellbeing? What cultural areas hold you back in maximizing your potential? What would you like to culturally change?	1 2 3 4 5 6 7 8 9 10 What would make this rating a 10? What changes would you like to make? What needs to happen to make the change?
Community	1 2 3 4 5 6 7 8 9 10 How impactful is community to your sense of wellbeing? What community-based areas hold you back in maximizing your potential? What would you like to change in your community?	1 2 3 4 5 6 7 8 9 10 What would make this rating a 10? What changes would you like to make? What needs to happen to make the change?

Part 4: Goal Setting and GROW SMART – Ready to Craft Your Goals

Step 5: Goal Setting from Passion to Action

The GROW Model[4] is best explained with a graphic.
In this section we consider three processes to inform goal setting:

    a. GROW Model - GROW is an acronym for *Goals, Reality, Options,* and *Will* (or *Way Forward*) used in business and coaching to help individuals or groups develop realistic goals and define measures for success.

b. SMART Goals – SMART is an acronym for your goals being *Specific, Measurable, Attainable, Realistic,* and *Time* bound. Though all these factors may not apply when crafting your top three commitments to self, they may help to inform what you are and are not willing to commit to.

c. Finally, for this goal setting section we will touch on decisional balance to be sure the goals you craft for yourself as a pathway for your personalized peak performance plan are those that will enable your long- and short-term visions to become your reality.

GROW (Goal, Reality, Options, Will/Way Forward)

Now that you have used your Wheel to help identify priorities, let's take a closer look at ways to maximize wellness and longevity by working through the GROW steps. You can gain clarity about your aspirations, current situation, identify possibilities, and define next steps to move forward.

G – Goal: Our goals embrace passion, inspiration, and commitment. Here are some common questions to consider to be sure you are on track with meaningful goals.

1. On a scale of 1-10, how important is this goal to you? (If you select 9 or 10, you are a go.)
2. On the same scale, how ready are you for change? Typically, there might be a small drop (8 or 9), but still strong.
3. On the same scale, how willing are you to put in the effort? This is where there is often a drop. Various circumstances may come into play; time being the big one. So, we can ask ourselves what it would take to move this up from a 5 or 6 to a 9 or 10 and explore further.
4. Importance, readiness, and willingness are key factors in setting a foundation for success before we move on. If you had a magic wand, what would your goal and vision look like?

R – Reality: Now let's recognize the reality, the backdrop, the context of our goal in our lives. What's your reality? Here are some questions to consider in exploring your reality.

- On a scale of 1-10, if an ideal situation is 10, what number are you now?
- At what number would you like to be?
- What are you doing that takes you towards you goal?
- What are you doing that is getting in the way of your goal?
- What are you most/least confident about?
- What are the main risks here?
- What resources do you already have?
- How much control do you have on the outcome?
- What are the rate limiting steps?
- What's been successful in the past?

Chapter 21 ~ Maximizing Wellness and Longevity

> *"The best way to predict your future is to create it."*
> ~ Abraham Lincoln

O – Options: There are many pathways to go from A to B. Let's investigate what those are. Consider brainstorming with someone on the pathways you've never thought of before and see which ones resonate.

How about discerning the options? Here are some questions to help you consider the options.

- If you had a magic wand, what would your goal look like?
- What could you do to get there?
- What ideas do you have?
- What alternatives do you have?
- What are the different ways you could approach the goal?
- What else could you do?
- What would you do if you had more time/control/money?
- What else could work here?
- Who could help you achieve this?
- What options resonate best to support peak performance?

> *"It always seems impossible, until it's done."*
> ~ Nelson Mandela

I'm going add another O here for "obstacles."

You may have heard the phrase "knowledge is power." Sometimes we can have deep knowledge about our needs, behaviors, goals, and a sense of the way forward, yet we are stuck in an obstacle. We are naturally resourceful, creative, and whole,[5] whether as a practitioner, student, patient, client, or simply a person focused on optimizing health. After reading the preceding chapters and with your life experiences, you have all the knowledge you need. Let's eliminate any known obstacles that may hold you back.

Whether you attempted your goal area or are focused on an area of the Wheel for the first time consider these questions.

- What obstacles did you face?
- What obstacles may still be there?
- What obstacles may emerge?
- How can you combat the obstacles?

- Who do you need to help you address the obstacle?
- What do you need to help you address the obstacle?
- On a scale of 1-10, how strong is the obstacle?
- What needs to happen for it to be a 1 or 0?

W – Will/Way Forward (What will you do)?

- How will you do that?
- When will you do it?
- How committed are you to this action plan?
- What will it take to increase your commitment?
- What option(s) do you choose?
- What have you learned about yourself?
- How will you measure success?
- What's the first step?
- If we were to meet again in a month, what would be different about your life?

> *"What you get by achieving your goals is not as important as what you become by achieving your goals."*
> ~ Zig Ziglar

SMART Goals: SMART goals are widely recognized as the way to reach performance goals and are 100% within your control.

S: Specific – Identifies the behavior
M: Measurable – Includes a measure – frequency, time
A: Attainable – Challenging but possible
R: Relevant - Builds on the current reality
T: Timeliness and appropriateness

The SMART goal process will focus on actions to be taken this week, in the next six weeks, three months, and future intervals that support your health or life plan.

> *"Setting goals is the first step in turning the invisible into the visible."*
> ~ Tony Robbins

Chapter 21 ~ Maximizing Wellness and Longevity

ACTION: Place your notes for the four parts of GROW in the P4 section on page 464.

ACTION: Place your top 3 commitments to self in the P4 section on page 464.

Decisional Balance

To round out your goal setting process, here are some decisional balance questions to consider. If nothing changes in your health or in your choices, what will likely be your health and longevity in 5 and 10 years from now?

- ?? What are the pros of making no changes?
- ?? What are the cons of making no changes?
- ?? If you make positive changes, what is the likely scenario 5 and 10 years from now?
- ?? What are the pros of making positive changes?
- ?? What are the cons of making positive changes?

PART 5: Positive Affirmations

Self-affirmations = Self-help

The acceptance of Freudian theories has ebbed and flowed for a century. Freud's topographical explanation of the conscious mind as the tip of the iceberg, with the subconscious and unconscious beneath, allows us to discuss affirmations and their impact on behavioral changes by accessing the subconscious to drive conscious behavior. [6]

Imagine for a moment that your subconscious mind is like a giant filing cabinet. It sorts every thought, action, and memory. Over time, the cabinet gets cluttered, and the "files" become corrupted, with some files appearing more dominant than others. In our subconscious mind, these files can relate to negative influences in our environment; messages from powerful authoritarian figures, bad habits we pick up over time, chronic stress, and ingrained habits related to food choices.

Science and Non-Science of Affirmation

Repeatedly being exposed to radio advertisements, TV advertisements, and billboards with key messaging could be considered an unconscious imbibing of affirmations, which if accepted by the subconscious, could influence decisions (positive or negative) towards the advertised product or service.

The self-affirmation theory[7] begins with the premise that people are fundamentally motivated to maintain their self-integrity or global perception of adequacy. Based on these findings, researchers hypothesized that awareness of self-affirmation benefits would undermine its impact when participants were instructed to self-affirm. Being told to self-affirm to attain specific benefits (e.g. to feel better about oneself) may challenge a recipient's sense of autonomy, undermining the affirmations' intrinsic appeal. However, researchers hypothesized that when individuals operated under the presumption that they had freely chosen to complete a self-affirmation task, its benefits for performance under threat could be restored.

In two studies, some participants were made aware of affirmation benefits for academic performance, and then they were either instructed to self-affirm (aware-affirmation condition) or given a choice about whether to do so (aware-choice condition). Thus, the two studies explored the boundary conditions under which self-affirmation sustains performance under threat. The researchers reported, "In both studies, affirmation benefits were negated when participants were made aware of its benefits and then required to self-affirm. However, these benefits were restored when aware participants perceived they could choose whether or not to self-affirm. In Study 1, aware participants experienced a boost in their performance when they chose to write about self-affirming concepts prior to a threatening test.[8] In Study 2, aware participants given a choice about which value to affirm experienced a similar performance boost. For these participants, a failure on one test did not lead to underperformance on the next, consistent with the ability of affirmation to psychologically buffer people against threat and foster resiliency." Evidence that led them to conclude that "if people benefit from deliberately choosing to self-affirm, perhaps they can learn to incorporate self-affirmation into their arsenal of tools for coping with everyday threats and thus become agents in the maintenance of their own well-being."

The above examples highlight some scientific relational direction in healthy subjects. However, does self-affirmation have any impact on ill health? For one study, 326 cancer survivors reported that participants with higher optimism reported better health, greater happiness, greater hopefulness, and lower likelihood of cognitive impairment, and concluded that given the malleability of self-affirmation, the findings are important avenues.[9] In another study, participants received either an insulting evaluation or a neutral evaluation from an ostensible peer. The researchers predicted that both neutral and insulting evaluations would increase cardiovascular activity, and that insulted participants would exhibit relatively greater increases. Furthermore, consistent with the self-affirmation theory, it was also predicted that thinking and writing about a core personal value after being evaluated would facilitate cardiovascular recovery.[10]

At the behavioral level, self-affirmation improves problem-solving performance on tasks related to executive functioning.[11, 12] Numerous studies highlight that thinking about self-preferences activates neural reward pathways. A group of researchers hypothesized that self-affirmation would activate brain reward circuitry during functional MRI (fMRI) studies.[13] Their findings suggest "that self-affirmation may be rewarding and may provide a first step toward identifying a neural mechanism by which self-affirmation may produce beneficial effects."[14]

In summary, it has been suggested by the scientists and behavioral care providers that self-affirmation reminds people of important aspects of the self, enabling them to view events from a reasonable, considered, and rational viewpoint.[15] By enhancing the psychological resources of self-integrity, self-affirmation reduces defensive responses to threatening information and events, leading to positive outcomes in various areas such as psychological and physical health, education, prejudice, discrimination, and social conflicts.[16] Thus, after being studied extensively by social psychologists, self-affirmation has now just begun to receive attention. Repeated use of affirmations in a meditative state can help to rewrite messages, but only if an individual is ready and willing to manifest positive change.

The subconscious mind, however, cannot differentiate between negative and positive or between what is real and imagined. For example, if we want to be successful, we cannot say things like "I don't want to be a failure." The subconscious mind will act upon the word "failure," ignoring the word "don't" and actualizing the undesired result. We must choose what we share with our subconscious mind carefully, and that is why positive affirmations are so critical. The subconscious mind is most open to helpful and beneficial suggestions while we are in the "alpha" brainwave state; our most relaxed state of mind. The alpha wave frequency is often achieved in a meditative state or just before falling sleep, creating an optimal time to receive positive affirmations. Music designed to create the alpha wave state or technology known as brainwave entrainment can also help if you are not an avid meditator.

Affirmations for Self-help and to Combat the Daily Grind

Affirmations are positive statements. When properly formed, affirmations can counteract some of our negative thoughts and habits, resonating with the alpha brain waves and enabling us to achieve empowerment. I frequently ask students and clients to give me examples of a positive affirmation. Some examples include:
"I am strong."
"I am healthy."
"I am in control of my life."
"I have set my goals, and I am moving towards them."

This is a great start, as affirmations with words and value phrases can be quite powerful, imprinting positive messages in our subconscious mind. These affirmations can help with rewriting the thoughts in the files where often negative messages that originate from a repeated phrase can be stored. The only barrier to achieving personal goals is oneself, and we often need to retrain our thought patterns to see the joys, opportunities, and possibilities in life rather than the limitations.

Our thoughts can drive our attitudes, our actions, and our behaviors. We can use this powerful chain reaction for empowerment, achievement, success, and self-actualization.

How to create powerful affirmations:
- Place your name in the affirmation.
- Phrase the goal in the present tense, to bring it into reality.
- Add a feeling to strengthen the affirmation (I feel, I enjoy etc.).
- Add a reward to reinforce what you are truly working toward.
- Be sure to balance the goal and reward so they are realistic, achievable, and meaningful.

Examples:
I, Jane, meditate ten minutes a day and I feel strong.
I, Sally, enjoy two healthy snacks a day, and I am healthy.
I, John, manage my time well, and I am in control of my life.
I, David, set daily goals, and I am empowered to achieve them.

Affirmations can be spiritual in nature or action and time bound orientated.

I _____ have mind body spirit balance, and I feel at peace.
I _____ enjoy aqua aerobics twice a week, and I feel fit.
I _____ devote two hours a week to art, and I feel creative.
I _____ release all negative thoughts, feelings, and ideas, and I move forward positively.

Remember to pick the right statement for your intention. Make it a daily habit to clear the clutter and reprogram your subconscious mind. Be aware that positive affirmations don't magically manifest results. What they do instead is open your subconscious to new channels of information and opportunities, so you must act on these in order for any major change to happen to your life.

Now try creating your own. I recommend repeating each affirmation 10 times. I also recommend that you create three affirmations reflecting areas for growth, improvement, and happiness. These affirmations can help you empower yourself to be who you truly deserve to be.

PART 6: Conclusion

Burnout: It might sound radical to consider burnout as an epidemic in the U.S., but simply think of your own practitioners and even ask them if their work-life balance is where they wish it to be. I share a case vignette simply to appreciate the gravity of burnout. Some might say it starts from the "Buried Life."

> **Case Vignette:** A medical practitioner, after a decade of practice, introduced himself as burned out. It was the first time I met a person self-diagnosing themselves with the condition of burnout. The practitioner left the practice to utilize their skills through teaching didactic and clinical classes. Over those few years the pace was more manageable but the fulfillment lacking. The practitioner, almost a decade later, returned to clinical practice, but this time their eyes were wide open as to the physical and mental limitations or boundaries that are necessary to identify, articulate, and live by in order to ensure health, wellbeing, and longevity.

Resilience: In today's fast paced society, the stress of simply existing (a pre-requisite to living) can be a fundamental drain on our mind-body continuum. The elements of nourishment described in Chapter 18 as well as the related physiological reactions pertain to food and nutrition. So why is it that some fare better than others under the same conditions; some survive, some are seemingly unaffected, and others still thrive?

Could it be our inherent resilience, our homeostatic ability to adapt to internal and external changes and the environment, self-concept, attitude, and values that combine to determine if we are in fight or fight mode; if we surrender to defeat or fear? Threats to our resilience are everywhere within our human anatomy and physiology, within the domains of our Wheel of Wellness and Longevity and societal expectations, too. Resilience is a topic that can go far beyond "what's in my shopping cart."

Blue Zone areas and are a testament to a life lived well; one beyond existing, embracing joys of community, achieving balance, and nourishing the mind and body. Ultimately, our self-care can swing between ill-ness and wellness and between dis-ease and wellbeing. When we listen, do we listen to understand, or to respond/react? When we listen, are we hearing the cries of the body, the torment of the mind, the weakening of the spirit, and thereby develop an awareness on the impact of resilience? A coach listens to understand, and we can coach ourselves or be coached by a professional to reconnect with our resilience.

Case Vignette: My mother lived 30 years beyond her medical prognosis with severe autoimmune disease. As I reflect on those years when she was frequently hospitalized (during my teenage years) and our lifestyle modifications as well as an array of natural medicine practitioners, I can't help but feel her resilience, wisdom, and spirituality kept a glorious smile on her face despite great pain and immobility. I am suggesting resilience is multifaceted, not just from our constitution but as a product of our emotions, attitude, and purpose. Anecdotally, I believe taking the best of all medicines provided my mother with longevity and a somewhat reasonable quality of life. My journey with her led to my mission 2B Well[17], which I share below.

The Power of Self-care

By completing the Wheel of Wellness and Longevity after careful consideration of each domain, you will have a sense of your areas for self-care and embark on the path to develop your health and life goals. Healers and practitioners often gravitate to the health providing professions either through a personal experience that made them appreciate the role of science/medicine as a healing art or simply out of a deep sense to care for others and positively impact the lives of others. Whatever your path to where you are now, it is a hard reality to accept that in the pursuit of healing others, we can easily lose sight of ourselves, and though it may sound extreme it can easily lead to burnout when boundaries are not set or observed.

If you take only one thing away from this chapter, may it be an adage my mother Rita frequently said, "Health is Wealth."

Our Journey with Food

Your Personalized Peak Performance Plan (P4) Starts Here

Step 1: Define your personal health vision.

[ ]

Step 2: Create your vision statement.

[ ]

Step 3: Create your mission statement.

[ ]

Step 4: Wheel of Wellness and Longevity – Where you are now; where do you wish 2B?

[ ]

Step 5: Goal Setting and GROW SMART – Ready to craft your goals

Goal

[ ]

Reality

[ ]

Options

[ ]

Will/Way Forward

[ ]

Chapter 21 ~ Maximizing Wellness and Longevity

SMART - Putting it all together

Commitment to Self #1

Commitment to Self #2

Commitment to Self #3

Coach Program/Coach Consulting  International Coaching Federation

1. Demonstrates Ethical Practice Definition: Understands and consistently applies coaching ethics and standards of coaching.

2. Embodies a Coaching Mindset Definition: Develops and maintains a mindset that is open, curious, flexible and client centered.

3. Establishes and Maintains Agreements Definition: Partners with the client and relevant stakeholders to create clear agreements about the coaching relationship, process, plans and goals. Establishes agreements for the overall coaching engagement as well as those for each coaching session.

4. Cultivates Trust and Safety Definition: Partners with the client to create a safe, supportive environment that allows the client to share freely. Maintains a relationship of mutual respect and trust.

5. Maintains Presence Definition: Is fully conscious and present with the client, employing a style that is open, flexible, grounded and confident

6. Listens Actively Definition: Focuses on what the client is and is not saying to fully understand what is being communicated in the context of the client systems and to support client self-expression

7. Evokes Awareness Definition: Facilitates client insight and learning by using tools and techniques such as powerful questioning, silence, metaphor or analogy

8. Facilitates Client Growth Definition: Partners with the client to transform learning and insight into action. Promotes client autonomy in the coaching process.

https://coachingfederation.org/credentials-and-standards/core-

1. https://2bwell.solutions/
2. GROW: The practical coaching model driven by a powerful coaching philosophy: https://www.performanceconsultants.com/grow-model
3. https://coachingfederation.org/credentials-and-standards/core-competencies
4. https://www.performanceconsultants.com/grow-model
5. What Is Co-Active? :https://coactive.com/about/what-is-coactive
6. https://2bwell.solutions/to-affirm-or-not-to-affirm/
7. Steele CM. The psychology of self-affirmation: Sustaining the integrity of the self. In Advances in Experimental Social Psychology L. Berkowitz (Ed.), 1988 vol. 21. pp. 261–302 New York: Academic Press
8. Philine S. Harris, Peter R. Harris, Eleanor Miles. Self-affirmation improves performance on tasks related to executive functioning Journal of Experimental Social Psychology 70 (2017) 281–285.
9. Jennifer M. Taber, William M. P. Klein, & Rebecca A. Ferrer, Erin E. Kent, Peter R. Harris Optimism and Spontaneous Self-affirmation are Associated with Lower Likelihood of Cognitive Impairment and Greater Positive Affect among Cancer Survivors. Ann. Behav. Med. 2016, 50:198–209
10. Self-Affirmation: Understanding the Effects David K. Sherman. Social and Personality Psychology Compass 7/11 (2013): 834–845, 10.1111/spc3.12072

Experimental Manipulations of Self-Affirmation: A Systematic Review Amy McQueen, William M.P. Klein. Self and Identity, 5: 289 – 354, 2006

11. David Creswell, Janine M. Dutcher, William M. P. Klein, Peter R. Harris, John M. Levine. Self-Affirmation Improves Problem-Solving under Stress J. PLOS ONE | www.plosone.org. 1 May 2013, Volume 8; Issue 5; doi: 10.1371/journal.pone.0062593.t001
12. Philine S. Harris, Peter R. Harris, Eleanor Miles. Self-affirmation improves performance on tasks related to executive functioning Journal of Experimental Social Psychology 70 (2017) 281–285.
13. Janine M. Dutcher, J. David Creswell, Laura E. Pacilio, Peter R. Harris, William M. P. Klein, John M. Levine, Julienne E. Bower, Keely A. Muscatell, Naomi I. Eisenberger. Self-Affirmation Activates the Ventral Striatum: A Possible Reward-Related Mechanism for Self-Affirmation. Psychological Science February 25, 2016; pp. 455–466
14. Robinson S. A Case Study of Self-Affirmations in Teacher Education. Journal of Invitational Theory and Practice Volume 20, 2014; pg. 27-36
15. Sherman, D. K., & Hartson, K. A. Reconciling self-protection with self-improvement: Self-affirmation theory. In M. Alicke & C. Sedikides (Eds.), The Handbook of Self-Enhancement and Self-Protection (2011; pp. 128–151). New York: Guilford.
16. Sherman, D. K., & Cohen, G. L. The psychology of self-defense: Self-affirmation theory. In M. P. Zanna (Ed.), Advances in experimental social psychology (2006: Vol. 38, pp. 183–242). San Diego, CA: Academic Press
17. https://coachingfederation.org/credentials-and-standards/core-competencies

Principles From OJWF 3

Introduction

1: Individuals can improve their health without drugs by changing their lifestyle and diet.

2: Food is foundational to culture and history, and understanding the power of food is essential to human wellness.

Chapter 1

3: Informed consumerism is the responsibility of the individual; reliance on government agencies, news sources or social media for reliable information is fraught with bias.

4: The priority of food manufacturers and marketing is growth; market share and profit, not health or equity. Due diligence is the consumers' responsibility.

Chapter 2

5. "There is a deep yearning for a human (whole) approach to medicine." Bill Moyers

6. The boundaries between conventional biomedicine and alternative health and wellness therapies are imprecise and continually changing.

7. Being open to sharing perspectives and beliefs can create collaborative relationships and improve communication.

8. Food connects us all.

9. Health-related changes in lifestyle are made incrementally. Results are seen if new behaviors are sustained over time.

10. In order to achieve and sustain wellness, multiple elements of each human's being must co-operate in good relationship and proper balance: mind/body/brain/spirit/environment/energy systems.

Chapter 3

11. The health and wellness of our bodies is dependent on consuming a wholesome nutritious diet; food is one integral component, but diet encompasses more than food. Diet is an entire way of life.

12. The same dietary approach does not suit everyone; the key is to find a pattern of eating that leads to metabolic balance for each person.

13. Nutritional needs are never static but constantly changing to accommodate the demands of normal processes (growth, development, and aging) as well as specialized needs for healing and recovery from illness, insult, or injury.

14. Local, organically grown, minimally processed whole foods are the proven choices for a healthful diet.

15: Diet matters.

Chapter 4

16. Our cells carry the memory of our ancestors. It is well to learn your family history: place of origin, cultural food preferences, and preparation so you can eat those things that will be familiar to the genetics of your body's cells.

17. Food is medicine.

18. A healthy gut is necessary for good health.

19. Medication use (especially long-term and polypharmacy) can contribute to nutritional deficiencies and degradation of health.

20. Dietary recommendations should be determined by individual needs: genetics, cultural background, beliefs, lifestyle choices, family and community norms, and available resources.

21. Bacterial DNA in the microbiome accounts for 90% of the DNA in a human body.

22. When using probiotics and fermented foods – more is not always better.

Our Journey with Food

Chapter 5

23. Normal physiologic processes in the body depend on complex, multifunctional biochemical reactions.

24. It is neither useful nor logical to pinpoint a singular chemical substance and posit either its absence or excess as the cause of a particular pathophysiologic problem.

25. Plants may contain substances that can be potentially harmful along with others that are beneficial.

26. Traditional and ethnocultural methods of cultivating plants and preparing meals often serve to mitigate the effects of harmful substances that may exist in raw foods.

Chapter 6

27. Nourishment must be redefined beyond only the diet to include the influences of culture, lifestyle, and the environment.

28. You are not what you eat. You are what your body assimilates from what you eat.

29. If a choice is available, always choose whole, fresh, and locally grown foods.

30. A "balanced diet" includes all the colors of the rainbow and all the tastes available to the human palate: sweet, salty, sour, bitter, and savory.

31. Antioxidants – GOOD; Free radicals – BAD

Chapter 7

32. If it takes a chemistry set to make or a chemistry book to figure out ingredients, don't buy it to eat.

33. Mushrooms provide unique vital compounds for health and vitality.

34. Sulforaphane and Kaempferol rich foods are the key ingredients in upregulating positive cell receptor sites and down regulating negative cell receptors.

35. There is no such thing as too many veggies, so "eat the rainbow" of colors in foods.

36. Eat organic: food should always be your first medicine

Chapter 8

37. Fiber is your friend. It feeds the gut microbiome, detoxifies and reduces illnesses.

38. Fat is necessary in a healthy diet, but all fats are not created equal.

39. Use fish oil and omega 3 and 6 oil supplements with care.

40. Epigenetic regulation in the body is related to what you eat.

41. Cholesterol is not a "dirty" word.

Chapter 9

42. Eating meat and/or eggs does not cause heart disease.

43. Not all proteins are created equal, and how much a body requires is related to age.

44. When (time of day) you eat protein is as important as how much and what type is eaten.

45. Nutritional deficiencies can result from all dietary patterns: vegan, vegetarian, meat/flesh-eaters.

46. Dietary protein is a key factor in gut microbiota functioning.

47. "Exercise is king, nutrition is queen; put them together, and you have a kingdom!" Jack LaLanne

Chapter 10

48. Vital minerals cannot be made by the body; they must be obtained through diet.

49. Bacteria and fungi play an important role in the processing of elements (minerals) to allow release of their nutrients in the body.

50. Minerals combine naturally with other elements; some act synergistically while some antagonize others.

51. Micronutrients from minerals play an essential role in proper growth and development of the body throughout the entire human lifespan; from embryo to death.

52. Ferritin, inhibits the ability of iron to cause some types of cardiovascular diseases.

53. "It is not the food itself, but how the food is made." Dr. Bill Schindler

54. Research is revealing that much can be done to avoid cognitive deterioration by eating a nutritious diet.

Chapter 11

55. Nutraceuticals and/or supplements do not replace REAL FOOD as nourishment. They are needed to fill nutritional gaps in daily nutrient intake.

56. Modern humans cannot physically obtain sufficient nutrients from food alone. Supplements are required to attain properly balanced nutrition.

57. The vitamins we know today were identified and isolated in the 20th century from research investigating whether the absence of a particular substance in the diet could cause disease.

58. Although there is a world wide epidemic of vitamin D deficiency, Western medicine promotes management through pharmaceuticals rather that nutritional supplements.

59. "When a civilization can no longer feed its citizens, it crumbles."   Reay Tannahill

Chapter 12

60. Many present-day medications originated as herbal formulas.

61. Herbs provide beneficial chemicals for health, but adequate knowledge is needed for safe use.

62. Herbs work best in combination with other herbs or plant substances. Many function as "adaptogens," which have no treatment corollary in Western medicine.

63. Herbal use is gaining popularity in mainstream medicine, largely due to research studies providing evidence of their effectiveness and safety.

64. Herbs strengthen the immune system; pathogens do not develop resistance to them, and they do not damage beneficial gut flora.

Chapter 13

65. To be healthy, humans need clean food, water, air, natural light, and a safe living environment.

66. The incidence of gluten sensitivity is increasing in the United States. It is a hereditary condition that is a delayed allergic reaction to proteins found in many cereal grains.

67. The brain is the body's "central computer" controlling all chemical responses, and it lives on sugar. 6% of the glucose converted from food goes to support brain functioning.

68. Make the time to enjoy your food, feel gratitude, and savor the flavor; dump the guilt, anxiety and fear associated with food. These "feelings" are as destructive as toxic chemicals.

69. Diabetes and heart disease go hand-in-hand.

70. Fasting has the potential to become an important health intervention.

Chapter 14

71. Chemical contamination is EVERYWHERE on the planet. The presence of chemicals in all of the above-listed requirements for life is making us sick and threatening lives with chronic and deadly illnesses.

72. Almost all drinking water in the U.S. contains "forever chemicals," so named because they do not break down naturally in the environment.

73. American military personnel and their families suffer the consequences of exposure to a myriad of dangerous substances.

74. Exposure to microplastics causes significant cellular (DNA/mitochondria) damage in every living organism on Earth.

75. Specific nutrients and herbs can help repair damage and eliminate toxins caused by chemicals.

Chapter 15

76. Water is the most important nutrient and the major component of a human body.

77. Water requirements vary throughout the life cycle depending on gender, age, physical activity, environment, and health status.

78. Adequate hydration requires a balance between water intake and output. Thirst is not a reliable indicator of hydration status.

79. Dehydration can kill.

Chapter 16

80. Alcoholic beverages/substances have been a part of human life since the Stone Age and are woven into the social fabric of civilization.

81. Results of medical research on alcohol use are conflicting and confusing. Moderate intake shows some health benefits, but no "safe" level of consumption has been established. Tee-totally is the only guaranteed health strategy.

82. Prolonged consumption of alcohol leads to a physiological state of "tolerance," increasing the risks of overuse, abuse, and addiction.

Chapter 17

83. Healthful nutrition is linked to fertility in both males and females of all animal species, including humans.

84. Nourishment available during preconception and gestation affects the health of progeny for their entire lifespan.

85. Optimal nutrition decreases risks for both mother and fetus during pregnancy, as well as improving birth outcomes for the neonate.

86. Fertility rates in the U.S. began a steady decline in the 1960s that continues today.

87. Nutrigenomics and epigenetics research data is accumulating to support the interplay of good nutrition and environmental and lifestyle factors on fertility.

Chapter 19

88. Unfortunately, attention to healthy food habits in relationship to general well-being does not usually occur until later in life.

89. A one-size fits all approach is not the name of the game when it comes to balanced individual food and nutrient needs.

90. Nutritional requirements change throughout the lifespan, and recommendations must be adjusted to meet specific individual needs.

91. Independent older adults may benefit from health coaching to achieve nutrition goals. Others may benefit from community meal service programs.

92. Healthcare providers must be attentive to interactions between drugs, their side effects, and foods as well as medication compliance, as these can have negative effects on nutritional status in elders.

93. Food choices carry consequences over time; both good and bad are amplified and magnified with aging.

Chapter 20

94. The whole is greater than the sum of the parts."~ Aristotle, Book VIII, 1045a.8-10

95. "Medicine is the art of maintaining a healthy body and once it has been disturbed by illness, to return it again to health."
~ Hedayat al-Motaallemin

Bibliography of Historical & Published Texts

Apelian, N. (2021). *The Forager's Guide to Wild Foods: The North American Edition.* Global Brothers SRL.
Archibald, A. (2019). *The Genomic Kitchen.*
Arloski, M. (2014). *Wellness Coaching for Lasting Lifestyle Change.* Whole Person Associates.
Ballantyne, S. P. (2017). *Paleo Principles: The Science Behind the Paleo Template, Step-by-Step Guides, Meal Plans, and 200+ Healthy & Delicious Recipes for Real Life.* Canada: Victory Belt Publishing.
Ben-Shahar, T. (2010). *Being Happy: You Don't Have to Be Perfect to Lead a Richer, Happier Life.* McGraw-Hill.
Bertha Harmer, RN, BS, AM - Columbia University. (1938). *Text-book of the Principles and Practice of Nursing Third Edition.* New York: The Macmillan Company.
Board, N. L. (1936). *Meat Tops the Menue.* Chacago: National Live Stock and Meat Board.
Bokelmann, J. M. (2022). *Medicinal Herbs in Primary Care.* Boise: Elsevier.
Breed, L. M. (1934). *The Human Machine.* Boston: The Alpine Press.
Briley, J. J. (2016). *Food as Medicine Everyday.* Portland: NUNM Press.
Brown, B. (2010). *The Gifts of Imperfection: let go of who you're supposed to be and embrace who you are.* Hazelden Publishing.
Bubbs, M. (2019). *Peak: The New Science of Athletic Performance That Is Revolutionizing Sports.* Chelsea Green Publishing.
Buhner, S. H. (1998). *Sacred and Herbal Healing Beers - Secrets of Ancient Fermentation.* Boulder: Siris Books.
Buhner, S. H. (2013). *Herbal Antivirals.* Storey Publishing.
Cannell, J. (2011). *Vitame D, Athlete's Edge Faster, Quicker, Stronger.* Here & Now.
Chokoisky, S. (2015). *Sex, Love, and Dharma: Ancient Wisdom for Modern Relationships.* Rochester: Destiny Books.
Cichoke, A. (1994). *Enzymes & Enzyme Therapy.* Keats Publishing.
Civitello, L. (2011). *Cuisine & Culture 3rd edition.* Hoboken: Wiley.
Collingham, L. (2012). *The Taste of War and the Battle for Food.* New York: Penguin Press.
Cressman, L. S. (1961, 1981, 2005). *The Sandle and the Cave - The Indians of Oregon.* Corvallis: Oregon State University Press.
D'Adamo, P. J. (2002). *Eat for your Blood Type Compleate Blood Type Encyclopedia.* New York: Riverhead Books.
Daniel G. Amen, M. (2015). *Change Your Brain Change Your Life.* New York: Penguin House.
Dietert, R. (2016). *The Human Super - Organism.* New York: Dutton.
DiNicolantonio, J. (2017). *The Salt Fix.* Harmony.
DiNicolantonio, J. F. (2019). *The Longevity Solution: Rediscovering Centuries-old Secrets to a Healthy, Long Life.* Los Vegas: Victory Belt Publishing.
Dukes, G. H. (2016). *A Short History of Eating.* London: London Press.
Edelstein, S. (2014). *Food Science and Ecological Approch.* Burlington: Jones and Bartlett Learning.
Edge, J. T. (2017). *The Potlikker Papers, a food history of the modern south.* New York: Penguin Press.
Ellet, M. E. (1972). *New Cyclopaedia: Domestic Economy, and Practical Housekeeper.* Norwich, CO: Henry Bill.
Ewers, K. (2017). *Solving the AutoImmune Puzzle.* Samadhi.
Fernandez, A. F. (2002). *Near a Thousand Tables a history of food.* New York: Free- Press.
Fishman, C. (2011). *The Big Thirst.* New York: Simon and Schuster.
Fitzgerald, K. N. (2016). *Methylation Diet & Lifestyle.* Medford: www.drkarafitzgerald.com.
Flandrin, J. L. (1996). *FOOD a culinary history from antiquity to the present.* New York: Columbia University Press.
Fogg, B. J. (2019). *Tiny Habits: The Small Changes That Change Everything.* New York: Houghton Mifflin Harcourt.
Gaby, A. R. (2017). *Nutritional Medicine Second Edition.* Concord: Fritz Perlberg Publishing.
Gazzaley, A. (2016). *The Distracted Mind: Ancient Brains in a High-Tech World.* Cambridge: MIT Press.
Gittleman, A. L. (2010). *Zapped.* New York: Harper One.
Greenfield, B. (2020). *Boundless.* Los Vegas: Victory Belt Publishing.
Haas, E. (2006). *Staying Healthy with Nutrition.* Celestial Arts.
Harari, Y. N. (2018). *Sapiens: A Brief History of Humankind.* New York: Harper Perennial.
Hawken, P. (2010). *The Ecology of Commerce Revised Edition: A Declaration of Sustainability.* New York: Harper Business; Revised edition.
Hawken, P. L. (2000, 2010). *Natural Capitalism.* New York: Routledge.
Hay, W. H. (1929). *Health via Food.* East Aurora: Sun-Diet Press.
Hesterman, O. B. (2011). *Fair Food.* New York: Public Affairs.
Hyman, M. (2009). *The UltraMind Solution.* Scribner.
Jenkins, M. (2017). *Food Fight.* New York: Avery.
Jensen, B. A. (1990). *Empty Harvest.* New York: Avery.

Kalanithi, P. (2016). *When Breath Becomes Air.* New York: Penguin Random House.
Kaptchuk, T. J. (2000). *The Web That Has No Weaver: Understanding Chinese Medicine.* Contemporary Books.
Karr, T. a. (2020). *Empty Plate Food Sustainability Mindfulness.* Summerland.
Karr, T. J. (2015). *Our Journey with Food.* Summerland Publishing.
Karr, T. J. (2022). *Our Journey with Food Cookery Book 2nd.* Summerland Publishing.
Katz, S. E. (2016). *Wild Fermentation.* White River Junction: Green Press Initiative.
Keith, L. (2009). *The Vegetarian Myth.* Flashpoint Press.
Kiple, K. F. (2000). *The Cambridge World History of Food vol 1&2.* Cambridge: Cambridge University Press.
Kirschmann, J. (2007). *Nutrition Almanac 6th edition.* New York: McGraw Hill.
Krimsky, S., Gruber, J. (2014). *The GMO Deception.* New York: Skyhorse Publishing.
Lama, D. (2009). *For the Benefit of All Beings.* Boulder: Shambhala.
Li, W. (2019). *Eat to Beat Disease.* Grand Central Publishing.
Lipski, E. (2020). *Digestive Wellness 5th edition.* McGraw Hill.
Lopez, D. A. (1994). *Enzymes The Fountain of Life.* The Nevelle Press Inc.
Lovegren, S. (2005). *Fashionable Foods, Seven Decades of Food Fads.* Chicago: The University of Chicago Press.
Mahan, K. ,. (2017). *Krauses's Food & The Nutrition Care Process, 14th edition.* St. Louis: Elsevier.
MD, A. J. (1921). *Nostrums and Quackery.* Chicago: American Medical Associastion Press.
MD, E. M. (2016). *The Mind-Gut Connection.* New York: Harper-Collins.
Medical Department of the General Confrence of Seventh-day Adventists. (1927). *Home Nursing.* Washington, DC: Review and Herald Publishing Associasion.
Michael Fossel, M. P. (2017). *The Telomerase Revolution.* Dallas TX: BenBella Books.
Minger, D. (2013). *Death by Food Pyramid.* Malibu: Primal Blueprint Publishing.
Minich, D. (2016). *Whole Detox: 21 Day Personalized Program .* New York: Harper One.
Minich, D. P. (2018). *The Rainbow Diet.* Newburyport: Conari Press.
Mintz, S. W. (1985). *Sweetness and Power.* New York: Penguin Books.
Morales, N. (2020). *The Native Mexican Kitchen: A journey into Cuisine, Culture and Mezcal.* Skyhorse Publishing.
Morse, S. (1908). *Household Discoveries: Encyclopaedia of Practical Recipes and Processes.* NY: The Success Company.
Moss, M. (2013). *Salt Sugar Fat.* New York: Random House.
Mukherjee, S. (2022). *The Song of the Cell.* Toronto: Schibner.
Nelson, T. (2017). *Food Fights And Culture Wars: Secret History of Taste.* Overlool Press.
Nestle, M. (2018). *Unsavory Truth How Food Companies Skew the Science of What We Eat.* New York: Basic Books.
Ni, M. M. (2012). *The Tao of Nutrition 3rd.* The Tao of Nutrition Press.
Niethammer, C. (2020). *Celebrating Tuson's Culinary Heritage: A Desert Feast.* The University of Arizona Press.
Norton, S. K. (2022). *Toxic Superfoods.* New York: Rodale.
O'Bryan, T. (2016). Betrayal the Autoimmune Disease Solution. New York: AutoImmune Group, LLC.
O'Bryan, T. (2016). The Autoimmune Fix. New York: Rodale.Owsley, D. W. (2014). *Kennewick Man: The Scientific Investigation of an Ancient American Skeleton.* Washington DC: Smithsonian.
Pacholok, S. S. (2011). *Could It Be B12?* Quill Driver Books.
Pearsall, J. M. (2006). *Sweet Deception.* Nashville, TN: Thomas Nelson Inc.
Perlmutter, D. M. (2015). *Brain Maker.* New York: Little Brown and Company.
Pestana C., G. (2020). *The World of Plymouth Plantation.* London: The Belknap Press of Harvard University.
Pizzorno, J. E.-B. (2016). *The Clinician's Handbook of Natural Medicine 3rd.* Elsevier.
Provenza, F. (2018). *Nourishment.* London: Chelsea Green Publishing.
Rakel, D. (2012). *Intigrative Medicine 3rd.* Elsevier.
Rakel, D. M. (2023). *Intigrative Medicine 5th edition.* Elserier.
Raymond, J. M. (2023). *Krause and Mahan's Food and the Nutrition Care Process 16th edition.* Elsevier.
Robinson, J. (2013). *Eating on the Wild Side.* New York: Little, Brown and Company.
Rodgers, D. R. (2020). *Sacred Cow: The Case for (Better) Meat: Why Well-Raised Meat Is Good for You and Good for the Planet.* New York: BenBella Books.
Rost, A. (2016). *Natural Healing Wisdom and Know-How.* New York: Black Dog.
Schatzker, M. (2011). *Steak.* New York: Penguin Books.
Schindler, B. (2021). *Eat Like a Human.* Little Brown Spark.
Scott-Dixon, K. P. (2017). *Genetics: The Universe Within.* Precision Nutrition.
Scrinis, G. (2013). *Nutritionism the Science and Politics of Dietary Advance.* New York: Columbia University Press.

Shanahan, C. a. (2009). *Deep Nutrition*. HI: Big Box Books.
Sherman, S. (2017). *The Sioux Chef's Indigenous Kitchen.* Minneapolis: University of Minnesota Press.
Shimer, P. (2004). *Healing Secrets of the Native Americans.* New York: Black Dog.
Shulman, M. R. (2007). *Mediterranean Harvest.* New York: Rodale.
Sinclair, D. (2019). *Lifespan.* London: Thomson Press.
Sitz, K. (2008). *Basque Heritage Cookbook.* Burns: Self Published.
Skidmore-Roth, L. (2010). *Herbs & Natural Supplements.* Mosby Elsevier.
Standage, T. (2009). *A Edible History of Humanity.* New York: Walker & Company.
Tannerhill, R. (1988). *Food in History.* New York: Three Rivers Press.
Teicholz, N. (2014). *The Big Fat Surprise.* New York: Simon & Schuster.
The W.T. Rawleigh Company. (1942 & 1943). *Rawleigh's Good Health Guide: Almanac, Cook Book.* The W.T. Rawleigh Company.
Thom, D. &. (2018). *Bioregulatory Medicine.* Chelsea Green Publishing.
Tips, J. C. (2014). *The Microbial Alliance.* Appleaday Press.
Wahls, T. M. (2020). *The Wahls Protocol A Radical New Way to Treat All Chronic Autoimmune Conditions Useing Paleo Principles.* New York: Avery.
Wilson, B. (2012). *Consider the Fork.* New York: Basic Books.
Wilson, B. (2019). *The Way We Eat Now.* New York: Basic Books.
Winston, D. M. (2007). *Adaptogens: Herbs for Strength, Stamina and Relief.* Healing Arts Press.
Wong, C. T. (2021). *Gastro Obscura.* Workman Publishing Co.
Wrangham, R. (2009). *Catching Fire How Cooking Made Us Human.* Philladelphia: Basic Books.

Index

2B Well, 431, 439, 443, 444, 445, 447, 463, 491

7-Up, 24

ABO Blood Groupings, 433

Acacia, 154, 155, 156, 182

Acetylcholine, 436

Acrylamide, 164, 184

Acupuncturists, 33

Acute Vitamin A Poisoning, 252

ADHD, 68, 333

Adiposity, 132, 168

Adrenal Cortex, 54, 238

Adrenal Fatigue, Xvi, 238

Aflatoxins, 164, 183

African American, 13, 123, 236, 374

Agent Orange, 319, 324, 409

Agriculture Data, 13, 29

AIDS, 120, 236, 256

Alcohol, Vi, 4, 20, 52, 68, 99, 134, 137, 229, 250, 251, 260, 273, 311, 315, 318, 338, 346, 349, 355, 361, 362, 364, 367, 369, 373, 379, 381, 401, 426, 435, 436, 440, 470

Aldosterone, 228, 230, 232, 266

Alfalfa, 162

Alkaline, 51, 52, 53, 59, 74, 190, 195, 258, 355, 356

Alkaloids, 104, 156, 295

Almonds, 89, 137, 179, 304, 305

Alopecia, 241

Alpha-Carotene, 101, 251

Alpha-Linolenic Acid, 167

Alpha-Tocopherol, 268

Aluminum, 24

Alzheimer's Disease, 103, 106, 121, 125, 134, 135, 146, 159, 175, 185, 186, 282, 283, 284, 288, 409, 410, 415, 416, 418, 420, 421, 422

Amaranth, 89, 158, 240

American Journal Of Gastroenterology, 77, 83

American Medical Association, 20, 44, 256

American Psychological Association, 443

American Red Cross, 16

Amines, 150, 194

Amino Acids, 73, 75, 85, 157, 158, 159, 190, 192, 193, 194, 198, 199, 202, 203, 206, 207, 212, 311, 338, 405

AMY2 Genes, 75

Amylase, 73, 75, 82

Amyotrophic Lateral Sclerosis, 258, 333, 415

Anaphylaxis, 147, 160

Anchovies, 334

Anemia, 56, 132, 169, 237, 238, 243, 247, 252, 259, 260, 323, 329, 381

Anorexia, 42, 57

Anserine, 207

Anthocyanins, 132, 146, 290, 292, 300, 325, 412, 420

Antibacterial, 76, 124, 133, 136, 146, 250, 279, 280, 283, 292, 293

Antihypertensives, 65

Antinutrient, 107, 108

Antioxidant, 16, 81, 101, 102, 103, 104, 105, 107, 112, 113, 118, 124, 125, 127, 129, 131, 133, 137, 143, 147, 148, 158, 161, 170, 227, 236, 241, 249, 250, 268, 272, 273, 283, 286, 288, 290, 291, 292, 293, 295, 321, 337, 338, 378, 416, 417, 418

Anxiety, 35, 39, 62, 66, 143, 265, 294, 299, 333, 391, 409, 411, 414, 418, 419

APOE Gene, 220

Appendix, 72, 81

Applejack, 364

Arabica, 142

Armamentarium, 157

Arrhythmia, 229, 285, 295

Arsenic, 121, 255, 329

Artichoke Leaf, 69, 179

Aspartame, 336, 343

Aspartic Acid, 194, 336

Astaxanthin, 105

Asthma, 54, 126, 127, 130, 144, 172, 221, 253, 281, 282, 283, 307, 333, 339, 340, 341, 372, 385

Atherosclerosis, 80, 127, 137, 168, 176, 177, 178, 186, 239, 243, 247, 260, 261, 268, 269, 270, 286, 289, 292, 361

Autism, 68, 103, 158, 182, 259, 275, 333, 373

Autoimmune Diseases, 163, 263, 267, 308, 349

Autonomic Nervous System, 430

Avocado, 152, 174, 180, 185

B Complex, 311

B Lymphocytes, 72

B Vitamins, 55, 69, 72, 76, 97, 249, 253, 254, 255, 256, 257, 275, 321, 364, 369, 416

B6, 69, 78, 87, 124, 125, 255, 257, 258, 259, 260, 262, 275, 416, 421

Back Pain, 66, 71

Bacteriophages, 226

Ballantyne, Sarah, 47

Barberry, 295

Bariatric Surgery, 86, 222, 254

Barley, 310

Basal Metabolism, 68

Basil, 123, 280, 340

Bayer, 14, 56, 306

Beans, 79, 82, 93, 98, 107, 126, 138, 139, 140, 142, 143, 151, 160, 161, 162, 163, 180, 183, 193, 200, 240, 272, 305, 311, 404, 405, 406

Bee Pollen, 341

Beef, 27, 29, 41, 69, 167, 168, 189, 193, 194, 197, 201, 202, 203, 207, 209, 210, 243, 253, 258, 272, 304, 317, 414

Beer, 4, 24, 105, 226, 310, 330, 361, 362, 363, 364, 365, 366, 367, 369

Beet, 89, 128

Beets, 71, 89, 98, 128, 129, 153, 240, 308, 317, 416

Beeturia, 129

Belief, 386, 395

Bell, Kathleen, Vii, Viii, X, 37, 345, 371, 490

Beneficial Bacteria, 61, 78, 321

Berberine, 179, 287, 295, 296, 299, 301

Bergamot, 179

Berries, 53, 71, 98, 132, 133, 135, 138, 154, 291, 295, 296, 352, 366

Beta-Carotene, 101, 104, 125, 147, 227, 251, 252, 286, 289, 338

Beta-Glucans, 151

B-Glucuronidase, 77

Betanin, 129

Bile, 70, 186

Bioflavonoids, 104, 341

Biomedicine, 31, 38, 297, 422

Biotin, 69, 78, 126, 364

Birdseye, Clarence, 9

Birth Control, 65

Bison, 189, 202, 209

Bisphenol A, 225, 334, 343

Bitter Greens, 138

Black Beans, 71, 161

Black Cherry, 69, 89

Black Mold, 339

Black Tea, 144, 238

Blackberries, 101, 105, 132, 134, 152

Bladder, 61, 72, 86, 121, 134, 262, 349

Blaylock, Russell L., 334

Blood Sugars, 56, 98, 99, 144, 151, 153, 161, 230, 284, 318, 320, 321, 322

Blood Type, 431, 433, 471

Blood–Brain Barrier, 335

Blueberries, 133, 148

BMC Public Health, 96, 109

BMI, 132, 350, 354, 359, 373, 377, 380, 381

Body Mass Loss, 353

Boswellia, 237, 281, 282, 284, 297

Botulism, 304

Bowels, 151, 152, 153, 295, 347

Brain Atrophy, 335

Brain Health, 322

Bran, 97

Breast Cancer, 103, 112, 125, 145, 161, 171, 224, 233, 264, 265, 274, 284, 289, 329, 361, 363, 390, 397

Breast Milk, 233, 287, 332, 338, 356

Broccoli, 112, 121, 122, 123, 146, 230, 338, 407

Bromelain, 73, 75, 82, 297

Brominated Vegetable Oil, 334, 336, 343

Bromine, 233, 336

Bronchitis, 124, 172, 294, 340

Buckwheat, 158, 159, 160, 182, 317, 407

Butter, Xviii, 14, 54, 71, 140, 168, 172, 177, 185, 210, 252, 253, 263, 272, 296, 306, 320, 376, 383, 412, 417

C. Difficile, 65

Cade, James Robert, 353

Caffeine, Xvi, 52, 68, 88, 93, 141, 142, 143, 144, 150, 317, 334, 373, 381, 417, 422

Calcium, 51, 71, 85, 86, 87, 88, 89, 90, 91, 92, 94, 121, 125, 129, 135, 159, 195, 217, 218, 219, 220, 221, 222, 223, 224, 225, 227, 228, 240, 241, 244, 257, 259, 264, 270, 271, 288, 289, 315, 351, 356, 372, 388, 403, 404, 405

Calcium Metabolism, 222, 270

California Institute Of Technology, 152, 181, 272

Calorie Intake, 403

Campylobacter, 304, 306

Cancer, 37, 50, 66, 68, 77, 102, 104, 117, 121, 125, 137, 143, 164, 177, 234, 271, 282, 356, 361, 392

Cancer And Vitamin C, 272

Candida Albicans, 79

Cannabinoids, 66, 67

Canola Oil, 167, 173, 175, 185

Captain Soup, 331

Carbohydrate, 44, 49, 56, 59, 69, 73, 75, 99, 100, 110, 111, 162, 163, 167, 197, 255, 256, 286, 317, 404, 406

Carcinogenic, 170, 268, 336

Cardiac Injury, 152

Cardiovascular, 49, 58, 60, 68, 100, 101, 102, 103, 104, 107, 110, 111, 112, 121, 127, 132, 134, 137, 141, 149, 156, 157, 163, 168, 174, 176, 177, 181, 182, 183, 184, 185, 187, 192, 203, 223, 224, 228, 229, 230, 239, 241, 244, 247, 259, 266, 270, 271, 275, 285, 289, 291, 293, 294, 295, 301, 321, 329, 337, 358, 362, 363, 364, 369, 371, 389, 390, 392, 398, 413, 460

Carnitine, 69, 173, 249, 272, 383

Carpal Tunnel Syndrome, 259

Carrageenan, 334

Cartilage, 101, 242

Cattle, 200, 201, 305, 409

CBC Lab Test, 238

CBD, 66

Celery, 89, 288, 289, 290, 299, 317, 352

Celiac Disease, 56, 77, 86, 158, 237, 238, 239, 252, 284, 308, 309, 310, 311, 312, 313, 315, 316, 323, 324

Cells, 311, 319, 321

Centers For Disease Control, 303, 317, 324, 337

Cephalic Phase, 61, 80

Cerebral Palsy, 270, 373

Cernohous, Sarica, Xviii

Chard, 89, 129

Chinese Buckwheat Liquor, 159

Chinese Herbs, 88, 105, 341

Chinese Restaurant Syndrome, 259

Chlamydia, 381

Chlorella, 338

Chlorine, 233, 333, 356

Chocolate, 42, 89, 139, 140, 141, 149, 150, 153, 240, 310, 414, 417, 422

Cholecalciferol, 263

Cholecystectomy, 70

Choledocholithiasis, 71

Cholesterol, Xv, 59, 64, 69, 70, 78, 79, 107, 119, 121, 127, 136, 141, 151, 153, 154, 156, 158, 159, 161, 167, 168, 170, 171, 172, 176, 177, 178, 180, 181, 186, 187, 191, 206, 243, 261, 263, 266, 286, 292, 316, 321, 325, 363, 404

Choline, 78, 106, 206, 214, 249

Chromium, 121, 126, 144, 207, 321, 329

Chronic Fatigue Syndrome, 120

Chronic Kidney Disease, 85, 86, 88, 91, 157, 182, 192, 212, 219, 351, 353, 369

Cider, 364, 365

Citrus, 75, 89, 102, 136, 146, 352

Coaching Process And Principles, 444

Coconut Oil, 168, 172, 173, 174, 185, 320, 419

Cod Liver Oil, 252, 253, 266

Coenzyme Q10, 64, 69, 72, 76, 384

Coffee, Ix, 9, 41, 88, 93, 142, 143, 144, 150, 200, 231, 235, 240, 246, 255, 256, 275, 286, 352, 355, 414, 417, 422

Cognition, 39, 66, 70, 133, 168, 174, 185, 192, 220, 282, 346, 412, 413, 417, 422

Cognitive Decline, 124, 308, 358, 361, 364, 416, 418

Collagen, 198, 199, 213, 257, 272, 292, 297, 311

Collard Greens, 123, 426

Collingham, Lizzie, 7

Colon Cancer, 151, 170, 220, 238, 361

Commensal Bacteria, 72, 77

Community, 451

Community Supported Agriculture CSA, 14

Concord Grapes, 134, 292

Conjugated Linoleic Acid, 168

Constipation, 51, 65, 78, 80, 107, 151, 153, 157, 161, 172, 220, 232, 255, 287, 289, 296, 316, 404

Cooking Processes, 85, 89

COPD, 340, 491

Copper, 51, 69, 119, 123, 144, 159, 227, 243, 262, 288, 315

Cordain, Loren, 46

Corn, 10, 12, 14, 15, 69, 98, 99, 111, 116, 117, 138, 139, 150, 153, 162, 165, 167, 168, 172, 193, 205, 206, 240, 252, 258, 262, 269, 310, 314, 317, 334

Corning Ware, 10

COVID, 27, 35, 56, 64, 69, 75, 80, 145, 149, 219, 227, 241, 245, 247, 267, 273, 277, 280, 294, 297, 301, 312, 374, 375, 391, 395, 398, 411

Cranberries, 101, 134

Cranberry, 89, 101, 111, 133, 134

C-Rations, 41, 334

Cretors, Charles, 165

CRISPR, 15, 29, 115, 116, 117

Crohn's, 2, 66, 86, 135, 229, 238, 239, 252, 257, 261, 284, 303, 317

Cruciferous, 98, 102, 107, 122, 123, 146

Cryptoxanthin, 101, 138, 251, 288

C-Type Lectin, 163

Cultural Gastronomy, 211

Culture, 8, 10, 29, 136, 324, 387, 393, 395, 451, 455, 471, 472

Curcumin, 282, 283, 284, 297

Cuyahoga River, 327

Cyanocobalamin, 259, 261

Cytokines, 63, 64, 170, 175, 289, 316, 397

Dairy, 14, 16, 52, 53, 54, 107, 116, 162, 168, 177, 189, 191, 192, 195, 205, 212, 213, 215, 224, 225, 226, 228, 235, 238, 245, 251, 256, 257, 260, 263, 268, 304, 306, 310, 311, 316, 332, 335, 382, 383, 403, 404

Dairy Substitutes, 195

Dandelion, 240, 287, 288, 289, 299

Davis, Adelle, 11, 414, 421

D-Chiro-Inositol, 159

DDT, 328

Dehydration, 144, 230, 232, 290, 348, 350, 351, 352, 353, 354, 359, 403, 412

Dementia, 134, 143, 158, 168, 182, 213, 220, 243, 294, 307, 331, 332, 335, 343, 361, 363, 409, 410, 411, 413, 416

Depression, 1, 28, 53, 67, 158, 163, 168, 171, 172, 221, 233, 238, 259, 263, 265, 289, 294, 299, 313, 318, 333, 335, 336, 369, 389, 391, 392, 418, 419

Detoxification, 36, 68, 77, 121, 129, 146, 232, 319, 337, 338, 354, 383

Diabetes, 1, 16, 29, 35, 37, 39, 45, 46, 53, 56, 58, 69, 75, 76, 79, 83, 87, 88, 99, 100, 101, 104, 110, 112, 117, 119, 122, 127, 130, 132, 133, 134, 143, 146, 148, 152, 153, 159, 161, 167, 168, 171, 178, 179, 180, 186, 187, 210, 211, 219, 221, 223, 224, 226, 231,233, 244, 252, 254, 257, 259, 263, 265, 266, 286, 287, 295, 298, 299, 308, 313, 318, 319, 320, 321, 322, 323, 324, 325, 329, 336, 337, 351, 353, 361, 363, 371, 374, 377, 380, 405, 409, 418

Diaita, 43

Diarrhea,, 78, 164, 241, 252, 256, 263, 287

Dietary Fiber, 132, 151, 153, 154, 158, 160, 316, 338, 404

Dietary Guidelines, 16, 420

Dietary Protein, 190

Digestive Tract, 61, 63, 71, 75, 76, 77, 78, 86, 107, 151, 260, 293, 296, 310, 316, 362, 415

Diuretic, 133, 141, 280, 288, 352, 364

Diverticulitis, 153, 165

DNA, 1, 6, 15, 76, 100, 101, 105, 106, 107, 115, 121, 125, 132, 147, 194, 205, 218, 236, 240, 280, 286, 324, 333, 337, 339, 375, 379, 385, 390

Dorsett, P.H., 8

Dysbiosis, 77, 157, 286, 415, 421

Dysentairy, 315

E. Coli, 201, 304, 306, 315

Edema, 288, 289

Egg, 172, 176, 177, 181, 193, 204, 205, 206, 207, 214, 240, 256, 272, 407

Elderberries, 133

Electrolyte, 220, 230, 231,236, 346, 348, 351, 353, 354, 356, 361, 384

Electromagnetic Fields, 44, 167, 384

Ellagic Acid, 102

Empty Plate, 29, 37, 39, 46, 296, 322, 328, 333, 356, 375, 395, 396, 397, 398, 412, 472, 490

Endocarditis, 257

Endocrine, Xvi, 1, 10, 29, 47, 70, 72, 117, 145, 229, 246, 334, 335, 337, 356, 372, 377, 383

Endogenous Retroviruses, 226

Endometriosis, 329, 337, 363, 377

Endosperm, 97

Environmental Toxins, 76, 153, 319, 338

Environmental Working Group, 138, 328, 329

Enzymes, 54, 56, 61, 70, 71, 73, 74, 75, 79, 82, 104, 154, 159, 161, 163, 169, 190, 191, 193, 218, 236, 240, 242, 282, 317, 337, 346, 364, 378, 471, 472

Epigallocatechin Gallate, 102, 152

Epigenetic, 106, 426, 427, 440, 468

Epilepsy, 49, 173, 196, 213, 361

Epithelial Barrier, 157, 272

Epithelium, 63

Epsom Salts, 218

Epstein-Bar Virus, 308

Essential Fatty Acids, 167, 207

Estrogen, 77, 103, 118, 224, 225, 264, 319, 363

Ethanol, 361, 369

Ethnobotany, 95

Eugenics, 34, 38

Euhydration, 353

Eukaryotic Viruses, 226

European Food Safety Authority, 251, 336

Excitotoxins, 334, 335, 377

Exercise, 43, 51, 66, 76, 93, 100, 147, 155, 173, 180, 181, 192, 194, 196, 197, 222, 348, 352, 353, 355, 381, 388, 392, 396, 397, 398, 406, 414, 429, 434, 437, 449, 452, 454

Fagopyrin, 160

Farsi Dari, 434

Fasting, 45, 49, 50, 59, 178, 213, 311, 321, 325, 421

Fat, 29, 94, 133, 151, 166, 167, 168, 212, 214, 249, 300, 319, 320, 332, 342, 404, 407, 412, 472, 473

Fatty Acids, 49, 50, 71, 72, 74, 75, 78, 79, 86, 90, 105, 132, 145, 151, 157, 158, 166, 167, 168, 170, 172, 173, 174, 179, 181, 185, 191, 206, 207, 223, 241, 244, 261, 268, 324, 405, 413, 416

FDA, 98, 116, 156, 157, 158, 182, 230, 254, 258, 265, 303, 304, 305, 310, 332, 376, 377, 385, 398

Fennel, 287, 299

Fenugreek, 287, 299

Fermentation, 55, 72, 78, 89, 108, 139, 140, 151, 153, 154, 157, 183, 195, 223, 272, 286, 315, 335, 362, 364, 368

Fernandez-Armesto, Felipe, 7

Ferritin, 69, 236, 237, 238, 239, 240, 246, 247, 257, 384

Fertility, 56, 135, 270, 329, 371, 375, 376, 377, 378, 379, 381, 382, 383, 384, 390

Fetus, 72, 222, 335, 356, 371, 372, 373, 375, 380, 381, 391, 393

Fiber, 71, 93, 148, 151, 152, 154, 155, 157, 164, 181, 182, 187, 404

Fibrinolytic, 75, 107

Fibrocystic Breasts, 234

Fibromyalgia, 137, 149, 168, 218, 238, 242, 428

Fibrosis, 173, 251, 291

Fish, 47, 53, 56, 71, 116, 167, 169, 177, 189, 193, 196, 202, 204, 205, 210, 214, 233, 251, 252, 256, 258, 260, 263, 268, 312, 317, 381, 383, 403, 404, 406, 407, 409, 412, 413, 416

Fish Oil, 168, 312

Fitzgerald, Kara, 3

Flash Fuel, 151

Flavonoids, 58, 101, 111, 140, 149

Flax, 118, 145, 179

FLG Mutation, 265

Flint, Michigan, 328

Fluoride, 137, 233, 235, 330, 333, 356

Folate, 106, 126, 135, 161, 195, 227, 343, 373, 379, 380, 384, 385, 416, 421, 427

Folic Acid, 69, 78, 121, 123, 129, 253, 257, 259, 260, 261, 275, 288, 372, 373, 379, 380, 416

Food Deserts, 11, 12, 37, 56

Food Of A Younger Land, 424

Food Sovereignty, 13, 210, 211

Food Swamp, 37

Foodborne Pathogens, 304, 322

Forever Chemicals, 10, 327, 328, 329, 330, 331, 342, 469

FOS, 78

Framingham Heart Study, 271

Fraser, Evan D.G., 7

Free Radical Theory, 105, 119

Free Radicals, 106

Fructans, 316

Fructooligosaccharides, 78

Fructose, 43, 69, 88, 89, 91, 98, 99, 111, 151, 172, 174, 185, 317

Fruits, 16, 37, 47, 71, 75, 94, 98, 101, 102, 104, 116, 132, 133, 134, 136, 137, 138, 149, 151, 164, 165, 180, 203, 205, 209, 228, 258, 268, 279, 287, 291, 292, 304, 305, 316, 317, 320, 328, 331, 348, 352, 362, 381, 389, 392, 402, 403, 404, 405, 413, 414, 416

Fungi, 47, 67, 75, 105, 112, 119, 120, 134, 189, 217, 260, 304, 318, 338, 344, 375, 387, 389

Funk, Casimir, 97

Gaia, 250

Galilean-Baconian, 281

Gallbladder, 61, 70, 71, 74, 81, 221, 289, 290, 294, 295, 296, 419

Garlic, 71, 78, 98, 105, 107, 123, 126, 147, 179, 279, 280, 285, 297, 340

Gastric Bypass Surgery, 265

Gastronomy, 387, 389, 390, 395, 424, 425, 449

Gatorade, 353, 354

General Mills, 27, 56, 166, 306

General Treatise On The Etiology And Symptoms Of Diseases, 254

Genetically Modified Foods, 115, 116

GERD, 143, 153, 295

Germanium, 104

Giardia, 315

Gin, 366, 414

Gittleman, Ann Louise, 44

Gliadin, 309, 315

Glucagon, 70, 153

Glucose, 43, 46, 49, 50, 58, 68, 82, 98, 99, 101, 105, 112, 120, 126, 130, 151, 153, 159, 168, 171, 173, 190, 194, 198, 232, 246, 255, 259, 263, 266, 286, 287, 299, 318, 319, 320, 422

Glucosinolates, 102, 146

Glutamate, 334, 335, 343

Glutathione, 75, 118, 119, 337, 338

Gluten, 308, 309, 310, 312, 313

Gluten Sensitivity, 68, 252, 266, 284, 308, 312, 316, 323

Gluten-Free, 16, 147, 158, 159, 193, 308, 309, 310, 311, 312, 314, 315, 316, 317, 323

Glycation, 85, 89, 287

Glycemic Index, 79, 107

Glycerophospholipids, 191

Glycogen, 68, 69, 98

Glycosides, 156, 293

Glyoxylic Acid, 86

GMO, 14, 15, 116, 117, 145, 166, 167, 199, 314, 361, 367, 383, 472

Goat Milk, 191

Gonorrhea, 172, 381

Gonzalez, Nicholas, 70

Gooseberries, 132

Gout, 283, 412

Grapefruit Seed, 78

Great Famine, 131

Green Tea, 69, 102, 105, 135, 152, 286, 338

Green Teasel, 279

Groats, 159

GROW Model, 446, 447, 455

Guptha, Leana Susan, Vii, 443

Guptha, Soneil, Viii, X, 176, 401

Gut-Brain Axis, 63, 170, 184, 415

Gymnema, 321

H. Pylori, 78

Hair Loss, 340

Hatch Act Of 1887, 14

Hawthorn, 290, 291, 300

Hay, William Howard, 52

Hazelnut, 172

HDL, 178, 179, 180, 181, 187, 243, 266, 286, 287

Headaches, 121, 142, 143, 153, 233, 238, 252, 263, 284, 336, 340, 349, 418

Health Coaches, 4, 33, 43, 445

Heart, 310, 321

Heart Disease, 53, 58, 67, 99, 100, 102, 104, 106, 119, 133, 143, 144, 152, 153, 161, 168, 171, 172, 176, 177, 178, 184, 186, 203, 206, 211, 214, 218, 228, 230, 231, 252, 263, 268, 269, 271, 272, 291, 321, 329, 361, 390, 409, 416, 418

Heart Rhythm, 351

Heavy Metals, 76, 87, 121, 255, 319, 321, 329, 331, 342, 361

Heme Iron, 238, 239

Hemicellulose, 151, 154

Hemochromatosis, 118, 236, 237

Hemorrhoids, 173, 252, 296

Hemp, 66, 168, 184

Hepatic Duct, 70

Hepatitis, 1, 69, 120, 164, 236, 237, 260, 283, 289, 295, 304, 364

Hepatitis C, 1, 69, 236, 237, 260, 364

Hepatoprotective, 124, 290, 338

Hesperidin, 102, 293

HFCS, 99, 110, 317

High Phenol Olive Oil, 171

Hildegard, 97, 363

Hippocrates, 43, 124, 133

Homocysteine, 257, 259, 261, 275, 416, 426, 427, 429, 440

Honeybees, 280

Horehound, 293, 294, 295, 301

Hormone Imbalances, 172

Hormones, 42, 112, 117

Horsetail, 279

Human Microbiome Project, 375, 385

Human Virome, 226

Hunt, Caroline, 16

Hydration, 403

Hydrochloric Acid, 106, 260, 354

Hydroxycinnamic Acids, 132

Hypercalcemia, 223

Hypercholesterolemia, 124, 176, 178

Hyperferritinemia, 236

Hyperglycemia, 101, 124, 263, 266

Hyperkeratosis, 273

Hyperlipidemia, 178, 186, 295

Hypernatremia, 232

Hypertension, 4, 43, 56, 91, 92, 93, 124, 128, 130, 144, 158, 224, 230, 232, 237, 244, 246, 261, 263, 266, 289, 291, 299, 329, 335, 361, 362, 369, 374, 380, 405

Hyperthyroidism, 256, 381

Hypocalcemia, 219, 223

Hypokalemia, 229

Hypomagnesemia, 219

Hypothyroidism, 87, 178, 234, 238, 251, 414

Hypovitaminosis, 251, 274

Hyssop, 280

Immune Function, 67, 153, 172, 190, 219, 234, 250, 259, 269, 273, 338, 348

Immune Responses, 64, 160, 163, 269, 329, 338, 388, 421

Immunoglobulin A, 72

Immunosuppression, 164

Implicit Bias, 35

Indigenous Peoples, 32

Infant Formulas, 191

Infants, 233, 345, 349

Infertility, 377

Inflammatory Bowel Disease, 63, 66, 226, 307, 308, 323

Insoluble Fibers, 151, 315

Institute Of Medicine, 229, 340, 344

Insulin, 43, 46, 49, 50, 51, 58, 69, 70, 79, 99, 100, 101, 111, 126, 127, 141, 153, 159, 168, 171, 173, 174, 179, 222, 225, 232, 241, 246, 286, 319, 320, 323, 337, 363, 378

Insulin-Like Growth Factor-1, 286

Intermittent Fasting, 50, 59

International Coach Federation, 447

Intestinal Hyperpermeability, 63, 80

Inulin, 151, 289, 316

Iodine, 118, 195, 199, 233, 234, 235, 236, 238, 246, 251, 264, 336

Iron, 51, 69, 72, 76, 78, 94, 97, 118, 119, 125, 129, 132, 137, 159, 207, 222, 227, 236, 237, 238, 239, 240, 243, 246, 247, 252, 255, 257, 262, 288, 289, 294, 296, 315, 323, 329, 404

Isoflavone, 103, 112

Jainism, 53

James Bond Of Beans, 142

Jefferson, Thomas, 368

Jerusalem Artichokes, 79, 80

Jiminez De Quesada, Gonzalo, 130

John Mcmonigle, 14

Journal Of Hematology, 312

Kaempferol, 113, 122, 146

Kellogg's, John Harvey, 7, 51

Kelp, 230, 233

Kernza, 13

Ketogenic Diet, 46, 49, 196, , 213 412, 429

Ketones, 49, 50, 194, 223

Kidney, 4, 85, 86, 87, 88, 89, 90, 91, 92, 93, 94, 112, 118, 120, 127, 134, 135, 144, 157, 162, 172, 174, 182, 185, 192, 208, 212, 218, 219, 228, 229, 230, 231, 233, 237, 245, 255, 259, 260, 271, 282, 285, 329, 351, 352, 356, 369, 403

Kimchi, 93, 107, 113, 362, 398

Kloss, Jethro, 1

Koop, C. Everett, 318, 324

Korean Ginseng, 69

Kroc, Ray, 23

Kuhne, Louis, 51, 52

L Glutamine, 312

Lactic Acid, 76, 107, 331, 362

Lalanne, Jack, 199

Lamb, 193, 202, 203, 209, 240, 243, 252, 305

Landsteiner, Karl, 432

Langston, Karen, 62, 63, 81, 82

Large Intestine, 61, 65, 72, 79, 151, 349

LDL-Cholesterol, 177, 178, 180

Lead, Xv, Xvi, 32, 44, 50, 64, 70, 74, 77, 82, 87, 99, 144, 153, 164, 174, 184, 199, 205, 206, 221, 223, 227, 239, 240, 259, 262, 263, 273, 283, 286, 289, 293, 304, 321, 328, 329, 333, 342, 354, 356, 361, 363, 371, 373, 374, 377, 378, 381, 389, 391, 397, 411, 413, 419, 420, 429, 433, 436, 437, 445, 452, 460, 463

Leaky Gut Syndrome, 63, 100

Lean Finely Textured Beef, 201

Lectins, 93, 107, 162, 163, 183

Lemon, 1, 69, 136, 137, 149, 296, 317, 355, 366

Lentils, 71, 151, 161, 162, 180, 193, 195, 240, 258, 311, 406

Leptin, 50, 69, 99, 133

L-Glutamine, 338

Lianhuaqingwen, 280, 297

Life Extension Labs, 266

Lifestyle, 36, 58, 113, 167, 185, 186, 324, 359, 401, 420, 471

Lightheadedness, 239

Lime Juice, 354, 355

Lindlahr, Henry, 52, 59

Linolenic Acid, 167, 195, 202, 324

Lipase, 73, 75

Lipoic Acid, 338

Lipoprotein, 79, 111, 168, 177, 178, 180, 181, 187, 206, 266, 268

Lipski, Elizabeth, 3, 80, 494

Listeria, 304, 305

Liver, 4, 37, 49, 54, 61, 63, 68, 69, 70, 77, 85, 89, 97, 99, 102, 110, 119, 120, 126, 127, 129, 133, 134, 137, 146, 159, 167, 170, 172, 173, 174, 177, 178, 199, 208, 218, 233, 236, 237, 239, 243, 249, 251, 252, 253, 255, 256, 260, 261, 262, 263, 264, 265, 266,268, 269, 281, 285, 287, 289, 290, 292, 295, 310, 313, 320, 332, 336, 337, 338, 339, 356, 358, 361, 364, 418, 422

Livestock, 29, 200, 210, 214

L-Theanine, 436

L-Threonate, 220, 221, 244

Lucky Strikes, 41

Lupus, 68, 267

Luteinizing Hormone, 127

Lycopene, 104, 181, 251

Lymphatic, 72, 173, 232

Lymphocyte Function-Associated Antigen 1, 219

Lymphomas, 336

Lyophilized, 79

Lysine, 158, 159, 194, 207

Macmickle, Virgil, 249

Macronutrients, 404

Magnesium, 51, 90, 123, 149, 159, 161, 195, 217, 218, 219, 220, 221, 222, 223, 226, 227, 228, 241, 243, 244, 245, 258, 264, 276, 288, 289, 315, 351, 353, 356, 364, 404

Maillard Reaction, 157, 164

Maize, 159, 165, 206, 262

Malabar Tamarind, 88

Malic Acid, 90, 136, 137, 149, 280

Malnutrition, 192, 212, 225

Manganese, 69, 123, 129, 134, 144, 159, 161, 288, 289, 315, 413

March Of Dimes, 374

Marjoram, 287, 299

Marubiinic Acid, 295

Massage Therapists, 4, 33

Max Planck Institute, 398, 427

Mayo, William, 328

McDonald, 23, 27, 172, 209, 214

MCT, 173, 185, 430

Mead, 113, 368, 393, 398

Meditation, 490

Mediterranean, 46, 48, 49, 51, 55, 58, 79, 83, 112, 113, 135, 136, 137, 142, 149, 170, 171, 172, 176, 193, 211, 286, 321, 335, 343, 380, 381, 390, 397, 413, 417, 418, 422, 473

Mennen, Frederick C., 166

Menstruation, 172, 224, 238, 378

Metabolic Disorders, 63

Metabolic Syndrome, 43, 44, 50, 59, 87, 89, 91, 127, 150, 163, 171, 206, 237, 265, 266, 299, 363, 369, 371, 373, 378

Methylation, 3, 69, 106, 318, 385, 471

Methylcobalamin, 260, 261

Methylenetetrahydrofolate Reductase, 427

Meyer, Frank N., 8

Microbiome, 37, 47, 56, 61, 62, 63, 66, 72, 76, 77, 79, 80, 82, 83, 101, 103, 110, 112, 117, 137, 154, 157, 162, 170, 175, 182, 222, 223, 226, 244, 276, 307, 311, 312, 319, 375, 385, 386, 387, 389, 393, 415, 421

Microflora, 76, 103, 151

Microfold Cells, 64

Micronutrients, 234, 245, 404, 469

Microplastics, 11, 63, 330, 332, 333, 356, 357, 412, 413, 420

Midwifery, 380, 490

Migraines, 1, 66, 127, 333, 418

Milk Fat Globule, 191, 212

Milk Thistle, 69, 238, 338

Mincemeat, 208, 214

Mindfulness, 490

Minerals, Xvi, 16, 51, 53, 54, 61, 69, 71, 88, 97, 100, 104, 105, 107, 118, 119, 125, 132, 137, 143, 158, 159, 160, 172, 192, 203, 206, 217, 218, 219, 221, 222, 223, 225, 227, 228, 230, 233, 243, 245, 250, 252, 288, 289, 293, 311, 329, 338, 347, 351, 355, 356, 369, 371, 402, 403, 404, 417

Minich, Deanna, 47, 133, 148, 357, 389

Mira Dessy, V

Miralax, 157, 158

Molasses, 69, 240, 366

Mold, 119, 319, 331, 333, 338, 339, 340, 344

Monosodium Glutamate, 334, 343, 335

Movement, 36, 319, 322, 387, 391, 395, 414, 449, 454

MRI, 35, 417, 422, 460

MTHFR, 318, 379, 380

Mullein, 293

Muller, Carl, 176

Multiple Sclerosis, 2, 3, 45, 103, 158, 258, 308, 415

Multivitamin, 350

Muscle Cramps, 242

Mushrooms, 104, 112, 118, 120, 145

Mycelium, 120

Mycosis, 338

Mycotoxins, 339, 344

Myers, 54

N-Acetyl Cysteine, 338

N-Acetyl Glucosamine, 338

Nanoplastics, 64, 225, 328, 332, 333, 356

National Association Of Nutrition Professionals, 85, 331, 490

National Congress Of American Indians, 327

Native American, 13, 31, 38, 130, 296, 342, 374

Native American Food Sovereignty Alliance, 13

Nature, 1, 52, 111, 213, 277, 323, 387, 390, 391, 395, 397, 398, 420, 439, 440, 450

Nausea, 66, 71, 142, 153, 173, 255, 256, 259, 263, 287

Nephrocalcinosis, 86

Nerve Pain, 66, 239

Neurocovid, 227

Neurodegenerative Disease, 104, 418

Neuropathy, 2, 258, 267, 309

Neuropsychiatric Events, 158

Neurotransmitters, 36, 67, 133, 319, 346, 386, 387, 388, 412, 415

Niacin, 97, 123, 125, 159, 227, 255, 258, 261, 262, 263, 288

Nicotinamide, 262

Nicotinic Acid, 261, 262, 263

Night Sweats, 2

NIH, 64, 65, 184, 246, 275, 318, 385

Nitric Oxide, 127, 128, 140, 273, 416

Nitrogen, 67, 102, 159, 194, 254, 268, 334, 378

NK Lymphocytes', 120
N-Methyl-D-Aspartate, 335
Non-Alcoholic Fatty Liver Disease, 69, 110, 172
Non-Steroidal Anti-Inflammatory Drugs, 169
NSAID, 285
Nurses 'Health Study, 271, 317
Nutrition Health And Examination Surveys, 348
Nuts, 49, 52, 89, 118, 141, 151, 165, 180, 181, 189, 193, 240, 255, 256, 258, 262, 268, 292, 305, 381, 404, 405, 406, 410, 412
O'Bryan, Tom, 308
Oatmeal, 71, 317
Obesity, 16, 29, 37, 41, 43, 59, 63, 69, 80, 82, 83, 87, 100, 101, 107, 110, 111, 112, 113, 117, 129, 133, 134, 152, 164, 170, 171, 172, 174, 187, 241, 265, 295, 307, 322, 325, 332, 335, 336, 363, 371, 373, 374, 376, 378, 379, 381, 385, 412
Oligomeric Proanthocyanidins, 321
Oligosaccharides, 107
Olive Oil, 49, 71, 141, 168, 170, 171, 172, 174, 176, 180, 181, 184, 185, 264, 272, 320, 404, 405, 406
Olives, 105, 312, 412
Omega 3, 155
Omega 9, 174, 312
Omega-6, 168, 206, 376
Onion, Vi, 10, 98, 71, 105, 123, 126, 127, 128, 138, 140, 141,147, 316, 317, 340
OPC, 292, 300, 321, 341
Oregano, 123, 280, 286, 287, 296, 298, 340
Oregon Grape, 295, 296
Organic Acids, 88, 132
Orthorexia, 41, 42
Osteoarthritis, 101, 228, 240, 242, 245, 263, 282, 296, 297, 298
Osteoporosis, 56, 77, 101, 103, 122, 127, 146, 197, 221, 223, 240, 244, 263, 270, 284, 288, 422, 437
Ötzi, 176, 186
Our Journey With Food Cookery Book, 14, 24, 52, 120, 129, 210, 233, 280, 296, 354, 472, 490
Ovaries, 234
Oxalate, 85, 86, 87, 88, 89, 90, 91, 92, 93, 94, 135, 259, 311

Oxalobacter Formigenes, 88, 92
Oxidative Stress, 337, 418
Oxysterols, 170
Paleo Principles, 47, 471, 473
Paleolithic Diet, 45, 46, 58
Palpitations, 143, 238, 239
Pancreas, 49, 61, 70, 71, 74, 75, 168, 310, 419
Pancreatic Enzymes, 70, 71, 74
Pantothenic Acid, 123, 125, 255
Parkinson's, 2, 121, 158, 163, 415
Pathogens, 63, 162, 163, 272, 303, 304, 305, 306, 322, 328, 375
Pauling, Linus, 112, 236, 272, 274, 275, 276, 363
Pavlov, Ivan, 62
Peaches, 22, 137, 138
Peak Performance Plan (P4), 446, 447, 449, 452
Pectin, 126, 151
Pellagra, 262
Perchlorate, 235
Peri-Menopausal, 236, 237
Periodontal Disease, 173, 263
Personal And Professional Development, 448
Personal Care Products, 349, 357
Personal Peak Performance, 443, 444, 452
Perspective, 494
Pesticides, 14, 106, 117, 134, 138, 139, 225, 319, 340, 361, 367, 377
Petroleum Byproducts, 167
PGE2, 269
Phenolic, 75, 107, 124, 126, 132, 134, 147, 148, 160, 170, 171, 286, 288, 289
Phenols, 148, 157, 364
Phenylethyl Isothiocyanate, 125
Phosphate, 218, 223, 259, 351
Phosphorus, 89, 119, 134, 159, 217, 221, 227, 228, 364
Phosvitin, 240
Phthalates, 337, 349
Phytic Acid, 93, 107, 238, 239, 240, 243
Phytochemicals, 315
Phytoestrogens, 103, 107, 118, 145, 199, 250, 363
Phytohaemagglutinin, 162

Phytonutrients, 47, 100, 101, 102, 125, 129, 389
Pink Slime, 201
Plant-Based Diet, 12, 42, 55, 56, 60, 82, 195, 206, 333
Plastic, 10, 11, 63, 167, 305, 319, 328, 330, 331, 332, 333, 334, 342, 356, 413
Pneumonia, 273
Polycystic Ovarian Syndrome, 286, 378
Polyethylene Glycol, 157, 158, 332
Polyphenols, 58, 75, 100, 101, 104, 111, 119, 124, 133, 135, 141, 148, 166, 170, 184, 193, 287, 311, 417
Polysaccharides, 98, 104, 112, 151, 158, 182, 285, 288, 299
Polystyrene, 80, 332, 333, 420
Polyunsaturated Fatty Acids, 167, 173
Pomegranate, 101, 135, 136, 149
Popcorn, 164, 165, 166, 184, 317
Pork, 69, 168, 189, 193, 203, 207, 214, 239, 252, 255, 258
Positive Affirmations, 459
Post, Marjorie Merriweather, 9
Postmenopausal, 58, 110, 144, 161, 223, 270, 417, 437
Potassium, 47, 90, 119, 123, 129, 135, 137, 159, 161, 217, 221, 222, 227, 228, 229, 230, 231, 232, 264, 280, 288, 289, 294, 315, 351, 353, 356, 364, 404
Potatoes, 15, 71, 79, 80, 89, 98, 123, 130, 131, 132, 138, 147, 163, 168, 228, 255, 274, 305, 310, 317, 320, 334, 407, 412
Pottenger, Frances, 7, 34, 54
Pottenger's Cats Study, 54
Poultry, 56, 69, 167, 168, 177, 189, 193, 196, 205, 207, 251, 262, 304, 305, 335, 403, 404
Prebiotics, 153, 396
Preconception, 56, 371, 382, 384, 470
Pregnancy, 56, 222, 234, 235, 240, 246, 247, 256, 257, 259, 260, 350, 358, 371, 372, 373, 374, 375, 377, 380, 381, 382, 384, 385, 390, 396, 397
Premenstrual Syndrome, 259
Prenatal, 80, 152, 253, 343, 371, 373, 374, 383, 385

Prescription Medications, 137, 155, 377, 438

Price, Weston A., 34, 53, 54, 252, 253, 263, 323

Price-Pottenger, 54

Primary Aldosteronism, 230

Proanthocyanidins, 104, 124, 134, 292, 300

Probiotics, 76, 77, 78, 83, 92, 119, 312, 321, 338, 415

Processed Red Meat, 201

Progesterone, 69, 78, 169, 264, 265, 319

Propylene Glycol, 250, 334, 438

Prostaglandin, 126, 167, 168, 273

Prostate, 37, 77, 117, 119, 120, 121, 127, 134, 135, 199, 224, 234, 271, 282, 292, 338

Protein, 16, 27, 44, 45, 46, 49, 51, 52, 55, 56, 58, 61, 73, 74, 75, 78, 87, 89, 97, 106, 107, 119, 127, 142, 146, 149, 157, 158, 159, 160, 161, 162, 163, 177, 179, 184, 189, 190, 191, 192, 193, 195, 196, 197, 198, 199, 203, 205, 206, 207, 208, 210, 211, 212, 213, 215, 218, 219, 235, 236, 238, 240, 246, 250, 260, 268, 280, 283, 291, 308, 309, 310, 316, 320, 323, 324, 334, 335, 336, 338, 353, 364, 379, 389, 403, 404, 405, 412, 418, 419, 422

Proteolytic Enzyme, 75

Prunes, 69, 317

Pseudo-Cereal, 158

Psychological Science, 152, 181, 466

Psyllium, 151, 154, 155

PTSD, 1, 66

Puberty, 375

Pumpkin, 69, 101, 123, 129, 130, 193, 240

Pumpkin Seeds, 69, 193, 240

Pure Food And Drug Act Of 1906, 15

Purpose And Mindset, 448

Pyridoxamine, 258

Pyridoxine, 87, 125, 258, 259, 260, 288

Qigong, 32

Quercetin, 112, 113, 126, 158, 181, 338, 341

Raspberries, 134, 148

Raynaud's, 261, 289, 409, 420, 426, 440

Razi, 113, 435, 442

RDA, 62, 153, 259, 263

Rehydration, 230, 348

Reinheitsgebot, 363

Reishi Mushrooms, 69

Relationships, 451

Renal Stone, 89, 93

Resilience, 462

Resistant Starch, 79, 80

Restless Legs Syndrome, 238

Retina, 125, 250, 288

Retinol, 251

Rheumatic Fever, 257

Rheumatoid Arthritis, 101, 242, 267, 284, 308, 313, 317, 323, 431

Rhinehart, Rob, 12

Rhodiola Rosea, 436

Riboflavin, 97, 123, 125, 159, 255, 256, 257, 258, 262, 288

Rice, 64, 71, 79, 88, 97, 98, 159, 162, 168, 179, 193, 228, 238, 240, 255, 256, 284, 310, 314, 315, 316, 317, 334, 362, 405, 406, 407, 414

RNA, 280, 339, 424

Roadblocks To Health, 439

Robusta, 142

Rodgers, Barbara, 376

Rosemary, 80, 280, 286, 298, 340, 407, 418, 422

Rudkin, Margaret, 8

Rum, 366

Rutin, 158, 159

Saccharin, 334

Sage, Xvii, 280, 287

Saliva, 55, 74, 75, 346, 359

Salmonella, 304, 305, 306

Salt, 41, 53, 88, 200, 208, 209, 219, 228, 229, 231, 232, 233, 234, 235, 246, 319, 346, 354, 355, 405

Sanskrit, 47, 67, 281, 355, 357

Sarcopenia, 105, 192, 212, 420

Saturated Fats, 42, 71, 137, 167, 174, 180, 203, 320, 376, 412

Sauerkraut, 272, 362

Scallions, 126

Schindler, Bill, 225

Schizophrenia, 158, 163

Schwarzbein, Diana, 44, 45

Schwarzenegger, Arnold, 42, 199

Scleroderma, 242

Scotch, 258, 365, 369, 426

Scurvy, 273, 277

Sears, Barry, 43, 197

Seeds, 12, 14, 16, 69, 102, 103, 105, 130, 135, 142, 151, 153, 154, 158, 162, 163, 165, 189, 202, 205, 268, 279, 287, 290, 292, 299, 365, 404, 405, 406, 410, 412

Seizure, 196

Selenium, 104, 118, 119, 134, 145, 159, 227, 257, 289, 321, 364, 384, 413

Self-Care, 463

Serotonin, 78, 141, 319, 336

Shallots, 126, 127, 317

Shanghai Declaration, 32

Sheep, 200, 202, 203, 256, 298

SIBO, 56, 77, 78, 86

Sickle Cell, 240, 381

Silent Spring, 328

Silicon, 333

Silver, 93, 341, 344

Sitz Bath, 290

Sjogren's Syndrome, 267

Skin Disorders, 349

Sleep, 325, 418, 436, 450, 455

Small Intestine, 70, 74, 77, 78, 79, 251, 255, 268, 269, 311, 323

SMART Goals, 458

Snap Peas, 79, 80, 320

Social Media, 15

Sodas, 100, 311, 318, 352, 355, 377

Sodium Bicarbonate, 70, 356

Sodium Deficiency, 232

Soluble Fiber, 78, 151, 154, 160, 338

Somers, Suzanne, 42

Soybean, 89, 172, 195, 269, 272, 276, 310, 314, 334

Soylent, 12

Specific Gravity, 350, 353

Sphingolipids, 191

Spinach, 89, 94, 125, 129, 240, 272, 304, 317

Squash, 98, 101, 105, 130, 138, 317, 407

Standard American Diet, 96

Star Trek, 11, 115

Starch, 75, 78, 79, 80, 82, 83, 89, 97, 107, 123, 158, 160, 183, 195, 310, 362

Steroid Hormone, 267

Stomach Acid, 56, 74, 221, 295, 419

Stookey, S. Donald, 10

Strawberries, 69, 89, 100, 132, 133, 134, 140, 152, 274, 279, 304, 317, 412

Strength Training, 437

Stress, Xvi, 32, 35, 36, 41, 62, 67, 76, 83, 91, 96, 101, 102, 104, 106, 112, 113, 141, 144, 146, 151, 167, 171, 179, 187, 221, 224, 227, 242, 253, 256, 257, 269, 271, 272, 273, 286, 289, 292, 308, 335, 337, 373, 375, 378, 381, 383, 389, 390, 391, 393, 401, 409, 410, 411, 418, 422, 459, 462

String Beans, 80

Stroke, 127, 143, 178, 192, 212, 228, 230, 252, 260, 261, 263, 269, 285, 291, 364, 389, 392, 398

Sucrose, 120, 136, 137, 141, 151, 177, 223, 336

Sugar, Xvi, 4, 11, 43, 49, 52, 53, 89, 91, 97, 98, 99, 100, 101, 111, 120, 126, 128, 129, 133, 134, 139, 140, 144, 152, 159, 162, 168, 176, 180, 186, 197, 209, 210, 225, 228, 266, 286, 287, 289, 295, 308, 316, 317, 318, 319, 321, 354, 363, 366, 369, 377, 378, 379, 383, 402, 404, 405, 412, 417, 432, 436, 469

Sugar Research Foundation, 176, 186

Sulfites, 334

Sulforaphane, 102, 112, 122

Sulfur Compounds, 69, 126

Superoxide Dismutase, 125, 257, 288

Supplements, 58, 146, 212, 239, 244, 249, 250, 276, 297, 299, 301, 321, 342, 473

Sustainability, 104, 189, 210, 211, 215, 387

Sweat Glands, 346

Sweet Potato, 130, 147, 317, 404, 406

Switchel, 354

Sylvester Graham, 55

Synovial Fluid, 346

Systemic Lupus Erythematosus, 247, 444

Tannahill, Reay, 7, 253

Tannins, 107, 133, 135, 293

Tea, Xviii, 89, 102, 111, 113, 140, 141, 152, 230, 240, 255, 256, 285, 286, 288, 289, 298, 295, 298, 352, 355, 407, 417, 436

Telomerase, 194, 285

Telomere, 285

Tequila, 367

Terpenoids, 104, 119, 282, 285, 288

Testosterone, 69, 127, 287, 299, 319, 381, 383

Tetrahydrocannabinol, 66

The 4-Cs, 440

The Anitschkow Dictum, 176

The Blue Zones, 284

The French Chef, 26

The Good Housekeeper, 55, 209

The Great Depression, 21

The Journal Of Toxicology And Environmental Health, 100

The Lancet, 100, 391, 421

The Rainbow Diet, 47, 58, 396, 472

The Wheel Of Wellness And Longevity, 447

Theobroma, 139, 140, 149

Theobromine, 141, 142, 150

Thiamine, 97, 123, 126, 161, 253, 254, 255

Thiamine, 254, 255

Thiamine Pyrophosphate, 254

Thrush, 79

Thyroid, 1, 69, 117, 121, 154, 199, 233, 234, 235, 236, 237, 238, 239, 252, 257, 264, 266, 286, 290, 292, 310, 323, 336, 337, 389

Thyroid Peroxidase, 238

Tight Junctions, 63, 311

Tincture, 280, 288, 295

Tobacco, 41, 67, 81, 273, 373, 379, 381, 426

Tomatoes, 71, 105, 116, 123, 138, 209, 274, 317, 320, 334

Totino, Rose, 8

Toxic Mold, 331, 338

Trace Mineral, 118

Traditional Chinese Medicine, 3, 105, 163, 267, 281, 357, 392

Traumatic Brain Injury, 428, 441

Trichloroethylene, 331

Triglycerides, 46, 50, 75, 120, 167, 173, 177, 178, 179, 185, 266, 316, 363, 419

Triocoachingacademy, 443, 491

Triterpenoids, 134

Tryptophan, 87, 194, 261, 262

Tuberculosis, 54, 173, 257, 263, 361

Tufts University Health Sciences, 96

Tupperware, 10, 29, 319

Turkey, 194, 206, 207, 214

Turmeric, 80, 282, 283, 297, 407

Turnips, 21, 98, 123, 426

U.S. Environmental Protection Agency, 337, 356

U.S. Food And Drug Administration, 24, 305, 336

Ulcerative Colitis, 78, 86, 120, 135, 155, 229, 238, 252, 266, 303

Undernutrition, 152

United Nations, 13, 29, 116, 395, 421

Unrefined Sea Salt, 233

Uremic Toxins, 157

Ureter, 72, 336

Urethral, 72

Utis, 78, 87

Vegetables, 8, 16, 37, 47, 52, 71, 91, 93, 94, 98, 100, 101, 102, 104, 107, 113, 116, 121, 123, 126, 129, 130, 133, 136, 138, 146, 147, 151, 162, 165, 172, 176, 180, 199, 203, 205, 228, 251, 252, 256, 258, 262, 268, 272, 287, 292, 304, 316, 317, 320, 328, 381, 389, 392, 398, 402, 403, 404, 405, 406, 409, 413, 414, 416

Vegetarians, 47, 56, 189, 196, 251, 261, 335

Virome, 226, 245

Vitamin A, 101, 125, 133, 137, 174, 227, 238, 251, 252, 253, 264, 266, 275, 289

Vitamin C, 71, 90, 123, 124, 125, 127, 130, 132, 133, 134, 135, 136, 227, 238, 241, 249, 269, 272, 273, 274, 276, 277, 288, 289, 290, 293, 321, 338, 369

Vitamin D, 106, 119, 177, 218, 219, 223, 227, 236, 237, 243, 263, 264, 265, 266, 267, 270, 275, 276, 288, 388, 391, 403, 416

Vitamin D Council, 263, 264

Vitamin E, 71, 123, 168, 227, 237, 267, 268, 269, 338

Vitamin K, 76, 78, 126, 135, 270, 271, 272, 276, 288

Vitamins, Xvi, 53, 61, 69, 71, 78, 97, 100, 104, 105, 118, 119, 121, 124, 125, 129, 132, 135, 137, 143, 158, 160, 169, 172, 177, 192, 195, 203, 206, 225, 227, 239, 245, 249, 250, 252, 253, 255, 256, 257, 263, 270, 272, 274, 288, 293, 294, 300, 310, 311, 321, 338, 341, 355, 371, 373,

378, 380, 383, 384, 402, 403, 404, 410, 414, 417

Voegtlin, Walter L., 46

Volstead Act, 20

Von Willebrand, 169, 184

Vulgaxanthin, 129

Wahls, Terry, 3, 45, 62, 183, 196

Water, Xvi, Xviii, 2, 4, 11, 12, 14, 43, 51, 63, 75, 89, 106, 117, 118, 126, 134, 139, 144, 151, 153, 155, 156, 163, 167, 174, 189, 193, 198, 231, 232, 233, 234, 235, 240, 246, 249, 254, 256, 259, 261, 262, 270, 272, 282, 285, 287, 290, 292, 304, 305, 306, 314,315, 316, 319, 324, 327, 328, 329, 330, 331, 332, 333, 338, 342, 345, 346, 347, 348, 349, 350, 351, 352, 353, 354, 355, 356, 357, 358, 359, 363, 365, 368, 383, 386, 403, 405, 412

Watercress, 124, 125, 146, 147, 230

Watermelon, 69, 129

Wavelength, 386, 395

Weakness, 172, 173, 231, 232, 238, 263, 273

Weight Loss, 41, 43, 46, 48, 49, 50, 52, 59, 77, 120, 151, 196, 241, 286, 316, 381

Weight Management, 59, 151, 168, 174, 355

Weil, Andrew, 31

Wellness Paradigm, 36

Wernicke's Encephalopathy, 254

Weston Price Foundation, 306

Wheat, 14, 71, 89, 97, 99, 150, 151, 158, 159, 162, 165, 183, 193, 205, 206, 240, 252, 255, 262, 268, 307, 309, 310, 314, 315, 316, 317, 323, 405, 406, 407

Wheat Germ, 268, 310

Whiskey, 365, 366

White Blood Cell, 72

Wild Asparagus, 426

Wild Cherry, 294, 301

Wilson, James L., Xvi

Wine, 4, 49, 85, 94, 105, 135, 140, 141, 142, 209, 296, 314, 355, 361, 362, 364, 365, 366, 367, 368

Wise, Brownie, 10

Wolf, Max, 73

Wolfgang Von Goethe, Johann, 281, 395

World Health Organization, 32, 43, 100, 175, 192, 238, 241, 251, 304, 324, 361, 377

World War II, 8, 10, 13, 14, 23, 41, 96, 166, 176, 207, 264, 331, 334

Xenobiotic, 271, 334

Xenoestrogen, 117, 319, 324

Xylitol, 93, 134

Yarrow, 290, 300

Yeast, 52, 76, 256, 262

Yoga, 32, 373, 383

Yudkin, John, 176

Zika Virus, 283

Zinc, 51, 118, 144, 159, 207, 227, 240, 241, 242, 243, 247, 257, 258, 288, 289, 312, 315, 383, 404

Zone Diet, 43

ZRT Lab, 236

Zygote, 372, 378

Your Author

TAMMERA J. KARR, Ph.D., BCHN®, CDSP™, CGP, CNW®, is an author, wellness educator, food historian, and clinician. She is an member of the National Association of Nutrition Professionals and Faculty at Pacific College of Health and Science. She has served as a nutrition advisor to wellness programs and presented at local, regional, and national conferences. She writes blogs, reviews, and contributes to national board exams.

Passionate about nutrition as the key to stopping many modern illnesses, Tammera authored *Our Journey with Food 3rd edition (2023)* and *Our Journey with Food Cookery Book 2nd edition (2022)*, adding to the story by filling in many gaps in our modern food knowledge for health. Believing "Traditional Foods" are all about community, Tammera invited colleagues, students, friends, and family to contribute to this work. Tammera and Kathleen Bell continued the journey with the third book *Empty Plate: Food~Sustainability~Mindfulness* (2020).

A native of Oregon, Tammera has over 50 years of experience with whole foods and the HOWs and WHYs of preparing and benefitting from the natural health properties of real foods. She currently resides with her family in rural central-southern Oregon.

Content Expert Contributors

KATHLEEN BELL, RN, MSN, CNM, AHN-BC, MSI-BC; Kathleen's nursing career of nearly 50 years encompasses maternal–child nursing, Nurse-Midwifery, education, integrative health, and holism. She has held many national certifications and is semi-retired. Kathleen trained in Primordial Sound Meditation and Ayurvedic principles for health/dietary practices with the *Chopra Center* and was certified to teach meditation by *The Center for Meditation Science*. In 2020 she completed her second degree *Usui Reiki* practitioner certification.

Retired from full-time academia — having taught nursing and midwifery at undergraduate and graduate levels in Utah, Oregon, Washington, and abroad — Kathleen is one of six holistic nursing faculty teaching the Integrative Healing Arts Program for the American Holistic Nurses Association (AHNA). She served on the Board of Directors with the Center for Meditation Science and a special advisor to the National Association of Nutrition Professionals' BOD.

Kathleen writes, research, and frequently presents on topics related to maternal-child/women's health, nursing and consumer education, meditation/mindfulness, integrative health, and holism.

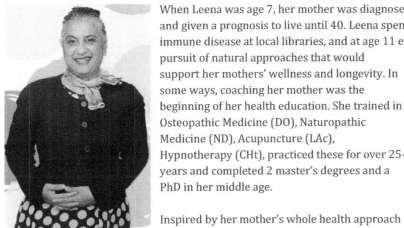

When Leena was age 7, her mother was diagnosed with an aggressive form of Lupus and given a prognosis to live until 40. Leena spent the next 4 years reading about auto-immune disease at local libraries, and at age 11 embarked with her mother on a pursuit of natural approaches that would support her mothers' wellness and longevity. In some ways, coaching her mother was the beginning of her health education. She trained in Osteopathic Medicine (DO), Naturopathic Medicine (ND), Acupuncture (LAc), Hypnotherapy (CHt), practiced these for over 25-years and completed 2 master's degrees and a PhD in her middle age.

www.2BWell.Solutions
www.2BWell-Edu

Inspired by her mother's whole health approach (and longevity to age 70) Leena's mission became clear "to educate and inspire a global community as to the value of personal peak performance health 2B Well for life." Similarly, her vision to "live in a world where allopathic and integrative therapies are offered with equal availability to all, where health care focuses on balancing mind body and spirit, utilizing the best of all medicines" is her way of honoring her mothers' spirituality and challenging life journey. Today Leena serves as President of 2B Well Education, 2B Well Solutions, Chief Learning Officer at Trio Coaching Academy and enjoys being a whole health practitioner and educator.   www.TrioCoachingAcademy.com

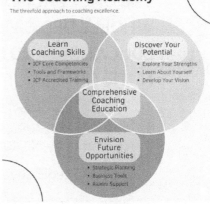

Dr. Guptha has more than 40 years combined experience as a practicing physician, a scientist in academia/industry/regulatory agencies and an educator for Medical School, Royal College, and Universities globally. His areas of specialization include cardiology; nephrology, lipids, diabetes, thrombosis, drug eluting stents and asthma/COPD. As an independent consultant he utilizes his expertise as an academician, clinician (interventional cardiologist), drug & device developer and educator in the USA, Europe, and Asia Pacific.

With a passion for whole health inspired by his mother's 50-year holistic practice as an Ob-Gyn, he trained in Acupuncture and Hypnotherapy. He has taught Naturopathic Cardiology, hospital-based integrative approaches to Cardiology, Oncology and Orthopedics and has developed fellowship courses in a range of integrative health and medicine areas. In his free time, he enjoys cooking and creating nutritional meals based on food science.

In 1999 he was awarded the 20th Century Achievement Award for admirable career achievements and contributions, USA and in 1998 he was awarded Outstanding People of the 20th Century, for exceptional contributor to Cardiology, Lipids. Internationally, he maintains a close relationship in educational activities of the at Royal College of Physicians, Kings College and the IFAPP Academy. He is published in peer review journals and has over 100 publications and presentations; as well as book chapters, book reviews and has been a course developer and director.

HN4U Our Journey with Food @ Yourwholenutrition.com

Who is this program for?

This course, while initially created for nurses eager to use food as medicine, is also suitable for anyone motivated to learn how to create delicious meals with health-promoting qualities.

Evidence-Based

Why You Want to Take This Program

> "Cutting edge science, practical application for clinicians and clients, history to add context and more… Incredible Value"
> ~Mary Hagood, FNP-C

Food and Health

There is a growing body of science supporting traditional food choices for sustainable health.

- Self-Paced Course with Instructor Access
- 12 Evidence-Based Presentations
- Over 20 Videos with Downloadable Tools
- 3 Exams to Test Knowledge
- Scientific and Historical Citations
- Group Interaction, Recommended Reading, Activities, Support, Tips, and Tools
- 25 credit-hour Approved Certificate of Completion for Nurses.
- 10 credit-hour Certificate for NANP Members
- CEs approved by the American Naturopathic Certification Board

This Course Will Cover:

- Nutrition Foundations
- Sustainability in Food Choices for Health
- Mindfulness in Food Selection and Lifestyle

Our Journey with Food

Books by Tammera Karr

Available through YourWholeNutrition.com and Amazon.com

"Empty Plate is a refreshingly original and insightful approach to true "Holistic" health. An enjoyable, thought-provoking blend of history, tradition, and science …. A must read for those with a serious interest in integrative approaches to health."

~Terry Wahls, MD
researcher, educator, and author of the Wahls Protocol

"Tammera Karr and Kathleen Bell feed body, mind, and spirit in *Empty Plate*. They teach us how to begin anew to fill our plate with food that nourishes, a mind that is calm, a world that encourages sustainability and a profound connection to nature. *Empty Plate* is personal with writings and poetry. It provides a historical and traditional perspective that you won't find elsewhere. It's also based on current research and provides practical tools throughout. This book will shift your attention and, ultimately, your actions. Gift yourself with a guiltless treat by reading *Empty Plate*."

~Elizabeth Lipski, PhD, CNS, FACN
nutritionist, professor, author of Digestive Wellness.

"Tammera Karr perfectly captured this book's essence in her poem *Hidden Delights* when she wrote, "*It is connection and preservation of knowledge*." That is precisely what they have created with this practical, relevant, and powerful book. These authors have done something incredible and created a resource that entertains, informs, and empowers all of us to get back into our kitchens, dust off our aprons, and prepare truly nourishing food for our families".

~ Bill Schindler, PhD
Author of *Eat Like A Human*, Speaker and Educator
Director of the Eastern Shore Food Lab and Executive Chef at Modern Stone Age Kitchen

"Tammera Karr's book, *Our Journey with Food-Cookery Book*, fills the gaps in our heritage and knowledge of food. This book is a unique blend of science, history, anecdotes, photographs, and wonderful recipes that begin to close the gap in our food knowledge. The book is logically arranged, beginning with explaining the benefits of staples in the kitchen and how to prepare and safely store many foods for later use. All these will reduce the risk of nutrition-related diseases such as obesity, diabetes, stroke, auto-immunity, and many others. The book is carefully documented, in contrast to many books of this kind, done logically and without malice or fanaticism. It is not only a good read but an essential part of our food history and the evolution of who we are".

~ Janet Ludwig, PhD, MS
Biochemistry and Nutrition
Professor & Dean of Integrative Health and Nutrition, American College of Healthcare Science

Made in the USA
Monee, IL
07 January 2024

50160241R00280